1969-1974 Bluemont News

1969-1974 Bluemont News

Evelyn Porterfield Johnson

1969-1974 Bluemont News
Copyright 2025 by Evelyn Porterfield Johnson/Lara Johnson Publishers
All rights reserved

ISBN: 979-8-9987569-0-0

Cover art by Clyde Beck, Bluemonter and artist
Image used with permission from the artist and appeared on the first Bluemont Fair poster.

Photo credit: Snickersville Turnpike hill, by Lara Johnson (Back cover)

Headers on top of pages - A decade of Bluemont News - not updated as caused many formatting errors.

The dates listed indicate when the column appeared in the Loudoun-Times Mirror newspaper. Name misspellings and typographical errors were corrected where known. There are a dozen columns missing from this 1969-1974 collection either due to the entire newspaper not found at the library or other; included are additional feature articles.

Acknowledgements

SPECIAL THANKS TO Mallory Craig for scanning the bulk of the columns from microfiche at the Thomas Balch Library in Leesburg, Virginia.

Thanks to Patsye Matthews, founder and owner of Thyme Books in Leesburg, Virginia for securing permission for cover art from the artist and for the book, "Rockin' with Porch Memories."

Thanks to Wren Begley for locating some of the columns at Clayton Hall.

Preface

THE FOLLOWING ESSAY captures the essence of this collection and appears in the book: "Rockin with porch memories", Editor: L. Claire Kincannon and Associate Editors: Linda Ankrum and Marty Potts, copyright, 2005.

THE PORCH AT CLAYTON HALL, BY EVELYN PORTERFIELD JOHNSON

I like to tell my children, "You had an idyllic childhood". Not only did I have the privilege of living it with them, I wrote about it weekly for seventeen years as the Bluemont correspondent for the *Loudoun Times-Mirror* and *The Clarke Courier*. And a lot of their growing up in our little village of Bluemont was played out on our big front porch. The concrete floor porch had been added to the 1797 stone house in the late '30's. It has a tin roof, flat though it has never caved in from a snow accumulation. Four columns frame the facade and originally it had a formal wooden ceiling which had developed a leak. One workman wanted to tear the roof off to correct the problem. Many times since, I have counted my blessings I said "No!" We just tore out the ceiling and now with the exposed beams, it works beautifully, thank you.

In essence the front porch is our extended living space from Memorial Day to after the Bluemont Fair, the third weekend of September. The number of birthday candles lit on cakes on the picnic table could never be calculated. As part of the early celebrations of the birthdays, the daughters would put on plays with entrances and exits from the hall onto the porch. A young neighbor came on one occasion, accompanied by his two pet goats, who gleefully mounted the ledges of the wide steps, the children screaming in excitement.

Dinner parties for adult friends have graced the big sturdy picnic table, made by a foster child in his vo-tech classes through Valley High School.

There have been parties for political candidates and a fond remembered steak dinner shared as raindrops fell on the tin roof.

The wicker and the hanging swing, bought from Nichols Hardware, go out in May. Red geraniums always decorate the ledges in window boxes.

In previous summer evenings, the children frolicked, catching lightning bugs on the lawn or sometimes helped churn ice cream for the Fourth of July celebration at the old school grounds in the village.

In fall we put out the pumpkins and stack the wood for the approaching cold, take down the swing and put out the old red school bench.

In winter, the sled and snow shovels go out. The prettiest sight I ever saw on the porch was a bough of freshly-cut holly dusted with snow, an early surprise Christmas gift from a neighbor. I have my bird house collection out on a tin-top table and there among some of my favorite things and blooming plants, I like to sit on the porch. Feeling the cool breezes from the swing in the summer, I recall special times with family and friends. But oh, how I wish, I could once utter to a passersby as in the days of another generation, "Won't you come up and sit a spell? I have the porch for it!"

1969

January 30, 1969

IT SOUNDS PREPOSTEROUS, I know, our being the latest newcomers to Bluemont, for me to serve as the correspondent, but Doris Allder after meeting many a deadline, wished to retire for a while and I thought it might be a good way to meet my neighbors.

In the first place, let me say we are absolutely charmed with Bluemont. As I pass the Hill Top Orchards on Rt. 7 and view the landscape of rotting pasture land and hills dotted with timber, I feel at peace with myself. Even though, we have been here but six months, we know we are "at home."

Others who were happy to return home for at least a weekend were David Spring, now of the U.S. Army and stationed at Atlanta, Ga. and Sadie Peyton, a freshman at Madison College, Harrisonburg, Va.

Tom Mann, son of Mr. and Mrs. Walton Mann, and his bride, the former Miss Ruth Ellen Kihlgren of Alexandria, were pleased to visit atop the mountain with the family over the weekend.

Tom and Ruth Ellen were married on Dec. 22 at the Mt. Vernon Methodist Church, Alexandria. Tom continues his studies at the University of Richmond while Ruth Ellen pursues her course of study at Strayer Business School in Washington, D.C.

Of course, everyone is delighted to hear of Mrs. Hazel Reid's return from the Winchester Hospital where she has been convalescing for several months.

Most of our summer and weekend people have deserted us but Mr. and Mrs. Herb Little and Miss Kathleen Nygard braved it last weekend.

Friends of Mrs. Wesley Carbaugh will be interested to know she is now a patient at Georgetown Hospital, Washington. Naturally we all anticipate a speedy recovery.

O.H. Nesmith had a fall and consequent burn at his home last week. He appreciates the kind attention of his good neighbors and friends in the community.

Recognition should be extended to Jimmy Campbell, a freshman at Loudoun Valley High School where he is a member of the school wrestling team. We hear he even missed his Thanksgiving dinner so he could remain in his 95 pound class!

Our traditional town meeting was held on Jan. 10, a reminder too, of the Methodist Church's meeting times, Sunday School at 9 a.m., church service at 10 a.m. with the Rev. Homer Hall presiding.

The grand social event of the week was the Mid-Winter's Dance of the Loudoun Valley Dance Club at the James Brownell's Whitehall Farm, Bluemont, on Saturday night.

You've all seen the commercial of the car running to the service station on its own, well, while Joyce Beck was brushing her teeth last Friday morning, her car got as far as the Butler's front porch. Maybe you better stop at the __ Station, eh, Joyce?

This is the weekly news of Bluemont that I've been able to scare up and of course, I would be delighted to receive a caller at the door or a telephone call bearing "news." Hope to meet you soon.

February 6, 1969

The mountain is a study in gray now; it's bleak but somehow comforting, the fog drifts in at night tucking the village in tight and we snuggle deeper into our homes, safe.

But danger lurked outside the door for a driver of a milk truck early last Wednesday morning. His truck went over the bank near all the Reids at the top of the hill and he wandered, dazed, to the Sam Joneses' who accommodated him for the night and helped him notify his family and employer. The rest of us slept, hearing nothing, not knowing, until the sun revealed part of the story and the grapevine spread the rest.

These "ice days" have brought some falls to some of our older citizens and some to the younger, too, for that matter, however, we are glad to report Mrs. Elsie Scott's arm is mending well after a fall she suffered several weeks ago.

There was quite a bit of visiting in the Bluemont limits over last weekend.

The John Carters entertained Mary Ann's sister, Mrs. Frances Sims and daughter, Teresa Ann from Landover, Md. on Sunday.

A family dinner party was given by the Clyde Becks for Joyce's father, Paul Grove of Lovettsville, in honor of his birthday on Sunday.

Other guests were Joyce's mother, two sisters and their husbands. Mr. and Mrs. John Minneci of Manassas, Mr. and Mrs. Dennis Settle of Oxon Hill, Md. and brother, Mike Grove of Lovettsville, plus Miss Margaret Grove of Arlington and of course, the Grove grandchildren which now number five.

Mr. and Mrs. Innes Saunders of Liberty Hill near Leesburg along with the Floyd Johnsons of Paeonian Springs were our guests on Saturday night. We bored them with our home movies which featured Bluemont last year at this time. There wasn't any snow then, either but there were plenty of weeds around this place.

Jean Dawson, daughter of Mr. and Mrs. Lawrence Dawson, spent a leisurely few days at home after her grueling exam week at Madison College in Harrisonburg.

Mr. and Mrs. James Walsh and family were reluctant to part from son, Jerry, who had spent a three-week Christmas leave at home with them. He returned to duty at Reese Air Force, Lubbock, Tex. a week ago.

Mrs. Marion Steele of Purcellville was a house guest of the Walshes this past week.

Mr. and Mrs. G.W. Townhsend took a few well-earned days off for a visit to their daughter's family, the Rothgebs of Beltsville, Md. this past week. They particularly enjoyed granddaughter, Karen.

Mrs. Sarah Chapman, Shirley Carbaugh's mother from Vienna, was their guest over the weekend.

A followww-up on Mrs. Wesley Carbaugh revealed she has returned to her home here and will not return to the hospital until March.

Mrs. Smyrna Holland of Bluemont attended the Artex Hobby Products Company Convention in York, Pa. several weekends ago. Mrs. Holland is an Artex instructor over a wide area of Virginia, conducting home parties at which the products are made available and demonstrations are given.

As far as we can determine the press had not formally congratulated the former Miss Verma Davis of Purcellville on her marriage to Clinton Hindman of Purcellville on Oct. 9.

They are now making their home with Clinton's uncle and aunt, Mr. and Mrs. Ralph Cochran of Bluemont. Norma continues her studies at Loudoun Valley High School while Clinton pursues the daily chores of farm life with his uncle. Consider yourselves congratulated!

We have missed our regular mail carrier, Bob Jones who fell under the flu influence, but his wife, Ellen knows "the mail must go" so she has been making rounds for him.

Bobby and Barbara Allder attended the funeral of his aunt in Herndon this past week.

The regular meeting time of the Methodist Church Junior Choir under the direction of Ralph Cochran is Thursday evening at 7:30, however, the youth wish to invite any interested adults for a combined choir effort at this same time.

When I asked Roy Virts what was the news of his family, he said he had gotten a hairrr-cut and his father would be glad to see that in print.

With that news item, I conclude; I'd call that progress in Bluemont for this week. Wouldn't you?

February 13, 1969

These are the mud days.

Big, heavy clods dried on the porch, oozing brown earth caked on the boots at the front door, muddy dog prints tracked onto the rugs and furniture, imprinted on the stairs and floors swished with wagging tails against the wall.

These are the mud days.

Pasture lands and lawn are gutted with tracks…animals are bogged down in the soft loam… Back roads are swollen with wet clay but the school bus pushes through, anyway.

There are the mud days.

And in my dreams I see grass, the tall grass variety that waves in the wind and hear the echo of Walt Whitman's image, "Grass is the beautiful uncut hair of graves."

Mr. Lloyd says if we sow the seed at the end of February, we can have grass this summer but as for now, these are the mud days!

The mud didn't stop quite a few visitors to Bluemont over the weekend, however.

The John Carters hold the record with guests streaming in all day Saturday and Sunday.

On Saturday Mr. and Mrs. Melvin Carter of Winchester plus James McCauley, daughter Charlotte, Gary Jewell and Margaret Powell of Bolivar, W.Va. all paid a visit.

Sunday brought Mary Ann's brother, Sonny Smith and wife Bonnie and three children from Cabin John, Md. and Mr. and Mrs. Jack Barber, Mary Ann's mother and her husband, along with Delamo Poland all from Purcellville. What a reunion they did have.

Mrs. Betsy Carter entertained her granddaughter, Mary Jane Carter and six children from Summit Point, W.Va. on Sunday.

A new family to the community, who is enjoying it as much as we are are the Don Bowmans. They are doing a remake of "Yours, Mine" and haven't quite gotten to "Ours" unless you want to count all those new puppies, lambs, and calves populating their farm these days.

His children visited this past weekend. They are Miss Debbie Bowman of Vienna and Mr. and Mrs. Robert Bowman of Fairfax.

Mrs. Don Bowman says she has heard from her son, Irving Havener, Jr. who is making his fourth trip to Vietnam as a Sergeant in the U.S. Army.

Her other son, Frank Havener is a Sergeant in the Air Force now seeing duty in Thailand.

Her daughter, Brenda, an eighth grade student at Loudoun Valley, resides with them here of course, at the farm. She is quite a horsewoman, too.

Another real rider among us is Steve Kelley, son of Mr. and Mrs. Stanley Kelley, Jr. He is already making plans to attend the Philomont Horse Show in April. It sounds like a great treat right in our own backyard. Father Stanley is a steward.

Barbara Jean Allder, daughter of Mr. and Mrs. Jack Allder, finally got home from Madison College after visiting with her boyfriend's family in Baltimore for several days.

Sonny and Jeanne Brown and children of Leesburg were our guests on Sunday and of course, I had to apologize for the mud.

Those leaving Bluemont for visits were Mr. and Mrs. Teasdale-Smith to see their son in his bachelor quarters in Washington and Mrs. Lucy Marks, Elinor and Elmer Anderson to chat with Bonnie and Peggy Marks in Vienna.

Pat Walsh celebrated his tenth birthday on the sixth with a dinner guest, Jimmy Lemon, son of Mr. and Mrs. James Lemon of Bluemont.

A royal welcome to the tiny female addition to the Richard Murrays.

Leading the sick list are Mr. and Mrs. Glen Lloyd with the flu, both Louise and Carl Gibson, she convalescing from an amputated limb, he a broken ankle and Mrs. Peggy Little who is a resident at Sibley Hospital Washington with a broken hip.

We are pleased to hear that George Freeman has returned from the Loudoun Memorial Hospital.

Congratulations to Mrs. Norma Hindman and Mark Brownell on their Honor Roll achievement at Loudoun Valley High School. If I have omitted a name, please inform me.

The Methodist WSCS met Wednesday at 10 o'clock at Shirlee Carbaugh's.

The Home Demonstration Club met on Tuesday this week, too.

Sorry, I had already put the column to bed when I got the news of the Citizens Association meeting which met last Friday night, featuring films on Virginia History.

Don't forget tomorrow is Valentine's Day. Why not remember your best girl who might even be your wife? Hearts and flowers to you all!

February 20, 1969

Hibernation was the order of the day over the several past weekends.

It was really a perfect country weekend with all the city people missing it and we were just relishing it ourselves our own way by staying close.

The kids rode the horses up through town on Saturday and then the snow kept us blanketed in on Sunday with church service even being canceled here.

I did see a few snow men and Alan Carter and cronies had a dozen sled rides in a field somewhere but mostly everyone stayed near the fire.

The family insisted on some snow-cream so we stomped up the hill to the Becks with the eggs and sugar and it turned out to be the best ever made.

Here's the recipe if you have hopes for another fall of the flurry white stuff and some of the town seers are calling for it:

Beat two eggs, a cup of sugar, a can of evaporated milk and a teaspoon of vanilla in a large mixing bowl, gradually add a gallon of snow (it must be the Bluemont variety that made it so good!)

This yields about a gallon and a half and you can top it with your favorite sauce. We blended in peaches and it was delicious!

Who am I to betray winter with thoughts of a golden bouquet of jonquils on the dining room table!

"Hawkeye" Reid says this is like March weather, bright and sunny one moment, snow flurries the next.

I do feel I unveiled a deep, dark secret this week for I learned the given names of the Reids; Hawkeye is Carl, Popeye – Gordon, and Buckeye – Marvin. I forgot to ask how they got the nicknames.

Nevertheless, they are doing a cracker-jack job on pointing up the stone behind the cinder-block garage which is next to go.

If you feel you missed the plane crash as evidenced by the tin in the front yard, that's the roof of the old kitchen.

I love the old wood shingles they found underneath but everyone in Bluemont has a shiny tin roof and not many are even painted.

David Spring who has paid several visits to his mother, Mrs. Barbara Spring lately will be on his way to Vietnam in about two weeks. Our sincere good wishes go with him.

Mr. and Mrs. Lloyd Loope of the beautiful Swiss chalet on the mountain road have just returned from a glorious ten-day stay in Mexico. Ah, wouldn't I like to be Acapulco bound!

Tom and Ruth Mann came for a visit again with his parents, Mr. and Mrs. Walton Mann. Mrs. Mann told me they had run Mann's Store for 21 years now. We sure couldn't do without them.

Donning their warmest winter clothes last Tuesday were a bunch of Bluemonters to pay a visit to their aunt and uncle, Mr. and Mrs. Clarence Grouch of Aldie. There was Martin Wilt, Mrs. Russell Peterson and son Robbie, Mrs. Russell Parks, Jr. and daughter Tina Marie, Mrs. Robert Allder and baby, Yvonne.

Mrs. Robert Allder entertained her aunt and uncle, Mr. and Mrs. Gordon Arnett of Arlington this week too.

Barbara and I had a wonderful chat on the phone while we incidentally swapped the official news.

Mrs. Bernice Manuel is visiting in Baltimore with her son, Clarence, Jr., or "Sonny" as we know him while Clarence, Sr. is confined to Loudoun Memorial Hospital. Let's hope his health returns soon.

Mrs. Ralph Cochran underwent dental surgery at Winchester Hospital last week but is home now recuperating.

Our condolences to Mrs. John Thomas who lost her brother of Indian Head, Md. this past week.

The Community Association made plans to re-sponsor Boy Scout Troop 959 and any boys between the ages of 11 to 18 with fathers who can assist occasionally should contact Mr. Leffingwell, the Scout master.

Well, I figured if Julie Nixon Eisenhower could do it so could I so I had an intimate little dinner party for my father, Roy Porterfield of Bethesda, Md. in honor of his Valentine Day birthday. Of course, Mother was here too, Jennifer, the twins, Wayne and…Very intimate, wasn't it?

Give me a buzz with what you know, 'cause I've been curled up with a good book and the hibernating fever!

February 27, 1969

It has occurred to me that life could be harsh for some of our neighbors when the temperature drops to icy depths and the wind whistles and manages to slip in a crack or two somewhere but then when I gaze from the window who do I see but Mr. Nesmith scurrying down the hill to the store at a rapid pace, Mrs. Nellie Powell scrubbing her long smooth porch and John Hyland vigorously chopping wood.

All live alone, none have central heat or indoor plumbing, all battle the elements daily and all keep hearty and hale into the 70 and 80 years in this rugged climate.

I hope the climate's the secret, so I can be telling the youngsters someday about what I remember of Bluemont in the '80s.

Despite the cold weather, there were a number of visits exchanged here over the weekend.

Justine and Brian Beck attended their cousin's birthday party in Manassas on Sunday. Barbara Jean Allder returned for a weekend visit with her family from Madison College where she is half-way through her sophomore year, also her next-door neighbor Jean Dawson was home from Madison.

More of the college crowd home for the weekend was David Loope from Duke University in Durham, N.C., and Robert Bowman now working on his master's degree at George Washington University in the District was a guest of the Don Bowmans the previous weekend.

Mrs. Lola Mann of Hamilton is staying with her son's family, the Walton Mann's, this week.

Wayne Hartwell, an art collector friend from Chicago spent several days with the Clyde Becks last week.

He and Clyde wined and dined in the nation's capital and made the round of the galleries. Sorta a vacation at home, huh, Clyde?

On Monday evening Mrs. Lucy Martz gave her Artex Products party where a number of the neighbors gathered and had a lovely time getting reacquainted while initially they were introduced to this liquid embroidery which can create many a beautiful object.

Mrs. Bessie Carter had as her overnight guests last Saturday, her daughter, Mrs. Juanita White and her children from Summit Point, W.Va.

The John Carters held open house again with Mr. and Mrs. Melvin Carter visiting on Saturday from Winchester. They had returned from a trip to Kentucky where they had settled their daughter, Mrs. Faye Wymer, with her husband, who is presently stationed there.

Mr. and Mrs. Donald White, Johnny's sister and husband of Summit, W.Va. were also guests.

In addition, Mr. and Mrs. Isaac Carter of Upperville, James McCauley and daughter, Charlotte and Margaret Powell of Bolivar Heights, W. Va. gathered at Mountain Shadow.

Mr. and Mrs. Lawrence Dawson spent a day last week with Lawrence's aunt, Mrs. Ora Mooney of Annandale, Lawrence's father, W.B. Lawrence Dawson, now 87, was just recovering from pneumonia and has been staying in his sister's home.

We will be glad when we can see him enjoying the big porch swing under the Dawsons' trees here in Bluemont again.

Henry Tumblin of near Bloomfield has returned from Loudoun Memorial Hospital this week.

Our deepest sympathy is extended to the Gibson family on the death of Carl's mother, Mrs. Kate Gibson.

The Methodists of the town saw each other twice on Wednesday with first a WSCS meeting at Mrs. Winnie Kelley's and then a meeting of the administrative board on Wednesday night at the Walton Manns.

Don't forget all those boys and fathers interested in reforming the Boys Scout Troop should meet at the school at 8 o'clock.

The troop has been discontinued for little over a year now but at one time boasted three Eagle Scouts, Pat McKay, Walter Loope, and Tom Mann.

There are mountains here that want "a-climbing" so why not join up, boys?

Speaking of mountain climbing, the big scoop of the week was the Lloyd Loope's report on their fabulous trip to Mexico City, Mexico.

In the first place, they were the guests of the Butler Manufacturing Company of Kansas City, Mo. Lloyd distinguished himself as the outstanding salesman of the year of the Jamesway Division of Ft. Atkinson, Wis. Only two other salesmen were thus honored.

They stayed at the beautiful Maria Isabelle Hotel of Mexico City, took in a Folk Lore Ballet and bull fight and highlighted their trip with an eleven-hour tour on Indian paths up between the two highest peaks of the country, Popocatépetl and Iztaccíhuatl.

Mrs. Loope said it was a breath-taking sight to see those snow-covered volcanoes that extended skyward for 17,000 feet and they went as high at 14,000 feet coaxing the automobile along to villages where the natives had never seen an auto before!

How delighted we are for them that they had such a unique experience. I know our little Bluemont foothills look very tame indeed in comparison.

Well as Mr. Nesmith says, less than a week till March dawns, so chirp up everyone!

March 13, 1969

March came in, pushed and shoved by the wind and snow and many more howling days are expected.

We are fairly sheltered here in the village but at the mountain estates it is high adventure.

About this time last year we visited the Rockwood Foster's "Rockwood" at the top of the mountain. With the roar of wind about us, we had the sensation that we were at the ocean front in a high gale.

Mrs. Foster says she loves it wild like that; last year they even got in some skiing.

I'm slightly disoriented this week, since through no fault of mine or the Times-Mirror, the column did not appear last week.

First I will give last week's items and then this. A special apology to Frances Ballenger who telephoned with this rather exciting item.

Natives of the village may recall Miss Mary Elizabeth Jones who spent summers here with her late aunt, Mrs. Nimrod Mercer. Mary Elizabeth, now Betsy Jones Moreland, makes her home in Hollywood Hills, Calif., and has appeared in television dramas and films.

Her first cousin, Ambrose Moreland is a Bluemonter yet and Betsy or Mary Elizabeth, as you like, appeared in a major role on "Ironside" this past week. I believe she must have been Judith who was the villain in the drama. Right?

Mrs. Gail Kelley was delightfully surprised by a group of friends including the school bus driving gang for her birthday last Friday.

Mrs. Barbara Allder celebrated her birthday last week too, with a dinner at Robert's mother's, Mrs. Margaret Allder of Herndon.

We can no longer claim Peggy and Jerry Lloyd as our own as they moved from their caretaking cottage on the mountain to Main Street, Round Hill, on Saturday. Of course, they'll still be close by and visiting a great deal in the Bluemont limits with Jerry's parents, the Glen Lloyds.

My telephone tingled with a number of soft, musical southern accents this week all issuing news.

First of all, we are most concerned that Mrs. Wesley Carbaugh underwent open-heart surgery last Thursday at Georgetown Hospital. Friends will want to encourage her with cards and letters, I know. We know she is receiving excellent care at this outstanding hospital.

Congratulations to the new grandparents, Mr. and Mrs. G.W. Townshend. Their daughter and husband, Mr. and Mrs. Wendell Rothgeb of Beltsville, Md., became parents the second time around with a boy to join daughter, Karen.

Mrs. Smyra Holland, the painting instructor, announces that another party will be given on Apr. 4 with Mrs. Lawrence Dawson as the hostess. If you have any questions about the new product, you may call Mrs. Holland at 226-4231.

The Robert Beetons attended the Republican State Convention in Roanoke last weekend. Mr. Beeton was delegate from Clarke County. The 12-inch snow in the Roanoke area detained them for a day but they returned Sunday having experienced a merry late-winter outing.

Featuring a lecture on Loudoun's Codes and Ordinances, the Home Demonstration Club met at Shirlee Carbaugh's last Thursday.

Two of the children returned home for a short visit to the R.M. Peytons this week. Son Ralph of Remington, Va. came for the day Wednesday, and daughter Sadie was home from Madison College over the weekend.

Doris and James Allder entertained Doris's brother and wife, Mr. and Mrs. J.D. Dawson of Arlington on Friday evening and Saturday evening they had dinner guests of Floyd Allder, Barbara Jean Allder and Ray Mauck who was Barbara Jean's special guest from Baltimore.

The monthly meeting of the Citizens Association was held on Friday night at the old school house.

Mrs. Judy Casey, the Glen Lloyds' daughter, now of Lincoln, gave a lovely "coffee" for all those members of the Women Sports Teams in the County at her home on Thursday evening.

It all sounds like a lot of fun with children and husbands rooting the ladies on; there are eight teams and Bluemont needs a pitcher, catcher and a few other positions, so if you can leave the dinner dishes in the sink this summer, join up with the Loudoun County Recreation League of Women Athletes!

"The woods are lovely, dark and deep,
The snow's so wet,
That it won't keep.
But March isn't through yet so beware!"

March 20, 1969

Oh, I know you've heard the birds chirping madly, "there's blue in the sky again and the sun is shining, but don't be fooled, spring comes late to Northern Virginia, late and sometimes never.

From winter to summer is often the story and many a blizzard has been known to blow in March; one of the worst storms in the east that downed power and telephone lines for a week occurred during the columnist's spring vacation.

There's a spring vacation coming up in our family this week, so…

Marvin Reid showed me a fascinating old post card several weeks ago. It was of the old empty store front in town, weather-boarded and with shutters. There was a barber shop at the back with a stripey pole, a general store and post office in the complex.

Horses were hitched under a beautiful shade tree across the corner where the present post office stands. A fashionable woman in a large picture hat and long dress was mounting the steps and several carriages stood awaiting their drivers.

Clayton Hall has a new fact now or maybe I should say an old one revisited. Apparently the old stone kitchen front wall has not been seen from the road for a number of years. An old photograph showed a frame room in front where the garage just removed stood with a frame porch to match across the front of the main house. Mrs. Dawson says she remembers the frame room and they have lived here for over 25 years now.

Roy McClaughry whose crew did the fine roof job seems to think the kitchen may have been the original cabin on the property. One workman found an old book up under the eaves; wouldn't it be interesting to know why it had been placed there and hence forgotten?

Of course, Mrs. Ingrid Jewell Jones is our own imminent historian and with her permission from time to time I would like to quote from her Old Bluemont Houses which she has recently compiled. Her research indicates William Clayton lived elsewhere in town before he built Clayton Hall.

Mrs. Wesley Carbaugh is making marvelous progress after her recent operation; also Clarence Manuel has returned from Loudoun Memorial Hospital.

The Citizens Association promises a travel film by Air France for its next monthly meeting.

Other meetings were the Softball League's organizational meeting at the school on Monday and the WSCA meeting at Mrs. Wayne Wynkoop's on Tuesday.

The Home Demonstration Club looks forward to a special meeting for April at Skyes Hall featuring an expert's comments on drug addiction.

Bluemont welcomed Tom and Ruth Mann again to the Walton Manns and son Willie of Gaithersburg, Md. to the R.M. Peytons this week.

The Robert Joneses paid a visit to their daughter and husband, Mr. and Mrs. William Anderson and grandchildren Valerie and Todd last Sunday. Ellen said they ran into a swarm of snow flurries on the way to Alexandria but it cleared into a pretty day by the time they returned to mountainous Bluemont.

The weather dawned bright for the Round Hill Women's Club Luncheon and Fashion Show last Thursday.

Our own Mrs. James Brownell did all the hard work of preparing delicious chicken salad and tasty treats while Bluemont guests of Mrs. Earl Virts, Mrs. Earl Iden, Mrs. Edward Willkie, Mrs. McCall (another one of those spry 86-year olds) and myself sat back and enjoyed the feast and show.

Commemorating their first anniversary, the chic fashions were supplied by The Door of Fashion, Purcellville.

If I could have motivated myself (the sleeping sickness has set in again) I should have saluted the Irish of Bluemont individually but since I didn't let me just say to all the Irish, I hope you had a happy "St. Patty's Day!"

March 27, 1969

This town is absolutely a hum with activity; the tractors groan on through the days and most of the women are convinced that the men are trying to burn the village by night.

The buds are a pink glow on the fruit tree and the jonquils and irises are pushing up through the now-thawed soil and at last grass in on the way.

It seems safe to say that spring is just around the corner and Bluemont is rejoicing in its own way.

Most of us are mourning the death of Miss Maria Copeland who was well-known in Bluemont even though she maintained the Copeland homestead in Round Hill.

Her true age was a mystery but her zest for life and boundless energy were a revelation to all who met her.

She visited here in the fall at the art show and declared that she would like to see Clayton Hall again before she died as she had been acquainted with Dr. Turner's daughters in her girlhood and visited here.

She was a most fascinating guest, relating legends of the house, pointing out craftsmanship with a quick wit and sense of humor.

Now we are pleased to hear that Mrs. Wesley Carbaugh has left the hospital and is visiting with her brother and sister-in-law, Mr. and Mrs. William Costello of Arlington for several weeks before returning to her home here.

Welcome to the Huffs who have just moved to our community.

The Softball Ladies met again on a county-wide basis at Valley High School on Wednesday. Thus far ten regulars have signed up for the Bluemont team but if you would still like to participate, Mrs. Joan Wilt can give you information.

There were two St. Patrick's birthdays this past week: Jack Allder and Wesley Carbaugh.

Wesley Carbaugh was entertained with a birthday dinner at his son's family, the William Carbaughs and Jack enjoyed a cake with Doris and James Allder.

Hazel Reed had a number of guests this week.

Mr. and Mrs. Robert Meredith of Richmond were our guests last weekend and we hardly had to leave Bluemont to entertain them.

April 3, 1969

The earth extends hope in its growing things this time of year and Easter with this same message of hope will be observed in our community this weekend.

Along with the Hillsboro charge, the Bluemont Methodist Church will sponsor a sunrise service at 5:30 a.m. at Pierrot's on the hill. Coffee and doughnuts will be served afterward and it should be a very inspiring occasion.

The four-day weekend for school children will afford a perfect time for softball practice and those interested in the Girls Ponytail League for ages 8-19 should meet at the Bluemont School on Apr. 7 at 4 o'clock. For any additional information, call Mrs. Alice Hays who will be the coach at 226-2521.

Already winning several practice games was our Men's Team who played the last two Sundays with Upperville at Marshall.

Featuring a discotheque atmosphere and taped music, the James Brownells played host to the Loudoun Dance Club in their lovely ballroom at Whitehall Farm several weekends ago. It was a very gay evening, indeed!

Area residents will be pleased to hear that Robert Fox Boxley, Jr. and his wife will be returning in the next week from Michigan State University in Lansing where Robert just earned his Ph.D. in Agricultural Economics. They will be making their home in Arlington where Robert is employed at the Agricultural Department in Washington. We anticipate many Bluemont visits.

All the Madison crowd is home for the spring vacation. Barbara Jean Allder, Sadie Peyton, Jean Dawson and Susan Brownell.

Also the Jay Kelleys are enjoying their visit with their son Sam who is home on his spring vacation.

On Mar. 13, the A.H. Martzs encompassed another member, when son, William, took as his bride Miss Joyce Crows of Kearnsville, W.Va. The couple are making their home in near-by Hamilton. Visiting the Martzs this past weekend were daughter Cindy and husband, Walter Core of Virginia Beach.

The Robert Joneses entertained son Carroll and family of Baltimore this past weekend.

The John Carters involved their guests in a fun game of horseshoes when Mary Ann's sister Frances Sims and family of Landover, Md., brother Sammy Smith and family of Winchester and Mrs. Ann Hill of Brunswick, Md. gathered at Mountain Shadow last Sunday.

Mr. and Mrs. Donald White and family were Mrs. Bessie Carter's dinner guests on Sunday.

There's another woman driver in our midst now; Miss Rosa Peyton is now a licensed driver.

Hope you didn't miss Loudoun County Day at Oatlands, and go easy on the Easter candy. Call me with your "coming-ins" and "going-outs."

April 10, 1969

The chocolate eggs have oozed into the tablecloth, the colored eggs have been consumed in a tedious week of egg salad, potato salad and hard-boiled breakfasts and the Easter bonnet has found its appointed box again as Easter has hopped on its way for another year.

Certainly though the holiday provided time for many family gatherings in Bluemont.

First of all, Justine and Brian Beck invited their cousins, Debby Lynn, daughter of Mr. and Mrs. John Minneci of Manassas and Karen, daughter of Mr. and Mrs. Dennis Settle of Oxen Hill, Md., plus grandparents, Mr. and Mrs. Paul Grove of Lovettsville, to a grand Easter Egg Hunt in the backyard.

Barbecue and baked beans were the fare for the day and it made for a marvelous family get-together.

The Lloyd Loopes welcomed home sons David from Duke University, Durham, N.C. and Walter from VPI, Blacksburg. I bet the beautiful Duke gardens are in full blossom now, eh, David?

All the Peyton children settled in at the homestead for a surprise birthday dinner for their mother on Easter. This included Willie and wife, Shirley from Gaithersburg, Md., Ralph and wife, Bobbie from Remington, Va., Delano and family from Mt. Jackson, Va. and of course, Sadie home from Madison and Rosa.

The James Walshes were pleased to have Alec who teaches in Manassas here for the long weekend and then they all went up to Philomont for Easter dinner with Mrs. Walsh's parents, the R.J. Lakes.

Another big family, the James Brownells, were together around the Easter table. Sons Jimmy, Bruce, Mark and Scott and daughter Susan home from Madison College were present besides Grandmother McCall. Jimmy will be departing for basic training in Ft. Jackson, S.C. on the 18th of this month.

The Robert Joneses entertained son Carroll and family from Baltimore for Easter dinner.

Sorry to hear Agnes Allder had to spend part of Easter Sunday in Winchester Hospital where she will undergo an operation this week.

Easter wouldn't be Easter to us unless Mrs. Johnson brought us a lemon meringue pie baked by Mrs. Robert Washington, one of those marvelous Lovettsville cooks. So we had the pie and steak here on Saturday, and Sunday went to Bethesda to Grandparents Porterfield for roast beef. I couldn't convince anyone to have a traditional ham dinner!

Some of the pre-Easter activities included a week's stay from Mr. and Mrs. Wallace Chappell of Atlanta, Ga. to Sonny and Betty Colbert. The Chappells had brought Wallace's mother, Mrs. Ada Chappell of Pine Grove home after she had spent the winter months with them. Daughter, Willa Colbert, a Valley High School student, just returned from the Southern Interscholastic Press Association Convention in Lexington.

Mr. and Mrs. Lawrence Dawson and Mr. and Mrs. H.G. Stearne made the trip last week to pick up Jean Dawson from Madison, also Mr. and Mrs. Ralph Peyton and daughter Rosa attended Parents Day last Friday at Madison with daughter Sadie.

Jim Walsh is teaching the 4-H electricity class at Banneker School near Middleburg and brought his class of thirteen last week to his Bluemont home to inspect his marvelous electric train layout and demonstrate the principles of electricity there.

The Clyde Becks appreciated a dinner at the Brown Mortons of Waterford who are restoring an old home there. Interestingly, Mr. Morton is an historical architect.

Mr. and Mrs. James Allder had guests of Mr. and Mrs. George Dawson of Hamilton, Doris' parents and her aunt, Mrs. Ethel Dawson of Leesburg on Thursday night.

The Citizens Association will meet this Friday, Apr. 11 at 8 o'clock at the school.

The softball ladies held another meeting on Monday evening at the school with manager Donnie McCarty of Pine Grove.

Speaking of teams, Libby and Henry Stearns along with Larry Dawson attended the opening game of the big teams, the Washington Senators and N.Y. Yankees at the Washington stadium on Monday.

Here's the line-up of that winning Men or Boys Team (they can't decide what they should be called). Managers are Denny Underwood and Robert Wines, Catcher Ray Goode, Pitcher Jimmy Emory, 1st B. Wayne Johnson, 2nd B. Jimmy Campbell, 3rd B. Robert Wines, SS Ricky Underwood, RF T. Bird Thomas (sounds like another one of those nickname stories!), CF Denny Underwood and LF Bobby Allder.

In the first practice game with Upperville, Jimmy Campbell and T. Bird scored a home-run and Denny Underwood slammed two over the fence.

We don't have a fence at the Bluemont field but it is an extremely pleasant spot with a lovely view of the rolling hills sloping up to the mountain. See you there! in June when the regular season starts.

April 17, 1969

Lofty spring temperatures and the accompanying fever struck our village this week.

There were bright forsythia in bloom on Mrs. Powell's fence-row, a pussy-willow tree laden down in the Dawson's yard, a dazzling clump of jonquils at Ruth's Home and a mass of beautiful red tulips bursting at the Becks.

The fever showed itself on Monday night with the lighting of the Christmas Tree at Ruth's Home and on Thursday with Mrs. Powell extending her spring cleaning to the porch roof while lawn chairs sprouted out in almost every porch and yard.

College students bid farewell to the spring recess and returned to classes.

The Madison girls spent their vacation in diverse ways; Sadie Peyton said she did a lot of sewing, Jean Dawson went here, there and yon and in particular looked for a summer job; Susan Brownell threw a party for some of her friends and Barbara Jean Allder rotated between Bluemont and Baltimore visiting those dearest to her.

If you wish to peer into these clear spring skies, a stop by the Richard Woolmans is a must.

Son Guy, a senior at Valley High School, has assembled a six-foot telescope that stands in the front yard. It was two years in the making as he even ground the lens himself.

Thus far, they have spotted Jupiter and the nails in the neighboring barn. Guy has been accepted for the fall term at VPI, Blacksburg.

Sorry to have overlooked another one of our teenager's entry in the Miss Loudoun County contest. Beverly Kelley, a junior at Valley High School, was sponsored by the

Loudoun Golf and Country Club where she has worked at the snack bar the past several summers. Although she didn't receive the title, she's a winner to us.

The Sewing Class sponsored by the Parks and Recreation Program began last Wednesday night at the school, Mrs. Shirlee Carbaugh played hostess to the Women's Missionary Society of the Methodist Church this past Wednesday morning.

The Ponytail League is reminded of their practice on Friday, the 18th at 6 o'clock at the school field. More participants are welcome.

I have just found out that the Mann store dates back at least to 1871 as Emma and Walton Mann found inventory lists when it was owned by a Mr. Silcox.

Another historical note brought out in the community was that a Dr. Evans had opened up a drug store in the present Lawrence Dawson home 50 years ago according to the Loudoun-Times column.

The old store front has added a new dimension to its history as it was deeded several weeks ago to the Robert Joneses. When are the weatherboarding and shutters going up, Ellen?

Allen and Billy, sons of the John Carters, escaped the slow pace of Bluemont for the stride of Purcellville and Bolivar Heights, W.Va. respectively when Allen took in movies and skating while visiting his grandmother, Mrs. Jack Barber and Billy saw new sights over the long weekend with the James McCauleys.

Grandmother Mrs. Bessie Carter is staying two weeks with her daughter and family, Mrs. Juanita White of Summit Point, W.Va.

Glad to receive David Spring's address and please drop a line when you possibly can.

Sp.-4 David W. Spring, HA529-17878, Battery A, 1st BN., 5th Artillery, 1st Infantry Div., APO San Francisco, Calif. 96345.

James Brownell's mother, Mrs. James V. Brownell of Key West, Fla. arrived on the tenth for an extended spring visit at Whitehall Farm.

I have never editorialized before but the time has come!

McCall's magazine tells of a town in Ohio called Dammit that posted a sign, Dammit Slow Down.

I've wanted to paint that sign for Bluemont ever since I moved here. How can Cinder Beck survive the summer? Next time it might be one of the children. So Dammit – Slow Down!

April 24, 1969

Last Friday was very special to me. Jennifer spent the day at Potomac School, McLean and while the twins napped, I took my solitary tuna sandwich and glass of ice tea to the front porch and watched the town go by.

What happened?

It was drizzling and every house, bush and tree was bathed in that incomparable soft green; several plump robins pounced by and nodded Hello, Allen Campbell went by in his new pick-up truck, there was a delivery of bread to Mann's Store, a station wagon slowly rounded the curve, the driver appreciatively gazing at our blossoming cherry tree and Mrs. Nellie Powell sat by her window watching too.

I was glad we didn't have to worry about the tourist traffic but at the same time, wondered if they only could know what they had missed in dear ole Bluemont.

Serenity was not the order of every day last week, however, as Miss Brenda Havener, daughter of Mr. and Mrs. Don Bowman, can testify as she was thrown from her horse last Thursday and suffered an injury of a broken collar bone.

Mrs. Joan Wilt has really been whirling with round after round of guests for the last two weeks.

Her cousin Mrs. Charles S. Swetnam of Alexandria has been their house guest, in addition she entertained on Thursday Mr. and Mrs. Charles Wood of Alexandria, Mrs. Russell Parks, Sr., Mrs. Robert Allder and daughter Yvonne, Mrs. Russell Pearson and son Robbie, Mrs. Donnie Hope and son Beecher, Mrs. William Kelley and son Lance and Lee Wynkoop at the Tastee-Freeze and Mrs. Hubert Sisk of Purcellville.

Sunday guests were Mr. and Mrs. Thomas Wynkoop of Hamilton.

There was a birthday party, snacks at the Tastee-Freeze and luncheon, at Battletown Inn during this time, too.

Martin and Joan along with Mr. and Mrs. Merle Gray and Mr. and Mrs. Donnie Hope of Bluemont attended the wedding of John Sleeter of Hill Top Orchards to the former Miss Mary Boyce of Round Hill. The wedding was held at the Purcellville Episcopal Church with the reception at the Laurel Brigade Inn. The couple will be making their home in Airmont.

Mr. and Mrs. Earl Iden and daughter Mrs. Earl Virts attended a wedding this last week too. Miss Jean Sarrew Iden became the bride of Doddridge Hewitt Biaeett, III at the Berryville Methodist Church, reception following at the George Washington Hotel in Winchester last Saturday.

The Idens, of course, are our terrifically energetic senior citizens.

Another future wedding announcement came this week when Mr. and Mrs. Leroy Thomas Virts of Bluemont announced the official engagement of their daughter Susan Lorraine to Warren James Spencer of Haymarket. No definite date has been set for the wedding.

Miss Jill Reed had two house guests for the weekend, Miss Charlotte Fitzwater of Purcellville and Miss Donna Underwood of Bluemont. They took in the boys' game at Upperville on Sunday.

Other sports news is that the women will be practicing on Mondays and Thursdays at 6 o'clock with their first game on May 24 here at Bluemont.

The Citizens Association voted to install a retaining fence at the ball field at the school and sponsor again the annual Fourth of July celebration with fireworks, cake and ice cream. Love those strains of small town, U.S.A.

The Sewing Class enrolled 17 students with Mrs. Nancy Cockerell from the County Agent's Office instructing.

To Agnes Allder, be assured we are all concerned and trust that your good health will return soon.

Jean Dawson and Barbara Jean Allder were home from Madison again this past weekend.

I saw a heart-warming sight this week; Mrs. Susy Neal's grandchildren were frolicking gaily on the green grass beside the drive and the apple tree in bloom behind them framed their merriment. Picture that in your mind and perform your own spring rites while these delightful days linger into summer.

May 1, 1969

At this time of the year with the apple, pear and cherry trees in bloom plus the beautiful native dogwood and violets, violets everywhere, I picture Bluemont as Snickersville.

It goes back to all those romantic tales we've heard of the Civil War and of course, Snickers Gap is linked with Mosby in the history books.

Mrs. Jones' history which she acknowledges to some extent came from Jean Herron Smith, former owner of the Scot Butler's stone home, says that Bluemont was officially Snickers Gap from Jan. 1, 1807-1824 at which time it was established by the Virginia legislature as a town and called Snickersville.

Snickers, Edward, that is, was an innkeeper, ferryman and plantation owner and according to Nichol's Legends of Loudoun, a captain serving without distinction in the French and Indian War.

Nichols goes on to tell the charming little story that Snickers being zealous for the American cause, rounded up some of his Quaker neighbors and marched them to Valley Forge where Washington was enduring that unforgettable winter.

Washington, however, dismissed them and said he would not want them to go against their convictions but rather they should remain on their land and grow crops which could feed the starving army.

Thus, we rambled from the Civil War period to the revolutionary but anyway can't you envision a young lad in blue presenting a sprig of lilac or bouquet of wild violets to his sweetheart before departing for the encounter with the enemy here in this rolling countryside?

So sympathetic to the Southern cause was this area that Mr. Nesmith's tale of a Davis who owned the present William Carbaugh house and was the only Snickersville resident to vote for Lincoln and vote against secession, is noteworthy.

Davis, prone to take evening walks, was never seen again after election eve promenade although wells and old foundations were searched and woods combed.

We still are designated as Snickersville precinct too when voting time rolls around.

Nevertheless, returning to Bluemont, 20th century, and fighting young men, David Spring called home from Vietnam, well and safe this week and Jimmy Brownell now finds himself with the National Guard at Ft. Benning, Ga.

Mrs. James V. Brownell, Sr. of Key West, Fla. underwent a cataract operation this week at Winchester Hospital. It seems she will be joining the Brownell clan here in Bluemont permanently.

Mrs. Barbara Spring's mother Mrs. Sadie Goss of Lucketts is spending several months here in our community with her daughter.

Also, Mrs. Spring had the pleasure of entertaining her young grandson Donnie Spring of Herndon this past weekend.

The Bluemont Home Demonstration Club was responsible for the bake sale at the Oatlands Exchange on Saturday. I know someone got some real goodies.

The Methodist Church has officially purchased a new organ and promise an organ recital for May with special choir music, too.

Visiting in our blossoming town over last weekend were Mr. and Mrs. Wendell Rothgeb, children Karen and Daniel of Beltsville, Md. who are the G.W. Townshend's daughter's family.

Tom and Ruth Mann were here again, the Herb Littles, Scot Butler, and Mrs. Louise Cauffman and brother Lewis Reed took to their mountain homes in Bluemont. Glad Peggy Little can return to enjoy her gorgeous dogwood trees dotting their piece of mountain after her bout with a broken hip.

Of course, a marvelous outing for any one this past weekend was the Philomont Horse Show and incidentally the horse population has swelled by one as Brenda Havener's horse foaled this week. This isn't the same mare that threw her by the way.

Clyde Beck is exhibiting several of his paintings at the Mall at the new Tysons Corner Shopping Center under the sponsorship of the Vienna Art League this week.

Word is that the proposed new Route 7 will provide a new access road to Bluemont eliminating the Coates' house.

I told the boys they must find another house here as we can't let an up-and-coming comedian like Alvin leave?

The railroad said that the name Snickersville wasn't appealing enough to tourists but I think it has character. Don't you?

May 8, 1969

Spring compels many of us to do something about the dingy walls, dirty floors and unkempt closets so Mrs. Brownell is cleaning closets, Mary Ann Carter is polishing floors, the Jack Allders have painted their house, the Sam Joneses built a patio, the Charles Tyrolers called the carpet cleaners and the Dawsons, Peytons, Martzs are planting gardens.

Then there are a few that despaired so that they moved on as the Charles Weedons who went to Lovettsville.

These are the ambitious ones among us but on the whole, the lethargy in this town is downright refreshing.

All last year, I suffered from a guilt complex as my energetic neighbors were refinishing, antiquing, fixing, scraping, planting while all I scraped was mud and grease off the rug (we had an old car then, too), all I fixed was baby formula, all I wanted to plant was a few winks of sleep in my eyes.

Living here in Bluemont I am content to know that Wayne and I got the windows washed this week.

What's that song "It's so peaceful in the country?" That's for me!

These weekends the weather has been so perfect that Bluemont drew Mr. and Mrs. Eugene Beck and Mrs. Anna Beck of Charlottesville here for a visit with the Clyde Becks. Of course, they are Clyde's brother and wife and his mother.

The John Carters and James McCauley and Miss Margaret Powell of Bolivar Heights, W.Va. ambitiously accompanied nine children on an outing last weekend to Keys Ferry, W.Va. where they swam, fished and soaked up quite a bit of sun. Right, Mary Ann?

Besides the Carter children there was Charlotte McCauley, Susan Dennis of Lazy Acres here and Dale Reed also of Bluemont.

Jimmy Campbell wishes to announce he is now a licensed driver and there's a Ford in his future. A 1950, that is!

Sorry to hear Donna Kelley injured her arm this week.

I heard the Boys were to play the Women last Thursday but someone "chickened" out. Anyway, the Boys start off the season on May 19 with a home game.

Mary Ann Carter celebrated her birthday Saturday night with a big party at their house, Mountain Shadow which was the one-room Bluemont school-house at one time.

Mrs. Elizabeth Kelley, whom you natives know well, attended school there and then taught there herself until the time it closed.

She has in her possession the old school bell which she believes to be about a hundred years old. She graciously wishes to have it returned to Bluemont.

Earl Bealle, formerly of Clayton Hall called last Sunday. He and his wife Lotta (Dr. Turner's daughter) now reside in Falls Church and have promised to pay us a visit soon. Now in their seventies, they lived here about fifty years ago and it charmed them then as it does us now.

Mrs. Jay Kelley told me this week she had a sampler made at the Snickersville Academy (Susy Neal's log cabin in 1826).

If we keep it up, maybe we can have our little museum and historic tour.

May 15, 1969

The snake tales are abounding in the village again and there are a few of the creatures showing themselves in garden plots and at back doors.

Even I saw a black snake (harmless, they say, a friend – in fact) in the back yard. Let a woman see a snake and her imagination goes wild, I've seen that snake in the baby's crib, on the stair landing and under the kitchen table but actually I think he is in the basement. I've never darkened the door yet and don't expect to.

Johnny Carter did see one in their basement.

The best story comes from Peggy Little who kept a pet black snake around their place for several years, feeding him milk in a saucer and naming him Junior. Peggy claims she got a name or two herself out of some workmen up there when she said, "Look at that sweet expression on his little face!"

Bud Canard's accounts last year of the ten rattlesnakes found on the Foster's stone porch, driving away the summer tenants, filled most of us women's hearts with horror.

Mrs. Mann too, is capable of a story or two, as she answered a visiting gentleman's inquiry about a piece of property he had purchased sight unseen. She gave him directions that included passing an old church foundation volunteering to him that during the summer months it was a den for rattlesnakes.

The man rather hurriedly left the store, remarking that he believed he might sell that property having never seen it.

My father, too, who delves into Civil War history, read that recruits talked of the rattlesnakes of Snickers Gap.

I know our population figures are low, and this might be one of the reasons. Maybe we better start counting the snakes.

The William Carbaughs went fishing this week and caught two colored carp, weighing five and ten pounds.

Of course, the big news of the week was the arrival of another Allder, Robert Eric weighing eight pounds, six ounces, born to Mr. and Mrs. Robert Allder. He kept us waiting for some time, right Barbara?

Two of our local girls participated in the annual Apple Blossom Festival in Winchester. They were Cheryl Ann Reid, daughter of Mr. and Mrs. Ralph Reid and Danielle Kephart, daughter of Mr. and Mrs. William Kephart. Both performed with the Loudoun County Marionettes.

The G.W. Townshends entertained a large group of guests last weekend. First of all was daughter Ann and husband, Mr. and Mrs. Wendell Rothgeb of Beltsville, Md. and their children, Karen and baby Daniel. Then William Townshend of Washington, D.C., Mrs. Naomi McCloskey of Port Charlotte, Fla., Mrs. Virginia Lyddome of Washington, D.C. and Mr. and Mrs. James H. Conklyn of Martinsburg, W.Va.

Also visiting last week with the Townshends were Mrs. S. L. Dodd and Mr. and Mrs. John Kreger of Moorefield, W.Va.

Tom Sixma and his family were here visiting his mother, Mrs. Alton Sixma. They came from Massachusetts where he is stationed with the Coast Guard.

The Sam Joneses enjoyed a lovely balmy Saturday with four Washington newspaper men and their wives with whom Mrs. Jones had been associated professionally until her December retirement.

Two ex-Bluemonters returned to their hometown last Sunday. Mrs. Jean Smith who you know owned the stone house next to Mrs. Powell from 1945-1966 was visiting her sister Miss Betty Herron of Washington, D.C.

Mrs. Smith, now of Dayton, Ohio drove out for the afternoon to see her former habitat. She searched old papers in both Philadelphia libraries and the Balch Library in Leesburg for historical information on Bluemont so you can see she was very much interested in our little community.

Secondly, we had an exciting visit with Earl Bealle, son Douglas, granddaughter Linda, and two friends from Falls Church.

He told me which rooms they had used, where two of his children were born in Clayton Hall, about the six horses he kept in the barn and then showed me a picture of himself at the age of 19 when he came to Bluemont and now at the age of 75.

He looked great both times! He came here as a railroad agent in 1916, snatched up Lotta Turner as his wife and reports of 2,000 people arriving here in the resort town on weekends.

He said the town looked about the same, of course, all the stores were in operation then and the post card that Martin Reid found must have come from about that time.

Hope they can visit again soon and bring Mrs. Bealle, a true Bluemont native, next time.

A word about some other local merchants, our William Kephart is the new owner of the Western Auto in Purcellville and Jack Grubb is exhibiting Clyde Beck's paintings along with his original reproductions in his new addition next to the present store. Clyde won second prize in the Tysons Corner Exhibit, by the way.

There was some more baking going on this week in town as the Methodist Church Women had a bake sale at the Safeway on Saturday to benefit the organ fund. Who made those delicious chocolate oatmeal cookies? I'd like the recipe.

I missed the County Garden Tour this year so I took my own in Bluemont. I know Mrs. Martz's tulips can't be equaled. Why not see for yourself?

May 22, 1969

What did I get for Mother's Day?

Well, I got two pair of orthopedic shoes, size 5½ D, and 4½ E, a pair of boy's sneakers, size 8½, a 1¼ wrench, and two boxes of animal crackers.

My egg money arrival coincided with the Mother's day weekend and everyone had plans for Mother's check.

Oh well, Tracey said Mommie consistently, for the first time, Jennifer said, "I love you very much," and Lara is always sweet so what more could a Mother want?

Hope you fared as well?

Isabelle Dawson said she was treated to a dinner at home when her four children whipped up some strawberry shortcake for her and Lawrence.

Mary Ann Carter got flowers and two dinners out on the town while Emma Mann was treated to a restaurant dinner too.

From my observations Bluemont seems to have either five or eight children families. Lucy Martz asked me if I just had four. I groaned yes as I felt twins were double-duty and she went on to tell of a relative who has 22, three sets of twins among them. Wherever she is – I hope she had a good Mother's Day, in fact they ought to honor her for about a month out of every year!

The Methodists are in a frenzy of activity raising money for their brand-new organ; the bake sale last week yielded enough for one month's payment and the MYF is currently selling those sumptuous candy bars with plans for pop and cupcakes to be sold at the ball games with the boys starting their season on Monday night.

An inspiring music dedication service was held at the church on Wednesday evening at 7:30 with visiting choirs of the Hamilton Youth Choir and Round Hill Adult Choir participating along with the Bluemont Choir renditions. In addition, Ralph Cochran, brothers, Phil of Purcellville, and Allen of Berryville provided special music.

Socially the Charles Tyrolers had the event of the week with their lovely party featuring delicious dips, tidbits and drinks in honor of Miss Phyllis Wright, Director of the National Humane Center of Waterford.

Miss Wright and her associates stressed the importance of being a responsible pet owner and that they have some lovable animals just awaiting a good home at the Center. If you have any problem with any animal, including a llama (Peggy Little said since it was the "In" thing, she might get one), call them. They are establishing a library and welcome visiting groups.

Carolyn's circle of white tulips two feet tall were another must on my self-selective Bluemont garden tour spots.

I raided my neighbor's yard for some flowers for my own front porch when I entertained Mr. and Mrs. Allen Carlsen and son Norman of Prussia, Pa., and Mr. and Mrs. Bill Thompson of Baltimore for a porch picnic. These were my college friends and spouses and we hadn't seen each other in ten years. Now don't try to figure out my age!

Sam Kelley was home visiting for the weekend with his parents, Mr. and Mrs. J.J. Kelley and sisters, Beverly, Gwen, Donna and brothers Hunter and Glen. See, another big family.

Mrs. Leon Brunelle of the Homestead at Skyline Orchards and neighbor and friend dropped by for a visit with more historical news on Sunday.

Thelma spoke highly of Mrs. Jane King, now deceased who owned the boarding house called Touchwood during Bluemont's peak years as a tourist trap. The name came from the Canadian meaning a touch of woods.

The William Deeley's, present owners have chosen their own name, Twinview, for the house built in 1919 that provided tourists with weekend and summer entertainment, even featuring a dance pavilion for Saturday night recreation. Thelma says she recalls visiting there as a child, having to sleep on the floor as the house was full to overflowing with guests in the summer.

Life was slower then, it was enough to sit around singing and chatting together and then eat a three-course meal before retiring in the cool mountain air.

But we are not a village to glory in our past; Jim Brownell says he will see Mr. Wiggins in Leesburg this week and give us details about the proposed road after he looks at the map, and have you caught that divine fragrance of the locust trees as the breeze drifts through the open windows?

May 29, 1969

The birds are in a frenzy building nests, capturing juicy dinners for their young and flying into my house!

There have been two delegations; one destroying a bottle from my collection on the window and two window panes.

It seems they resented the large amount of copy devoted to the snakes (by the way, Wayne almost stepped on a big black snake in front of Mrs. Virts' on Tuesday night) and requested equal time.

Well, I will say they are the friendliest bunch of birds I have ever seen; Mrs. Dawson has a nest right under her roof too. There are nests behind our shutters in the porch pillar and in the attic ledges but I believe the living room and kitchen ought to be off-limits.

Natives and former students will be pleased to know of a reception to be held in honor of Mrs. Elizabeth Kelley at the time of her retirement at the Round Hill School on Sunday, June 8 from 4 to 5:30 p.m. You are invited and we hope to see her visiting among us more next year when she is free from the pencils and the books.

If it is labeled Bluemont, I look again so I see there was a quarter horse show at the Bluemont Center, five miles from Rt. 7 on Rt. 50 on Sunday. Did anyone go? Tell me all about it.

Mrs. Glen Lloyd's family reunion was held last week at Lovettsville Game Club. Most of the children of the John Neffs now live in Loudoun County and there were close to a hundred at the clan gathering.

Kay Costello, the future daughter-in-law of the Lloyds, was honored the same day with a wedding shower. Larry Lloyd and Kay have set the date for July 26 at the Upperville Methodist Church.

All the neighbors are at their neighborly best with Shir Carbaugh passing out mint plants and Mrs. Peyton donating some lettuce and radishes to the Johnsons. She also has some delightful strawberries she's selling.

I had a lovely Thursday afternoon visiting my former Leesburg neighbors, Mary Lou Hook, Jean Brown, Shirley Boltz, Ada Slavens and Helen Lewin who lunched with me at Clayton Hall.

If you ask enough people, long enough around here, you're sure to get an answer so I finally found out the tall trees with purple flowers now and pods all through the winter are called Paulownia or Princess or Empress Trees named after a Russian princess. They extend as far as New York state and are very plentiful in Harpers Ferry, where tourists keep asking the same question.

I'm still kind of a tourist in Bluemont myself, so please bear with me.

The Boys Softball Team took a hard fought defeat at the hands of Hamilton with a score of 4-3 on Thursday night.

Guy Woolman took a picture of the moon with the aid of his telescope this week so you see whoever we are, Bluemont or Snickersville, we're space age!

June 5, 1969

The birds chirped softly, the honeysuckle fragrance evoked nostalgic youthful days in the country to the correspondent, the haying season was in full spring at the Brownells. L.W. Robey and Bud Canard floated some lyrical guitar notes on the breeze while the Summers and Coates teenagers danced in the street to welcome the long, hot summer to Bluemont.

Shir Carbaugh celebrated her birthday with a surprise cake and family softball game which included the grandparents. I didn't quite get it straight who opposed whom but Lynn's team won!

John Campbell, four-year-old son of Mr. and Mrs. Allen Campbell held a gay birthday party with his local young friends.

The Fourth of July will be rolling around soon and with it will be the annual ice cream and cake festival.

There will be games at 6 o'clock and fireworks at dark.

The Methodist Church which furnishes the ice cream and cake is asking for a loan of an ice cream freezer or a donation of some homemade ice cream. Call either Mrs. Roberta Underwood or Mrs. Ralph Cochran. Contributions for the feast will benefit the organ fund.

The Citizens Association meets this Friday night, June 6 at eight o'clock at the school.

You've heard the expression, "flat on your back." Well, that's just what the doctor ordered for Lawrence Dawson as a cure for an ailing back. Let's hope the cure took for his sake. Sorry Clarence Manuel had to return to Loudoun Memorial this week.

The only visitors in town that I heard of this week were the Townshends guests of William Townshend and Mr. and Mrs. Robert Bean and daughter Janice of Washington, plus the Cochrans' guests of Mr. and Mrs. Robert C. Hindman of Hamilton and Mrs. Pearl Olson of Indian Head, Md.

Debbie Carter spent the long Memorial Day weekend with her friend Susan Dennis at Lazy Acres Farm, Bluemont, and Donnie Spring of Herndon was back again for a visit with his grandmother, Mrs. Barbara Spring.

The Madison girls all came home, one by one, after exams for the summer recess this week and wasn't it exciting to see Guy Woolman's picture on the front page last week?

The Boys' Team won over the Leesburg Adriannes on Monday by a score of 12-4 and then dropped a game to another Leesburg team on Thursday while the Women have a home game this Saturday night.

Jim Brownell has the proposed road map now and it's a fascinating document about erosion plan A. Mary Elizabeth Jones still owning property here (our movie star, you recall) and higher elevation for the new road.

Cinder Beck, may be saved as Rt. 734 is to be dead-ended thus no more pace-setting dump trucks; Hunter's Store is to be taken in exchange for a clover-leaf at the top of the hill but you better look for yourself as this is one of those fuzzy feminine approaches to the subject. The map will be at the Brownells.

In conclusion, I want to give my own little dramatic critique of the week. If you missed "You're a good Man, Charlie Brown" at the Shady Grove Music Fair, you passed up some terrific entertainment and besides we all have a little Charlie Brown in us, you know. This light musical was to run one month but stayed the entire winter season due to its extreme popularity.

And as for Shady Grove near Gaithersburg, Md., it was just a shady spot in the road where we high schoolers bought ice cream and sandwiches after football games and now look.

Of course, we've already hatched the idea of the Bluemont Summer Theatre in the barn. Wouldn't it be perfect? All we need is what is commonly known as a backer. Oh well, we don't like traffic problems in Bluemont, anyway.

June 12, 1969

"No more pencils, no more books, no more teacher's dirty looks." Yippee! School's out!

That's one point of view, the students' and teachers' but a few mothers are groaning with the prospects of muggy days of kool-aid mixing, bathing suit wringing and sand sweeping amidst the gleeful screams of children on vacation.

Oh well, the inevitable cookouts on paper plates will lighten the dish washing load at least and the children will be most helpful too. Gulp!

Our public school teachers and staff welcoming the stay-at-home days will be Mrs. Vedith Teasdale-Smith, assistant principal at Valley High School, Mrs. Alice Hays, secretary at Valley, Mr. and Mrs. Scott Douglas, he teaching Health and Physical Education at Valley, she teaching at Hamilton Elementary, James Deegan of the English Department at Valley and Mrs. Joyce Beck and Mrs. Jack Lightner, teachers at Round Hill Elementary.

Our hardy bus-drivers relaxing with their own brood for several months are Mrs. Gail Kelley and Mrs. Shir Carbaugh, so you see the school recess changes the lives of quite a few of us here in the village.

Several of our college crowd are lining up summer jobs, Susan Brownell will be employed at the Loudoun Memorial Hospital in the nursing line and Jean Dawson will be in the "salad" line at The Portals restaurant at Dulles Airport.

Sadie Peyton is taking some summer courses at Madison and Barbara Jean Allder will be visiting with her boyfriend's family in Baltimore for the next week.

Exciting news is of the graduates.

Miss Marguerite Verloop, daughter of Mr. and Mrs. J.H.H. Verloop of the Mt. Weather Road, after three years at Madison finishes this year at the Medical College of Virginia at Richmond.

Graduating from Valley High School were Sharon Ann Lee and Frank Robert Wilhelm, daughter and son of Mr. and Mrs. Richard D. Wilhelm, Kenneth Howard, son of Mr. and Mrs. James Howard and Guy Woolman, son of Mr. and Mrs. Richard Woolman.

A number of Bluemonters were honored at the Athletic Awards Assembly at Valley High School. Jimmy Campbell received a letter in wrestling, Timmy Reed, a letter in cross-country and track with recognition as the outstanding senior in track.

Jan Woolman was awarded a school letter for outstanding participation in the Girls Athletic Association.

Academically, Guy Woolman received a monogram which is earned by maintaining a B average while remaining active in school activities.

Jan Woolman was privileged to be one of the two juniors to receive the coveted D.A.R. Citizenship Award while Nancy Gray of near Bloomfield received a scholarship in pursuit of a nursing career.

If others have been distinguished, please inform me as we would like to share it with the community.

The Community Vacation Bible School for the Round Hill-Bluemont vicinity sponsored jointly by the Methodist and Baptist Churches will be held from June 16-20, 9-12 a.m. for ages four through Junior High age with the Rev. Homer Hall acting as principal. If you wish more information, you can call him at 338-7287.

As for the sports news, the women have a 1-1 record losing to Round Hill 10-3, and winning their first game over Middleburg 4-3.

The boys' record is 2-2, winning Thursday night over Purcellville 15-4 with Jimmy Emory's pitching.

Joan Wilt's aunt, Mrs. May Swetnam of Alexandria returned for an emergency visit when Joan injured her toe while cutting the grass. I'm beginning to get that guilt complex again as I notice a number of the Bluemont women keeping the lawns trim.

The Charles Parks had a luncheon last Saturday entertaining the family, Mr. and Mrs. Russell Parks of Pine Grove, Mr. and Mrs. Gordon Arnett of Arlington, Mr. and Mrs. Clarence Crouch of Aldie, Mrs. Nell P. McMullen of The Plains, Mr. and Mrs. Melfore Parks of Round Hill, Bobby and Barbara Allder and Joan and children while Martin kept our Safeway running efficiently.

William Kephart has just been elected new Post Commander of the V.F.W. Post 4468 in Purcellville.

Wasn't it marvelous to see the activity around the old stone house of the Scot Butlers while their daughter took part in the Upperville Horse Show?

I'm on tour again with my little red wagon piled with the kids behind.

Aren't Mrs. Campbell's roses lovely on the bank? And the Carter's vegetable garden is a real beauty.

Johnny Carter told me it was the custom some years ago to have garden contests and their family won a contest one season. Let's have one here in Bluemont.

I'll be glad to be the impartial judge, of course, I'll have to sample all of the products!

And the cherries are ripe!

And to the Dads, Happy Father's Day.

June 19, 1969

Now I know why the Southern Railroad prevailed on the powers that be to redesignate Snickersville, Bluemont.

When the summer heat descends, it is usually ten degrees cooler here in the mountains and the green foliage on the hill deadens the glare of the sun and you feel cooler somehow.

It's a wonderful summer town and the blue haze of the mountain in the distance apparently gave some railroad man about 1900 an inspiration.

One of the most beautiful views in Bluemont of the blue haze is on the yellow schoolhouse road where the Underwoods, Parks, Peytons and Walshes are bathed in the shadow of blue.

Mrs. Townshend, our postmistress, tells me we are the only "Bluemont" in the country too.

A decade of Bluemont News

Life ought to be cleaner, fresher here in the country, but tragedy struck our town this week as we are all horrified that someone would wish to harm gentle, generous Luther Starkey. Naturally, we are all hoping for a miracle that Luther may return from Winchester Hospital in our citizenship again.

This must teach us to band even closer, if anyone sees anything afoot, call the police or another neighbor. Indeed we are our brothers' keepers. We want no big-city indifference here.

Regretfully, we have several others in the hospital this week. Agnes Allder has returned to Winchester Hospital and Baker Bayles was rushed to Loudoun Memorial Hospital with a ruptured appendix last Thursday night.

The Round Hill Elementary School honors were passed out the last day of school and the Bluemonters captured a number of them.

Special congratulations to Donna Kelley who received the Best Citizen of the Seventh Grade Award and to Lynn Carbaugh who won the D.A.R. Virginia History Award. Our own Mary Elizabeth Lightner, a member of the D.A.R. and Round Hill teacher presented the award to Lynn.

Donna Kelley also was the recipient of the DECO Mathematics and Science Cash Award.

Desiree Allder distinguished herself with the best poster for the Cancer Research contest.

Perfect Attendance Awards when to Donna Kelley, Desiree Allder, Jeannette Glass, Sandra Mitchell, and Jay Allder.

Timmy Dawson and Hope Lloyd were presented handwriting certificates for improvement in handwriting.

Representing Bluemont on the Student Council next year will be Hope Lloyd, a seventh grader as Donna Kelley presided as President this year.

Congratulations to those seventh graders graduating to the eighth grade and consequently high school next year; I was not able to obtain a complete list.

At last with the official announcement of Barbara Jean Allder's engagement to Ray Mauck, we can give our fondest regards for happiness.

Did you know Bluemont has a new industry? Bruce Brownell's saw mill right on Whitehall Farm and visible from the ball diamond will be filling orders very shortly.

I saw a number of my neighbors hauling treasures away from the highly successful Round Hill Fire Department auction and sale. Clyde Beck had paintings, chairs, dishes. Radcliffe Bell bought a nice set of dishes for his attractive yellow house on the hill, and Frances Ballenger towed away several loads of antiques. I've always said what Bluemont needs is a nursery (trees, that is), an inn and an antique shop and it looks like the latter may be forthcoming soon. Right, Frances?

What's sweeter than a puppy? Nothing to me, so we adore our newly acquired little dachshund whom we named Snickers of Snickersville. Mrs. Jones pointed out the highway department erroneously left Snicker singular so we have put the plural on our doggie. Won't you come and meet Mr. Snickers?

Keep in mind the Democratic Party Primary Day on July 15 for Governor opposing the Republican candidate in the fall. Candidates are Howell, Pollard and Battle. Voting will be held at the schoolhouse.

Tom Mann leaves this week for Indian Town Gap, Pa. for the University of Richmond R.O.T.C program.

Miss Florence Maitland, a former resident and retired teacher, is back from St. Petersburg, Fla. for the summer, enjoying the greenery surrounding the Waldrops' summer place.

Mr. and Mrs. Lawrence Dawson and daughter Jean paid a visit to Lawrence's father, W.V. Dawson and aunt, Mrs. Ora Moody of Annandale this week.

The Boys dropped two games to Lovettsville and Lincoln so they now stand at 4-2 record-wise.

Most of us take pride in our community so the peppering of the schoolhouse window violates our good neighbor policy and threatens the continued public use of the schoolhouse.

Utopia doesn't exist anywhere but we've got a plait or two on the drawing board here in Bluemont so let's keep it that way.

June 26, 1969

Wildlife abounds right here in the corporate limits.

Now the bug-life has flown, crawled and buzzed-in in legions.

First, the gnats claimed Bluemont as their own, then the wasps and bumblebees, then in the earth, there were ants – big, black ones and the beetles that roll into a ball that we loved as kids and now the friendly lightning bugs baffling scientists with their cold light and delighting us all, are profuse on these warm evenings.

The butterflies aren't too plentiful; they like dark, dank mossy areas but the mosquitoes find the village an apt environment for raising their young.

Remember to empty rusty tin cans of water if you wish to discourage the mosquito population.

Life has generally been very serene; the Glen Lloyds were feeding 19 for dinner the other night as daughter Linda is home with two guests, Miss Leatha Otey and Miss Carol Ann Dillard of Roanoke and all the family came for a get-together.

With Frances chauffeuring, Vicki and Randy Ballenger and guests Wayne Johnson, Marsha Dodson of Berryville and Sandi Longerbeam of Pine Grove spent Monday at Colonial Beach.

The women's team suffered a set-back when short-stop Shelia Tapscott of Pine Grove was injured by a ball that broke her nose in several places.

The boys lost twice this week so maybe a little Bluemont rooting section would cheer them on to a victory in their new uniforms that finally arrived.

Virginia Woolman at the Purcellville Library guided me to a fascinating little book this week called Loudoun County and the Civil War which I noted with in…Continued… Part II missing.

July 10, 1969

Bluemont's "glorious Fourth" has come and gone again for another year and what could be a more appropriate way to show our appreciation for our American heritage than by meeting at the old schoolhouse in the shadow of the blue mountain with friends and neighbors and to consume gallons upon gallons of homemade ice cream (the chocolate flavor even washed out of Jennifer's dress!) and rounds of Methodist Women's cakes and then when darkness came to "ooh" and "ah" over the Citizens Association fireworks?

We were please to become acquainted on this occasion with our new superintendent of schools and his wife, Mr. and Mrs. Robert Butt, now of Country Club Hills near Purcellville.

Everyone was there and didn't Jill Reed look terrific in her red, white and blue outfit?

Head Start swung into action this week and now thanks to my guide, Mary Ramey, I've been meeting my neighbors in Howardsville, Unison, Bloomfield, St. Louis, Willisville and several other little spots in the road that all boast an official name. We're at Banneker School and would welcome any visitors or volunteer workers who might like to share a hobby or interest with us sometime before the closing, middle week of August. Call me if you are interested.

There's lots of activity here in Bluemont too now with the Parks and Recreation program on Monday and Thursdays from 9-12 a.m. featuring drama, dance and music and arts and crafts and an afternoon session on Monday and Wednesday of sports from 1-4 p.m. for ages 6-18.

Speaking of sports, the Boys lost one and won one last week and the Women had an All-Star game on the 7th at Purcellville under the lights.

Keeping the town hopping again over the weekend was L. Robey and Friends who provided the music for a lively dance at the schoolhouse Saturday night and the Methodists held their annual picnic at Camp Highroad just down the road on Sunday.

June was the month of birthdays and weddings, each of which occurred some years ago for several of our citizens.

Our Wayne notified Uncle Sam that he had become 18 and celebrated with a little strawberry shortcake amongst local friends on the 29th.

The Martz's celebrated their 47th anniversary on the 30th and son Ronnie and family treated them to a dinner at Battletown Inn while the Lawrence Dawsons admitted to 28 years of married bliss on the 29th as their children entertained them with a cook-out.

Big news around town last week was that Kathryn Frye had won the Mustang at the Purcellville carnival. Congratulations.

Emma and Walton Mann put on their walking shows and hiked from Front Royal to home on the Appalachian Trail last week. They met a fellow traveler who had started from Georgia a month ago and was fast approaching Maine. Wouldn't that be a marvelous adventure?

Sorry to hear John Hyland had a fall this week and is still resting at the Loudoun Memorial Hospital.

Mrs. Brownell has found a beagle-type dog if anyone has lost their pet.

The Carters and Wilts have been visiting and receiving guests this week.

Debbie Carter is spending several weeks with her uncle Norman Smith and family in Cabin John, Md. while guests to the John Carters, were Mr. and Mrs. Jack Barber of Leesburg, Frances Sims of Landover, Md. and Mr. and Mrs. Ike Carter of Upperville on Sunday.

Last Sunday the Martin Wilts entertained Mrs. Martha Wilt and his sister Vallie Wilt of Timberville, Va. along with Mr. Haruyuki Yoneda of Japan.

Joan's uncle and aunt Mr. and Mrs. Robert McDonald of Clearwater, Fla., were houseguests last week along with her aunt, Mrs. C.F. Swetnam of Alexandria.

Now that the sun has set again behind the mountain I wish I had another bowl of creamy homemade ice cream. See, I told you we ought to have our own ice cream parlor, right here in town.

July 17, 1969

The clouds blacken…the thunder rolls…the tree tops toss gently then angrily in the wind and then the hush falls as we wait for the summer storm. To me, there is always a great deal of excitement and adventure, waiting till the last possible moment to shut the windows against the cooling breezes and driving rain.

In Bluemont the mist on the mountain and the soft patter of drops on the tin roofs are a welcome summer phenomenon.

Traveling on the back roads, watching the rabbits spring from the gravel, catching a glimpse of fertile green rolling hills or the golden glow of a sunflower, I appreciate anew our beautiful Loudoun County. When I was exclaiming about the beauties of the countryside complete with grazing sheep one day while traveling on the school bus Alvin Coates asked me, was I "from the city or something?" Whatever the "something", I'm grateful for what my eyes can behold in our Bluemont backyard.

Now that the showers have freshened the gardens again, Mrs. Peyton has green beans for sale and Mary Ann Carter keeps on canning in the wee hours of the morning.

Libby Spinner turned 30 or so this week with two cakes, one baked by Elaine, and then there were presents from the children, too.

Mrs. Cochran and her committee wish to thank those who donated ice cream and cakes to the highly successful Fourth of July celebration. Did you know 24 gallons of ice cream were consumed that night?

Gone are the Clyde Becks this week to the celebrated Virginia Beach Art Exhibit where Clyde will enter his work along with entries from all over the country. Of course, a lot of sun and sand will be on the agenda too for the family.

Don't you like that light-colored gravel of Perry Engineering Company which the Brownells put to good use on their road leading from the farm to the lower part of town?

Donnie Spring of Herndon had a pleasant visit with this grandmother, Mrs. Barbara Spring, last week.

Naturally we were all very saddened by the death of Richard Underwood of our community whose children and their families live among us.

Young Debbie Carter has changed residence again as now she is visiting with her aunt and uncles, the Whites of Summit Point, W.Va. for several weeks.

Nature's own, housed by Clayton Hall for so many years, are reluctant to make a change of address so now the bumble bees have put up a resistance when we attempted to invade their nest in the porch roof but "progress" we will.

Our summer people are swelling the population these days; Mrs. Kathryn Hatcher and grandson William are up from Delray Beach, Fla. for several weeks; the Littles and Waldrops are here for the weekends and Mrs. Browning of Arlington joined the John Thomases for the Fourth as Delores Murray and her sister have been putting in weekend appearances.

The Seidenspinners, too, one of our nice young families on the mountain, say they can see the Washington Monument with a telescope "on a clear day."

All the Manuels are off for several days to Myrtle Beach, S.C. Where else would mountain people go but to the shore?

Now to any butterfly, moth expert, whatever your technical name – please come to our rescue. Patsy Arthur of Bloomfield, our Head Start driver, found a huge butterfly or moth right at the Banneker front door this week. Retaining it in a jar overnight, the next morning we were amazed to see a mass of newly-hatched eggs. On the advice of the Becks, we have administered cotton soaked in sugar water. Can you tell us what to do?

Call me at 226-2051. Ignorant teacher in distress.

July 24, 1969

It all came back this week…Do you remember the radio serial, Jack Armstrong, the All-American Boy?

Well, now it's Neil Armstrong, the All-American Boy conquering the moon! What a week in history!

Snickersville held its Democratic Primary on Tuesday and only forty-two out of a registered 160 Bluemont showed up. Let us do better on Aug. 19 when the run-off between Battle and Howell is held.

Although the heat has been extreme, villagers have been beating it with splash parties and escapes to the beaches.

Justine Beck had fifteen guests Monday to celebrate her sixth birthday in the cooling waters of her pool in the back yard.

James and Doris Allder and children spent a day at Hershey, Pa. – chocolate town, you know – and then went on to Cacapon State Park, W.Va., where they were joined by some other members of the family including special guests, Doris' sister, Mrs. Cynthia Wagoner and son Craig whose permanent address is Kinshasa, Africa. A Bluemont native, Cynthia, will be spending the summer here and will be joined in August by her husband and other son before returning to Africa in the fall.

Col. and Mrs. Taylor Holt are entertaining their four grandchildren, Markus, Adam, Seth and Sarah of New Haven, Connecticut for the summer.

The Walshes have a full house with sons Alec of Manassas and Jerry of the Air Force joining them for most of the summer.

Mrs. Walton Mann hosted a lovely wedding shower for Miss Barbara Jean Allder, daughter of Mr. and Mrs. Jack Allder on Friday night.

Barbara Jean was married to Ray Mauck, son of Mr. and Mrs. George Mauk of Baltimore, Md. on Saturday at Faith Baptist Church, Baltimore.

Another wedding in the community was that of George P. Freemans's granddaughter, Billy Joe Freeman, who was united in marriage at the Unison Methodist Church on July 20.

Mrs. Harry Dennis just returned from Arlington Hospital where she underwent a foot operation; meanwhile Libby Stearne is at the Loudoun Memorial Hospital.

Young Keith Arthur celebrated his ninth birthday last week with a barbecue and movie session of "The Swiss Family Robinson" among friends including sister Lori's guest, Nancy Wright of Cleremont Farm and Thomas Rose of Middleburg.

The Arthurs also entertained the Lynn Wilsons of Chattanooga, Tenn., and the John Elkins of Bluemont on Sunday for dinner.

Joyce Ann Cross is visiting her grandmother in Purcellville for the summer.

We're all missing the Spinner family, which has moved to Lovettsville.

Put Aug. 9 on your calendar as the day of the Methodist Rummage and Bake Sale to benefit the organ fund down at the schoolhouse.

Have you seen Bessie Carters's string beans strung on a line? It's an old West Virginia recipe, I hear.

A half-dozen tired Boy Scouts hiking from Harper's Ferry on the Appalachian Trail found Bluemont a fine spot at the end of the line on Saturday.

Well, our butterfly departed this world, leaving behind hatching larvae and no one has rescued me with the needed information. Help!

July 31, 1969

Air conditioners run day and night, multiple salt tablets are sold over the drug counters, evening rides are taken to the country and mountains and that's where Bluemont's story begins and ends because it's sweltering.

Our twins Lara and Tracey celebrated their second birthday Sunday with Grandparents Johnson of Paeonian Springs. The next six months are crucial with four little hands grabbing, grabbing and my threatening to post a sign in the front yard, "Beware of Mad Woman."

Two births right here in town – the Harry Coates became the parents of a daughter, Harriet Charleen, and Connie and Wayne Wynkoop now have a new son.

Coming home from the hospital this week was Libby Stearne but John Hyland remains at Winchester Hospital.

Herb Little said it looks as if he will have to postpone his Bluemont vacation till September but he and Peggy did get in a long weekend just passed.

Johnny Cowgill of Winchester, Jimmy Campbell's nephew who interestingly is the same age, has been visiting his uncle the last several weeks.

I've heard of stray dogs, stray cats, stray cows, even stray kids but the Brownell's stray buzzard was a first for me. Bruce, rescuing the injured fowl, kept it on a string when a Westerner showed up at Whitehall farm and began to wonder about these crazy Virginians. The Human Society of Waterford volunteered to confine "Buzz" until he could make it on his own so now the Brownell family must ask about visiting privileges.

I see the new apartment in Airmont is practically ready for occupancy.

Little Unison was making the scene politically last week and it certainly is a pretty little spot with the red geraniums dotting the landscape. I saw a beauty of another old stone house over there too.

After my recent first visit, I asked Mr. Nesmith how it got its name. He said there were two stories, but the one he favors was that during the Civil War it was composed mainly of Union sympathizers and thus their uniting or standing in unison behind their cause provided the village name which leads to the two spellings, Unison (on the store sign) and Unision on the country road map. The map is a handy document to have in your possession on your first visit too.

Readers may be interested in Cynthia Wagoner's comparison of Africa living versus State side existence. She said food was frightfully expensive there but the native fruits like bananas are so superior that her children refuse to touch the store-ripened variety here. They have their skyscrapers like our cities but due to the political unrest, their quarters are guarded. Help has not gone out of style there and Cynthia has the equivalent of a maid and butler and of course, they must have air conditioning in such a climate.

Maybe it's not really so hot here after all.

August 7, 1969

Do you have that "soup-bowl" feeling?

These daily showers keep the atmosphere moist but still we won't complain as August can be a long and hot month yet.

Walton Poston in Unison is already saying it's drier than last year but his tomatoes certainly aren't proof of it. The plants are five feet tall already and the tomatoes are gigantic. Last year he said they weighed two pounds and Mrs. Poston put up 100 gallons of produce.

The big event in town this weekend of course, is the Methodist Church's rummage, bake and miscellaneous sale starting at 10 o'clock Saturday at the schoolhouse.

Kitchen utensils are being solicited too and if Bluemont women can clean out their attics and closets and pass the treasures on to any of the women of the church, the organ fund will advance.

Visitors in town this week were Bessie Manuel and children of Fayetteville, N.C. visiting with her in-laws, the Clarence Manuels and the Robert Hindmans of Hamilton who celebrated their 54th anniversary on Thursday with their daughter, Mrs. Ralph Cochran.

Mr. and Mrs. John Milleson of Berryville entertained the James Walshes for a good ole get together before Jerry leaves for Da Nang this week.

Two birthdays this week, Lynn Carbaugh who already is trying to keep it a secret and O.H. Nesmith on the other hand, pleased to be able to admit to his 86 years.

Almeata Reid of Howardsville recently returned from a three-week stay in New York City and Linda Underwood and Jill Reed are back after a fabulous trip to their cousin's wedding in Nashville, Tenn.

J.S. Reed of Leesburg was wed to Patricia Fitts of Nashville before some 700 guests.

On the return trip Jill and Linda toured the Smokies and visited the Cherokee Indian Reservation in North Carolina.

The Reeds had houseguests Mrs. Estelle Reed of Gwynedd Valley, Pa., and Mr. and Mrs. James W. Marcus and family of Gwynedd Valley last week. We're pleased to know that Grandmother Reed keeps up in Pennsylvania each week.

Libby Stearne is really quite a news-liner. I knew she had been to the hospital but missed on informing readers of the outstanding honor paid her in a special ceremony conducted by Major General Robert B. Shera, Chief of Army Dental Corps.

Libby is fulfilling her position as dental secretary to Deputy Chief of the Corps. Col. John C. Kepper and was distinguished for her outstanding rating and sustained superior performance.

She wishes to thank all those who remembered her with cards and gifts while she was in the hospital.

In our rural setting here, we love our pets so the nine little piglets in assorted colors of the Carbaughs and Sue Dawson's new puppy, Chuck are most welcome.

I was fascinated to hear of Ralph May's collection of civil war relics found mostly in the locality of Snicker's Gap and Pine Grove. We must get a picture for the Times-Mirror soon.

Aren't these old piled stone fences lovely? They always bring back a mental picture of the Civil War to me. I see so many on my travels but our own Wilts have a beautiful one just outside of town.

Think on Stevenson's little lyric and be delighted with our present weather.

"The rain is raining all around
It rains on field and tree
It rains on the umbrellas here
And on the ships at sea."

August 14, 1969

After last weekend's storm, came that delightful weather of bright skies with big, cumulous clouds, the kind that are shapes of a sheep's body, a horse's head, a pig's foot. There is a noticeable briskness to the air. This weather I choose to call Canadian summer as the colder northern influence seems to be felt.

Summer days still linger but not for long; Head Start concludes this week but not before we had a marvelous visit with the James Walshes exhibiting Jim's fabulous electric train layout this week.

While shifts of children watched trains whizz by, others romped on the lawn and I admired Betty Walsh's seven-foot sunflowers growing in profusion and the blue mountain vista.

Again I was sure the people on the yellow schoolhouse road had the best view in Bluemont including the Roy Santmyers whom I met the other night. They are two of our oldest natives but very youthful in appearance and spirit, he telling me of the mail carrier's duties in horse and buggy over 25 miles of rough road in 1926.

The Glen Lloyds are sitting back on their comfortable front porch now after seeing son Larry to the altar in the Upperville Methodist Church on July 26. Jamie and brother-in-law Bill Casey were ushers and Mary Jo was the flower girl for Upperville's Donna Costello's wedding. Larry having built a home there is now an Upperville resident and what a quaint pretty little town it is. Of course, that is where many of our horse people reside and this week was the exciting Saratoga Horse Sales.

Hospitalized now is Agnes Allder at Winchester Hospital and John Hyland is now in residence at Shawnee Nursing Home. John Carters game of "horse" got Bluemonter's attention, I'm sure.

Not so exciting as the "horse" sales but fun anyway, was the John Carters' game of horseshoes with dinner guests, Frances and Eddie Sims and children Theresa and Scottie on Monday.

Mary Ann's brother, Norman Smith and son Timmie were weekend guests from Cabin John, Md. joined by Mr. and Mrs. Jack Barber of Leesburg and Melvin and Judy Carter of Winchester on Sunday.

Mr. Nesmith had a Bluemont bake-sale cake and ice cream among friends, the Waldrops, Florence Maitland and son Bernie on the Clayton Hall front porch last week to celebrate his 86th birthday.

The Waldrops are off to Asheville, N.C. now but plan to end the summer in Bluemont for the Labor Day weekend.

George Parker of Wheaton, Md. came out last week to improve his Bluemont property where he sees deer occasionally. George, a dear school friend of the Johnsons discovered the charm of Bluemont first and then we followed close on his heels a year later.

Another who joins the ranks of Bluemont admirers is Mrs. Mary Carter now of Statesville, N.C. who has just departed our village after a month's stay with son Robert's family welcoming a new grandson, David Mason Carter born on July 8 in Winchester Hospital.

A Loudoun native she leaves Bluemont with thoughts of meadows of dandelions and daisies, pitchers of cool lemonade, porch-screened voices, lawn-locked laughter, crickets' rusty cackle, vines of roses climbing up trellis and the wide blue sky, which seems to be just a little bluer here.

What could be lovelier than to be remembered so poetically by letter?

I'm getting closer – to the ice cream parlor – that is. Got an old churning freezer this week and Shir Carbaugh has supplied me with the Pine Grove recipes, the Methodist Ladies', the Carbaughs' and I'm still looking for the good chocolate I had on the Fourth. I'm learning a few secrets, the finer the ice, the smoother the cream.

Now that the June apples are here (even though it's August) here's a simple recipe we love at our house.

To make a quick delicious cobbler, melt a half stick of margarine in a flat cake plan (butter if you wish to be affluent), add a cup of flour, a cup of sugar, a cup of milk, two teaspoons baking powder mixed together.

In a sauce pan, cook pared apples over low heat with sugar and cinnamon till softened.

Pour hot fruit (will work with any substitute, of course) on dough mixture.

Bake in oven till dough is done (it bubbles up around the fruit) at about 400 degrees.

Don't forget to cast your vote in the Democratic run-off on Tuesday, Aug. 19. Let's improve that record.

August 28, 1969

Now the Bluemont gardens are yielding up their high quality fruits; the Brownell's corn couldn't be sweeter, Mr. Martz's lima beans couldn't be bigger and the Carter's tomatoes couldn't be more flavorful.

Of course, Mr. Martz is really a grand champion in his own right with ten-foot tomato plants, an exquisite trellis of lima beans and plump Bermuda onions.

At the age of 71, he's still going strong with five gardens.

Besides his garden growing this week, he killed two rattlesnakes in one day at the Tyrolers' mountain home.

The Tyrolers are the envy of us all now with their new swimming pool.

Bluemont's claim to fame has always been the simple pastoral life it seems, as Florence Maitland says even during the tourist peak days, post cards of Bluemont pictured grazing cows.

Had a nice chat with Karlton Monroe of near Unison last week. He interestingly has a collection of antique farm implements and relics that spell country living of yesteryear.

Guests taking in the country living of present day Bluemont this week were Charlie Gee of Bethesda visiting Bill and Winnie Kelley and Beth Miehm now of Alexandria visiting with Donna Kelley. The Miehms are sorely missed as they were such active members of our community for a number of years.

Vicky Hart, the Martzs' granddaughter from Florida, has been here for about a month.

Jill Reed entertained her friends Donna Underwood of Bluemont, Judy Sibel and Ann Williams of Berryville last Saturday night at a slumber party.

The Lucien Reed family also hosted a cook-out for the recent bride and groom, J.D. and Patsy Reed now of Emory, Va. and included Linda and Donna Underwood last week.

Mr. and Mrs. Burvie Arthur of Bloomfield attended a farewell party at Quantico Creek for friends shipping out to Vietnam last weekend.

"Stop the World, I want to get off" means I need a little change of scenery so several of our families are vacationing; the William Carbaughs in Canada (I told them to take their warm clothing), Gail Kelley and offspring Donna, Sam, Hunter and Glen joined by Rhonda Underwood to Hershey, Pa., and the Louis Underwoods brushing up on their history in Williamsburg for the week.

We had an urge "to talk with the animals" so Jennifer's fourth birthday and Grandmother Johnson's birthday were celebrated at the Washington Zoo on Sunday.

As usual the humans visiting proved as fascinating as the animals visited. One gentleman had a large shopping bag full of assorted treats for the various animals, he calling each one by name and they responded instantly so it was plain to see he was a frequent visitor.

The James Piersons of Bloomfield are proud new grandparents of a baby girl born on July 16.

Congratulations to John and Jamie Dodderidge, sons of the Robert Dodderidges of Myrtle Hall Farm, on their excellence in the tennis matches sponsored by the Loudoun County Recreation Department carrying them to the finals in Purcellville this week.

Well, in case you're interested our Head Start butterfly was a Black Walnut moth, very rare to this part of the country and last Wednesday a groundhog popped his head in the door so you see it's about time we dropped this expression, "Dumb Animals."

September 4, 1969

The days have been pleasant, the nights lovely with the bright patches of moonlight warming the rooms and a dark silhouette of a mountain hung low in the sky here in petite Bluemont.

Talk in the town this week has mostly centered about two tragedies, the destruction of hurricane Camille to our neighbors in Richmond and Charlottesville and the sudden death suffered from a heart attack of our Stanley Reid.

We can contribute in the Red Cross fund and extend a helping hand to Bonnie Reid in our typical small-town-way to show concern for those who suffered these losses.

We are also distressed to hear that Herbert Martz encountered a fall from his tractor sending him to the hospital and that Beverley Kelley had an operation on her arm which has been bothering her since she fell from her mount last year and that Baker Bayles and Lee Cook are patients at Loudoun Memorial and Newton D. Baker Hospitals, Martinsburg, respectively.

With the Labor Day weekend just passed and the opening of school, families were out for a last summer fling, some visiting Bluemont and others leaving for their winter homes elsewhere.

Florence Maitland took off for Florida, detained by a day when her cat wished to linger, finally he was found and they were on their way from Dulles preceded by son Bernie and Gilbert Dawson motoring ahead, hoping to enjoy some days of surfing before summer was done.

The Walton Manns had a trip to Cleveland, Ohio last week, the Loopes had their usual fabulous camping trip to the West and the Becks came back from Charlottesville with reports of the awful sights of flooding, ruined property and loss of life.

Ada Cook, daughter of Mr. and Mrs. Lee Cook, has just returned from a month's visit in Hartford, Conn. with sister, Rosie.

Coming to marvel at our clear skies this week were the Robert Joneses and son Carroll and family of Baltimore, Mr. and Mrs. Jonas Hose of Moorefileld, W.Va., visiting the Lee Cooks, the J.C. Stallards of Virginia Beach to see us and Ruth Alley's mother from Washington nestling in at Ruth's home.

You can take the girl out of the country but you can't take the country out of the girl, so the Townshends' daughter Ann and children came for the canning season, finding the local peaches, tomatoes, and apples just the right size for a quart jar. I, too, figured it was the thing to do if you're going to live in the country and if I can find some alum for Elizabeth Kelley's seven-day pickle recipe from the Bluemont Cookbook, I ought to have a few spicey treats this winter.

Speaking of treats, Mrs. Lloyd sent up some of her homemade ice cream and that heavy cream must give it that special "Bluemontness." Even with Bob's excellent churning, the evaporated milk version didn't come up to the Bluemont standard.

Another Bluemont institution may be pony rides. Milton, Alvin and Donald Coates after breaking a pony for the Leffingwells enroute to Stanley Kelley's stopped off here delighting Jennifer and the Beck children with a bareback round.

Junior Sisk's tomatoes perched on the windowsill look as big as pumpkins. Mrs. Townshend says, one slice would equal two regular-sized ones.

Happy School Days!

September 11, 1969

"There she goes, Miss America,
There she goes, My Ideal."

Every year it's an absolute must on my social calendar; I guess I get a vicarious thrill out of it all. Well, I have three daughters who might be on their way to Atlantic City someday. Who knows? Bluemont ought to be represented, don't you think?

Now that the kids are shut up in school, the days here are fairly quiet and one can watch the wild morning glories and abundant marigolds grow (they were Senator Dirksen's choice for our national flower, you know) for amusement and at night the mosquitoes sting and the groan of the trucks keep the evening eventful.

There's really just a trickle of news; Lawrence Dawson's 87-year old father is visiting from Alexandria, sporting a marvelous tan and quick step; Mrs. Bessie Carter seems in good health after her involvement in an automobile accident where the car overturned.

The Lucien Reeds returned just in time for school and Mrs. Reed's school bus route after a visit with Mr. and Mrs. Bill Marcum of Gwynedd Valley, Pa.

Jill got some more cute fashions in the Philadelphia stores.

Herbert Martz was exhibiting his community pride this week by clipping the road frontage, bouncing right back after his fall from his tractor a week ago.

A few of the college crowd are turning thoughts to study as departure time looms on the horizon. The Loope boys will find themselves at the University of Utah and Duke. Walton continues his study for a Master's in Utah and Lloyd pursues a Ph.D. while David goes on with his undergraduate work at Duke. There must be a pretty impressive library in that pretty chalet on the mountain.

John Hylands' niece and family have been out trimming down weeds while John remains at Shawnee Nursing Home unable to climb stairs yet.

The Herb Littles sat behind their perfect big windows admiring the valley view again this weekend while the rest of us must beat off the bees if we want a peek at the mountain.

I informed the Becks that news was scarce so Clyde volunteered to produce some so he and Brian took a lazy boat ride on the Shenandoah River on Saturday but hurried home to beat the storm.

Mr. Nesmith likes to count the seconds between the thunder clap and lightning strike. These country pastimes give Bluemont its flavor that we appreciate so much.

Really, we aren't completely crazy, the additional canine you see prancing through the yard is just Barnaby, a Golden Retriever, vacationing in Bluemont while his family went further north to Massachusetts. Puppy-like he relished any stray garment as well as his Kennel-Ration. Yep, he loves it here – probably he'll want to bring the family out for weekends from now on.

September 18, 1969

Is it the height of Bluemont's Indian summer (the setting for every good horsie teenage novel) or nippy Autumn? The days debate but Autumn begins in earnest, I declare it to be the most delicious time of the year.

The signs are here – the Dawson's swing is down, the stick-me-tights or beggars' lace cling stubbornly to dog fur, cat fur and we human beasts, wood has been stacked handily for a morning fire and those beautiful yellow flowers blanket the fields.

The earth may be preparing its vegetation for a long winter's nap but the bite in the air sets the blood-a-tingling and it's great to be alive!

The nation and Loudoun County lost a dear friend last week in Senator Everett Dirksen.

Enjoying his ranch-style home, "Heart's Desire" on the Potomac River with his "Chipmunk Crossing" sign on the driveway, his beloved marigolds and diverse other flowers, we were pleased to see his chauffeured car pass almost daily, he raising his hand if we were near the road and generally being a good neighbor in Broad Run Farms.

Whatever he uttered was elegant and what a marvelous sense of humor combined with a sincere interest in and love for people.

With the season came the opening football game of Valley High School and Charles Town on Friday night and what's a game without the band, our own Maurice Gibson and Donald Coates joining in the music-making?

More of the college crowd departed this week. Jean Dawson, Susan Brownell, and Sadie Peyton are back at Madison and Guy Woolman begins at VMI.

The Citizens Association started the year anew with an election of officers and discussed plans for community use of the schoolhouse. Serving as president will be Louis Underwood; vice-president, Robert Jones. Remaining as secretary will be Mrs. Ingrid Jones and treasurer, Ellen Jones.

A workday for cleaning the grounds and schoolhouse is on the agenda near the end of the month.

I would like to propose a little Bluemont Fair, an unsophisticated day in the country with pony rides, dried arrangements, local art, antiques and homemade foods.

Wouldn't it be fun? How about next fall?

A few of our citizens have joined John Hyland at Shawnee Nursing Home; Luther Starkey and Bill Reid are also residents now.

Sam Kelley returned to his school, St. Benedictine in Maryland this week and Cynthia and Sydney Wagoner and two sons after a drowsy summer in Bluemont and Hamilton left via jet to Africa anticipating a lay-over in Europe before arriving "home."

The Robert Hindmans of Hamilton, parents of Ivy Cochran are spending some time with the family on their pleasant farm.

Walton Mann's mother from Hamilton is visiting with the Manns on the steep mountain road.

Mrs. Essie Carter suffered another accident, breaking her shoulder, and is now a patient at Winchester Hospital.

Cheryl Reid and Danielle Kephart relished the annual picnic of the Loudoun County Marionettes held atop Bull Run Mountain last Sunday. Mr. and Mrs. William Kephart and Ruth Reed were guests of the girls.

Do you like the TV talk show? Well, Chet Huntley with this talk on preservation on the David Frost Show inspired me to pick up the beer cans cluttering our school grounds. My little two-year old twins were enlisted to help "Mommie" pick up these few cans. Rapidly we had the little red wagon overflowing. It was really quite perfect there with the swings, green grass and mountain-view except for the cans poking up all over the place. Once the countryside is tarnished, there will be no getting it back.

Feel inspired yet?

September 25, 1969

Is there a hint of yellow and red on the mountainside?

The fire blazing cheerily in the fireplace feels good tonight.

Do you know what I do religiously every Sunday? Yep, I go and pick another grand bouquet of those yellow flowers.

It's the time of year we weed-women go crazy, gathering our weeds and arranging them in any handy pot.

Don't forget the Waterford Foundation dates for exhibitors and Sept. 29, 30 and the tour and exhibit will be Oct. 3, 4, and 5.

The Becks have their pine-cones bagged and the bitter-sweet a-hanging.

Some delicious baked goods will be available in front of the Safeway in Purcellville on Saturday, courtesy of the Methodist Women's Society.

The visitors are coming, the visitors are coming.

The Herb Littles have socked in here in the mountains for a three-week vacation and their daughter from New York is also filling her lungs with some fairly unpolluted air.

George Harrison, nephew of Mr. and Mrs. Marion Kerrick is here for a visit after having just returned from duty in Thailand.

Mr. and Mrs. John Thomas, Jr. from Texas settled for several days with Mother and Dad Thomas, Sr.

Barbara Jean and Ray Mauck, the newly-weds were here from Baltimore seeing the family, the Jack Allders.

The John Carters entertained Mr. and Mrs. Donald White of Summit Point, W.Va., last Saturday while Mrs. Bessie Carter is still suffering with her arm.

Congratulations to Jamie and John Dodderidge, sons of Mr. and Mrs. Robert Dodderidge of Myrtle Hall Farm on their championship in both the singles and doubles in the Loudoun County Recreations Department's Tennis matches.

The boys are now back at school at St. Paul's in Concord, N.H.

Libby Stearne had an operation this week at Loudoun Memorial Hospital and will be confined for about a week. Friends may wish to visit or send cards.

Glad that Thomas Martz has returned from Newton Baker Hospital in Martinsburg.

The Home Demonstration Club met last week at the school with reports of their progress of their achievement record. The second Wednesday morning of every month is their regular meeting day.

Clyde Beck took a little river safari in his boat on the Shenandoah, traveling from Front Royal to Berryville. We may see more of this adventure as he took his sketch book along.

The stick-me-tights are still sticking. They've been through the washing machine and vacuum and now have settled into the rugs and furniture, all to declare that Autumn is here and I saw three snakes (dead, that is) on the road this week so look out.

Met Mr. O'Brien of antique fame this week and told him Bluemont needed an antique shop and of course, ice cream parlor; his place would be perfect.

October 2, 1969

This Bluemont weather is down-right intoxicating.

Clare Booth Luce in her little talk on the David Frost Show this week said the industrial revolution caused men to take over the traditional home industries of the women and generally I'm sure that's true but the women in this town are absolutely terrific!

Shir Carbaugh is always on some creative enterprise, now refurbishing several pieces, Emma Mann molds candles, Isabelle Dawson sews and bakes, Betty Walsh is painting gourds and hanging her Indian corn, Linda Lloyd is using milk cans as end-tables in her new venture in housekeeping near Norfolk and to top it all June Lloyd is making apple butter in her yard in a big copper kettle!

Joyce Beck's aunt says the secret to storing apples is to arrange them in layers of newspaper in a basket or barrel.

With all the talent not to mention Ivy Cochran's decorative cake making, surely we could have a little fun with a Bluemont Fair next fall.

The Community Association meets tomorrow night so why don't we discuss it?

Henceforth any group wishing to use the schoolhouse must make a fifteen dollar deposit to the treasurer to be refunded if the school is cleaned within a week after the event.

Anyone wishing to meet the Democratic candidates for Governor, Lt. Governor, and Attorney General are welcome to attend the Democratic Party Barbecue on Sunday, Oct. 5, at 5 p.m. at the Purcellville Fireman's Field.

It was too pretty a weekend to stay on campus so Jean Dawson and Sadie Peyton along with six other Loudoun girls headed for the hills of home last weekend and the

Valley students are involving themselves in extra-curricular activities. Timmy Walsh was elected vice-president of the sophomore class and Larry Allder is now a member of the Future Teachers of America who plan to teach classes and observe teachers in other nearby schools. J.K. Cornwall plays guard on the J.V. football team with two wins thus far.

News of the servicemen is that Jerry Walsh just departed Bluemont after a week's visit with his parents, the James Walshes of Berkley Farm enroute to Da Nang but was pleasantly surprised with a stop in Hawaii. I hear they have some rather nice mountains there too.

David Spring, son of Mrs. Barbara Spring, now serves near the Cambodia border and just asks Mom to send some sardines and mustard. We always called those packages from home the "care" packages when I was in college and amazingly I always had a number of male escorts volunteering to assist me with my package to the dorm!

The great weather drew Judy and Bud Anderson of Alexandria out for a visit with the Robert Joneses, Judy's parents.

The Littles are finishing their final week of relaxation, having enjoyed many side trips in the area.

Scot Butler of McLean found the weather right for improving his lovely stone house by leveling the front yard and putting in a walk-way.

The Kenneth Cooks of Partridge Farm on the mountain top still delight in spending their leisure hours there, even though they have just completed their tour of the fifty states, ending with Alaska. I'd say that was quite a recommendation for old Bluemont.

Mr. and Mrs. Larry Seward of Richmond and Mrs. Lizabeth Cox of Surry County, were our guests on Sunday.

Alvin Coates is sporting a broken leg and Jerry Summers says he had something to do with it but I didn't quite get the story straight.

Granny Jones is now convalescing at Shawnee Nursing Home after falling and breaking her hip.

Wayne See has been confined to Winchester Hospital now for three weeks, undergoing tests.

Libby Stearne returned from Loudoun Memorial this week.

Lucky Lawrence Dawson won a Porter Cable and Skil Drill at the J.T. Hirst Lumber Company open house.

The Methodist Church is winterizing with a new furnace and storm windows, the walnuts are falling and now that the persimmons are on the tree, we're all waiting for the frost, warning the children as mothers warned us, as their mother warned them all down through history. There are better reasons to pucker up!

October 9, 1969

Suddenly it was Autumn.

The day was dark and rainy but the glare of the golden trees shone through the window and suddenly it was Autumn.

The corn stalks stood stark against the sky, the pumpkins sprouted overnight at the roadside stands; suddenly it was Autumn.

Talk was of frost, oil was in the tank, wood was in the bin, Denver got six inches of snow. Suddenly it was Autumn last week.

The chrysanthemums are budding, some of those golden-bronze are already out (my favorite – Mrs. Martz gave me a bouquet for my hallway now that the yellow flowers are gone), the potted plants are still on the outside window sills but there is some worry and Grace Dawson's night blooming cereus of 14 years blossomed out for its annual September show. Only blooming once a year all at one time, Grace acquired it from a friend who bought it from Trinidad; it even came out this year in the heavy rain beating the frost.

The animals were restless this week with one of Jim Brownell's beautiful Holstein heifers leading them on a merry chase back and forth across Rt. 7 and an Airmont pig has gone Marine.

Richard Jeffrey, son of Capt. and Mrs. K.L. Jeffrey of Lucketts and son-in-law of the Karlton Monroes near Unison, called home this week requesting a low-slung hog. The whole family has been enlisted to locate a suitable representative (he was found in a forty-acre field of the Dutrows in Airmont), design a marine outfit including harness for leading in the parade for Richard's O.C.S. graduation at Quantico. Karlton said he (the pig, that is) absolutely wasn't riding in the front seat of the car to the ceremony.

It brought to mind a comedy I saw once where some sailors were confiscating a pig for a Christmas dinner when they were stopped by the officer on duty.

Quickly they jammed a sailor hat on the pig's head and when the officer asked his name, he was identified as "Oink Smith."

The pig let out a grunt and as they drove off, the officer shook his head and muttered that Oink Smith is the ugliest sailor I've ever seen!

Of course, you did read Animal Farm, did you not?

Whether you want to face it or not, it's time to juggle the clothes in the closet again, swapping the cottons for the woolens and it might be a good time to rummage about at the annual Loudoun Hospital Rummage Sale today and tomorrow. I got a darling antique wooden tray there one year.

Interestingly, Grace Dawson who like us all complains of never being remembered on her birthday, received 46 cards this year.

Mrs. Pauline Cook near Bloomfield received her sister and husband, Mr. and Mrs. Frank Miller from Moorefield, W.Va. this week along with her father, Ashley Mongold for a visit.

Frances Ballenger and children Ricky and Vicky have joined us now in the village occupying the former Baker Bayles residence.

The town meeting was postponed until this week, still time to talk about the Bluemont Fair (aren't you already sick that you didn't take something to Waterford?) and the annual Halloween party. It's at eight o'clock, Friday evening at the schoolhouse.

Elva Cook, daughter of Mr. and Mrs. Lee Cook spent several days with her aunt in McCoole, Md. last week.

Our deepest sympathy to the many relatives in the area of J. William McCarthy of Airmont who passed away last week at the age of 83.

What is the little purple or lavender flower adorning the fields now? Could it be heather?

Newsweek says (it claims to be the country's most quoted magazine, so I'll quote it too) that the most contented people of the middle class are those who live in the country.

Inspecting a tree, flower, or brook is slightly more uplifting than watching the ants on a concrete slab. So you couldn't take a vacation this year, what is lovelier than a Bluemont autumn?

October 16, 1969

People say Bluemont is a summer place but it was this autumnal weather that attracted us to Clayton Hall and its stand of trees changing colors set in the midst of a sleepy Sunday village.

Yes, at last the Thomas Wolfe weather has come in earnest. It was always fall in Wolfe's books with marvelous descriptions of the beautiful scenery in mountainous Asheville, N.C. complimented by a breakfast of ham and eggs and fried green apples. Always it was Autumn and always he was hungry. What poetic language he put in prose.

The natives are out celebrating the rites of fall, now tramping the woods, riding the trails, and entertaining other natives.

A big family reunion and birthday party for Mrs. Georgia Payne of Frogtown on her 84th birthday was held last Sunday. Here's the list of those who partied: her sisters Miss Betty Elsea, Mrs. Katie Weekly with her daughter Evelyn Bly and Pauline Farmer and Mrs. Edna Hummer. Also present were Mr. and Mrs. Gerald Payne and daughter, Eunice, Mr. and Mrs. Julian Christ and daughter, Lisa, Mr. and Mrs. Tyson Payne with daughter Margaret Fincham and granddaughter Pamela, Mrs. Walter Heflin with her daughter Brenda Lloyd and grandson Darrin, Mr. and Mrs. Michael Payne and son Brian, Mrs. Gene Payne and son Ty, Mr. and Mrs. Joe Royston, Mr. and Mrs. Michael Santini with children Judy, Michael and Victor, Mr. and Mrs. Ronnie Graham and son Kenneth, Joe Royston, Jr., Mrs. Al Burgess, Mr. and Mrs. Drew Payne with children Kimberly and Crawford, Mr. and Mrs. Robert Alan McAllister with children Wanda Jean and Alan, Mr. and Mrs. Paul Downs, Mr. and Mrs. Paul Downs, Jr. and daughter, Dana, Mrs. Brenda Lowenbach and son Mark, and Steve Wynstrub.

Mrs. Gene Payne and son Ty near Philomont have been doing some of that horseback riding on the trails and it sounds like she's the perfect candidate for organizing our Bluemont Fair Pony Rides.

The Community Association met this week and reported it was all for it and busied itself with many plans.

The annual Halloween party is set for Halloween night at 7:00 o'clock at the schoolhouse with games, cakewalks, door prizes and prizes for costumes.

Chairman of the party is Mrs. Roberta Underwood. Mrs. Betty Walsh should be called at 226-4191 if you can supply some cookies for refreshment.

There was some discussion of providing a library for the community in the schoolhouse as a generous gift of many books, particularly history has been offered to Bluemont.

There will be films again this year and James Walsh was authorized to investigate the cost of providing central heating for the schoolhouse.

Walton Mann has the key for any group wishing to use the school and he will collect the deposit recording their name and date.

The Home Demonstration Club met last week, attempting decorations for Christmas trees and of course, on Monday "A Peek at Christmas" was held at Skyes Hall.

Betty Walsh gave her secret for preserving gourds; she just uses liquid wax.

The Birthday girls this week were Desiree Allder and Mary Jo Lloyd.

Mary Jo had a family party on Wednesday with eighteen and then on Friday her debut at age five with her young friends.

Guests were Tracy Rose, a cousin from Hamilton, nephews Chip Lloyd of Round Hill and Scott Casey of Lincoln plus Jennifer Journell of Lincoln, Pam Jenkins of Berryville, Bob Kelley, and Jennifer Johnson. It was a great party, complete with hats, honks, candy baskets, masks and polaroid pictures of every guest.

Judy Casey announces the opening of her knitting shop in her home in Lincoln, featuring free knitting lessons. If interested call her at 338-6057. Start your project now for the Bluemont Fair next October!

Mr. and Mrs. Martin Wilt entertained Mr. and Mrs. Joseph Everly of Alexandria, Mrs. C.F. Swetnam of Alexandria, Mr. and Mrs. Robert McDonald of Clearwater, Fla., and Mr. and Mrs. Russell Parks, Sr. of Bluemont last Sunday.

I admire ingenuity so J.K. Cornwall's homemade goal-posts are terrific and Lynn Carbaugh is active serving groups of hungry guests at both Waterford and at a banquet for the Milk Producers Association at Loudoun Valley High School as a member of the F.H.A. Yes, even a hot dog can be quite a challenge if the patron is fussy.

Of course, we all realize our own personal loss with the death of Luther Starkley this week, directly resulting from the beating he received supposedly by juveniles here in the middle of town this summer.

Education has been abandoned in four spots in our Bluemont limits – the Snickersville Academy, a quaint log cabin now inhabited by our dear Suzy Neal, Mountain Shadow – the abode of the John Carters, the old stucco structure now leased to the Bluemont Citizens Association and the yellow schoolhouse, frame now, replacing a stone structure so Mr. Nesmith says. All of them possess a good deal of charm.

Another interesting historical note brought to my attention this week was the fact that the concept of transporting milk by tank trucks was hatched right here in Bluemont. I want to find out more about this. Who knows?

Got a new slogan for Bluemont: Bluemont – the village that nature claimed. Of course, it probably wouldn't spoil the slogan, if we chopped a little of the jungle back along the road. What do you think?

October 23, 1969

"His stronghold was situated on the banks of the Hudson, in one of those green, sheltered, fertile nooks in which the Dutch farmers are so fond of nestling. Hard by the farmhouse was a vast barn, every window and crevice of which seemed bursting forthwith the treasures of the farm. Sleek porkers were grunting in the repose of their pens. Stately squadrons of geese and ducks were riding in an adjoining pond; regiments of turkeys were gobbling through the farmyard.

The schoolmaster's mouth watered as he looked upon this promise of sumptuous winter fare. In his devouring mind's eye, he pictured to himself every roasting pig running about with a pudding stuffed within it and an apple in its mouth; the pigeons were snugly put to bed in a comfortable pie and tucked in with a coverlet of crust; the geese were swimming in their own gravy; and the ducks pairing in dishes."

Recognize it? It's that perfect Halloween story of Washington Irving's "The Legend of Sleepy Hollow." Time to get it out again and become reacquainted with Ichabod Crane, Brom Bones, Katrina Van Tassel and the Headless Horseman.

Our own setting here in Bluemont is rather reminiscent of this description of the Hudson Valley.

You see, there's a lot of English teacher in me yet.

We think we have a pretty nice bunch of teenagers up here, too; Lee Ridgeway and Donald Coates came to my rescue this week when Snickers hauled in a dead chipmunk on the family room floor.

I hear the Halloween party in town will be competing with the Clarke County-Loudoun Valley football game for fans' attendance. Oh well, see you next year at the Halloween party!

Jean Dawson was home for the weekend and last Sunday Mom and Dad, sister Sue and Aunt Pearl Slye of Philomont visited at Madison in Harrisonburg. Libby did the chauffeuring to work on Monday after her post-operative period.

The Lawrence Dawsons also went to Annandale last week for a visit with Lawrence's father, W. B. Dawson and he will be returning their visit here this week.

The Clyde Becks had a houseful of guests on Saturday, the Becks of Charlottesville, Matriarch Anna Beck, sisters and spouses, Mr. and Mrs. Earl Graves and Mr. and Mrs. Lewis Herndon and brother and wife, Mr. and Mrs. Carlton Beck.

I saw a rather interesting record this week called the The Cavalcade of 1953. That was the name of the Lincoln High School Yearbook.

The county had four high schools then, one at Aldie, one at Leesburg, one at Lovettsville and at Lincoln.

Superintendent O.L. Emerick, at the time, proposed the consolidation at Leesburg and now with the dedication of the Broad Run High School we're almost back to four again.

What revelation those pictures were – Barbara Parks (Mrs. Robert Allder, now the mother of five), Tommy Wynkoop, Dickie Potts were the impressive Seniors. The underclassmen – "Billy" Carbaugh (he'll probably want to kill me for that), Dolly Manuel, Mary Virginia Allder, Benson Lightner (her picture was cut out for some reason) and the teachers – Mrs. Whitley looks just as she did then, Louise Whitman began her career there that year and we were collegiate at Herndon High (Lincoln's old football rivals), Mrs. Dillon now at Valley and the book was dedicated to their King Arthur, the beloved late J. Lupton Simpson.

The most popular club was the Keen Teen Club (a social group, I take it and advertisers were Anett Electric Shoe Shop – "Not the best, but good as the rest", Mann's General Merchandise – Bluemont, Freeman's Store – R.F.D. Bluemont, Patterson's Pharmacy, White Palace Restaurant, Hill Top Gardens - "You can't live forever – our specialty funeral flowers."

It was quite a sentimental journey – even for someone who went to Gaithersburg, Md. and I'm not going to tell you what year.

My garden spots around town now are the most edifying of sights in trees- all massive and beautiful yellow, orange, and red. See for yourself- the tree at the top of the village by Bessie Carter's, the giant oak in the corner of the Robert Jones' yard, the golden glow between the Dawsons and Jack Allders and the view must be perfect now at the top of the mountain road and up at the Littles.

Tourists will relish these sights next year at the Bluemont Fair.

If I don't get the heat on soon, I'll have air pollution from my own fireplace!

October 30, 1969

"And the goblins will get you, if you don't watch out."

How we loved my grandmother to recite that James Whitcomb Riley "piece" when we were kids.

Have you "Jackie" (that's our Jack-O-Lantern's name each year) grinning on the front porch?

See you at the Halloween party tomorrow night at 7 o'clock at the schoolhouse.

The trees have been rather disappointing this year, the colors seemingly washed out. My parents, Mr. and Mrs. Roy Porterfield of Bethesda, Md., on their visit last Sunday thought it was due to the fact that we hadn't had a killing frost as yet.

Well, we got it Thursday night. "Popeye" Reid said it was 15 degrees at Oatlands, 16 at Waterford and Lucy Martz claimed it was 22 here; the Lawrence Dawson's Princess tree just shed its green leaves in a hurry and Clyde Beck's miniature gourds were lost to the bite of Jack Frost.

"Crazy" time is here again, that's what the farmers call the change from Daylight to Standard but I could never get it straight which was the "Crazy" time.

It seems a shame to have the twilight hours gone before one can get an after-dinner stroll.

No excuse now, not to turn out the vote here in Bluemont, remember it's this Tuesday, Nov. 4 balloting for Governor, Lt. Governor and Attorney General.

Jerry Hummer, son of Mr. and Mrs. Harry Hummer of Airmont spent a few carefree days at home before shipping out for Germany with the U.S. Army.

Sorry to hear Billy Boxley was confined to Loudoun Memorial Hospital this week with appendicitis.

Bluemont's favorite grandmother, Granny Jones, is back from Shawnee Nursing Home just in time to celebrate her 91st birthday with a big cake.

The Walton Manns took a little spin to Richmond on Sunday to see son, Tom and wife and we finally got around to celebrating Grandfather Johnson's birthday with a steak dinner.

A new course in sewing is being offered at the Valley High School for any woman interested.

Yes, it's time to coax the ghosts out of the closet and snatch another bite of the candy apples (what a perfect taste combination, sweet with tart). Hope we have a lot of them at the Bluemont Fair, apples that is, not ghosts.

"And the goblins will get you, if you don't watch out." Boo!

November 6, 1969

The sky is dark now brightened some by the yellow leaves but we know soon winter will wrap us in again and we'll be that remote little village at the foot of the mountains in Loudoun County but we will enjoy our pumpkins now as we may.

In Circleville, Ohio, they hold Pumpkin Week with pumpkins, more pumpkins and pumpkin dishes. One pumpkin weighed a hundred and ten pounds, the local bakery features the "world's largest pumpkin pie" weighing three hundred pounds.

That's alright, we don't have to have one at the Bluemont Fair next year.

Isn't Halloween fun here?

With our small number of treaters we all recognize the neighbor children instead of strangers bussed in from other areas as is the practice in most heavily populated sections.

Everyone is cordial and generous. The Sam Joneses treated splendidly with a large assortment of treats on a beautiful pattern of china.

The Halloween party under Roberta Underwood's chairmanship was a great success with Winifred (love that name) doing a marvelous job with the games – Pin the tail on the donkey and 1400 grains of corn in a small coffee jar (my estimate -500) with prizes for the winners of each age group.

Roberta wishes to thank all those who assisted.

A trio of judges awarded Kimberly Orrison first prize for the ugliest costume, Tammy Dawson, a prize for the prettiest, scariest to Jay Allder (I never did see his face behind that horrible mask) and most original when to Justine and Brian Beck for their boxes, the Queen of Hearts and a silvered robot.

The only vandalism around here was Snickers quick onslaught on Tracey's cat mask, but I did get a fright out of an eerie sound booming through the darkness that turned out to be Furka (the Dawson's boxer) with a cough.

Earlier in the week, a harvest moon smiled down. It was perfect weather too, for a wiener roast with Mrs. Edith Middleton and son Brook of rural route Leesburg in our grove of trees.

"Trick-or-Treat" night found some of the Madison girls in the Lawrence Dawson's front parlor, awaiting rides to upper Loudoun, of course Jean was arriving home for the weekend.

Sorry Mrs. Clara Riley of Bloomfield has to celebrate her 77th birthday at the Loudoun Memorial Hospital. Hope she'll be home soon with her family, the Arthurs of Bloomfield who have four generations living together.

Dale Reed (by rights I should have had a cute freckle-faced red-headed boy like that) acquired a new puppy this week from the Arthurs.

Got an encouraging word from Mrs. Murray Pearson of Pine Grove this week; her mother was raised by the late Rosa Turner Wynkoop. I figured Rosa's grandfather Townshend Osborne must have resided here during the Civil War, was said to have buried his gold in the Clayton Hall basement but since it became town gossip, he went and dug it up again.

We did find a small canning jar with a four-leaf clover and the words Good Luck imprinted on it and a 1920 soft-drink bottle called "Try Me", so you see there are still some treasures in that basement but forget the pick and candle routine. I read a story once of Edgar Allen Poe's about someone being walled up in brick – underground.

This could get worse – so better call me with some news for next week.

November 13, 1969

From October we turn the corner and run head-on into Thanksgiving, the last of the fall rites.

With all the good cooks in the area, it's a cherished occasion for family gatherings; already a wild turkey was sighted by the passengers on Shir Carbaugh's school bus.

The Rockwood Fosters always gather the clan of their four sons now scattered in schools in the east, including Charles the youngest who left this year for St. Paul's in Concord, N.H. at their mountaintop estate.

Karlton Monroe called this week to admit he had created a big stink all the way from the Gulf of Mexico to tiny Unison. The Monroes on a three-week tour of Florida picked up a trunk-load of starfish and a big mud turtle which sent out a heavy scent, especially when they stopped for overnight accommodations but the collection is intact and no one has been complaining around here.

Incidentally, Karlton has graciously agreed to exhibit his other collection of antique farm tools at the Bluemont Fair next October.

Ever been to an apple bee?

Well, there were all the Lloyds (which is quite a number by themselves) and the Roy Santmyers, peeling, cutting, cooking and adding spices for fabulous home-made apple butter this week.

Glen operated an old peeler that came from the old Purcellville cannery and then the apples were transported upstairs for cooking – a regular assembly line. Seven bushels yielded 21 gallons and that's a lot of cutting plus they made two batches.

The town meeting was held this week and a committee was appointed to set up rules for a home decorating contest for Christmas. Clyde Beck, Mr. Leffingwell, Mrs. Sam Jones and Mrs. Winifred Kelly will serve on the committee.

A lively discussion of plans for the Bluemont Fair to be held next Oct. 24, 25 ensued and we'll leak a few of the surprises weekly.

Meeting also this week was the Home Demonstration Club on Wednesday morning with the program, Services in Loudoun County. The Club should be congratulated on its second prize in achievement awards and it's attainment of an outstanding merit rating.

Sorry to hear Ralph May of Pine Grove is ill.

Joyce Beck celebrated her birthday with a little family ice cream and cake this week.

Got a great little note from Columbia, S.C. this week from the Diedricks who plan to retire next summer at their place near Unison and will bring a little life to this part of the country, I know.

As Dean Martin would say, "Keep those cards and letter coming" and watch out for the birds, they're migrating down chimneys these days.

November 20, 1969

There were a number of bright star-studded nights this week; a light November snow fell as everyone predicted and now it's swag time again.

Swag time is kinda an "in" Bluemont thing. In case swag doesn't ring a bell with you, it's sorta an outdoor horn of plenty, without the horn but with boughs of evergreen and fruit. Clyde Beck makes one every year just before Thanksgiving but I wait till Christmas.

I heard the latest statistics on Loudoun this week, there's 500 plus square miles (of course, that hasn't changed) with 43,000 people. Any guesses on how many square miles in Bluemont and how many square people? (Those half people always get me in the statistics).

Not square are our young people, that's for sure.

Jan Woolman is taking karate lessons and doing a research paper on Bluemont History and Beverly Kelley was a princess in the Homecoming Court of Valley High School on Friday night.

The Methodist Church grounds were tidied up this week by the men.

Louella Robey is hospitalized and young Pam Carbaugh is confined with pneumonia.

Seven of the 13 members of the Home Demonstration Club were awarded reading awards for reading five or more books this year. It's a perfect way to spend the winter in Bluemont.

Miss Ruth Alley gave me some history on her place: built about 1900 when the railroad came to town, the 22 room home was a hotel and then in the winter months a girl's school was held there later joined by some boys from an academy in Middletown.

The Bluemont Fair will feature a historic film next year and if you can dig up any old photos of the town or scenes nearby, let me know please. Winifred Kelly has already volunteered some from her late father's album.

Mrs. Sam Jones is in charge of the history presentation and would be most eager to know of some relics that might be displayed the two days of the fair.

Another film maker in town is Mr. Taylor who will show his travel films from exotic lands at the next Association meeting.

I have just read the Home Demonstration Club safety hints for Christmas and was glowing in my assurance that I ran a safe home when it happened.

Lara (one of the twins) yelled, from her room where she was supposedly napping, "Mommie, get me" and there lay a diaper pin, a charred electrical outlet and a burned little finger on a chubby sooted hand.

Whoever coined that phrase Double-Trouble knew what they were talking about.

So gather in the nuts, the fruits, the sage and the bird, Grandma and Grandpa, the aunts, the uncles, the cousins on roller skates and be ye thankful there can be a Thanksgiving Day.

November 27, 1969

"Over the river and through the woods to Grandmother's house we go." It all sounds terribly picturesque, does it not? And if you were coming from Berryville to Bluemont, the description of this Thanksgiving song would fit the ride.

Golden brown roasted young Tom turkey, fluffy mashed potatoes with giblet gravy, oyster dressing, green beans with onion rings, cranberry sauce, sweet potatoes with marshmallows, home-made hot rolls, baked squash, (I have the Battletown Inn recipe, if you ever want it) and of course, mince-meat and pumpkin pie for dessert.

What's your menu?

Mrs. Mann says lots of people in the area have oysters, she scallops hers; my mother always makes oyster dressing and the Wesley Carbaughs are sure to serve them some way for their family gathering with Bill and family plus sons Eugene and I.W. and grandmother Viola Carbaugh.

The Lawrence Dawsons are gathering in the flock with all the daughters, Jean home from Madison, Sue, Libby and son-in-law, Homer, son Larry and Grandmother Dawson for the traditional 35 pound turkey served again on Sunday following Thanksgiving with a few more guests.

Lucky Homer Stearne has won two turkeys, a hundred pounds of beef and 24 chickens already this year so the freezer is brimming over.

Not too many knew their definite plans as we went to press but guests last weekend were Carroll Jones and family of Baltimore to the Robert Joneses and Victoria and Andrew Knight visiting Clyde Beck from Washington plus Ruth and Tom Mann dropping in on Mom and Pop Walton Mann from Richmond.

The children were enchanted with Mrs. Townshend's Thanksgiving arrangement in the post office and the afternoon crowd on Shir Carbaugh's bus spotted a striking pair of pheasants this week.

The Bluemont post office department asserts there are approximately 250 people in the village but up to 1200 who have a Bluemont address on the sixty mile mail route.

Sorry to hear Johnny Carter had to undergo an operation on his hand at the Winchester Hospital this week.

Winifred Kelley played hostess to the Methodist Women's Missionary Society at her home on Wednesday.

The lights now on Iden's and Mann's stores in the early evening seem to make the village twinkle but now that hunting season is here, the sound of gun shots makes me involuntarily shudder.

Although some people I love dearly gather their gear and take out after game, especially the deer at this time of year, I still can't see the "sport" of hunting a defenseless animal with a high-powered firearm.

Yes, I read Bambi and it's no child's book but a beautifully written argument by an Englishman who detested man's inhumanity to his fellow creature.

In the story, Bambi's brother became a pet of man and then was turned free with a collar to show his trust in man but still the huntsman's bullet cut him down.

When one creature has put his faith in another, it is not a trust to be taken lightly, though the creature be animal or fellow man.

I know in a rural setting, we must expect this and of course, at one time in our history manhood was judged by adeptness with a gun but with the death of Joseph Kennedy, father of two sons who met their early demise by a gun, it's an especially bitter pill to swallow this week.

The Grandparents Johnson and Porterfield plus Uncle Jim Porterfield and his intended have promised to celebrate Thanksgiving with us at Clayton Hall this year so I prettied up the house a bit with a dried arrangement now that most of the fresh flowers are gone, although Mr. Martz still has some dazzling yellow chrysanthemums and turned my thoughts to the dried arrangements for the Bluemont Fair to be handled next year by Betty Walsh.

Start saving containers for arrangements. What do you think of Clorox bottles with the tops cut off? Betty wants fresh flowers, seeds, and paper flowers, too.

Not fancy enough for Thanksgiving but a quick perk-up for green vegetables is two tablespoons of mayonnaise, one teaspoon of mustard and a squirt of lemon juice. If you work fast, you can drain and remove the vegetables from the pan, then mix the sauce in the same pan and no additional heating is required.

Hate washing any extra pans, don't you?

"And hooray for the pumpkin pie."

December 4, 1969

No, it couldn't be – but yes, with Thanksgiving behind us, it's time to think of the holly greens, the tingling bells, the glow of lights on a tree plunked from the woods and Bluemont is playing it low-key, but it's creeping up on us anyway.

The monthly town meeting will feature Mr. Taylor's films and discuss final plans for the Christmas decorating contest tomorrow night, Friday, the 5th at the schoolhouse at eight o'clock.

The WSCS will hold its annual Christmas bazaar with baked goods, homemade items, decorations and gifts on Saturday the 6th at the schoolhouse at 10 o'clock.

Emphasizing the Christmas theme again will be the Home Demonstration Club's social at 1 o'clock, meeting at my house, Clayton Hall on Wednesday, the 10th.

Thanksgiving was a pretty gala affair here in Bluemont with Mrs. Barbara Spring feeding turkey to 16, her daughter's family, the Ralph Sullivans of Great Falls with five children and son Thomas and family from Leesburg with three children plus young Donnie Spring, grandson from Herndon who spent the long weekend on the Spring's side of the hill.

David, although far away physically was close in their thoughts and he reports, "Yes, Virginia, there is a "Bridge on the River Kwai" as he saw it on his R and R leave to the golden city of Bangkok recently.

The Walton Manns had niece Estelle Williamson and daughter Debbie of Baltimore for the Thanksgiving feast.

I'm beginning to realize Virginians love their country hams for Thanksgiving and Christmas as well as the popular turkey as the Jim Brownells served both along with scalloped oysters in elegant style to the clan; including Susan home from Madison and Jimmy from the University of Richmond plus Mr. and Mrs. John Broome of Arlington.

Barbara Allder served two dinners, the first to the family including Mr. and Mrs. Charles Parks and Mrs. May Tumblin at Noon and then that evening they were joined by the Clarence Manuels and daughter Ruth for more turkey and then Billy Journells and four children sailed in from Hamilton for Barbara's homemade pumpkin pie. Cards followed up dessert with the women beating the men but I didn't hear who had to do the dirty dishes.

Col. and Mrs. Holt were pleased to have their daughter's family the Rauffs of Connecticut with three grandchildren for the holiday up at their place.

The Jim Scots really had a crowd; all the children and their children, our own Harry Coates, Virginia Lincoln and her family from Round Hill, Jerry Lincoln, eldest son from Washington, Ruth Butler and her family from Washington and Ted Scott of Purcellville. All the usual Thanksgiving trimmings were the order of the day.

The Martin Wilts entertained Mrs. Robert Wynkoop of Hillsboro.

Grandmother's house is in Charlottesville so off went the Becks for a grand Thanksgiving day and poor Cinder had to contend with his usual fare with no turkey garnishes.

We were mighty glad to have Grandfather Johnson of Paeonian Springs here after his recent operation. Who else could carve our turkey?

Walton Mann's mother is visiting in the community this week from Hamilton.

Mr. and Mrs. Robert Allder attended the funeral of Mrs. Margie Pyne of Middleburg this week.

Have you seen a cat-tail shed? I'm speaking of the plant variety, of course. After eight years, one started blowing in the wind in the bedroom so I led it to the wastebasket where it literally foamed, filling the container. It was a most interesting sight.

All I wanted for Christmas was to get rid of my old sofa and I got that for Thanksgiving so…and Hawkeye Reid says he knows where yon grows the running pine.

December 11, 1969

Ah, the romance in these changing seasons.

Although winter doesn't begin officially until the 22nd the bitter winds and frequent snow flurries convince Bluemonters that winter is here.

The nights are "lovely, dark, and deep" with bright stars. The air is fresher, the fire a greater comfort and the promise of holiday gaiety is stirred in with the common cold.

It's time for toys for tots but Grandmother's homemade stocking doll, made from scraps of old long-johns and odd buttons still seems to be the nicest doll yet. Granted she didn't sparkle with Barbie's sex appeal or ask questions in a high pitch-pipe voice but yet in our imagining she became whatever we wished and she felt warm and soft on the pillow beside the small tousled head on a cold night.

Loudoun Memorial Hospital now confines one of our villagers, Mrs. Leffingwell. May she return in our presence soon.

The south room of the old school was a cozy spot on Saturday with the aroma of coffee and bright displays of the WSCS annual Christmas Bazaar. June Lloyd's apple butter was gone by 11 o'clock: the early bird catches the worm, I guess.

"The prettiest sight you'll see is the holly that will be on your own front door," so says the Christmas decorating committee headed by Clyde Beck.

The contest will be open to villagers and to those homes in a two-mile radius and will be judged from Dec. 21 to Jan. 1. If in doubt, call Clyde who has arranged for two Leesburg judges and use your ingenuity. It's not the amount you spent, but rather the amount of creativity you show. There will be a first prize of fifteen dollars, second-ten and third-five.

Going back to Thanksgiving, the R.M. Peytons had a nice family gathering with Sadie home from Madison and son Willie and wife Shirley from Gaithersburg, Md. joining them along with neighbor James Sheffield who shared a five-pound turnip he had grown in this good Bluemont soil.

Mrs. Townshend has added a little tree, choir and manger to the Thanksgiving scene at the post office and it shines brightly for the children when we go to pick up our bills. Oh, well maybe a few Christmas cards will lighten the vista soon.

Trash collection will be in the next two Saturdays.

The James Allders welcomed guests Mr. and Mrs. William Sargent and son Lee from Leesburg last Sunday and Brian Beck held up five fingers pronouncing his ever-approaching manhood to me this week.

A family party was held Sunday with Grandparents Grove of Lovettsville, aunts, uncles and cousins from sundry places.

The pink house near the yellow house exchanged occupants over the weekend with the Ralph Saunders moving to Philomont and Beverley and Russell Powell moving in.

"Christmas at our House" – that's what we want to know – call me and tell me of your family traditions. How does a small town say Merry Christmas? Let's find out.

Now about Mr. Nesmith's passing; he was Mr. Bluemont to me. He symbolized the dignity of the individual as respected in a small town.

He had a quick wit and great zest for life up to his last days; he had his dreams; he was not a practical man; he knew he would be kept warm and fed at a nursing home but asked more from life than that.

He lived at the side of the road and became a friend to man and in return he had good neighbors who will miss his radiant spirit and rare sense of humor and wish that Jennifer's words of comfort were true: "Don't cry, Mommie, he'll undie tomorrow."

The walrus's tough, hairless hide cloaks a six-inch layer of blubber that keeps the animal warm in icy polar waters, the National Geographic Society says.

December 18, 1969

Holly branches strewn in the back of the truck… the Jack Allders' beautiful candles glowing in the windows… packages mysteriously slipped in after the small fry are in bed… these are the scenes in Bluemont these days.

The ham has arrived, the nuts, candy, and fruit cake gathered in and according to my favorite magazine, we can all expect to gain five pounds over the holidays so you might as well choose your most delectable sweets and forget the calorie counting.

The Home Demonstration Club started the fattening process with a perfect assortment of Christmas cookies, punch and spice tea at their Christmas party here last week.

Oh, what a bunch of clever ladies; Ruby Payne had made a lovely decoration of the tiniest pine cones gathered in Louisiana arranged in star-shaped Styrofoam and Betty Walsh's homemade knitted slippers which I was lucky enough to receive, give the feet a foam-rubber lift.

Here's the spice tea recipe, essential as the egg-nog to our celebration. Put three teaspoons of cinnamon, two teaspoons cloves in a tea pot, make pot of tea your usual strength, add one and one-half cups sugar, add large can of orange juice, large pineapple grapefruit juice. Makes about two gallons.

The Brownells have done it again, now a large owl moved in with them, sitting in the dining room allowing members of the family to pat him on the head. Dr. Laing verified that they make wonderful pets. Someone must have slipped up a sign, Bird Sanctuary in a tree somewhere at Whitehall Farm, huh?

Just heard the song, "My Home Town" for the first time this week - sounds like Bluemont, alright. If anyone knows all the words, please let me know.

Just imagine this – one morning you fetch your mail from the box and read that you are a grand prize winner in a contest you didn't even know you had entered.

That's exactly what happened to the M.J. Klingensmiths who feed the wild birds at their home near the Shenandoah River, buying sunflower seed in fifty pound bags.

Taking a picture of the golden evening grosbeaks and taking it to Peoples Drug Store for their picture Christmas card they were automatically entered in the contest, winning a two-week trip for two to Europe.

Who says there isn't a Santa Claus?

We've had our traditional trip to Winchester with Grandfather Johnson followed by his rendering of the oyster stew; the next week we'll go with Grandfather Porterfield to see the awesome President's tree and the fantastic windows in Washington.

Time to read again the touching tale of the Littlest Angel. May I quote? "The littlest angel trembled as the box was opened and there before the Eyes of God and all His Heavenly Host was what he offered to the Christ Child."

"And what was his gift to the Blessed Infant? Well, there was a butterfly with golden wings, captured one bright summer day, a sky-blue egg from a bird's nest, and two white stones found on a muddy river bank where he and his friends had played like small brown beavers. At the bottom of the box was a limp, tooth-marked leather strap once worn as a collar by his dog."

"Why had he dreamed that such utterly useless things would be loved by the Blessed Infant?"

"There was a dreadful silence complete and undisturbed save for the heartbroken sobbing of the Littlest Angel."

"Then the voice of God spoke saying, 'Of all the gifts of all the Angels, I find that this small box pleases me most. Its contents are of the Earth and of Men and My Son is born to be King of both. These are the things My Son, too, will know and love and cherish and then leave them behind Him when his task is done. I accept this gift in the Name of the Child, Jesus, born of Mary this night in Bethlehem.'"

December 25, 1969

The enchantment and excitement of Christmas-time is creeping in on small feet to Bluemont.

Families are polishing up their memories of a perfect Christmas, generally spent right here at home.

The tiny post office is overflowing with bags of cards and packages for neighbors sending and receiving Season's Greetings.

It's time to put the final touches on the tree and front door decorations; the judges will probably be here on the 23rd.

The William Carbaughs find tramping for the tree in woods their kind of sport; they will seek one at a Christmas tree farm near Charles Town.

They are making cookies, admiring the Christmas sights at Tyson's Corner and shopping for Mom's and Dad's gift along with one name they have drawn among the four sisters.

The Burton Leffingwells say they will spend Christmas day in Alexandria with friends, the William Crewys, but observe midnight mass here in Loudoun and decorate their tree with their own handmade ornaments.

The Lucien Reeds have a grand celebration with all the family, Grandmother Estelle A. Reed from Gwynedd Valley, Pa., Lewis and Lester Underwood's family from Round Hill and Gordon and Helen Reed from Leesburg.

Everyone brings a dish for the big dinner of turkey, ham, and fried oysters and lots of salads. Roberta Underwood bringing her specialty, the beautiful Christmas jello ring.

All the children bring one of their toys to try out around the tree so truly there is much merriment.

The Louis Underwoods decorate their house with colored lights and cautiously place a twenty-year old ornament, a reindeer, near the top of the tree.

The R.M. Peytons, along with daughters Rosa and Sadie, will spend the day in Gaithersburg at son Willie's, while Sarah Campbell's family joined by her daughter's family, the James Fishbacks and four children of Winchester, will be sure to devour every crumb of Mother Campbell's traditional apple sauce cake.

The Ed Reids will have a turkey dinner with the immediate family while Ruth visits her sister, Grace Canard, over the school holiday in Marshall.

Sadie Peyton celebrated her 20th birthday by welcoming her sister Rosa and Billy Piggott of Bluemont last weekend at Madison where they attended the Christmas dance and a Christmas concert by Bob Marshall and the Crystals and the Swinging Medallions. Rock groups, for those who aren't in the know. Sounds exciting, doesn't it?

Barbara Jean and Ray Mauck of Baltimore were visitors to Barbara Jean's parents, the Jack Allders last weekend and John and Jamie Doddenridge arrived home for the holidays from their school, St. Paul's in New Hampshire.

The Methodist Church will hold an inspiring candlelight service on Monday evening, the 22nd at 7:30 with special music.

Two rituals we have in our family every year – Christmas morning with the Johnsons here, presents under the tree, stopping while Daddy poses us for the movies and Christmas breakfast – brown-sugared grapefruit browned in the oven, muffins, scrambled eggs and sausage filled out with fruit cake and stocking pickings, then dinner at the Grandparents Porterfield in Bethesda where Santa always manages to leave a few more items for the Robert Johnsons and there are "lots of chocolates for me to eat."

But Col. and Mrs. P.S. Teasdale-Smith have topped us all with son Bob from Washington bringing two guests and Mrs. TS (as the Valley students like to call her) serving their crowning glory, the flaming plum pudding. Ah, what a spectacular tradition!

"And it came to pass in those days that there went out a decree from Caesar Augusta that all the world should be taxed. And all went to be taxed, each to his own city. And Joseph also went up from Galilee from the city of Nazareth to Judea to the city of David, Bethlehem because he was of the house and lineage of David to be taxed with Mary, his espoused wife, being great with child.

And while they were there, the time came for her to be delivered and she brought forth her first-born son and wrapped him in swaddling clothes and laid him in a manger because there was no room for them in the inn.

And it came to pass there were shepherds abiding in the fields, keeping watch over their flock by night.

And to the angel of the Lord shone upon them and the glory of the Lord shone round about them and they were sore afraid.

But the angel said unto them, 'Fear not, for behold, I bring you good tidings of great joy which will be to all people. For unto you is born this day in the city of David a Savior which is Christ the Lord and this will be a sign unto you, ye shall find the Babe wrapped in swaddling clothes, lying in a manger.

And suddenly there was with the angels, a heavenly host praising God and saying, 'Glory to God in the highest and on earth, peace, good will toward men."

Is this not the true and beautiful tradition of Christmas?

May we keep it and ponder all these things in our hearts as Mary did.

1970

January 1, 1970

Time to ring out 1969 and roast and toast in the New Year. Always I have preferred the even numbers but claimed seven as my lucky number, all my children have a seven in their birthday and I have two in mine so welcome 1970.

Just to look backward for a moment, however, 1969 was a very special year to me, mostly due to a place called Bluemont as an opportunity to be called the Bluemont correspondent enabling me to meet many of my neighbors and receive the well wishes of my dear readers who may not live so close.

Sixty-nine closed on a perfect note in Bluemont with snow, a full moon, carolers at the door (Snickers joining the crowd for several stops) some lovely sprigs of holly left on the doorstep by a thoughtful Karlton Monroe, a plant I thought I had killed spouting a big new leaf on Christmas morning and the village and countryside springing alive with colored lights for the first Christmas decorating contest.

Little did we know we had engaged such a professional judge as Col. Wayne Cecil who had served as a judge in Taiwan and Korea. His wife Mary and Clyde Beck assisted him.

First prize went to the James Walshes who had a red candle in every window and arches of blue lights across the porch, the Herbert Martz's took second having endeared the judges with their small blinking tree bringing to mind a mint tree, and third went to the Russell Powells now in the pink house.

Honorable mentions were paid to the Clarence Manuels (I particularly liked their red-lighted Christmas tree frame), Mrs. Sarah Campbell and the Lloyd Loopes who really got my vote with that beautiful colored tree dripped by nature's touch of snow.

Of course, the children were enchanted with the Robert Jones's Santa and reindeer on the lawn and Miss Ruth's display. Be assured Miss Ruth your lights will be strung next year on yours, the biggest tree in town and so beautiful last year.

We'll have a town trimming with hot chocolate and popcorn too, you'll see.

A glittering party for about 100 guests was hosted by the James Brownells at their Whitehall Farm home last Saturday night. A roaring fire in the fireplace and a 12-foot tree in their splendid ballroom along with many delectables served by the lady of the house, made it an evening to remember. We relished the Glen Miller records too.

The Clyde Becks entertained the Charles Tyrolers and Sam Joneses for an intimate candlelight dinner that night also.

Larry Allder, son of Mr. and Mrs. Jack Allder, recently attended the annual FHA Convention in Richmond at the John Marshall Hotel along with three other Valley High School students and Mom and Pop celebrated their 22nd wedding anniversary last week.

I got a wonderful old postcard of Clayton Hall in a Christmas card from Louise Cauffman of Washington who along with her brother still own their home place, "The Reeds" right behind us. What a pleasant surprise.

Now it's time to say a blessed Happy New Year to our neighbors, summer people and readers wherever you are, but especially to the real Bluemonters, forgive me if I leave anyone out. To the families of the Allders, Jack, James, Floyd, Clyde, Bobby (and any others – about half of Bluemont's population, I think), to Miss Ruth Alley, to the Andersons, Arnolds, Ballengers, Baxters, Bayles, Beaklers, Becks, Beetons, Bells, Bowmans, Boxleys, Brownells, to the Campbells, Allen, Mother Sarah and hers, Carbaughs, Wesley and William, Carters, John and Mother Bessie, Clarks, Coates, Cochrans, Colberts, Coles, Conleys, Coopers, to the Doddenridges, Dennises, Dutrows, Dawsons (all three families – two related, one not), to the Elseas, Embreys, Evans, Ewings, to the Fancuillis, Fergusons, Finchams.

Fletchers, Foersters, to the Franciscan Friars of the Atonement (it's such a beautiful sport), to the Gibsons, to the Harrises, Hendricks, Hitchcocks, Hollands, Howards, to John Hyland in Shawnee Nursing Home, to the Idens and there's another Johnson in town (the country's most common name you know), but to the Joneses, Sam and Robert, to the Kelleys, James, John, Stanley, to the Kerricks, to the Longenbecks, Leonards, Lloyds, Littles, Longerbeams, Loopes, to the Mailliards, Manns, Manuels, Mayos, McClures, McClaughrys, Robert, Ray and Roy (twins too, you know), McElhinneys, Miss Florence Maitland, Mitchells, Murrays, to Miss Nygard, Miss Susy Neal, No O's, guess there's only a few Irish in Bluemont, to the Parks, Russell, Jr. and Sr., Paynes, Pearsons, Perssons, Peytons, Powells, Pierotts, Peggotts.

Popes, Postons, to Mrs. Nellie Powell, now to the Reeds and Reids – both clans too numerous to mention and besides I'm not sure I have everyone straight yet, a special greeting, Reynolds, Robinsons, to the Santmyers, Savages, Scotts, Summers, Sheffields, Sisks, Smallwoods, Smiths, Sowers, Springs, Stearns, Strangs, to the Townshends, Tatums, Taylors, Teasdale-Smiths, Thomases, Tibbs, Tinsmans, Tomlins, Tyrolers, to the Underwoods, Lester and Lois, to the Verloops, Vezenas, Vinkes, Virts, to the Waldrops, Wills, Walshes, Mrs. Willie, Wilsons, Wines, Woolmans, Worleys, Wynkoops.

We have no Y's or Z's, granted I don't know you all but by 1971–let's be sure we can say Hi Neighbor. My warmest wishes for a Happy New Year.

January 8, 1970

"The snow is snowing.
The wind is blowing.
But, we can weather the storm."

In fact, it was downright disgusting the way Bluemonters had dug out even before the machinery came in.

The male animal, homo sapient variety, that is, just can't resist a struggle against the elements.

Herbert Martz, age 71, was gleefully plowing away with this tractor, while ours was stuck in the drive, but Clyde Beck and Bootsie Stearne were only too glad to lend a helping hand while I was cursing the darn automobiles and threatening to post another sign, "Sleds Only."

It was great to hear the ring of sled runners on the long hill at the side of the house: the wonderful stories we've heard for a year now about the slides that could be had down that hill and last year with only the light snows, I was a kid again receiving a sled at Christmas when there was no snow and a bicycle when the little white stuff made cycling impossible.

Seeing the second snow of their lives were the Peirott's grandchildren from Mexico visiting for Christmas; of course, we know their protected hill is the best place in town for a coast.

The schoolhouse was still snowbound as the Citizens Association meeting was cancelled this week.

What is the news around town? I got one call and one caller and I haven't been anywhere to find out anything.

Mrs. Edith Reid called me to tell of their marvelous Christmas gathering with their children and families, Marvin, Melvin of Falls Church, Carl, oh Popeye – what is your given name? Anyway – Popeye, Mr. and Mrs. Andrew Lawrence of Fairfax, Mr. and Mrs. Marshall Campbell of The Plains and patriarch Thomas, of course.

Yep, you guessed it, everyone in town is on a diet after the stuffing (admit it, that's the accurate description). I believe I'll go the grapefruit way, myself; grapefruit, lean meat, grapefruit, boiled egg, grapefruit, yogurt. Ugh!

My caller was Mrs. Jean Smith now of Dayton, Ohio, but formerly our very precise historian occupying the stone house next to Mrs. Powell. She brought out some fascinating information about businesses that once thrived here and gave Mrs. Sam Jones an ideal reference for securing some early photographs. Mr. and Mrs. Sam Jones were her host and hostess for the evening and furthermore she said she didn't think she could resist the Bluemont Fair so you see we really should be starting on those long-term projects now.

The new look fashion-wise is going to be knitted and crocheted flairs so we might as well capitalize on it and those maxi-coats, don't they bring the nostalgia?

A few other travelers around town were the Clarence Manuels who spent several days with their daughter-in-law and grandchildren in North Carolina while the Charles Tyrolers spent Christmas day in Charlottesville. Donnie Spring, Mrs. Barbara Spring's young grandson from Herndon spent last weekend with Grandmother here and lucky Willa Colbert whisked herself off to Florida for a week's stay before Christmas.

Even Cinder Beck got away from it all and enjoyed the comfort of the Groves' easy chair in Lovettsville for an overnight visit. You wouldn't expect a dog of his refinement to sleep on the floor now, would you?

Now I really ought to give everyone their projected horoscope for the year but I'm strictly a novice in interpreting the signs of the Zodiac, about all I know is a lot of stars are paying sky-high prices to some Zodiac advisor to tell them about their personal sign in the stars.

Can you settle for your sign? If your birthday falls between Dec. 21-Jan. 19 - Capricorn, Jan. 20-Feb. 18 – Aquarius – they are the creative bunch – Clyde Beck is one. Feb. 19-March 20 – Pieces (The fishes), March 21-April 20 – Aries (Ram), April 21-May 20 – Taurus (Bull), May21-June 20 – Gemini (Twins), June 21-July 21 – Cancer (Crab), July 22-Aug. 21 – Leo (Lion), Aug. 22-Sept. 21 – Virgo (Virgin), Sept. 22-Oct. 22 – Libra (the Balance), Oct. 23-Nov. 21 – Scorpio, Nov. 22-Dec. 20 – Sagittarius (Bowman).

I believe the land animals are supposed to be good matches, the fishes made for one another but all I know is I'm just a poor little Capricorn (goat, the almanac calls me) and I have to live with a bull and three lions.

Anyway, watch the slippery pavements – you might have a bad fall if you don't exhibit extreme caution. Now there's a horoscope for everyone.

January 15, 1970

The temperatures swooped to new lows, the wind raged and life approached a facsimile to grandfather's day last week in Bluemont.

With Allen Campbell reporting 4 degrees below at 6 o'clock Friday morning and Mrs. Markle announcing that it had finally reached 0 at three o'clock in the afternoon on the mountaintop, natives spent a better part of the day in discomfort or chatting beside firesides about the severity of the cold front.

The auto just wouldn't go in some instances; Jack Allder's Mustang wouldn't even give a snort though coaxed by jumper cables and neighbors' tugs; sleds were parked at doors, in front of the general stores and beside the post office and there was much talk of a sleigh being found, the village longed to hear the music of the prancing feet and sleigh bells again.

In my childhood neighborhood, a sleigh was an unknown; it was a new neighborhood of frame two-stories and bungalows, differing only in appearance with the individual color of shutters.

But there were hills, good ole 72nd Street is where I had my first and last flying leap over a snow-covered ramp and there was a safe pasture hill nearby with a creek at the bottom, a creek since covered with asphalt and more new homes. Robert Frost wrote a poem about a creek like that once.

Lawrence Dawson's car was struck by a Volkswagen as he was turning at Clarks Gap last week but no one was injured.

Central heat was unreliable at best, the Beck's furnace stopped twice in a space of two days. Sarah Campbell's quit twice in a day and here we had the fiasco of the stove.

Not being able to secure a temperature above 62 degrees on either floor, the head of the household proclaimed that we would haul the oil stove out of the old unused kitchen and install it in the present kitchen.

Of course, ye old stove rebelled, shooting soot all over the place, which in turn was tracked onto the rugs and furnishings and now I know what it means to be a Cinderella (in fact, there are four of us in the house) and if you're coming to visit how about bringing a good rug cleaner?

My bottle collection suffered again with the colored water in the bottles set in the window turning to ice thus shattering the glass.

School remained closed for three days while youngsters wrapped in bulky sweaters, heavy socks and wool slacks (the fashion of the uni-sex reigned) set off down long hills of snow.

I had the best birthday ever, getting my ride down the hill at the side of the house, I started at the Becks and went all the way past the John Carters (about a mile, I'd say) with just a kick of the feet at the corner; I stuffed a big turkey and had cake and ice cream with the Johnsons of Paeonian Springs. OK, so I'm off my diet!

A wonderful surprise birthday party was given for Mrs. Harry Dennis, Sr. by her daughters JoAnn and Barbara plus Shirley Russell of Round Hill at the home of the Robert Joneses recently.

Other guests were the Walton Manns, the Harry Dennises, Jr., Mrs. Allen Campbell, Mr. and Mrs. Ray Drewery, Mr. and Mrs. Robert Dennis, the Steven Russells, Mrs. Pearl Jones, John Riggleman, and Mrs. Frances Kuykendall.

The Robert D. Beetons received their engraved invitations to Governor Holton's Inauguration Reception and Ball for Saturday, the 17th in Richmond and the Thomas Reids will celebrate their 52nd wedding anniversary on the 17th. Imagine that?

Ralph May of Pine Grove had to return to the Veterans Hospital in Washington, D.C. after Christmas and would appreciate any news from home, I'm sure.

The latest attraction in town is Mann's Store's candy love beads, mounted on an elastic string. You can wear them and eat them too.

I had about concluded the bitterness of such a climate might discourage any creativity but then I was reminded of the Russian writers. Yep, I guess Tolstoy's War and Peace and Dostoyevsky's Crime and Punishment are rather good arguments against such a theory!

The thaw is bound to come soon but before it does, why not take a tramp on the snow-covered roads beneath the bright stars, admire the beauty of the countryside combined with the warmth radiated by lights in the windows and maybe you'll conclude as I did, it's a pretty nice little place to be despite the harshness of the weather.

January 22, 1970

Now that we are well into the seventies, it's time we realized we must face and solve the problems of the decade or man's actual survival on the planet we call earth may be threatened.

I put my antenna out in every direction at the end of the 60's listening to the commentators, viewing the television specials and reading, reading the numerous magazine and newspaper articles and mainly hearing the concern by my neighbors and friends in Loudoun County.

One expert said the problems of war, famine, pestilence and pollution must be met whereas three are foremost in my mind. First the war in Vietnam, it seems to be until this conflict is stopped our nation will remain divided and our energies consumed while we should be focusing attention on the other problems of secondly, pollution and all its related aspects as proper land usage, improved city dwelling and preservation of natural resources, wildlife, and old structures so dear to us in Bluemont, and thirdly the problem of human rights when every man will be judged and respected as a fellow human being regardless of his color or creed.

Look Magazine's Nov. 4 issue was a terrific presentation of the dangers inherent in polluting the atmosphere – imagine our nation setting off underground two nuclear bombs a month for testing? I look to see the combustion engine condemned and certain types of heat outlawed for individual homes as well as extensive factory clean-up.

More open spaces must be preserved, Loudoun's greatest problem in the next few years, Will we push the farmer completely out? County Agent Jack Brown says he has seen over a hundred farmers leave farming in the last 15 years here simply due to the tax rates.

Will the bulldozer destroy ancient buildings and plant life and leave animal life without a natural habitat all in the name of progress?

On Christmas Day in Bethesda, I saw literally thousands of starlings roosting in small woods behind my parents' home, simply because their natural roosting places had been taken down by a developer.

Naturally the developer is not an ogre for he is creating homes for those that wish to move away from the city however, man needs uplifting natural realms for his soul as well as shelter for his body.

Look's quote, so beautifully put, "But we need the wilderness as a personal, as well as a scientific reference if we ever hope to discover what we are. There is as much mystery for man in an acre of living wilderness than in all of mortuary space. For whatever else we may be, we are wild creatures, under the veneer of civilization. There are tides in us that answer to the moon. If we have anything like a racial memory or soul, its natural context is wilderness."

Too, what will we do with our new scientific knowledge? Will we allow Brave New World to become a reality with test-tube babies conditioned for a certain strata of life? Already we have the knowledge to endow the embryo with made-to-order features and intelligence quotients. Will our grandchildren be a standard model only distinguished by a name tag as in one of Rod Serling's "Twilight Zone?"

We are a people who appreciate the old and beautiful objects and homes forged by our forefathers and know the unspeakable joy of life in a rural setting where we know our neighbors and like them and find inspiration by casting our eyes toward a small mountain which registers a change of seasons with a blinding snow storm, a dazzling green hue of spring and summer or flaming autumnal glow.

We have found out what we are and must fight to preserve that good life in our little wilderness.

Yes, Virginia, there is a Bluemont but we're not sure we want to be found.

January 29, 1970

It was another one of those weeks in Bluemont…sub-degree temperatures…more snow…falls…illness…accidents…pipes freezing and furnaces giving up the ghost.

Mrs. G.W. Townshend our postmistress was out a week with the flu…Bill Carbaugh was stricken, then here at Clayton Hall the bug "flu" in and struck the Johnson patriarch but still the news had to be delivered so off we set about 11 o'clock Monday morning when enroute our dear little Tracey hit the electric doorknob in the car and fell at the side of Rt. 7. After a few stitches and a night of observation at Loudoun Memorial where we watched another baby fight a 104 degree temperature with pneumonia and a five year-old take the cure for a nose-bleed that wouldn't quit, we were home again before the next light snow fell.

Grace Dawson's baby shower went ahead as scheduled, her mother falling and bruising her arm the same day, when J.K. Cornwall hurt his foot while Shir Carbaugh stood in the 0 degree weather waving traffic when her school bus succumbed for the second time in a day.

The Pearson's pipes froze in their house while they procured a blower to keep the rest from going…the Becks' furnace went off again at four in the morning Wednesday and ours repeated the act the next day. While we waited the six hours for the repairman, we prepared for the next onslaught, finally rounded up two wood stoves; Darr's Hardware in Round Hill said he couldn't keep them…and then for the next commodity, fire-wood. Brownell's Saw Mill had sold out twice during the cold snap but finally Russell Parks, Jr brought us a rich cord.

The struggle for survival has kept us busy, in fact we're almost physically spent but then I saw Betsy Jones Moreland, our Bluemont movie star on "McHale's Navy" and the next day I met her cousin Ambrose Moreland.

Ambrose said this weather was merely a snap compared to the 45 degree below temperatures he experienced in the northland as a boy. He said wood was brought fifty miles by sleigh, coal was mostly burnt in little stoves or fireplaces and up on the mountain the Seidenspinners and Howard Robinson have taken the hint, finding a supply in Berryville, they use it now in their fireplaces and individual stoves.

Mr. Robinson has the old red house over the West Virginia line minus all the 20th Century conveniences, using instead kerosene lamps for light and little coal stoves for heat; he wouldn't have it any other way.

The Brunelles, Seidenspinners and Mr. Robinson have a great little society there at the end of the road with "Roby" promising to show his slides soon of his recent Virgin Islands trip.

Besides her oil freezing in the pipes, Miss Ruth Alley completed her tenth year of volunteer work with the Red Cross serving at the Newton Baker V.A. Hospital in Martinsburg, W.Va. as of this week.

History-wise, what treasures were unearthed!

Mr. Beeton was kind enough to lend me a most fascinating history by Dr. George Plaster written in 1902 bringing the town from Snickersville 1769 to Bluemont – 1900. He says, "The arrival of the mail coach caused more excitement among the scores of horses and horsemen lining the streets, as well as among railway train of the present day. Horsemen, galore, from all parts of the wide district receiving mail at this point were on hand to greet the incoming stages. With what pleasure the writer recalls those scenes. The spirited steeds, the glowing faces."

Secondly, I am indebted to Florence Beans of Round Hill who sent a 1951 clipping from the Washington Star about Bluemont written by Solange Strong, author of the out-of-print Old Stone Houses of Loudoun.

February 5, 1970

You heard it. I felt it, we all sensed the rhythm of spring's drummer this week even though February has been said to be the cruelest month yet in these parts.

The birds were actually warbling and on Saturday I sighted a yellow convertible with top down while the optimistic ones among us were calling for an early spring.

Exams were over for Berryville High and Valley students of our area and a birth and death spelled the cycle of village life.

Charles and Grace Dawson are now the parents of baby boy born Jan. 23 at Loudoun Memorial. The baby was sent to Children's Hospital in Washington with an oxygen problem but all seems to be well now.

Saddened were we all by the death of Grafton Tumblin who was stricken with a heart attack before he could call for help. A number of the neighbors served as pallbearers for the funeral held Saturday at Berryville with interment at Sterling. Winter is so hard on our dear older citizens.

The flu is raging, teachers are calling for substitutes and the absentee lists are growing. Wanda Reid and James Allder are both ill.

Now that the snow has gone after a month's stay, the monthly town meeting will be held this Friday night, the 6th at 8 o'clock at the schoolhouse.

Congratulations to the Methodist Church which in less than a year paid for its new organ.

Mrs. Townshend was still ill this week but she passed on the names of all the past postmasters starting in 1907 and it seems they served then on a part-time basis using their residence as the post office. John Hyland's place was used twice at a little shed behind, the first postmaster lived at the Sam Joneses, also Becks' home, Clayton Hall and Scott Bulter's were used as the post office.

Too, this week William Osborne James, raised in Bluemont, gave me a delightful call relating that he had a map of the town with about 30 dwellings dating back a hundred years. Sufficient to say, there hasn't been much new construction since.

All will be pleased to know that Mr. Nesmith's cat is safe, taking up residence with the Becks' other numerous felines. If you would like a pet, please give them a call this week.

With the landscape so barren, now is the time for a Sunday drive in the country, revealing some beautiful estates, a drive to Boyce with its charming, solidly built railroad station now housing the post office made me wonder if its history may be similar to our own with the railroad pulling out and a profitable livelihood vanishing with it.

If you can remember your sign of the Zodiac, I found at last the attributes prescribed to the personality, they were coded on the side of a trash can, no less.

If the shoe fits, wear it! See what you think.

If you're a Capricorn like myself and Joan of Arc and Ben Franklin we are supposed persevering, reserved, ambitious yet diplomatic type. We take life seriously and have a high regard for tradition and authority. (Another source says we like the glittering and new – so there you are,) We're suited to Taurus, Virgo and Libra.

They say this age of Aquarius – the broadminded, amiable, popular, honest, humane, unbiased, open-minded bunch who are free of prejudice or superstition. Yep, it does sound like Abraham Lincoln and Franklin Roosevelt. Suited to Libra, Gemini, Aries. Wonder what Mary Todd and Eleanor were?

Now for the Pieces (fish), they are sensitive, often melancholy; they prize solitude and are under the sign of the poet. Michelangelo and Einstein were Pieces and they are suited to Cancer, Scorpio and Virgo.

Watch for the next exciting disclosures of the horoscope in the Bluemont News and don't forget those projects for the Bluemont Fair.

February 12, 1970

It was almost as if a plague had struck our area as misfortunes were legion this week.

Foremost in everyone's mind was the sudden untimely death of young Ruby Leffingwell due to a heart attack suffered at her home here in the village. She is survived by her husband Burton and five children; also Mrs. William G. Ballenger of Pine Grove passed away without warning, having been admitted to the hospital for a routine check-up. Her two brothers George and David Bell and sister Mrs. Jessica Payne are all citizens of our community.

Words are never adequate but we all greatly share these families' losses.

Mary Elizabeth Walsh was still fighting the flu while I found the classroom a warm friendly place for the endurance of the rainy days at the first of the week. What's more fun than a game of eraser tag and a discussion of the forthcoming Bluemont Fair with enthusiastic youngsters?

Birthdays seemed to be the order of the day with two in the Walsh family, Patriarch Jim and youngest son Patrick; and Russell Parks, Sr. was treated to a grand celebration when his daughter and husband, Joan and Martin Wilt, threw a card party with three tables of competitors.

The Lucien Reids were there, the Russell Parks, Jr., the William Kelleys, the Robert Allders and Gordon Beavers to nibble at the shrimp egg roll and other great edibles and to declare Groundhog Day the perfect birthday.

A little barking outside the door last week revealed that Jean Dawson and Sadie Peyton were receiving loud good-byes from the canine crew as they proceeded back to Madison College after a semester break.

At the Citizens Association meeting, it was pointed out that the new year of light dues had begun: Mrs. Ellen Jones can receive your payment any time. At the same time Bob Jones cleared up the Dr. Plaster matter, his son George is the one who operated the dance hall built in 1920 and at the same time the building was used as a car dealer thus explaining the big garage doors beneath and the large windows in the front; there was also a barber shop there at the same time and later auctions were held in the building.

More plans were made in connection with the Bluemont Fair and an organizational meeting and covered dish supper will be held at Clayton Hall on Feb. 25 at 6:30 for activity chairman.

Fulfilling my promise, here's the next installment of the horoscopes. The Aries are pioneers, captains, leaders of men, full of enthusiasm and energy, however, they must be aware of their impulsive nature. Houdini and Leonardo da Vinci were Aries and they are suited to Leo, Sagittarius.

Now for the Tauruses (bulls) – this is the sign of the builder, they are stubborn but kind-hearted, steadfast, systematic and unshaken in the face of adversity. Suited to Capricorn, Virgo, Cancer – Catherine the Great and Ulysses S. Grant were Tauruses.

The Geminis – exuberant, expressive, artistic, clever, versatile in dealings yet restless at times with an obvious impatience with sameness. Walt Whitman and Frank Lloyd Wright (two of my favorites for their respective field of creativity). Suited to Aquarius and Libra.

The last of the plagues here, another starling in the living room. A sick child, a broken piece of furniture, three glasses of spilled milk for three meals daily, dog piles to be shoveled out every morning – ok – but a bird in the house sets my limbs shaking and my teeth-a-chattering. Bluemont's Bird Man, Clyde Beck came to the rescue.

Question of the week – Would a Taurus send a Capricorn a Valentine (like a dozen long-stemmed roses – if fantasy's your bag – you might as well go the whole hog)?

Hope you can realize your impossible dream. Happy Valentine's Day!

February 19, 1970

We are a mountain town…snow-covered, remote, possessing the highest elevation in Loudoun County, bordered by the mountain state, West Virginia, intertwined with Clarke County, quiet, mundane, serene; we are a mountain town.

The school bus struggles up the rutted back roads dropping its passengers safely at their homes while the sheep blend into the background. We are a mountain town.

Most of the news around town was bad; more of the neighbors caught the flu; Shir Carbaugh had to give up the school bus route for three days while Mrs. Faye Willkie was hospitalized and about the same time lost her companion of many years at Oakland Farm. Alida Bokker, originally from Germany, passed away on Feb. 2.

Round Hill Elementary School voted for their King and Queen of Hearts and our own Sandra Mitchell, Debbie Carter and Hunter Kelley were capturing a goodly number of votes.

Sunday, Feb. 22 will be Heart Sunday; Mrs. Mann and her committee will solicit the community for contributions.

Of course, the 22nd always brings to mind our first president, George Washington.

Snicker's Gap as we were called then, had George as overnight visitor at the pink house (then log) at the crest of the hill in the village, as recorded in his diary so legend says and his brother owned investment property here before the town sprung to life.

The Home Demonstration Club was scheduled to meet Tuesday at 9:30 at the schoolhouse.

With the recent snow, it's a good time for reading; Mr. Beeton says he takes 33 periodicals per month, the Manns keep busy while store tending reading their numerous magazines and papers, and the Becks' mailbox is always bulging with magazines.

Right now I have an article going in Geographic, the current Newsweek, a back issue of Life on the 70's, the Christmas issue of My Baby magazine (it looked so tempting when I picked up Grace Dawson's shower gift in a local shop) and just finished February's McCall's and Dreiser's An American Tragedy. I have a feeling it beats television most of the time.

The horoscopes this week are the Cancers, Leos and Virgos.

The Cancers are prophets, teachers, sensitive, sympathetic and patient but too easily influenced by others. Ernest Hemingway and Helen Keller (a terribly remarkable person) were Cancers. They are suited to Pieces, Tauruses and Scorpios.

Now for the Leos – Mrs. Mann says she is one along with our three little girls – Napoleon and Henry Ford. President, King, proud, trusting, energetic, with a tendency to be authoritative and domineering. (Wheh! you're telling me). They set others off toward fulfillment.

The Virgos – methodical, exacting, intelligent, industrious with great powers of discrimination. They pay strict attention to the rules – sounds like they would be great lawyers. Queen Elizabeth and William Taft were Virgos and these should mate with Tauruses and Capricorns.

Keep the home fires burning and the sleds sliding. Remember all this snow is great for the vegetation – think of the exquisite flowers and grass we'll have this spring and our little town will abound with sweet violets.

February 26, 1970

"Whenever the moon and stars are set,
Whenever the wind is high,
All night long in the dark and wet

A man goes riding by.
Why does he gallop and gallop about?
Whenever the trees are crying aloud,
And ships are tossed at sea,
By, on the highway, low and loud,
By at the gallop goes he,
By at the gallop he goes, and then
By he comes back at the gallop again."

Stevenson's little poem, "Windy Nights" aptly describes the Bluemont weather here at the end of February and the expected gusts of the kite flying month of March.

With shutters banging and cracks around windows hissing, some are sure specters are roaming and a good number of people in town are convinced Clayton Hall is haunted. A mystic I must not be because try as I might I just can't get one of the white-sheeted fellows to appear although one night when a fever raged within my head, I thought I heard old William Clayton stub his toe in his secret closet just above my bedroom.

And about the dead Confederate soldier, Solange Strang in her '51 articles claimed it was at the Nesmith place (the old homestead, I assume) where he was shot while trying to hide in the stone chimney.

No – the spookiest place in town to me, is on the porch of Mann's Store on a windy night with that Coca-Cola sign creaking in the breeze and shadows from the swaying boughs playing against the street light. Boo! "And the goblins will get you if you don't watch out."

Now to clear up another legend: Ingrid Jones who is the most accurate researcher says that George Washington's reference to a stop at Snickers' Tavern "under a hill" was actually at a spot in Frederick County (now Clarke) along the Shenandoah River, the tavern being operated in conjunction with Snicker's Ferry of that time.

Mrs. Jones even knew the source of the legend; you can't beat that for accuracy.

Even though Jerry Walsh can't be home to celebrate as he serves in the Air Force in Da Nang, we are thinking of him on his birthday, another February date for the James Walsh family on the 24th.

Of course, our Bluemont Fair meeting will be held this Wednesday and I hope I'll glean some news then as it has been rather scarce lately.

In connection with the Fair, June Lloyd requests village homemakers to save mayonnaise and quart-size jars for the apple butter project.

The Karlton Monroes report they are anticipating a trip to Canada in April where they will find more snow and ice but they like that free, rugged countryside.

Bet you missed the eclipse of the moon Friday night; if you had been up from 2 in the morning till 6 a.m. you could have seen it.

Keep in mind the Thrift Shop in Leesburg benefiting the retarded children of Loudoun County is now open for business; my mother-in-law is having a great time carrying articles in and out.

For your amusement I offer the following teacher contract of Chatham, Va. in 1915 clipped from the Chatham Star-Tribune with a salary of $100 per month. Men needn't apply, I take it.

> Not to get married. (This contract becomes null and void immediately if a teacher marries).
> Not to keep company with men.
> Be home between the hours of 8 p.m. and 6 a.m. unless in attendance at a school function.
> Not to loiter downtown in ice cream stores.
> Not to leave town at any time without permission of the chairman of the board.
> Not to smoke cigarettes (This contract becomes null and void immediately if the teacher is found smoking).
> Not to drink beer, wine, or whiskey. (This contract becomes null and void immediately if the teacher is found drinking beer, wine or whiskey).
> Not to get in a carriage or automobile with any man, except her brother or her father.
> Not to dress in bright colors.
> Not to dye her hair.
> Wear at least two petticoats.
> Not to wear dresses more than two inches about the ankles.
> Keep the school room neat and clean: (a) Sweep the floor at least once daily (b) Scrub the floor at least once weekly with hot water and soap (c) Clean the blackboards at least once daily (d) Start the fire at 7 a.m. so the room will be warm by 8 a.m.

And now you know why the "Roaring Twenties" followed, Baby.

March 5, 1970

Nature played havoc with our emotions; promising spring with smiling skies one moment and then blowing in the bitter winter breezes the next as February crossed into March this week.

Nevertheless, there was a light-hearted air about the village as citizens met to plan for the rosy days of Autumn when the Bluemont Fair would come to town for the first time.

Characterizing the generosity and enthusiasm of Bluemonters, most everyone brought two dishes instead of one to the covered dish dinner and planning meeting last Wednesday.

Frances Ballenger in charge of antiques was on hand with the most delectable cottage cheese salad, she mixed in fresh fruit, coconut and tiny marshmallows and Emma Mann was kind enough to bring her delicious banana bread.

Ivy Cochran brought us another cake and fried chicken too and Sam Jones favored us with a savory beef stew.

We had plenty of hot rolls, meat loaves, salads and vegetables too and about 40 cups of Shir Carbaugh's coffee was consumed. The sample of homemade pickles and relish that Shirley Poston's mother sent is bound to be a big seller at the Fair.

Slides of old photographs and post cards mostly from Winifred Kelley's father's album were shown and everyone marveled at the western appearance of some of our structures and the mud road pictured in front of the old stone church.

Serving on the history committee with Ingrid Jones will be Mrs. Elizabeth Kelley and Mrs. Virginia Woolman.

Clyde Beck will have the art, of course, Ralph Cochran – the produce, Betty Walsh – dried arrangements, seeds and cut flowers, baked goods – Doris Allder, candy apples, popcorn will be Joyce Beck and both Louis and Roberta Underwood along with Emma Mann will handle the sale of crafts.

Promising to demonstrate ceramics for us is Shirley Poston, Mrs. J.H.H. Verloop of our beloved ridge will do weaving and we think Ruby Payne can show us caning and a broom man is waiting in the wings, we hope.

Stanley Kelley says pony rides there will be if he can break several this spring; Louella Roby will play country music and the Lloyd family will be there turning out the apple butter in a big kettle.

Winifred Kelley and Burton Leffingwell are to work on the program and Walton Mann, James Walsh and Ellen Jones are our financial advisors.

James Brownell will act as host and help solve the parking problems and Lawrence Dawson will help us with the construction of the stands.

The Methodist Women's Society has agreed to serve a turkey dinner with all the trimmings in the old ballroom of the James Brownell's.

Mrs. Brownell, Ivy Cochran and Shir Carbaugh are in charge of this.

The teenagers are going to be rounded up for waitresses, busboys, short-order cooks, pony trainers and money-changers.

We're just starting to recruit help so look out!

Everyone should turn out for the Citizens Association meeting on Friday, Mar. 6 so we can finish tying the knots we started last Wednesday night.

Sorry to hear that Mrs. Lula McCarthy is very ill in Winchester Hospital and glad to know the Leffingwells are again part of the Bluemont family now occupying a house on the Cochran's farm.

As Julian Truesdale, the correspondent for the New York Times who settled here atop the ridge a goodly number of years ago once said, "When you invest in Bluemont, you invest in life."

March 12, 1970

Fog crept in on little cat's feet as Carl Sandberg said and a foggy day in old Snickersville town had Bluemonters "low, had them down, they viewed the morning with much alarm" (Mrs. Freedman of Twin Oaks said she couldn't even see off her front porch) but to me it was a serene, snug experience, a special day, a day for peanut butter and banana sandwiches for lunch and fried mushrooms for dinner, a day for reflection and long thoughts.

The weekend came with the celebrated eclipse of the sun; the Becks traveled to Bethany Beach, Del. for a better impression of the total eclipse while Kevin Summers and Dale Reid, winners of the Dribble and Pass Contest at Round Hill School competed at Loudoun County High School on Saturday.

Mary Jo Lloyd was the victim of chicken pox and great was our rejoicing to hear that David Spring is back from Vietnam and will be stationed near Fredericksburg for some time.

We're pleased to know Mrs. Powell is home after her winter's stay at Philomont.

The Citizens Association met this week; better come and get in on all this policy-making for the Bluemont Fair to be held the 17th and 18th of October.

It has been decided the Association will take 20 percent from exhibitors and charge an admission of 50 cents for adults, 25 cents for children and children under six will be admitted free. Exhibitors should call the chairmen mentioned previously for additional information.

The grand campaign for old photographs and post cards is still on; even if you only have one, it would be greatly appreciated if you could contact me. The Sam McMichaels had several of interest and in addition two lovely paintings by the Airmont artist, Lucien Powell known as the American "Turner" who was commissioned by Senator and Mrs. John Henderson of Henderson's Castle, Washington, D.C.

Finally the mystery of those round stone pillars fronting on the road at Airmont is solved for me; these were Powell's entrance posts copied after his elaborate employer's house, Henderson's Castle.

Then we had two delightful conversations with the former Clayton Hall owners and heirs, Earl Bealle of Falls Church, the ticket agent here in 1916 and nephew Landon Wynkoop of Leesburg. Mrs. Lotta Bealle, Dr. Turner's daughter, is now in a nursing home near Falls Church.

Mr. Wynkoop said Dr. Turner had one of the first automobiles and first telephones in use in Loudoun County.

Also Sam McMichael says he believes the round trip fare by train to Purcellville when Purcellville had its famed "Bush meetings" was 32 cents. Well, of course, Earl Bealle would know for sure. We have several great pictures of the train now, both the old steam engine and the later electric.

Now about my Christmas decoration on the door, well it really is some artificial tomatoes that sparkle more on the front door than on the kitchen wall, granted I still have my evergreens by Ingrid Jones who joins me with a bough of pine at the door, says it is staying till something else green comes along and Shir Carbaugh had her Christmas dinner for all the relatives this Sunday due to all the snow-outs. So we're a little behind the times here in Bluemont and provincially proud of it. Tsk! Tsk!

March 19, 1970

Spring begins on Mar. 20 at 7:57 p.m. so the Almanac says but up here in mountainous Bluemont, we adopt the Missourian slogan, "Show Me" and those snow flurries last Saturday showed winter's intention to linger a while longer.

Nevertheless, the chocolate eggs have hatched in the stores and Jennifer now of the technical age between four and five is questioning if the Easter Bunny will make it past our dogs safely.

Even amidst the snow flurries, the Door of Fashion Show sponsored by the Round Hill Methodist Church blossomed in gay array with Ethel Hall and Evelyn Pearson (she stole the show with her antics) modeling some very smart numbers. Of course, dear Mac Brownell and Mrs. McMichael dished up the delectable chicken salad for the occasion.

The big question now is, will it be midi or mini and it seems knee length is the safe approach – right where the average American woman keeps her skirt. Only time will tell whether Madame Pompidou will be the leader of we "so called" American sheep.

The fire engine roared by the house several days this week and the Seidenspinners were up on the ridge flying kites last week with weekend guests, the Wiley Marshalls of Silver Spring, Md. They are all working on some articles for the Bluemont Fair.

It was girl talk involving dog talk where Mrs. Verloop, Mrs. Strang and myself were entertained warmly by Mrs. Helen Freedman at their charming Twin Oaks on the ridge last week. We kindred spirits found we were all dog lovers, the Strangs and Freedmans with their unusual Great Pyrenees, the Verloops with their basset hound and us with our dachshunds and collie.

Mrs. Freedman had old catalogs (now there was the midistyle – 1938) an old tour book featuring a Twin Oaks ad and postscript stating that Bluemont was one of Loudoun's most historic towns with Louis Phillipe traveling through here on a visit once, and a marvelous old wooden sign lettering Twin Oaks Tavern.

The Twin Oaks telephone number was Bluemont 14 and Mrs. Verloop explained it all to me. You ran the operator with that jingling sound and gave her the number and she responded with "I'll try it but I know Grace just went to neighbor Nellie's for the day, shall I try there for you?"

Virginia Woolman has been digging up some great books for historical reference and Harrison William's History of Loudoun County is very readable plus Rails to the Blue Ridge had all kinds of pictures of our Bluemont Local 41.

Anthony Dawson, son of Mr. and Mrs. Charles Dawson, entered the National Guard this week and his grandmother, Nellie Tibbs was kind enough to undergo the task of covering an old cherished quilt of mine.

This project led to my first visit to Coiner's Department Store, Berryville and suddenly there was warmth again in the marketplace; the cashier sat above while the receipts clanged up to her on the cable and another customer told me of the days when there were low stools along the wall for waiting your turn (how the children relished these, he said.).

There were Easter baskets for a nickel and some great ice tea glasses (like antique glass) and a terrific selection of material and wooden salt and peppers and…Yes, I know they have been in business for about 100 years, but still I feel a little like Columbus with my new discovery. I could use a pair of those Wranglers, too.

Believing the calendar, Johnny Carter is putting out onion sets now and has plans for potato planting next week, hope he doesn't have to shovel away the snow to do it.

For those who really have the winter birthdays – here are the last of the horoscopes – Libra – well-balanced with a sympathetic nature, alert, artistic, affectionate, multi-sided. They are best suited to Aquarius, Gemini. George Gershwin and Sarah Bernhardt were Libras.

The Scorpios – this is the sign of the inspector or governor. They boast a passionate, independent, determined nature. They have strong likes and dislikes. They should stay with Cancers and Pieces. Marie Antoinette and Theodore Roosevelt were Scorpios.

Lastly, the Sagittariuses – restless, impulsive, candid and generous. They have extraordinary mental activity. They should mate with Aries and Leos.

Oh, that one of my Leos could meet a Beethoven or Mark Twain. Twain (Samuel Langhorne Clemens), who wrote the great American novel, Huckleberry Finn, and said some of our greatest truths humorously.

Ah, to have had a billiard table and been able to offer him a good cigar and a stiff draught as a preventive of toothache. He never had a toothache, he never expected to have a toothache. He was one of those "Show Me" Missourians too, you know. He might have been right comfortable here in Bluemont.

March 26, 1970

I told you so! About the snow, that is, and now Jennifer has the solution. Santa Claus will bring the Easter Bunny.

Many Bluemonters have been struck with sickness; the Tony Reids had the flu as did Roberta Underwood, Walter Peyton and the Floyd Rossess have been ill and Mary Carter and her husband have just joined our community, temporarily staying with their son, the Robert Carters, but first she was admitted to Winchester Hospital for tests and possible surgery while Lula McCarty has been released from there and has taken up residence in a nursing home in Falls Church.

With the snow, Donnie Mann slid across the road in their car, uninjured fortunately.

There was a light side of the weekly news, however, those guests at the Bill Carbaugh's Christmas dinner were Mrs. Turner Wiley and Mrs. Edith Rogers of Boyce, from Front Royal – Mr. and Mrs. Douglas Chapman, Mr. and Mrs. Walter Gore, Mrs. Ella Stead and Mrs. Irene Marlow from Vienna. Shir's mother, Mrs. Sarah Chapman, and of course, our own Wesley Carbaugh.

Wesley Carbaugh found himself the center of a surprise birthday party on the 17th.

Christmas kept on right here again; when my parents from Bethesda bought us the gifts left at their house for Christmas; the Easter candy came in another package and two pregnant sprigs of pussy willows completed the paradox.

Jack Allder celebrated his birthday on the 17th too, while Flora Carbaugh heard the strains of Happy Birthday on the 23rd.

The nippy weather brought Jean Dawson and Sadie Peyton home from Madison College for their spring vacation; the worst blizzard I remember was during a March Spring vacation, power lines being down for five days.

Some of the Bluemonters left the community this week – Anthony Dawson reported to Ft. Polk, La., with the National Guard serving from four to six months, when he can return to us and his present position with the Fairfax County School Board; David Spring – home on leave persuaded Clyde Beck that a spring fling or a trip to Texas to visit his brother C.W. Spring would be in order so they were off while Ingrid Jones drove to Richmond to haunt again the libraries researching her book on Virginia history.

Before the grand exodus, the Becks entertained Andrew and Victoria Knight from Washington, who brought some other Englishmen to see the Bluemont countryside and our beloved friend, Earl Bealle returned for a too-short visit with son Gordon and wife this time. What an attractive family.

Mr. Bealle introduced us by phone to Clarence Tallman, telegrapher at the former Bluemont Railroad Station. Now of Vienna, he sent a wealth of pictures and post cards of Bluemont scenes that promise to be an essential part of the historical film.

Very exciting was the Freedman's news that their Renaissance Roulette, their 13-month old Great Pyrenees, placed first in her first show at Harrisburg at the State Farm Building from their Renaissance Kennels at Twin Oaks on the ridge.

Rosa Peyton distinguished herself by appearing on the Valley High School Honor Roll again.

The Citizens Association has changed its meeting time to the first Wednesday of every month making it Apr. 1. By popular request another showing of the old pictures being collected may be shown including a gem lent by Mrs. Lightner showing their home prior to the Civil War with a distinguished group arranged on the front lawn.

Every day people say, "You know, we live next to the old Throckmorton farm or it's next to the old Paxton store." Well, I don't know since I wasn't raised in "these here parts" so since the census-taker finds everyone, I applied for the job.

I'm just out to find my neighbors and be assured nothing of your private business will appear in the Bluemont News, so please don't sick the dog on me and I'll see you soon. Happy Easter even if it isn't a Spring holiday this year!

April 2, 1970

First the rain and sleet came, then the wind blew…a few jonquils popped their heads up through the cold earth, children dyed eggs and fingers simultaneously and new outfits were hemmed, pressed and cleaned for a Sunday-go-to-meeting as another Easter came to Bluemont.

The forsythia was out in Charlottesville on Wednesday when we finally got a little trip away from the village and the Becks found even more of the crocus and hyacinth out when they spent Easter Sunday with Grandmother Beck there.

Not only were bunnies sighted about the village but a raccoon walked down the sidewalk in front of the John Carters last week.

About the Easter dinner, I haven't heard; our ham still hung in the Berryville Locker Plant awaiting the last week of curing so we had to settle for roast beef and our traditional lemon pie.

Guy Woolman was pleased to spend his spring vacation from VPI with his parents the Richard Woolmans while sister Jan won a $500 scholarship with the candy stripers and has been accepted at Alexandria School of Nursing for next year.

The most startling thing to happen in Bluemont this week was the spring clean-up by the youth of our community. Armed with gunny sacks, they spent one of their two holidays picking up trash by the side of the road. Ten bags were collected from the post office to the church.

Somewhere in Louisiana there's a homesick Bluemont boy now known as Private Charles A. Dawson, so how about dropping him a line. His address: Pvt. Charles A. Dawson, Company A, 4th Battalion, 1st BCT Brigade, Second Platoon, Ft. Polk, La., 71459.

Ah, the romantic aura of the railroad, most of our trip to Charlottesville we discussed with our friends, Dr. and Mrs. A.E. Jackson, the pleasant experience of a jaunt across the southland in a Pullman car.

When the children were young they would board the train in the evening, have an enjoyable meal in the dining car and then bed down in the berth, sometimes awakened by the jerk of a stop revealing a small charming station perhaps, with a name like "Bluemont."

Mr. Kerrick this week told of the fun days at the Bluemont station when "Blondy" Tallman with his talent as a ventriloquist would throw his voice outside the station, calling the name of a passenger who would run looking for the caller while he and Earl Bealle, the ticket agent would enjoy the joke.

Our friend, Bob Meredith of Richmond, gave us a surprise visit on Monday and told us of a concern who is buying old railroad cars, converting them into diner cars. It could happen here all over again, you know.

Then we met this week Mrs. Benedum, whose father J.B. Throckmorton ran a livery, hiring out horses for carriage rides up through the scenic mountain trails and Mrs. Beatty's Willow Brook Academy catalog quotes James Head's History of Loudoun County asserting that Loudoun is one of the healthiest sections of the world, "as is" proven by statistics which place the death rate at 8 ½ per 1,000 the very lowest in the table of mortality gathered from all the parts of the habitable globe.

So, put that in your pipe, but don't smoke it. Our statistics might be outdone with lung cancer, you know.

April 9, 1970

Wind, Rain and Mud" or "The Misadventures of a census-taker in Northern Virginia's April Weather" might be the title of a sketch either Frances Ballenger or myself could write as long as we battle the elements looking for the neighbors.

The first day, I found Radcliffe Bell disassembling his attractive house for a new location in Clarke County but still a Bluemont address as the Road Department has declared Apr. 25 as D-Day; he pointed the way for me when I only hit a few boulders in the long lanes; Mr. Vinke, Mrs. Verloop's father was utterly charming and the Beetons were kind enough to supply me with needed information on the next trip.

Owen Thomas was gracious enough to pull me out of his field with his tractor where I mired down on the second day (I know it sounds fantastic but it's a long story) and the third day the McDaniels pointed out the Scotland Heights railroad stop where the trains once paused briefly for a milk stop and only a few fallen limbs and the infamous Yatton Road challenged me with a new set of obstacles.

Everyone has been lovely and I'm having a great time exploring the territory just a few miles from home.

Mrs. Deale of New York came for a visit with a carload of youngsters when her auto failed her about 11 o'clock at night on the ridge road and Mr. Beeton came to the rescue again.

Now I think I know what the substantial prosperous Virginian calls a comfortable way of life.

His property is off-the-beaten path (it might be a rather muddy path this time of year), sheep may be grazing in the fields, Black Angus chomping the pasture grass, a swollen creek runs through the sloping hills – the house is stone – the field variety with flecks of green shining through when it rains, hams hang from the rafters in a first-floor kitchen and everywhere now the bulb flowers are sprouting up through the rich earth.

Sickness and death knocked at the homes of some again this week.

Especially were we saddened by the loss of two sisters in one day, Mrs. Lola McCarty of Airmont and Mrs. Pearl Slye of Philomont last Thursday. These two natives leave a number of children and loved ones in our community bereaved.

Mrs. John Thomas fell and broke her hip, undergoing an operation in Winchester Hospital last week; Mrs. Allen Campbell is now home after her operation and Harry Dennis was confined to the hospital this week.

Last weekend visitors were Joe Cobb and daughter Diane from The Plains and son Willie and wife Shirley from Gaithersburg, Md. to the R.M. Peytons while the Loopes entertained Alice's brother and family from Wisconsin.

William G. Ballenger, Jr. of Pine Grove celebrated his 29th birthday on Easter Sunday with dinner guests, Mrs. Marie Baabsen, son and daughter Gary and Gail of Arlington, Mrs. Janet Earman, son and daughter, David and Deanna of Winchester and Barbara Watt, Edward Diez and Herman Concho of Berryville formerly from Jamaica and Chile respectively, plus of course, patriarch William G. Ballenger, Sr.

The Jim Brownells were off for a 25th anniversary trip that started on April Fool's Day; the year they got married it was Easter Sunday. They were to roam as they liked but take in the Smokies.

Son Mark preceded their trip by a jaunt to Key West, Fla. picking up Grandmother Brownell's belongings. She will be making Bluemont her home now.

In my browsing among the old Loudoun-Times tucked away in the airy Purcellville Library attic, I read with interest the "Bluemont Breezes" of 1919. The writer C.S. wrote a marvelous sketch about residents, the names of their homes and renovation of the properties.

The Idens dominated the news and by far Earl Iden had the snappiest ads in the paper for his General Store. Those appealing items advertised – if only they could be offered at those prices again.

Sam McMichael has agreed to assume the responsibility for collecting the relics for the Bluemont Fair exhibit. Rosebud James had several Civil War medals worn by members of her family.

Willie and Shirley Peyton of Gaithersburg and brother Ralph and wife Bobbie of Remington returned this weekend and accompanied Rosa Peyton to the Country Music treat at Valley High School on Saturday night while our own Mary Elizabeth Walsh competed for the Miss Loudoun County title.

And there's a tint of green to the grass and the red, red robin can be seen bob, bob, bobbing along again.

April 16, 1970

"Spring has sprung,
The birds have sung."

Lara has poison ivy and my freckles have popped out again, Mrs. Powell and Clarence Manual are sowing in their garden patches, the birds are nesting, nesting in the eaves, house repairs and polishing and painting have begun again in earnest, Herbert Martz is mending a wall at the Kulgrens, the Browns are anticipating the pink glow on the orchard near their house but I'm still not convinced, there's still a sting to the wind that hurts and the picnics on the porch may be a long time coming yet.

The memory of the snow-bound winter was still fresh in Mrs. Sullivan's mind as we chatted this week and the wind rattled doors and windows so, some didn't hear the census-taker's knock. In April '70 I know I'll hit Windy Hill Farm on my rounds in its peak season. At least I hope it doesn't get much worse.

Anyway, I'm beginning to get the clans straight and find the homes of the dog visitors at Clayton Hall several weeks back.

I have canvassed Bluemont proper, a three-day assignment. It was a walking tour and when I hit Reeds' and Reids' hill, I knew I was in a mountain village.

Hazel Reed is truly remarkable with her great determination to overcome her terribly crippling accident. She told me of the days when she and brother Llewllyn Robey played regularly on WTTF in Alexandria, meeting Arthur Godfrey, another Loudouner with red hair and freckles, as you know.

Speaking of red hair and freckles and the Reeds, another one down here in the village celebrated his birthday this week – young Dale Reed, son of Bonnie Reed had a family party with some small friends several weeks ago.

Clyde Beck is causing excitement again with his house painting party at his intended studio in the former Lake Store now owned by the Robert Joneses.

I considered showing-up with my three kids but decided finger-painting wasn't quite what he had in mind.

There were two chimney fires last week – the John Carters and the Piggotts on the ridge frightened most of the neighborhood but each was extinguished quickly.

Reports were that Linda Lloyd, daughter of the Glen Lloyds looked stunning the night she participated in the Miss Loudoun Contest.

The J.J. Kelleys had Friday night guests of the Lyle Fitzgeralds from Buena Vista, Va., and Lois Parenteau, formerly of Silcott Springs visited in the area a week, staying with the Kelleys and the Charles Hummers of Airmont. She claims Desert Hot Springs, Ca. as her mailing address.

Also Sammy Kelley just left after his spring vacation for his school in Maryland.

The Tyrolers were jet-setting again this week – Carolyn for a few days in New York and Charles to Vietnam and Thailand.

Returning to the beautiful Bluemont ridge are Bertrand H. Bratney and his sister to their home, Bouldercrest who have been wintering in Charleston, S.C. (where the Civil War began, you know).

Oh, to have hours to talk with Rose James and hear all her wonderful Bluemont tales. Now there's a book title for you!

Mrs. Kulgren had the most perfect crocus in the area until she laughed and revealed their source – Woolworth's but Mr. Martz has his usual display of the real McCoys and lovely jonquils.

And now the sales and auctions fill Saturdays of the weekends and if I could find a round table for the kitchen and a pretty pie safe, my heart would skip a beat!

Oh, you're looking for the same thing – Yep, I was afraid of that!

April 23, 1970

There's a new melody in Bluemont these days, it's the tune of rushing water. With the heavy rains, the mountain streams are pouring their waters into village properties and village streets. The one at the side of our barn is a delight to the Murray and Summers children and my own trio found a bottle that had floated down, no message in it however.

The census continues with its new set of obstacles – a lost tread on a tire, another day of walking while waiting for the new tags while standard attire for the feet are boots.

I hear the Clarke County enumerator drives a jeep and that should be standard equipment. The roads have always been notorious in this area. According to an Englishman's journal kept prior to the Revolution, the traveler bogged down in deep ruts and opened gates on private property to make his way toward his destination.

Oh, the charmers I've met this week who claimed their birthday to be between 1890 and 1899. They were above being suspicious, gracious, offering a cup of tea, showing me their home and antiques and chatting about local history. J.J. Kelley certainly knows everyone that ever lived here and every place where they ever lived.

Some of these felt as I do that Snickersville was a name worth preserving.

Mrs. Louise Gibson showed me her quilt patch-work and promises some for the Fair and Mrs. Tibbs returned my old security blanket with a pretty new cover that I carried about a tri-state area during college days, semester breaks and shore summers and it's good to have it at the foot of the bed again.

Bob rang up Mr. Tallman and Mr. Bealle again and heard the stories about Mrs. Weadon's boarding house when she served big platters of fried chicken, home-made rolls, buttermilk at one end of the table and sweet milk at the other and for dessert, you had your choice of five different pies all for fifty cents.

Well, the Bluemont Fair dinner won't be quite that cheap but for one thin dollar and a half, you'll have a home-cooked turkey dinner with dressing, hot rolls, apple sauce, green beans and homemade pies for dessert. Mac Brownell has it all arranged where while you wait, you can sit on benches on the porch and appreciate the view up the rolling hills.

Then Mr. Bealle told about the movie house he and Earl Iden operated and lo and behold, Mrs. Dawson had a picture of another one in town plus several terrific scrapbooks she has saved over the years of newspaper clippings featuring Bluemonters. I saw Roberta and Louis Underwood's wedding announcement, a picture of Donald Hope, Sr. in his baseball uniform and Ivy Hindman Cochran's high school graduation picture.

Home-made ice cream was a big seller before in Bluemont at the movie houses on Saturday night according to Jim Scott.

Jean Dawson was home from Madison sporting a pretty red shawl on Saturday and Robert Carter, a resident of Whitehall Farm, is confined to Winchester Hospital.

With the sunny days, it was time to trot the horse and Mr. Snickers' first encounter with the hoofed beast was a frantic affair.

My neighbors were particularly generous as I made my rounds this week, Mac Brownell insisted on sending a Col. Sanders barrel full of big apples home to the family, Mrs. Overton presented me with a bouquet of dark-faced daffodils. Justine Beck picked me some bright sprigs of forsythia, and my dear babysitter Lynn Carbaugh purchased me a silver necklace from a traveling saleswoman and my other dear helper Mary Ann Carter, treated me to an afternoon of ironing and the Becks remembered me when they came across some old bottles.

Do you ever wonder why I adore Bluemont? I thought not.

April 30, 1970

The violets are out, the violets are out. I'll be the town crier to announce the news. A scant showing of the flowering fruit trees has begun and that tint of pale-green is lighting up the mountain vista.

If I could write a sonnet, I'd write about being 17 and discovering a gigantic patch of violets while on a spring tramp with three other young lasses, about how we plopped in the clump and plucked and plucked the sweet violets. Perhaps that marks the difference between a poet and a "picker."

Anyway, the 1970 Census is all over but the counting and analyzing, at least for me. My trusty Ford took me through a few more rough lanes and brought me back to the good graveled drive at Clayton Hall, a good many friendships and acquaintances richer.

I was all set for a bright day on the ridge but the Clarke County man beat me to it, mystified by the district line between Clarke and Loudoun, he sailed through the Nashes and the Bratneys, only losing out the Manns, with Emma knowing her territory as she is our Snickersville registrar.

Very well, I strove on to the yellow school house road, relinquishing Roy Santmyer's sense of humor, Mrs. Peyton's anticipation of the strawberries, and Mrs. Parks' kindness and the usual lovely view of the hill.

Then appropriately, I shifted into low, and took my first incline up Pierrot's hill. From there I could survey my travels, the Wesley Carbaughs lending me binoculars and pointing out the sights. Indeed what a lush terrain.

Then I dipped by the Scipio sisters, a darling pair, and called back to Virginia Woolman, our Bluemont enumerator of 1960, saying a grateful yes to an offer of a glass of sherry and then two days of rain when I stayed in close, pulling off the plastic from the windows so I wouldn't miss the blossoms this season.

The herring are running and Bluemont men have gone "dipping" in area waters, sharing their catch with just about everyone in the village. Mrs. Wesley Carbaugh even preserved some in a jar.

Karen Underwood told me she had celebrated her seventh birthday this week and recent guests of Mr. and Mrs. Kenneth Reid of Pine Grove were their daughter and grandson, Mrs. Bruce Costello and Bruce Costello of Alexandria.

The Englishmen from the Embassy returned for a visit at the Becks who are redoing just about everything and I met two other delightful English ladies on my travels. Mrs. Courtney and her sister are now in their eighties and as usual, terribly energetic. Mrs. Courtney and her late husband once operated the famed Courtney Inn in Purcellville. The English have denied this area is like England, as one article stated that I read recently, but they quickly added, "We like it, anyway."

Young Donnie Spring of Herndon, Barbara Spring's grandson was back for a romp in the creek, field and woods of Bluemont this past weekend and J.K. Cornwall, Randy Ballenger, and Allen Carter heralded spring with a camping trip on the trail.

The Thurston Potts exhibited the cherished "The Loudoun" catalog – a school for selective young ladies housed at the present Miss Alley's. She told of her brother Owen and her rides by sleigh to the school once upsetting in a deep drift.

Time to sow some grass with the promise of more rain, dust the volume of Robert Frost off and find a quiet stream somewhere and woo the Goddess Spring to our mountain village.

May 7, 1970

Some call this delicious hot spell summer but whatever it is, the warmth of the sun urging blooms on red-bud, dogwood, pear, peach and our particularly native apple trees convinces me Virginia is one of the fairest spots in the northern hemisphere.

But what a time of year. One wishes for new furnishings – indoor and out, a new patio, a pool, shubbery, gardening tools – a trip, a nice little party with some perfect watercress sandwiches, some new fashions, perhaps even a new home or piece of property.

Men want motor-cycles, sports cars, new mowers, tractors – farmers desire more stock, new machinery – Americans seem to want to invest in everything but new stocks right now but most of us settle for a little paint to brighten up the dreary walls and take to the front porch or backyard for cookouts on last year's grill.

Mrs. Irma Fuller and her sister Mrs. Brown of Berryville whom we had the pleasure of meeting over the weekend, told of Mrs. Santmyer's mother's lemonade, cake and ice cream stand when a round dance above the old Lake Store and a square dance at the stone structure across the street were held simultaneously and it sounded like there were many gay times in the old town.

The Hatchers of Del Ray Beach, Fla. knew it was the right time for a visit to their Virginia property here on the hill above the village and they kept Mrs. Powell company several evenings at her wonderful roomy house.

Jerry Lloyd and his family managed to relocate back in Bluemont, buying the stone house next to the John Thomases up on Route Seven.

Yep, you guessed it, those long wiggily creatures are back in Bluemont, too, Mrs. King sighted one in her yard and Mrs. Dawson almost put her hand on one out at the Ebenezer Church graveyard where epitaph reading should be great these sunny days.

Spring seems to produce a sign hoax to our village each year. Remember last year's "Hyland Hilton Hotel" and my "Beware, Mad Woman" poster? Now we have "John Week's Birthplace 1821." If we are discrediting a great unknown hero, better let us know because all the local historical experts say they never heard of the gent.

Clyde Beck is now exhibiting a number of new works in the Dupont Theatre in Washington where you can also take in the show, "They Shoot Horses, Don't They?" I fully expected Jane Fonda to win the Oscar for her performance in it, didn't you?

The Donald Bowmans had quite a little mishap when they arrived home last week to discover all the electricity off on the farm; one of the sturdy calves had knocked down a utility pole.

Bessie Carter's grandchildren, the White's of Summit Point, W.Va. spent the weekend basking in Bluemont's agreeable weather with good-natured grandmother.

We lured a former Miss Loudoun, Pat Fagge Jackson and her two children from Reston to Bluemont on Friday too, took her for a wade in Little's creek and oohed and aahed over the red-bud and dogwood on the hill and then the country cousin, Jennifer went back to the city with the city cousin and we all ended up there on Saturday night, taking the plunge on the elevator in the big apartment house (highest building in Fairfax County) there and getting lost on the way to the rest room again. Guess I'm too simple to live in a city.

Our babysitter Lynn Carbaugh was down with a case perhaps of ulcers and our sympathy to her.

A big surprise birthday party was held for Wendy Kelley at Gail Kelley's last Tuesday with Ivy Cochran creating another cake special with a wishing well and Wendy hoeing a garden of flowers. Joan Wilt and Doris Allder helped with the calling of the 23 guests and some 13 pre-school offspring.

It's time to worry about those hatching mosquito larvae again and a new experiment shows garlic deposited in the water will kill the pests. Next time you want a mosquito free outdoor supper – serve a real spicey Italian dish and pass the mints.

Happy Spring Fling!

May 14, 1970

Little League has begun, the lilac's fragrance is everywhere, even the dormant-appearing Empress trees are displaying their lavender blooms as activity teems in little Bluemont.

Mr. Beeton, my thoughtful reporter on the ridge writes "For the past week there have been numerous automobiles parked along the Appalachian Trail. No persons have been observed in these cars but nearby they can be seen in the woods looking at the ground in search of something. As a native mountaineer told it, they are looking for 'Mushy rooms' or 'Mushorooms' (Mushrooms to you). What are these mushyrooms being looked for, well Larousse Gastronomique, a French encyclopedia of food, wine and cookery, translated into English puts it this way: 'Morel pronounced morille – a fungus, one of the best growing in France. Found in the Spring on the fringe of the woods. Various species, the most highly prized being the little black pointed morels found in the mountainous country.' This is what is being looked for and the cause of the parked cars and they are growing here in our beautiful Blue Ridge Mountains."

He also notes that a John McInerney and his dog both from Ireland were trampers on the trail last Thursday and the Oscar Veninas and dog Honey took in the Apple Blossom Festival reporting a fine time.

Back to the ridge were the Tom Holmes last week and Father John Whelan, former head of Catholic University and now vice-president of that institution was host to a group of nuns from CUA last week at his retreat on the ridge. (Thank you, Mr. Beeton).

Karlton Monroe called to let me know he and Mary had returned safely from their great trip to Canada and back, escaping a disaster of a sunken ocean-liner the Patrick-Morris which they were slated to board but luckily changed their minds – the captain went down with the vessel when 70 mile winds endangered the ship that was seeking to rescue a fishing craft.

Karlton said they saw 15 foot ice drifts and sunlight at 4 o'clock in the morning and learned that it costs $50 a day just to put out the lobster pots and the price of lobsters in Canada was low but in Maine – high. Oh, how I'd love some lobster tails in melted butter right now.

The Earl Idens celebrated a quiet 62nd anniversary (they shouldn't be quiet about that) with their daughters and spouses, Mr. and Mrs. Howard D. Sprague of Purcellville and of course, the Earl Virts of Bluemont too last Sunday.

The Robert Allders are displaying a nice new fence. Now if we had a neat sidewalk to match, it would be perfect.

The Townshends had a goodly number of guests all for a sit-down dinner last Saturday. Pre-sent were the Wendell Rothgebs with grandchildren Karen and Danielle of Beltsville, Md., Mrs. Mary Baughman of Winchester, Mr. and Mrs. Charles Brill and son Charles of Gore, Va. and Mr. and Mrs. Walter Quick of Lynchburg.

Mary Ann Carter celebrated a birthday last week with her sister and husband Mr. and Mrs. Ed Sims of Landover, Md., her brother Norman Smith of Cabin John, Md., and Jack Barber of Leesburg plus aunt Ada Cornelius from Arcola.

She and Johnny spent Saturday at Keys Ferry Acres in West Virginia with James and Margaret McCauley.

Glad Lynn Carbaugh is back from Winchester Hospital and can take to some real-live food again.

Graduation announcements are going out now and Bluemont's Larry Allder, Jill Reed, Beverly Kelley and Willa Colbert are sending out theirs. Willa threw a gay party for the occasion here on Saturday night.

Having just purchased two handsome 450-pound Hereford steers last week, the Don Seidenspinners were dismayed to realize they had broken out shortly after they were put in the corral on the ridge.

If you see these babies with six-inch horns, a blotch of green paint on their back and a collar with numbers eight or nine, please call 226-4331. These were to be the children's pets.

I've dreamed about it since we moved here and finally it happened – there was a snake under the dining room table last week.

Quickly Jack Allder came to my rescue, my dear little Gretchen giving me warning it was in the house earlier when she literally tried to tear the baseboard heat duct apart.

Jack proclaimed it to be a "house moccasin" and Agnes says I can keep all the snakes over here and so a light burns bright in old Clayton Hall these nights. Bare feet on a bare-snake rug in the dark. No thanks!

May 21, 1970

Now the ever-encompassing green has completely conquered the brown hue on our mountain-side, the irises are showing purple and the snow-balls have fluffed up the landscape.

The Bluemont women are back at the softball diamond into their second game here against Purcellville on Saturday night.

Joan Wilt, the pitcher was also entertaining her aunt Mrs. Mae Swetnam of Alexandria for a few days.

Charles Anson of the English Embassy was back to see the Becks on Saturday along with a journalist friend from the Baltimore Sun hoping to find a suitable weekend retreat in Bluemont.

Everyone is sporting numerous mosquito bites: the sixth Lord Fairfax, Proprietor of the Northern Neck had the same complaints in 1730 about Virginia's mosquitoes according to Berryville's Stuart Brown's book lent to me by our historian Ingrid Jones.

Young Master Robert Morris Carter celebrated his third birthday on the 15th with a party, also the Robert Carters of Bluemont entertained Mr. and Mrs. John P. Carter, Miss Lisa Ann Carter and Mrs. Henry Russell of Alexandria.

Sorry to hear the Robert P. Carters were unable to locate permanently here in Bluemont and have returned to Statesville, N.C.

There was a Californian visitor in town this week, a former Miss Reid whose father operated a store on the present Mann's Store premises; she promised to return before departing for good after a visit to her daughter in Baltimore.

"The Wizard of Oz" was performed by the sixth and seventh grade of Round Hill Elementary this week with a number of fine actors from Bluemont participating. A cast party was held on Saturday. Desiree Allder, Hunter Kelley and Debra Dawson were three of the triple threat.

The Seventies Club was extremely active this Friday; Frank McComb was grooming the Virts sidewalk frontage, Walter Peyton was hoeing his advanced potatoes, tomatoes and cabbages, Jim Scott was applying the cycle to Ruth's grass and Earl Iden in the eighties club was doing a little concrete patching.

Have you seen Herbert Martz's absolutely exquisite display of tulips? He picked off 19 dozen last week and there still are plenty more.

Poor Carolyn Tyroler was stricken with mumps and around went a recipe chain letter, promising 36 recipes in several days.

The whole community was sorely grieved to hear of Ralph May's passing. Mr. May who operated a general store and service station in Pine Grove for many years was a kind, friendly man who took pride in his neatly-kept property and rare collection of Civil War relics all recovered from local areas.

Feature writer Jean McDonald gave a coffee on a dewy Saturday morning and when her son placed his petite Dutch rabbit among the empty coffee cups, visions of Alice and her tea party and unbirthday party came to mind. Lewis Carroll was a bachelor who wrote the tales to amuse his niece, Alice. It was somewhat of a satire so the English professors tell us too.

Mrs. Willkie looked pert and when we got on the subject of my snake she volunteered that she kept several black snakes in the yard. I wonder if a sign, Beware of Snakes is posted?

Mac Brownell reported her energetic crew of off-spring has just dug out the old original cellar pouring a new floor so they might have a secluded "pad" at old Whitehall Farm.

"Something there is, that doesn't love an air-conditioner – That wants it out."

Pardon my paraphrasing Robert Frost but before any sweet spring breezes can blow across the bedstead, the air-conditioner is put in place and things are closed up tight.

In winter, the thermostat is turned up, then down, in the summer the air-conditioner flips on and off – it's the old battle of the sexes – I guess nature knows what she's doing but even with our extra layer of skin, we women can shiver at 60 degrees and the noise pollution of it all. Watch out. A little feminist lurks in every woman.

May 28, 1970
"At the Senior Prom we danced till three"

A full yellow moon shone down…the sweetness of mock orange sauntered through the open windows… all spelling a sentimental romantic time on the calendar.

Wedding bells rang all around us; entertaining for their own Junior Bridesmaid, the William Carbaughs held a ham, chicken salad buffet supper for about 20 guests last Saturday to honor Miss Kay Hoff of Boyce and her fiancé Robert Sell of Greencastle, Pa., a student at Shenandoah Conservatory who will take those steps down the altar the first week in June.

"Mutter" Brownell is elated that her first-born, Jimmy will bring his bride from Richmond after a Memorial Day wedding to spend this summer at Whitehall Farm.

All the Manns, including Tom and Ruth were down from Richmond for the weekend attending the wedding of William Mann and Brenda Null in Frederick, Md. last Sunday.

If you haven't met Helen Freedman yet, you've missed the Hostess with the Mostest. Up we went to see those adorable Great Pyrenees puppies and she has special treats of candy, cookies and black cherry soda for the children after having just overseen the whelping of a litter of seven, plus playing hostess to Roy and Jane Newlin and nine-month old baby Dierlin for seven weeks. The Newlins were some of the "doggie" people (Mrs. Strang's cute expression) too whose foreign-born Pyrenees was boarding at the Freedmans till they could pick him up after a two-year hitch in the U.S. Army spent in Germany. Now they are California-bound with furniture, three pets and baby equipment. The courage of some people.

Now I adore those dogs, mostly because they're like bears in their appearance without any of the frightening aspects of bearhood. "Monty" who stays on the Twin Oaks front porch just kept giving me his three-pound paw.

So when I heard at the lovely craft luncheon at Emma Mann's last week about the appearance of a brown bear to their side-door about seven years ago, I really perked up. He was on the Kerrick's roof as well on his sojourn to civilization. I guess we villagers shouldn't complain about a few snakes.

Back to Mother's Day several sunny Sundays back, Edith Reed was pleasantly treated to a picnic at Old Ebenezer Church in Clarke County when all the children gathered to say, "We think you're terrific." The Marshall Campbells of The Plains, Andrew Lawrence of Fairfax, Melvin Reed of Falls Church, then Carl, Gordon and Marvina and family from Bluemont, also Sonny and Betty Colbert were all there.

The community will be pleased to know that a new craft shop called The Country Craft operated by Ann Van Deventer and Katie Smith has opened its doors for business in the old store across from the Esso Station on Rt. 7 in Round Hill. Art and crafts will be sold there on a 20 percent commission basis for interested craftsmen.

The Bluemont Methodist Church announces that the Sunday School picnic will be at Camp Highroad again this year on July 5 followed by our glorious fourth's celebration here in Bluemont. I can taste that ice cream now.

Don't forget the important town meeting the first Wednesday in June.

Now Memorial Day is almost here again – the day that unofficially heralds in the summer season at shore-points.

While a student, I learned this the hard way – taking a calculated risk I got a ride with friends to Ocean Grove, N.J., a Methodist Camp Ground where autos aren't allowed on Sundays with about eight dollars in hand. In a matter of hours, I found a job at the "Cozy Cottage" as a waitress, a place to stay in the top-floor dormitory of the an old hotel which my parents called a fire-trap for five dollars a week, all right before Memorial Day one "fifties" summer.

One day of customers' smiles and snarls and then the onslaught, Jim, an old waiter pro and myself walked, ran and crawled carrying hot plates of rib roast, filet of flounder and corned beef and cabbage to an over-full house till closing time, realizing I had made good when the penny pinching proprietor offered me a free dessert for a job well done.

Memorial Day in the countryside, however, is a service at Old Ebenezer Church, a right and just setting for laying down one's earthly cares and where a thoughtful friend or relative might bring the fullness of a peony bud on a hot Memorial Day.

June 4, 1970

School days are numbered, daisies are pushing up through green fields, cherries are almost ready for picking and robins are ever on stage performing their curtain-call ballet.

Health and happiness to our graduates. They are Vicky Ballenger from Clarke County High School, Gilbert Dawson, Larry Allder and Jill Reed, both seeking government business jobs come June 11, Jan Woolman – the recipient of a nursing scholarship to Alexandria School of Nursing plus Willa Colbert – college-bound all from Loudoun Valley High School in Purcellville.

The locusts are making life a little unpeaceful on the ridge but I haven't seen a one in the village. They're eating and chirping reports the Strangs, Verloops and Freedmans and in France they're being lacquered and sold for costume jewelry. The arrival of these insects is a new phenomenon to many but somehow 17 years ago is vivid in my mind when my high-school friend and I would stroll after cheerleading practice to her old Victorian frame house in the then farm-town of Gaithersburg. Chatting of dates and summer plans, the locusts would hum and fall upon us when we passed under the laden branches along her long sidewalk.

Mrs. Owen Thomas reminds the community of the annual Vacation Community Bible School in Round Hill sponsored jointly by the Baptist and Methodist Church held at the Baptist Church this year beginning on June 15. Miss Ann Crouch will serve as superintendent.

The Bluemont Home Demonstration Club meets this month on the second Wednesday at 9:30 a.m. at the schoolhouse featuring a demonstration on dried flowers. Anyone interested is invited.

Proud Grandmother Reid wanted everyone to know her granddaughter, three-year old Pam was at the Mother's Day picnic, too.

The owners of Bear's Den are up for a visit painting and restoring the lovely stone property with stone picnic pavilions and rock cylinder-like gatehouses on the long lane to the rocky view over the valley. This is the spot where long-skirted ladies had their pictures taken after a delightful carriage ride up from the quaint Bluemont Railroad Station.

Another spot with a strange sounding name was "Shirt-tail Hollow" up there on the ridge somewhere where the late McCarthy's (Roberta Underwood's parents) first started housekeeping.

Clyde Beck was traveling with the international set over the Memorial Day weekend not by jet, but good old bicycle down the tow-path at the canal. Englishman Charles Anson and a Frenchman rounded out the trio.

Ralph May's son and wife dropped by last week to talk about the Civil War relics. May, an avid collector reports he found many breast-shields and minnie balls at near-by Retreat where troops camped for a month.

Two birthdays of two illustrious Bluemont leaders occurred this week. Shir Carbaugh and Walton Mann and we promised not to reveal the age of either.

I was about to pronounce Lynn Carbaugh as the original feminist as she helped me open windows that wouldn't budge for helpless "little ole me" but alas, we had to call on Larry Allder for assistance and Memorial Day wasn't a flag-flying day here at old Clayton Hall at all but a window-washing one.

The Men and Women's ball teams are engaged in a lively season with Larry Allder and Dickie Costello coaching the women.

Some neighbors promenade with governors and heads of state but my children and I find our bi-weekly jaunt to our post-office stimulating.

There are Routes A and B; A takes us by the Dawsons where we might find an Empress pod for a dried arrangement, by Mann's Store, a stop for penny candy on special days, by the Robert Allders where a talk with Yvonne is in order, a glance over the Carbaughs, speaking to Hector and Buss, the small canines behind the picket fence, then by the Virts admiring the iris and across the street to peek in the window at Mr. O'Brien's antiques in the old dance hall, then past the old store arriving at our destination.

The kids dip into the trash while Mrs. Townshend and I try to exchange pleasantries and we're homeward bound on Route B.

Up the rocky road by the Joneses and Mitchells we go treating our eyes to Herbert Martz's ever-blooming flower garden, a pat for Queenie, a quick side-step to Ruth's swings, a moment with Walter Peyton at the old telephone office, across the lush field behind the Allders sometimes sighting a rabbit and into the graveled drive of home again.

Yes, this is a marvelous walking village, and wouldn't some renovated sidewalks be nice? Plug! Plug!

June 18, 1970

The mood of your correspondent is rather melancholy tonight: often as I worked on a summer night the sound of the cackling laughter of Donald and Alvin Coates and companions in the street below would drift through the open windows but they were forced to abandon their home here today along with the Murrays, Summers and Gibsons to go soon. A new road coming through – progress they call it, we will be a weaker community without them.

On the bright side – in season came back on local menus. First the blueberries – Mother and Daddy bought three quarts from a Bethesda outlet to Bluemont and I was a child again, chilling them – dishing them out in blue-print bowls with sugar and cream, next morning there were blueberry pancakes and a few saved for a fruit compote over sherbet.

Then Mrs. Peyton called to say the strawberries were in. This is a special trip every year for the children and me too (I'll admit it). We just had a piece of sticky-iced cake, see the pigs slopped, pet the new kittens, inspect the baby chicks and pick some young lettuce and as ever – admire the view before getting back to the village proper.

Then on Wednesday, a pick-up truck of watermelons pulled into the store and the Carbaughs and Becks had a feast and of course, the cherries are prime for picking and tasting now too.

Mrs. Boxley, the dearest of gracious Southern ladies entertained her brother-in-law Miller Petty from Roanoke and his daughter Mrs. Charlie Morgan for a fried chicken country dinner before driving them to Dulles Airport where they will be flying to Spain, no hijacking involved we trust.

Cheryl Anne Reid, daughter of Mr. and Mrs. Ralph R. Reid, a member of the U.S. Twirling Association took part in the State Championship Contest on Memorial Day at Langley High School.

Sorry to hear Mrs. Reid was a patient at Winchester Hospital recently.

With the closing of school came the retirement of Mrs. Betty Lightner from teaching at Round Hill Elementary where she taught for five years and she was the beloved principal at the Bluemont School when it still operated. She was entertained at a luncheon and presented with a lovely piece of luggage by the Round Hill faculty. As an appreciated patron said, "Whatever Betty Lightner undertakes, she does well."

The Bookmobile will be making summer stops here on June 16 and 30, July 14 and 28 and Aug. 11 and 25 in the afternoon. What better way to spend a hot summer day than with a book propped above you in a hammock on the front porch.

Speaking of front porches, doesn't the Plaster place look inviting with the rocker the Baker Bayles have placed there?

The Loudoun County Department of Parks and Recreation has announced its schedule and Bluemont will have a half-day session Monday through Friday from 9-12 with Arts and Crafts, Drama, Dance and Music and Sports and Athletics for ages 6-18 at the old school grounds.

Pretty Linda Virts of Leesburg was here for a two-day visit with her grandparents, the Earl Virts.

I was right the first time, Gilbert Dawson graduated last Thursday night and expects to be employed with the telephone company.

Charles Anson of the English Embassy and Al Serber of Baltimore will be making the Bluemont scene on weekends at the Waldrop place. Miss Florence Maitland decided against spending her traditional summer in Bluemont and with Mr. Nesmith's death, the characters have changed in the old setting at the end of the lane.

James and Evelyn Pierson of Bloomfield graciously invite anyone interested to some iris bulbs, colors – black purple, two-tone purple, and light orchid and if you don't get them now – maybe the Piersons will bring them to sell at the Fall Fair.

There will be no local Home Demonstration Club meeting for July and August.

Now I take it all back – a dead locust fell down the chimney this week. Their drone in the morning hours is overwhelming at times but the cricket's chirp in the long evening is always a pleasant lullaby as hours go dreamily by here in the summer haven under the mountain shadow.

June 25, 1970

There's something terribly exhilarating about a country sale and the Bluemont neighbors, the Lawrence Dawsons with their auction in Philomont added a dimension of excitement to the usual quiet pace of both villages on Saturday.

Not often does a general store go up for sale, but what a way to have to shop for groceries.

While the crowd was still small, I finally got the courage to try this bidding business against myself, but I still think I got the bargain of the day with 40 cans of spices, six small bottles of turpentine and five of sweet oil for 50 cents. Of course, 10 were pumpkin spice and I never made a pumpkin pie in my life and sweet oil – well, maybe we'll have a lot of earaches.

Shir Carbaugh came back with a whole basket of glassware for $3 and I put the old pro Shir on some blue dishes for me and she brought home the bacon.

Dishes should be blue to me and that lovely bright set of pottery reflects Mrs. Slye's gaiety and congeniality on the one occasion that I met her about a year ago so I believe I have the perfect fond remembrance.

The antique sales on Friday in Lincoln drew a lot of the Bluemont neighbors too – love to hear of your purchases.

I was pleased to meet Lucien Reed's mother who has been visiting from Pennsylvania. She said she had her first ice cream cone right here in Bluemont and did all her Christmas shopping here at one time.

Ah, what a revival this place is getting – the painting of the old Lake Store by Clyde Beck gives the spot a new face and Herbert Martz is improving lots with his mowing.

Up on the ridge the David Freedmans were pleased to welcome his mother from New York and she brought a sample of that city's pastries with her. Yum! Yum!

On a diet – forget it – the sacrifice is just too great with homemade ice cream time fast approaching.

Great champions of that art are the Glen Lloyds and all the Lloyds had a grand annual family reunion last Sunday at the Berryville Horse Show Grounds with 120 in attendance.

Glen is the baby of the even dozen and he comes closest of tying the record with his nine off-spring.

The Robert P. Carters of Statesville, N.C. were up for a visit last weekend and still hoping to locate around Bluemont in September. If anyone knows of rental property available please write them at: 1108 Boulevard, Statesville, N.C.

The Bluemont Women's Team is going great guns with a 4-3. Winner of the hundred dollars (sold to benefit the uniform and insurance fund) was Roger Thomas of Hamilton.

The Loving Service of the Berryville Baptist Church met with Mrs. G. W. Townshend on Friday, June 12 and the Townshends entertained her sisters, Mrs. Oscar McCloskey of Port Charlotte, Fla. and Mrs. Stanley Lyddane for the weekend.

The school children continued their leisurely summer pursuits – catching crayfish, putting lightning bugs in a jar, climbing trees for sour cherries and sitting barefooted sipping a coke in front of Mann's Store.

And then Father's Day went sparkling by - in the south he's Daddy, whatever his age or ours, and old-fashioned I may be, but there still is no one quite like my Daddy – hope you told your pop, dad, father but never "old man" the same on Father's Day.

July 2, 1970

Now the orange tiger lilies and perky black-eyed susans are here to brighten the verdant landscape.

The Becks English friends are treating their tastes buds to lily roots, shoots (like nuts) and blossoms (for frying) and "the lilies" creeping quality presents me with a border bouquet through the efforts of the neighbors' planting.

"Something there is that doesn't love a wall, that wants it down." Frost's words come through every time I observe this phenomenon.

But there is more going on in Bluemont this week than blossoming flowers.

In the first place, great plans are being made for the glorious Fourth. Starting at seven on the school grounds there will be games and feasting on homemade ice cream and cake and then the exciting fireworks at dusk.

Those who are contributing ice cream have been asked by Chairman Ivy Cochran to put their name on their freezer and parts including the finger-licking dasher. Contributions will benefit the Citizens Association this year.

Guests are requested not to bring individual fireworks as a real danger to eye and limb is involved.

A grand Bluemont Fair meeting will be held the following week, July 8 at 7:30 at the school. All chairmen are expected to attend and give a progress report.

Electioneering time is here again and the Democratic Primary will be Tuesday, July 14.

Dorothy McDermott of Fairfax has made several long stops in Loudoun feeling at home in the county where she spent childhood summers at Philomont and Lincoln, recalling a winter sleigh ride from Lincoln to Purcellville and Darrel Stearns is sending-out personal letters publicizing his professional work as city planner; Alvin Zeiset and David Gardener are the other two candidates for the House of Representatives for the Eighth District. The winner will oppose Republican Congressman William Scott.

Then for Senator is Milton Colvin, Clive L. Duvall, II and George C. Rawlings, Jr. to run against neighbor and now independent Harry Byrd, Jr. of Winchester. Of course, the latter is hardly a new name in Virginia politics.

"By the sea, by the sea, by the beautiful sea" – Snooks Campbell, Willa Colbert found Florida the ocean spot for them last week and the Martin Wilts along with the Russell Parks, Sr. of Pine Grove and Karen Parks of Airmont fathomed the waves at Ocean City, Md.; meanwhile the J.H.H. Verloops are looking forward to two weeks on old Cape Cod. Ah, I can almost sniff the sea air now, see the trim lawns and bright-blue shutters on seaside cottages and pick a handful of primroses traveling up an Oceanside trellis, not to mention the sight of sailboats and vast ships on the golden horizon. And oh, the lobster, to be able to stop and have lobster salad in a bun in any little snack shop.

Oh well, a green mountain is an inspiring scene too and my evening walk last night revealed a string of soft purple morning glories clinging to the side of the Butler's wonderful old stone house.

The indomitable Earl Iden along with daughters, Mrs. Earl Virts and Mrs. Howard Sprague and husband of Purcellville were off to Emporia, Va. to Mrs. Iden's Morris family reunion last Sunday.

At the same time Mrs. Mabel Virts, Earl's sister came for a weekend visit in Bluemont.

Always a marvelous host and hostess, the Charles Tyrolers are enjoying the company of Carolyn's son and family, the Edmund B. Games of Dedham, Mass.

Lynn Carbaugh says she will get away from it all and escape to Boyce to spend the week with her great-aunt Mrs. Frances Wiley.

Clyde Beck wishes the public to know his new studio at the Old Lake Store will be open for inspection the weekend of the Fourth.

A good letter came my way this week – its greeting was "Dear Lover of Loudoun."

An organization whose purpose it is to "Keep Loudoun Beautiful" (a noble goal, indeed) needs money, time and interest.

Contributions can be sent to "Keep Loudoun Beautiful", P.O. Box 5, Leesburg, Va 22075 and if time can be given for services contact Mrs. B. Powell Harrison.

To hear the birds chirp, to breathe fresh air, to feast the eyes on nature's coolness may be merely a memory to relate to our grandchildren unless we act now, "dear lover of Loudoun."

July 9, 1970

Indeed, it's rather heart-warming to realize that a whole town is bent on creating delectable homemade ice cream and cakes just prior to the Fourth of July every year, but that's what happens here in Bluemont annually.

The 29 gallons of the leading favorites – chocolate and vanilla plus banana, strawberry, raspberry, pineapple and cherry-nut were consumed before the crowd swelled to the estimated 300.

The Bluemont Fair promotional balloon stand, constructed by Mark Brownell was a favorite with the small fry. Graced by Rosa Peyton and provided by the blowing action of the kind Seidenspinners on the ridge, the light flimsy articles went within the first 45 minutes.

The girls and women battled it out on the softball field while an energetic crew of local boys tapped out some good tunes with their guitars and drums and then, of course, came the fireworks.

A vote of thanks to Ivy Cochran and her committee for such a memorable Fourth.

A good number of the citizenry gathered again the next day at Camp Highroad near Aldie for the annual Methodist Church Sunday School picnic. There was swimming and splashing and lots of good food as usual.

Talk about a swimming party, Friday night the Becks provided drinks and sumptuous fare on the patio, then summoned guests to the studio for a jam session and adjourned to the Charles Tyrolers for a midnight dip.

Special guests were the English and French again who are enjoying the Waldrops' retreat for the summer along with their guest British actress Angela McDonald sporting a beautiful tan having just come from Jamaica.

Hope Lloyd's tan looks good too as she spent a week at the bay recently.

The Walton Manns took Wednesday off from the store and took in the Amish Fair in Kutztown, Pa. along with Emma's sisters, Mrs. Ruth Simpson of Purcellville and Mrs. Alma Arnold of Lovettsville.

The James E. Piersons of Bloomfield welcomed the grandchildren Holly and Shelley and son James Jr. and wife from Lanham, Md. who always come for the fireworks and Sunday School picnic each July.

Sorry Mrs. Chapman, Shir Carbaugh's mother couldn't join us for all the socializing. She is confined to Winchester Hospital and would appreciate hearing from her Bluemont friends.

Life will settle back to its usual quiet pace as the wilting days of July and August advance but before the tigerlilies are gone, why not try an arrangement of lilies with Queen Anne's Lace as I saw at the Battletown Inn this week?

The baked squash is as good as ever and by the way ladies, how about paying up with those recipes from the chain letter? Promised 36, I got one!

Happy Dog Days!

July 16, 1970

"Raindrops keep falling on my head," the Academy Award winning song could well have been inspired by the area's weather this week.

The downpours threatened bridges and made a mess of the Brunelle's new driveway and coaxed a black snake up on Mrs. Powell's porch but being a farm community, it's hard to turn down a summer shower even if it's something of a storm.

Still thinking back to last weekend, Ivy Cochran wished to thank all those who helped with the arrangements for the Fourth of July celebration.

Some special guests at the celebration were Mr. and Mrs. David Thomas of Pennsylvania and their coming is kinda a Bluemont success story to me.

Mrs. Thomas was known to Bluemonters as Delia, a charge of Miss Alley's for some 20 years. As is Miss Alley's way, she was loved and nurtured tenderly, the neighbors were part of Delia's family and the whole community her concerned friends.

Delia left Bluemont several years ago to attend vocational school and then met David Thomas, a linotype operator for a Philadelphia paper.

Now as his wife she lives a full and fulfilled life, also serving society as a nurses' aide.

He was thrilled to meet Delia's family, the kind neighbors of Bluemont and so when Alfie asks his question, "What's it all about?" that's the Bluemont answer, "Brighten the corner where you are."

The William Carbaughs had a great trip to Hershey, Pa. – Chocolatetown – this week and Pam and Sharon were chosen as candy tasters – good work if you can get it!

Lisa Cornwall and Tammy Parks are off for a delightful week or two at nearby Camp Highroad which boasts a wonderful pool and a real deep-woods location up from Philomont.

The Kenneth Reids of Pine Grove had a good crowd of weekend guests over the Fourth. Daughter and grandson, Mrs. Bruce Costello and young Bruce and their other daughter Carole, husband John and their child Alisa.

The Bluemont Community lost two families this week, the Leroy Virts and the Edwardses moving to Winchester.

The Parks and relatives had a big picnic on Sunday to celebrate Yvonne Allder, J.K. Cornwell and Mrs. Russell Parks, Sr.'s birthdays this week.

Now about that homemade ice cream, young Yvonne Allder won the prize on the half-gallon of ice cream at the Fourth of July festival and I have a few tips from my two batches. That mix with eggs, milk, sugar, and cream is terrific – then you just add your favorite flavor, use plenty of ice and the rock salt makes the freezing quicker.

Sunday night wasn't too soon for another batch but Monday morning found Bob coming down from the attic with an antique gear. When I asked, "What's that?" he replied he was going to rig it up to the freezer. I got the old-fashioned turn kind for fun but since he got the job of churning, this was his modern answer.

After several meals out on the town last week, Jennifer asked if the breakfast was "Corn Flakes Virginia?"

Mrs. R.M. Peyton has fresh vegetables for sale now, either by the pound or bushel.

There was a good turnout to the big Bluemont Fair meeting last Wednesday night and chairman should contact me in the next two weeks to tell me what they want for their stations – chairs, tables, stands – let me know.

Colorful curtains enhanced the appearance of the meeting room thanks to Shir Carbaugh, Ingrid Jones, Betty Walsh and Ivy Cochran.

George Washington's picture hangs in the old room, too and Mrs. Elizabeth Kelley says she remembers when her students won that for selling the most pencils some years ago.

Citizens are reminded that trash collection fees are due to the treasurer, Ellen Jones.

If it's poetry, you're wanting,

I have it not
My head is aching
And a lot! Burma Shave!

July 23, 1970

"Inevitably there comes a time when the longing for the open, sun-lit country, gently undulating valleys, fresh green meadows, mountains which softly blend into the azure of the sky and the cool, healthful breezes, cannot be further unheeded."

So began the Washington and Old Dominion Railway's enticement to take their train to Bluemont in the early 1900's.

The little booklet, "Resorts" was unearthed by Mrs. Owen Thomas this week and included a fascinating list of boarding houses and hotels with guest capacity and rates. Earl Iden had the Blue Ridge, John Chapin – the Loudoun, Simpsons – Bluemont Heights. Lone Oak Farm, Rose Villa and Virginia House and the Miller and Humphrey Boarding houses were our principal eight.

A decade of Bluemont News

This would have been the height of the tourist season with our now warm days and pleasant nights.

Quite a bit of activity was going on in the old burg this week.

The gardens were coming in hot and heavy: Mary Ann Carter has already canned over a hundred quarts of beans, Mr. Horning on Rt. 709 just below Thelma Best and Gertrude Beatty has the most succulent blackberries – see him if you wish to pick your own or have him pick – Mac Brownell said she made a six-quart cobbler the other night.

The Home Demonstration Club sponsored a refurbishing class and some adorable pieces showed up and progressed nicely under Ruby Payne and Dot Heasley's guidance. Both these ladies are helping us with the Bluemont Fair craft exhibits.

Ruby said any piece of furniture made before 1930 was considered an antique and that a tree should be 75 years old before it is suitable for furniture-making.

William G. Ballenger, Jr. had as a weekend guest, Miss Hilda Grant of New York City, formerly from Guantánamo, Cuba and the Lucien Reeds entertained the A.P. Gotschs of Norristown, Pa. last weekend and then included Sunday dinner guests of Mr. and Mrs. Gordon Reed of Leesburg, Mr. and Mrs. J.D. Reed of Emory and Mrs. Frankie Hardy and son of Charles Town.

News from the Robert Carter family was that little David Mason Carter celebrated his first birthday with a family party last week and the Carters entertained Mr. and Mrs. James Bruce Carter, Miss Jacqueline Carter and James Bruce Carter III all from Statesville, N.C. for a week.

Those two pretty blondes visiting in town are the Herbert Martz's granddaughters, one from Florida, the other from Hamilton.

The church news is that the Bluemont Methodist Youth Fellowship has been reorganized for youths, aged 10-15 and the officers elected were Lynn Carbaugh, president, Pearlina Leffingwell – vice president, secretary – Belinda Dawson, treasurer – Deborah Dawson, adult leader – Ivy Cochran and assistant – Rosa Peyton.

Their next meeting will be at the Ralph Cochrans July 28 at 7:30 p.m.

First Baptist is planning for their big annual rally held the fourth Sunday of July here at the church in Bluemont. The Rev. Ottis Jasper of Washington, D.C. who also serves the Purcellville, Hamilton, and Airmont charges will be the guest speaker and dinner will be served after the service at 3:30 p.m.

Fair meetings were going on right and left last week and a pre-registration day has been set for Sept. 30 from 1-8p.m. at the schoolhouse in order for exhibitors to receive their numbers. Hope you're filling in the leisurely summer days with fair projects.

A grand mall water battle raged between Hope Lloyd, Hope and Sharon Carbaugh and Bootsie Stearne was sighted with flashlight in tote – deep in the grass, looking for night crawlers as another summer week eased by in 70-year old Bluemont.

July 30, 1970

Mark off those lingering cool breezes from the calendar now as summer has ripened into a real heat wave as August envelopes Northern Virginia.

Can summer be two-thirds gone?

I'm afraid so but before it passes a lot of fun is packed into the weekly schedule.

First of all, back on the local scene is Anthony Dawson after his hitch with the U.S. Army at Ft. Polk, La. Ivy Cochran did him up right with a welcome home cake complete with jeep and flags.

Visiting here with the Leffingwells last weekend was Paul and Ursula Leffingwell from California and due on the first is the other side of the family Pearl and Ray Garcia and son Victor from Texas.

The Senior Robert Carters and Miss Lisa Ann Carter of Statesville, N.C. plus Mrs. Elizabeth Wilson and son Bradley Mason of Alexandria were weekend guest of the Robert Carters again.

Here visiting with us is George Parker of Wheaton, Md. who bought the old Fox place. He had plans to stay there until he sighted two snakes in the house. Ahem!

There is a grand cleaning-up project down there with other guests Jim Parker and Robert S. Jones known as Casey of Falls Church lending a hand and Bob Johnson lending a leg that became infected putting him in Loudoun Hospital.

More excitement here was the twins' third birthday complete with a homemade ice cream and cake party with both sets of grandparents on Sunday.

Lynn Carbaugh became sweet "fourteen" with a family party of homemade peach and cherry-nut ice cream and two kinds of cakes on the 23rd.

The John Carters were really struck this week when on the same day and hour practically, Stevie fell from his bicycle and Debbie collided with another ball player and both were stitched up by two different doctors simultaneously.

Now back to those snake stories: I met William Milhollen, the former dentist's son who maintained an office on the site of Bessie Carter's abode and he said Dr. Turner who lived here kept a big seven foot black snake in the barn and when someone accidentally ran over it, he almost had the man arrested.

He had some marvelous tales about his travels with Dr. Kilgour on his house calls all over the snow-laden countryside.

Sorry to hear of his cousin's death, Hirst Milhollen of Philomont who gave us a good tip on the collection of old civil war photographs for the upcoming Fair.

An enjoyable day was spent at Hershey, Pa., by Belinda, Debra and Pam Dawson with the Truman Hawes of Philomont and their three daughters, Wanda, Betty and Jean.

Donna Kelley and Norman Sowers were the guests of Mrs. Dorothy Wiltshire on a trip to Virginia Beach and Petersburg for about a week recently.

As for us, we went the tourism route, took in the Leesburg Museum, Monda's Craft Shop, Irvine Gallery and the Washingtons' garden in Paeonian Springs on Monday. Mrs. Washington promises some pumpkins and the Irvines promise some paintings for the Fair and Mrs. Moody of the Museum is promoting our endeavor.

The relic committee is in great need for an opportunity to either borrow or rent some showcases or glass china closets. Please call me if you can help us.

The berry-picking business is still in full swing at Mr. Horning's charming Victorian spot straight from an illustrated Robert Louis Stevenson, complete with geese, and an artisan spring-fed lake and acres of sweet berries on Rt. 709 outside of Round Hill. See him after four during the week and all day weekends. People as far as Herndon and Vienna have picked a pack, a peck - one lady picked 60 quarts.

This week brings Herbert Little's retirement from the Voice of America so now he and Peggy won't have to rush back to the city on a Sunday afternoon and can give the hammock a few extra licks and drink in more of their perfect view.

After dining the kids out, leading them in the "zoo" parade, laying presents at their feet, they bubbled the most over the time at the bookmobile and the picking of the black-eyed susans on the school grounds and the penny bubblegum at Mann's Store.

"Cinderella" – saturated somehow the familiar, homely things seem the dearest this week in Bluemont.

August 13, 1970

"Beauties, wondrously bright," is a phrase that can aptly be applied to the Bluemont vegetables these days.

The neighbors are sharing the fruits of their labors and the glow of the squash, cucumbers, carrots, corn and tomatoes make one of nature's most beautiful arrangements.

Last year, the Glen Lloyds gave us a zucchini squash and I found it too pretty to eat, keeping it in an arrangement for about three months; the 4-H Fair has such glorious vegetable arrangements this year. Of course, a good many find their way to the dinner table too.

Speaking of corn, the Brownells had it in abundance and upon their invitation, we were led by our trusty guide Jim, Jr. through the waving 20-foot jungle. There was a path in the middle where the planter had missed, leaving way for the motorcycle. What a way to farm?

Others enjoyed the corn on the cob, barbequed chicken, potato salad, watermelon at the picnic hosted by the Loudoun Board of Supervisors at Whitehall Farm on Saturday evening for Loudoun employees.

Mark Brownell can now rest from his summer-long project of creating his own pad and what a pad it is! Dug out from the old basement, it now boasts a new floor, ceiling, painted walls, built-in benches, psychedelic posters and music and a pool table! How sweet it is! Every young man should have such a retreat!

The James Allders are back from a perfect week at Myrtle Beach, S.C. where Doris found about 40 shark teeth, had her portrait done in charcoal and won 25 games of bingo bringing home dishes, a clock, stuffed animals, towels as well as soaking up the sun and surf.

Doris and her sister also gave a highly successful birthday party with about a hundred guests for their father George Dawson of Hamilton on his 72nd birthday on the 26th of July. They even had a band along with the traditional cake.

The Bluemont Methodist Church is anticipating its annual homecoming on the 16th. Guest speaker will be the Rev. Eugene Thayer, a former pastor here about 20 years ago when he handled six charges at the time.

He now makes his home in Oakland, Md.; the service when he will speak will be at 2 o'clock at the church, lunch will be served at 12 on the school lawn.

The Robert Joneses have become grandparents again – Judy and Bud Anderson welcomed a son to their family last week.

Now what should every good little Bluemonter be doing these days? Thinking and planning for the Fall Fair, of course. Half-way gone is August now, then September will scurry by and crisp October will be here when the anticipated tourists will once more abound in Bluemont.

Donning my leather gloves the other evening, I started my thistle collection, how about drying, knitting, antiquing?

The categories for exhibitors again are antiques, art and sculpture, handcrafts of any type (none made in Hong Kong variety, please), baked goods (no mixes), homemade jellies, jams, pickles and relish, apple butter, popcorn, candy apples, dried arrangements, fresh-cut flowers, seeds, bulbs and produce (if you grow it, we'd like it).

A delightful letter came my way this week from a lady who visited our village 47 years ago in 1923. She and her parents and brother came here in their Buick touring car, spent the night in one of the boarding houses and were impressed by the friendly people, pretty flowers and attractive homes here.

Certainly, paying the community the highest compliment, she told her father she wished she could live in Bluemont.

August 20, 1970

It seems cruel to even mention the fact but summer is slipping quietly by us; the public school teachers will commence their meetings this week and the children will return to the classrooms on Aug. 31.

Somehow it seems too soon to be anticipating early-morning eggs, packed lunches and school-bus good-byes but Bluemonters with one foot in summer and the other in fall are still filling the days of splashing and romping and nights of flickering lightning bugs with visits, barbecues and games.

Sadie Peyton had as her guest this week Miss Judy Fattoine of Arlington while younger sister Rosa spent the week at Beverley Beach on the Chesapeake with the Haskins.

Sadie also attended the wedding of former Bluemonter Kathy Miehm to Mike Fields in Arlington last weekend.

The Earl Dutrows of Airmont were pleased to welcome their daughter and son-in-law the Larry Phillips of Del Ray, Fla., for a two-week visit.

Burton Leffingwell and children entertained weekend guests again, Burt's mother, Mrs. Burton C. Leffingwell and sister Mrs. Susan Bebbe and daughters, Linda and Janet, all of New Canaan, Conn.

The younger children Pearlina and Earl will be returning with them to attend school in Connecticut this fall.

Due to Pearlina's leaving, Sharon Carter was elected the new vice-president of the Methodist Youth Fellowship.

The Recreation Department closed up shop this week but not before the staff awarded good citizenship trophies to Pam Carbaugh and Alton Ramey.

The community wishes to express its great appreciation to the fine instructors who kept our children busy and contented this summer. They were Anne Cockerill, a teacher and neighbor, Babe Sampson of Purcellville, enrolling in Bridgewater College for her first year, and Carry Dawson of Lovettsville continuing his second year in college.

Sports-wise the Girls Pony Tail team is doing very well, tied for first place in the American Division; Donna Kelley distinguished herself by hitting a grand slam homerun in a recent game with Round Hill.

Jamie Lloyd is spending the week in Roanoke as a guest of sister, Linda; the Glen Lloyds also relaxed with a barbecue the other night with their guests, the fun-loving Roy Santmyers who had been shucking lima beans with them for several nights running.

Sister Hope says things are quiet with just Mommie, Daddy, Mary Jo, Kelley, and herself at home and sisters Judy, Anne and brother Jerry dropping in occasionally with the grandchildren.

Mary Monroe called at the top of the week with news of a marvelous reunion of the Diedricks – her family scattered here, there and yon – at the Monroe's Unison home. About 30 came to the garden picnic and swapped old tales of growing-up days together.

Mary said too that the neighbors, the Glen L. Ballengers, were doing very well with their horse at local races and were on the big trip to Saratoga this week.

Kay Seidenspinner always has the nicest guest and this time Mrs. Elizabeth R. Parker spent Monday here driving about the country and relating to me that this wasn't her first trip to Bluemont as she had come here about 1916 on the train from Washington.

She said in those days resorts had to either be reached by rail or boat; they also would go down to the Seventh Street Wharf and take a boat to Colonial Beach where the content of the water was more salty then than now and spent days away from the hot concrete of the city.

Working for years at the National Headquarters of the American Red Cross, her stay on the front porch was much too short, the fall fair will bring her return though she said.

Pets and people in the news are Brenda and Debby Bowman's winning of a blue ribbon for obedience at the Dog Show at Frying Pan Park several weeks ago with their lovely border collies.

Alas, our Mr. Snickers was struck by the telephone truck and is recuperating from a fractured pelvis, and half of the waiting room at the vet's were the Bluemont neighbors.

There were the Teesdale-Smiths and their adorable Scotties and Mrs. Eugene Payne with her wonderful mother Weimaraner and two of the nine puppies, now about three weeks old. The one puppy had accompanied the other for company and Carol Weedon was there with a beautiful young German Shepherd in tow, explaining they were now building a new house in Lovettsville.

You know the traditional Englishman's love for their pets; there was an attractive English lady declaring all the dogs lo-ve-ly!

Several new cars are now in town – the Jack Allders and Llewllyn Robey are looking prosperous.

Everyone is talking about and sniffing Bluemont's pure air these days.

George Parker, our two-week guest upon a return Sunday visit, said he could hardly breathe in Wheaton by contrast and Helen Freedman said even their dogs having panted the whole New York trip, laid down in the back seat and relaxed when they hit Purcellville, and the air was decidedly more breathable from Leesburg on to home in unpolluted Bluemont.

So take a sniff – windows will have to be closed against the bitter wind soon enough.

August 27, 1970

Heavy is our burden this week to learn of the untimely death of young Connie McClaughry, daughter of Mr. and Mrs. Roy McClaughry of Pine Grove.

The terrible automobile accident that claimed her life occurred one rainy day near the Berryville Horse Show Grounds killing the drivers of both cars involved in the collision.

Connie had just completed her work on her master's degree and was coming for a surprise visit to her parents' house. Two of Mr. McClaughry's sisters live in our village proper, Mrs. Frances Ballenger and Mrs. Ellen Jones.

Earlier in the week we had caressed the adorable five dachshund puppies now six weeks old and ready to be adopted by a good home at Frances's house across from the old schoolhouse.

Frances told us the house had been built under Earl Bealle's direction with blocks of clay formed from the creek below the house probably making it about 50 years old now.

Another prominent Bluemont family, the Underwoods held their annual family reunion on Sunday at the Fireman's Field in Purcellville; Janet Reed said she was frying chicken and baking a cake for it when she called to report the news of their fabulous week in the Poconos with Lucien's sister and husband, the Bill Marcuses of Gwynedd Valley, Pa., who visited here first.

Surrounded by a lake and mountains the party could watch deer in the evenings nibbling the apples in the orchard. They spied 18 in a day.

Janet said the weather was superb; my experience there had always been a bad case of chattering teeth till about nine o'clock in those crisp mornings that were bathed in a heavy haze.

Jamie Dodderidge was back this week from a month's stay at a Dude Ranch in Montana many adventures richer.

Sorry to hear Peggy Little fell bruising a few ribs this week and a few of the local boys have been taking some tumbles practicing football for the Loudoun Valley High team. They are Young Scott of Airmont, Tommy Gray and Jamie Lloyd. If there are others let me know, please.

August birthdays were commonplace in Bluemont, Emma Mann had hers two weeks ago and Louis and Roberta Underwood added a year; you know they must be perfectly matched – the Leos –affectionate when they get their way. Hmm.

Here the summer birthdays are over now, Jennifer had her first party with the neighborhood children becoming five on Monday and then she and Grandmother Johnson celebrated together on Sunday with just the family.

The younger set enjoyed Ivy Cochran's circus cake and each other's company. Guests were Pam Carbaugh, Justine and Brian Beck, Mark Allder (a little later that evening but…), Mary Jo Lloyd and Brook and Robert Middleton and Jennifer Brown of Leesburg.

The W.S.C.S of the Methodist Church met at the Ralph Cochrans this week for their monthly afternoon meeting, and the C.H. Townshends entertained for the Rev. Eugene

Thayer who brought the address for last week's homecoming. Guests were Mrs. Elizabeth Kelley, the Ralph Cochrans, Miss Ruth Alley and the Marion Kerritts.

Donnie Spring spent last weekend here with this grandmother, Mrs. Barbara Spring after having enjoyed a Texan summer. Mrs. Ralph Peyton has tomatoes and potatoes now for sale and when you scrub those potatoes it's good to know that's our rich Bluemont soil going down the drain.

Before the books returned to the bookmobile for the summer, the children and I made the final reading of that beloved "Casey at the Bat" written in 1888 soon after baseball began.

"Ten thousand eyes were on him as he rubbed his hand with dirt,
Five thousand tongues applauded when he wiped them on his shirt,
And somewhere men are laughing and somewhere children shout,
But there is no joy in Mudville, mighty Casey has struck out."

Happy Football Season!

September 3, 1970

One more week and summer will be officially over but now it's very much a summer evening in Bluemont with a band amplifying nearby and the dogs barking at one another over a noise they thought they heard somewhere.

Nevertheless, the acorns up at the Freedmans are falling and our Empress tree is already shedding, the girls becoming my second generation weed women, arranging them for the front porch.

While talking about a use for the acorns, Clyde Beck promptly got out his "Wild Asparagus" book and read – "Acorns – an ancient food of man." This was followed by a recipe for acorn bread made from acorn meal, so you see, you could invite a few two-legged creatures over for lunch in addition to the squirrels.

The more customary edible – the potato being gathered this week – Allen Campbell got in about 20 bushels and we figured that the average family uses about 15 bushels per year, so they can sell their surplus at the Fair.

Squirrel-like the village women are canning, canning – peaches and tomatoes seem to be on the top of the list right now.

Of course, this was the week of both the Clarke and Loudoun County 4-H Fairs.

The Don Bowmans have a lot of ribbons exhibited above those sheep and six-year-old Julie, daughter of Stanley Kelley got a third place in suitability of mount, seat and hand astride "Little Angel", one of the ponies to be ridden by young riders at the Bluemont Fair, coming soon.

Great news this week saw the return of John Hyland to his home here from Shawnee Nursing Home and the reassurance that Mrs. Maude Alton formerly of our ridge was not seriously injured in the accident that involved her car last week.

The road construction is pushing ahead: a great bare river of sandy soil makes for a new terrain at the approach to the Shenandoah Bridge.

Abandoning their business and home here, the Donald Hunters and Mrs. Della Hunter, owners of the general store at the Snicker's Gap sign have moved to White Post.

The Robert B. Barkers have now made their attractive residence on Rt. 601 their permanent home.

The Deale family with friends were up for a week's stay from New York a week ago and Mrs. Harold Spivacke, a music professor at the University of Maryland is now lecturing on music in Buenos Aires, Argentina.

A great event this week and rather rare to Bluemont was the birth of a daughter to Andrew and Sandra Sisk at Loudoun Memorial on Saturday, Aug. 22nd.

You can bet the Andrew Seniors were pretty proud of their first grandchild, too.

The Eugene Clarks entertained Sharon Slate, a senior at Hagerstown High School and pre-schooler Linda Sweeney from Hagerstown this week.

We enjoyed meeting the Littles' guests, Peggy's daughter, Nancy Martin and two other New Yorkers who spent a week drinking in one of the best views around Bluemont with them.

The Walton Manns got a few days of well-earned relaxation this week while the Kerricks minded the store and when Mr. Kerrick slipped over to see the slide show of old Bluemont scenes, he told a fascinating tale of a flu epidemic many years ago when the best a doctor could do was prescribe aspirins and a good stiff drink of whiskey.

Some of our young people are anticipating their first year at College, Ricky Underwood, son of Mr. and Mrs. Lester Underwood, is enrolled as a student at Stephens City College, Stephens City, Va.

Mary Elizabeth Walsh will delay her departure to a Georgian school until second semester. Her mother and I said, "Great, you'll be here to help with the Fair."

Bear in mind the Citizens Association meets the first Wednesday of every month at 7:30 at the schoolhouse.

Moving down the road a piece to the pink house this weekend were Homer and Libby Stearne who formerly occupied the apartment above Mann's Store.

September 10, 1970

"All's right with the world" – the wild yellow flowers dot the roadsides again and a mellow bouquet catched the tilt of the sunlight on my windowsill.

The evenings are cool, the sun sets close-by eight o'clock now and though a blanket of humidity caused five pictures to escape their gummy hook on the wall in a space of a half hour this week, the songwriter's lyric, "it's autumn, somehow I know it's autumn," rings true.

Arriving to glimpse the last of summer were two Dutch students, Dirk Loeff of Leiden University studying law and Maas de Quay of Groningen University studying medicine who paid a surprise visit to the J.H.H. Verloop family of our ridge.

Sporting wooden shoes and an identifying sign, they hitch-hiked their way over the country and were impressed by everyone's helpfulness and were fascinated by state-side city living, meeting Senator Edward Kennedy on their first trip to Washington, D.C.

The Verloops really have the prominent news item this week as they announce the marriage of their eldest daughter Margerite to Fred Nelson Smith of Little Falls, N.Y., on Saturday, Sept. 12 at their home here.

Officiating will be our own Markle's son-in-law Edgar Mayse, a ministerial student at the Presbyterian Seminary in Richmond.

The bride and her husband are to make their home in Chicago where Mr. Smith will pursue graduate studies at the University of Chicago.

The younger Verloops, the twins: Maurice and Edith turned seven with a splash party at Retreat a week ago.

More guests arriving in time for the wedding were the Vinke's guests, Mrs. Valstar, Mrs. Vinke's sister and her sister-in-law, Mrs. Adriaansen who came by boat from Holland, docking in New York and then taking the train to Washington last Friday.

Too bad the Old Dominion Railroad can no longer leave them at Bluemont's door-step.

Putting the railroad out of business of course was the auto and Bluemont's younger generation is pleased to be part of that scene as Rhoda Underwood became a licensed driver this week and Jill Reed is flashing by in her new yellow Mustang.

The Ralph Cochrans found last Sunday's weather perfect for the annual Hindman-Markle family reunion, the two sides of Ivy's family.

They came a 125 strong and of course, you know their reputation as good cooks.

September 17, 1970

The brightness of September's late afternoon filtering through the dogwoods and pines on the shaded lawn made the perfect setting for the marriage of Miss Margerite Verloop of Bluemont to Fred Nelson Smith on Saturday.

It was marvelous to greet some of the ridge dwellers and those wonderful Dutch people and I promised to keep all the remarks off the record. Such wonderful champagne!

With the arrival of the promotional post cards from the printers, our Bluemont Fair seemed thoroughly launched this week. Clyde Beck's sketch of the village turned out beautifully and the posters are to follow on their heels.

Bear in mind that June Lloyd needs your pint and quart jars for the apple butter.

Just prior to our event is the worthwhile opportunity to take a train excursion sponsored by the National Historical Society. The train will leave Winchester bound for Baltimore and its unique railway museum on Sept. 27. Tickets and information are available through our own Jim Walsh. The purchase price of $15 for adults and $12 for children must be secured by the 18th. So hurry!

The G.W. Townshends entertained a house full of guests again last weekend. Pre-sent were Mr. and Mrs. Gene Stringer and children Krehl, Philip and Catherine of Fort Wayne, Ind., Mrs. Virginia Lyddane of Silver Spring, Md., Mr. and Mrs. Wendell Rothgeb and children Karen and Daniel of Beltsville, Md., William Townshend and Marvin Jenkins of Washington, D.C.

Mrs. Nellie Tibbs is spending about a month with her sister, Mrs. Frank Lambert in Bland County, Va.

Sorry to hear Robert Allder had to spend several days in Loudoun Memorial Hospital this week undergoing tests.

Big news this week was the grand success of our Girls Softball team. They are the champions of the Loudoun County Recreation Department's summer program.

Winning the American Division over the Lovettsville team and then beating Ashburn of the National Division, they were victorious last Monday night celebrating over the Labor Day weekend with a big picnic at the J.J. Kelley's here.

Coaching and managing the team were Alice Hays, Clara May Thomas and J.J. Kelley with Mrs. Gaines as the scorekeeper. Miss Thomas provided transportation and the Ralph Cochrans were their most loyal fans.

Here are those illustrious players: catcher, Donna Kelley and grand slammer many times over; pitcher, Candy Jones; first base, Wanda Hawes and Gail Hurst; second base, Betsy Lemon and Debra Dawson; third base, Glenda Knutson and Ethel Leffingwell; short stop, Vicki Oliver; right field, Barbara Smith, Belinda Dawson and Stephanie Leffingwell; centerfield, Wendy Smith; left field, Sherree Gaines and short field, Norma Sowers and Linda Knutson.

We have lost the Edward Sowers family formerly of Bloomfield to White Post – the Post was erected by George Washington as a landmark to Greenway Court, residence of his friend, Lord Fairfax.

Jan and Guy Woolman departed our village for school this week. Jan is beginning at Alexandria School of Nursing and Guy takes his second year at Blacksburg's VPI.

The Walton Manns found some treasures in the attic this week – an old scale, cheese cutter, tobacco cutter, and ledgers, one dating to 1861 listing the account of a Capt. Glasscock who served with Mosby's Rangers. There was a Porterfield too, so maybe I have some roots in old Bluemont after all.

Mr. O'Brien was in town several weeks ago too carrying some raw flax and explaining the process for readying the raw material for spinning.

He will be exhibiting some of his rare antiques at the Bluemont Fair.

Charles Anson's sensational Pimm's blend at Clyde Beck's art showing convinced me he was the man for our hot cider stand and he graciously agreed.

The Loudoun County Guidance Center is sponsoring again its annual sale of pecans. Five pound boxes are available through Emma Mann. Delivery will be before Thanksgiving and they can be frozen too, you know, for year-round use.

Ah, the mellowness of the sunlight's tone these days! See you at the Bluemont Fair.

September 24, 1970

Life was altered. The pace has quickened. We have joined the ranks of mothers chauffeuring children.

Jennifer is enrolled at Jane's Kindergarten and June Lloyd and I make the twice-daily trip to Hamilton to Miss Jane Roger's home and school. The beautiful gracious home was once Baldwin House, a luxurious boarding house during the days of the train.

The Becks are on the road with Brian at Miss Crocker's.

Morning comes early, evenings are spent in readiness for the next day and telephoning, telephoning.

Is there anyone left in Bluemont or even Loudoun County I haven't called about the Bluemont Fair?

Meanwhile people here in the village and on the ridges are busy moving dirt, discing, planting seed – preparing for next year's lawn.

The geraniums are at their prettiest now and that volunteering tomato plant of mine is turning both corners of the house and engulfing the budding chrysanthemums.

Bees are taking over rafter spots; Clyde Beck felt the wrath of a wasp on the top of his head and consequently couldn't see for an hour or two and the Charles Tyrolers reported seeing a bob cat in their backyard. I don't know about those evening swims now, do you?

One more backward look to summer, the coaching and managing staff for the ladies softball team composed of Dickie Costello, Donnie McCarty, Eddie Wines and Larry Allder would like to thank the 1970 team for its fine team effort and outstanding season.

Players were: left field, Cindy Fincham; center field, Ruby McCauley; right field, Jill Reed; shortfield, Evelyn Tapscott; first base, Joy Hawkins; second base, Peggy McCauley and Doris Allder; third baseman, Geneva Hummer and Donna Underwood; shortstop, Shelia Tapscott; catcher, Barbara Embrey and pitcher, Joan Wilt.

The M.Y.F. of the village stone church is active with projects and parties.

A surprise party for their sponsor, Mrs. Ivy Cochran was held last week at her pleasant home framed in the mountain vistas.

Their next meeting on Sept. 29 is to be given over to a clean-up of the old school grounds for the upcoming Fair.

Every Tuesday is to be clean-up day at the school until the Fair or if you can help anytime, stop by Mann's Store for a key.

Oct. 10 has been set as town clean-up day of sidewalks, road-sides. Come armed with clippers, swing-blades, rakes and gloves. Shir Carbaugh has promised homemade ice cream for the workers.

Of great importance is the Sept. 30 Pre-registration Day for the Fair. Exhibitors will get their tags and numbers from registrars, Ivy Cochran and Betty Walsh, from 1 o'clock to 8 p.m. at the Bluemont school. That way, items can already be tagged with price and number for Oct. 14, 15.

Ethel Leffingwell turned 15 this week with an exciting skating party at the Purcellville rink on Tuesday night.

Singing Happy Birthday about the cake were some 80 guests.

Bob took in the usual Lovettsville's Farmers' Club luncheon meeting as guest of Jim Brownell on Saturday. Showing the Bluemont slides to an appreciative audience and feasting on that good Virginia ham, he proclaimed again the goodness of the Lovettsville women's cooking.

I had a Thanksgiving dinner there in Lovettsville one year and oh those delicious German noodles! Their pies at Oatlands were sumptuous too. Maybe they will bring us some wares to the Bluemont Fair.

The time is drawing close – maybe too close but Bluemonters brace yourselves – here comes the Bluemont Fair, Oct. 17, 18. See you there!

October 1, 1970

I'm worried.

Will there be a fall this year?

I hung the Indian corn on the front door to usher in the season, but thus far the 80 and 90 degree temperatures have continued.

Bill Spencer and Isabelle Dawson are reassuring me that the Bluemont Fair will be held amidst the turning of the leaves' colors, but still I'd feel better if some of that hot oatmeal weather were here.

Anyway, the next 17 days will tell the story.

The Sam Joneses played it smart, waiting now to take a trip to the beach, they spent this "fall" weather in comfort, oceanside.

Ah, the happy reunion at the James Walshes this week, son Jerry has returned from Da Nang and will be here on an extended visit.

Willa Colbert was back in town after her first week at Madison College as a Freshman.

The Colberts are painting the exterior of their frame home and plans are being made for everyone to get in on the cleaning-up act on Oct. 10.

Let's get some of these roadside weeds down so we won't miss any of our lovely views.

A four-year-old Great Pyrenees needs a home so the Johnsons report. Please someone – give the Animal Shelter a buzz – this is too nice a pet to be lost.

We are sad to report the death of Mrs. Virginia Lyon of Purcellville formerly of Bluemont. One of her homes here was Mountain Shadow, the one-room schoolhouse that was expanded into a dwelling. She was well-known and loved in this community.

Sorry too that Miss Beatrice Scipio has been confined to the University Hospital in Charlottesville for several months. We trust she will be returning home here soon with her sister, Mrs. Valentine.

They had some wonderful old post cards of Bluemont dated 1903 and 1909.

We were pleased to hear that Mr. and Mrs. Robert J. Carter and sons, Robbie, Jerry and Mason have been able to locate close-by at the William Cockerill's farm near Airmont and the Robert Carters, Sr., and granddaughter, Lisa Ann are now living in Berryville.

The G.W. Townshends were able to get away and spend a pleasant weekend as guests of Eugene Thayer of Oakland, Md. last weekend.

Now for my own press reviews – Didn't the Loudoun-Times give us a nice write-up? Jean McDonald did a beautiful job. She said she was inspired.

Thanks to Mrs. Earl Brown and Mrs. E.G. Fuller of Berryville, better known in Bluemont as the Costello sisters, I have just spent a pleasant hour with the March 7, 1925 copy of the Loudoun-Times.

On the front page was the announcement of Dr. George P. Plaster's death at the age of 98.

A long article ensued about his history as a major in the civil war and his adventures as a gold prospector in addition to his good deeds as the beloved country physician.

I suspected after reading his history of Snickersville written in 1902 that he was a brilliant individual and this article confirmed it.

In the same paper there appeared the Washington and Old Dominion train schedule to Bluemont. There were four trains daily then, the first one of the morning left the Rosslyn Terminal at 9:10 a.m. and arrived in Bluemont at 10:05 a.m.

But an even more glorious time according to Dr. Plaster in his history were the days of the stage-coach and unfortunately there is no one left who can tell us those marvelous tales.

They had a picture too of Mrs. Molly Weadon who ran the Virginia House. She was dressed in her Gibson-girl blouse and long skirt just as the Bluemont ladies will be clad at the Bluemont Fair.

So come, invite your friends to see the old pictures at the Bluemont Fair.

October 8, 1970

Everyone is talking about this fine autumnal weather and all's well until you step inside Clayton Hall.

There the temperatures indicate there are cooler days ahead, lots of morning of hot oatmeal ahead.

And as for the oatmeal, I wasn't raised on the stuff by my husband was and our children have taken to it, taking a cue from the commercials, I doctor it up with plenty of brown sugar and raisins and it isn't half bad.

The birds are back, two flew down the chimney in the twins' room early Saturday mornings and the Dawsons had to come to my rescue.

A real sight was the pouring in of about 30 swallow swepts (that's what Clyde Beck called them) to Mrs. Powell's chimney last week. What a fright that would be if they all came tumbling down.

Jim Birchfield in his visit here took a fancy to that house as I always have.

The Pre-registration for the Fair went well – now all that remains is to clean up and decorate this burg.

Bring your cutting equipment, and gloves along with a sandwich on Saturday, Oct. 10, this week to the old store (Beck's studio) at 9 o'clock. Drinks and dessert will be provided. We're counting on you. Don't let us down. The faithful few have done the work at the school, now let's do the rest.

Some Indian corn and a pumpkin or two on the porch would delight our visitors, don't you think?

We were saddened to hear of the death of Mrs. Ada Reid who had spent the summer here with her daughter-in-law, Bonnie Reid. She was a lively, dear person until she suffered a stroke a month ago when she returned to Shawnee Nursing Home.

The Karlton Monroes had their Canadian friends as guests for five days last week. They were Mel and Dot Badger and 18-year-old daughter, Ethel. Among other spots, they saw Harper's Ferry and Skyline Drive (Karlton said the leaves weren't turning there either) and generally loved Virginia.

Another personage to become hooked on Bluemont is Mr. Carbone who has just bought a home on the ridge. He makes the daily long trek to McLean but says it's worth it, to live here year round.

I saw lots of traffic while I cleaned the wall of weeds on Saturday and was particularly pleased to see the Girl Scouts from Round Hill who had hiked to Bluemont and then gone on the Appalachian Trail. I could have used some of their energy for my task.

The Lucketts Home Demonstration Club royally entertained the Bluemont Club this week at a luncheon in Lucketts. Shir Carbaugh, Bluemont President said they had roast beef, hot rolls, loads of salads, topped off by peach or apple cobbler and whipped cream! They all indulged, deciding you only live once.

Mrs. Thomas J. Holmes of the ridge was delegate to the Ikebana Flower Convention in Japan and spent a month there.

Mrs. Ann N. Arnold and family are finding times pleasant here at their vacation place on Bluemont's mountainside.

Now for one half of the ending of the tale about the Seidenspinners' lost beef. One swam the Shenandoah to join a herd of Angus, about 200 pounds heavier he looks very happy they report.

As for his companion, I just wonder if some hiker on the trail near the Seidenspinners didn't get a real scare one night.

I got a nice letter from Mrs. Elsie Elwers Isbell of McLean who told me of her mother-in-law's (Mrs. Alice Isbell formerly Alice Virginia Pearson) interest in the Bluemont Fair.

Now 86, she attended the yellow schoolhouse and still recalls vividly points of interest in the vicinity.

She will be coming to the Bluemont Fair. It will be one grand reunion. See you there.

October 8, 1970, additional feature article about the Bluemont Fair

A unique country fair, in the foothills of the Blue Ridge Mountains in the famous village of Bluemont, will be held Oct. 17 and 18. It is sponsored by the Bluemont Citizens Association.

The fair will highlight the history of the countryside, Revolutionary and Civil War events, and the time when a regular daily train served Bluemont as a thriving summer resort and residence for leading Washingtonians. Two illustrated sound-slide films on this background will be shown at frequent intervals during the fair.

A printed history of the area's earlier years by Jean Smith, a long-time Bluemont resident will be available. Collections of Civil War relics and of antique farm implements will be on view. And country music will be in the air from morning on.

The town of Snickersville, which changed its name to Bluemont early in this century was the sanctuary of the legendary "Grey Ghost," Colonial John Singleton Mosby, and his Confederate guerilla. Today old Snickersville lives on in memories, histories and faded newspaper clippings.

Other activities of the Fair will be craft demonstrations and sales at the old schoolhouse. These will include weaving, spinning, beekeeping, tinware, stained glass, feather-making, silk-screening, paper flowers, candles, knitting and the method of making old-fashioned apple butter.

Colorful art and antiques will be on sale opposite the Post Office in the unique studio of Bluemont's famous artist, Clyde O. Beck.

Farm produce – pumpkins, apples, Indian corn and honey will be on sale in the old barn of historic Clayton Hall.

A home-cooked turkey dinner with all the trimmings will be served each day in the ballroom of the Brownell's old plantation home, Whitehall Farm. Price: $2.00.

Found on sale at the old schoolhouse will include hamburgers, hot dogs, candy apples, popcorn, hot cider, baked goods, jams, jellies, relishes, pickles and other home-made delicacies.

Other attractions available include pony rides, and on-the-spot professional portraits of visitors to the fair.

Admission including parking and all regular activities of the fair, will be $1 for adults, 50 cents for children 6-12. Children under six will be admitted without charge. One admission will cover a full day's activities.

Bluemont is right off Rt. 7 approximately 15 miles west of Leesburg, about four miles west of Round Hill and 11 miles east of Berryville. For those coming from Route 50, take State Route 734, Snickersville Turnpike near Aldie, which goes directly to Bluemont. Bluemont is 55 miles from the White House in Washington, D.C.

Come to beautiful Loudoun County and visit Bluemont –with the enticements of the slow pace of a mountain village during the peak of the autumnal colors.

October 15, 1970

After the Fair…I'll finish my piece of refurnishing I started this summer…I'll scrape the paint off the upstairs windows…I'll mend the stacks of clothes that have piled up…sort out garments for next year's hospital sale…scrub the crayon marks from the wall (the kiddies have been quite busy during my many telephone calls)…engage Herbert Martz to make my tulip bed for next spring. Best of all, I'll settle down with my magazines and books on long winter afternoons, and start preparing for Bluemont's annual Halloween party. After the Fair…

The colors are beginning to wax elegantly and it's all going to be perfect for the Bluemont Fair.

I want to thank those who lent their time and muscles on Saturday for clean-up day. Our appreciation to the Manns and Carbaughs who treated the workers to soft drinks and dessert.

It was a good feeling to know we were united and a team.

The Reid family was stricken again this week as Ada Reid's son, Bill who also had been a patient at Shawnee Nursing Home passed away. Our deepest sympathy to this bereaved family.

We all suffered a loss with Malcolm Davis' death. His nature column in the Loudoun-Times was always so beautifully done.

Great News for the Freedmans on the ridge was their Great Pyrenees Renaissance Montserrat (better known as "Monty") winning the Best of Winners and Best of Breed giving him a four-point major for his championship at the Virginia Kennel Club Show on Sept. 26 in Richmond. Monty may put in an appearance at the Bluemont Fair, too. You'll love him!

More show winners in Bluemont were Clyde Beck and Steve Kelley at the Waterford Foundation Art Show. Clyde won First Prize – Best in Show and Steve won first in the Junior Art Division.

Other painters in town now are the Glen Lloyds experimenting with a yellow that was brighter than they thought.

We had the same experience but now on this dark side of the house, it is so rich and beautiful in the late afternoon sun, we're glad we stuck to the color.

We have lost Mr. and Mrs. John Thomas as they have moved to El Paso, Tex. where they will be near their son. Miss Alley accompanied them on the plane and then returned here last week.

The G.W. Townshends had a number of dinner guests on Sunday. They were Mr. and Mrs. Jerry Strong and son Michael of Quantico, Va., Mr. and Mrs. R.D. Leake of Charles Town, W.Va., and Mr. and Mrs. Charles O'Connor of Hagerstown, Md.

"Mac" Brownell has a lot of friends and if you have ever met her, you would instantly know why. A goodly number of her dearest friends got together last week and gave her a surprise birthday party complete with a three-tiered cake and many wonderful gifts. It couldn't have happened to a nicer person and the work she has done for that turkey dinner!

Whether the Bluemont News makes next week's paper, may be determined by the amount of popcorn I must pop on Saturday night and indeed, whether I'm pooped to pop myself.

Anyway, it has been quite a year of planning: citizens, please park your cars other than on the roadsides and what more is there to say. See you at the Bluemont Fair!

October 22, 1970

Wasn't it all just too grand and glorious!

Ah, what a wonderful sweet smell of success is in the air!

Neighbor united with neighbor to accommodate and entertain our nine thousand guests.

The atmosphere was friendly, the weather perfect and the guests patient and relaxed, glad to visit our pretty countryside that we at times take for granted.

Here are some of those "in" stories, fifty people were turned away from the dinner Saturday night, Mac Brownell rushing to Winchester for hams for Sunday. About 500 people felt the warmth of the flicking fire in the fireplace and tickled their palate with a filling delicious meal; Bob Johnson's bulb blew out right after the last showing of the slide show for the workers and the coke wagon gave out of gas right at the crucial lunch hour on Saturday and Jerry and Timmy Walsh went to Falls Church banks and filling stations for change for the Fair to operate on Saturday, the banks being closed here.

I saw "Hawkeye" Reid having his sketch done, Edith Verloop in the most adorable outfit made by her mother and that barn crammed to full capacity with lovely flowers and weeds.

As for that country music, Llewllyn Robey and his Blue Valley Boys were absolutely the best I've heard.

It is being aired in Bluemont that Bill Spencer of WAGE Radio is second only to David Frost as the best interviewer in the country. Our great thanks to them and the Loudoun-Times Mirror and Clarke Courier for their coverage.

Amidst all of the excitement, we were all stricken with the death of a life-long resident and one who owned some of the most beautiful land in upper Loudoun for many years, J.J. Kelley, affectionately known as "Jim."

How we grieved that his sons and their families, Bill and J.J. Kelley had to undergo this sorrow.

Brenda Bowman took a few hours off from helping with the pony rides on Saturday to go to the Oakton Dog Show where she received a first and two seconds with her marvelous border collie, Twiggy.

Desiree Allder spent her 13th birthday "keeping Bluemont beautiful" on clean-up day preceding the Fair.

The comments I kept hearing all through the Fair "Did you ever think you would see four deputies directing travel in Bluemont?" And what a wonderful job they did for us!

Now is the time to get down off the clouds. Halloween is almost here and the kids will expect their party. Can you believe a year ago, the Halloween party was the biggest social event of the Bluemont calendar?

So you see Virginia, there is a Bluemont after all and we rather favor the climate year round but for those who just like to visit – see you at the Bluemont Fair! Next year – that is!

October 29, 1970

Autumn is finally here and when goblins are stirring and ghosts are hooting next Saturday night, she should be decked in her brightest finery.

It's a time for apple-picking and there were strains of our ancient name being resurrected this week as the story goes that Bluemont, or Snickersville, was once Pumpkin Town due to a carriage loaded with pumpkins overturning and pumpkins went rolling through the area. Well, this week a truck carrying apples headed for Sleeter's lost its wooden side just this side of Bill Kelley's road on Rt. 7, and a reenactment seemed in order with apples instead of pumpkins.

Yep, you guessed it, the Johnsons have a few now in cold storage out in the old kitchen. Once you've read Steinbeck's Grapes of Wrath, you hate to see fruit rotting and besides the adventure rather appealed to my latent pioneer spirit, plus what can't be done with an apple and a little brown sugar – candy apples, apple-sauce, apple pie, apple-butter, cider (wasn't that hot cider great at the Fair?), apple fritters, apple crumb, fried apples, baked apples, stewed apples – desserts and main dishes.

Still on the subject of apples – 75 gallons of cider were sold last weekend (that's a lot of cups), 1052 candy apples and an Australian guest told the Lloyds they had never heard of "apple" – butter, just cow's butter.

There were Canadians here and a 96-year old lady who spoke only Russian but who was intrigued with the primitive tools on display and used in demonstration.

Isn't it great to be able to delve into Jean Smith's book, Snickersville. Some are still available at Mann's Store.

The costumes were such fun. Jack and Betty Lightner looked tremendous, he with his derby and perfect side-burns and she with her authentic linen and lace dress with fur piece and upswept hair style.

Roy Santmyer and James Pierson who like to recall their school days at the yellow schoolhouse and those frolicsome sled rides down the long hill, were joined by several other mates so it was a grand time for embracing former comrades.

I got a delightful telephone call from Frances Iden of Berryville and she reports Dr. Iden was quite pleased to see his former teacher, Miss Eliza Lunsford's picture in front of his during the slide shows.

Also Lola Bealle sent us her best: somehow it didn't seem right that they couldn't join us. Friends may be pleased to know her address, lliff Nursing Home, Dunn Loring, Va.

There will be one more sociable time in connection with the 1970 Bluemont Fair. A covered dish dinner (everyone bringing one dish and his own silver) will be held Nov. 8 at 6 p.m. at the schoolhouse. All those who served at the Fair are welcome; the historic slides will be shown and an evaluation session will be held.

Of fun and games this week is the annual Halloween Party to be held in the school auditorium at 7:30 Saturday evening. This year there will be cartoon movies, a contest for the best costumes and cider and cookies. See you then "incognito."

A great congratulations to our Home Demonstration Club which won Outstanding Club of the Year for the second straight year. Their table placed third with their display from Vietnam at last week's Skyes Hall activities.

We were saddened to hear of Leonard Sowers' death last week. He is survived by his two brothers of our village.

The Becks left quiet Bluemont (see everything has returned to normal) for Charlottesville where a grand birthday party was thrown for Clyde's mother.

There's a beautiful sound of serenity here again – the phone isn't ringing – I actually had time to run the vacuum and bake a cake and take a jaunt to the schoolhouse grounds where we removed the Bluemont Fair sign and found the last of the Black-eyed Susans, Jennifer kept them clutched gently in her hands all the way home. We had time again to wander the land we love in dear old Bluemont.

November 5, 1970

Halloween is always a fun time for both children and adults in Bluemont.

Here we have just the right amount of population to guess who's behind that sheet or witch face. The ghost at Clayton Hall was kept right in my pocket this whole trip since Tracey said she couldn't see out of those small holes.

The setting was just right this year, dark and dismal but nevertheless, there was a great deal of gaiety.

After the trick-or-treating, everyone met at the schoolhouse for flicks, cider, lots of cookies and the costume contest. The funniest prize went to Kathy McCauley in a sort-of-space outfit, the most original to her brother Greg in a marvelous crepe-paper fox outfit, prettiest to Mary Jo Lloyd who made a lovely child bride, smallest to Jennifer Wynkoop in a mop of a hairdo. The best witch was Debra Dawson and the ugliest was Jay Allder behind the terrible white mask.

Hope Lloyd had everyone guessing who she was in her blond wig, fur coat and "groovy" glasses and the Verloop twins dressed as leopards were offered a piece of raw meat at their grandparents Vinkes.

Justine Beck in her Campbell soup can and Kelley Lloyd in his girlie outfit were a big hit at the Round Hill school judging.

Autumn is such a creative time of year for teaching and Miss Jane Rogers came up with some brilliant ideas as always at Jane's Kindergarten, the other mothers at the co-op nursery said you were supposed to dry out the pumpkin seeds from the jack-o-lanterns, toast them, sprinkle with salt and snack.

Friday found me at Valley High where between the new dress codes and costume day I had a looking-good time.

The art students working on humorous photo montages kept complaining that the paste didn't taste as good as when they were in first grade. See nothing stays the same!

Mixing in another special day this week were the Jones family with "Granny" or Pearl Jones celebrating her 92nd birthday. Isn't that terrific?

One of her gifts was a copy of Jean Smith's book Snickersville. The Rev. Melvin Steadman said as far as he knew we were the only town in Loudoun County to have our own history.

Two great entertainments to be brought to Loudoun stages before the pumpkin pies are to be popped into ovens is "Harvey" with our own Landon Wynkoop as lead. Even though Landon doesn't live here anymore he cherishes his days in the neighborhood and his family will always be a part of Bluemont. His grandfather was Dr. Turner of Clayton Hall, his mother was born here and was quite an entertainer herself as she played the piano beautifully. The play will be presented at the Waterford Elementary School. Don't miss it!

Secondly, benefiting the new hospital fund is the musical, "There's No Business Like Show Business" to be performed on Nov. 20, 21 at Loudoun County High School. You'll hear all those great show tunes again and I'm glad my friend, Pat Jackson will be doing several of them.

Come on Bluemonters, let's take in some "theatre"!

Mrs. Barbara Mauk, daughter of Jack and Agnes Allder took her first jet flight on Saturday to spend the weekend with her husband, now Pvt. John R. Mauk stationed at Ft. Leonard Wood, Mo.

Hope everyone exercised his rights as American citizens this Tuesday, Election Day, and don't forget the evaluation meeting and social time on Sunday, Nov. 8 at 6 o'clock in the school auditorium.

Everyone is to bring a covered dish and his own plates and silverware and the pictures of "Snickersville, 1864" and "When the Train Came to Bluemont" will be shown.

November 12, 1970

Now here in the middle of November rather than October our countryside is at the peak of its autumnal flavor and there are still quite a few green leaves.

I was ready to yell "uncle," the gloom of so many dark days hung despair as curtains on the old place but at last, the sun shone again and reflected a few silver linings on the horizon.

One of the nicest things to happen this week was the appearance of Spur Magazine on newsstands in Berryville with a lovely story on Bluemont by Elizabeth Wertz. Pictured along with the article were Whitehall Farm, the old train station, the Waldrop's place, Clayton Hall and our unique stone church. Be sure to get a copy, call me or Kenneth Levi at the Blue Ridge Press in Berryville. This is really a collector's item.

Our history must be interesting: one individual who bought two copies of Jean Smith's Snickersville at Mann's Store left them on the seat of her car while she picked apples in Byrd's orchard and when she returned they had been stolen.

They are still available for buying, that is, with Jean at 1245 Uhlwood Dr., Miamisburg, Ohio 45342.

The weather was ripe for a visit from relatives, Carolyn and Charles Tyroler entertained her sister and family from Long Island. Carolyn says she always goes by the Hagerstown Almanac and fortunately we seemed to sneak in the best days for October for the Bluemont Fair.

In fact, in a lovely complimentary note on the Fair from Kathryn Wilson of our ridge, she said if we had anything to do with the weather that weekend we really ought to be congratulated.

The Becks entertained guests too from Washington and the week before were gathering the Grove clan together on some cold damp days, stirring apple butter in the backyard.

Peggy and Jerry Lloyd managed to slip away for a pleasant weekend without the children to visit sister Linda Lloyd in Roanoke.

The dog population in Bluemont has risen the last several weeks; Queenie, Bud Mart's dog gave birth to seven lovely little creatures and Trixie, Mary Jo's doggie had two. Is there anything cuter than a puppy?

I know of a red two-year-old dachshund (male) who needs a home.

Then on Sunday evening we had a wonderful turnout for our Fair evaluation meeting and dinner; the next Association meeting, the first Wednesday in December will decide whether there will be a 1971 Fair and who will be the new chairman. Please plan to come.

The Home Demonstration Club met this Wednesday and admired Christmas "nothings," creations out of spools, old Christmas cards, walnuts sequined – all for hanging on the Christmas tree.

The children and I got an early peek at Mrs. Townshend's collection that was so attractive.

About these sunless days, at least one doesn't have to wear sunglasses. Not that I mind wearing sunglasses but they might be lost and I hate to lose anything.

Thus we have the logic of the feminine mind. Happy Autumn.

November 26, 1970

A dazzling heavy frost flashed in the early morning sun on Mrs. Powell's field, the mountain showed just a few golden trees with leaves left and the calendar turned again to Autumn's last holiday, Thanksgiving.

The William Carbaughs were ordering their oysters for the feast up at the Wesley Carbaughs with great grandmother Carbaugh and the two uncles where the view is the best over the Bluemont countryside.

The pumpkin pies were being prepared at the Cochrans, the Dawsons, the Allders while the Harry Dennises were rejoicing that they could gather the family about the Thanksgiving table in their newly-completed home.

The G.W. Townshends looked backward with fondness on their visit with their daughter's family, the Wendell Rothgebs in Beltsville, Md. last weekend and Nellie Tibbs was visiting again this time in Philomont with the Bobby Longerbeams.

The Methodist Church ladies were putting final touches on their items for the annual Christmas Bazaar scheduled for Saturday, Dec. 5 at the schoolhouse while Stephanie Leffingwell was inviting friends to her 16th birthday party on Nov. 23 at the Purcellville skating rink.

Perfect for the season is a cup of spice tea and Ann Gregory at Valley High offered me a cup that lifted my day. The dried recipe came from Peggy Stout of Round Hill whose roots on her maternal side are to the Mordecia Throckmorton family of Snickersville. Ingredients – a cup of instant tea, two cups of tang, a package of Wylers lemonade mix, one teaspoon cinnamon, one teaspoon cloves. Stir two heaping tablespoons into a cup of boiling water.

Although village life drones on at its usual pace, bulldozers above the village are changing the terrain and making Bluemont a different place.

When a time is set to discuss the plans for using the Fair funds, maybe we should give serious thought to the eventual future of our community. Do we want progress as evidenced in shiny modern shopping centers or can a new face be put on the village by restoring older buildings to house new shops?

It is time for all those who hold Bluemont dear and hold memories of Bluemont as the quiet spot at the foot of the Blue Ridge mountains to think seriously indeed.

Even youth now know the joy of sighting a deer on the fringes of town or a rabbit in the backyard. Somehow this seems like the gifts we should give our children.

Indeed "let Bluemont bloom" but may it be among grass and trees and flowering things, not asphalt.

Savor the setting along with the turkey and trimmings and Happy Thanksgiving.

December 3, 1970

A damp coldness set in for several days last week and it was a signal to all creatures that snow may be pending.

In a mountain village like Bluemont, the feel of snow in the air sets preparedness in motion.

Up on the mountain the Tyrolers had the snow fence in place, the Verloops had covered the shrubbery with canvass and Herbert Martz tucked the last tulip bulb into its cover under the earth before the real freeze came here.

Wood was gathered in to a protected spot near the house and the birds munched apples from the trees while most of the villagers settled down to the inevitable winter routine.

Thanksgiving was particularly quiet this year, there weren't many big celebrations.

The James Allders entertained the George Dawsons, Doris' parents from Hamilton for the day and the Earl Dutrows of Airmont had the William Wallers of Lynchburg as guests.

The Herbert Martzs held Thanksgiving two Sundays ago so all the family could be together and they were 28 strong and the David Freemans on the ridge had 15 for dinner. Daughter Wendy and husband Richard Blumberg from Poughkeepsie, N.Y. were there along with Mr. and Mrs. Manny Blumberg and son Larry joined by other daughter Evelyn and husband Tom Huntingham of Waydon, Md.

Friends in Southfield, Mich., the Arthur Larsens and the local friends, Dorothy and Ed Smith of Round Hill and Paul and Edith Strang of Rt. 601 came too.

Grandmother Mollie Freedman had been here for a visit and she baked apple pies for the occasion and Helen served up the 24 pound turkey and eight pound capon to make Thanksgiving a memorable time at the foot of the Blue Ridge.

Of course, you know too this was the week Santa Claus came to town, Leesburg, that is, by helicopter.

It was all very exciting; I got a wink from Santa myself and WAGE radio entertained the tots royally (one of the gift records to the children was actually a slow number) and there was Karolyn McKimmey taking pictures for the Loudoun-Times.

Then just incidentally we stopped at McDonald's and there was a handsome young Santa who said, "Hello Mrs. Johnson" which convinced Jennifer of the amazing omniscience of this jolly chap in his red corduroy suit.

Of special importance this week is the Bluemont Citizens Meeting at 7:30 Wednesday night at the old school and the annual W.S.C.A. Bake Sales and Christmas gift sale on Saturday.

This year there will be handmade gifts and jellies, pickles, pies and cakes for sale along with an added feature of a grab bag.

Beginning at 10 a.m. to 3 p.m. on Dec. 5 at the school, the sale will benefit the many worthwhile projects of the Methodist Woman's Missionary Society.

We were glad to know Harry Dennis, Jr. was back from the hospital after having undergone surgery for a brain tumor and Mrs. Erma Hill had returned from seeing her son who was involved in a car accident in Clintwood, Va.

Tragically we lost another one of our Sowerses, Emory and our Bluemont brothers from the monastery, the three Fathers who were killed instantly in a head-on collision on Route 7 this week. Our sympathy to those who knew and loved them.

Bluemonters may be interested to know I had a nice visit with Lotta Bealle at the Iliff Nursing Home last week but was sorry to hear of Earl Bealle's confinement to Arlington Hospital.

I hope to incorporate some of their delightful tales in a little book along with other stories natives may kindly relate to me.

I still have a few more "Spurs" if you are interested.

So look out, Christmas cookie baking time is fast approaching and there are whispers of many good times in store for those who like to proclaim, "Christmas comes but once a year, But when it comes it brings good cheer."

December 10, 1970

Everything around here is still a mixture of fall and the approaching Christmas.

The kitchen mantle boasts the pilgrim and turkey candles along with the Christmas plates the children got in the grab bag at the W.S.C.S. Christmas sales; the hall holds a dried arrangement decorated with Lara and Tracey's homemade Christmas ornaments.

The buffet still displays the horn of plenty and Jennifer's pine cone turkey but the calendar dates are leaping toward the big day, only two weeks away.

There are a few signs in town, the Christmas novelty candy is in the general stores and packages are being sealed tight in the post office.

The Methodist Church will present a Christmas play on Dec. 22nd at 7:30 p.m. on the school stage and they will have their regular Christmas Eve Candlelight Service at 7:30 at the old stone church.

The M.Y.F. will serenade the villagers with Christmas carols and Clyde Beck promises to see that Miss Alley's tree is trimmed and the second annual decorating contest will be held with the judging on Dec. 26, and 27 with Mrs. Betty Walsh acting as Chairman for the judging.

There will be a 1971 Bluemont Fair – Oct. 16 and 17 headed by a trio of Mrs. Ralph Cochran, Mrs. James Walsh, and Mrs. Jack Lightner.

The Loudoun Board of Supervisors has requested that the Virginia Employment Commission conduct a detailed survey of Loudoun County's manpower resources.

The purpose of the survey is to acquire an accurate, up-to-date picture of the county's manpower resources so that local leaders can try to attract new industry and plan for the overall economic growth of Loudoun County.

Every resident, 16 years of age and older – employed, unemployed, housewives, students and retired – are urged to take part in the survey.

An interviewer will be at Mann's Store on Thursday, Dec. 10 from 9:30 a.m. to 6 p.m. for the purpose of registering the residents of Bluemont.

And at last I found my antique round table right next door at Shelly's Antique shop in Round Hill. This new little shop is helping Round Hill put on a new face – he has a great collection of bottles and old newspapers in the old store across from the railroad station. How I envy their rail station.

It was a week for straying cows – the grass was probably greener on the other side of the fence – up at the Tyrolers, two calves were at pool-side munching the tender new roots and on the Paxton road past Windy Hill Farm, a big Angus stood steadfast in the road and we didn't argue, so went the pleasures of a Sunday drive on the winter afternoon in the country.

December 17, 1970

Time to gather in the greens, address the last of the Christmas cards, finish the baking and rush out again for a few more gifts.

Wanting to catch the glitter of Tyson's Corner's decorations, we appreciated the animated dolls and flowing fountains, then moved on to the lights of Leesburg and Purcellville but nothing compared to the beauty of Miss Alley's lovely tree that shone so brightly right here in our hometown, Bluemont.

Set out about 30 years ago by Jim Scott the seedling was just about two feet tall, so it has thrived in our rich Bluemont soil and was kindly strung with lights by Clyde Beck.

Doris Allder's sister, Mrs. Sydney Wagoner and sons Scott and Craig formerly of Kinshasa of Africa will be able to have a real American Christmas this year as the family is returning to the States permanently. They will be locating in this area soon but are visiting Cynthia's parents, the George Dawsons of Hamilton until Sydney can join them.

Mrs. Dawson's six children also threw a special birthday for her this week at the Aldie Fire House.

A shipment of Jean Smith's book, Snickersville arrived in town this week and is available again at Mann's Store. The book will make a nice Christmas gift.

The always perfect Christmas program at Jane's Kindergarten with Mary Jo Lloyd and our Jennifer was staged this week in Hamilton. Everything was perfect even down to the Santa Claus soap in the bathroom, naturally with twins I made a double trip to the scene.

The Lawrence Dawsons had an enjoyable trip up to Madison in Harrisonburg to see daughter Jean last Sunday and their wreath and red lanterns make an attractive ornament for villagers to enjoy.

The Home Demonstration Club had its Christmas party at the schoolhouse at their regular Wednesday morning this week while the W.S.C.S. Christmas program will take place at Emma Mann's this week.

A housewarming party at the new home of the Harry Dennises was frequented by villagers over the weekend while the chicken pox flew into town as Justine Beck spent the week Bluemont-bound.

A sudden disease claimed the life of a former Bluemonter, Mrs. Leroy Virts this week. Four children still remain at the family's present home in Herndon. Would we could comfort them in their time of need.

Maybe the world is not totally sophisticated yet; while shopping at Nichols Hardware last Saturday, two little girls of about eight or nine years of age came in to see the dolls. The dolls weren't curvy but rather soft and cuddly, well, like a baby and that was their choice to grace the bottom of their Christmas tree.

I don't believe Sen. Spong would mind my reprinting a phrase from his Yule message which he borrowed from the poet Max Ehrmann in his selection, "Desiderata."

Advice for a full life and my wish to you, "Especially do not feign affection. Neither be cynical about love; for in the face of all aridity and disenchantment, it is as perennial as the grass."

Merry Christmas!

December 24, 1970

"It's beginning to look a lot like Christmas."

Ah, the smells, sights and sounds of Christmas.

Floating on the air is the aroma of cookies and cakes baking and lifting notes of carols sung by the professional choirs on record and our own Methodist Church group.

The sights are getting better by the day, the new couple above Mann's Store have a lovely red-decorated door and those favorite candlelights of mine at the window as do the Jack Allders. The Becks have the traditional swag again and a lovely arrangement intertwined in the porch slants and Miss Alley's tree is glowing over the countryside with "Popeye" Reid's and Clyde Beck's efforts of trimming the tree being appreciated by all those who love to gaze on its beauty.

Randy Ballenger says Santa can bring him a sled and our two inches of snow last week added just the right touch of season atmosphere.

Mann's Store has cards, gifts, icicles for the tree, red and green candles; there was a time when folks could do all their Christmas shopping right in the village, you know. A drop-in at the William Carbaughs really shows preparation at its best. Shir has made the most exquisite boxwood wreath with a big red velvet bow, there were apple sauce cakes in the oven and plans for the making of glass candy and more cookies plus old Santa Carbaugh himself pulled up in a new red chariot, a beautiful LTD. How much brighter can the season get?

The snow birds are fluttering from branch to branch in the old evergreens here. In front of the house reminding us not to forget our feathered friends this time of year and the holiday can proceed now as Karlton Monroe made his generous holly delivery again. I believe Karlton has a smell for snow, last year he arrived head-on in it and this year he beat it by about eight hours.

The village tonight will ring with merriment as the MYF group will present a play for the community at the schoolhouse at 7:30 p.m.

Mrs. Ivy Cochran has directed the play with Gwen Kelley as co-director and Belinda Dawson playing the part of the mother, Larry Cochran and Hunter Kelley – the sons, Mark Cochran – the grandfather.

Lynn Carbaugh will be the announcer and Hope Carbaugh will play Connie while Steve Carter and Glenn Kelly will portray Luke and Isiah.

Rose Peyton has prepared a piñata for the younger set and the performance will benefit the Children's Home in Richmond.

Sorry to hear Ivy's mother, Mrs. Robert Hindman has been bed-ridden with a bad back for several weeks at her Hamilton home.

Home for the holidays are our growing number of college students, Susan Brownell of University of Virginia, Guy Woolman from VPI, Jan Woolman from Alexandria School of Nursing, and Willa Colbert, Sadie Peyton and Jean Dawson from Madison.

And now the freshening scent of evergreen marches through the door and Tracey wishes for a doll and her two front teeth and all I don't want for Christmas is three cases of chicken-pox – so may the Bluemonters and the readers of the Bluemont column have the most joyful of Christmases and perhaps you might appreciate these thoughts from the conclusion of Peter Marshall's (the preacher-poet) sermon, "Let's Keep Christmas."

"We long for the abiding love among men of good will which the season brings, believing in this ancient miracle of Christmas with its softening, sweetening influence to tug at our heart strings once again.

We want to hold on to the old customs and traditions because they strengthen our family ties, bind us to our friends, make us one with all mankind for whom the Child was born.

So we will not "spend" Christmas…nor "observe" Christmas. We will "keep" Christmas – keep it as it is…in all the loveliness of its ancient traditions. May we keep it in our hearts, that we may be kept in its hope."

December 31, 1970

Now about that Christmas past – 1970 – it seemed to have been a good one for most of the villagers.

Beginning with the well-done MYF play on the old school house stage on Tuesday and culminating with the discovery of the contents of those packages under the tree early Friday morning, it was a most pleasant early winter holiday.

Pre-Christmas activities included a gracious birthday dinner party given for our well-liked politician neighbor, Jim Brownell by his wife, the always perfect hostess.

The Burton Leffingwells were off for a long trip to Connecticut to be reunited with the rest of the family; the Becks entertained here with a turkey as big as the young lad in Dickens' A Christmas Carol inviting all the Grove clan, Mr. and Mrs. Paul Grove and son Mike, Miss Margaret Grove, the John Minnecis and the Dennis Settles while here the chicken pox arrived Christmas Eve but we went to Bethesda anyway for the traditional gift-gathering at the Grandparents Porterfield.

Tom and Ruth Mann were up from Richmond for the day as was Walton's mother from Hamilton and this brought Mrs. Susy Neal back to her cabin for a visit with her cat, Tommy, who meowed his happiness about the reunion in a most enthusiastic way.

Charles Anson and friends weathered it out over at the Waldrops last weekend with no central heating and lots of Charles' marvelous hot cider while Louis and Roberta Underwood were still sandwiching and snacking on the big ham and turkey left from Christmas, while their children were mixing up a fresh pizza.

About half the village were sighted down at the Moorcones Theatre on Sunday evening taking in the flick made from the biggest selling novel of the year, Airport.

The new couple are Carl and Peg McClelland, a Purcellviller told me, so I guess it's time we got acquainted.

Betty Walsh, Chairman for the Christmas Decorating Contest, reports the winners were first prize – The Martin Wilts, second – the Clyde Becks – third – the Frank Voiths in their beautiful new home on the yellow schoolhouse road.

Once a year, I indulge myself in a little editorializing – ok – maybe twice a year but anyway I hope many of you share my concern over the misuse and pollution of this planet we call home – the earth.

I'm afraid it's the best of all possible worlds for earth creatures. Probably each of us feels what we do is insignificant but we have a chance to save a world. Let us use the channels of communication open to us in our free system – let us write our congressman and senators and let us write Senators Spong and Byrd today and stop this super-sonic transport that may very well destroy the natural life cycle.

Think big by writing a little letter so each of us and those unborn children and grandchildren and great-grandchildren may be wished a Happy New Year – year after year, after year.

Thank you for making 1970 such a good year for me. Happy New Year.

1971

January 7, 1971

NECESSARILY IT WAS a quiet New Year's even in Bluemont, well on the entire eastern coast, for heaven's sake!

The 18 inches of that fluffy white stuff drew the couples and families closer to the hearth and Toby Rickards' friends beat the storm and stayed on up at the Little's hilltop for some good times of sledding down the big dip and partying.

It really couldn't have happened at a better time, no one had urgent business anywhere the next day so Herbert Martz just kept "worrying the snow out" with his chained cub as Walton Mann said, and most everyone was content to stay close one day.

Come Saturday, it was impossible to move through the village by wheeled vehicle, sled or on foot. Everyone was stuck including the snow plows and Jim Brownell's hay truck and the telephone men – oh, the troubles they had.

There was still some talk of Christmas, the Robert Allders, it was revealed entertained 22 for dinner and more for dessert while the Earl Dutrows entertained the James Dutrows for dinner along with the Keys of Lovettsville.

The G.W. Townshends spent the long weekend with their daughter's family in Beltsville, Md.

A late card pictured a scene that I wished might be recreated in Bluemont, a horse-drawn sleigh loaded with gifts is pulled up to the rail station and the feel of festivity is in the air.

No longer will the big orange school-bus cover the roadside in "beautiful downtown Bluemont." Shir Carbaugh tearfully has resigned her duty in order to assume a position at Hazelton Laboratory. Ruth McCauley over on Rt. 719 near Round Hill will now cater to Snickersville small fry.

We are greatly distressed to hear of the serious nature of young Jennifer Wynkoop's condition. Hospitalized in Winchester, she is the young daughter of Mr. and Mrs. Wayne Wynkoop.

Care to do your part for ecology and earn some money at the same time?

Neighbor C. Nelson Hoy up on the far side of Rt. 601 is looking for typists to stuff envelopes and address letters from Smokey the Bear to school children who will be requesting the information.

It would be an 11-month job ideally requiring four hours a day and employees must live in a close radius of his home and the village.

If interested type him a letter indicating the number of hours you could give to the project daily at P.O. Box 167, Rt. 2, Bluemont.

I'm craving sweets and our neighbors' Monastery fruit cake is certainly a sumptuous sweet and the spice tea is just right for cold evenings and besides it supplies that needed vitamin C to keep the good ole common cold at bay.

Time to toast the toes by the fire, store the Christmas decorations in the attic again and think what a perfect time for a winter carnival. The sledding sounds right outside the window and with roasting chestnuts and baking turkeys in the oven…Don't be alarmed, it's just an idea for the seventies, sometime.

Snow sculptures would be fun, too and…

January 14, 1971

Ah, the security and comfort that this little mountain village offers with its continuing hard crust of snow and icy blasts.

There are meat and bread in the freezer and if the delivery trucks can safely arrive other luxuries such as milk and eggs are here at the two general stores.

There are logs on the front porch and additional kindling in the barn and as long as there are no electrical blackouts, there is television entertainment at night.

Somehow the forecast of more snow with its silent descent from the heavens brings a hush to problems of the Twentieth Century too. The battle with the elements comes first, we are pioneers again!

These are the days of the Capricorns – two brand new ones swelling the lists of grandchildren from the Earl Dutrows and Karlton Monroes arrived this week.

Kathryn Hope Dutrow was born on Jan. 3 at Loudoun Memorial Hospital, her parents being the James Dutrows of Airmont.

On Dec. 28, Richard and Betty Jeffreys became the parents of a son making Karlton and Mary Monroe of Unison, proud grandparents again.

Mrs. Edith McCall, "Mac" Brownell's mother celebrated her 88th birthday on Jan. 3. Long ago as a young girl, she came to Bluemont on the train and summered with friends here and then amazingly she returned, now to make her home here with her daughter's family. She's everything a grandmother should be and in such marvelous health.

The Townshends slipped away last week before the storm to visit S.L. Dodd and Mrs. Tom Bergoll in Moorefield, W.Va and how happy we are to report that petite Jennifer Wynkoop has been able to return from the hospital.

We trust Mrs. Bessie Carter has now fully recovered having suffered what was believed to be a mild stroke and Herbert Martz was under the weather with the flu bug too this week.

Susan Brownell was another of the young people of the community entertaining guests for New Year's Eve with about 15 left at dawn due to that snowed-in feeling.

One out-of-town guest was James Starling, a resident in surgery at the University Hospital in Charlottesville.

An old movie was playing locally, how old I found out later. Gone with the Wind with Vivian Leigh and Clark Gable was made in about 1936 according to a few of my neighbors. I saw it in the '50's and assumed it was brand new then. I have heard scenes were shot at nearby Llangollen Farm. Does anyone know for sure?

Then last Wednesday, Ivy Cochran and I were invited to give a few pointers to a group from Front Royal who were considering sponsoring a festival or fair. Some charming ladies from Luray shared their experiences too and then someone suggested that a train ought to be chartered for a trip through the valley and I was sold. Oh, if only Bluemont could have its train back, a non-polluting type, of course.

Senator Byrd or I should say his assistant answered my letter and pointed out that he had made several statements on the subject of the SST opposing it mainly on an appropriation basis.

The next vote will be in March, so "keep those cards and letters going."

Friends of the train and trainmen will wish to know that Clarence Tallman, the former telegrapher, lost his wife suddenly recently and has gone to be with her people in Pennsylvania for a while.

The Bluemont Citizens Association will attempt to meet this Wednesday, the 12th if a lane to the school can be cleared.

And now the Stowe's story.

Just before Christmas, Clayton Hall was the scene of an interesting discussion involving several members of the writing club sponsored by the Loudoun County Parks and Recreation Department and our near neighbors on Route 711, the Sam Stowes.

The Stowes, both writers, who say they have retired, gave pointers to the struggling collectors of rejection slips.

Sam went on to tell his fascinating tale of his part in the terribly successful musical South Pacific by Rodgers and Hammerstein.

Noticing a small clip announcing Hammerstein's intention to write this play, Sam promptly wrote Hammerstein offering background tales and pictures on the Seebees.

He was invited to New York for a luncheon date, stayed on to dinner time, related humorous incidents and exhibiting his pictures, one being of a homemade shower and two months later, he and Betty saw the first-run show in Connecticut in fifth row seats and the big hit, "I'm going to Wash that Man Right Out of my Hair" was the direct end result from viewing Sam's picture.

Don't think you have to jet-set the world over to meet fascinating people, they're here right in your Bluemont backyard.

January 21, 1971

Snickersville, The Biography of a Village by Jean Herron Smith, a former Loudoun resident, has sold out the initial 500 copies and gone into a second printing.

Mrs. Smith whose love for her old stone house in the mountain village now known as Bluemont was prompted after some years of commuting to her Washington government job to find out the history of this house whose windows framed the Blue Ridge Mountains.

Acquiring a knowledge of its history from old deeds found at the County Clerk's office and records at the Balch Library, she unearthed along with its past, the past of the village.

Her research went on for three years when she says those former founders and dwellers of Snickersville became real people, not just names upon a deed.

She began work on a manuscript but feeling no publisher would be interested, she laid it aside.

Then early last year her friend Mrs. Ingrid Jewell Jones, a retired newspaper woman and historical chairman for the Bluemont Fair wrote her at her present Miamisburg, Ohio address presenting her with the suggestion that copies of her history be available for visitors to the two-day event.

Mrs. Smith then went ahead, procuring the services of a Miamisburg artist and printer and the 500 copies complete with pictures and genealogies of prominent villagers was ready.

Bringing the books herself from Ohio to the Fair, Mrs. Smith autographed copies and gave a fascinating interview over the local radio station.

The book was an obvious success in Loudoun selling 350 copies at the Fair and orders were filled in following weeks by Mrs. Smith in Ohio while an available copy was not to be found in Bluemont. The Tri-State Trader gave it a review, the Miamisburg News and Dayton News carried features on Mrs. Smith's accomplishment as did the Federal Times which mistakenly located Bluemont in Ohio.

At the time of her interview here, she confessed that the selling of her home necessitated by her agency's move to Ohio, was a traumatic experience, for 14 years she had known the comfort of its thick walls, the beauty of its low window sills that afforded a view of the mountain, the security of her rocker by the hearth.

The house built in 1820 by Timothy Carrington on a lot purchased from Martha Clayton, daughter of Bluemont's architect, William Clayton became in subsequent years a tavern and general store as well as the fond-remembered Virginia House.

Virginia House operated by Molly Weadon in the famed railroad hey-days in Bluemont's history drew hungry employees of the Washington and Old Dominion Railroad to her backyard suppers of fried chicken, hot rolls, pies – "all you could eat for 50 cents."

Now the old house, the tavern addition in stone ruins and abutted a frame house owned by the Robert Colberts enjoys perfect up-keep by its present owners, Mr. and Mrs. Scot Butler of McLean.

While anticipating the Butlers' retirement when the house will be their permanent dwelling, the Timothy Carrington house, Virginia House or Jean Smith's house stands lonely awaiting another chapter in its history and that of its village to unfold.

January 28, 1971

The sleds fly again as January drags its heels and daydreams of tropical scenes come to mind.

More disconcerting than the outdoor weather was those low temperatures indoors with chill winds keeping it a cool 61 degrees here. Former owners have always commented that Clayton Hall was a great summer house and January and February weather in Bluemont make their point well.

Villagers scurry about hauling wood for the fireplaces and popular wood stoves and there is much talk of batteries and jumper cables and maybe Ford better get a "better" idea for these winter mornings but in the great tradition of this burg, there is always a helping hand available for the lady in distress.

For others who moan a breakdown on their foreign-made cars, a neighbor, Bill Oscanyan of Route 601, has started a new service of maintenance and repair primarily for Volkswagens, Porches, Volvos and Landrovers.

He calls his business Greyrocks Ingenuity and says he likes to solve problems. Buzz him at 226-8228 for quick service on your foreign-made cars.

Just what has been going on in Bluemont? I feel I have been elsewhere all week.

The League of Women Voters' meeting on air pollution was most informative. It was pointed out that transportation (mainly autos) put 63.8 million tons of pollutants in the air per year and then the mechanic in Winchester who worked on my polluting vehicle this week said after the speed of 62 miles per hour, it took more gas to operate a car and thus the pollution level would be higher. See, I knew we all needed that sign, "Dammit, Slow Down!"

The question was also raised at the meeting, how willing were we to make sacrifices for a cleaner environment? Would we pay higher taxes, use mass transportation? Then I said, Great, let's get the train back.

This week is the organization meeting for the April Clean Up under the auspices of Keep Loudoun Beautiful and I believe Bluemont is already leading the way with Jim Brownell's fine proposal of limiting drinks to be sold only in returnable containers. Yes Sir, I'll drink to that!

Fashion-wise, a Winchester store clerk told me bell-bottoms were on the way out just when I thought I might buy a pair and former Miss Greece now returned in her Loudoun home after a pleasant winter vacation said it was the midi and boots on the islands and in Athens that were in.

The heart specialists on the David Susskind Show say to stick to the low cholesterol diet so that big he-man breakfast of two eggs, bacon and toast with plenty of butter is not the best of all healthful starts for the day after all.

Sorry our friend Herbert Little is hospitalized at Washington Health Center while Emma Mann, local registrar reports that Jimmy Campbell was the first eighteen year-old to register in the Snickersville Precinct.

If you are interested in the Loudoun Craft Club now forming, call Nancy Cockerill, your Home Economics Extension Agent.

The students are here again for the semester break, Susan Brownell stuck close by while her parents slipped away for a weekend trip while Jean Dawson had her car out for a Sunday spin.

The Jack Allders sped away to Baltimore for a visit with their daughter Barbara Jean Mauk and Charles Anson and company came for a winter stroll through the Bluemont lanes.

The children raided the attic again and so when the bouquet of artificial jonquils came out of hiding, I draped them in my blue crock in the hall so when wistfulness overcomes me, I can imagine the fragrance of their backyard counterpart now very much asleep under the frozen earth.

February 4, 1971

"Tis bitter cold, Tis Bitter cold, says Files on Parade
And they're hanging Danny Deever in the morning."

This refrain of the poet's goes round and round in my head as we confine our movements to that of log-cabin living – everything in one room about the fireplace.

The children's small table and chairs are placed there before the hearth and the old-fashioned school-desk serves as my seat for our morning repast while the little bit of winter sunlight streams in the front windows.

Then as the shadows deepen, I try to practice those tips I was given on fire-building.

Place the kindling on the andirons, then twist wads of paper under the kindling for slow burning, put a good dry log on top and be sure it has plenty of air.

Goodness though, it seems little could have been accomplished in colonial times but cooking and the keeping of the fires going and washing the smoke-odor out of one's hair.

Had another bird this week, I believe he just came in for a little warming-up, Isabelle Dawson was my bird-woman this time. In the last several days, I found some dried crusts of bread near two of the fireplaces and I have just surmised a bird took my left-over breakfast offerings up the chimney for a snack when it got away from him.

The threatening weather scared Mr. and Mrs. Thomas Reid away from their 53rd anniversary dinner to be given in their honor and at the same time, it was to celebrate their daughter's birthday, Mrs. Leola Lawrence of Fairfax and they were to be entertained at their other daughter's Mrs. Gladys Campbell of The Plains, but the snow flurries on the 17th were flying thick and furious here so they stayed home.

The French Club at Valley High School was making some great plans this week for their Paris trip in April and who is to be chaperone but our own Mrs. Teasdale-Smith.

Our sick list is growing, Mrs. Robert D. Beeton of Rt. 601 is confined to Loudoun Memorial Hospital with a crushed vertebrae, Mr. Beeton was most appreciative to the Round Hill Rescue Squad who came quickly and efficiently to assist in transporting her to professional care.

Elsie Scott is also at Loudoun Memorial but hopes to return home soon.

Now Bluemont is in for another project – an important one.

Keep Loudoun Beautiful is sponsoring the April Clean-up which will be observed all over Virginia the week of April 12-25.

We need workers, trucks and money. Everyone should be willing to do his part in some way.

The organization wants local dumps cleaned out and refuse along the roadsides cleared and funds to pay for services that can't be acquired through volunteers.

The Boy Scouts will lead the nation on March 20 in tackling this problem and then all citizens should be prepared to help about a month later.

Tony Carbone reports a dump on the Appalachian Trail near his home.

All trash should be taken to the new sanitary land-fill that is to be opened on March 15 on Evergreen Mill Road.

I'm sure the Bluemont Citizens Association will want to back this project and a committee meeting to organize personnel will be called in several weeks.

Be eating your Wheaties, Cream of Wheat or whatever it takes so we might have a "beautiful down-town Bluemont."

February 11, 1971

We're well into the second long week of February, the month of hearts and flowers and the presidents' birthdays, Lincoln and Washington.

Every time I see Washington's birthday as the 15th I see red and it's not the reflection from a valentine. How can a birthday be changed? It was originally the 22nd for the record, although years from now our children won't believe us as the calendar will clearly show his birthday on a long weekend. Bah! Humbug!

The week brought us low, low temperatures, freezing mist (they called it), fog and then a warming trend and Sam Stowe reports a rare sight of three flocks of out-of-season birds, robins, bluebirds and cedar waxwings. They were using the mountains here as a fly-way before either flying north or south. As Sam said, the originator of that flight-plan may as well cancel plans for re-election next year.

Not deterred by the cold, the large earth machinery still groans and snarls at the hillside for the new road.

Up near the Route 7 turnoff to Bluemont, villagers appreciate the remodeling of the one remaining house left on what was called Summers Hill owned by Herbert Pearson of Leesburg.

More restoration is being attempted amidst 40 degree temperatures in the small log cabin near the Ralph Cochrans' farm.

Marvin Watts, a freelance writer formerly of Georgetown, is now calling it home.

The three chairmen heads and myself met at the James Walshes one of those icy days last week to begin plans for the 1971 fair. In the warmth of that good coal-burning heat, it was decided Mrs. Jack Lightner would officiate as acting chairman and Mrs. James Walsh would be the official registrar and co-chairmen.

While at the Walshes I learned Jerry is permanently home with us, having finished his requirement with the U.S. Air Force.

William Ballenger, Jr. of Pine Grove just returned from a marvelous trip out to Denver where he attended the National Western Stock Show and Rodeo and then went on to see friends in Santa Fe, N.M. and Evelyn Levi is on her way to Africa. I'm perfectly pale with envy.

Now about the most exciting experience I had this week was my reading of "A Night to Remember" by Walter Lord.

Now there was a gal on that unsinkable ship listed as Mrs. J.J. Brown, a Denver millionairess who became known to film fans a few years back as The Unsinkable Molly Brown. A great story.

The first page of the book mentioned a first class passenger. Clarence Moore of Washington, D.C. who had purchased fifty foxhounds in England for the Loudoun Hunt. Fortunately, he did not send the dogs on the Titanic as he perished that April night in the Artic Sea in 1912. It makes for fascinating reading under the covers here in Virginia far from the sea in February.

Sorry to hear Stanley Kelley suffered an attack of appendicitis last week.

Miss Mary Jo Lloyd was pleased to entertain her classmate from Jane's Kindergarten, Miss Jennifer Page Love of Hamilton for an overnight visit this week.

Margaret Fincham threw a big anniversary party for her parents, Mr. and Mrs. T.L. Payne of Bluemont last Sunday.

Married in 1927 in the Berryville Baptist Church, the couple received a congratulations from Mr. and Mrs. Oliver L. Payne, son Gary, Mr. and Mrs. Mike Payne, son Brian of Winchester, the C.E. Paynes and son Ty of Bluemont, Mrs. Walter Heflin and son Dennis of Boyce.

Joining this party also were Mr. and Mrs. Grantland Lloyd, Terry Elizabeth and Gary Michael and Mr. and Mrs. Dennis Lloyd and son Darren.

Three-year old Pamela Ann, youngest grandchild of the Paynes, just had to share the secret that Mommy had baked a big cake for the celebration and hidden it at the neighbors, the Andrew Sisks.

February 18, 1971

February continues her flirtation, promising spring one day, delivering icy winter the next. Patches of sod are visible, driveways are still coated with ice from the thaw-freeze cycle. Nature dazzled this week with its full moon and silver mountain display here in Bluemont.

The trees outlined with ice caught the rays of sunlight and it was a spectacular sight and our Apollo boys splashed down, always the best part of the flight to old cautious me.

Jay Allder turned nine this week, asked a friend Glen Kelley over for a birthday ice cream and cake and St. Valentine was said to have sparked a few tender messages between lovers and some fattening pounds of chocolates were passed out.

The children and I settled for the heart candy necklaces at Mann's Store.

One of the most festive sights spotted was the big doily Valentine on Jane's Kindergarten door where registration for next year's classes of nursery, kindergarten and first grade are going on.

Sam Kelley came from his Maryland school for a long weekend with Mom and Dad and siblings five.

Ray and Louise McClaughry and Kenneth and Mary Lee are spending their traditional month of February at their cottage in Largo, Fla.

After a great deal of remodeling Bud and Judy Anderson, the Robert Joneses' daughter and son-in-law, are permanent residents with us at Lazy Acres Farm. This is the spot where Volney Osborne counted the Yanks who were surprised by a Confederate command that resulted in the little Snickersville skirmish at what is now the Springs' and Sam Jones' doorsteps.

Wasn't it exciting that some of our neighbors and neighboring properties were used in the national television special on Lincoln last week?

Our community was terribly saddened to hear of the death of the William Robeys' infant, Theresa Ann.

Women are social creatures. Whatever the excuse to fight pollution, study the Bible, make a quilt, women like to get together and what better way to ripen a friendship than over a cup of tea.

Most of us find the friendship the richer with a cup of spice tea so here's the dried version recipe again. I'm thinking of dubbing it the Throckmorton blend since Peggy Stout, descendant of the Throckmortons of Bluemont began the proportions.

Mix together one cup of instant tea, two cups of Tang, one package of lemonade mix with one teaspoon of ground cloves and one teaspoon of cinnamon. Add two teaspoons of the mixture to a cup of water.

The Home Demonstration Club is meeting this week. Caneing classes are being taught. The Methodist Church has choir practice and their annual board meeting, while I'm trying to sandwich in a Clean-Up committee meeting and the Fair chairman heads have met again and are now calling department chairmen for next year's Fair.

It's a fairly busy little burg under its placid exterior and of late, I've been reflecting on that surprise package of tulips that Mr. Martz put out in front of the old barn last Fall. A sign ought to be posted, "Do not open until Spring," but like a child with the premature arrival of the Christmas package, I can hardly wait.

February 25, 1971

Life continues to throb to the rhythm of the washer and dryer. A virus of epidemic proportions is sweeping the county's three high schools and everyone seems to have a touch of the mid-winter blues.

Hailing from Missouri originally, these sunshiny days don't fool me. March can be a wild time in Virginia particularly in our little mountain hamlet but if you want to put the convertible top down – go ahead. Nature may spring another of her surprises – Spring in February.

Anyway with the top surface of white gone, the litter seems to be more in evidence.

We had a very productive meeting last Wednesday night, appointed a publicity person, chose crew leaders for different sections and hope to discuss the rest of the picture with the Bluemont Citizens next Wednesday night, Mar. 3, the first Wednesday of the month.

Likewise, the Bluemont Fair chairman heads had a meeting so they will want to give their report.

"Hawkeye" and "Popeye" Reid are already beginning plans to carry out their war against litter on their designated strip of town.

The Home Demonstration Club is already looking ahead to Easter and Easter eggs. Their meeting the third Wednesday of the month at 7:30 at the schoolhouse will feature a work-period for decorating the emptied shells.

Lucy Martz with an attractive new hair-do was celebrating her birthday with a number of her children and grandchildren last Sunday.

Sorry Lisa and Yvonne Allder were stricken with this virus making the rounds.

Bill Ballenger, Sr., is out visiting again. Last week he was the guest of Mrs. Myrtle Shelton of Richmond. They took side trips to Williamsburg, Jamestown, Norfolk, Petersburg and Colonial Heights.

Mr. and Mrs. William Ballenger, Jr. spent last Thursday in Orange, Va. as the guests of Harry Sear and Mrs. Estelle Reed made the trip down from Gwynedd Valley, Pa. with Mr. and Mrs. Bill Marcus for a pre-spring jaunt to the Lucine Beeds.

Janet Reed reports the back roads have been quite treacherous with all the flooding for the big orange school bus.

The weather change stirred up something even in my old show-me attitude 'cause I burned up the evergreen decorations from the front door in the fireplace and even thought about washing the windows. I do hope I see a kite soaring in the blue soon in Bluemont.

March 4, 1971

Everybody thinks it's spring, bees, birds, flies, not to mention the two-legged creatures out washing their cars, tidying up lawns, refinishing pieces of furniture on the front porch.

There's that wonderful sense of euphoria here, all's right with the world.

Bruce Cochran distinguished himself this week by winning third prize in the annual Lions Club Band Memorial Contest. Bruce won with a vocal number in the instrumental, vocal contest.

Bud Anderson got his transfer for Sterling Post Office from Alexandria so he's much closer to his Bluemont home now.

Mrs. Herbert Martz had a pleasant week visiting her brother and family in Charlottesville this week.

I received a real treasure in the mail from Bill Ballenger. Having seen that I had an interest in Molly Brown, he sent me a post card of her Denver mansion. He had a recent trip there, you will recall with plans to return in July. He also has a large collection of post cards from all over the world.

Those post cards people were kind enough to loan for the Bluemont slide show proved to be the best specimens for copying. Since the Fair, we were loaned another, a great one of the big hotel at the top of the hill and now with the road work going on, the main gate posts are most visible. Unfortunately, also visible now are the hundreds of cans and bottles dumped there too.

Keep Loudoun Beautiful met again Tuesday and Mrs. B. Powell Harrison was most gracious to supply me with reams of material. Do you know the state of Virginia spent $800,000 last year just to pick up the litter from the roadsides? Surely, our tax money should be spent in more vital projects.

Three of the four Carbaugh girls are now down in the mouth with this flu, Lynn, Hope and Pam and Shir had her bout last week.

Mrs. Robert D. Beeton is progressing slowly but she has had a terrible siege with this crushed vertebrae, being unable to move from a flat-on-her-back position for 28 days at Loudoun Memorial Hospital.

Suffering from a broken shoulder was Mrs. Joseph Smith too but she is now well on her way to recovery.

Mrs. Beeton was even unable to read, a most terrible fate to me. Oh, how I love to read. Books, papers, magazine, letters, diaries fascinate me.

After sinking in the Artic Seas on the Titanic, I went on to climbing Annapurna, became the Sensuous Woman, learned how to read Body Language and now with the appearance of the new Geographic, McCall's, and Reader's Digest, I don't have time to read my textbook for the current course being offered at Valley High School from University of Virginia on How to Teach Reading.

I guess I ought to rise early like Ivy Cochran at five o'clock in the morning when she gets in her daily reading.

Another early riser is the Cochrans' new neighbor, Marvin Watts who begins the day reading his own writing at the same hour in the morning.

Mm! it makes me tired just to think about it.

Anyway, rest up Bluemonters, Clean-Up Week is coming and stalks of green are pushing up. See, everybody thinks it's spring!

March 11, 1971

Bluemont is shifting into gear and gaining momentum in motivation for the first involvement of Loudoun County in the state-wide Clean-Up Campaign to be carried out Apr. 12-25.

The organization Keep Loudoun Beautiful has recruited district chairman for each community and then that individual picks his committee who are free to meet their own local needs.

The April campaign is mostly a war on litter and Mt. Gilead's supervisor, James Brownell is leading the way by this proposal to pass an ordinance that will ban the sale of non-returnable bottles and cans throughout Loudoun County.

The Bluemont Citizens Association at its March meeting went on record to support their supervisor's proposal.

Keep Loudoun Beautiful chaired by Mrs. B. Powell Harrison suggests that each individual first clean his own property, then extend himself to his church and school and then as a group of individuals a community project may be tackled.

Bluemont's committee who expect the same from their citizens is composed of Mr. and Mrs. Ralph Cochran, Mr. and Mrs. Walton Mann, Herbert Martz, Mrs. James Brownell, Anthony Carbone, and Mr. and Mrs. Glen Lloyd.

Crew-leaders have been assigned by the committee to enlist workers to clean designated strips of town property.

They are Walton Man, Tony Carbone, Mr. and Mrs. Ralph Cochran, the Glen Lloyds, the William Carbaughs, Mrs. Robert L. Johnson, Clyde Beck, Herbert Martz, Jim Walsh and Mrs. James Brownell.

Feed bags were recommended over plastic bags. These will be supplied by the Glen Lloyds and Louis Underwood will be in charge of assisting local pick-up trucks to certain areas.

The local trucks will deposit the rubbish behind the school where the state and county trucks will be collecting the bags for the expected opening of the new land-fill near Leesburg.

Tony Carbone will handle publicity, anticipating a door-to-door flyer either sent by mail or hand-carried, informing citizens when they may expect pick up of their individual anti-litter efforts.

The committee in the tradition of another national organization, Clean It, Paint It, Fix It pointed out eye sores in the village proper of overgrown lots, unpainted buildings and unusable sidewalks which may be corrected in a future community effort.

Certainly the enthusiasm radiated at the Bluemont Citizens Association meeting and among the members of the Methodist Youth Fellowship was most encouraging.

March 18, 1971

"Spring is here, I hear" or so the calendar claims as of this Sunday and Ralph Cochran says you can plant potatoes any time now, "any time after Washington's birthday, whenever that is" he added with a chuckle.

Mrs. Thomas Reid's comment early in the week was "March is tricky" and she ought to know as she has been celebrating her birthday on the second of March for 74 years now. She says she got lots of cards this year and her vigor is certain proof of the goodness in this pure mountain air up here.

Another birthday celebration this week was for young Chip Lloyd, son of Jerry and Peggy Lloyd now in the stone house up on Route 7. Chip turned five with two parties at each grandparents; and two of the most adorable cakes I've ever seen baked by his mother. One was a cat, the other the candy house straight out of Hansel and Gretel and the best part for the Johnson twins was that they were around to lick the mixing bowl.

The great event of the week for the twins was the buying of new shoes – saddle shoes. Ah memories – black and white saddle shoes and dirty bucks were in when I was hopping around leading college cheers and when Elizabeth Wertz assured a somewhat younger man who happens to be meeting the payments of Clayton Hall that even the Harvard men wore them, he couldn't believe it. Yep, they wore crew cuts too.

Peggy Lloyd was telling me that the present Route 7 in front of their house should be like a country lane because the four-lane job will be behind the house. When all this will come to pass no one seems to know, however.

All in all, it hasn't been a bad winter – the fruits of my neighbors' labor were on our table most of the time – we still have plenty of Shir Carbaugh's green peppers (mm! those sloppy joes were good the other day). Mary Ann Carter's tomatoes were a great plus in all those beef stews and Herbert Martz's potatoes filled out every meal with the day starting with the Lloyd's milk on the breakfast cereal.

I hear we're going to have a garden this year. Mm! Charlie Waddell will indulge my little story about our gardening experience together when we were neighbors in Broad Run Farms. The land was plowed on our lot, Charlie planted the seeds, kept out the weeds, diligently and I harvested it. Bob and Marie wanted no part of the project. This went on for two seasons, the third summer, Charlie said he didn't think he wanted a garden that year!

Now about our supervisor up here, we're all so sorry to hear Jim Brownell has been confined to Winchester Hospital with a blood clot in his leg.

Another friend and native Bluemonter, Sam McMichael is also a patient there having undergone an operation this week.

Mac Brownell is stewing chickens and dicing up celery again a la chicken salad for the third annual Fashion Show sponsored by the Round Hill Methodist Church. Expanding this year to Emerick Elementary School in Purcellville, it will be held on Saturday, Mar. 27 with the Door of Fashion, Purcellville supplying the fashions. For additional information or reservations for a group, call Mrs. James Brownell, Bluemont.

Jennifer entertained her little friend Aillen Laing of Purcellville for lunch this week and Clyde Beck was over at Atoka picking land cress – three bushels full. Joyce says you can blanche it and freeze it but then you can't make sandwiches, right?

Surely, Carolyn and Charles Tyroler ought to be able to dream up another reason for a spring fling so we can have some more of those "yummy" watercress sandwiches and right gin and tonics.

Lynn Carbaugh made the sick list this week when her foot became infected – after encountering a splinter.

Ruth and Tom Mann were up from Richmond poking around in the mountain junk yard as I did about this time last year. We agreed it was great fun and Clinton Hindman admits that's where he has found most of his antique bottle collection at similar spots.

And you know Bluemont could have bought an absolutely adorable red caboose in Rosslyn for $1600. It was auctioned off this week. Happy Spring!

March 25, 1971

The wind's howling, snow flurries are dancing in the glare of the street light at the corner and over at Mann's Store grass seed and pussy willows peek out the windows and many Bluemont homes have a tall vase of forsythia brightening up a dark corner.

It's just typically March in Northern Virginia and I haven't seen a single kite soaring yet.

Gardens are going in, the Robert Allders have in their potatoes and when Bessie Carter's grandson from Summit Pt., W.Va. came around Saturday with seeds for sale, I knew I couldn't pass up the zinnias.

A wrong turn down a dirt road near Hillsboro revealed a big sign, Ecology Gardens. When we asked a neighbor what it was all about, we found it was garden plots that were being rented to city dwellers.

Bluemont has been anything but a quiet spot this week. On Monday, a three-car collision occurred at the turn-off from Rt. 7, the political pot boiled over with the announcement of Mrs. Carolyn Tyroler's intention to oppose James Brownell for the Mt. Gilead representative on the Board of Supervisors on Wednesday and a small plane crashed out near The Troppe on Saturday. Miraculously, none of the four men from Harrisburg, Pa. were seriously injured.

The John A. Bardons are pleased to know that both their daughter and son are dean's listers. Michael is earning his honors at Baptist Bible Seminary, Clarks Summit, Pa. while Jeanne is a sophomore at Madison College, Harrisonburg.

Roberta Underwood and Shir Carbaugh are operating the candy apple concession for the Association this year at the Bluemont Fair and are calling for good recipes.

Molly Freedman of New York City is visiting her son and daughter-in-law, the David Freedmans for several weeks while they all are awaiting word from the Freedman's daughter, Wendy who is expecting her firstborn.

We enjoyed a visit from the Jasper Richards of Lovettsville last Sunday. Jasper was telling us his grandfather served at the White House under three Presidents, Grant, Hayes and Garfield and that his own father as a young child was allowed to ride in the dumbwaiter and breakfast with the President many mornings.

Clyde Beck took his children Justine and Brian along with Susan Potts on a wonderful sight-seeing tour to Washington recently. Right at Easter is such a wonderful time to see Washington.

There isn't a more breathless sight than to see the Cherry Blossoms across from the Jefferson Memorial in full moonlight. And the Botanical Gardens are so lovely with azaleas and lilies and one can sit quietly in the Art Gallery patios and smell the fragrance of sweet flowers and then roam the galleries of great masterpieces. Then one should dine at night at one of the wharf restaurants on lobster and the best hot lemon meringue pie you ever ate and then take in a play at Arena Stage. That's what we all need, an occasional day and night out on the town.

Wesley Carbaugh had a St. Patrick's birthday again last week and Grandmother Viva Carbaugh now turning 86 is entertaining her children, grandchildren and great-grandchildren herself for her birthday, doing the whole meal herself with her specialty, twice-baked potatoes with cheese.

Glad to hear that Mrs. Robert D. Beeton and James Brownell are each home from the hospital now.

The MYF went on a mission of goodwill this week, delivering new sheets and pillow cases to Paxton Home.

Of course, we're all waiting to see our neighbors acting as models in the third annual Fashion Show sponsored by the Round Hill Methodist Church this Saturday at Emerick School at 12:00 noon.

Bill Scott's opinion poll of 30,000 respondents shows that 72 percent thought the SST should be subsidized through cooperative efforts of private industry.

The Bluemont chapter of Keep Loudoun Beautiful will meet this week and then we will announce when you may expect pick-ups. Several of the neighbors have already gotten started.

Ah, to be floating down the Mississippi on the Delta Queen next month on the National Trust Expedition.

April 1, 1971

There will be no surprises in April for me. Since the 1970 census in Loudoun County, I will know what to expect. Showers – yep, MUD, Snow, Fog, Blue skies, dells of daffodils.

Herbert Martz says he has checked my tulips he planted last fall and two are pushing up through the still cold earth.

The old burg is fairly lively these sunny Saturdays. The teen-agers have a Snickersville Pike basketball court and there Alvin Coates visiting with his grandparents, the James Scotts, shoots a few baskets with his former neighbors. Brother Donald's here too up at the Beetons planting grass seed.

The Carbaugh girls gave me a hand with collecting for the Red Cross and we gleaned the weekly news as we went along.

Our first clean-up was accomplished by June Lloyd's group on Saturday. They cleaned from the yellow school house down to the Trappe Road, about a half mile, filled 36 bags and turned in about 20 returnable bottles.

The enthusiastic crowd of Robie and Mike Pearson, Steve, Timmy and Judy Dawson, Belinda and Tammy Dawson, Desiree Allder, Glen Kelly, Mary Jo and Kelley Lloyd, along with the adults Dorothy and Grace Dawson and Ann Lloyd Wilson then roasted wieners at the schoolhouse for lunch. Jerry Lloyd made the hauls in his truck.

Officially, we want to repeat the performance on Easter Monday with Ivy Cochran's section from the Trappe Road to the Church, the Carbaughs' section from the Church to

Iden's Store. Mr. Martz's group on his road, my section from the old store to the corner and Mac Brownell's from the corner to Rt. 7.

We wish to enlist the aid of the youth that day and another wiener roast is planned.

If anyone can furnish us some bags, let us know. Ralph Cochran has donated 50 and they are here at the old barn if you wish to begin before the April dates.

Clyde Beck says his Washington friends including Charles Anson are to help him the week before Easter.

Pick up for the outlying neighborhood will be Apr. 24.

There's that great Bluemont community spirit in action again. Don't forget our monthly meeting is the first Wednesday of each month; Apr. 6 is the date for the Bluemont Citizen's Association meeting at 7:30 p.m.

The end of winter brings lingering illnesses. Glad to hear Sam McMichael is home from Winchester Hospital.

Bessie Carter was out for a Saturday stroll, looking spry again and John Hyland has returned to Shawnee Nursing Home.

Mrs. Powell says she believes her house is sold to a retired Army colonel and his wife. I told her if anyone should receive a beautification award, it ought to be her as she keeps her property immaculate.

Bonnie Reid had a pleasant surprise visit from her parents, Mr. and Mrs. W.B. Coates of Glen Island, Alaska. They visited here for a week and then they all went down to Berkeley, W.Va to see Grandmother Coates. They took in a delightful barber shop quartet concert and daughter Wanda celebrated her sixth birthday.

Sam Hatcher is up from Florida at his mountain property here for the week.

Don't forget the program to benefit the Blue Ridge Speech and Hearing Center on Apr. 3 at 8 o'clock at Loudoun County High School. Tickets are one dollar at the door.

Boy! Clinton Hindman and Ralph Cochran really found a rare treasure in an old bottle this time. Printed on two three-inch clear bottles was the name, Dr. Charles Turner, one with Bluemont at the bottom, the other with Snickersville. You will recall Dr. Turner lived here at Clayton Hall and maintained his office across the street, now the Lawrence Dawson home which also was a pharmacy. Now there's an item for the relic display at the Bluemont Fair!

On sleeping late in the morning at Clayton Hall, two words summarize the happening – Forget It!

Inevitably an early riser teams up with a Lazy Bones and as the dogs are released from their sleeping chamber by the early riser the Lazy Bones' chances of rest completely vanish.

First Snicker, our male dachshund pushes open the door with his nose and lands on my stomach, then Gretchen, the female dachshund, whines at the side of the bed, demanding a lift up to a place under the covers. Parrish the collie excited by all the activity barks, one of the twins awakens, banging at her door, the other cries out and Jennifer appears dewy-eyed at bedside. The day has begun again at 7:30.

Ok, so you rise at 5 o'clock. As Mark Twain said of exercise, What's the advantage of being tired? Ho! Hum!

"So if it's raining, have no regrets…"

April 8, 1971

"While visions of cherry blossoms danced in our heads" and the grass is getting greener every day.

Mary Jo Lloyd has caught the spirit of the season with a new beautiful, white, red-eyed rabbit named Clover.

Natives are longing for Spring weather but the chill persists while the James Brownells can look forward to a short visit to Puerto Rico next month and the Robert Ewings can think back to their March trip to sunny California.

Historic Garden Week in Virginia ushers in this month but according to Connie McElhinney the east is acquiring longer winters and all these Spring rites may eventually have to be moved to May.

Nevertheless, Herbert Martz's tulips are about eight inches high and he has crocuses in bloom while the Becks' forsythia is casting a dazzling yellow reflection this way.

Ann Van Deventer says her County Craft Shop in Round Hill will open on the 15th and the Dawson girls, Libby and Sue, caught the fever by purchasing new cars.

Spring projects abound: Jack Lightner has devoted many hours to building a new fence at Locust Grove while Keep Loudoun Beautiful is formulating its final plans for the Spring clean-up, Apr. 12-25. The youth will begin work here on the 12th at 10 o'clock.

The circus is in town and Mr. and Mrs. William Ballenger, Jr. of Pine Grove took their two children into Washington to see the 100th Anniversary show of the Ringling Brothers, Barnum and Bailey Circus.

Charles Anson, back from wintering in Mexico, was here again on the weekend over at the Waldrops as was Al Serber and their usual guests.

The Loudoun Valley French students and chaperones, our Mrs. Teasdale-Smith among them flew to Paris for a ten-day trip on Monday. Gwen Kelley was one of the students who will experience April in Paris.

Bruce Cochran was among a group of journalism students who attended a conference in Charlottesville on Friday.

The James Brownells celebrated their wedding anniversary on the first.

Out at Oatlands on the same day, I met a neighbor, Harlee Pate of Bloomfield, who is circulation manager for the Loudoun-Times Mirror. He sees the potential of Bluemont as the great little tourist trap, too.

Also there with the Senior Citizens of Sterling Park were Mr. and Mrs. Redmond, and he is a former native of Bloomfield. He said he often frequented Iden's Store when it was located at the large stucco building known as Lake's Store originally.

There's really quite a bit of action at these little general stores. A Mr. Thompson came in Mann's the same day, looking for silver dollars and gold coins. I heard him give the offer of $500 for an 1861 gold coin in perfect condition. He said last year he had found a young boy down at Iden's who sold him several coins. If interested, he says to call him, at 771-1801.

The Methodist Church will hold a sunrise service at 6 o'clock at Pierott's Hill, weather permitting next Sunday, Easter.

Ralph Cochran, his sons, Larry and Mark and nephew Clinton Hindman, did their cleaning strip, from their house to Payne's corner almost two miles, last Saturday. They collected 33 bags in a half-day's work. Most of them were Black Label beer cans they report.

Please don't forget the united effort on Easter Monday and then the general pick-up on the 24th.

Have a happy Easter.

April 15, 1971

Life in Bluemont, weather-wise, is fantastic. Last week when everyone was sure Spring had come at last, the village proper got eight inches of snow while on the fringes of town at the Brownells, the Cochrans, the Lloyds, there was maybe two inches. Up at Mt. Weather thirteen inches was reported. Yep, we live in a mountain village.

It didn't seem to hurt the forsythia or jonquils, however, just freshened them up a bit but most of our old apple tree came down and a good many branches were strewn in other yards.

Oozy chocolate fingers and artificial grass tracked from one end of the house to the other along with the traditional ham and lemon pie dinner with both sets of grandparents completed Easter '71 here while the Walton Manns entertained their son and daughter-in-law, Tom and Ruth from Richmond, along with Mrs. Mann, Sr. of Hamilton for a turkey dinner.

The Lawrence Dawsons went the turkey road too with all their clan and the college crowd came in from Madison. Willa Colbert and Jean Dawson and Susan Brownell from University of Virginia, while Sadie Peyton became Mrs. Pigott at a lovely little church wedding at the old stone church all over the Easter vacation.

The David Freemans became proud grandparents with a six pound 14-ounce granddaughter. Helen, spent several days last week burping baby and changing diapers at her daughters' side in Poughkeepsie, N.Y.

Elsie Scott remains at Loudoun Memorial Hospital.

The Lucien Reeds entertained the Gordon Reeds of Leesburg and Mr. and Mrs. J.D. Reed from Emory on Saturday and delivered daughter, Jill to Winchester Hospital on Sunday and she will be minus her tonsils as of this reading.

So you were going to pick out a buy for Easter. Wouldn't you settle for a sweet Airedale puppy? He was abandoned here by his former owners and has the dearest disposition. Please call me at 225-2051 if you would like this little dog as a pet. I don't even require a fence.

Justine Beck reported a splendid trip to Washington to view the now ripened cherry blossoms and then greeted us with Happy Easter accenting it with a gift of some incomparable sprigs of forsythia.

Elizabeth Wertz still hoping to find a suitable spot nearby for herself and her three German Shepherds was out for a country drive from Arlington last week and she made the rounds of country sights.

Such a lovely weeping cherry tree next to Klingersmiths at the Shenandoah Bridge. We adored the red shutters now on Thomas DeLashmutt's cabin as Marvin Watts greeted us with paint brush in hand, admired yellow on barn, shed and house on several farms.

Bennie Lightner and I said it would be a nice color for the schoolhouse. Russell Parks, Jr. is making repairs and painting there this week and Clyde Beck is investigating the possibility of new sidewalks as part of the outcome of the Citizens Association meeting last week.

Spring brings change, often reflected in real estate transactions so there appeared an ad for Leaven Stevens' house in Bluemont this week. It's most charming, as you know.

Of course, it's the Sam Joneses talking of deserting us for a warmer climate (I guess they have a point there, what a winter!).

But really I hate to think of a time when Ingrid won't be here to keep the most precise minutes possible at the Bluemont Citizens Meeting, cheerfully writing tactful letters that get action bettering our community. I hate to think of Halloween without her treats, Home Demonstration Club functions without her support, ice-cream festivals without her dishing-up and of course, her specialty, who will enlighten us when it comes to Snickersville history?

At least Sam, give us that good beef stew recipe before you leave.

Did you know there was a full moon the night the Easter bunny made a few stops in Bluemont?

We always lock the dogs up, put out a carrot and leave the front door open for him. How he turns that tricky knob, I never question.

Actually I was hoping Harvey would drop by! Wouldn't life be beautiful if we all had a Harvey and a voice like Jimmy Stewart's with which to articulate?

April 22, 1971

The mountain hasn't gone green yet but warm rays of sun and April showers have coaxed buds into blooming and even a few fruit trees into lacey magnificence in the village this week.

The Herbert Littles assumed the weather was warm enough to begin their spring, summer days here at their mountain retreat but they were literally snowed in for a day during our little Spring snow last week.

Col. and Mrs. Taylor Holt spent the weekend in New Haven, Conn. with their daughter's family, the Rauffs. Mrs. Holt lingered on with the grandchildren for a while as their daughter Jane undergoes surgery.

The clean-up is still going-on here. Monday, a great onslaught was accomplished on the village with close to forty young people and adult leaders working. The Citizens Association treated the workers to a wiener roast with Betty Walsh acting as cook.

Ivy Cochran engaged the MYF from the corner of Route 606 to the church, the Carbaugh girls took their strip from the church to Iden's Store, Clay Ratcliff led a group up the dirt road, Mac Brownell recruited five Round Hill boys to clean the Route 700 strip and finally I rounded up Dale Reid and companions to clean up an actual dump on the grassy patch next to the old store, Jim Walsh and family cleaned the school grounds, even grooming trees.

Just before the rain on Saturday, Clyde Beck's group loaded two pick-up trucks stacked full of refuse off the long hill. Laboring there were Hawkeye, Popeye, and Buckeye Reid, Ambrose Moreland, Sonny Colbert and all the Becks.

Walton Mann finished his mile from Route 7 to the Clarke County line on Route 601. The Paul Reislers of Skyland lent a hand along with Popeye again. They collected thirty bags there.

Next Saturday, April 24, citizens are encouraged to clean up in front of their own property, particularly down the yellow school house road and on the other side of Route 601. Pick ups will be made by the Bluemont Citizens on that day.

It is pretty terrific to think that our entire county is involved in this massive effort to rid our lovely by-ways of ugly litter.

Jerry Walsh returned home this week from an auto trip to Oklahoma City.

The Robert Carters are back in residence at Whitehall Farm again. They entertained Robert's parents, the Robert P. Carters of Berryville for Easter.

Friday, I went gaily out forgetting entirely that the new tags had not been put on the car. When I was "pulled over" the policeman discovered my operator's license had expired. Now to cram in the rules of the road and hope I can figure out which car has the right-of-way in that awful little diagram.

Wouldn't it be simpler just to walk, staying right here, patronizing the general stores, the butcher, the baker, the candle-stick maker? No, let's don't go that primitive!

Happy Motoring!

April 29, 1971

A high wind ripped our old drain loose and balmy days brought the first picnics of the season all in the same week of Virginia's aging April.

As Wesley Carbaugh said on Saturday he had removed his sweater and then put it back on with the chill a dozen times that day.

Mrs. Roy Santmyer said those warm days were too hot for her but Emma Mann and I said we would stick to that 80 degree weather.

Cool Saturday marked our last day of clean-up, the James Walshes did a super job on their Berkley Farm and Louis Underwood made pick up on the right side of No. 601, if my count is correct from the crew leaders' reports, 75 people were involved in the cleaning, 173 bags and three pick-up truck loads of refuse were collected.

The Paul Strangs' kind donation covered the expense of the luncheon served to the youth workers on Apr. 12.

Our picnic spot was near the old Snickersville Academy, this week. On that hillside there, one has a marvelous view of the village cluster. Somehow I felt like Emily from Thornton Wilder's Our Town as I watched a lone figure make his way to the store then begin the long trudge back up the steep hill. It was a good place for reflection until I saw three pairs of saddle shoes drenched by the rapid-flowing creek and I was forced to ponder that motherhood and reflection do not often walk hand-in-hand.

Anyway I do hope we can tackle that area for a clean-up before the Bluemont Fair. Old refrigerators, stoves, shoes are strewn everywhere.

Tom Furr is a most remarkable man. He made his rounds on Saturday for the usual two-month trash pick-up and he kept pushing in another large container of cans and bottles. It was an astounding sight.

Herbert Martz came along about that time, lending his usual cheerful assistance when he revealed he had celebrated his 73rd birthday last Thursday. Who has more industry or energy than he at any age in town? His tulips are in full magnificence now.

Scot Butler spent many hours this week beautifying his old stone house. The house built by Timothy Carrington was patterned after the Samuel Washington house, Harewood near Charles Town, which I noted with interest on the Jefferson County Garden Tour this year.

At Harewood in 1794 James Madison married Dolley Payne Todd, whose sister Lucy Payne Washington was mistress of the handsome home.

Jean Dawson was home for the weekend from Madison and another Dawson, Roger of Falls Church came by to show me his Lee photograph in the April Civil War Times. It turned out perfectly lovely.

Mrs. Kitty Manuel gave a wedding shower for Miss Linda Fowler of Unison at her in-laws home here, the Clarence Manuels on Saturday night.

Betty Walsh and Roberta Underwood in connection with the Home Demonstration Club traveled to Skyes Hall this week where they created a lamp shade for their homes.

May 6, 1971

Rainy days are soothing to me. I love the green mist, the quiet, the chirping of the birds and the cessation of that incessant howling wind. A few rainy days came to Bluemont this week reinforcing the serenity of the spot.

Rainy days are what Spring is all about – it's budding trees, green grass and robins looking for worms in the damp earth. Spring is late this year. The Herbert Littles say the dogwood haven't opened yet on their hill but Peggy says many of us forget it's colder here and flowers appear later.

The native rosebud is full now and daffodils, iris shoots and lily heads are rising.

I discovered a fact about tulips quite by accident this week. The twins and I had just agreed we wouldn't pick the tulips until they bloomed, we had many green buds. Two minutes later they appeared at the door, laden with short green tulip buds. I let loose a few emotionally-charged words on the couple and half-heartedly stuck the buds down in a kitchen cup. By the end of the week they had all turned lovely hues in the warmth of the kitchen atmosphere but my pansy plant is wilting fast in its little pot. Is it too early to put them in the soil outdoors?

There's been lots of talk of real estate changing hands in town but then I'd find out it wasn't definite. The Sam Joneses and Mrs. Nellie Powell have sold. More about the newcomers later.

The Bluemont Citizens are meeting Wednesday night at the freshly painted school at 7:30 p.m.

Miss Ruth Alley is to be honored for her ten years of service at the Veterans Hospital in Martinsburg, W.Va. as a Red Cross worker next week. She has contributed 5000 hours, entertaining the shut-ins, taking them for drives, for luncheon and even to the Charles Town track to watch the horses exercising, telling them, "See you went to the race track and it didn't cost you a cent!"

How pleased we are to hear that the William Ballenger, Jr.'s are new parents of a baby girl, Bibi Mae born April 9.

Mr. Ballenger is keeping me up with the Molly Brown doings in Denver, Colo.

The Rocky Mountain News reports an endeavor is underway now to raise money to save, restore and make her brownstone house into a museum.

In my opinion, it's about time a group got started on a "Save the Old Hotel" in Leesburg campaign. Let's get some comparative figures on preservation and demolition and thus reconstruction.

Really what's new in Bluemont other than the beginning of lawn-cutting, I hardly know except what my immediate neighbor next-door could tell me.

The Clyde Becks entertained at a dinner party for Charles Anson and friend Nancy, Al Serber, Marvin Watts and Paeonian Springs artists, Gloria and John Irvine on Friday night.

Charles will be leaving our country in July; he and his friends have been such a bright weekend addition to Bluemont.

I know it's not too pleasant a topic but a reporter must report all of the news—I spied a dead snake on Route 7 this week.

Mrs. Richard Wilson up on the ridge believes as I do when she says she doesn't appreciate the habitation of snakes behind the kitchen cabinets. Of course, Peggy Little is still moaning the loss of Junior, the pet black snake up at their place. Anyway, I'm not adventuring to my dark, earthened stone-foundation basement these days.

May 13, 1971

The whole valley is now bathed in a soft green, the wind has calmed and as the weekend transpired there was more hope that summer would return again this year.

Anyway, Mrs. Nellie Powell's sale on Saturday began at 1:00 p.m., proceeded until the spring shower started in earnest at 2:15. Most of the neighbors were there, Roy Santmyer, Jack Allder, Dot Heasley from Purcellville, Dolly Manuel Journell from Lincoln with her absolutely beautiful twin daughters and those who love a sale, the Glen Lloyds, Shir Carbaugh, Frances Ballenger, Clyde Beck, Lawrence and Isabelle Dawson, Libby and Bootsie Stearne.

Lucy Martz came along and told me she had had a fall this week.

Gail Kelley was there – Boy! What a prize she got that time they found the Snickersville Academy Sampler at a local sale.

Miss Susy Neal was back down at her cabin, saying how she would miss Mrs. Powell as a neighbor.

Packing up too are Ingrid and Sam Jones. The community will have a covered-dish supper in their honor this Saturday evening, May 15 at the schoolhouse at 6:30 p.m. Be assured the entire community is invited and urged to come.

Activities are definitely picking up: Roberta Underwood, Betty Walsh and Miss Ruth Alley represented the Bluemont Home Demonstration Club at the district meeting in Woodstock this week and the Club is sponsoring a special meeting open to the community on May 19 with guest speaker, Howard Sprague, who will speak on "Loudoun and Its Future." This certainly is a timely subject so let's make Mr. Sprague welcome in his wife's hometown.

We have been hearing some nice compliments on Bennie Lightner's participation as a model in a Lovettsville fashion show last week.

Mr. and Mrs. H.G. Stearn entertained Henry's mother, Mrs. Margaret Griffith at a dinner birthday party on April 18. Guests at the buffet supper were Bill and Carol Griffith and son from Fairfax, Dr. and Mrs. Curtis Shockley and three daughters from Manassas, Carl and Karen Davis and Mrs. Dorothy Phillips from Woodstock, Johnny and Gloria Stearn from Alexandria and of course, Bob Griffith, husband of the honored guest.

Johnny Carter is now hospitalized at Loudoun Memorial pending an ulcer operation and their home, Mountain Shadow is up for public auction at the Leesburg courthouse this Saturday. Here's hoping they can still be its tenants.

The Robert Jones' granddaughter, Valerie Anderson, turned eight on Saturday with the biggest birthday cake I've seen in a while. It was devil's food and decorated with yellow roses, too.

The talented Cochran family brought the special music at The Harmony United Methodist Church Revival in Hamilton this week. Brothers, Ralph, Phil and Allen sang accompanied by Ralph's son, Bruce, on the organ.

Mrs. Townshend was sharing the beauty of the blooms from her perfect Japanese cherry tree with all the post office patrons this week and now the flowering dogwoods dot the hillsides.

Mrs. Richard Wilson reports that she was actually reading the comment in the news about her disliking snakes when her husband came up and announced he had just found a black snake in the furnace room! Mrs. Wilson reminded me that one mustn't dare harm a back snake – they keep down the mice and rats – this is the code of the country!

Who got treated for Mother's Day – no one was telling on Saturday when the Bluemont news went to press. Later, I heard Libby Stearne treated her mother and the Lawrence Dawson clan to Sunday dinner down at her pink house but the girls here, ages three and five went to cleaning and dusting with gusto all for the love of Mother for about five minutes, when Jennifer, the oldest, called for a coffee break!

Oh, the ways of the world!

May 20, 1971

Mrs. Powell Has Kept Beauty Alive in the Village
Bluemont Recognizes A Citizen's Efforts

For 21 years Mrs. Nellie Powell has been Bluemont's "white tornado."

The 79-year-old has continually scrubbed, mopped, and polished her spacious 17-room house and trimmed, planted, fertilized, and mowed her half-acre lot entirely by herself for 17 of the 21 years.

Ever amazing and inspiring her neighbors, Mrs. Powell was presented a framed certificate this week by the Bluemont Citizens Association in "grateful tribute for her efforts in beautification and upkeep of her property."

Her large frame house, rumored to have been built in 1897, has an unspoiled view of the foothills of the Blue Ridge in the back yard and fronts on the famed Snickersville Pike. The house has been sold to an English couple who saw in the old house a facsimile of the rambling farm homes in the English countryside.

The original clapboard structure on the back of the house was the office of Dr. Henry Plaster whose father, Dr. George E. Plaster, was hailed as the "dean of Loudoun physicians" practicing medicine in the village and making house calls on horseback in a large section of upper Loudoun before the turn of the century.

The house served as did many others in the village as a boarding house during the years the Washington and Old Dominion railroad carried tourists for weekends and summer vacations to the pastoral scenes around Bluemont.

Mrs. Powell herself hasn't gone too far from her birthplace north of Round Hill. She says hard work has been her way of life – on the farm there were pigs, cows, and chickens to feed, gardening to be done, and daily household chores to be undertaken.

A large patch of her backyard in Bluemont yields bushels of tomatoes, corn, lima beans, carrots, beets and peas which she has canned seasonally along with making apple sauce for her city daughter's family, the Floyd Fischers of Vienna.

Two other daughters, Mrs. John D. Reid of Round Hill and Mrs. Homer Pierson of Hamilton and 11 grandchildren reside close-by but she calls on neither family nor neighbors for favors. Amazingly, she has been most independent in a house with no central heat, plumbing, telephone or television.

A neighbor, Baker Bayles, would stack her wood in the basement, then with the first sight of a snow flake, she would be out, hauling the wood to the front porch for her small wood stove – her only source of heat.

Having endured many Bluemont winters but without complaint, she has undertaken precautions. For years, she has conducted her own boycott on cans and bottles, telling a neighbor she bought all her vegetables and meats in disposable wrappers. Practically speaking, "What would she do with all those empty cans and bottles?"

Years ago she rejected an offer for an adjacent lot from one who intended to build a service station. Her unselfish action preserved the country atmosphere so desirable to Bluemonters.

Year after year she has contributed to the good of the community in her own way, demanding nothing from the neighbors, asking only that the rich soil bring forth the flowers she loves, and the still air catch the fragrance of the miniature lemon trees she planted next to the white board fence years ago.

As she leaves the village, her plans are to maintain her independence. She may seek home nursing or a "little place of my own" where the cycle of Nellie Powell "doing her own thing" will go on.

May 27, 1971

There was some moisture around the edges of the grass and the second bird in two days made his appearance down the chimney on Friday, as I pulled away from Bluemont.

I was on a sentimental journey, a college reunion near Philadelphia. It sounded enticing! "Those Were the Days" – was the program's theme.

I chose to take the Old Pennsylvania Railroad ride from Union Station, Washington. I thought I would have to say the scenery was the same "spoiled" countryside but it looked fairly lush and green but there were billboards and of course, industry has a way of growing along the tracks.

The neighbors had done their part to see that I had the opportunity to make the trip, the Glen Lloyds took Jennifer and the Lawrence Dawsons and John Carters took shifts with the twins while Elizabeth Wertz and dog, house-sat.

Meanwhile back at the town, the James Brownells were entertaining the local Republican Party for Sunday dinner at Whitehall Farm in the old ballroom.

Linda Lloyd cruised in from Norfolk for a visit with the home folks while young Robert Morris Carter spent the weekend with parents, the Robert P. Carters. Robert M. had celebrated his fourth birthday earlier in the month on the 15th with a family party.

The John Carters have to give up their Mountain Shadow property and would be glad to have any leads on a close-by rental.

Of course, Loudoun's big news this week was the passage of the ordinance prohibiting the sale of non-returnable bottles and cans.

Back to renewed impressions of Philly, the first thing I saw when I got there were the soft pretzels for sale to be dipped in mustard and the pigeons on the concourse – they were at my feet there and it was alright but here flying through the rooms of Clayton Hall…

Then there's the way the commuters read their newspapers on the locals, folded down in the center in half. The train makes its two-minute stops at each little town just as the old W&OD made its way up through Loudoun County, terminating here years ago.

Then at the reunion itself, there was the same warm, affectionate crowd, all telling one another we hadn't aged a bit, admiring pictures of children or the live specimen and exchanging dreams and plans for the future.

The Canadian geese were swimming in the lakes, the ancient weeping willows were bending green again to the surface of the water, the old paths of romance and adventure were recalled, "Those Were The Days", indeed but that's in the middle of suburbs and I'm a happy villager now.

The reception upon returning was the same domestic country round, the dogs had hauled some type of dead animal to the door, Elizabeth reported a bird had flown in again and the twins proceeded to unstuff a stuffed animal, scattering the insides all over their bedroom floor.

I was home.

June 3, 1971

The sun glimmers on the green Victorian paint on the roofs of Bluemont while there is talk of strawberry picking and school closings as the long Memorial Day weekend ushers in the beginning of summer.

Having just met a late deadline two days ago, I was amazed at the news that came my way just two days later.

Luckily I spoke to the right garrulous people. Visitors to our mountainside and fertile valley for the long weekend are the daughters and families of the David Freemans and the four children of the J. Dennett Guthries.

Taking in the view at the Freedmans are the Richard J. Blumbergs of Poughkeepsie, N.Y. and that brand-new granddaughter, two-month-old Amy.

Other daughter, Evelyn and Thomas Cunningham from Lothian, Md. will be on hand with son, three-year-old Butch.

A wonderful time is to be had at the Guthries with son John in from Hampden-Sydney and daughter, Nancy just graduated from Wellesley, near Boston.

Two other daughters, Mary Franklin who will begin her residency this month, having completed pre-med at the Medical College of Pennsylvania and Elizabeth, now Mrs. Keith Rowan, of Inglewood, N.J. will also be present for the grand reunion.

Mary Franklin lives in Haverford, Pa., the same spot where I hung my hat for two years and in this crew are twins, so I think I really ought to drop over for a things-in-common chat.

More uniting going on will be the June 5 wedding of Bruce Brownell and Diana Blake at the Waterford Presbyterian Church. The Senior Brownells will entertain them and their young friends at a buffet dinner at Whitehall Farm following the ceremony.

Had a great chat with the incomparable "Uncle John" Lloyd, Glen's uncle who will celebrate his birthday soon at the annual Lloyd reunion at the Horse Show Grounds in Berryville on June 13.

I hadn't heard before but he walked nine miles last fall just to meet a ride to Bluemont to help with the stirring of the apple butter for the Bluemont Fair.

What's even more remarkable is that Mr. Lloyd lost his vision in both eyes some years ago but he can't be lost in his own territory and what a silver tongue! He and Glen both have a way with phrases that makes conversation with them a rich experience.

A little bird told me June Lloyd's birthday is the third.

High school graduation is just around the corner at Loudoun Valley High School on the ninth with Rosa Peyton and Norma Hindman representing the village.

The delightful "Sound of Music" was presented at the Round Hill Elementary School last Thursday evening. Justine Beck played the part of the youngest child, also in the cast were Debbie, Sharon and Stevie Carter.

Please let me know if there are other graduates and show personalities that I haven't heard about.

Unfortunately we also have had illness in the fold; R.M. Peyton just returned from a two-week stay at Loudoun Memorial Hospital.

Then as we went to press, we had news that the ambulance had taken Ray Payne from the old Costello place where he had been helping us with the remodeling, after he had suffered a heart attack. Ambrose Moreland also suffered a mild heart attack and was admitted to Winchester Hospital.

Sadie, the R.M. Peyton's daughter, and her husband, William Piggott have bought a home in Winchester and Sadie will complete her degree next year at Madison.

Also Paul and Ann Wilson (the Glen Lloyd's Ann) are building a new home in Berryville.

Now my mother is a great newspaper-clipper on any topic which she thinks may interest me, antiques, old-home restoration, child-rearing, safety hints for Mothers and I believe this last category is important to readers who might have purchased the Royal Blue China from the Safeway earlier this year.

I'm a sucker for a blue-print in dishes; these with the unicorn on the back sold also at Food Fair and Pantry Pride may cause lead poisoning. According to Action Line of the Evening Star (May 20, 1971) telephone Li.3-7474, the Food and Drug Administration are conducting tests now. I will call in several weeks and give you the word.

Another bulletin she passed on from the U.S. Department of Commerce reports a surprising number of deaths from people ingesting poisonous plants.

Watch your children – among the list are poinsettias, oleander, hyacinth, narcissi, daffodil, berries of mistletoe, leaves and twigs of wild and cultivated cherries, wisteria, lily-of-the-valley, jack-in-the-pulpit.

Mrs. Earl Virts has a glorious array now of peonies, iris and even a few lingering tulips. Admire them but don't think they look good enough to eat.

June 10, 1971

How divine it is. The long-awaited summer weather is here but of course, already I've heard complaints that it's too hot.

How pleasant to have the window open again – those that can be pried loosed from the old casings – then held open with a stick. Oh the conveniences of an old house!

Just as I was relishing the cool draftness of the night in the bedroom – winter started all over again – the window unit of the air-conditioner must be installed I was informed and we're back to stale air again and blankets – Burr.

It's vacation church school time again. The Community Vacation School sponsored jointly by the Round Hill Baptist Church, the Mt. Zion Baptist Church, the Bluemont, Round Hill and Roszell Methodist Charge will be held June 21-25 at the Round Hill Methodist Church from 9-12 a.m. Ages from kindergarten through Jr. High, a nursery will be provided for children of the workers.

Strawberries are in, Mrs. Peyton picked us some for eating and freezing and Mrs. Lightner reminds Fair exhibitors to put up their preserves and jellies in screw-type lids as there was some lost last year due to loose lids.

Ella Bell of Pine Grove sent over a fascinating old record called the Loudoun-Mirror printed in 1909. This solely commercial issue described the many thriving enterprises in Bluemont and other county spots at the time. Complete with pictures!

As usual Miss Jane Rogers climaxed a year of many special days at Jane's Kindergarten with a wonderful closing-school picnic for mothers, younger peers and students in her grand backyard in Hamilton. Bubble-blowing, pin-wheel flying, treasure hunts and treats galore were part of the festivities all enhanced with Raggedy Ann and Andy providing the decorating theme.

The James Bruce Carters from Statesville, N.C. spent the weekend with the Robert J. Carters at Whitehall Farm. All came to visit the hospitalized Sr. Carter, Robert P. of Berryville. He is still a patient at Winchester Hospital.

Boy! Did I goof! Three of our most popular young people are among those graduating from Loudoun Valley High School this week. They are Mark Brownell, Mr. Fix-It, Donnie Mann and Barbara Dennis.

The Lawrence Dawsons with all their children reunited as Jean returned from Madison last week entertaining Lawrence's nephew, wife and two children from Farmington, Mich. on Sunday.

Keep Loudoun Beautiful members were graciously entertained at the home of chairman Mrs. B. Powell Harrison of Waterford this week. Plans were considered for continuing motivation for anti-litter efforts through the summer. Radio spots, place-mats and brochures were to be aimed at the tourists passing through our borders, encouraging them to feast their eyes on our lovely terrain and reminding them to do their part in keeping Loudoun beautiful.

New sidewalks are coming to Bluemont soon too hopefully.

Nature made her visitations this week – a turtle arranged himself on a gravel drive, cottontails pranced through the tall grass and a black snake sat quietly taking in the view just behind the house.

Jennifer was all for calling a neighbor to do the snake in, but I educated her to the code of the country!

Hope I won't have to call the snake doctor soon about a pest in the house. Happy Summer!

June 17, 1971

Bluemont Has Become A Haven for Artists

Bluemont is fast becoming a real haven to artists and summertime promised an opportunity for the public to meet the artists, see, hear, and appreciate their artistic accomplishments.

This Saturday evening June 19 at 8:30 p.m. resident painter Clyde Beck will invite the public to a concert of classical lute and guitar music performed by Bluemont neighbor, Howard Bass of the ridge's Skylands.

Cleveland-born Bass resides there with other music students, the Paul Reisters who make and play ancient instruments.

Beck's second-story studio referred to locally as the Old Lake Store will provide ample room for the event as it originally was built as a public hall for dances, movies and the like entertaining the tourists who flocked to the cool temperatures of Bluemont at just this time of year, fifty seasons ago before the W&OD Railroad ceased operations.

Mr. Bass majored in music at American University, studying with John Marlow. In the summer of '69 he studied under Jose Tomas in Alicant, Spain and has mostly been concertized on the east coast in Boston, New Haven, Atlanta, Huntsville, and Birmingham.

Last June found him in concert at the National Gallery, Washington, D.C. and since then he has appeared at Barter Hall, Washington, D.C. and in Alexandria.

The rest of the summer will be taken up in concerts at Ogunquist, Me., and the Georgetown Musical Festival, Washington, D.C.

Bass's Saturday performance will be divided into two segments, one devoted to the renaissance stringed instrument, the lute and the other to the guitar.

Many of the renditions of renaissance music were written originally for the lute but have been transcribed for the guitar.

He will play music from the countries of Spain, Holland and England of the Elizabethan period in history with one number by Bach transcribed from the lute for the guitar.

His only contemporary piece will be a composition by Spaniard Juan Manen.

It is the hope of the artist that other area musicians will make themselves known and that Bluemont might provide the spot for an airing of their talent these summer nights.

A silver offing will be accepted at the concert while refreshments will be served as the cooling mountain breezes of the summer air come in the open windows, the serenity of the music's tempo will float into the village streets. Then Bluemont will throb again in its most celebrated season. What could be more pleasant?

June 24, 1971

Summer is officially here now, calendar-wise; it's time for daisy-chains, trips to the river and some Father's Day picnics.

I'm sure the Carbaughs had a whooper-do Father's Day. I'll have to let you in on it later.

The lazy summer pursuits here are the Lloyds swimming at the Grays near Bloomfield and the Cochran boys hunting arrow-heads in Maryland and raft riding on Boxley's pond.

Of course, there's a lot of hard work going on too with hoeing the gardens, picking the yield, canning the results.

The tarring of the road has made the biggest appearance change in town and caused the most cussing among village housewives with the tracking in.

"Safety-first is a very good rule" – was old Dick Mansfield's, the safety cop's slogan back when preaching and chalk artists were popular and I will lend my advice for what it's worth. Why not try on a tetanus shot for size? With the ever-bare-feet a rusty nail is bound to be encountered; our Jennifer's experience over the weekend.

The Glen Lloyds still have two adorable black fluffy puppies to be adopted. If interested in these healthy little darlings, call them at 554-8207.

David Freedman is just in from his continental business trip. Good work, if you can get it!

While there he visited the French kennel where one of their Great Pyrenees puppies was sired and informed the kennel master the dog was now an American champion. Congratulations are in order to both kennels, the dog is the first French import to become a champion here.

More honors coming to Bluemont young people is a typing certificate earned by Belinda Dawson for being among the top three in speed writing in the beginning class.

Other seventh graders who would have traditionally graduated to high school before the advent of the new middle school concept in Loudoun County are Sharon Carter, Brenda and Janice Church and Bertha Payne.

Howard Bass's classical lute and guitar concert at Clyde Beck's studio drew an estimated 150 or more.

Clyde and Joyce had put all the right touches on at the studio, flowers in antique crocks and wonderful punch with Mrs. Peyton's Bluemont-grown strawberries and pound cake. I believe Bluemont could be called colorful but hardly cultural, the sounds drifting out the windows were most high-toned but the sounds coming in were the old down-to-earth cries of a baby and hot-rodders roaring through the streets and no one enjoyed the concert more than Cinder Beck, the doggy character who went around to all the audience for a good healthy head-patting.

Bret Harte would have had a hey-day in Bluemont.

July 1, 1971

Summertime…a restless time…time for a vacation, a change.

The neighbors were finding new times this week.

The Becks and Toby Richards went camping with friends, the Lawrence Dawsons, Sue, Jean and son-in-law Bootsie Stearne and wife, Libby were all off to Detroit, Mich., and Canada, the Walton Manns motored to Florida, Bill and Shir Carbaugh went camping on Skyline Drive.

Last week's Father's Day news was the children of the Townshends were out for a day, William Townshend of Washington, and Ann Rothgeb and children from Beltsville, Md., were there to pay tribute to Dad.

Carroll Jones and family from Brunswick, Md., were all over to honor Bob Jones.

The Cochrans began a busy Father's Day rather disastrously when neighbor Burt Leffingwell, helping with the milking, fell and broke his leg. As Ralph was returning from the hospital, he found his nephew Clinton Hindman at the side of Route 7 unhurt but in his battered car that had just been involved in an accident.

At least good news at the Cochrans was that son, Larry, a student at Banneker School won the mathematics plaque presented by Westinghouse.

The David Freemans really had news announcing the birth of eleven Great Pyrenees puppies. Champion Mother Roulette is doing fine.

Keep in mind it's time to line up the ingredients for the homemade ice cream and dust off the freezer. This Saturday our just plain home town will celebrate the Fourth in our traditional home style, fireworks, ice cream and cake. See you there at the old school grounds.

I know I harp on the same theme, but we had our change Sunday, down to Lake Fairfax; the crowds were tremendous, the food lines staggering, the heat oppressive and the glare of the sun devastating.

Weekend house guests of Mr. and Mrs. Raymond A. Potts were Joe Stephens of Roanoke and Drew Francis of Chesapeake, Va., who were members of the Potts-Price wedding party.

Miss Kay Thompson, and Mr. and Mrs. B. Lawrence Thompson attended the wedding of Miss Cathy Talon of McLean to Gordon Taylor of Oklahoma on the 18th in McLean. Miss Thompson was a bridesmaid for her college roommate.

About 60 friends and family were out on June 20 for a 5 o'clock Vesper Service held on the lawn at the home of Mr. and Mrs. William Van Doren to celebrate their 50th wedding anniversary. The Rev. David Voss was in charge and was assisted by the Rev. Jennings Hobson of Luray, Mrs. Earle O. Baker, and Loyal D. McMillin of Middleburg.

A social hour under chairmanship of Mrs. Walter Duncan, president of the Women of the Church, St. Andrew Presbyterian, of Purcellville, was held later.

Mrs. Frank Fleming entertained at a small family picnic in her home on Monday, June 21 for her nephew, Randolph Chancellar Seay, his wife Barbara and four children of LaSalle, Calif., who are visiting relatives in the county.

Tom Watson of Minneapolis, Minn., was an overnight guest on Wednesday of Mr. and Mrs. Donald L. Hopkins.

Mrs. Shaler Aldous is home after spending three weeks visiting in England and Scotland.

Mr. and Mrs. Edward Bark have returned from vacationing in Florida. They attended the wedding of Miss Judith Paylor, daughter of Mr. and Mrs. Sam Paylor of Fort Pierce, Fla., formerly of Beacon Hill Farm in Loudoun. Several other Loudoun residents were at the wedding. The Barks spent several days at the Paylors' Ranch and on Florida beaches.

Steven Quinn of Hillsboro Sr. Honor 4-H Club attended the Jamestown Senior 4-H camp June 14-19.

Mrs. Frank Spencer of Salt Lake City, Utah who is visiting a sister in Arlington was a weekend guest recently of Mr. and Mrs. Hobart Rowe.

Luncheon guests on Wednesday of Mr. and Mrs. Hobart Rowe were Mrs. Norman Hewson and a friend, Mrs. Paxton, of Washington.

Miss Mabel Virts and her house guests Mr. and Mrs. Lloyd Cooper were dinner guests of Mr. and Mrs. Earl Virts Sr. on the 27th. The Coopers left on Tuesday for their home in Orlando, Fla.

Shumate Legard, who was an usher at the wedding of cousin Holmes G. Walsh was in Norfolk for the weekend of the 27th.

Recently Mr. and Mrs. Ernest DeCorte entertained at Windcrest at a farewell party to honor Col. and Mrs. Charles Spence. About fourteen other guests from the metro area were out for the party.

Rod and Guy DeCorte entertained the members of the pony Club Monday afternoon the 21st at a swimming party at their home, Windcrest.

July 8, 1971

Arms were aching with turning the old crank on the ice cream freezer in preparation for the annual homemade ice cream festival and fireworks display on Saturday night as we went to press.

The local post office was participating in the beginning celebration of a change called the U.S. Postal Service which is an independent arm of the government.

Our efficient and friendly postmaster of many years, Mrs. Bessie Townshend explained that this was the first change in 200 years and now the governing body for the postal service will be a board of governors appointed by the President rather than Congress.

How pleasant on a hot day to be greeted with lemonade and cookies and have the opportunity to purchase the collector's item envelopes postmarked Bluemont.

Wallace W. Giglio of Purcellville, a Fairfax County teacher is the instructor. The theme of the week is Hollywood; the children put on an impressive skit with a few props found in the old auditorium. All community children from ages 6-18 are urged to join in the program.

Lynn Carbaugh went on the day's excursion to New York with the Loudoun Valley Home Economics students.

A great splashing time is being had by Carolyn Tyroler's grandchildren up on their cool spot on the ridge.

In from California with their mother, Mrs. Ronald Forster are Tracy and Dean and from Dedham, Mass. are Alison and Timothy Games.

Charles has suggested sweat shirts with Camp Granny! Obviously everyone's having a great time, riding lessons included too.

The Herbert Littles entertained Peggy's daughter Nancy from New York City last week, Nancy's grown-up twin I enjoy.

Two of our girls have joined the Round Hill Pony League team. Sharon and Debbie Carter report a victory over Leesburg in their first game on Monday.

The fine Blue Grass Music floated through the air again at close-by Watermelon Park on the Shenandoah over the hot July 4 weekend.

One of the nicest things about Miss Reid's anniversary party at the Loudoun Times-Mirror building was the opportunity to meet some of the other correspondents.

Of course, Mary Alice Wertz I've known from junior high days in another state, and Lillie Darnes of Ashburn, managed to see that I gained about 10 pounds one year when I was teaching at Ashburn Elementary School as she is one fabulous cook.

Sandy DiFilippo and I have had some good talks via telephone but never met in person until last week and she sent me an interesting little reminiscence of C.E. Davis' which appeared in the January 1966 Civil War Times which might shed light on our village in the days it was known as Snickersville.

It was entitled – Church – A Good Place for Sleeping:

"Mile after mile of this weary march we counted off, until at last the little stone church in Snickersville, at the foot of the mountain, appeared in sight, lighted as if for a special gathering. The temptation to stop was very great, and many there were in the brigade who availed themselves of the opportunity.

What a scene was presented to view upon entering the door! Men were lying on the seats, under the seats, in the aisles, in the pulpit: every available spot large enough to stow a body, was found to be occupied, until they were packed as closely as sardines in a box. Though every lamp in the church was lighted, there was noone awake to enjoy it; all were snoring away like so many pigs, reminding one of a pond of bull frogs on a summer's night. 'Behold how good and how pleasant it is for brothers to dwell together in unity.'"

And now they tell us our Mt. Gilead designation has been changed to Blue Ridge. Progress! Bah! Humbug!

July 15, 1971

The children fight and dirty another clean outfit; it's the long, hot summer – the screen door goes thump, thump, thump again, the mosquitoes whine around the ears and the lightning bugs flash their mating call and the front porch is the place for perching in the evenings – it's the long, hot, summer!

Back to the Fourth, what a chill settled in this valley; fireworks spectators wrapped themselves in blankets and sweaters for the annual display as a large crowd gathered for the ice cream and cake eating. Ah – that raspberry! and the cakes – I never saw so many cakes.

Among the guests were Douglas and Nancy Chapman and Mr. and Mrs. Walter Gore of Front Royal, visitors to the William Carbaughs. A big welcome to Shir's mother, Mrs. Sarah Chapman now retired from her work at Weakley Nursing Home, Vienna. She will maintain permanent residence here now with the family.

Lynn Carbaugh gave me the low-down on her New York trip. The Home Economics Class and 4-H group stayed at the Taft Hotel and took in the celebrated sights of the U.N. Building, Times Square, the Statue of Liberty and Chinatown. They even saw a show at Radio City Music Hall and went shopping at Macy's, catching sight of Dick Clark doing the same.

Barbara Dennis celebrated her nineteenth birthday with a family party on the fifth while Nellie Tibbs went on a great visit to her grandson's and great grandchildren's home in Layton, Utah. She accompanied her son and wife, Mr. and Mrs. James Moyer of Crozet, Va.

Libby Stearne and Frances Ballenger gave a baby shower in honor of Beverley Underwood Powell on Saturday evening with about 20 relatives and neighbors in attendance.

Stevie Carter, son of the John Carters, is visiting his aunt and uncle in Brunswick, Md. and former Bluemonters, the Carl Costellos were down at the Carters for a Friday night visit.

Our best to their son, Mike, who is serving with the Armed Forces in the Panama Canal Zone.

The David Freemans are entertaining Dave's brother, Bernard from Concord, Calif., for several days.

Mrs. Norman Hindman gave a party at her home on the beautiful farm once called Moorland, now owned by the Ralph Cochrans last Wednesday night.

We're glad to hear Rosa Peyton is doing well after an eye operation.

Of course, the village was greatly shocked by the sudden death of Mrs. Nellie Powell. No one worked harder to keep her corner of the world a beautiful place than she.

Fortunately Mr. and Mrs. Hatcher from Florida were staying at her home when the end came. How we all worried for years about her being there in that big house by herself.

Charles Anson is relaxing here at the Waldrop place before his final departure from our shores for his native land, England come the nineteenth. He entertained the Becks and town friends Friday night for dinner and Saturday evening the Becks did a turn-about with country ham, and homemade ice cream for Charles and his date, the Christopher Wilsons of Leesburg, and the Brown Mortons of Waterford.

Now the Fourth has been wrapped up for another year – I know I ought to forget it but I go back to my childhood Fourths when Grandpa, a special local-color character went all out to celebrate.

His finest hours had been as an American soldier in the Spanish-American War and the Fourth was the time to remember and give thanks for this golden country of his.

First the mounting of Old Glory had to be done, he would recite all the rules for displaying and honoring the flag to us grandchildren, then the most costly and showy display of fireworks in the neighborhood would be set off next. He would purchase a case of orange pop (that was the finest of treats then) for us children and a case of beer for himself just to ensure the proper beverage for a real celebration and a big, ice-cold watermelon was served before the tired, too full tummies were laid to rest.

Now, "Pa-Pa" plays a part in our sacred celebration – he brings a bucket of Col. Sanders' chicken, a watermelon and then escorts us to the homemade ice cream and cake festival as fireworks explode before a mountain back-drop. It's not a bad heritage being repeated – not bad indeed!

July 22, 1971

All's quiet on the eastern front; it's 10:30 on a Saturday night and the drone of motorcycles and zooming cars up the long hill at the side of the house has subsided.

"The children are nestled all snug in their beds" and the village is peaceful – so welcome after a busy day.

Village pursuits have come in assorted pursuits this week.

First of all Lucy and Herbert Martz's 16 year-old grandson William Poston of Frogtown let a 4-inch rattlesnake have it up at Chamblin Acres on Route 601. The snake was six inches around and had eight rattles and one button, his other grandparents the William L. Postons of Unison are right proud of him too.

Mr. and Mrs. John Fowler and daughter Virginia of Unison just returned from a week's stay in Atkins, Ark. visiting a friend, Alex Corbett, on leave from the armed services and his mother. They also stopped by to see Mr. and Mrs. Romaine in Russellville, Ark. and saw the local tourist attraction, the Dardanelle Dam on the Arkansas River.

The Robert Carters celebrated some more young-fry birthdays last week. Jerry is now three and Mason – two.

Roberts's parents the Robert P. Carters and granddaughter Lisa Ann of Berryville along with Bradley Carter of Alexandria, Va. were guests at Whitehall Farm on Tuesday.

Young Ty Payne, son of the Charles Paynes, is organizing a Pony and Horse Show for Aug. 3 at 10 o'clock on the H.G. Langert's property, Grasslands out Route 765, the road by Myrtle Hall Farm.

It will be a schooling show for all ages. For more information, call 554-8290.

New additions to the village population are seven adorable piglets, the William Carbaughs' sow's pride. No that's lions, isn't it?

Justine Beck turned eight this week with a party for the cousins and schoolmates, 14 in all in their pleasant backyard. Then two of her friends, Susan Potts and Pam Carbaugh stayed for a slumber party that night.

There's been lots of talk around town about Bluemont Fair plans this week. June Lloyd is soliciting jars for the apple butter again this year and Mary Lou Markle is making plans for a food stand at the Baptist Church where the slides will be shown.

Shir Carbaugh is testing recipes for candy apples and I saw some of our craftsmen who are eager to return at the Farm Craft Days at Belle Grove on Saturday.

The woodcarver is working on a beautiful ensemble of a general store complete with potbelly stove and two men playing chess. He has the shelves lined with old jugs and frying plans and he expects to bring the display here the third week in October.

It was really a fun day; I can hardly wait to hear that country music again here in little Bluemont.

July 29, 1971

"Fish are jumping and the cotton is high" may be the refrain for the deep South but here in Virginia it's just Summertime and the living is "busy", not necessarily "easy."

There are lots of projects going on and the birthday parties are frequent.

Clyde Beck engaged in a building project in his backyard using the old timbers from Ambrose Moreland's former home, which the highway department saw fit to remove from its "before" spot.

Hawkeye is lending a hand and Popeye is reporting that the countryside is free from litter on his side of the mountain. Wasn't it great news to hear of Keep Loudoun Beautiful's second place in the state for beautification efforts this year?

Lynn Carbaugh, Brad Campbell and our twins all celebrated another birthday this week.

Brad turned eight with a party at his house with guests, Jeanette Glass, Sandy Mitchell and Wanda Reid beside brother, John.

Lynn had about four family parties with different sets of relatives and the twins enjoyed the Carbaugh's homemade blueberry ice cream and Peggy Lloyd's gingerbread house cake with Debbie and Sharon Carter, grandparents Johnson and Porterfield on the front porch on Sunday.

I saw another set of twins – the Journells of Lincoln were back in town visiting their grandparents, the Clarence Manuels this week.

More homemade ice cream being whipped up was by the Mann lads, Tom and Donnie. While Emma and daughter-in-law Ruth took in the Craft Day at Belle Grove, the boys did the honors. The Walton Manns are always glad to get that visit from Tom and Ruth when they can get away from Richmond.

The Hatchers are now here for the month of August from their Florida home.

Sorry to hear Robert Carter's mother from Berryville is in the hospital now.

There was a real swinging time over on the Whitehall Farm property last week, I'm told.

Mark, the real entrepreneur of the family, built an elaborate platform, hired a band and charged admission to a real orderly "happening."

The children of the community involved in the Parks and Recreation summer program provided a real little carnival to the neighborhood last Friday. They set up all kinds of games and raised $60 to be used for needy children's school clothes.

Our new neighbor, Linda Corley is continuing the tradition of Snickersville women's good cooking with her sumptuous blueberry cake which she shared with us the other evening. We were all getting in the spirit for the 1971 Bluemont Fair with another Bluemont slide show.

Another classical music concert will be presented this Saturday night at 8:30 at Clyde Beck's studio. Returning artist Howard Bass will perform on the guitar and lute will be accompanied by Bo Leydon of Aldie on the recorder. Leydon has acted as apprentice to the John Shortridges of Philomont who built their own harpsichord.

And Herbert Martz has some mighty delicious homegrown vegetables now – oh, those beets and little new potatoes! And the lettuce has gone to seed, four feet tall with a yellow bloom on top!

Summertime convinces me all over again that nowhere are the neighbors kinder, more generous, more tolerant than right in our little mountain village.

August 12, 1971

It's subtle but there's a change in the temperature of the days and nights now.

A beautiful golden harvest moon appeared on the horizon this week and the length of daylight is shortening.

The gifts of the neighbors' produce and spirit have been so dear to my particular family this week – human kindness has flowed in buckets to my door.

One especially delightful treat was Helen Kulgren's cold cucumber soup made in the blender and combined with a can of split-pea soup, scallion juice and dash of ginger – so exotic!

The Robert Colberts' house has taken a marvelous new appearance with black shutters and a new door frame.

Some visitors who enjoyed our weather with us were Mr. and Mrs. C.W. Spring of Texas visiting his mother Mrs. Barbara Spring and his son, Donnie Spring, of Herndon, was also a guest for the day.

The Robert J. Carters entertained Robert's uncle, Clifford Carter from Richmond and Robert's brother, James from Statesville, N.C. this weekend and had their usual Sunday dinner guests of his parents, the Robert P. Carters of Berryville.

The Clyde Becks didn't let Sunday go by without bringing city dwellers Leonard and B.J. Pack of Washington to Bluemont for a final visit before they move permanently to New York.

A permanent resident of our own now is David Spring having finished his stint with the U.S. Army.

Frank McComb played host to the Catoctin Farmers Club at his home on Tuesday night with the unsurpassed June Lloyd preparing the delicious ham and chicken dinner for the twenty guests. It proved to be a very pleasant occasion for all, I've heard.

Glen Lloyd's uncle John is walking and re-walking up his mountain road for a distance of 20 miles without benefit of sight to further the Clarke County Recreation Development program and from the stories I've collected on the subject, there would be no chance of getting him lost – the story goes – one person even put up his barber shop in a wager once so great was his faith in John's sense of direction.

The Charles Dawsons had a wonderful week's stay near Cherry Point, Grantsboro, N.C. on the Neuse River with Grace's sister's family, the Marshall Bennetts. A highlight of the trip was their first experience in crabbing.

Don't forget your opportunity to hear some fine Blue Grass music this Saturday night, Aug. 14 at the Bluemont School at 8 o'clock. Admission is one dollar which includes refreshments at Clyde Beck's studio later. The Becks drove the rain away on Thursday by escaping for the day to see Clyde's mother and sister and brothers' families.

We have lost three outstanding citizens in the last several months and I'm sorry to report your correspondent has just learned of their passing.

Our sympathy to the bereaved family of Calvin Cooper at the top of the ridge. Mr. Cooper was killed in an auto accident over a month ago. Also another kind cliff dweller, Thomas C. McEwan passed away suddenly from a heart attack and dear to natives was Louise Kaufman who maintained a summer and weekend home here called the Reids (their home place). She was helpful and eager to assist at last year's fair and had quite a collection of old post cards that documented the Bluemont train era.

Our community grieves their loss; each one was a very special human being.

Now we all know of the Jim Brownells' way with animals – Here's the latest – on a recent vacation trip to an old tramping ground of Jim's boyhood days near Elmira, Pa. out on the mountain trail, Mac and Jim ran almost head on into a large black bear. Jim judged it to be about 800 pounds. He came as close as seventy-feet, took a sniff in the air, stared at them, they at him, and beat a hasty retreat. Needless to say the Brownells retreated in short order too.

Of course, very exciting news was Sue Dawson's engagement to local neighbor, Philomonter Charles Hall. Now we missed Libby's courtship days having moved here too late but watching the cars bring male guests across the street to see the other two girls takes me back a little or up too far with three daughters with blond tresses who at age four and five talk of boyfriends already – it's bound to be quite an adventure!

A November wedding –how nice– "Shine on, shine on Harvest moon."

August 19, 1971

Blue grass growing and blue grass singing – Bluemont got both this week.

My critic's comment on the Cameron Blue Grass Band – "The best live entertainment I've heard in several years" and I just walked down a block from my house – plucked down a dollar and enjoyed a marvelous three-hour show with refreshments thrown in right in little Bluemont.

In another month another treat is in store for music lovers as Paul Reisler and Clyde Beck sponsor the fourth offering in their Bluemont series.

Now that Pony Show on the third was some sporting event too. Sponsored by young Ty Payne at Grasslands, home of the H.G. Langerts, there were fifteen categories in the schooling show and Julie Iselin of Unison on her pony Escalibur was the grand champion winner.

Wanda Rose's Spot did very well winning Pleasure Champion. The judge was Kappie Beach of Windsor Farms, Upperville, a lovely spot I got to know on my Head Start jaunts several summers ago.

The Langerts' granddaughters from New Jersey participated in the Lead Line event along with young Pamela Fincham of Bluemont.

The icing on the cake was Mr. Langert's generosity in offering fried chicken prepared by our Maggie Basil, cokes and watermelon to all the participants and guests at the show.

In addition to this show, Ty showed his two ponies Demitasse and Haunt Fox at the Clarke County Horse Show at Berryville recently. Demi won a second and third.

Now about those vacations. Floyd Allder and his children were off for a week to Myrtle Beach, S.C. while brother James and family just returned from the same fun and sun spot.

The J.H.H. Verloops had a great camping trip to Mt. Mitchell in North Carolina – up 7,000 feet where the wild life was plentiful and friendly. They didn't stare down any bears, however.

The Walton Manns joined later by son Tom and wife Ruth camped at Ocean City, Md. Walton said the water was fine but I didn't see any souvenir salt-water taffy in the store.

Linda and Don Corley took in the Pennsylvania Dutch Days while Lynn Carbaugh continued her two-week recess from pit-feeding here in Bluemont for a visit with great-aunt Mrs. Frances Wiley in Boyce.

Weekend guest here were Clarence Manuel, Jr. and his family from Baltimore visiting with his parents the Clarence Manuels, Sr.

A real little visitor soon to be a permanent resident is Russell and Beverley Powell's new addition, a baby boy born on Aug. 15. Congratulations!

The ambulance made two trips down to the John Carters over the weekend. MaryAnn's step-father, Jack Barber of Purcellville had a fall on Saturday night and daughter Sharon was carted off as we went to press with no particulars forthcoming on Sunday.

Larry Allder reports the softball season is over with the men finishing fifth, defeating the second place winner Sunrise American 4-2 in their last game.

The Women were eaten up by eight defeats and one win – sounds like a team I coached once at Herndon High School.

Fair exhibitors should be planning for the first registration date of Sept. 8 from 1-8 p.m., at the old store front. It won't be terribly long now.

Someone or should I say everyone has been trimming grass on village roadsides this week and the town looks to be a cleaner, more orderly place. And all Hail to the Blue Grass Band. They made us forget our troubles – what better recommendation could there be?

August 26, 1971
Bluemont Fair to Have Model Train Layout

An elaborate model train layout prepared by the Winchester Area Model Railroad Group will be a main attraction at the second annual Bluemont Fair Oct. 16-17.

The group, which usually meets once a month, is now devoting one to three nights a week to the mammoth project of building track and scenery on a large raised platform in a classroom in the former Bluemont School.

Originally they had hoped to duplicate according to scale the old approach and scenery that made Bluemont a popular terminus for the Washington and Old Dominion Railroad during the early 1900's but spokesman James A. Walsh of Berkley Farm, Bluemont, said that would have required two years of effort.

Nevertheless Richard Woolman, Bluemont resident, is building the model train station on the scale of the nearby Purcellville station, which is still standing.

Now Walsh, along with Claude Strickler and Franklin Barley of Winchester, say the plastering of the scenery is the next step of construction of the O gauge track layout.

Materials have been donated by the Berryville Lumber Company and Galladay Building Supply, Stephens City, as well as by individual members of the Model Train Club. In addition to the moving display of trains, there will be static exhibits on shelves in the train room.

Next door, in another classroom, the Winchester Chapter of the National Railway Historical Society will show slides of the Washington and Old Dominion Railroad, particularly of stations on the former Rosslyn-Bluemont run.

Additionally, equipment used by the W&OD from its conception until its demise in Bluemont in 1937 will be displayed.

September 2, 1971

Oh Boy! Summer's over! At least vacation-wise the end has come for kiddies.

On the other hand, I'm the weeping mother in Norman Rockwell's sketch sending her first little bird out of the nest up the long flight of stairs to P.S. 96 and then with mixed emotions I'm gleefully handing the child her lunchbox deducting there's one less fighter on the home battleground for a few hours.

There will be three orange buses leaving the area for Valley High School, Round Hill Elementary and the new Blue Ridge Middle School this year and then our mountain friends of course head for the three Berryville schools. Bluemont, between two states and two counties has some mixed-up geography at times.

The village and mountain news alike was lots of rain one day last week – threatening, indeed and another hoax played on the sheriff's department as someone reported a robbery in town.

Things weren't really quite that exciting although the William Carbaughs entertained some of the mountain neighbors for a cook-out on Sunday. Shir Carbaugh was looking all over for a "red" pepper for a salad and of course, trusty Herbert Martz, our produce man, was able to turn up one for her.

Lynn says the roller coaster rides up at Hershey, Pa. were pretty exciting too when the whole family took in the Pennsylvania Dutch Days earlier in the week.

The G.W. Townshends took a trip all around Petersburg last weekend visiting Mrs. S. I. Dodd and daughter in Moorefield, Mr. and Mrs. Winton Hyre and Mrs. Grace Letherman in Petersburg and the John Aylors in Wardensville. If my memory serves me right, Petersburg was the spot where they built an elaborate trench for a civil war battle that took place there.

The James Walshes entertained the Richard Jones' from Wilmington, Del. as overnight guests this week while matriarch Ellen Jones was given a grand birthday celebration at a dinner party at the home of her daughter and husband, the William Andersons of nearby Lazy Acres with other offspring and their families Carroll Jones of Brunswick and Robert Jones, Jr. of Winchester in attendance.

Ah, do I feel pampered! Some of my dear Bluemont friends surprised me with a baby shower at a lovely sit-down luncheon prepared again by June Lloyd and daughter Hope in their superb catering style.

The old washing machine can have a rest as everyone showered me with "Pampers." No one will ever convince me there are nicer neighbors anywhere on the habitable globe than the environs of Bluemont!

Belinda Dawson, daughter of the Charles Dawsons and her cousin Wanda Hawes of Philomont celebrated their sixteenth birthdays together at a combined skating party at the Purcellville Rink last week.

Grace's brother and family the Willis Tibbs were up from Roanoke over the weekend while her mother, Mrs. Nellie Tibbs, our expert quilt-maker is off again on another extended visit to her sister's, Mrs. Frank Lambert in Bland County.

A spready fallen branch provided the kids with Christmas ideas, somewhat out-of-season, as they gaily trotted to the attic for the tree ornaments, thus garlanding the front porch with a festive appearance on Saturday.

Heavens Forbid! Let's get the Bluemont Fair behind us first.

See you there!

September 9, 1971

So what's the "talk of the town?" From what I can determine, it's fall weather, sidewalks or no sidewalks, and election gossip.

Whatever the talk – Sept. 14 is an important election day as the Democratic Primary is to be held.

Readers should give attention to these names on the sample ballot – for State Senate, 33rd District – Henry C. Mackall, Charles L. Waddell, for House of Delegates, 20th

Legislative District (vote for three) – Stanley A. Owens, William A. Murphy, Lucas D. Phillips, Charles W. Rector, for Commonwealth's Attorney – Donald W. Levin, Thomas W. Murtaugh, for Justice of the Peace for Blue Ridge Magisterial District – Marvin a Holder, for Precinct Committeeman, Precinct 12 – Elizabeth K. Gibney.

Ah, there's the rub – that Precinct 12 – what character does a number possess? Our Snickersville precinct designation endured for 70 years after the Southern Railway christened the spot Bluemont and so now all that's left on the Snickers tradition is his name on the gap above the village.

Mrs. Gibney says she fought to preserve the name but was out-voted.

Bluemonters must vote in Round Hill at the town office next to Roy's Grocery (Paterson's Pharmacy for years).

For those who get the news on Wednesday, today is the first for registration for exhibitors to the Bluemont Fair, hours from 1-8 p.m. at the old store just freshly painted by Jack Lightner and Clyde Beck.

Tonight is a discussion meeting with Philip Bolen of Parks and Recreation and James Brownell – Mt. Gilead (has that changed as of now?) Supervisor, concerning the community use of the school building at 8 o'clock at the school.

There wasn't much of a great exodus over Labor Day weekend since most vacationers had settled back in the area before the week was out due to region children's Aug. 30 school day beginning.

Janet Reid hurried back from the Poconos to pick up her school bus last week. Again this year they relaxed in the Pennsylvania mountain spot with Betty and Bill Marcus.

Gail Kelley is back driving the big orange crate to Valley High School while June Lloyd has joined the driver's union packing her Bluemonters, the duPonts, the Verloops, and Towes near Round Hill down to Leesburg's Loudoun Country Day School. Bluemont is fairly well represented there with Col. Teasdale-Smith acting as Assistant Headmaster and newcomer Linda Corley becoming a teacher there while husband Don has gravitated to Clarke County public schools along with Alice Loope of the mountain road.

Before sending the college students off, more vacationers were the John Markles with their month's stay on a boat on the Bay joined by their daughter and husband and Jill Reid cavorting at Clearwater Beach, Fla., for two weeks. She says she likes those tropical scenes or maybe it was "where the boys are."

Susan Brownell was visiting in Vermont for a week. That's another of those "green mountain" areas.

Now to pack the students' bags – Mark Brownell is beginning at Tennessee Tech University, Cooksville, Tenn., Donnie Mann at Shenandoah College, Winchester, and Timmy Reid at Luther-Rice College in Alexandria.

Returning to the higher hall of learning are Willa Colbert back at Madison, Guy Woolman at VPI and Jan Woolman at Alexandria School of Nursing.

Jean Dawson will commence her senior year at Madison by engaging in her student teaching experience taken at Reston Elementary School.

So the world's a little wider than Bluemont but most of the time I wish it weren't.

September 16, 1971

Indian summer is here again. Hot, sticky days relived by a soaking rain and then followed by even more humidity is usually the pattern.

Whatever the weather, Fair fever is really in the air here in Bluemont. Labor Day was spent laboring over the Fair, the chairmen are blue with meeting and re-shuttling of plans and the first registration was a busy time.

"My dear 'Mr. Robinson'" and all others – the dates for the second annual Bluemont Fair are Oct. 16, 17. Will we have leaves turning then?

Guess who was here? Jean Smith, our Snickersville biographer brought her autographed copies of her successful book in readiness for Fair guests in case Uncle Sam says "Yankee, Stay Home" back in Ohio when Fair times rolls around.

Florence Maitland and Clarence Tallman have written and say they hope to be here for the festivities.

The Shenandoah River celebrated in song and legend was our choice for a Labor Day picnic last week. The children fished with sticks, felt the sand through their toes and the threat of a bee sting when the chocolate cake was uncovered – would that every child would have these nature encounters often. It was good to know we could often go "down by the riverside."

Meanwhile a few more of our residents finished up vacations.

Bill and Judy Casey, Bluemont's second generation who are returning to build their new home here took Judy's brother Kelley Lloyd and their son Scotty on a southland jaunt. The first day out they visited with Linda Lloyd in Roanoke, then went on to Atlanta where they saw the Crutchfields, former Loudouners. There they took in Stone Mountain with its huge carving of J.E.B. Stuart (we had his lock of hair last year at the Bluemont Fair, you know), and its frontier train ride with a western town burning and Indians attacking. Scotty wasn't at all sure it wasn't the real thing! Then down at Miami, Kelley landed a dolphin and then a very rare catch of a blue marlin which got away due to improper equipment. These weigh about 300 pounds. So it was quite a trip!

The John Fowlers of Unison, with son Randy, daughter and husband, the Ernest LaFehrs of Fairfax and Mrs. Margaret Allder of Herndon went on a grand trip to Garden City, Mich. where nearby they climbed the country's longest Indian trail with cut-in steps up a steep cliff. They went fishing at a five channel dam in Canada, took in the African Lion Safari in Rockland, Ontario and started homeward by stopping by one of America's greatest tourist attractions, Niagara Falls. But do people really still go there for their honeymoon?

A few guests came to Bluemont other than to register for the fair – they were Mrs. Mame Bryant and son from Cleveland, Ohio visiting the Walton Manns over the weekend.

Even though it's hot some are calling it, the Fall. Anyway football season has begun at Valley High and one of our senior players, Bruce Cochran broke his arm. As he is a talented organist too this is a real handicap for the time being.

Now what's more beautiful than a jar of home-canned tomatoes or peach preserves or plum jelly basking in the sunlight on a deep window-sill?

Such was my satisfaction this week when the neighbors shared their tomato yield but double must be their joy to know they sowed, hoed and picked their own produce.

And best of all – the yellow flowers are back. Ellen Jones says they are called Golden Glow.

September 23, 1971

Should it be wool or cotton, sandals or knee-socks, shorts or slacks, umbrella or none – thus the fickleness of the season flirts with our intentions.

News is slim other than what's being planned for the Bluemont Fair.

Our Lucketts friend Sandy DiFilipo will have helium balloons for the kiddies, the Carrington House where Jean Smith researched her material for her book Snickersville will house the historic book shop, the old stone church appropriately will be the spot for the slide-showing of the Civil War skirmish story and the train era. Since Confederates once slept in the pews, what better place to show what transpired when the Blue met the Grey near the church site in old Snickersville?

A Richmond poet who once made his abode in Bluemont has promised a reading of his poem, "The Coach Road", a lyric about the Snickersville Pike and along with the Blue Ridge Express, the Loudoun County High School majorettes, will provide Sunday entertainment.

There will be more ticket booths, more parking spaces, more eating facilities and more "johnnies" than last year. So come-we promise a bigger and better Fair and oh, if we could promise comparable weather to last year's!

Shir Carbaugh and Roberta Underwood are requesting those who volunteered to sell the country-ham sandwiches and candy apples to call them so shifts of work-hours may be assigned. This is a good hint for all department chairmen.

I had a delightful talk with our Philomont-Airmont neighbor with a Purcellville address, William Cockerill this week. Of course, for years he served as County Agent and he knows some wonderful tales of the area.

His own home was built in 1881 by his grandfather.

He recalled how they brought apples from their farm in big barrels by horse and buggy to the Bluemont train depot and from hence they would go to Alexandria and other ports. We marveled over the change in mode of transportation over so short a time from horseback to moon rocket!

We're sorry to know that the Cockerill's son, Thomas had a bad burn about six weeks ago and still remains at Leesburg Hospital.

Well, the big news at Clayton Hall was the appearance of another snake in the house – a tiny, ribbon specimen. He got away as I was phoning a neighbor for help and I hasten to add I'm counting on his permanent disappearance.

Clyde Beck's cabin is really looking good with most of the roof up and "Popeye" and "Hawkeye's" beautiful stone fireplace coming along nicely.

The Karlton Monroes have just returned from a pleasant ten-day trip on Chesapeake Bay.

The J.J. Kelleys made a visit with a former Loudoun music teacher, Miss Bessie Conner last week. Now, Miss Conner works in Grenada, Miss. at the Conference Office of the Methodist Church and came this way for her annual vacation.

The death of George Freeman who operated his store in Bloomfield was a great personal loss to so many of his neighbors. Young people particularly knew they had a friend in George Freeman.

More about the yellow flowers – Ralph Cochran says they grow in marshy spots and the dried weed is prickly and undesirable for a dried arrangement.

And as for the road construction-Saturday's blast sent my best antique bottle shattering on the floor!

Homer Hall, our beloved Bluemont Methodist pastor, points out that mountains must be special places because the good in life is called a mountaintop experience and I feel that mountains offer a feeling of security. Maybe this is just another reason why Bluemont seems such a special place to us "Mountaineers" who live here!

September 23, 1971, additional feature article
Village's Landmarks Are Schools

In a village that's only one street long and two side-streets wide, it's surprising that the four main landmarks, all still standing, are schoolhouses and that one life-long resident, Mrs. Elizabeth Kelley has a close link with three of them. This is the case in upper Loudoun's Bluemont.

The first school, supposedly built about 1807 on land donated by Amos Clayton is the Snickersville Academy, a log structure occasionally used now by Miss Susy Neal and owned by the Samuel Hatchers, residents of Florida.

Dr. George Plaster's history, which he recorded in 1900, says this school operated until 1872 when it was replaced by "the existing public school." Now it is used as a residence and is still designated as Mountain Shadow.

This one-room building expanded to a roomy home is where Mrs. Elizabeth Poston Kelley began her education. She recalls about 50 students gathered around the pot-belly stove being instructed by the beloved, well-remembered Miss Eliza Lunceford. Miss Lunceford was responsible for teaching grades one through seven, employing the older students to help with the younger.

Perhaps here is where Mrs. Kelley acquired her love for learning and instructing. Two years ago she retired from the Loudoun County Public School System after having nourished, loved, and taught scores of upper Loudoun children for 35 years.

She recalls there was a belfry built for the bell at Mountain Shadow and one of the older students would ring it at 8:45 a.m. Miss Lunceford would yank on the sturdy rope herself at nine o'clock as the final signal for school's beginning. "That bell could be heard all over town," Mrs. Kelley says.

The same bell and Mrs. Kelley became linked along with another Bluemont school known as the "yellow schoolhouse" during World War II. At that time she and her late husband, Otto lived on the well-known Rose Moor farm which included a small wood structure called the yellow schoolhouse.

The bell was removed by then from Mountain Shadow School, which closed in 1922 with the erection of the new stucco school. The school, now unused except as a community meeting place, is to be the center of activity for the up-coming Bluemont Fair, Oct. 16-17.

Otto mounted the bell in a tree and was responsible for ringing it in case of an enemy air attack. Fortunately he was never called upon to ring out that fateful news.

This yellow schoolhouse located at the end of the village, operated simultaneously with Mountain Shadow. It closed its two doors (Mrs. Kelly says one was for the boys, the other for the girls) about 1930. Students felt free to interchange schools according to their liking of the instructor at the time.

In Mrs. Kelley's adult years while living at Rose Moor, her husband had the occasion to call a Berryville doctor, William Barlow for his ailing wife. His directions for finding the spot was "Look for the yellow schoolhouse." However, at that time the building was "bright-white" and the good doctor was greatly delayed and confused because of the change in color.

Though he spent the entire night at Mrs. Kelley's side in the hospital, he asked for no fee but requested they take the money and "paint that damn building yellow."

Two years after the stucco school opened Mrs. Kelley joined the faculty of two—Miss Eliza Lunceford acting as principal and teacher of the upper grades and Mrs. Ruth Schulke, who retired in 1969 being responsible for the middle grades, Mrs. Kelley, instructed the first three grades.

There was no water at the beginning, Mrs. Kelley remembers, and the community more than the school board took the initiative in bettering conditions.

The parent group, then the Community League, sponsored dances and raised money for all the kitchen equipment and maintained an excellent cafeteria with Mrs. Rebecca Iden as cook for many years.

Even the James Osbornes who had no children in school worked diligently for the cause of better education and curiously today the auditorium of the old building is dedicated to the community and built with funds given by Dr. Rufus Humphrey, former owner of Berkley Farm now the home of the James Walshes.

Sadly, Mrs. Kelley bade farewell to the community and school in 1960 when the county closed the Bluemont School and with her husband's death, she moved to Round Hill where she taught until two years ago.

Now, however, the revitalization of the school under the auspices of the second annual Bluemont Fair is bringing native interest back and Mrs. Kelley is serving with the James Piersons of Bloomfield in gathering memorabilia for a display at the fair. To be housed at the Bluemont School the display will proudly include the old school bell salvaged by Mrs. Kelley and lovingly returned to Bluemont.

There's been some talk of fair funds going toward the purchase of the Snickersville Academy where a permanent museum could be maintained.

There the bell could find it's perfect setting again and Mrs. Kelley's link with all Bluemont's public schools would be a complete chain.

October 7, 1971

The apple-butter bee down at the Glen Lloyd's took place Saturday – Yum. That rich brew of June's: the cider has been ordered and most of the activities for the Fair are in-doors so maybe everyone will have a good time regardless of the weather.

Our congratulations to Clyde Beck on winning first prize in the art again at Waterford this year.

We're very glad to hear that Tyson Payne is back from Winchester Hospital after three weeks recuperating from a heart attack.

The Robert J. Carters had some weekend visitors again. They were Mrs. Alberta Morris, Mrs. Louis James and son Tommy from Alexandria.

Unfortunately, the bad news down there was that four-year-old Robert Morris fell and broke his arm last Saturday.

Sandy Mitchell reports that she became a teen-ager this week, celebrating with a friend over for dinner.

We're sorry to hear that Agnes Allder is a patient at Winchester Hospital.

Tony Carbone gives us his news that his menagerie is growing. He acquired three kittens from Willie Littleton and although they are for adopting Sam, the Great Pyrenees as mother, he moves away from their licking advances.

Right before the Fair there will be another music special with Amateur Madrigal Singers appearing at Clyde Beck's studio, next Sunday evening, Oct. 10 at 8:30 p.m.

And if we can get the grass cut, everything is about ready for the Bluemont Fair.

With these rainy Sundays, many a picnic has been spoiled but the William Carbaughs' event of last Sunday was a smashing success. Shir's family along with the Wesley Carbaugh's brought such salads, pickles, rolls, fried chicken, hamburgers and hot dogs, brownies and cakes as I have ever seen. It was just as good or even better in-doors!

Roberta Underwood, a proud grandmother and daughter Beverley Powell and new six-week old son went visiting this week to Beverley's old office which she will frequent again in several weeks, while little Powell is tenderly cared for by Isabelle Dawson. Then they stopped for lunch at Roberta's sister's family, the William Kemps of Arlington.

Lester Blackiston, the poet who will make a tape of his poem, "The Coach Road" to be played at the Fair says John would tell him tales about the travels on the Snickersville Pike.

He agreed Mr. Nesmith was a beautiful human being too. We do cherish our older citizens here.

Helen Freedman and I made a real discovery this week – there's an honest-to-goodness Chinese restaurant in Leesburg. The cook and the waitress are Chinese – the vegetables are fresh – not over-cooked, the amount of shrimp in the chow mein and the pork in the fried rice is generous and even the twins thought the egg-drop soup was tremendous – the thickest I've ever had.

So if you're a little tired of country-ham, chicken and beef – try the China King Restaurant on S. King Street. Having savored Chinese fare around the Philadelphia, New York areas for years, Helen and I found the food exceptional.

Someday I'll have an inn at Clayton Hall or an ice-cream parlor and maybe train whistles will blow here again. Well, at least as Worthy Caulk says, miniature whistles on the model trains will be heard at the Bluemont Fair. See you there!

October 14, 1971

Pitter, patter, pitter, patter – there's that now too familiar sound again – rain on a tin roof.

Comforting but….

We've heard the Waterford stories – now we wonder what nature combined with human nature has in store for us this weekend.

Bluemonters are an industrious lot – they don't keep every blade of grass trim like city-folk but they throw themselves whole-heartedly into this, our community project, the Bluemont Fair.

They have done all the work of erecting a pole-tent themselves, painting the old store, cutting weeds and setting up the relic display, the train exhibit, and in addition, they have done all the organizational work, are manning the stations themselves and to boot producing a goodly number of saleable items.

The William Carbaughs are picking money-plant till their fingers are sore, dipping candy apples. Ivy Cochran has put up about 70 pints of jams and jellies for sale, turning out banana bread and many batches of fudge; Bessie Townshend besides supplying many jars of home-canned goods has the greatest assembly of "nothings' she calls her Christmas tree ornaments made out of pill bottles, tops of plastic containers, walnuts as I have ever seen.

The final hours of preparation are here now and is Libby Stearne the best secretary in the world! She is so thorough – she has been helping me with the press releases. Through it all the neighbors still seem to have time to do nice things for their neighbors. I'm mighty proud of them!

This weekend promised to be very full with other activities too. Loudoun Valley High School is having its Homecoming celebration – parade, dance, and game and we're very pleased tiny Bluemont is represented twice on the Homecoming Court in Rhonda Underwood and Gwen Kelley.

Gail Kelley says Sam will be home for a visit from his eastern shore Maryland school and there's a wedding to attend while J. has promised to take pictures for us of the happenings here.

Last Sunday amidst nature's showers, Miss Sue Dawson was showered by her relatives Mrs. Eston King and Miss Hilda Payne in anticipation of her Nov. 20 wedding. She got lots of bowls and towels – so she can mix and mop up the mess if need be.

Mary Jo Lloyd had a small gathering over for her birthday while the whole family was recuperating from their major project of last weekend, canning 24 gallons of the genuine article, rich apple-butter for the Bluemont Fair. The sale is a donation to the Bluemont Citizens Association.

The Clyde Becks entertained at a buffet supper at their home before the Madrigal Singers performed at Clyde's studio on Sunday evening.

I'm looking forward to entertaining the Retired Teachers Organization sponsored by Loudoun County Parks and Recreation on Tuesday for a preview of the Bluemont Fair.

The books for the Carrington Book Shop are coming in very well. We have "The Battle of Ball's Bluff", "Snickersville", "Loudoun County and the Civil War", "Spur Magazine" with its special history article on Bluemont, "The Ketoctin Chronicle", "Old

Courthouses of Virginia", Dorothy Givens' lovely little book of poetry plus Mary Alice Wertz's cemetery inscriptions from Ebenezer Church.

Our number of exhibitors has risen to about 370 thus far.

Donna Seidenspinner now can claim to be a teenager too, having turned thirteen this week and they felt the proper way to celebrate was with an outdoor slumber party. Fortunately, that was one of those non-rainy evenings, whenever that was!

I'm indebted to J. Terry Hirst of Purcellville who sends me this week a copy of an 1832 Winchester paper that advertised the public auction of Clayton Hall. It described the property, number of acres in pasture, orchard and timber and the inclusion of the barn and house as it still is today, making note of the stone kitchen attached. It went on to mention the outbuildings, stopping at two with etcs., corn house and meat house. The meat house regretfully we removed ourselves fearing it was a haven for snakes. Well, it didn't mention the "outhouse" we found here too – it was a five seater!

There will be plenty of Johnnys on the spot here too for the Bluemont Fair – so come one, come all. We're ready for you!

October 21, 1971

Everything was really quality and as Mark Twain in his book, Huckleberry Finn said and "when you are with the quality...." meaning the aristocrats of his day. Now I don't know if ours were "aristocrats" but they were "quality."

The whole fun of the Fair has been in the opportunity to meet so many nice people.

Our sales seemed to have doubled over last year, whether this means we have more people or not I can't say, no one including the sheriff's department would estimate a guess but I'm so proud of our chairmen heads who did such a marvelous job of organizing everything so there was very little confusion.

The baked goods, jams and jellies took in $1,200 on Saturday and that's a whole lot of stirring and mixing worth.

Marvin Watts, our writer friend out in the cabin in the countryside got together some of these nice folks and I had a marvelous chat with the balladeer who entertained impromptu at Waterford and here on Sunday. He is an Australian and has been seeing the country just simply by meeting a person who takes him a certain place there he meets someone else who takes him another place and from these experiences he has a acquired a wonderful inherent trust in his fellow man.

Oh! I was so impressed with the maple-sugar people. They had the genuine article – the wife had poured up a batch that morning before they came – it took me back to my childhood when a relative brought me a souvenir maple-sugar man. Now my children can have the same memory from the Bluemont Fair.

There was little news other than what happened at the Fair. After having tried to reach the John Markles and Tony Carbone on Fair business for five days, I found each had taken a great trip.

The Markles had a fabulous trek northward to Nova Scotia where Mary Lou said the leaves were just at their peak and so lovely and Tony sent a mountain view postcard from New Mexico where the scenery was glorious.

The Kenneth Reids of Pine Grove had weekend guests of their daughter and son-in-law, the Peter Carters of Alexandria with their grandsons Bruce and Brian Costello.

Well, in fact just about everyone had weekend guests for the Fair, the G.W. Townshends had a houseful, the Brunelles up on the mountain were trying to bed down about eighteen and Marvin Watts was soliciting blankets and mattresses for a camp-in around the fireplace in his non-centrally heated abode.

The balloons that Sandy DiFlippo bought were the best I've seen but a few got away from the Johnson trio.

And Abe Lincoln came – our White Post friend who played the part in the television special last year. He says to look for him again in March in another special, Surrender at Appomattox. His long, lank frame was costumed in an old black suit and he wore that identifying tall stove-pipe hat, of course. The kids thought his arrival wonderful.

The sun didn't shine on us, but the rain didn't rain on us either and so we roll up the streets of old Snickersville, of days of train whistles and tourists and get back to the daily routine. It is time to think about treating our children at the Halloween party and approaching Thanksgiving and Christmas holidays and next week should be the time for getting the apples and wrapping them in newspaper before the big freeze.

Farewell tourists-Hello serenity.

October 28, 1971

"Didn't it rain, children." "Raindrops keep falling on my head." "Singing in the rain, just singing in the rain." There are lots of songs on the subject and there has been plenty of subject matter for the song writers these autumn days in Loudoun County.

Fall has really been spoiled with the rain shedding the turning leaves before their time and it's so mild – at least that helps with the heat bill.

Everything is back in place now, put away except for the staff parking sign – although there is quite a bit of talk yet about last week-end's event.

For those looking for a nice Christmas gift, I will keep here at Clayton Hall through the month of November some of the local histories available. Anyone interested in the "Ketoctin Chronicle" (a history of the Ketoctin Church), "Snickersville", "Loudoun County and the Civil War", Patch's "Battle of Ball's Bluff, Spur Magazine with its history of Bluemont and the Methodist Church's attractive cloth calendars can call me at 554-2051. Mary Alice Wertz of Purcellville has the Ebenezer cemetery inscriptions if you are interested.

We wish to thank our new neighbor Thomas Grubisich of Hillsboro for the nice write-up in the Washington Post.

His closing statement about the small number on the roll at the Methodist Church is well taken because just about that small number of citizens put on the Bluemont Fair. We do want to thank our Round Hill and Purcellville neighbors who helped us serve and sell. This feeling of unity is alright, isn't it?

Another thanks to Moore and Dorsey who furnished the four bushels of apples that became sticky, gooey candy apples and sold out in the two days' time.

Now back to the regular news – some of last week's visitors are lingering on – Mrs. Estelle Reid of Gwynedd Valley, Pa. is still here with her son's family, the Lucien Reids, as is Miss Ruth Alley's mother from Washington, D.C.

The Tyson Paynes entertained Miss Marie McDale of Houston, Tex. and Mrs. Lucy Payne of Bluemont during the two days of the Fair and then on Sunday they served dinner to Mrs. Walter Heflin and son Dennis of Boyce, Mr. and Mrs. Dennis Lloyd and son Darren of Falls Church, Mrs. Michael Carroll and son Jeffrey of McLean, Mr. and Mrs. Charles Payne with son Tyson of Bluemont plus Dough Rasnick of Vienna.

The Joseph Smiths entertained Mr. and Mrs. Talbert Young from Martinsburg, over the weekend too.

Now some very nice news is that Ellen and Bob Jones are grandparents again. Son Carroll and his wife welcomed a new daughter Sherrill Lynn on Oct. 22, nine pounds, ten ounces.

Shir Carbaugh and Emma Mann invited some of the office crew and neighbors to a wedding shower for Miss Sue Dawson at the Mann's on Saturday night. The big event is fast approaching, Nov. 20. Our lovely little stone church will be the setting.

Our former neighbor, Mrs. Ruth Miehm who still visits her son regularly and who has taken over the old homeplace out the yellow schoolhouse road is off on a pleasure trip to London. No one deserves a vacation more.

We all are missing Mrs. Connors who is the regular organist at the Bluemont church.

There are some important dates and functions for Bluemonters in the next several weeks.

Of course, first of all the annual Halloween party will be held next Saturday night at 7:30 at the schoolhouse. Eastern Standard Time comes in then too.

There will be cake walks, refreshments and the annual judging of the prettiest, most original and ugliest.

Don't forget to vote on Nov. 2, so you have to drive to Round Hill. Don't neglect your rights as a U.S. citizen.

The town meeting will be the next night, Nov. 3, the first Wednesday in the month at 7:30 at the school-house.

Then on Nov. 14, plan to attend the covered dish supper for all those who worked as the staff of the Bluemont Fair. This is always a pleasant evening and well-deserved for all those hard-working citizens.

Now the best story I've heard to come from the Bluemont Fair was passed on to me by Clyde Beck, our dear village helping handyman, and artist when the neighbors don't keep him busy with community projects.

He said one patron of the turkey dinner at Whitehall Farm said that it was one of the best dinners she had ever had, the service was so lovely and when she complimented the young girl serving her, the girl replied that since it was her first time in doing such a thing, she wanted to please her!

And that's why we have a Bluemont Fair. It seems to bring out the best in us. Happy Halloween!

November 4, 1971

Can we stuff in any more candy, cookies, cakes, popcorn, apples, cider? Oh, the Halloween Fall treats.

Every time I see all those different cakes at the Halloween party my mind travels to Washington Irving's perfect Halloween tale, "The Legend of Sleepy Hollow." He talks about all the different cakes set out for a Dutch tea-party in the Tappan Zee area in New York State. I was privileged to have had a trip there once at just this time of year. It was golden Autumn and sublime just as it is in Bluemont now!

Joan Wilt directed a fun Halloween party down at the schoolhouse with 200 people in attendance.

The judges had a rough decision this year as there were many excellent costumes.

Mrs. Ruby Parks, Mrs. Shir Carbaugh, and Mrs. Roberta Underwood selected the Ugliest costume prize to go to Jennifer Case, the Funniest to Steven Furr in a bear outfit complete with apron and matching bonnet, Best Witch was Mary Jo Lloyd and Most Original were the twins – Maurice and Edith Verloop in a horse outfit - they had sculptured the head themselves in papier mache.

Prettiest went to my Lara thanks to the Jane's Kindergarten birthday crown of last year and a drapery we pinned with a sparkling brooch so she could be a queen! Her prize – a rubber snake – needless to say a little boy got a gift since I had killed another just this week. I didn't need an imitation to give me another fright.

There were ten cake walks which gave quite a few of the villagers a chance to take an additional treat home.

A number of our youth won prizes at their respective schools. Hope Lloyd won the prize for the funniest at Valley High School in big over-grown boots and a braid sticking straight up on the top of her head; she used a wire to secure it.

At Round Hill School Brian Beck won third prize for his Hippy Ghost outfit and Pam Carbaugh took first in the Ugliest category with her Hunchback of Notre Dame garb.

The Verloops with their horse again took second in the funniest category at Loudoun Country Day. They had twin jack-o-lanterns on their gate posts for Halloween night too.

There were more parties around the neighborhood this week. Everyone wanted to get in on wishing Ivy Cochran Happy Birthday. The MYF surprised her at the first of the week and then a large group of her friends offered congratulations at a party at Mrs. Ann Draisey's on Thursday.

Ivy herself did some entertaining over last weekend.

The Youth group from the Landover Christian Church had a picnic at the farm, made homemade ice cream and watched the football game on television on Saturday and then on Sunday her parents, Mr. and Mrs. Robert Hindman of Hamilton celebrated their 79th and 80th birthdays at a dinner party at the Cochrans. Ironically they have the same birthday.

Shir Carbaugh wishes to remind everyone of the Home Demonstration Club meeting on Monday, Nov. 15 at the school at 7:30. Extension Agent, Mrs. Nancy Cockerill will be the guest speaker.

Frank McComb was welcoming his brother and sister and some of their family from North Carolina over the weekend.

Miss Ruth Alley celebrates a 25th anniversary this week on Nov. 3. She has operated her school for retarded children here for 25 years. She was first associated with Miss Gundry in Falls Church who was one of the pioneers in establishing a home for the retarded. After her death, Miss Ruth bought most of the wards here.

Politicking was abounding over the weekend, Jim Brownell was passing out combs and Charles Tyroler was sporting a William Jennings Bryant button as wife Carolyn sought to capture the Blue Ridge district seat away from incumbent neighbor James Brownell of Whitehall Farm.

November 11, 1971

With November the story of the Grasshopper and the Ants comes to mind: One can't ignore the fact of approaching winter much longer.

The balminess of October's days convinced us winter was far off but now we know it's time to winterize.

Ray Paine has been here at Clayton Hall most of the week caulking and putting the plastic on the windows; there's hardly anything Ray can't fix. Happy Birthday to him too as Saturday marks the day he made his entry into the world.

It was an exciting week with Tuesday's elections; congratulations to my neighbors, present and past – Jim Brownell and Charlie Waddell. And condolences to Bluemonter Carolyn Tyroler who campaigned so vigorously.

Now we look forward to next weekend's Sunday covered dish supper for all Fair workers and their spouses.

It will be held Nov. 14 at 6:30 in the school auditorium; mostly salads and side-dishes are being solicited as some left-over "Fair turkey" is forthcoming. Mrs. Emma Mann, Mrs. Roberta Underwood and Mrs. Shir Carbaugh are the arrangement chairmen.

Jim Walsh is planning an extra treat for the day too; the model train display will be operating again for the benefit of the interested public who missed the demonstration during the Fair. This will be provided from 2 to 5 p.m. Sunday afternoon and then just prior to the dinner Fair workers are invited to view the display.

The original slide shows "When the Train Came to Bluemont" and Snickersville – 1864" will provide the entertainment for the dinner.

On Nov. 15, Monday evening, Mrs. Nancy Cockerill, Extension Agent will present a talk on "Projecting Yourself to Others" at the monthly Home Demonstration meeting at the school at 7:30 p.m. The men of the village are to know they are invited too.

November's Bluemont Citizens Association meeting was a lively affair with guest Lawson Cowart discussing drainage, water and sewer.

It appears the new highway is going to contribute even more gushing waters into the village streets and some village basements.

December has been set for the month for election of the Association's new officers due to the pre and post Fair "hang-over."

Regretfully I cannot mail any of the books I have here; I will try to bring some to the Fair dinner for those interested. The very nice cloth calendars of the Methodist Church are still available too.

The weather was finally right for apple-butter making and so the Becks stirred last weekend and the Lloyds this weekend; meanwhile the Ray McClaughry's entertained Mrs. Paul E. Shultz and Miss Beth Miller from DeBary, Fla. last week.

November 18, 1971

The leaves have all but lost their color, some still drab green, others are arrayed in darkened colors and too many are skeleton-appearing, standing bare against a changing sky.

It was a good country weekend. Friends from Philadelphia came, our city cousins we chose to call them – they bought games and books and some good store grapes and a cherry cake from another friend and returned with an antique table and a skateboard found in this terribly junky attic.

There was just enough time to gather the firewood, inspect the Becks' new cabin and ride down the country lanes getting a little of the local folklore and history of the land and then to see the Great Pyrenees up on the ridge.

There's another one there now by the way – Tony Carbone has acquired Nero, another of the giant beasts to keep Sam company.

The David Freemans spent their weekend away with their dogs, showing them at two different shows. With Dave acting as handler their Renaissance Randolph (Randy) won Best of Winners at the Salisbury, Md. show on Saturday.

Sandy Mitchell got in a visit to her cousin, Dawn Allder, in White Post, before the big Fair dinner on Sunday night where everybody seemed to show up.

Mr. O'Brien, a bachelor who hadn't had lunch, expressed concern that the food wouldn't last but the most delectable dishes were in abundance. Someone made the best winter compote with apricots, raisins and apples. How we are enjoying our bushel the Carbaughs gathered for us from Bryd's orchard.

Mrs. Marion Kerrick, Mrs. Elizabeth Kelley, Mrs. Bessie Townshend were seated together – all having loved and lived in the environs of Bluemont for some time. The Kerricks' guests Mr. and Mrs. William Coates is Marion's sister and a longtime owner of the house the William Carbaughs now occupy. She is also the mother of our Bonnie Reid and Connie Wynkoop and Grandmother Kerrick joined in the visit returning to Alaska with the Coates from her Berkeley, W.Va. home.

Many have lent me a helping hand in preparation for the new Johnson addition slated for November. Ray Paine hammered the last of the rungs of the crib together (it had taken an almost unrepairable beating from the twins), another bed was delivered from Bethesda by my brother and with the pampers piled high in readiness – the event can take place anytime as far as I'm concerned – anytime!

The local histories are to be returned so if you are still interested, the Clerk of the Court has Loudoun County and the Civil War, Potomac Press of Leesburg has the Battle of Ball's Bluff, Jean McDonald of Round Hill post office has the Ketoctin Chronicle and Kenneth Levi at the Blue Ridge Press in Berryville has the Spur Magazine with its attractive Bluemont history write-up.

The outlet for the book Snickersville by Jean Heron Smith now of Miamisburg, Ohio will again be at the Mann's Store, Bluemont.

Well, next weekend our neighbor, Sue Dawson will be taking the wedding vows down at the little local stone church and the couple happily for us all will remain in town, renting Frances Ballenger's apartment and then the pumpkin pies will be stirred up in earnest and the year will be making its final turn, but sufficient it is to live each day for itself.

Now there's this talk about the beautiful people – they are the glamorous, glittering jet and cocktail set – I know I'm small-town minded – but I've found the most beautiful people in the world right here in Bluemont. They are concerned about their neighbors – this is the kind of beauty I want to surround me and in the friendly shadow of "our" mountain.

November 25, 1971

November is somber, October – bright, December – crisp but November tucked between brightness and crispness, nevertheless sparkles on Thanksgiving Day.

China, crystal, silver, whether under the advantage of "Lemon Joy" or not, adorns the festive table and the cranberries and roasted turkey are a delight – Thanksgiving dinners are all "sweetness and light" except for the year I undercooked the country ham and the turkey. Oh, well – the rolls and oyster dressing were still good and my brother loved the onion rings topping the green beans a la mushroom soup?

What I'm saying is – it's that time of year again and a few are making their plans as of this writing.

The David Freemans will be going to daughter Evelyn's family, the Thomas Cunninghams in Lopian, Md., and then entertaining here on the weekend the Arthur Larsens of Southfield, Mich. who acquired a Pyrenees puppy from this last Renaissance Kennel litter.

The G.W. Townshends too are spending the day with their daughter's family in Maryland; Lynn Carbaugh says she plans to take in three dinners, one at the Wesley Carbaughs up on Pierrot's Hill, one at her home, the William Carbaughs and one with her aunt Mrs. Frances Wiley in Boyce.

The rest of the Bluemont families will have to let us know what eating took place where after the record.

Speaking of facts, I heard of another Bluemont institution that had existed back in 1908. Karlton Monroe told me there was a band wagon with about 20 Bluemont musicians including some of the Starkeys and Wynkoops. They traveled through the streets of town entertaining and took part in local Fairs and dances. How colorful can you get!

Mark Cochran had a birthday this week and I'm sure we're ready for another initial one around here soon.

The Bluemont Methodist Church will join in a community Thanksgiving program at the Round Hill Methodist Church this Wednesday evening at 7:30 p.m. with the Rev. Fred Parish of the Round Hill Baptist Church bringing the message.

The Becks entertained at a dinner party again last Wednesday night and last week chestnuts were roasting on the stove that will keep The Helping Hand Shop in business through the winter so the seasons are blending into one and someone here is talking about Santa and a talking doll.

Happy Thanksgiving!

December 2, 1971

It was a Thanksgiving most of us wouldn't forget for some time.

Snowbound and electricity deplete for 14 hours, Bluemonters drug out the logs, turkeys were roasted in gas stoves and the stork dropped in at the Loudoun Memorial Hospital just before the big storm to bring Virginia Clayton to the Johnsons of Clayton Hall.

Even from the Loudoun Hospital window there was a beautiful mountain scene with snowy peaks and a golden tree laden down with white.

The world is a very small place indeed. Neighbor Mrs. Clifford of Pine Grove, supervisor of the nursery at Loudoun Memorial cared for "Ginger" through the first days of life and then stayed stuck in after the snow and as usual the neighbors looked out for the Johnsons, Lara reporting she had pumpkin pie and turkey at Libby and Bootsie Stearne's along with the rest of the Dawson clan.

Lawrence Dawson celebrated his birthday at the same time with a big cake.

The Dawsons had just sent off daughter Sue on her honeymoon the Saturday before with a perfect country wedding. Ivy Cochran had made the most beautiful four-tiered cake imaginable for the affair and other neighbors took part, too. Ruth Manuel was one of the bridesmaids and Louella Robey brought his country music group to entertain at the reception.

The Glen Lloyds were planning Thanksgiving dinner for 19 but I'm not sure who arrived due to weather conditions.

My Bethesda-based parents couldn't believe the stories about the snow, but they don't know upper Loudoun like the rest of us, now do they?

Mrs. Sadie Piggott, daughter of the R.M. Peytons of Bluemont, came from Madison College to her home at Clearbrook near Winchester for the holiday and earlier in the month sister, Rosie Peyton had celebrated at her sister's home on the eighth of November.

Herbert Martz was lending his usual help to villagers in snow-laden driveways and Santa arrived via helicopter in Leesburg again this year with a few Bluemonters greeting him.

Way back in October, Clyde Beck mailed a letter to Santa from Justine and Brian and the Johnson trio so they really see no need to bother the fellow with the long, white beard with details. They are assured he got their message.

The William Carbaughs are already talking of hiking to find their tree in a special place they frequent each Christmas.

Bloomfield neighbor Jim Pierson was also a patient at Loudoun Memorial this week undergoing tests.

Mary Alice Wertz, when giving me a buzz, got a gentleman patient. Needless to say, he was quite taken aback when she said she thought she had the maternity ward.

Even though the storm threatened, plans went on for the usual festive Thanksgiving dinner at the James Scotts' with children and grandchildren attending.

Mary, John and Carmen Campbell, from Landover, Md., plus Martha, Harry, Donald, Alvin, Edith and Harriet Coates, now of Ryan, came for the day. How we miss our old neighbors, the Coates, who were displaced by the highway construction!

Deer have been spotted all over the Bluemont environs. Ivy Cochran and I saw one take to the field next to the Russell Piersons last week and my parents reported seeing a fawn at the top of the hill by the Brownells and at least four Bluemonter freezers will be storing some venison this season since Louis Underwood got a six-point deer. Merle Gray and Russell Parks of Airmont bagged one along with Clinton Hindman all on our Bluemont mountain.

It's good to be home again – back to Clayton Hall – among our neighbors where our roots go deep in the garden of human kindness.

December 9, 1971

Here in the Bluemont countryside there's a lot of crisp December in the air and still a lot of white on the pasture land and on the village lawns.

With snow and the first of December, thoughts and plans turn to Christmas naturally.

The local Methodist Church says they will have a Candlelight Service Christmas Eve and aren't sure about a Christmas play as of this date.

Choir practice has started again on Thursday at 7:30 p.m.

It's time for someone to think about plans for helping Miss Alley decorate her tree which was so very beautiful last year but meantime birthdays, engagements and meetings have dominated the Bluemont news scene this week.

There was still a great deal of talk about the "hammy" Thanksgiving most of the village celebrated due to the power shortage.

The J.H.H. Verloops welcomed two of their children home. Emily came from Richmond where she is a student at VCU and was later joined by a friend John Thomas of Randolph-Macon on Saturday.

The whopper of a story came when son Michael was returning to Indianapolis by plane. A conversation between him and his seatmate developed and when she inquired about where he was from, he was dumbfounded to find she was Jean Smith, author of Snickersville.

That just about tops those "the world's a small place" stories, doesn't it?

Now when it comes to the birthday news let me first make the correction that Larry Cochran had the birthday last week, not Mark.

Debbie Carter entertained guests for her birthday on Dec. 1 with two cakes, home-baked by her dear mother.

Brian Beck turned seven with a group of friends in for games and fun on Saturday.

A visit to the Robert Hindmans, Ivy Cochrans' parents in Hamilton was a pleasant experience.

There in a cozy atmosphere you can enjoy the beautiful wild birds that habitate their porch pecking at their feeders and here the old stories of Bluemont from Mr. Hindman who spent his early manhood in Bluemont sleeping at Berkley Farm now the home of the James Walshes in the ice house where if he didn't cover his clothes, they would freeze during the night.

My old news nose told me there was a scoop at the Brownells but I neglected to call. Congratulations to Susan on her engagement!

The Bluemont Citizens Association elected new officers at its regular monthly meeting this week. Clyde Beck was elected president; Louis Underwood, vice president; secretary is still vacant, and treasurer, Ellen Jones.

Please keep the John Carters in mind if you know of a place for rent nearby. We sure hate to lose them in Bluemont.

Mary Ann has been here all week – how can we manage without her, I don't want to find out and then at night Hope and Lynn Carbaugh helped in the greatest tradition of good neighborliness, getting Jennifer off to school, fixing dinner and doing the dishes.

There have been soups and salads brought to my door, cakes (and I can't have any chocolate), meat, baby food, formula, Pampers, cards and greetings of congratulations.

Thanks neighbors – you make life so rich and good and ah, finally Ginger succumbed, at first I thought she would endure through the writing of the Bluemont news.

Judging for the annual Christmas home decorating contest will be from 7-9 p.m. Dec. 22 and 23.

December 16, 1971

Did you have that fogged-in feeling last week? Or sometime the children call it "frog" and they go together somehow to me.

I didn't get far from Clayton Hall but when I did I made it count. With a new baby, you have that "prisoner in your own house" feeling and that little joke about the slip found in the fortune cookie that reads, "Help, I'm a prisoner in a fortune-cookie factory," keeps going through my mind.

When I dipped out into the rain for a Tuesday visit to the doctor in Purcellville, it was just the right time to have my first visit to Demory's, the general store with the 8,000 pounds of Christmas candy.

The place is pure delight, immaculately neat and clean with those really marvelous antique counters and such reasonable prices plus a white-haired Mrs. Demory, Sr. who might have passed for Mrs. Claus.

Louise Hall of Round Hill, an assistant I needed badly, treated us to some pink coconut bars (I'm still giving up chocolate but not for long, I hope) and with a fruit cake in tote, we all had a warm seasonal feeling.

Saturday night the Cameron Street Grass Band returned minus their rhythm guitarist to Bluemont. We still don't know if the road construction kept him lost or not but they were as good as ever and I had a chance to chat with one of the members and his wife. This is an avocation with them not a vocation but with their talent they really ought to be on top.

I also had an opportunity to meet Jack Barber and his daughter from over near the Shenandoah River. He and Mrs. Barber just returned from a two-month European tour and are enjoying retirement there beside the river celebrated in song. The group managed a song too about the Blue Ridge Mountains of Virginia.

There have been lots of little signs of the approaching Christmas season this week.

The apartment above Mann's Store is done up in style again this year; the Lawrence Dawsons have put out a pretty wreath, the Jack Allders have their lovely candles and right now efforts are continuing on Miss Alley's mammoth tree which is always the town sensation each year.

Clyde Beck, J.K. Cornwall, "Popeye" Reid and the children Justine and Brian Beck joined by Jennifer and Donnie Spring from Herndon up for a visit with his grandmother, Barbara Spring, did the honors.

The Walton Manns had a visit to Philadelphia this week to see Tom and Ruth, their son and daughter-in-law and Timmy Reid's family took in a basketball game down at Tim's school, Luther-Rice in Alexandria.

Tim, a first-stringer on the five had unfortunately injured his hand but the cheerleaders hadn't forgotten him with a big sign about "Hurry back" and a bag of pre-seasonal treats.

Tony Carbone has been spotted in town with a new jeep that sports a snow-plow and there are rumors that he may be available to lend a neighborly blade when the next coverlet clothes the driveways.

Although I can't get out for many visits, certain creatures are still visiting me. Two very small harmless field mice (Ugh) frequented the upstairs this week, one crawling right by me when I was on the telephone and into my closet (you can bet I shut that door fast).

As usual I yelled "Help" up the Becks' way and every time they give me the creatures' motives, "They are just trying to get warm." Nevertheless, I resent their invading my privacy!

Anyway, we'd welcome a visit from any other two-legged creatures and if you don't want to get some colicky stories and the like, better give me a buzz with some news.

Happy pre-seasonal activity!

December 23, 1971

Time to ring in Christmas, 1971.

In Bluemont, Christmas is a very tender feeling of real love and concern being exchanged between neighbors and friends this year.

Karlton Monroe made his traditional holly delivery on Monday, then the Carbaugh girls in the lineage of the "Little Women" story helped me and my four girls decorate the tree.

All the lights were strung perfectly when in popped a friend with a gift for under the tree but alas next morning the tree with broken canes and ball greeted us.

"Don't feel bad," Grace Dawson said, theirs fell three times!

Something very special happened this year; I saw people were throwing aside the idea of lots of commercial buying but instead they were sewing clothes for an old doll, freshening its dress, putting a new hair ribbon in its hair.

They were sharing these things with us and then in turn the girls wanted to do the same for someone else in need.

The doll could never be new again but yet with its scars and the touch of love, she had become even more of a cherished object for the giver as well as the receiver. Isn't there a parallel here for us humans?

The Earl Virts now have a lovely little English tree decoration on the door as the decorating judging contest nears on the 22nd, and 23rd from 7 to 9 p.m.

Things were bustling in the post office when Ginger got her first visit downtown Bluemont last week – she fell asleep on the way home!

Then later in the week, Mom wished to share her love of the smell of printer's ink so in we trotted to the Times-Mirror to greet some of the staff and our friends there.

The MYF carolers will be here after a round around the village on Wednesday and then Friday evening at 7:30 will be the annual inspirational Candlelight Service at the Methodist Church.

Tom Sixsmith is here from Rhode Island visiting his mother and all is winding down to the day celebrated by the Christian world as the birthday of the Christ-child.

Having a new baby in our house to hold and embracing the love of neighbors for the newborn and our family has made the Yule particularly inspirational this year.

With a heart overflowing with gratitude may I wish all my dear Bluemonters and readers everywhere the joy expressed in that life that began in Bethlehem centuries ago. May I claim for you the fulfillment in his purpose in coming, "I came that you might have life and have it more abundantly."

So in the fullest sense of the greeting, Merry Christmas!

December 30, 1971

What a Christmas!

How our neighbors, friends and loved ones remembered us! It's been the best we've had in years!

The people of Bluemont take others into their family; blood kin is not what counts.

Herbert Martz has been playing Santa for years with candy treats from Demory's store. He has an elaborate bagging and sorting system, counting out so many pieces of mixes for his 26 grand-children and other neighborhood children. We got a couple of the hundred and ten pounds he distributed this year. How I love our Bluemont characters!

We saw friends this year we hadn't seen in years; the Jerry Stallards once of Broad Run Farms and previously of Berryville now of Virginia Beach came with their three girls and granddaughter Christmas night.

How we loved the Tom Murtaughs' tree at their new place by the Shenandoah River in the perfect idyllic setting. The bubbling brook and the mountain view about makes it the perfect spot for one of the David Freeman's Great Pyrenees pups. Might as well keep him in the Bluemont family.

Thinking about our friends on the ridge; all the Verloop children managed to make it home for the holidays and our dear nurse friend, Jessica Clinton in Pine Grove welcomed her son Shepherd from Miami-Dade College in Miami for a winter visit here during the Christmas vacation.

Most of the village turned out for the Candlelight Service at the Methodist Church and all the cards about the Blessed Babe held a special message for me this year with Ginger on my lap. How glad we were to know Jim Pierson was released from the hospital in time for Christmas.

Ethel Hall's remembrance to the Johnsons took me back, it was tangerines wrapped in red cellophane and had a magic that could go on my "these are a few of my favorite things" list.

Then there were so many kind Mr. and Miss Clauses around town this year and enjoying simple things in the country as we do, the burning of the wrapping paper in the fireplace produced the most beautiful flames of pink, violet, blue and green and thus was a special delight.

A ride around town was a must. Here are the critics choice – the Clyde Becks – first prize for their elegant simplicity – white lights on the porch pickets with a red ribbon looped at intervals. An interesting historical note was that those pickets once graced the porch here as proven by an old photograph and then their turning up in the barn.

The James Walshes again distinguished themselves with candles in the windows and blue lights on the posts for second prize; third went to the Louis Underwoods for their well-balanced display – candles in the windows and a wagon wheel with greens and a string of lights.

Honorable mention to the Russell Piersons and Bennie Lightner said she particularly like the Carbaughs' doorway with the reindeer over the threshold too.

Clayton Hall is still in the colonial, tradition – mostly in the dark, but we're glad our neighbors all make the effort in such good taste.

Anyway thanks to Karlton Monroe, I can almost say as in the song "But the prettiest sight you'll see is the holly that will be on your own front door."

Since Ingrid Jones isn't here this year to keep me company, I guess I'll have to take my decorations down on time.

Town meeting time has rolled around again, the first Wednesday of the month at 7:30 at the schoolhouse and now it's time to haul out all the sweets again for the New Year's celebration and just between you and me, I wouldn't be sorry if I never saw another paper doll again, even if it is Betsy Ross in colonial outfits.

Happy New Year!

1972

January 6, 1972

1972 – THE even numbers seem more complete to me – presidential year – it holds the promise of excitement.

Some of the Christmas lights of the village still dazzle.

The Carbaughs believe in the twelve days of Christmas and the celebrating they have done!

Beginning on Christmas Eve with a buffet supper at their house that included the Wesley Carbaughs, Mrs. Frances Wiley and Mrs. Edith Rogers plus us, they next went to the traditional Christmas Day dinner at the Wesley Carbaughs and then entertained office friends and neighbors, the Dickie Potts, on New Year's Eve.

Part of the family, Lynn, Hope and Grandmother Chapman brought the New Year in at Boyce as guests of Aunt Frances Wiley.

Now last year's end was quite another story if you will recall; we had a near blizzard that kept motorists stranded and party-goers home.

Whether a bell clanged, a gun-shot or a pan banged at the appointed hour this year, I wouldn't know. Too many early feedings have curtailed any taste for the excitement of staying up late for me.

Justine Beck and cousin, Debby Lynn, of Manassas, were exchanging visits back and forth over the holiday and where has the school vacation gone? Now back to that alarm ringing and the routine of winter mornings.

The Glen Lloyds reported all the children and grandchildren there for Christmas Eve and then returning for Christmas day dinner.

I'm in a daze struggling with that first year of life – forgotten soon but numbing at the time so you better chance some news my way or my frustrations will be leaking out in print.

Happy undecorating – remember to feed the birds and the tree makes good firewood and you can freeze just about anything, milk, nuts, pumpkin bread – there are my helpful hints for '72.

January 13, 1972

Now the coziness of winter evenings has set in; a fire may either roar or flicker on the hearth and the football games rage on and on via television as the family visit becomes closer knit.

Nevertheless, a day of substituting at Valley High School and attendance at the Bluemont Citizens Association meeting reaped a number of news items.

Clyde Beck, our new president presided at this first meeting, and Libby Stearne was welcomed as the new secretary.

Mr. Taylor brought films from his travels and now you'd think the Moorcones of Purcellville would see all the films they could stand but we were glad to have them join us in Bluemont, home-movie style that night.

The February meeting will be devoted to discussion of the use of monies earned from the Fair and election of a new chairman.

Shir Carbaugh announces that the Home Demonstration Club has changed its meeting night to the third Tuesday of every month with the program this month to be on "old glass."

I found out the Stearnes were doing a lot of entertaining down at their end of the village over the holidays.

First in December they had a birthday party for Libby's sister, Jean Dawson and then Christmas Eve they had a family dinner with the Lawrence Dawsons, the newly-united Charles Halls (sister Sue) joined by Linda Galaiti of Alexandria and Mike Hoggett of Unison.

And New Year's morning they had everyone back for breakfast.

The Leffingwells enjoyed a Christmas visit to Connecticut and look forward to the younger children's return visit in February.

Mrs. Lucy Martz underwent an operation on Friday and Herbert reports she is doing fine.

News from the Harry Dennises is that his uncles from both sides of the family came for New Year's Day. They are John Kuykendall and Alvie Dennis of Baltimore.

Donna gave me the J.J. Kelley news. Beverley was home for a visit from Bridgewater College where she is now a sophomore and young Sammy was there from his boarding school in Maryland.

The mail brought me good news from the Robert J. Carters at Whitehall Farm. Their latest addition, a daughter Sarah Rhonda Michelle, was born Dec. 15 at Loudoun Memorial Hospital.

Some of the older ones of the younger set there spent the day with their grandparents, the Robert P. Carters in Berryville. That was Robert Morris, Jerry and Mason.

The Kenneth Reids of Pine Grove had a houseful of guests for the holidays. Son Jerry was home from Alberta, Canada where he is a college student; their daughter and son-in-law, the John Smallwoods and daughter Alisa of Charles Town, were present along with their other daughter's family, the Pete Carters, sons Bruce and Brian of Alexandria.

A particularly nice piece of mail came from Beulah Gray now of St. Paul, Minn. who claims kin to the Demorys of candy fame. She keeps up with her former neighbors weekly, subscribing to the paper. Isn't it wonderful to know distance doesn't really separate us in kind thoughts from one another?

It was this time of year the stork hit some town somewhere some years ago. As for me I'm not telling how many, but Hope Carbaugh became fourteen and I ahem! the seventh of January.

Grandmother Carbaugh brought down the cake and ice cream for the family celebration and here we were content with cokes and popcorn until the candles, cake and ice cream came on Sunday with the folks who made it all possible, my parents, the Roy Porterfields of Bethesda.

A semi-city slicker who milks her own cow every morning and bakes all her own bread for her family of nine children asked me an agricultural question this week about the reason the farmers were plowing now and I thought I had the right answer but I just thought I better check with an expert like Ralph Cochran.

Ralph says the soil is easier to work with now – in the spring it can be terribly wet – plus this is a lax season – it's a time one could be whittling at the general store, trying out the old barrel the Manns have placed next to the oil stove.

So curl in your toes; it's a good reflective time of year for all.

January 20, 1972

Now the winter winds howl, the balmy days are over and snow talk persists.

"It's too warm, we need snow, the water table will be low unless there is 'snow in the mountains', snow in the mountains." Thus proclaimed a Leesburg apartment dweller last week but as one who lives where that snow in the mountains accumulates – hurray to fair skies and forsythia blooming.

Ever since "baby care' has been my main occupation, avocation and just plain drudgery, bottles of milk the doctors and books say can be served at room temperature. That was all well and good with the previous summer babies but now wintering at Clayton Hall especially in the back bedrooms, it's a pretty cold drink for a mid-winter morning meal so I must brag on my ingenuity – tripping down the stairs at 2 o'clock waiting for a bottle to warm on the stove – no indeed! – I just placed the night's supply on the radiator!

And car talk…is there one auto in the country that is dependable on a cold morning? I suppose horses went lame and were temperamental and certainly the ride in freezing weather must have been a horrible ordeal but it wasn't mechanical. After you've had the battery, the choke, the distributor, the plugs, the wires replaced…

I got word indirectly again from our friend, the former Bluemont telegrapher, Clarence "Blondie" Tallman, who is wintering in Fayetteville, N.C. where it isn't any too warm, as I know having spent two winters close by at Wake Forest. In fact, I went by way of North Carolina to Virginia having met a Virginian there who brought me back to the Old Dominion.

Blondie would welcome some mail: c-o Mrs. Hazel T. Davis, 425 Lancaster Road, Fayetteville, N.C. 28303.

Here on the home front, Mrs. Erman Hill had her son Leonard and his family from Clintwood as weekend guests. Returning after a two-week visit from Clintwood is son, Kenneth.

The Harry Dennises entertained Harry's sister, Mrs. A.C. Ball of Jacksonville, Fla., last weekend.

Particularly at this time of year, I think of our ridge people – the real pioneers weathering the stormy blasts. Welcome back to Mary Agnew who had been for a visit to her sister's in Philadelphia.

The Pyrenees at the Stangs, Freedmans and Carbones should be welcoming the colder temperatures with their heavy white coats. This is a far cry from the Alps – but it can get rugged!

And how about the Brownells' official trip to Europe?

So wish for what you will – weather-wise. I believe I may be going with the Tahiti syndrome, and to think I passed up a trip to Barcelona, Spain one time because I didn't want to leave my baby!

Yep! You guessed it. I haven't changed!

February 3, 1972

A forecast of snow changed the village scene this week – the children fully expected to have a sled ride down the big hill and a dish of snow-cream before retiring on Saturday night, but when the weatherman call for it – I forget it.

There were lots of trips to the store and Walton Mann made more deliveries than usual.

Any Bluemonter can tell you to rely solely on your own feeling and bones but the icy roads on Friday gave the students and teachers a delightful long weekend.

Of course, my children were up a half-hour earlier than usual. These are the real mysteries of life – the unlocked scientific secrets – the only justice in it is their children will repeat the tradition.

It was a good day for baking – cleaning is futile with the mud time here. Mrs. Molly Freedman, visiting from New York at Twin Oaks sent down some nostalgic cinnamon rolls. Grandma always made them when she baked a pie. The left-over crusts are rolled out in a straight line – filled with sugar and cinnamon. Mrs. Freedman put in raisins too – then rolled back up and browned in the oven. What a treat!

The storeroom of jellies and relishes from the neighbors are particularly precious these days, too.

Dave Freedman was the guest speaker last week at the Army Food Service Worldwide Seminar at Fort Lee.

In attendance were the European Pacific, Alaska and Southern commands along with Army Material and Combat Development Commands, and a goodly number of generals- major, brigadier and lieutenant. I don't know enough about the ranks to know who should get my best salute.

Over Pine Grove... W.G. Ballenger, Jr. celebrated her birthday on Jan. 11, (so did my mother!) and then later in the week the Ballengers entertained the Richard B. Smiths III of Berryville and Hyattsville.

Friends and neighbors will want to remember Ambrose Moreland who lost his foot due to frost-bite during the preceding terribly cold Sunday. He is now a patient in Winchester Hospital.

This is the week of the Bluemont Citizens meeting, Wednesday at 7:30 p.m. at the schoolhouse. The spending of Bluemont Fair money will be discussed.

County organizations are reminding citizens that they are alive and kicking even though much of the activity is indoors. Individual membership in Keep Loudoun Beautiful are being solicited at $5.00 and group memberships at $25. Respond to Box 5, Leesburg.

The Loudoun County Extension program is sponsoring a school on Feb. 3, 10, 17, 24 from 7-9 p.m. on animal management, sewing and foods.

Now the stillness of a winter evening settles on the village. Happy sled-riding, and Mrs. Peyton, the last batch of your strawberries for the snow-cream are right on top in the freezer, but not a snowflake can be heard!

February 10, 1972

The traditional January weather has now advanced into February, the bitter winds blow, the flu has receded to be replaced by the common cough and sniffles while seed catalogs arrive and housewives do a bit of scrubbing in pre-spring clean-up style.

Last week's mid-week light snow provided the long awaited sled riding for some of the village children, the Becks and Carbaughs found a field perfect for sliding up above the village, indeed a spot where Emily from Our Town could look down.

This time of year marks the end of the first school semester and how pleased we are to know our Jean Dawson got an A in her student teaching and made the dean's list at Madison College in this her Senior year.

John Carter is admitting to a birthday this week; he didn't even mind telling his age.

Sorry to hear Mrs. Sarah Chapman fell this week and broke her toe.

Shir Carbaugh reminds Home Demonstration Club members of the meeting the third Tuesday of every month at 7:30 in the schoolhouse. The leaders this month are Emma Mann, Hilda Dutrow, and Ruth Alley; their topic is professional sewing.

At the Wednesday night Bluemont Citizens meeting president Clyde Beck appointed the three acting Fair chairman, Mrs. Jack Lightnor, Mrs. Ralph Cochran, and Mrs. James Walsh to suggest three to take their place for the 1972 Fair.

It was voted to spend some of the Fair profits on another shed for the school grounds and reconstruction of some sections of the sidewalks.

The C.E. Paynes now have found an idyllic spot on Road 619 around the corner from Grasslands. With ten acres of cleared land, it's a good place for horses. They have dubbed it Foxwoode.

Tippy got a belated Christmas gift of a trip to see the Lipizzaner Stallion Show in Fayetteville, N.C. last week. Too bad they couldn't have met "Blondie" Tallman wintering there who writes that the weather has been very pleasant.

The picture he took about 50 years ago of the water tower overburdened with ice will tell him of our weather.

Another visit over the river revealed some fascinating information about the goat world as lawyer Tom Murtaugh enlightened me.

The old idea of goats eating anything holds true in that they will eat prickly "pears" and other spikey fare but will not eat vegetation actually in the ground thus they avoid worms unlike our other grazing animals.

Amazingly goats manufacture their own vitamin C; Tom says it was thought that man had this capacity at one time.

The thin-legged mammals resemble the deer in many ways, climbing quickly over rocky terrain: one of the Swiss breeds had the beautiful markings of tan and black like our dachshund but in reverse.

And their milk, it really doesn't taste like leather if it's cooled immediately after milking; the little milking station is cute too.

So with the promise that the old car will start, there may be other horizons to conquer, other paths (perhaps snow-laden) to follow but it's a secure feeling to know one can make the return to Bluemont.

February 17, 1972

One bright winter day follows another as Shir Carbaugh continues to fume, grieving that no snowy visitations have descended upon the village.

It's been a fairly quiet week here – at last the ice has been chipped from those treacherous front steps and sidewalks and the mind can only occupy itself with reading and spring plans.

Students at Valley High School are ordering class rings, is it possible that Ethel Leffingwell and Allen Carter will be seniors next year?

So time has a way of adding another day, month, year to life and Jerry Lloyd had his official birthday last week with a big buffet dinner at his parents, the Glen Lloyds. Twenty-one people were on hand to take a slice of the birthday cake.

It was good to see Marvin Watts again who has really been adventuring, skiing in the west, and then tripping to Europe where unfortunately he became ill and had to be hospitalized in Vienna for several days.

The old town will get a little winter variation next week when Clyde Beck and Paul Reisler play host to three gentlemen who will sing a Renaissance Mass at Clyde's studio at 8:30 p.m. Saturday, Feb. 19.

Amazingly a good bit of construction is taking place in Bluemont these winter days; we are pleased to know the John Carters will be staying in Bluemont, occupying the old Costello place.

Clyde Beck and a healthy crew are working on several houses on the property across from the old Throckmorton place and Bluemont will be welcoming the Thomas Ogdens of Great Falls at the end of the month at Mountain Shadow. They have renovating plans for the former schoolhouse.

Any leak to the press about any stirring of villagers would be appreciated; it won't be long when those flower and vegetable seeds Janet Payne is peddling will be tempting indeed. Happy thoughts of tulips budding and robins warbling.

February 24, 1972

All in all it was sorta coziness personified - the days of the February snow, that is.

Early Saturday morning the fireplaces were laid, the wood stove placed in the flues, the coal, gas, and oil appliances set to bubbling.

Here in our colonial house, I checked out the temperature by candlelight about 6 a.m., crawled back in bed, waiting for the reassuring hum of civilization's necessity – electricity.

We were to wait six hours for the return, I had settled for a cold breakfast of cereal and oranges but out at the Cochrans they had their hot chocolate on the gas stove before the milking chores, Ralph hooked up the generator to the barn, the Freedmans on the ridge used their Coleman stove for bacon and eggs and Tony Carbone and the Becks had their gas stoves cooking and heating at the same time.

As our little wood stove went up, someone suggested beans and franks at 10 o'clock a.m. and by the time it was prepared, it was a tasty lunch – wheh! the life of the colonial maid.

And traffic – you should have seen downtown Bluemont – Mann's Store opened for a while and one waited in line in vehicle in the one-wayed cleared path made by a friendly jeep. As of this Sunday morning writing we have yet to see the snowplow.

Of course, most of the townsmen had the freezers full and at least one gallon of water in readiness. With the electricity's return, people began to prepare for another onslaught and Marvin Watts said he just thought he would fill the bath tub as a ready source of water.

The biggest projects of the day were getting the wood in off the porch, rounding up burnable, old magazines, boxes (the children quickly employed them as marvelous carts), making a big pot of home-made soup for the evening meal and putting a longer rope on the sled.

And the making of snow cream – the strawberries went in first, then a gallon of snow, two eggs, real Guernsey milk from a friend's cow and a cup of sugar.

With the evening all thoughts of the Renaissance Mass were abandoned, even Sunday morning church service was foregone although the lovely blooming plants supplied by Estelle and Helen King have been appreciated during these non-blooming winter months.

Lucy Martz was to celebrate her 67th birthday on Sunday with her family but again plans were changed. Lucy has had to spend 25 days in the hospital since the first week in January.

Right before the snow, Mrs. Sarah Chapman was a patient in Winchester Hospital but fortunately an operation was ruled out.

I noticed too Allen Campbell's new home is well under roof. He has a lot between his mother's and Lew Robey's; it's amazing what you can see when you get a chance to get to your own backyard.

It was good to see the Virginia state flag being raised each morning at Valley High School last week and a letter to the editor in defense of the flag.

I have been engrossed in an article on child-rearing, Life, December '71 (Yes, that is about my present speed in keeping up with things). Studies show now that a child's intellectual capacity is mostly set between the ages of 10 months and a year and a half. The mother or mother substitute should give some minutes of undivided attention to the child each day, encouraging creative thinking with the playthings by showing another approach to the block building or pot and pans hammering and confinement to a play pen discourages learning stimulation. (The boxes here now are desks).

Now more problems of "snowbound" how to deliver the copy with no Monday mail and a reluctant auto minus snow tires in the deep-drifted drive and to think a poet was stranded here over the weekend plotting an immediate escape route back to Washington. Now what if John Greenleaf Whittier had thought that way!

March 2, 1972

As a cold Monday dawned for many in the area still without electricity most of Bluemont was blessed with heat, hot water and cooking facilities but Wednesday marked the first day most everyone was able to get out, waiting in long lines in the supermarkets, swapping stories of the ordeal.

The only Bluemonter rescued by helicopter was Mrs. Esther McCuen, thoroughly chilled who has decided she will winter elsewhere next year.

Ironically Tony Carbone who had purchased a jeep and blade just for such an emergency was stuck himself at the side of 601on the ridge for two days.

Also ironically the sled-riding crew all happened to be snowbound out of the village.

Lynn Carbaugh had gone Friday evening to visit her aunt Mrs. Frances Wiley in Boyce (all of Clarke County maintained current), Pam Carbaugh went nearby to the Byrds just off Route 7. Sharon and Hope stayed over up at Pierott's Hill with grandparents Wesley Carbaughs and Justine Beck went to Manassas to visit cousin Debra Lynn while Brian Beck really caught the power failure in Lovettsville with his grandparents Grove.

Come Thursday morning with the additional light snow the night before, the legions of sled-runners down the old Snickersville Gap road were thick, however, the sledders were home and off and running.

The mid-winter week vacation for school children was a grueling one for Mom and Pop; there were finger-painting projects on the bedroom rug, picture and card sorting over every floor, puzzle-construction in the middle of the family room floor and an ever-blaring television fare of kiddy repeats.

The wood piles are low now and so are the aspirins in the big bottle – it was quite a week!

Just before the big storm, the two youngest Leffingwell children came in from Connecticut for a visit. They reported they have had more snow there, but no snow-days off from school.

Of course, the death of Mrs. Owen Thomas was a terrible shock. It was always pleasant to see her on election day acting as one of the registrars. She had a thorough knowledge of local history. Our fullest sympathy to her family.

Keep Loudoun Beautiful is laying plans for the annual clean-up campaign scheduled for April 3-19. An assistant district chairman is being recruited for each area; I know Bluemonters will cooperate as they did last year. Loudoun's efforts last year placed them second in honors in the state. Let's be first this year!

The regular Bluemont Citizens Association meeting is scheduled for this Wednesday, Mar. 1 at 7:30 p.m. at the schoolhouse.

The Renaissance Mass will be re-scheduled for some time in March.

Isabelle Dawson always leading the way, has cleared a path to both her doors while here I'm waiting for Mother Nature as usual to eliminate the four-foot drift on the sidewalk, the trash has piled up, finally the vacuuming has been accomplished and there's but one more load of clothes now ready in the dryer and tomorrow the film, "The Song of the South" beckons as it did years ago when someone else was doing the driving. Zip..Ba..Dee..Do..Da!

March 9, 1972

Brooks were bubbling, streams were fast flowing, rivulets were full brimming – it was all part of the spring thaw – folks said – and then a curious thing happened – the temperatures dropped again.

Take down the wood stove?

Not on your life – not until March passes in Northern Virginia.

Only too well do I remember a college spring vacation spent in the Washington area. As I left the Library of Congress late one afternoon, snowflakes were falling and they kept falling, the fury of a blizzard was upon us in several hours. We were five days without electricity. The boys and Dad spent the days chopping wood – Grandma spent her time simmering a pot of coffee on the one fireplace in the house and kept calling for a partner for a couple of hands of Gin Rummy while I attempted to compile a term paper on a long narrative poem by Edwin Arlington Robinson and Mother kept buttering bologna sandwiches with hot mustard.

The Porterfields never fared too well at going primitive – in fact – that NBC news report that "thousands were stranded in Loudoun County" during the recent storm had them phoning Bluemont.

Nevertheless, plan and promise that the spring cycle will return here has motivated the organization Keep Loudoun Beautiful to hold its first organizational meeting of the District Directors for the spring clean-up this Wednesday.

Jim Brownell has agreed to be the assistant Director for Bluemont and Marvin Watts already demonstrating his interest by collecting bags of cans thrown near his wayside in the off-season will attend the meeting on our behalf. June Lloyd says she will take her strip littered badly already again and Clyde Beck will tackle the disgraceful big hill. I know "Popeye" Reid can be depended on to help.

Ellen Jones says she will recruit for her road and the Carbaughs say they will help with the middle of town and Emma says she thinks Walton will collect on their side of No. 601 again so it's "a hunting we will go."

A little run-down on what transpired at the Bluemont Citizens Association meeting is that we have contracted to have the sidewalks from the post office to Jerome Fanciulli's redone for the cost of $1800 and hope to mount a flag pole in front of the schoolhouse so we might fly our state flag.

The returning Bluemont Fair chairs made a recommendation that the new administration for the Fair be handled by the officer of the Association acting as a board of directors. This was accepted by the members.

Our Virginia Clayton is considering a cast-signing party. She's hip-deep in two casts on her tiny legs so she can avoid the hereditary pigeon-toes of her mother and Sarah Chapman has spotted a robin while the lady selling bread crumbs on the Mary Poppins record keeps echoing her admonition "Feed the birds, Feed the birds" and so another winter week bites the "mud" in the Bluemont countryside.

March 16, 1972

March froze, thawed and refroze the ground, snow flurries threatened and frightened the populace several mornings and tones of somber light reminiscent of a Rembrandt painting became the Bluemont scene this week.

New signs are popping up in town, a new welcome mat at the Lawrence Dawsons' front door and a good job of lettering on the old wooden sign at Mrs. Powell's now dubbed the Snow House are in evidence. The new neighbors have been here over the weekend, transforming and transfixing the 1-room former boarding house.

Marvin Watts, true to his promise, attended the Keep Loudoun Beautiful meeting where it was pointed out that both the Governor and Loudoun's Board of Supervisors have asked that all citizens cooperate in the spring clean-up, April 3-17.

Everyone is expected to pick up in front of his house. Feed bags for hauling are available locally at Whitmore and Arnold and Southern States.

We will arrange again to have the Highway Department take our collection from the school grounds. Place bags near the old incinerator there if you are working on an individual basis.

Gen. B. C. Harrison has the name of a gentleman who will haul away those miserable junked autos for ten dollars apiece. Be thinking about getting rid of these extreme eyesores.

The Loudoun Valley High School students have been operating paper recycling centers in Purcellville at the shopping center and the former Safeway store near the Shell station. Hours are from 10 o'clock to 2 o'clock on Saturdays. Their representative pointed out it takes 17 trees for oxygen-making and eye-edifying.

Easter Monday will be Youth clean-up day in town, the other leaders may choose their own time. The MYF has agreed to help again.

A sign of the season is noted in special services planned by the Methodist Church for the 20th, 21st and 22nd at Round Hill Church.

Right now there are five Easter baskets adorning the dining room table with drawings of carrots and the inscriptions, I Love You for the Easter bunny. Just in readiness, you see.

The weekend brought visitors and visits away for Bluemonters.

The David Freemans took in the Detroit Dog Show sponsored by the Detroit Kennel Club and specializing in the Great Pyrenees this year. Tony Carbone and Paul Strang were dog-sitting so they couldn't get away for the event.

Our guests, Mrs. Elwood Shoemaker, son Douglas and daughter Brenda of Bowie, Md. returned Saturday evening to take in the Dog Show in the National Armory.

Things haven't really quieted down here yet; Claire and I were college roommates so when a wrong number rung here at 1:15 a.m. we were undisturbed, naturally we were still up talking – you don't think you can get in a word with five children running around, do you?

Most visitors like antiquing. Wow! Have the price of straight chairs gone up but Mr. Kirk has two marvelous round tables at a good price. It was crisp and clear at the Murtaughs where we showed the city kids the goats having kids and there's been a lot of talk about trailblazing on the Appalachian Trail on a later visit.

The Kenneth Reids of Pine Grove were glad to have their daughter's family the Peter Carters with sons Bruce and Brian of Alexandria for the weekend.

March 23, 1972

Oh, the wind doth blow is March's lament but rain has come too, to the village and on the mountain top it's snow.

Lucy Martz and Trudy Verloop would be good Missourians – they are reminding us of last April's snow so don't hurry to put away the woolens yet.

The fun began last Sunday, however, after I had put away the Bluemont news, the warmth of the day perpetuated a stroll around town.

First down the lane to the Snickersville Academy, across the swollen creek to find Mrs. Susy Neal's cane on the porch. She was there for the weekend, reporting the news that her granddaughter, Libby Spinner had a new daughter about Ginger's age (three months).

Then back up to the Snow House where the children were getting acquainted with the new neighbor children out for the weekend with their parents who were engrossed in the grand job of renovating.

Down to the post box, up to chat with the Herbert Martz's where we were joined by Janet Payne and then up that lane to see Walter Peyton spading his garden and J.K. Cornwell shining up his new car.

I was on my way home for sure when I spotted the usually ambitious Sarah Campbell digging in her front yard while son Jimmy was washing his blue "wheels", then back to join the children at the house when Miss Alley hailed me and really crowned the day with glory by presenting me with a bouquet of pussy willows and a baby carriage (needless to say, Ginger's 12 pounds plus with casts weigh heavy on me now).

Down the bumpy drive now to be summoned again by Mrs. Campbell, Snooks Campbell would give me a tour of her and Allen's new house still in construction. How lovely it is going to be with a wonderful view, big basement and beautiful stone fireplace compliments of "Hawk" and "Popeye" Reid.

So went a sunny Sunday Bluemont stroll.

Wasn't it good to see our center of commerce, Mann's Store in the limelight last week? The Manns themselves too are such wonderful citizens.

Of course, Mr. Iden's Store would make a good feature too. Isn't he remarkable to still be operating his store and enjoying such good health as he gets close to his ninetieth birthday?

Speaking of ninetieth birthdays, Miss Alley's mother has been visiting her again and celebrated her 91st birthday this week and among her congratulations was a birthday greeting from President Nixon.

Oh, so I didn't say a word about the wearing of the green - Well, I hadn't thought much about it until J.J. Kelley brought the Bluemont Fair pictures by for inspection and spoke of daughter Gwen's new job as receptionist at WEAM Radio Station.

It seems a short time ago. Paul of Peter, Paul and Mary was in and declared Gwen to be an Irish Lass before he even heard that purebred last name.

Two birthdays every year for St. Patrick's Day are Jack Allder and Wesley Carbaugh – Pisces – they would be.

The other two Aries in the Wesley Carbaugh family – Mrs. and son on the 23rd and 29th had a big celebration down at the William Carbaughs on Sunday with Shir's new recipe Heavenly Hash and birthday cake, of course, and no one is counting the candles.

I don't believe the Paul Draiseys of Round Hill, our dear neighbors who extend to us a helping hand when we need them, visited Ireland on their recent three-week trip to Europe but they saw many marvelous sights and missed the big storm here.

Mrs. Wesley Carbaugh will undergo a major operation this week so let's remember her in our prayers.

Best wishes to Lloyd Loope and his new bride who were united in marriage in Ohio and will reside in Wyoming where Lloyd is employed by the National Park Service.

Gather your feed bags as you may and get ready for the big clean-up and let's hope we don't have to dig for the cans and bottles in the snow, right, Lucy and Trudy?

March 30, 1972

More shades of gray, no blue skies and Easter Sunday fast approaching marks the Bluemont scene this week.

Weren't all childhood Easters bright and warm when we wore our new light-weight short coats (they were called toppers), white hats, white gloves, white shoes?

We hunted for colored eggs in the green grass as the warm sun beat down and the dog ate up the egg a week later that we had forgotten about behind the full forsythia bush… and when high school days came there was always a spring hike where one found violets in mammoth clumps or was it all only a dream?

Bluemont Easters that I recall have been raw and it seems this year will be no exception but robins have been spotted on the wing (headed south, I'm sure!) and two weeks ago I almost ran off the road practically blinded by the dazzling sprig of forsythia Mary Ann Carter held behind Trudy Verloop's windshield.

Anyway the spring clean-up for youth will take place Easter Monday at 9 o'clock.

Down near Miss Susy's is a bad spot; Marvin Watts urges us to clean up a dump out his way and frankly the trash down the dirt road in town is "enough to make a body sick" as Huck Finn would have expressed it.

Tony Carbone kindly brought a goodly number of feed bags here on Saturday, compliments of Adams Seed Company.

As we glean the area, everyone will notice the number one offender – beer cans!

Maybe Americans will become more aware of the third leading disease in the country – alcoholism. One in every ten households has a family member in this category.

About the most newsworthy item I've heard or observed this week was the grand discovery by the new neighbor children of a half-dozen frog in their creek, cold but with a decidedly green hue and the children claim the Becks have a new pet lamb, what Cinder Beck thinks about this I've yet to hear.

The Methodist Church has purchased a new piano and so the organ fund will be replaced by the piano fund. Perhaps you would like to contribute.

And if my guesses are correct Ethel Hall the Reverend's Mrs. was a stunning model in the Fashion Show held down at Whitehall Farm this week.

Between diaper changes there's little time to put my ear on the ground…

Life can be frighteningly routine at times:

Every morning feed the baby the early bottle, drag the school-age children out of bed, shove them out the door at eight with a hurried breakfast, nagging, nagging – "You'll be late; then put in a load of clothes in the washer, unload the dishwasher, make the beds, dress yourself, feed the pre-schoolers breakfast, respond quickly to the baby's cry, give her her bath, bottle, cereal and fruit.

Hurry to take some meat out of the freezer for the evening meal, then put in another load of clothes in the washer, start the dryer – maybe time for dusting or ironing – lunch time rolls around, another baby feeding – fold up the clothes from the dryer, the school children are home, baby gets meat, vegetable and fruit, hurriedly cook dinner, do the dishes, prepare the baby bottles for another 24 hours, television "repeats, repeats" – bedtime for the children – more threats – then another baby feeding – at last a telephone call to a friend – exhausted you call it a day.

Oh, no – I don't have Spring fever!

Break the monotony with the Round Hill Fire Department Women's Auxiliary on April 8 for a roast beef dinner at the firehouse beginning at 5 o'clock. Tickets at the door are $2.50 for adults, $1.25 for children. The proceeds will benefit new firefighting clothing equipment for the firefighters – our kind neighbors who provide this service to us freely.

Even though Easter is not a spring holiday this year, the observance of the occasion – "He is Risen" reminds, bringing hope and life to mankind.

April 6, 1972

A fire on the hearth on Easter Eve? Well, I really hadn't meant it to turn out that way but there's the little matter of destroying the evidence and the brightness of the sun during the day precipitated a little cleaning on the porch and while clearing off a few of the smaller logs, where else to store them but in a convenient place – the fireplace – so here I am tending fire and awaiting the appearance of a "Bugs" relative.

No – he's not coming down the fireplace! "How does he get in?" "Well, we just don't discuss that here!"

"Is he going to tip-toe by Gret, the dachshund and hide an egg next to her bed?"

"Well, we'll just have to wait and see."

Anyway he'll be in slicker and rain-hat and will have to follow the Clyde Becks down to Charlottesville to Grandmother Beck's to catch the children there while their pet goat (not a lamb, these city slicker children of mine don't know the difference) waits here.

The neighborhood was most communicative this week with some phone calls coming my way of news.

First of all, the spring clean-up got off to a great start here with June Lloyd's group collecting 45 bags on Rt. 734 (the Old Snickersville Pike) from the end of town to the Wilts' and down the yellow schoolhouse road a ways.

June enlisted 21 people, adults – Dorothy Dawson and Betty Pierson, their offspring, the J.J. Kelley's boys, the Charles Dawson children, the James Allder children and Dickey Ramey and Gene Clark.

They had a cook-out at the school and stored a dead skunk in one of the bags for good measure.

You can count on a Neff (June) to do it right! That's her sister, Mrs. Jasper Rickard in Lovettsville who always cooks the barbecue for the clean-up crews there.

I just had the pleasure of meeting the new neighbor, Shirley Lynn, who with her husband is occupying the newly renovated house right at the Bluemont turn-off from Rt. 7 on Tuesday at Round Hill School where she is currently teaching third grade when on Saturday they dropped by for more bags for their collection of beer cans, which they gleaned from their house up to the road (five bags). With neighbors with this kind of community pride, how can we lose?

More news of the Lloyds – they were celebrating all their April birthdays and Easter too on the April 2 date.

In addition, daughter Judy Casey bought an airplane ride for Mary Jo and Kelley Lloyd and son Scotty on the Auction of the Air so they had their first flight over Leesburg's crowded skies, taking off from Godfrey Field.

When I called Trudy Verloop about the clean-up on their mountain road, I got the news she and children Emily and twins Edith and Maurice had gone for a visit to older son Michael in Indianapolis while Pop was bravely managing alone at home.

The John Carters had Mary Ann's sister, Frances Sims, and her two children from Adelphia, Md., along with Frances' mother-in-law, Mrs. Ann Hill, over for Easter and son-in-law, Lt. Richard Jeffery from Camp Lejeune, N.C. were here for the weekend, staying on for the celebrated cattle show at Kenslee near Lucketts, the Kenneth Jefferys' homeplace.

It promises to be quite an event with delegations from Japan and Russia in attendance.

Emma said son Tom and wife Ruth dropped by from Philadelphia enroute to a best man's wedding in Hampton last week.

Sorry to hear Tyson Payne suffered another heart attack but gratefully he did not have to be hospitalized. Mrs. Wesley Carbaugh is recovering nicely from her recent operation and the Herbert Littles are both patients at Georgetown Hospital.

I'm really not much of a reporter since Jim Brownell had to tell me about the three-car collision that occurred right in front of my house.

Robert Carter was driving a car when the brakes failed, hitting Walton Mann's car parked in front of the store, knocking it into Stanley Kelley's car.

Other bad news for the Carters was both of his parents, the Robert P. Carters of Berryville, are hospitalized in Winchester Hospital and his grandmother, Mrs. Lola Carter died in Galax, Va. on Wednesday.

Another death in our Bluemont family was that of Mrs. Frank McComb, a patient at Herndon Nursing Home and wife of our dear neighbor who owned Whitehall Farm for many years prior to his retirement from dairying, selling the place and building a new rambler south of Purcellville.

Mrs. Townshend kept up her creativity with a delightful egg tree at the post office and attended the Executive Post Office Conference in Blacksburg last week.

I have placed some feed bags under the trees in the driveway for anyone needing them and in case of rain on Monday, Saturday will be the group clean-up day.

Easter Sunday dawned bright and the Methodist Church was full to over-flowing. Herbert Martz said there were more people than he remembers in the adult class since he's been coming these twelve years. Many children were in attendance with infant baptism administered. The Andrew Sisks, Jr. presented their daughter and the Russell Powells their bouncy baby boy and several others that I must meet and then we passed the Scipio sisters on their way to First Baptist.

April 13, 1972

Who laughed? Who snickered in Snickersville about rooting our beer cans in snow in April?

The "spring" clean-up lost ground over the weekend with sleet on the sidewalks, roadsides, greening grass and daffodil heads.

The long hill clean-up will be rescheduled for this Saturday at 9 o'clock a.m.

Monday's clean-up went very well with excellent cooperation on the part of the young.

In the middle of town I had plenty of help with Gary Ross holding the dust pan while I swept the broken glass from the old store front. The Paynes, Dillows, Campbell boys, Sandy Mitchell, Jeanette Glass, Wanda Reid and Carter children worked hard with a good spirit and much to my delight found me a whole little red wagon full of antique bottles for my collection.

Frank Comb and helpers gathered up 75 bags behind Iden's Store and Herbert Martz did a beautiful job of raking on both sides of Miss Alley's lane while at the same time treating youngsters to rides to the school in his laden-down tractor wagon.

Ralph Cochran and sons cleared their road and combined with the MYF's efforts collected 29 bags from the end of town up to the church and around the school grounds.

Marvin Watts got 28 bags in a long stretch of road out Rt. 606 and told me he even picked up a "ditch dog." He educated me to the term, it meaning a dead dog that was lying in the ditch.

Bob and Ellen Jones kindly lent their truck for hauling the collection to the school.

Our assistant on this detail, Miss Barbara Dennis has since become Mrs. Donald Hill as of Thursday. The couple will continue to reside in Bluemont.

A lovely wedding shower was given for Barbara on March 25th at the home of the Harry Dennises.

The week went swiftly by at Valley High School for me when I filled in for Mrs. Alice Whitley, retiring Latin and Math teacher who had the marvelous opportunity to accompany a student group to Greece.

Mrs. Whitley is a special friend to the Bluemont community as she has graciously lent her valuable limited editions and photographs on Stonewall Jackson and Robert E. Lee each year for display at the Bluemont Fair.

The fair plans too are beginning again; Tuesday night there will be a meeting of the new chairmen with those who served in the same capacity last year.

And hurrah! The Jack Lightners are back from their glorious month-long trip to Hawaii! Having lived there for a number of years previously, they thoroughly enjoyed a grand relaxed reunion of old friends.

Sorry to hear Tony Reid has been a patient in Winchester Hospital and that the Herbert Littles still remain at Georgetown Hospital.

Too, we have lost Laura and Paul Reiser to Keyser, W.Va. They left Skyfields on the mountain where they had been raising goats and gardens.

Other enhancing appearance features in town are the now newly completed sidewalks from the post office down to the school grounds and the Lawrence Dawsons' house undergoing indoor and outdoor improvements.

After an ever-extending winter, social plans are beginning again.

April 22 will mark the date for the re-scheduled Renaissance Mass at Clyde Beck's studio at 8 o'clock.

Likewise, the Bluemont Citizens ordered the fireworks for the annual Fourth of July celebration and voted to invite the Blue Grass Band back for entertainment that night along with the traditional home-made ice cream feast.

A grand discovery in Bluemont of late has been a marvelous old family Bible belonging to Granny Jones's grandmother originally which dates it to 1837.

The births and deaths of Osbornes, Humphreys, Throckmortons are recorded with our Bob Jones' birth being the last entry.

The Bible was found in an old wardrobe the Joneses had passed on to the Cochrans as a throw-away and when son Larry pried open a drawer, he found the treasure.

Both the Joneses and Cochrans, farm owners could profit from a vacation plan I read about this week.

City people pay country dwellers money to be boarded and entertained country-style as was the mode in the making of Bluemont years ago. It was enough just to be in the country, feasting on home-made rolls and pies and taking in the simple amusements like the Bluemont fireworks and home-made ice cream festival.

If I had the cows and land, I believe I'd be in business.

There is a long face in town these days, young John Campbell lost his pet toad as it disappeared out of its box when he parked it on the Becks' living room floor.

The Becks may have a long face too when it makes its re-appearance beneath the sheets some night.

And these twins here are really a team.

Tracey awakened us all at 6:30 this Sunday morning but I turned them all over to the babysitting cartoon theatre while I settled down for a few more winks but then Lara kept coming to the bedside, requesting breakfast.

Then when they hit the teenage years it will be a fight to get them out of bed! Happy dreams to all the Bluemont readers!

April 20, 1972

Yes, the grass 'tis green – 'tis very green and forsythia is out and daffodils, and one of the children picked a sole violet this week and the robins keep up that unique strut behind the still plastic-plastered windows here and some of the neighbors wish to declare that it's spring!

Watch it – it's pneumonia weather as young Pam Carbaugh can attest having been confined for two weeks.

There's a good bit of talk about those "dang" rototillers and "getting the hang of it" and "the soil is mighty wet yet" and the dairy farmers report the heifers are straying these days being sure the grass is surely "greener on the other side of the fence."

Everyone slated to help has done his bit for the Keeping of Loudoun Beautiful.

Jim Brownell brought a crew down the grade from Rt. 7 turning in his six deposit bottles Walton Mann reports and Clyde Beck enlisted about 12 people for the long hill on Saturday; they collected old bed springs, car parts and 55 bags of mostly bottles and cans; a good 90 percent of the collection, Clyde says.

Maybe that 20 percent statistic of the bottling and cans lobby holds true at the Tastee-Freez but on the roadsides of Loudoun County, we trash pickers aren't buying it.

Tony Carbone got two bags up his way on the right side of Rt. 601 and the four Verloops and Lloyd Loope collected four bags farther down while the Marion Kerricks collected 17 bags up to the Clarke County line and Walton Mann collected another seven near his home on the left side of the road.

Hawk, Buck and Popeye Reid were Clyde's helpers along with Frank Reid, Sonny and Betty Colbert, Don Corley, Gene Wade and Tony Rickards plus Joyce and children who spotted two "dead" garter snakes already.

Back to the social scene, Brenda Havener Bowman was married to Richard Aronholt in a lovely Friday evening wedding at the Round Hill Methodist Church while Tony Carbone entertained a college friend and wife, John and Amy Lyon Gatdos from Morristown, N.J. for the weekend at his mountain retreat.

I was pleased to meet at the wedding reception William Cravens, our Bluemont neighbor, who claims a Round Hill address and hear of some of the history of their old stone house.

Mr. Cravens has read some fascinating old papers that had belonged to the original owner of the 800-acre tract who had two stone houses built on the property.

How we need an up-dated, more encompasing "Old Stone Houses of Loudoun" book.

A reminder to all that the Renaissance Masses will be performed this Saturday evening at 8 o'clock in Clyde Beck's studio above the Old Lake Store.

With spring my old delusions of grandeur re-occur.

The Bluemont News would go syndicated and with an extra income, the things I could do!

Did you ever think about what you would do if you had money?

Retire to a tropical isle and never be seen again?

Not me, I would change my lifestyle very little and I wouldn't save it for a rainy day – oh no – I would spend it.

First of all, though it might not be sound business (I couldn't deduct for interest), I'd give First and Merchants the cash in exchange for Clayton Hall. Fair enough? And then I would redo it and hire the services of my neighbors and pay them well.

In line of priorities, I'd have Allen Campbell tile the bathroom, get Leon Brunelle to plaster in the holes in the ceilings, retouch up some of the walls, have Russell Parks or Bobby Allder repaint every room with a wonderful Williamsburg red in the family room and a mellow blue like the Sam Grahams have in their dining room in mine and then I would do that old kitchen!

Every touch would be right with cabinets made of old boards, a brick floor, a beautiful solid piece found for a mantel on the big fireplace with the hook, the old beams would be refinished and I'd have Hawk, Buck, and Popeye Reid point up all the stone work and lay down a stone patio and install a bird feeder outside near the kitchen window so I could watch the birds.

I'd get Herbert Martz to lay out a beautiful formal garden with boxwood, tulips, jonquils, mums, geraniums and rose bushes and pile up rock for an old piled rock wall up the Becks' property.

And then if money kept rolling in, I'd buy antiques from Mr. Kirk, paintings from Clyde Beck, some oriental rugs and then if the funds really came, I'd have a chauffeur to worry about new tags, auto break-downs, new tires and flat tires and traffic – someone who could take me everywhere in safety – Ethel Hall wouldn't be a bad candidate.

Then I'd get Toby Rickards to fix the color television (to buy a new one would be just a waste) and I'd add a downstairs bathroom and have freshly cut flowers in every room and take an occasional jaunt to Acapulco and maybe treat the kiddies to DisneyWorld.

In general I'd live the good life right here in Bluemont.

And the pear tree is in full bloom behind the Virginia House here in the village!

April 27, 1972

April showers brought the automatic rote verse to mind - "April showers bring May flowers" while the flowers of April came springing to newness of life too.

All through the lawn there were violets and most of the flowering trees were smiling with blossoms and in general it was a most innovative week.

Here off went the plastic from the windows, a winter's accumulation of ashes from the fireplace were scattered in spots in the grass for fertilizer, the wood was hauled from the porch, a sand pile went in the backyard – all in the name of spring energy.

Most of the neighbors felt the grass needed its first mowing of the season while Herbert Martz reported on Friday he had plowed his 25th garden.

Turning 74 on Saturday, he and Lucy were treated to dinner in Winchester by son Gilbert and family.

The spring clean-up statistics for our community topped last year's, I believe with 99 people lending a hand in the clean-up and 334 bags of trash collected.

Frank Combs deserves a real deal of credit for bagging 75 bags from behind Iden's Store.

More news of bottle finds – the Carbaughs found an unseamed gem that floated down the stream in Saturday's down-pour and the new neighbors at Mrs. Powell's former house have found pharmacists bottles which they assume came from the days that the first part of the structure was occupied by Dr. Henry Plaster.

I noted that the Hecht Company in Arlington was selling new glass bottles for $2.50 so why are we selling our antique ones for 50 cents here in the country?

Continuing with history news, everyone will want to get the new engagement calendar put out by the League of Women Voters. Evelyn Adams has done some lovely sketches which includes our Bluemont; they would be so suitable for framing.

The Paul Strangs and David Freemans of Great Pyrenees fame have been making the dog show rounds and the Freedmans' Renaissance Kennel's Suzanne gave birth to two pups this week.

J.K. Cornwall is joining Uncle Sam's Navy, reporting Thursday to Great Lakes, Ill., and we are pleased to know the John Kulgrens will now be registered residents of Loudoun County as John is retiring after 31 years with the Department of Defense Intelligence.

How marvelous to know Al Serber who frequents Bluemont in the summer occupying the Waldrops' place is now a bonafide author of a book on Washington tourism.

Mrs. Nellie Tibbs, with her sister Mrs. Fred Gore, of Purcellville, and Mr. and Mrs. Leland Lambert and son Eddie of Fairfax Station spent last weekend with Mrs. Tibbs' daughter and family, the Marshall Bennetts in Grantsboro, N.C. While visiting there they attended the Centennial celebration in Pamilco.

The James Brownells had a nice day even with the rain at Quinn's Island at the mouth of the Rappahannock River where the Executive Committee of the Virginia Association of Counties met, Jim being an official member, and then on Sunday they stopped off to see son, Jim and wife in Richmond.

At the store on Saturday Marvin Watts and I were exchanging similar experiences involving the reappearance of rodents that have decided it's still a little cool outdoors, so they are moving back inside. The Marian Kerricks who were minding the store for the Walton

Manns who were on a fabulous Caribbean cruise said, to drive a rat outdoors simply spray some cheap perfume about. Now that was a new one on me. Believe I'll stick to D-Con.

Then on Saturday evening the two Renaissance Masses were sung beautifully by the three male voices and the occasion gave the Becks an excuse to have a pre-concert buffet supper.

Everything was so special, they served a ham they had cured themselves; the pigs were grown here and the recipe was Allen Campbell's.

Paul Reisler made some great homemade bread; the watercress for the salad came from our good earth over on the Hoffmans' farm and Shirley Lynn was telling me there was quite a trick to the art of wine-making. Whether you have to stomp on the grapes in your bare feet she didn't say.

With the rainy days, the attics have been revisited.

How wonderful that the children can play there; always as a kid I had this romantic idea my house should have an attic with trunks of old clothes and boxes of old love letters and diaries and now my children can have that.

Ah! but the junk there. Lamps and overgrown beds and pans and kitchen utensils not needed now and jars (have I ever thrown one away?)

There's only one thing to do – have a sale – of course, that's a big project – especially when you have to read all the old letters and yearbook autographs first.

"Roses are red.
Violets are blue
Skunks stink
And so do you."

I had forgotten how popular I was!
Happy April Showers!

May 4, 1972

Le ceil est bleu…I could go on but my French is so rusty, I dare not.

It was one of those all-together days on Saturday.

While the mowers hummed here in Bluemont, Ethel Hall and I escaped to the serenity among the absolutely beautiful flowering trees, the perfectly clipped grass, the rare treasures in the old stone and brick homes of Clarke County.

Ah, the lovely rugs in those homes and that Burwell-Morgan Mill in Millwood is a real wonder; the wood on the structure is so beautiful, the mammoth wheels so awe-inspiring.

And the box lunch at Powhatan School was a real delight, a fried chicken leg, a ham salad sandwich, some homemade dessert and a fruit cup with fresh strawberries all in a decorative little basket which can serve as a memento of the day for years to come.

It's the time of year for all the senses to awaken.

Particularly smells have become powerful, the soap that arrived in the mail this week filled the bath with a marvelous fragrance and one of the best of nature's scents, the lilac appeared in many arrangements.

When the tour bus went by, I realized anew the advantages of living in the country where one can avoid one of the other scents from those pollution vehicles.

The days are starting earlier and earlier and with the arrival of daylight time, the dark tones of winter will be left in the shadows indeed.

Dorothy Givens says the birds go off at her house about 4:02; here I figure it's about 5:30 and then Virginia Clayton goes off about six and the other children always manage to arise extra early on weekends while you can't pry them out of bed on school days.

Saturday morning about 6:30 Jennifer was scurrying to the attic to fix the television antennas, being sure there was something wrong with the set when she couldn't get her favorite Metro-Media (at that hour they weren't even broadcasting)! Ah, kids! "Why can't they be like we were, perfect in every way? Oh, what's the matter with kids today?"

The merry month of May is fast filling with events as everyone wishes to spring from his and her cocoon simultaneous.

Keep Loudoun Beautiful luncheon is at the Laurel Brigade on Wednesday. Friday is the Apple Blossom Parade in Winchester. Then the circus is coming to Leesburg and the Round Hill Brownies are having a tea and the Women's Auxiliary of the Round Hill Fire Department invite the public to their food and rummage sales on the 13th at 9:30 at the Firehouse. Those wishing to donate items are asked to call 338-7057.

The tulips Mr. Martz has planted for sundry neighbors are rising majestically, filling the rooms with beauty here in a vase and the dogwood dot the mountain while paint brushes emerge.

The long hard winter is o'er!

May 11, 1972

Ah! May, it was time to be one with nature. Whether your style was pushing or riding a mower trying to down the invincible grass or hiking on top of the mountain on the trail or just cruising the auto, the warm sun felt fine and there were yellow violets, May apples, ant hills six feet long to be discovered.

A Mr. Fowler from Unison said he was afraid it was too late for mushrooms as he scanned the ground near poplar trees on the left side of Rt. 601.

On Sunday the Shenandoah ran swift and inviting to campers and picnickers at Watermelon Park – the inevitable fishing pole made its appearance and our young guest Doug Shoemaker from Bowie, Md. was proud to have caught a frog on his first overnight hike on the Appalachian Trail with his father while mom and daughter preferred the luxury of hot water at Clayton Hall.

Marvin Watts pursuing nature in his own way has adopted a raccoon dubbed Racquel who dines on hamburger (ground round) and eggs and makes her nest under the old logs under the porch in his cabin.

Gardens are beginning to send up tops of vegetables; the Robert Allders' rows look perfect and young son Eric turned three with a banana cake on Tuesday and older brother J.K. is now home from Loudoun Memorial after his pneumonia bout.

The stop gap on Friday after the torrents of rain from Tuesday on sent all the mowers sputtering but mine wanted to give up the ghost as Janet Payne gallantly undertook the task of attacking the jungle.

First Clyde Beck came to the rescue, cleaning out the choke, Lynn Carbaugh, Ruth Reid, and Lawrence Dawson put their muscle to cranking, then Russell Powell drew out a screwdriver and did something about the gas mixture and then when it conked out again, Marvin Mitchell found the trouble, a small spring on the choke assembly was missing.

Where else but in Bluemont would neighbors lend such a willing helping hand?

And aren't the dandelions thick this year?

The Robert Joneses are happy to announce the birth of another grandson, Herbert Harold Jones, born to Robert V. Jones, Jr. and his wife on April 21. The Winchester family have one other boy, Robert V. Jones, III. See that's how we get all those Bob Joneses in the telephone book.

Now at last we can officially congratulate Jean Dawson on her engagement to Mike Hoggott.

Shir Carbaugh announces that the Home Demonstration Club Meeting scheduled for May 16 has been postponed. Their guest speaker, Deputy Keyes will be very much involved at that time directing traffic for Transpo '72.

If anyone doubts Loudoun County is not growing, take a look at that!

The MYF invite all to their rummage and bake sales to be held this Saturday, May 13 at the Purcellville Firehouse. Donated items can be given to Belinda Dawson.

The Women's Auxiliary of the Round Hill Fire Department will make the same offer, the same day at the Round Hill Firehouse from 9:30 to 4 o'clock.

Marvin Watts doesn't have a monopoly on new pets. Miss Alley's new boarder is Ralph, a three-year old collie and the Becks' goat is still bellowing MAA (sounding like my children yelling Mom!) at the side door.

Howard Bass has just returned from a three-month concert tour of Europe and wishes to relocate in Bluemont or anywhere in Loudoun County.

I know the students and teachers have the days all counted out but only about a month of school remains and can you believe Tim Walsh, Rhonda Underwood, Ruth

Reid and Bruce Cochran are graduating from high school? Only yesterday they were freshman, it seems.

With more rainy days in sight, Mothers might welcome this recipe for home-made finger paint.

Combine one-half cup any detergent or one capful of liquid detergent; two tablespoons of liquid starch; poster paints or food coloring.

Beat detergent and starch with an egg beater until it is like thick marshmallow frosting. This makes enough for three or four pictures.

Divide mixture into jars and add different colors.

If mixture thickens too much to paint, add a little more starch and beat it in with a spoon.

Collages are fun too and a sunny day activity can be to collect the materials for a nature collage to be put together on a rainy day.

How's that for an idea of keeping the kids busy and beware ticks are back but with that light-green diffused over the countryside, who can complain about anything?

May 18, 1972

Suddenly the season had changed, no longer could one delay in putting out the shorts, the sandals, the short-sleeved shirts; the grass had to have another cutting, the caulking needed to be chipped out, the screens in the old windows put in place.

The gardens needed weeding, time to get a flea collar for the dog and there were meetings, classes, trips, births, sales and plans for meetings, classes, trips, births and more sales.

A tick came in with a bough from the woods and a big jack rabbit hurried by in his "I'm late, I'm late to a very important date" fashion in the backyard on Saturday evening.

The traffic swirled up the long hill at the side of the house and generally everyone was all in a flutter about something.

Beginning the week was our Supervisor's open meeting at the Purcellville Recreation Center.

I venture to have observed that 80 percent of the interested citizens were in their sixties, owning fairly large tracts of land.

They concentrated their gripes on increased taxation but I wondered if they caught James Brownell's vision that once the land is lost, there's no retrieving it. There was talk of the gas line earning a revenue of $100,000 a year for Loudoun County but isn't our mountain worth more than this?

Living here at the foot of the mountains, I am reminded of Hawthorne's story "The Great Stone Face." The hero Ernest felt he had a friend in the face etched in stone on the side of a mountain and we who live within the shadow of our rolling hill share that kinship with nature. Surely there's no price tag on this.

It's up to each individual citizen to express his sentiments to our supervisor, only we can save our county from desolation, suburban style – let's hope that we will see we must keep this open land intact for future generations to enjoy.

Some of the younger generation, students in Mrs. Scott's English classes at Valley High School collected litter and strung it together in a giant pyramid with a sign, "Litter Towers Over Us" to demonstrate the need to clean up the environment.

It's clean-up time again at the Ebenezer Church, Bloomfield in preparation for the annual Memorial Day Service. Friends and interested parties are asked to bring tools and meet at 8 o'clock on May 20 with an alternate rain date of the 27th. The Unison United Methodist Church women are treating the workers to lunch on the grounds. Sounds like a fun day to me!

A class to go right along with my "creative" people sale is being offered at Waterford by the Foundation beginning on May 22. The instructor Charles Harris of Baltimore will bring his antique tools and show participants how to repair wood antiques. Missing parts can be made, blending in with the original piece. For more information call Mrs. Charlotte Laing 338-6024.

Speaking of antiques I am indebted to Dorothy Smith, Round Hill of antique button-collecting fame for a book on antique bottle collecting, another of Dorothy's hobbies. According to the book, there are a half million of us antique bottle collectors in the country.

Of course, the hand-blown bottles without any seams, all in one piece, are the oldest, but then the next rule of thumb to determine the age of the bottle is to remember the closer to the top of the bottle the seams extend, the more recent was the production of the bottle.

Karlton Monroe, the prize collector of them all, says he saves all glass, metal and wood items and in years to come they become antiques.

I found out Herbert Martz is a coin collector; he has 200 Kennedy half-dollars still just worth 50 cents but he claims the Eisenhower silver dollars are already worth a dollar and a half.

And at my sale I'm offering old sheet music for sale, it seems they would be darling for framing with the old sketches on the cover.

The W.S.C.S. of the Methodist Church is planning a Flea Market for June 24. Maybe we can combine forces and have a really furious day in Bluemont with the MYF selling sandwiches on the lawn. Clyde Beck offering art in the barn, while vendors hawk their wares at the schoolhouse.

I never did get back to all the Jack Bardon's news as I was dashing for the door when the call came about their fabulous three-month trip to Central America.

Their daughter is a dean's lister at Madison again this semester while son Michael already having earned a B.S. from California State Technological College graduated May 8 from Pennsylvania Bible Seminary.

When I saw Rhonda Underwood in the halls the other day at Valley High School she told me there were 14 more days of school for the seniors and after graduation a goodly number of the class were heading for Virginia Beach for one grand beach party!

Sorry about leaving Jimmy Campbell out in my senior list last week.

Saturday evening found Rhonda hitting a homerun for the Bluemont Women's Team in their first softball game of the season, taking a 11-9 loss to the visiting team.

The Robert D. Beetons spent a delightful weekend in Lexington, enjoying a particularly delicious meal in the Greek restaurant there. Upon arriving home Mrs. Beeton looked up the recipe in her many cookbooks, another collection and collector among us.

Al Serber and a host of friends from the Washington area relished the greenery at the Waldrops' place over the weekend, they themselves spent Saturday here and Miss Susy Neal came for a sojourn in her old cabin at the turn of the mountain lane while Justine and Brian Beck led the children in the store and back for a Mother's Day gift, wrapping it in a special package with yellow feathers and the purple flowers of the Empress tree burst into bloom as another May week matured into summer.

May 25, 1972

In fertile Northern Virginia this week not only does the grass look greener on the other side of the fence, it looks greener on this side of the fence. In fact, just where is the fence? The grass, weeds if you like, have engulfed the fence, walls and gravel paths.

Bluemont is looking a bit raggedy around the edges but unless your mower is going full blast the two sunny days of the week, there's no chance to catch up.

Waiting for a pleasant day in May in order to stroll over with the baby and poke my nose in the new neighbors' business, I've waited in vain for about a month so rain or shine, we were introduced this weekend.

The two ambitious couples who are literally redoing Mrs. Powell's house, replacing indoor, outdoor walls and ceilings are Leslie and Ken Hutchins and Mary Lynn and Curtis Budny presently at a Hyattsville, Md. address.

They hope to be permanent residents as of July 1.

Of course, I had to get the story behind their sign, "The Snow House." Young Kenny about five years of age always referred to it as the snow house because each time they came for a viewing there was snow on the ground, not at all uncommon for Bluemont. Finally that name seemed more suitable than Willow Brook, Mountain View, etc.

So welcome!

On two of the nicer days the Women's Team took a defeat and Herbert Martz told me he had rewarded the "Underwood" girl with five dollars for hitting a home run.

A decade of Bluemont News

Only in a small town could such a mistake be made as Mr. Martz was just a generation behind, the Underwood girl was actually the mother of our present star, Jill Reed. Her mother, Janet was an Underwood and so it was Rhonda Underwood's first cousin who really hit the homer.

More softball team news was that Donna Kelley entertained the Loudoun Valley Girls High School team last week for a big picnic down at their home, the J.J. Kelley's.

Valley had a 8-2 record with Donna playing catcher and former Bluemonter twins Glenda and Linda Knutson filling important positions.

These girls plus Valley player Barbara Smith will hopefully help bring in the victories for the Bluemont Girls Team this summer.

On one of those other sunny days this week, we had a sorta surprise baby shower luncheon for Harriet Murtaugh now of the Bluemont countryside.

I hearken back to the Biblical injection that if your neighbor has a guest, lend him food and drink so he may entertain graciously because that's just what I did.

The Becks loaned me chairs, June Lloyd brought flowers for arranging, Helen Freedman made her specialty, the cheese cake made from the recipe of Lindy's Restaurant in New York and Janet Payne and Gary Ross helped me cut the grass.

And definitely one of Bluemont's unsung heroes is Martin Mitchell. Always he is so gracious, lending a mechanical hand to a neighbor in need.

Incidentally, I sure wish someone would lend a helping hand to The Helping Hand who will be forced out of business as of June 1 if they can't find another location.

If you have a barn or unused house or building you would be willing to lease, call William Steward, Purcellville.

Bruce Reed, son of Mr. and Mrs. Lucien Reed will graduate June 9 from the Navy Recruit Training Center in Orlando, Fla.

Brother and sister Jill and Timmy will make the trip down to see the ceremony after which Bruce will report for further duty in Memphis, Tenn.

We'll be glad when he can return for a visit up North way here in the heart of the Confederacy, Virginia.

Bruce remembered mom on Mother's Day with a long distance call and having had a week and a half to reflect on the occasion, it's a pretty good time for us matriarchs.

Blessed be the convenience of Mann's Store where the children found me a lovely washcloth and secondly, everyone should have a mother like mine.

For Mother's Day she brought a Swiss steak, strawberry shortcake dinner to me and my family along with the accumulated clippings on poisonous plants, craft ideas, child-rearing clues plus magazines, lipsticks, containers for dried arrangements and a fresh geranium plant.

I have a pretty rich heritage to pass on to my own children in the cycle that is the only thanks a mother wants, for her child to be a kind and loving to their own siblings.

Another fine occasion we don't want to overlook was the 65th wedding anniversary of the Earl C. Idens celebrated in April with the family group, daughters Mrs. Howard Sprague of Purcellville and Mrs. Earl Virts of Bluemont along with their families.

Now the Idens have been prominent in the Bluemont news for a number of years.

Among my treasured old song sheets was found a copy of the former Purcellville newspaper The Blue Ridge Herald, May 2, 1940. This paper included the Bluemont column with the news item about the Earl C. Idens attending the Iden reunion of New York, Pennsylvania and Virginia at the Willard Hotel on Sunday afternoon.

Our sympathy to the Dean family of Round Hill on the loss of their son.

More local color is the secondhand story on gardening tips coming from Mary Ann Carter repeating Herman Vincke who says in order to prevent mice from destroying your tulip bulbs, plant daffodil bulbs in between.

Secondly, Herbert Martz and I agree on a number of things, namely there's no place like Bluemont for pleasant living with the best neighbors in the world and a strong feeling that a gate ought to be kept closed.

His words, "I always felt a gate wasn't any account, unless it was kept closed!"

So come for a visit but close the gate behind you!

Exciting news is the report of television star, Betsy Jones Moreland visiting on the mountain with her cousin, Ambrose Moreland.

Miss Moreland was noting the desolation of the land with the new road construction and other signs of city growth.

Perhaps Loudoun's problem could be solved if we could somehow have people say, "Loudoun's a nice place to visit, but I wouldn't want to live there."

Let's accommodate the population we have but provide no additional city services.

If you want to rejuvenate an old house – fine – but please no sub-dividing.

What's uglier than a little brick rambler on every lush hill?

And the Transpo signs dot the major roads.

Welcome visitors!

June 1, 1972

A full moon hung brightly over the village mid-week as the big Memorial Day weekend approached.

Bluemonters generally are stay-at-homers – whether we claim lack of traveling expenses or just contentment where we are, we stick close by the wildly growing grass, mowing, clipping, filling up the gallon jars from Idens' pump, sighing with relief that another four-day growth has been conquered.

It was a week here of sorting clothes, sale items and then in logical order came laundry – you know that's that tedious washing and ironing.

My mother-in-law (bless her seamster heart) had helped with the fitting from all the downstairs trunks on Saturday when something prompted me to go up to the attic on Monday and there was a whole new wardrobe for three growing children.

Hand-me-downs! How I loathed them as a kid (that's what we called children then, too) – how I love them as a parent!

It's the time of year for students to show off their talents and so last Sunday Mrs. Judy Lewis' piano students gave a lovely recital at the Purcellville Library – our Lynn Carbaugh played The Wedding March and The Beating Song.

Then the young artists of the village exhibited some of their works at the Blue Ridge Middle School Art Show.

Kelley Lloyd, Larry Cochran, Desiree Allder and Debra Dawson represented Bluemont.

On Wednesday, the first and fourth grades at Round Hill Elementary School presented The Little Red Hen and A Trip Around the World, two musical productions.

Bluemonters really shone there with Wanda Reid, Brian Beck, April Wilt, Mark Allder, Jennifer Johnson, Pam Ross, Donna Lowe and Bobby Lee participating in The Little Red Hen play and Pam Carbaugh, Polly Riggleman, Stevie Carter, Glen Kelley, Jimmy Payne, Steve Dawson, Jimmy Whirley, Debby Ross, Jay Allder singing and dancing in a Trip Around the World.

Pam Carbaugh really stole the show as a white lady cat and a special honor went to Jay Allder who was chosen as one of the four best citizens in the fourth grade. In a lovely gesture they passed out long-stemmed snapdragons to the audience as a finale.

They brought back a good memory, my mother always had a bed of them each summer and how my brothers and I used to love to pick them and make them snap, tormenting and chasing one another around the side of the house.

Only too soon, the latest addition to the Bluemont family will be an elementary school student.

Norma and Clinton Hindman are proud parents of their first child, a boy born May 24, weighing seven pounds, four ounces.

I didn't delay to ask the tired new auntie Ivy Cochran more about him, but she did tell me a shower was given in Norma's honor several weeks ago with about 30 guests with one of her special cakes at her home.

Another cute story to come from the Cochran's confines concerns the appearance of their old black car we all assumed was a new blue car. In actuality, the black car had a new blue paint job.

Not only were the villagers fooled but when our neighbor mechanic Russell Powell now at Allder's Esso in Round Hill looked the car over he said, "Funny this car has the same trouble that old black Buick of yours had!"

Another very important graduation is at Madison College, Harrisonburg where we are proud to acknowledge our neighbor, Jean Dawson's concentrated four-year effort earning her B.A. degree.

Al Serber was back in town for the weekend announcing that his book which includes Clyde Beck's sketch of the famed Pandas will be off the press in two weeks.

Bill and Shir Carbaugh went for a two-some hike up at Big Meadows, Skyline Drive over the weekend while Mr. and Mrs. Joseph Smith entertained the Talbert Youngs from Martinsburg.

The Walton Manns slipped a trip in up to visit son and daughter-in-law, Tom and Ruth, in Philadelphia and it was spring cleaning time at the Methodist Church and the report all over town was that Walton Mann personally put the finishing soap touches on the beautiful old windows.

The Methodists are on the move again and there isn't a dry eye in Bluemont – Homer and Ethel Hall are moving on – fortunately close-by to Broad Run Farms.

They have led us well, now we must prove our wings without them to lean upon – we must fly alone – richer and wiser for our relationship with them. They have prepared us for this day – now we can stand on the strength they have helped us see that we can possess with God's guidance.

Plans are formulating for the W.S.C.S. Flea Market at the schoolhouse on June 24; I'll have my barn sale at the same time – so come bring your lunch or buy some goodies here and picnic on the lawn with us and if it rains, we'll let you eat on the porch. Of course, there couldn't be any possibility of showers, especially on a Saturday.

Now May puts away her finery for another year, counting on June to ripen the cherries and float the intoxicating nectar of the peonies on the still warm night air.

June 15, 1972

The calendar registered the middle of June but a cool Canadian air flow enveloped our mountain village over the weekend sending natives to the wood piles so a fire could be laid on the hearth, and a fresh pot of hot coffee was set to spluttering on the back burners.

The heavy quilt mother had lovely covered years ago when she sent her innocent child to the big wide world of college felt right on Saturday night and teeth were seen to chatter among the spectators of the Women's Softball team game that evening.

All this news came my way when I attempted to find a babysitter for Sunday evening; first of all, three sitters were eliminated when the William Carbaughs took in the Craft Fair at Harpers Ferry, a worthy event, I'm sure.

Mrs. Clarence Manuel told me the cool air was Canadian and that Ruth was still visiting in Herndon, then Glen Lloyd was the fellow making the fire and lending the coffee pot, anticipating the big Lloyd reunion on Sunday in Berryville.

A very special creature by nature, he speculated on a good time, pronouncing it fun when you could visit and eat all the finest of delicacies at the same time.

My Bethesda-based parents had to give me the news that our neighbor Jim Brownell had been seen on a television newscast. I'm too busy generally writing the Bluemont news or talking to the neighbors attempting to gather the Bluemont news to watch the television news.

Emma Mann gave me the progress report for the W.S.C.S. Flea Market slated for June 24.

The Hamilton Craft Shop ladies will be demonstrating and selling their California crafts, Harry Dennis with lamps and that type item will have a booth while the Women's Group of Pine Grove Episcopal Church will have a rummage stand.

William Morris of Hamilton with antiques, and a little bit of everything will be here while Barbara Sheldon of Round Hill will sell jewelry.

Frances Ballenger is to have her antique shop open in the old store and I have two saddles, a horse trailer, chairs, lamps, building supplies, auto parts, television tubes and five hundred balloons that must go!

This week brought the roses, more strawberries, honeysuckle (that divine fragrance), lightning bugs and even more birds.

A wild canary flittered in my pear tree on Wednesday while village young hummed with delight over the school closing for summer vacation.

Jimmy Campbell among the high school graduates will begin work on a fulltime basis at Doubleday while Sam Kelley reunited with his family, home from boarding school for the summer.

The teachers among us were glad to relax too after so many "students' dirty looks." Shirley Lynn from Round Hill Elementary was seen on a Bluemont Walking Tour with her husband Tom and about five other couples last Sunday, pursuing the Good Humor man who had stopped for a Coke on Mann's Store porch.

We saved our baby food jars for Hilda Dutrow who was fast filling them with strawberry jelly and Nelson Foster of Richmond wrote reporting that his aunt dated the Snow House, place of his birth, at 1840.

Now yard work has never been my tour de force but the axiom, "Necessity is the Mother of invention" applies here and it was a pretty good feeling to spade up the earth, rocky soil that it is.

The Carbaughs' generous gift of the tomato plants needed attention and if the plants do well as the stray seed that fell on rocky ground a season ago, the Johnsons' many jars will be filled with the citrus acid of tomatoes, a good substitute for orange juice in the winter so I've been told.

This all leads me to pass on the secret of peeling an onion while maintaining a dry eye in the house.

As you begin, turn on the cold tap water, wetting your fingers and the vegetable – I haven't cried in years over onions – that is!

One television series that always leaves me blubbering is "Hazel." If the world were made of such straight-forward loving persons as she, it would have to be a better place.

Jennifer always asks why I'm crying and when I tell her I just like "Hazel," she always wants immediately to engage her as our maid. Who wouldn't? Shirley Booth really made that comic strip so believable!

"I'd like to teach the world to sing in perfect harmony…!"

June 22, 1972

The fire engines screeched and roared through town Saturday evening, cars sped by and this pace like a house a-fire has been the pattern of the week in Bluemont.

Here at Clayton Hall I've investigated every nook and cranny in this old house searching successfully for saleable items.

The "lofty" room above the old kitchen had a piece of marble just like Trudy Verloop ordered, the barn held treasures like a fine Victorian bed, a soft leather trunk, a quaint old scale, two fireless stoves, an old mirror all from the days when Donald Clayton occupied the barn instead of the house.

With the wind blowing there, it can be an eerie place but the workmanship in the high rafters and giant timbers make it a pleasant spot too, to put in some "dusting and hauling" hours.

If the tropical storm doesn't develop that Emma Mann heard was scheduled for the day, this Saturday, June 24 promises to be a really eventful one in Bluemont.

The W.S.C.S. has their Flea Market lined up for the schoolhouse and there they will be serving lunch too.

The M.Y.F. will have available baked goods and drinks here at the barn and the kids are starting their balloon blowing. Lara so far is the champion blower-upper!

The summer schedule is somewhat frenzied already.

Back to the J.H.H. Verloops, they gave a lovely party for daughter, Emily and her fiancé John Thomas, last Sunday evening.

John's family was represented by his grandmother from Falls Church, a charming lady who knew Bluemont in its train-whistling days. John's parents formerly Baltimorians have moved to Greenville, S.C. so it was a little far to come for a cool June Sunday get-together on top of the mountain.

The Purcellville Library Bookmobile will be at the Bluemont School on Tuesdays, July 4 and 18, and Aug. 1, 15 and 19 from 10 a.m. until 11 a.m.

It's always fun to see the Paul Strangs again and the John Markles, Mrs. Faye Willkie and it was nice to meet Col. and Mrs. Hilary who have enjoyed their mountain retreat here now for about 25 years.

He told me of their fire shortly after they had moved in and how he knows how to spend his retirement taking a daily early-morning walk on the mountain side.

Mr. McClure said the Mountain laurel was beautiful up at their place as on the trail and I got an invite up there.

If one would take up the neighbors' invitations, there would be no need to travel widely, the sights right here in Bluemont are some of the most edifying in the state.

There was talk of Bear's Den and Betsy Jones Moreland got a wonderful letter this week from Mrs. Maud Alton, formerly of the mountain and now of Purcellville, reminiscing about Betsy's aunt churning her butter, gathering the eggs she sold to close-by neighbors. There aren't too many places left where the day brings such chores as those now.

Last weekend the Louis Underwoods were treated royally to a 27th anniversary dinner at Peter Pan Inn in Urbanna, Md. by daughter Beverley and husband Russell Powell.

Rhonda Underwood, graduating from Valley High School just last week has won a full scholarship to the Vienna Culture School, also Belinda Sue Dawson, a Junior won for the second straight year, the typing award at Valley High School.

Other news at the Dawsons was that visiting with Charles and Grace and Mrs. Nellie Tibbs on Saturday, June 3 were Mr. and Mrs. W.P. Lambert, son Emory, of Philomont, with Mr. and Mrs. Leland Lambert, Mrs. Belle Fincham of Fairfax and Elmer Lambert of Bland County, Va.

This past weekend brought son, Anthony, and Miss Melody Howard as guests to the Dawson home.

There was lots of news at the Brownells.

Diana, Bruce's wife, got a vacation away from the kids and the domestic round, spending a week with her sister in Georgia.

Susan Brownell Vondel is now graduated from the University of Virginia and in the fall she and hubby will be with the Department of the Army in Texas.

Mark has completed his first year at Tennessee Tech and this summer will be taking a six-week course at Officers Candidates School at Quantico.

Mac's sister, Rosalie Shipmen arrived for a visit this week from Charlotte, N.C. and I heard about the divine wedding reception for Joyce Nichols, daughter of Mr. and Mrs. Edward E. Nichols, Jr. from Purcellville on the lawn at Whitehall Farm.

It had a romantic tale connected with it as it had been the meeting place of the couple last Fourth of July.

Another wedding anniversary the town is buzzing about is the upcoming 50th of Herbert and Lucy Martz to be celebrated on July 1.

At the Bluemont Citizens Meeting, Wednesday night there was much talk about the Fourth of July celebration and Bluemont will stay traditional and set off fireworks on Tuesday, the 4th!

Beginning at 7 o'clock, the homemade ice cream and cake will be served, Lou and his Blue Valley Boys will give that country music we all love and then at dusk – the piece de resistance – the fireworks!

The flag will wave from the schoolhouse and Marvin Watts promised a surprise to villagers for a return to the really traditional style of celebrating.

Clarence Tinsman of Middleburg, is now picking up our trash once a month, the third Saturday. He couldn't have picked a better time for me! Today the attic, the old kitchen, the barn, tomorrow – the world!

The Department chairmen for the Bluemont Fair will meet Monday – time to get the machinery rolling again for the Oct. 21, 22 event.

This upcoming weekend couldn't be fuller with more activity than if the Fair itself was running.

Saturday are the sales, Saturday evening Howard Bass on guitar, John Shortridge on flute and Thad Barter singing will present English Folk Song arrangements at Clyde Beck's studio at 8:15 p.m.

Sunday, the community is invited to a reception honoring Homer and Ethel Hall, our beloved friends who will be leaving the Bluemont, Philomont and Round Hill Methodist charges for residency in Broad Run Farms where at one time I was thick with all the good Baptists.

All are invited to come from 7-9 p.m. to the Round Hill Methodist Church Social Hall.

I hear too Lincoln High School will have its reunion at the Round Hill Fire Department Hall on Saturday night.

When all this activity dies down, I'll want to start my Bluemont Garden Tours again.

I did manage to get one in last week. Well, I should say two, the John Carters have an upper and lower garden and my do the beets, onions, tomato plants, potato plants look healthy and in plowing Mary Ann is finding miniatures for a bottle collection at the same time.

Things were so busy here last Sunday with a visit from my parents, I didn't get to chat long with Miss Frances Gavens who dropped by with a delightful poem about Snickersville – the last part poetically describing Bluemont's decline after the railroad demise:

"Genteel Bluemont
shabby and spent
vacant houses
stores for rent,
porches sagging
railings bent."

If Marian Holland, the poet could only see it now! See you on Saturday.

June 29, 1972

Agnes – they called her – with the biggest capital A to ever hit the country.

Rivers, streams, creeks raging out of control – as far as Ohio the storm roared, as northern as Maine, as southern as Florida where the disaster first made its tremendous force known on the coast-line.

The worst flood in the history of the country to have hit such a wide area so the reports went.

Bluemont had its problems naturally, the Robert Joneses lost their freezer due to basement flooding, the Vinckes' property was floating in their cellar high up there on the mountain, the David Freedmans' pump was underwater but probably the worst disaster was the terrific gush of water that spilled and spilled and spilled into the Robert Allder's basement.

The sight of that water streaming underneath their cars in the drive was one of the saddest, unbelievable sights I have ever seen.

Something must be done about this drainage problem heightened by the construction of the new road.

"Tales of the Shenandoah" is a whole other book that could be written so I hear, houses and furniture floating down river and for my former Broad Run Farms neighbors, I truly lament.

Pumps were burned up. One dealer informed Delores Hall of Round Hill who was looking for such an item that he had sold 47 Thursday morning and the Round Hill Fire Department, bless their hearts, were on call, pumping, pumping, pumping in the most congenial rescuing manner.

Most of the community so involved with problem-solving did not know that Robert Hindman of Hamilton, father of our beloved Ivy Cochran had passed away on Tuesday.

Mr. Hindman had spent his youth in Bluemont and with his passing went many unrecorded tales of places and people of the area 50 years ago.

The Hindmans are unique; people like that don't come down the pike every day.

Right before the heavy rains Ethel Leffingwell came over for a chat, lingering till about four when I was to drive her home on my way to the Cochrans and then did it pour. Ethel was convinced she would spend the night in town and then we went colonial style here as the electricity went off just as the report of the flood damage came over the television.

Ethel reports that she is the only Senior Girl Scout from Loudoun County to serve on the Advisory Council for the District of Columbia, Maryland and Virginia. The council works as a right-arm to the Board of Directors who decides policies and programs for the organization.

Too, before the excitement, Jack Bardon and I had a pleasant chat, he telling me of his and Claire's recent participation in the music activities at the Glenville State Folk Festival in West Virginia. It was a banjo and fiddle concert and uniquely Jack plays the harmonica and guitar together without a prop for the harmonica.

Sounds like the perfect program for the next Bluemont music presentation.

Beating Jack to the strumming, however, will be the anticipated Bluemont Fourth celebration with Lou and his Blue Valley Boys.

There will be homemade ice cream and cakes as usual and fireworks and guess what? Five hundred Bluemont Fair balloons did not go on Saturday so there will be balloons for the kiddies and bell-ringing and all on Tuesday, the real honest-to-goodness Fourth of July!

The festivities will begin at 7 o'clock. You all come!

Now about the Flea Market and Barn Sale – Emma Mann warned us she had heard about this tropical storm.

Nevertheless, there were some treasures at the Flea Market. I found a lovely little luncheon set made in Switzerland with a teapot, cups, saucers and luncheon plates – dishes – my weakness and the Corleys had some great items. I love my enamel ware coffee pot and the Hamilton California craft shop lady was just great telling us a fascinating story of her friendship with the niece of Charles Schultz, creator of Peanuts. The niece's name is Pat and her personality is the basis for her uncle's Peppermint Patty.

And talk of talent, Larry Cochran had some marvelous oils of pastoral scenes.

There was a Grandfather's Day reunion in honor of Tyson Payne in Bluemont, last Sunday. The list of guests went on and on – the O.L. Paynes of Winchester, the C.E. Paynes and Ty of Bluemont, Mrs. Deila Heflin and son Dennis of Boyce, Mrs. Margaret Fincham and daughter Pam from Bluemont, David Heflin of Boyce, Brenda Wisecarver – Richmond, the Julian Christs and Liza from Falls Church, the Richard Roystons of Maryland, Dorothy Lloyd and children from Falls Church, the Dennis Lloyds of Falls Church, Gary Payne now stationed in Parris Island, S.C., his bride-to-be Pam Dyke of Winchester, the Mike Paynes of Winchester, Luther Royston of Washington, the Robert Millers, Winchester, Miss Eunice Payne, Bluemont, William Hunt, Maryland, and Mike Gossom, Falls Church.

The week before Sandy DiFilipo had been here full with the plans for the first Lucketts Farm and Church Tour.

It sounds just terrific – just what Betsy Jones Moreland and I ordered. Besides the tour, the old school grounds will have an art exhibit, 1912 vintage classroom recreated, Indian artifacts, ham and turkey dinners on July 22 and 23. Tickets, $2 block, $4 a family.

A hay ride and corn on the cob – What could be more fun?

A farewell reception for the Rev. and Mrs. Homer Hall and daughter Janice was held Sunday evening in the Round Hill Church when the three charges presented them with an engraved silver bowl. No one is saying goodbye – just we'll be seeing you!

So passed a perilous week for villagers and mountaineers, generally assured they were high above flood water territory. Perhaps we all should be thankful no real tragedy in our community took place.

July 6, 1972

The rains came again and then on Saturday, it was hot – a July hot – a day Northern Virginians could cope with – this they had known before.

Air-conditioners were cranked up, long tresses pulled into pony tails and up-swepts and all were home free, on familiar ground, complaining about this terribly hot weather!

Here at Clayton Hall, the windows are still caulked – it's about like cave-living in an old stone house-50 degrees year-round.

The big event of the week was the 50th wedding anniversary of Herbert and Lucy Martz. And was it a golden affair!

The old auditorium of the school was festooned in gold and white crepe paper, there were three bride and groom cakes, sandwiches (2000 to be exact), cookies, punch, chips and rings for everyone, party favors, and Richard Nixon sent a congratulatory greeting.

The gifts were legion with ne'er a duplicate.

Gold clocks, gold watches, gold necklaces, gold pins, a silver creamer and sugar, golden silverware, towels, sheets, bedspreads, quilts, vases, glassware, ceramic ware, an electric bean pot, candle stick holders, golden salt and pepper shakers topped off by Bill and Judy Casey's gift of a new straw hat and bright red handkerchief for Herbert.

The Martzs are one grand family and we only wish we could wish them another happy 50 more years together.

It was moving day here too – Charles and Sue Hall were moving out to Leesburg while the Hutchins and Budnys finally were taking over the former Powell House for good while reconstruction goes on.

As we go to press, the ice cream list grows longer at Mann's Store, Marvin Watts debates about the flavor to make in his gallon and a half freezer – "Raspberry probably", he says, adding he had some with whipped cream for breakfast.

He is oiling the old bell, lining up bell-ringers.

Clyde Beck was transporting chairs to the school grounds and here we must start the balloon blowing again.

The William Carbaughs' house will be decked out in a new color for the occasion – a lovely gold siding is going up.

While life was hardly serene at Whit Haven, the Tom Murtaughs place near the river as the water continued to rise, Harriet waited till it was all over and slipped to Columbia Hospital and had a healthy seven-pound, 14 ounce boy. Thank heavens, the water subsided so they didn't have to go by boat!

Glad to hear Brad Campbell is back home after a stay in the hospital.

Congratulations to Shephard Clifton, son of Mrs. Jessica Clifton of Pine Grove who graduated with honors from Miami-Dade College this June.

Some years ago a fellow student wrote a poem, "Strangers and Pilgrims", which caught the essence of the destruction that now is invading our county.

His area was the now suburban sprawl of Philadelphia, now he's a professor at the same little college we attended and with his permission I quote some of these beautiful lines.

He speaks of land before it was sub-divided when his grandfather came to pick out the site for his home on the then hundreds of undeveloped acres of woods and pastureland.

"He wasn't sentimental, but he knew what a landscape does for a man's soul,
When he's tamed it in spots, and sprinkled his sweat and memories over it,
And then steps back to watch the sunset bless it.

Somehow that's the part of this place that I think of,
When I think of it all at once,
How I used to harvest armfuls of those flowers,
And dance back, wet footed across the stones that always had a traitor among them.
Then, with my cheeks burning in their blue springtime smell,
I'd dump the treasure in my mother's arms,
She always improvised another mason jar,
To vase the dying beauty.

It was a kingdom, a place to exercise dominion in, like God told Adam to do,
Where I could test my own ideas without crawling up a neighbor's back,

And make him the bother of having to catch up with my latest idiosyncrasy,
To keep from running short of good conversation at the club,
When the pennant race wasn't hot enough to get interested in.

It was a place to teach my children how to live,
With plenty of object lessons handy,
We're strangers and pilgrims, all of us,
We're looking for a home, a home we can keep."

July 13, 1972

The mowers whine, the birds titter, the children shout, scrapping – these are the sounds of summer that come in the open windows.

July and all the country's a vacation-land – time to raise prices for the tourist trade – toot the horn at a big truck on the turnpike – some of the Bluemont family have slipped away on trips – the farmers begin their busiest season, planting, reaping, canning, freezing.

Brad Campbell let me in on their over-night stay to Baltimore where the Allen Campbells took in the Baltimore Orioles game.

The Fourth was very well celebrated in Bluemont this year with our guest list estimated at 650 and happily we sold 150 Bluemont Fair balloons and ate our way through 27 gallons of ice cream.

Ivy Cochran wishes to thank those who contributed the ice cream and cake for the event; the country music by Louella Robey and his Blue Valley Boys put just the right touch on the occasion.

With the busy Fourth behind us, Mary Alice Wertz proposed a trip to Kutztown Folk Festival near Allentown in Pennsylvania.

We dared it with seven children, returning to Loudoun County convinced it was a mistake.

The crowds were unbelievable, as we rode along a country lane to the approach to the fairgrounds, we delighted in the scenery only to find the ground edged by a sub-division with parking concessions on every lawn.

The hosts were great, the crowds frequenting the fair – a good sort but too many human beings in one spot is bad news – Clyde Beck, I believe, is right – let's keep the Bluemont Fair at a reasonable size.

The best part of the trip was the individual touch we got by staying overnight in a young couple's old brick farm house. You don't get a comfortable mattress in an old brass bed in a motel!

And then dinner at the Memins Hotel, an old stone structure with antiques hanging on the mantle, arranged on the wide window sills and a friendly small-town atmosphere run by one family for seven generations was perfect with a Pennsylvania Dutch dinner of chicken pot pie with thick, savory dumplings and big chunks of chicken, slaw, ice tea and homemade bread for $1.85.

But then it was good, hitting Route 15 in Loudoun County, no more billboards enticing the kids – the greatest consumers in the world, seeing the black-eyed susans at the side of the road, stopping for a milkshake at McDonald's in Leesburg – we were home!

The Bluemont Citizens met this week – To build a shed or not to build a shed – that is the question!

The debate goes on. More citizens are needed at these meetings to decide these issues; we would like to know the wishes of all the citizens.

A special committee is meeting with the board of supervisors on our drainage problem.

July promises some special delights – here we are anticipating the Lucketts Farm and Church Tour with a hayride and corn on the cob slated for July 22, 23 and on the 22nd our own Citizens Association will host another wonderful Blue Grass Group, Johnnie Whisnant and the Courtrymen at 8:30 at the old school auditorium with a paid admission of $2.

Shir Carbaugh invites the women of the community to the Bluemont Home Demonstration Club meeting on July 18 at 7:30 p.m. led by the Sheriff's Department on the topic, "Self-Protection for Women."

Next Sunday is the Methodist Church picnic at Camp Highroad with members meeting at the church at 1:30 p.m.

A reminder to villagers of the trash collection this Saturday, the third of each month.

In expectation of Jean Dawson's Aug. 5 wedding, Miss Hilda Payne, Mrs. Eston King and Mrs. Mary Ellen Simpson gave a lovely bridal shower at the King's home on Sunday afternoon.

Grace Dawson tells me Anthony is now scheduled for training in New York State near the Canadian border where the nights promise to be cool and crisp, year-round.

July 20, 1972

The flicker of the flame in a campfire, a guitar strummed on the front porch, rich homemade ice cream being eaten on the cool lawn – the intense July heat is here again and the activities that made Bluemont an attractive spot for vacationers are being re-enacted.

As Saturday night started off, it was still hot and Bluemonters were socializing, talking of the days of Bluemont's glory, drinking in the mountain breezes.

Harold provided a fruit salad with blackberries he had picked at his doorstep, marshmallows for toasting and wonderful company.

The Leon Brunelles were there (Thelma and I could talk for hours about the Bluemont of yesteryear) with their guests. Dr. Leonard Kephart, a fine gentleman who frequented

Jane King's boarding house years ago, and Thelma's niece, Lynn Donaldson, and fiancé, Chuck Kuhn of Hyattsville.

Chris Deale, now a student at Catholic University was up at her parents' place that was that same boarding house years ago.

Of course, Don and Kay Seidenspinner were there and their four girls with their guests, Don's sister, Mrs. Patsy Roberts and son Tom and Kay's mother, Mrs. Ruth Townshend.

The mountain breeze was divine – the whole evening a delight!

And lo and behold as I came down the mountain road home there was Betsy Jones Moreland and Ambrose Moreland in their big mobile home trying for a breeze on the top of the ridge and down here next door the city folks from Georgetown were trying out the Becks' patio while the Becks were trying out theirs in Georgetown, exchange style.

They quickly absorbed the Bluemont way of thoughtfulness – Jack valiantly starting my lawnmower for me again, and again on Sunday.

The Glen Lloyds were cranking up their usual super ice cream, that rich cream makes it so good!

Hope, Kelley, and Mary Jo will be going by auto-train to Florida with older sister Ann and husband Paul Wilson come next week.

Scot Butler was out trimming up his grass while Ken Hutchins with his guitar serenaded the close neighbors, the Lawrence Dawsons rocking in their green wicker rocking chair on their front porch.

Ginger Spring of West River, Md., and daughter of Tom Spring came for a visit to her grandmother's, Mrs. Barbara Spring, this week.

Sad word was received too that Charles Westley Spring, father of our Tom, David and Jane passed away last week in Alexandria.

The James Allders are back from their glorious two-week vacation at Myrtle Beach, S.C. and Doris as usual is sporting a tan that makes the rest of us mountaineers look sick.

They also stopped by the Hatcher's in Del Ray, Fla., took in Cypress Gardens and Disneyworld and they still can afford to put that autumn-gold siding on their house!

Back too from a Florida trip are Emma and Walton Mann looking tan and healthy.

Here we are looking forward to the Lucketts Farm and Church Tour on July 22, 23, the Blue Grass Music next Saturday night at the school at 8:30, Justine Beck's birthday party, the twins' and Lynn Carbaugh's birthday.

July in Bluemont is a time for fun and games and the canning of 20 gallons of beans by Ivy Cochran.

Sunday brought rain not on our "parade" but on our picnic.

Bluemont Methodists settled in the roofed-in shelter while Emma Mann and I had a nice chat with former pastor, the Rev. Lupton Simpson who amazingly was picnicking on the land that his father sold to the Methodists in the forties – well, partially gave away as he says, 125 acres went for $1400 and they sold $300 worth of timber off it in the first year.

The wonderful rustic setting of Camp Highroad holds out a hope that not all of our land is sub-divided yet.

After such a full weekend, Monday morning comes early. See you at the Lucketts Fair!

July 27, 1972

Intense…blazing…brilliant…adjectives to describe a new book or play? No – here in Bluemont, the countryside and village – this is the language personifying the sun's rays. The asphalt is melting, major roads are buckling. Thelma Brunelle says the forecast is the same through Tuesday.

Through the heat this week, cabbage came to full growth; berries in the thickets were ripe for picking.

Herbert Martz as usual has a good crop of cabbage, squash and onions and next week, he says there will be tomatoes.

Mary Lynn Budny and Leslie Hutchins were delighted to find the raspberries abundant in their uncleared backyard and so they're stirring up jam.

It was a week of breakdowns – Herbert Martz and I are both having 'tractor trouble" while Martin Mitchell has spent his week up and down a ladder adjusting the pump – with gallons upon gallons of water needed each day – what a time for it to blow!

The creatures of the sky and earth are still making their visitation to the village homes.

I knew things were to be leisurely Sunday after a week of University of Virginia extension classes in Leesburg, an exciting trip to the Lucketts Fair on Saturday and a full evening of Bluegrass entertainment the night before, so when the baby began fussing at eight o'clock Sunday morning, I resolved I would get her a bottle and settle down to the writing of the Bluemont news while the other girls continued to sleep. Ahem – "The best-laid plans of mice and men go astray!"

There stretched out in the hall to greet me was a four-foot blacksnake that Clyde Beck pronounced as mean!

Serenity – thou art a light year away!

Mary Lynn Budny reports she let out a screech or two too when a bat flew down into the living room early in the morning as George McGovern was making his acceptance speech.

At the top of the week, Justine Beck celebrated her ninth birthday with cousins and neighbors, a few remaining all night and into the next day for a "slumber" party.

Wednesday, my aunt and uncle from Lorton, Va. brought their niece from Florida here for a cooling drive to the country only to find weather rivaling the tropical heat waves of her native state.

Thursday, the Bluemont Girls Softball team took a defeat from Lovettsville placing second place of the Western Division of the Senior Ponytail league.

The real Bluemonters on the team were Ethel Leffingwell, catcher, Donna Kelley, third base, Debra Dawson, second base, Karen Ramey, right field, and Belinda Dawson, left field.

I had gotten all the particulars down about the John Fowlers' guests when I found the note with a big hole cut in the middle—one of the twins was practicing the fine art of cutting, but around the edges I can read that Mr. and Mrs. Vinson Harrold from somewhere in Iowa came for a visit while their daughter, Virginia went to visit the Le Fehrs in Eastland, Mich.

Of greater intrigue is that the Fowlers are the ones responsible for Mike Higgott meeting Jean Dawson; Mike and several other Marine friends rented the Fowlers' cottage for weekends and when a party was given with some of the local girls invited, bells rang at the church for three couples. How's that for combining "The Dating Game" with "The Newlyweds?"

Saturday was a great treat for us. Grandmother Johnson accompanied us to Lucketts where we found the scenery even much more beautiful than before realized.

The tours to the four old churches and the modern farms were outstanding. At Bob Arnold's we saw pigs just a few hours old and when we got to Faith Chapel we met Bob's sister from Bethesda who really knew the genealogy of most everyone who ever lived in the Lucketts community or in Loudoun County practically!

The New Valley Church, the Old School Baptist stone structure was probably my favorite with the old bamboo fans available for worshippers and a big pile of wood stacked in the corner for burning in the stoves. There too were two giant boxwoods putting out that scent that always spells melancholy to me.

There we met a charming gentleman, a Philomont native who knows Rosa Turner and Elizabeth Poston and sundry mountaineers who still claim residence in Bluemont.

And the hayride in a field, with mountains all around for viewing – Perfect!

Topping it all off the twins made the Channel 7 news show – showing off some of the crafts exhibited in the school.

A goodly crowd weathered the heat for the fine "singing and picking" by Johnny Whisnant and The Countrymen; the Don Corleys had a dinner party and evening's entertainment there with about ten guests.

The order of the day, find a stream or pool, submerge heated limbs and then relax while in my brain round and round goes the lyric, "We're having a heat wave, a tropical heat wave!"

August 3, 1972

"Then God made little green apples in the summertime."

It's that time of year, the corn's about ready and so are the tomatoes – the best eating in the world – fresh vegetables with a little salt!

And in my childhood memory, one of the most elegant meals I ever ate was somewhere in Virginia when our family went to the mountains – my father loved them so and in a shiny restaurant somewhere in this state, I had a breakfast of sausage and fried apples served by a handsome black man in a white coat on blue dishes, too, I believe.

So the little green apples are back – green apple pie, apple sauce, apples with crunchy topping, cobblers, tarts, apple crisp, main dishes and desserts – just waiting there for picking and eating.

With the apples came a real cool spell and gnats – up at the Brunelles they have the gnat hats lined up for guests – they're the big straw floppy kind – the kind you could win years ago at the local carnival if the midget couldn't guess your age and weight.

With the week's end, Betsy Jones Moreland was tearfully bidding Bluemonters adieu and with her parting I fondly remember her words, "I can't remember what happened yesterday in Hollywood, but in Bluemont the memory of what happened is always fresh!"

Lynn Carbaugh had a real celebration for her 16th birthday – jewelry, clothes, a cookout and two cakes were on the agenda last Sunday and then the twins had a real wing-ding here with our new neighbors, the Hutchins, Budnys, the Grandparents Johnson and Ethel Leffingwell supplying the music, our favorite, "The Candy Man," of course and Lynn helping out again with the youngest Johnson while I poured out the punch made with some of Mrs. Peyton's strawberries, Mr. Horning's delicious huge blackberries and Hill High's peaches.

Ken Hutchins, hailing originally from New Hampshire, got on the subject of a sugaring-off party, which sounds utterly divine – you have it in the spring when the sap is running right and there is still snow on the ground and you pour the maple sugar out on the snow and naturally have corn chowder, a little bit of New England in Virginia – wouldn't that be heavenly?

Up on the ridge, the David Freemans' Renaissance Bridgette gave birth to four sweet Pyrenees pups sired by the Paul Strangs' Simoun de Pontise, son of an international champion from France.

How's that for a Bluemont happening?

The Freedmans also had some guests during the heat wave of Al and Lucie Warren and daughter Pat from Plymouth Meeting, Pa., and just a little further up the hill the Charles Tyrolers are entertaining Carolyn's grandchildren, Tim and Allison Games from Dedham, Mass.

Then up near the trail the Robert D. Beetons had an interesting experience last week when a young couple hiking with their dog stopped for water.

The dog was carrying his own pack of food on his back and thus far they had walked 150 miles. Enjoying their company, the Beetons persuaded them to stay for lunch, dinner and after hiking for a ways they came back to spend the night.

Now I'd call that Southern hospitality!

As Sunday dawned rainy and cool, Shir Carbaugh was creating her own little shower for Jean Dawson, a bride-to-be in just one week.

Now Joyce Beck and I haven't gotten that blacksnake's motivation for coming into Clayton Hall yet – there must be a rhyme and reason for everything, our teacher-background tells us but nevertheless, upon encountering Jim Scott at the counter at Mann's Store on Saturday, he had a good snake story in tote.

He said at one time there was gas lighting in all these Bluemont houses (I see the evidence here) and the hole left by the removed pipe at Miss Alley's left a place for mice to squeeze through so an elderly lady on the top floor supposed.

She set a trap by the hole and hearing the trap spring, she looked for the mouse only instead to see a big black snake caught in the trap and then as we feminists are prone to do, yelled for help, Jim being the rescuer then.

So in Bluemont as July turns the corner into August, it's donning the flannel night clothes, pulling up the heavy comforter, stirring up hot chocolate and oatmeal for breakfast with sausage and "little green apples in the summertime!"

August 10, 1972

As the cool mountain breezes continue to sail through the windows and are slammed out by shivering occupants, the talk in town, on the mountain and in the countryside is the same – where has the summer gone?

Fall seems just too close even as the katydids keep up their chatter on the hill.

The giant machinery up on the road project above the village shakes us in the morning and though the sign up the big hill says "Closed to Through Traffic," there is much driving up and backing down by the side of the house.

Itch, itch, scratch, scratch is also a cadence in town as the poison ivy comes on; Jennifer and Mrs. Isabelle Dawson are suffering.

Gloriously though this was the week that was for vegetables.

The gardens yielded up pure eating delight; at last for lunch a tomato sandwich which can be savored.

Without a check in sight (summer is rather the long duration for substitute teachers) and the budget plan for a mammoth fuel bill staring me in the face, I was dejected until I went by the in-laws, picked some apples, squash and corn and arrived home to find a bag of cucumbers and tomatoes from Herbert Martz so with a tuna fish salad, we had a banquet fit for a king.

While conversing on the subject of vegetable dinners, the Budnys and Hutchins reminisced on "All corn" dinners and lo and behold Saturday night, they put it into practice inviting the Johnsons to participate, sixty ears were slurped down, Ken devouring a dozen or more himself.

With the talk of the tomato sandwiches, come discussion of other sandwiches, unheard of to bologna and cheese makers in suburbia.

Did you ever have a pork and bean sandwich, a potato salad sandwich, a cottage cheese sandwich?

Mary Lynn said her grandmother would go find anything in the refrigerator and put it between two slices of bread.

But the sandwich that has endured here in the south that horrified my Pennsylvania friends is peanut butter, mayonnaise, and banana. Try it, it's good!

Over in the Bluemont countryside Jack Bardon was recalling "good ole days" at a high school reunion in South Dakota several weeks ago.

"Funny," he said, "what people remember about you." Folks kept coming up and referring to his "moon car." Jack says he wishes he had it today; it would be worth a great deal. There were very few made on the order of a Rolls-Royce.

Too he said he saw the girl he had first danced with and he further commented she having spent her years since high school raising a family, still looked "Danceable."

At the Bluemont Citizens Meeting this week there was much talk of the upcoming Bluemont Fair.

This year, our feature will be the Indians who performed on the Mall in Washington in the spring.

Leslie Hutchins is researching our own Indian lore and the Cochrans, Ralph, Larry and Clinton Hindman have a fine collection of Indian relics all ready for a wonderful display.

The Winchester Chapter of the Historical Railway Association was at the school Wednesday night adding special touches to the elaborate train exhibit.

Guy Woolman has had a pleasant summer in Austria pursuing his studies under VPI, and of course, taking advantage of the foreign sights.

Bill Stewart has announced that "The Helping Hand" will reopen at the old Poland Building across from the old train station in Round Hill in another week.

Shir Carbaugh invites village women to the Home Demonstration Club meeting on the fourteenth at 8 o'clock at the school.

Jean Mock of Gel Mil House of Hair will discuss wigs and hair pieces.

The Glen Lloyds are pleased to announce the birth of a new granddaughter born two weeks ago to Judy and Bill Casey of Purcellville. The baby came a little early so she is still growing at the Loudoun Memorial Hospital under the excellent care of our Pine Grove neighbor, Mrs. Jessica Clinton.

Socially, Saturday was full, Lawrence Dawson rendered up for the last time his response to the question, "Who giveth this woman to this man?" when youngest daughter Jean was married to Mike Higgot at the little stone church in town.

Bruce Cochran played the organ, Ralph Cochran sang and Ivy made one of her most beautiful cakes.

Then that evening Allen and Snooks Campbell invited friends over for a house-warming and their new house is just lovely with new furniture, too.

"Now I'll tell you what I'm going to do" – I'm going to have that barn sale again since it was so highly "unsuccessful." The Murtaughs have promised to bring a hutch and I'm going to reduce everything half price and I might even consider a little New York bargaining procedures.

This is all in benefit for the Loudoun Memorial Hospital (I have a huge bill there) and Southern States (Clayton Hall is one great consumer of fuel oil!) So you all come on Aug. 19 and 20.

Back to Lucketts and its success, one of my very favorite stops was the authentic country store there with the old-fashioned panes in the windows advertising Coca-Cola and a unique treasure on the wall of a marvelous etching of the head of a Gibson girl type, her hair style framing a question mark with the caption underneath The Eternal Question.

See before Women's Lib, we had mystique!

August 17, 1972

The summer nights return, the crickets' song is stronger than ever; natives sense the summer's end, vacations fill in the season's last days.

The last game of the current women's softball season terminated Saturday night and Larry Allder, coach along with Bill Martz sent a fine report.

Larry says the team never gave up, even when losing and had a much improved record over last year's 13-1.

The gals treated themselves to a party after the game Saturday night as players for this year were Eleanor Anderson and Louis McClaughry, pitchers; Geneva Hummer, catcher; Brenda McClaughry and Jill Reed, first base; Doris Allder, second base; Shelia Tapscott, short stop; Donna Underwood, third base; Evelyn Tapscott, right field, Joyce Martz, short fielder, Joyce Shephard, center field and Cindy Fincham, left field.

The team and coaches wish to thank George Littleton and Johnny Wilson for their fine umpiring this year.

Don and Linda Corley had a marvelous trip to some of the New England states and agreed with me that Concord, Mass. made for one of the loveliest stops plus they were the ones to leave me the bag of tomatoes and cucumbers.

I have so many good neighbors, don't know who to thank.

The Clyde Becks returned home Sunday evening from a week in Nags Head while Hawkeye Reid goat-tended and Pam Carbaugh kept the cats and Cinder Beck fed.

We were glad to see Lucy and C.W. Spring visiting from Texas and C.W.'s mother, Mrs. Barbara Spring.

Lucy is a most creative gal; we poked our noses into The Helping Hand now back in business where she found an alligator bag for 50 cents and I found a dresser for nine dollars.

Lucy drew me a beautiful barn for my poster reminding folks of my barn sale this coming weekend, Aug. 19, 20 from 10 a.m. to 4 p.m. I hope to have some of Clyde Beck's paintings and Curtis Budny's work (he did a beautiful copy of an old train station) and Clinton Hindmans's old bottles plus I have canning jars and plastic containers.

Mrs. Nellie Tibbs is back after a six-weeks visit to her sister's in Southwest Virginia and Grace Dawson's sister from North Carolina has been here for a visit.

A really adventuresome crew visiting has been Mrs. Walter Hatcher and her seven daughters from Miami, visiting the in-laws the Sam Hatchers who own the beautiful mountain property directly behind the village. They have merely pitched a tent and are camping in the green field.

George Dawson of Hamilton turned 74 last week with his traditional birthday party down at the old school in Bluemont.

Over a hundred people attended the party thrown by his eight children. How many grandchildren practically defies counting but there were three great grandchildren there.

Unfortunately, Mrs. Dawson was taken to the hospital the next day but is now recuperating at home.

Desiree Allder, daughter of the James Allders and one of the grandchildren has been enjoying a visit with Doris' brother in Fairfax.

Now the tractor and car breakdowns take turns and the poison ivy keeps off the boring times as an Army friend kiddingly said the boys tried to keep a good case of athlete's foot going so there would be something to wile away the slow-moving evenings of island-based duty.

Summer's lament is almost spent and the sparrows' soft groans in their shutter nest supply the Lindbergh fly routine to a tiring columnist.

August 24, 1972

Motor-bikes whirling past, banjo strings crying, dogs frantically barking, the nights are far from still – summer is having its last fling in Bluemont.

The vacationers have returned. The Clyde Becks came with sea shells and shark teeth and souvenirs for the neighbors from Nags Head. Young Brian remembered me with a ceramic piece from the Williamsburg pottery factory. Yep – it had a blue print!

The Lawrence Dawsons and daughter Libby and husband Bootsie Stearne got in a couple days visit to Williamsburg too before the season called it quits.

Isabelle Dawson and I are still scratching the poison ivy. Helen Freedman joined the list of sufferers but I got a couple of home-made remedies.

Joyce Beck sent down a couple leaves that really did do wonders overnight; you bend the leaf in half and rub the membrane on the wonderful mess and Mrs. Ogden says she takes liquid detergent and makes a paste with cleanser when the first few bumps appear.

Next I need to get a cure for some kind of bite – what hit me, I don't know but the way my eye is swollen, I'd make a good Dracula!

Ah summer and all the world's one mammoth insect hatchery!

Well, now the majority of summer birthday parties are behind us.

Christopher Budny turned four this week and our Jennifer seven with a party that featured melodrama at its finest. The Little Pigs (Rosemary Murtaugh, fourth grader was giving us the etymological background of the folk tale) and this was combined with the highest quality of homemade ice cream – June Lloyd variety.

Then Jennifer found out our good mechanic friend Russell Powell had the same birthday. We have been seeing a lot of Russell these days – four road calls and a new battery for the car and a tractor that won't go in first.

Mrs. Teesdale-Smith rescued us at the Safeway, four children, groceries and all. I'm beginning to think she is rivaling the late Miss Liza Lunceford in educational popularity in these parts as she assumes the principalship of the new middle school at Purcellville.

The Beck and Hutchins were auto-fixing too. Give me a horse and buggy and a driver! See I'd still want a chauffeur.

It was time this week for something new for the tastebuds so I asked Lucy Spring to give me a Mexican recipe before she and C.W. left for Texas.

She said she liked Chiliquillies with the price of meat rising – the main ingredient is eggs.

You put in grease as you would to scramble eggs then add a package of ten-cent corn chips (crushed) to six or more eggs, about one-fourth cup catsup, and one-fourth cup grated cheese with hot sauce to taste. Serves five or six.

I tried it and thought the hot Mexican chili beans would fill it out as a main dish. We had it with a fresh tossed salad and some of the Monk's whole-wheat bread and honey.

How that whole-wheat bread and honey came our way is most heart-warming.

The Daggits of Falls Church came on Friday to see the stuff in the barn and left the treat with us, being devoted readers of the Bluemont news every week.

Small world that it is – they had worked with our Oscantayans of No. 601 on an Appalachian Trail shelter in Pennsylvania several years ago. It was quite a project involving a two-year search for the appropriate site and then cutting trees and notching the logs correctly – plus building a stone foundation.

A barn sale is fun!

First it was the calls when I took an ad in the Post.

Did I have old dolls, men's jewelry, a health relaxer, musical instruments?

Then a dealer wanted to deal and a Hillsboro neighbor wanted to know if I would like to trade a goat for a saddle?

The four girls from Washington were fun! They bought the scales (old grocery style with the date 1903), the Victorian mirror (she was to convince the airlines to put it in with the luggage for her flight back to Colorado), a gunny sack what was to be a dress and fourteen pieces of the old sheet music.

Gosh – they are cute! There is a young Perry Como and Ozzie Nelson and Dale Evans pictured on the cover and the song titles with the Flapper sketches are so perfectly "campy."

August 31, 1972

"Where has the summer gone? Where has the summer gone?" is the wail heard 'round the village.

Can it be that Monday morning alarms with awaken school children and mothers who must arise to pack lunches and cook a good nutritional breakfast for the reluctant student? Is the day to begin again to the sound of the heavy groan of the school buses shifting into second at the corner in front of the iron gate?

But then will the day be more serene with one less child at home, demanding a drink, a peach, a cracker, a cookie, a nickel to spend at Mann's Store? Yes, all hail to the resumed school bell ring!

At this time of year, I'm grateful I'm an unemployed teacher, too many summer chores left undone, vegetables and fruits to be canned, lingering chats with the neighbors would have to go unsaid.

Where has the summer gone? Miraculously I think I know.

Two weeks of hauling from attic stair to cellar well to barn door and then Hurricane Agnes. After that my course with U.Va, and then Ethel Leffingwell painting the twins' bedrooms while Lynn Carbaugh baked and baby sat for the Johnsons, then Lucketts had a successful farm tour, the summer birthdays of the Leos here were celebrated, Jean Dawson was married, the Allen Campbells moved in their new house, a number of the villagers got away for trips, returning to find Loudoun County a pretty nice place to live and today summer turned on the heat in honor of Emily Verloops marriage to John Thomas.

It was very lovely indeed with the ceremony down at the little stone church and then a wonderfully lavish reception under a tent at the J.H.H. Verloops home, Mintwood.

The drinks and delicacies were divine and the breeze and pink and purple petunias on the back porch which affords a wonderful panoramic view made the perfect spot for chatting with the Bluemonters present; Carolyn Tyroler, Col. and Mrs. Hilary, the McClures, the Paul Strangs, Bessie Townshend, Emma Mann, the Lloyd Loopes, Mary Lou Markles, whose son-in-law did himself proud as the officiating clergyman, George Dawson, Faye Willke, whose wonderful fan kept me cool at the church since I drew a seat behind her.

Such handsome families the Verloops and Thomases, with John's father making a very good double for Charlton Heston. Our best wishes to the bride and groom.

It was good to see the other Verloops, Marguerite and Michael again and of course, the twins, Edith and Maurice have gotten quite professional having been the youngest attendants in their sisters' weddings in the last several years.

Natives will be sorry to hear Blondie Tallman, one-time telegrapher with the W&OD Railroad situated here in Bluemont, had to celebrate his birthday in the hospital as he fell and broke his hip a week ago.

Friends can drop him a card at this address: Clarence Tallman, Fairfax Hospital, Room 656, 3300 Gallows Road, Falls Church, Va. 22046.

The William Ballengers Jr. went to a fascinating event in National Chimneys, Va., where they attended the annual jousting tournament which claims to be the oldest consecutively held sporting event in the country.

That must have been some sight indeed, after which they visited friends in Moscow, Va.

Col. and Mrs. Taylor Holt, Jr. of Route 601 have had a jolly houseful of summer guests with their four grandchildren.

Adam, Seth and Sarah Reuf came from Buffalo, N.Y. joined by cousin Penny Welton of Calabasas, Calif.

Is that any way to run a summer vacation for parents? You bet it is!

The C.W. Townshends aided with the grandchildren too, a week ago when they spent the time with their daughter's family, helping them get settled in an apartment as they build a new house.

The William Caseys' house is almost ready here, down that beautiful road on which the William Kelleys live.

Congratulations to Rhonda Underwood on her engagement. Now with the Bluemont Fair and Rhonda's wedding, October will be a full month for the Louis Underwoods.

The William Carbaughs took in the Pennsylvania Dutch Days last week and the girls have been visiting grandparents and aunts away from the village, with Sunday being the last big picnic day before school began, at the Wesley Carbaugh's up on the hill.

Marvin Watts has returned from a three-week trip to the West Coast, toting in marvelous salmon he caught in Puget Sound. He had it salted and in a special pine box which he had made for the purpose when the children and I had a chance to inspect it before the butcher carved it into steaks!

A call from Betsey Jones Moreland in Hollywood gives us word that she finished filming a part in "The Doctors" and is auditioning for a regular series part.

Wouldn't it be nice if we could see Betsey every week? Preferably we would like to see her in the real but we'll settle for celluloid.

Bruce Cochran leaves next week for his first year at Eastern Nazarene College, near Boston while brother Larry is facing early-morning football practice at Valley High School.

It was great to see Mark Brownell this summer, who will return soon for his second year of school in Tennessee.

And what were the week's adventures here?

There was another snake story: a friendly black snake wiggled his way through a loose brick in the fireplace over at the Snow House as excited children and two frantic mothers called on Lawrence Dawson, vacationing, to come to the rescue.

And we went to the spring house. Brian and Justine Beck showed us the way up the Little's lane, among the high white birches, to the clean enclosure with the wonderful clear water flowing out, cascading over the mossy rocks, cooling the feet refreshed for the spiraling stroll to the top of the road to inspect the old Route 7, closed now to through traffic.

How perfect to wheel the baby leisurely in a stroller on the section of road where the heaviest and most whirling of traffic had once sped.

And then on Thursday it was time for our traditional summer trip to the city. With Grandmother Johnson back from her South Boston, Va. trip, we took in the big shopping center at Tysons Corner where an occasional fruit stand was the extent of the commerce twenty years ago.

There we had a great lunch with a Dixie Land band strutting by, rides up and down the escalators (Lara called them the rolling stairs), found items we most wanted on sale and topped the day with a real feeling of smugness when we saw the city kids paying a quarter to see a rabbit, duck, pig and goat.

Sassy and Little Bit, the Becks' goats got an extra pat that night. Oh, yes, we were smart to be in that privileged class who live and work in the country.

September 7, 1972

Indian summer droned on with the most delightful days, cool in the morning, hot in the afternoon, cool at night: September's song is now being sung in Bluemont.

The school bus crowd has swelled at the stop across the street, young Master Wade is a first grader now at Round Hill School and the Wilson children meet the bus here as Mrs. Dawson cares for them before and after school hours.

John and Brad Campbell catch the bus at the end of their new lane to their new house but walk downtown every morning first to check out the action.

And action – there seems to be a lot of it here – I'm reminded of a slogan "It's not the size of the dog in the fight, it's the size of the fight in the dog."

Life in Bluemont is rarely dull.

Plans are stirring now for the annual Bluemont Fair to be held Oct. 21, 22. Those of us on the publicity committee know we must get started.

Bennie Lightner reminds exhibitors that the first registration is Sept. 13 from 1-8 p.m. at the old school across from the post office.

New exhibitors can get a Fair number, all exhibitors can pay the registration fee of 50 cents at that time and pick up their tags.

And I'm ready to talk shop – Clayton Hall Book and Craft Shop, that is.

I've spent this week sweeping, dusting and moving furniture again, clearing out my old kitchen in readiness for the grand opening of this permanent shop in my home.

Primarily I will sell the local histories (aren't we glad to see Mrs. Dirksen has written a book!) along with the placemats and note cards we sold last year at the Fair and then I invite the Bluemonters to sell their small antiques, old bottles, any type of crafts and home-made products, jams, jellies, produce and I could sure use some dried arrangements to hang from the rafters.

Be thinking about what you can sell; Mrs. Barbara Spring already has a beautiful afghan and Leslie Hutchins makes the cutest Barbie doll clothes you've ever seen plus she led the children in creating decorated jars with fringe, perfect for pencils or a little dried arrangement and everyone has been telling me it's a good year for bittersweet.

More news about Mrs. Spring is that she has retired from the government and has her lovely old home up for sale. The Porterfields after a trip to the mid-west like the looks of Loudoun County so we had a look and that large old spring house on the property is most unique.

With an early dead-line the only other news to come my way is that John and Emily Thomas are having a marvelous honeymoon in Bermuda and Libby and Bootsie Stearne spent the week at Virginia Beach while here Sassy and Little Bit, the Beck's goats are doing the most fantastic job on the weeds on my fencerow.

It's unfit for human cutting as Ruth Manuel can also attest as she now is doctoring a terrific case of poison ivy contracted while cutting the weeds at the Manuel's domain.

I once thought a good slogan for Bluemont would be – Bluemont – the town that nature claimed!

Take heart – only eight more weeks of grass-cutting left in 1972!

September 14, 1972

It's rather crisp around the edges, the weather, that is, as September cools its way toward October and Glory! Glory! The yellow flowers are back!

All the talk is of the Bluemont Fair now, slated for Oct. 21, 22.

Daily the Fair is expanding to include some wonderful added attractions.

The Ebenezer Church will be open again, there will be a musket shoot on Saturday at 2:30 in the area of the Snow House.

One team is the Louisiana Tigers from Berryville with our personification of Abraham Lincoln of last year's stovepipe hat fame participating.

No stove-pipe hats this time but real Confederate uniforms.

There will be lots of music. Mrs. Ruth Miehm will give an organ recital at the United Methodist Church, alternating with the slide shows shown as last year.

Louella Robey and his Blue Valley Boys will play along with Joe McDonald's country music group as well as Jack Bardon and his extraordinary talent and some spiritual singers.

Fifteen cars from the Shenandoah Division of the Antique Cars of America will be on display behind the school and calls are going out for jars and apple cooks for the apple-butter. June Lloyd should be contacted for help in this endeavor.

The posters are going to be something very special indeed but we'll wait on that story.

The forecasted arrival of the Indians seem to interest many and I found out J.M. Mauk, vice-president of Blue Ridge Middle School is some kind of an expert, having found an Indian graveyard some years ago, the finds of which are now in the Smithsonian Institution.

The children in town are delightfully excavating; finding pieces of broken pottery and china and some really old bottle finds so they started their own museum out on a board next to the Snow House. Proceeds to go to Mann's Store for ice cream and the like.

Death knocked at three community doors last week.

Our sympathy to the family of Mrs. Alta Sixma and Tony Reid whose widow and three sons, Hawkeye, Popeye and Buckeye are a vital part of our community.

Also Bill Casey, the Glen Lloyd's son-in-law lost his father last week and the Porterfields and Lardies laid Grandma to rest at Arlington Cemetery on Tuesday.

She left me the richest heritage any one could have in a Grandma.

That was just what she was – to everyone who knew her.

She baked pies and made stocking dolls and recited "pieces" for the grandchildren wearing always simple oxford shoes, her hair in a bun, a printed apron and a hearing aid.

She never met a stranger; she lived for others, asking little for herself. She was Grandma!

Bright news for the Casey family is that the new baby girl was able to come home from the hospital and in a matter of weeks they expect to be in their new home, a really elegant structure that Judy designed herself.

Sorry to hear the Courier publisher, Kenneth Levi has been hospitalized this week.

We are all congratulating Martin Mitchell on the winning of a new Pontiac. No one deserves it more.

I was very pleased to meet Ruth Lee Holler. She and her husband and two young children, Brian and Amy have recently bought former Walter Allder's home near Mr. Iden's

Store. She has great energy and was a wonderful help to me in arranging the furniture in my shop.

Now I'm really counting on you neighbors to supply the trappings, crafts, old bottles, jams, pickles, art and antiques.

When you're coming to register for the Fair on Wednesday, bring a few items for Clayton Hall Book and Craft Shop.

I convinced Harriet Murtaugh it was a fine weed-picking day and when we asked Father Francis at the Monastery if we could pick the weeds, he was rather mystified but congenially agreeable. If the weed find wasn't worth the trip, the view was. I know of no other spot so close that offers such a landscape of the Blue Ridge Mountains in every direction.

While calling about for help for the Fair, I got news of the Robert Dodderidge's sons.

John begins as a freshman at the University of Virginia this week while the younger of the boys continues his studies at St. Paul's in Concord, N.H.

Taking in mountain living for the month of September are Mr. and Mrs. Charles Hoge of Ft. Myers, Fla. at the Brunelles at the end of No. 601.

Charles is a real native son of Loudoun, reared in Unison and having a sister Mrs. Mildred Shackelford in Purcellville who both claim kinship to the dynamic Plaster family, formerly of Bluemont, with doctors George, Sr. and son Henry, who both practiced locally, making house calls on horseback, no less.

In fact, one of my next projects would be to see Dr. George Plaster's history of Snickersville, 1902 put into print.

"When the dog bites
When the bee stings
When I'm feeling Sad
I simply remember my favorite things
And then I don't feel so bad."

September 21, 1972

Indian summer combines dried arrangements with marigolds, geraniums and even some gladioli I saw in the Colbert's' backyard; signs of a mouse invading the house have been spotted in the kitchen while still the children romp in the grass barefoot.

The apples are perfectly ripe – time to get a ladder to pick the yield – Sonny Brown from Leesburg pronounced them good for cooking but not so great for eating.

Even with the greenness of the grass – Autumn was here, there and everywhere – especially in Waterford where the weather always seems golden.

With the shops open now on weekends before the Fair, Sunday was too perfect a day to be closed inside so the mill and country store in Waterford beckoned. Such beautiful crafts in the mill (a magnificent old structure) and ah those Tiffany lamps handcrafted by a resident of Hillsboro!

Then at the first of the week I took a quick visit to the Craft Club that meets monthly in Skyes Hall and then spent a marvelous morning in Lincoln at Mrs. Wood's, whose lovely surroundings with that incomparable boxwood makes for an inspiring time long remembered.

Bluemont Fair (Oct. 21, 22) details are being completed; I feel I've written a million letters this week trying to round up all the Loudoun writers and historians who might wish to have their work for sale at Clayton Hall Book and Craft Shop, the only place I know where all these can be found at one shop.

If I have missed someone who would like to be included, please call me.

I told Mrs. Evelyn Adams I give the credit for getting these writers' creations together to her as about four years ago she gave a fascinating talk to the Senior Women's Club on Loudoun authors, numbering about 30 at that time.

Of course, we're very happy to have her book, Old Courthouses of Virginia with her sketches of each county's courthouse and human interest stories making a unique presentation.

Also her sketch work on the League of Women Voters' undated calendar will be here.

Ann Van Deventer who once had the County Crafts in Round Hill has certainly been helpful and she is a most artistic person herself, doing oils and etchings.

The weather has been perfect for the Joseph Deals of Dumont, N.J. visiting on the mountain, seeing the sights with the Leon Brunelles as Thelma says she is on her mini-vacation.

Tearfully we had to bid some of our young people adieu. J.K. Cornwall reported to Uncle Sam's Navy on Friday headed for Ann Arbor, Mich. Our prayers and love follow him and Willa Colbert has returned for her Senior year at Madison while Beverly Kelley took to Bridgewater College and young Sam Kelley returned to the Benedictine School in Ridgely, Md.

The Marian Kerricks had a pleasant visit with Mrs. Delia Hunter whose home was once in our neighborhood at the top of the hill but the highway saw fit to use the land so she vacated to Winchester and we are sorry to receive the news that she fell and broke her arm.

Over Pine Grove way the Ballengers have interesting news again.

The William Ballengers, Jr. spent last Sunday in Flintstone, Md. tramping on the Warrior's Path, one of the longest Indian trails in North America.

Wonder if it intersected with Snicker's Gap?

Then the Bill Ballengers, Sr. along with Mrs. Ella Mae Greenwald of Leesburg and Mrs. Madge O'Brien of Baltimore motored to Troy, Pa. visiting with the Ronald Raupps.

Before returning home they visited with Eddie Butler in Elmira, N.Y. and saw Mr. Ballenger's nephew Mark Ballenger pitch for the Elmira Indians, farm club of the Cleveland Indians.

Now I had heard Harold Miller, Democratic candidate for Congress was to start a march down Rt. 7 Saturday morning at Bluemont over at Mann's Store.

Yes I thought I might get across the street by 8 o'clock; I would like to see my old neighbor Charlie Waddell, now our distinguished Senator in the Virginia legislature but come eight o'clock on Saturday morning with the baby on a second bottle, sacked in, I "clean-plumb" forgot it.

Sorry about that but at this juncture in life, I need all the beauty sleep I can get.

Funny thing about creating those dried arrangements – the first couple – the price is low – this is fun –there's nothing to it – why charge a lot for weeds?

Then by the time you've pricked your fingers a couple of times, forgetting the gloves – the baby is fussing for dinner – the price shoots up. After all I had to wade in mud and stickers to get them and my time is valuable plus there are some rare specimens of different varieties here you can't find every day and I did have to buy the string for tying (ok, so Emma Mann did give it to me) and the white wrapping paper and darn if I didn't put the wrong number on them and they have to be tagged all over again.

Grand opening – Sept. 30 – who's got Indian corn and pumpkins.

September 28, 1972

Autumn – the bees are stinging, the snakes are pausing up by the barn, the mice are tiptoeing into the kitchen, the porch roof is sagging and the electric bill doubled over the last month but still life seems golden and especially fine – it's autumn!

The children particularly seem to sense the fun of the season. How they love to skin up a tree for an apple and fill their shirt tail with the fallen pears. Since the horse trailer has been sold, the planks stored within make perfect boards for a house propped up by a former Bluemont Fair Balloon stand. And what avid bottle collectors we have here. John and Brad Campbell and Jennifer found three big boxes full that washed down by the creek.

The Bluemont Fair posters are here now; their designer, Joseph Boswell, Jr. was named on a list of ten top young men in the country. Because of their distinction, these silk-screened creations will be on sale at the book shop and with the art display by Clyde Beck's studio during the Fair.

The visitors streamed to Bluemont this week; our Lucketts neighbors, Sandy DiFillipo, along with Martha and Samuel Hopler came. Sandy brought blackberry jam and watermelon pickles for the shop and Martha put one of the old pieces of sheet music in an artist mat to show the effect of framing.

Dot Givens brought two lovely beer steins and her book of poetry, Jeannie Brown sent Virginia note cards and cookbooks from the Junior Woman's Club, and Mary Whitmore and Barbara Cochran are promising some dried arrangements.

Kay Seidenspinner brought some darling children's crafts, belts and purses, pencil spools and hand puppets, and each day the fun grows as we anticipate what will march in next.

Some came for inspection, Isabelle Dawson, young Rusty Powell, Agnes Allder and Linda Johnson deButts' delightful parents from Richmond and Waverly, Va.; and everyone is promising to come back for the Fair, Oct. 21, 22.

Mac Brownell with 10 turkeys in tote from the Berryville butcher began the cooking of the birds for that wonderful home-cooked turkey dinner served at Whitehall Farm.

It was good to see Susan before she departed for San Antonio, Texas with her husband David Vondle.

Good news came that Bruce Cochran is well and happy at Eastern Nazarene College near Boston, and continuing the tradition he started here, he will be playing the organ for a small Methodist Church near the college.

Our little stone church will receive visitors for the morning church service during the Sunday of the Fair, and if you have never worshipped there, it is a blessed experience to which you may like to avail yourself.

Ivy Cochran tells me the interior was not always so attractive. A brown painted floor and drab pews were once the main features – now a lovely red carpeting, a new organ and piano and beautifully refurbished pews create a serene feeling of worship.

Speaking of preservation, it is my understanding the Loudoun Historical Society recommends to the Board of Supervisors that a building with the same façade of the old hotel in Leesburg be erected in its place. Let us hope this will be carefully considered and the charm of the center of our county seat will not be destroyed with a glaring modern building, not in keeping with our Virginia heritage.

The only bit of unpleasant news to come my way this week is that our beloved June Lloyd is hospitalized at Winchester Hospital, probably remaining there for another week. Friends may send greetings to Room 1417.

The Women's Auxiliary of the Round Hill Fire Department will hold an open house Oct. 2 at 7:30 p.m. at the fire house. The Bluemont ladies are to know they are most welcome too.

And over in Berryville they were picking, singing, I guess you don't say jamming with guitars, banjos, dulcimers and the like in the best Blue Grass tradition over the weekend but they had nothing on us; an old college friend came by serenading us with "Country Road, Take Me Home."

Come and have a cup of tea with me. See you at the Clayton Hall Book and Craft Shop opening this Saturday, 11 a.m. to 4 p.m.

October 5, 1972

The weather nipped, tanged and generally chilled the village and mountain folks as a storm over the weekend blew in the coldest moist air yet this Fall season.

Mary Lynn Budny pronounced Clayton Hall cozy as compared to the Snow House now fast filling with new interior walls but no electricity for heat.

We'll weather it here for a while yet, the kindling is stacked in the family room fireplace if the air becomes too brisk.

Life's cycle was most evident in our Bluemont family this week.

There was much scurrying about with individual projects and then we got word Ambrose Moreland had died.

Betsy Jones Moreland, his cousin had just called here on Wednesday full of plans for sending for Ambrose to spend the winter with her in Hollywood, informing me of his approaching birthday, Oct. 5.

Now we extend our sympathy to her but gratefully they had had that wonderful visit together this spring and summer in Bluemont.

Betsy had news that she will appear on Oct. 6, 9 on the show in the daytime, Days of Our Lives, channel 4, NBC.

Then as in the rightness of time, the James Brownells of Whitehall Farm became grandparents again with son James R.'s second child, Faith Brownell arriving on Sept. 29.

One of our favorite teenagers Sandy Mitchell turned 14 on Saturday and Desiree Allder bought her a macramé belt of Kay Seidenspinners right here.

Desiree's reminding Sandy her birthday is just a week away.

Then we're glad to receive word that Blondie Tallman, former telegrapher with the W&OD Railroad that terminated in Bluemont, has been released from the hospital and is at Stalker Nursing Home, 112 Ayr Hill Avenue N.W., Vienna, Va. 22180.

And the weekend brought some congenial history buffs Bluemont way.

Paul Sheehan of Hamilton and I had a chat about the young Englishman's journal that he kept while residing in Leesburg prior to the Revolutionary War. Admittedly he was consuming pints and pints and quarts and quarts of ale, no doubt the local home brew!

If the whole journal is in published form, we'd like to know about it and a good number of natives would like to see Nichols: Legends of Loudoun reprinted.

Even though we may be liberated generally we gals like to still please a man so when the male population put their stamp of approval on Clayton Hall Book and Craft Shop, I was highly complimented.

The Clyde Lamonds of Alexandria and now Bluemont came by; they have built a beautiful rail fence on the front of their property located on that invincible "yellow schoolhouse" road with the best view ever of Pierott's Hill.

They all have taken to our country living; producing a great garden and feeding some cattle shared with Louis Underwood.

Being neighbors of the Roy Santmyers, they have caught a little of his infamous teasing as has Rhonda Underwood now awaiting that trip down to the altar next Friday evening.

A reminder to all that wish to sell crafts, art, baked goods, jams, dried arrangements, produce at the Bluemont Fair Oct. 21, 22 that this week Oct. 4 from 1-8 p.m. at the old store is the second registration.

You must pay your fee again this year for tags and have them in your possession at the two days the week of the Fair, you can bring your items already tagged and ready to set into place.

Now about that picture in the paper, I really don't have a shot gun behind my back even if the expression on my face seemed to conjure up images of a fierce pioneer woman chewing tobacco, feuding, fussing and fighting ready to protect her young against any ornery low-down critters that might be meandering by.

It's a cinch I won't be out Betsy Jones Moreland's way trying my face out on the running footage.

The Becks entertained Al Serber and some Washington friends on Saturday evening for drinks and dinner and I'm betting there was a fire on the hearth there then.

And Mrs. Kulgren (bless her heart) says she would pay 50 cents for my spice tea recipe but rather than suffer the slings of printers fees or a mimeographing machine's tricks, here it is free for the clipping: the real recipe calls for three sticks of cinnamon, two teaspoons of clove, boiled in water till tender and poured over tea leaves. I sprinkled in some cinnamon and cloves in the tea as I would make a regular pot then add one and half cups of sugar, a large can of orange juice, a large can of pineapple juice and grapefruit juice and several slices of lemon, squeezing in the juice. Brew for about an hour. Makes a gallon.

Now I propose a toast – Here's to you and October's best!

October 12, 1972

The chill has decidedly set in…is it time to get anti-freeze in the car, take in the plants?

The wind is coasting by the corners of the house, gusting forth with a howl now and then.

I should consult with Mary Ann Carter, she always has the foreboding weather reports and the pros and cons in the furnace debate raged on here through last Monday.

I asked Marvin Watts's advice, he said, "No, just lay a fire in the fireplace" and then when Scott Brownell came by I asked him if they had taken the plunge at Whitehall Farm and he said, "Oh, yes, we had to!" Further evidence for the case, Scott seemed in the best of health while Marvin has had a terrible flu bout.

The tradition of women enduring the cold at Clayton Hall has been a long one apparently as Elizabeth Kelley colorfully recalled seeing Lotta and Rosa Turner placing a bedspread – blue on the floor to keep off the chill and then of course, at that time there was no central heat.

The starlings too are back, one night this week just as I had flicked out the light there came a terrible thud upon the roof.

Now I can be dramatic! At first I was sure it was a wild cat but then my best detective self put two and two together and came up with about four birds, landing on the eaves for a pre-winter's nap.

It was a full week with lots of good telephone chats and visits with the neighbors.

Jack Bardon called relating a great time he and Claire had spent in a small town in Ohio who had a fest of some kind with old Swiss music instruments being aired by the musicians. Next he was making plans for squirrel hunting and while I wanted to take it all in a professional reporter's manner, the kids were crumbling crackers on the kitchen floor, so pardon me and the details, Jack.

Barbara Allder brought reassuring news that J.K. is well and happy in Uncle Sam's Navy but certainly he would appreciate a letter from home to SR James K. Cornwell USN Company 416, Recruit Training Command, Naval Training Center, Great Lakes, Ill 60088.

Rosa Peyton is now enrolled at the Northern Virginia Community College and will pursue studies there leading to an eventual nursing course.

We're proud to hear that Andrew John Murtaugh distinguished himself by showing his French Alpine goat, Whitehaven – Clytie's Susy at the Virginia State Fair, winning second prize against 11 other outstanding entries in the Junior Doe Class.

Also the Renaissance Kennel of French Pyrenees of David Freedmans brought home enough points for our beloved "Monty" with the beautiful head to be declared a champion now.

Now as of this writing it is but two weeks until the Bluemont Fair; everything seems to be in readiness. The hams and turkeys are baking, the new shed is finished on the school grounds while Louis Underwood painted the interior stairway. The model train enthusiasts are preparing another delight, a circus train with an accompanying appropriate display.

A reminder to villagers to please clean in front of your own property and park the cars off the street the days of the Fair, Oct. 21, 22.

Additionally, I will be a guest on Loudoun Chit-Chat this Friday at 9:30 a.m. on WAGE Radio and Clyde Beck will answer a few questions of Bill Spenser's on the 19th on the Village Shopping Center program.

The musket shoot teams are both Confederate, one called the Louisiana Tigers, the other the 17th Valley Infantry which sounds particularly interesting as Mr. Beatty has a limited edition book on the History of the 17th Infantry here.

Although the heavens poured, there wasn't a more radiant bride than Rhonda Underwood last Friday night when she was united in marriage to Jan Marcus.

After a visit here, they will make their home in Montana.

Ivy Cochran made the perfect cake again, Judy Lewis played the organ beautifully and Shir Carbaugh and I talked again about how we should have ridden together.

It was nice Mark Brownell could be home for the weekend from college in Tennessee. He tells me he has a part-time job milking—it's a cinch, they couldn't have gotten a more experienced hand. And Jennifer says, "Mark is so handsome, too." Modest too, I might add.

All is fairly serene. The animals invaded the village – domestic this time – a pony was tied to the Snow House fence on Saturday and a goat has joined Little Bit and Sassy. She is Little Bit too.

Sassy's animal nature led him eventually to my geraniums—the human nature exhibits this tendency on occasions too—the forbidden fruit is so delicious! And Walton Mann just cackled on his store steps while I tried to maneuver my blooming beauties away from the critter. Back to the weed patch. Boy, you have a little more nibbling to be done before the Bluemont Fair.

And the leaves are turning. Tra La.

October 19, 1972

Bewitching is the season…For years I've asked myself what is the magic of autumn? Why is it we bubble, we are dazzled, in short we enjoy life a little more when the trees flash in a brisker atmosphere? Part of it must be the mellowness of the sunlight – in the late afternoon it baths the earth in softness – mellow is the only word for it.

Next week at this time the story will be told on the third annual Bluemont Fair.

Certainly today the neighbors are out, sprucing up lawns, and lugging unsightly piles of rubbish aside. Walton Mann did a fine job of cleaning the fence row near the Marshall Place and I have promised to do this corner, all before the traffic flows in next Saturday at 10 a.m.

Those in surrounding communities who wish to sell their crafts, dried goods, antiques, produce, jams and jelly can bring their items on Wednesday, Oct. 18 and Thursday, Oct. 19 from 10 a.m. to 8 p.m. to the old store across from the post office. Baked goods come the morning of the event.

Our other "crafty" friends remind us and invite us to an Early Peek at Christmas held at Skyes Hall in Leesburg, Nov. 2, 3, and 4.

Emma Mann, also in preparation for Christmas, tells us the pecans sold to benefit the Loudoun Guidance Center, should be ordered now from her at 554-8174, or at Mann's Store at 554-4421. These will be delivered between Nov. 15 and Thanksgiving so the

Christmas baking can begin in earnest. Ah, for a big bite of a rich pecan praline right now or a piece of pecan pie! I haven't made one in years and they are really easy if you can make a crust. Now there's the rub for me.

Stanley Kelley tells me there's a new little girl in town, he and wife Barbara are the proud parents of a seven pound, seven ounce daughter born Oct. 13 named Kristina Elizabeth.

And the newlyweds, Rhonda and Jan Marcus arrived at their Montana apartment Thursday evening to find it 20 degrees and snowing.

Then the Brownie troop of Round Hill had a grand day Saturday at Howard's Nature Nook near Hamilton.

Our own Joan Wilt is one of the leaders this year with her April and Katrina in the troop, and did I luck up with her chauffeuring my Jennifer from meetings. If Jennifer has the story straight, Katrina celebrated her birthday on the Saturday outing with ice cream and cake with others pledging, "I will help someone every day, especially at home." Now I'll vote for that every time.

In honor of the Bluemont Fair, and crafts and "back to nature" and the whole program, and to "Albert" who will be demonstrating soap-making at the Fair, I want to share this soap recipe given to me by Lucketts correspondent, Sandy DiFilippo, who says it is so easy and the greatest for getting out "ring around the collar" marks.

She thought this was too long to put it in the paper so I won't go into rendering your own fat.

For nine pounds of pure, hard smooth soap, combine one can lye (13 oz) with two and one-half pints of cold water, (rain water is best) with six pounds clean fat (about six and three-fourths or 12 standard cups).

Pour the lye into the cold water and carefully stir until the lye is dissolved.

Let mixture cool to correct temperature.

Melt fat into clear liquid and let cool gradually to correct temperature.

As to the correct temperature this is the key! – use a dairy or floating thermometer. When soap is made from sweet, rancid fat the lye solution should be held at room temperature of 75 to 80 degrees Fahrenheit and the fat at 97 to 100 degrees at the time they are mixed together. Sweet lard and other soft fats call for temperatures of 70 to….Part II missing.

October 26, 1972

All thoughts now in Bluemont are of the fine day we all had at the Bluemont Fair, visitors and hosts alike.

I suppose one of life's greatest satisfactions is to bring pleasure to others and how gratifying it is to hear our guests say what fun they were having.

It only takes a perceptive person a short time to sense the beauty and richness of the lives of the good people I'm fortunate to call my neighbors.

One guest put it so beautifully to me – "the weather may be cold" she said, "but this town is warm. The people here are alive: people are dead in the city."

As usual everyone pitched in doing their specialty.

Mrs. Elizabeth Kelley was stirring up fruit cakes from Mrs. Molly Weadon's recipe. Natives will remember her for her wonderful Virginia House where she served the best of meals for 50 cents.

And if you don't remember, you could have seen it recaptured in the slide show, "When the Trains Came to Bluemont."

Another interesting fact that Mrs. Ruth Blackburn of the Potomac Appalachian Trail Club pointed out to me was that a 1934 folder she read said overnight accommodations for hikers at Snicker's Gap were available at Clayton Hall.

Plus a Clayton came by from Georgia whom I missed while viewing the Beck's cabin, which was absolutely adorable with Mrs. Verloop giving a marvelous spinning demonstration.

Because of the real chill this year prior to the Fair, some kind of classic things happened.

Thursday morning found me sweeping the snow off the pumpkins – I've heard of frost upon the pumpkins but this was ridiculous!

In addition, the old kitchen here had a fire on the hearth probably the first time in at least thirty years thanks to Marvin Watts who experimented successfully with it Thursday night and then "Hawkeye" Reid laid a roaring one each morning of the Fair while a nice import, Tom Brown of Paeonian Springs, kept it going all day.

Curt Budny with the Indian display exhibited his real sense of humor when he pointed out the circus train and Indian presentation were the most popular of the exhibits at the schoolhouse due he said to the room that contained the best heat from the only stove in the vicinity.

The train display was even more elaborate than last year. Linda deButts and visiting family seemed to really like it.

Then the musket shoot was extremely colorful – the uniforms were bright red – those of the Louisiana Tigers, and having four daughters I got a full report from my oldest who was particularly fascinated by the event, bringing home a real musket bullet and a story about one of the soldiers losing his keys – to his house she claimed.

The setting there was perfect with the turning foliage as a backdrop.

We wish to thank our neighbor, Joseph Leith from White Post for bringing the group. He's our personification of Abraham Lincoln, you know and it was a real jolt to get a call from his wife last week when she jokingly identified herself as Abe Lincoln's wife. Her costume was marvelous too!

Another wonderful guest who spent the night in the village was our talented poster artist, Al Boswell from Norfolk.

A decade of Bluemont News

And the craftsmen who came did such quality work, those demonstrating in the new shed had lovely, lovely items.

Of course, there was lots of other news – most everyone had house guests.

The R.M. Peytons' daughter Sadie and husband William were here from Winchester for the weekend and when Mrs. Tyson Payne called me about her Oct. 7 visit to the Oliver Paynes in Winchester, I nailed her down to help in the book shop.

She went to celebrate their son's birthday who was home on leave from the Marines stationed in Jacksonsville, Fla.

Then on Sunday of that week they celebrated her young great grandson's birthday at the Grantland Lloyd's near White Post.

The William Ballengers were entertaining again with weekend guests, Bill's aunt Mrs. Marie Baardsen and children Gail and Gary of Arlington, along with Mrs. Ballenger's cousin, Mrs. Annabel Mathias of W.Va. and cousin Mrs. Anita Whetzel and sons Byron and Jeremy of Linville, Va.

Up at Happy Place last week, Mrs. Taylor Holt, Jr. had as her house guest a girlhood chum, Mrs. R.A. Hicks (nee Nell Jones of Boyce) from Front Royal.

With Mrs. Hicks as her guest of honor, Mrs. Holt gave a buffet luncheon attended by several other of her schoolmates of earlier days in Boyce. The guests were Mrs. Mozelle Henson, Miss Ruth Toyston, and Miss Retha Gaunt of Berryville, Mrs. Louise Langbeim of Pine Grove, Miss Mary Thompson of White Post and Mrs. Helen Welch (nee Helen Shumate of Boyce) of Lincoln who had taught all these ladies when Boyce had a high school.

Col. Holt who was on KP says the various reminiscences were both revealing and delightful to hear.

There was talk of the old days in Boyce when the "drummers" got off the train there, spent the night at the hotel, rented a rig from Sam Edison, Mrs. Holt's father who happened to be the owner of the hotel, and the livery stable.

Sounds like some stories about Bluemont I've heard when every general store sold the finest of merchandise this side of New York.

Now as always on the heels of the Bluemont Fair, comes the annual Halloween party at the schoolhouse set for Tuesday night, from 7:30 – 9 o'clock.

There will be the usual cider and cookies, the cake walks, a door prize and prizes for the prettiest, ugliest, the most original, the best witch and the best ghost costume.

And our good young friend Paul Draisey of Round Hill gave us a fine on-the-spot reporting for WAGE radio and was the hot cider popular this year, but best of all was the natives' conversation. "Oh, yes you married Katherine Hummer, lived out here by Bloomfield. You turn on that dirt road, there was a barn that burned there at one time."

See you at the next Bluemont Fair!

November 2, 1972

We were socked in…the soaking rain kept the colorful leaves fluttering to the ground and the children left to their own resources captive indoors, were incorrigible!

Two visitors came to the shop but otherwise the day was drab, the loud ticking of Grandma's clock marked tediousness even though the aroma from the oven of the oatmeal cookies for the Halloween party lifted our spirits somewhat.

We were to carve our big pumpkin into a shining Jack-O-Lantern tonight but one more project with this crew after a day like today was unthinkable.

All the talk the week through has been of Halloween costumes.

Tracey remembered there was a clown suit around here in one of the trunks somewhere and Lara was agreeable to don a sheet for a ghost and Jennifer said she would be the Confederate drummer boy complete with gauze bandage on her head.

The talk was the same at the Snow House; Mary Lynn Budny recalled for years she was content to be a gypsy with lots of bracelets on her arms and necklaces about her neck.

That led me to think back to childhood Halloweens and all I could remember was how ghastly to have to wear a mask, stumbling up some neighbor's steps for a treat.

We lived in one of those perfectly horrible suburbias where Halloween literally was a nightmare with kids swarming at the door but I do recall the parade on Halloween night was something pretty great with hot dogs for all the kids and there was bobbing for apples and the judging of the costumes on one street of the neighborhood called Taylor's Court.

Then during college days, I was always a flapper. My mother had made me a costume of a black sequined dress and classmates actually threw pennies when I did the Charleston. Maybe that's my repressed desire – to be a frivolous flapper!

Well, enough of Halloween's past – here's hoping it's a pleasant night.

Before we leave George Cochran and the pumpkin subject, I wish to add that I was unaware of their other two children's existence when I wrote up the feature last week.

Their oldest child is Barbara Lee Melton of Annandale who holds a very important position as Secretary of the Joint Chiefs of Staff at the Pentagon and tragically they lost their youngest, a son Steven Allen at the age of 18.

Now before the Jack-o-Lantern can wipe his grin away (I wrote an editorial about that years ago), everyone is talking Christmas.

Of course, these local bazaars are very pleasant affairs.

Mrs. Frances Iden gives us word that the Parish House of Grace Episcopal Church in Berryville is holding a Christmas bazaar on Nov. 16 from 7-9 o'clock and Nov. 17 from 10 a.m. to 3 p.m., lunch being served that day with many beautiful hand crafted gifts for all ages, Christmas decorations, baked goods, jams and jellies, toys and attic treasures. It sounds charming, indeed.

A decade of Bluemont News

Naturally too this week Nov. 2, 3, 4 from 11 a.m.-9 p.m. on Thursday, and Friday and 11 a.m.-5 p.m. on Saturday is the Early Peek at Christmas at Skyes Hall near Leesburg sponsored by the Loudoun County Craft Club, the show them being Christmas, R.F.D.

The country ham and biscuit lunch sounds divine, too.

It's that time of year all right. Elizabeth Kelley had her bucket this week for gathering black walnuts which she claimed were in abundance at the side of the Airmont road.

Giving credit where credit is due, Herbert Martz assisted Walton Mann in cleaning the fence rows in town for the Fair. Herbert said it was a 17½ hour job.

Thanks to everyone who helps us put this affair over every year. We appreciated our help from Purcellville, Round Hill and Leesburg.

And while we're giving our bouquets, June Lloyd wanted to thank everyone for their cards while she was in the hospital. She said she got about 100 remembrances plus flowers and dried arrangements.

I told June she proved the old saying, "No one is indispensable" wrong, There was no Bluemont apple butter this year due to June's inability to make it.

Now generally there is a harmonious tone between man and beast in Bluemont but you've all heard of the Hatfields and McCoys, the Shepherdsons and Grangerfords, right now there's a full-blown feud between me and a certain goat named Sassy.

First time was the geraniums but then as the end of the season, one can overlook it, then the rosiness of my cheeks paled the other night when I went to feed the dog on the porch only to hear a clattering of hoofs, jumping to and fro on the picnic table, that could be taken in stride but when I caught him munching my gift chrysanthemum from Mrs. Ogden, having already devoured Thelma Brunelle's bittersweet hanging on the shop door, it was too much! And to think I'm a Capricorn myself.

Other doings beside the Fair last weekend in Bluemont, was a fantastic Great Pyrenees dog rally up at the Paul Strangs; a few gravitated down this way with the news and the William Ballengers, Jr. and Sr. along with Mrs. Ella Mae Gennade toured the marvelous Shenandoah National Park from Front Royal to Afton when the leaves must have been at their peak.

Next year we'll get there with a pot of chili in tote; time to get the Thanksgiving invitations out and the wood in.

November 9, 1972

The large golden maple framed the brown bottles propped on the window ledge as the days rotated dark and bright as November knocked at the door this week.

October went out in grand style – a fun time was had in Bluemont Halloween night before the rain descended.

The costumes were the best I've seen in years. The judges fount it most difficult to pick the best in the designated categories at the annual party down at the schoolhouse but at last they said, David Keyes was the ugliest, the best ghost was David Anderson, the best witch was April Wilt who also won a prize with her costume at Round Hill Elementary School, the prettiest was Tammy Dawson in a fairy god-mother outfit while the most original went to Greg McCauley whose mother had done it again this time with a marvelous bird out of crepe paper.

The neighbors across the street had created some darling costumes, Chris Budny was a monster with four arms and a multi-colored mop for hair while his little sister Heather was the cutest little witch you've ever seen. Leslie Hutchins had made son Kenny a magnificent clown costume with big hat and suit of stripes and polka-dots.

Additionally, Pam Carbaugh was outstanding as Abraham Lincoln and Mary Jo Lloyd was a cute Frenchman in beret and striped shirt accented with a painted-on mustache.

What would we do without Jane Rogers' props? Beecher Hope wore his fireman's hat from Jane's Kindergarten and last year Lara won with Jane's birthday crown.

And don't we all love the cake walks?

Almost every family won a cake, Maurice Verloop, the twins here (they wound up being a doctor and nurse). Kelley Lloyd and Brian Beck won the beautifully decorated cake at Round Hill Elementary School for guessing what was inside (a candy pumpkin) and the right number.

In like manner, Roberta Underwood won the cake door prize for adults at the Bluemont party by guessing the right number.

Walton Mann always gets the best cider to go with the homemade cookies so it was a pleasant evening, indeed.

We're all happy to hear that Bruce and Diana Brownell have now finished their new house and are maintaining residence down a lane off Rt. 7.

There's little news now in the countryside, villagers are winterizing – Mary Lynn Budny (brave soul that she was) took a five-day trip to Georgia to visit her parents with the two young children.

It's election time again and I know it's extremely terrible of me – but when are the American people going to get some real caliber leadership again?

Sorry 'bout that-guess the Kennedys and the promise they held out to this nation got in my system. Name -calling is not my kind of campaign!

The standard time ushered in more fatigue to me—the children and I awake on the old time, now it's 6:30 instead of 7:30 and we go to bed by the old so I figure I'm missing an hour of sleep!

Round one of the Capricorn fight is over, Sassy retired to the mountainside where I'm sure a good weed patch exists for his munching and good company, instead of an irate lover of flowers.

The natural playthings this week seem the best, the children handle sticks and ropes for jumping over and leaves for jumping in.

They gather the fallen pears and apples and load the semi-logs for the fireplace in the little red wagon. I think some people call it work!

Whenever I feel poverty stricken and I got a pang near the end of the month with very little teaching behind me, I always reason that I should make bread pudding.

You see you take those scraps of bread you throw in the garbage or feed to the birds and whip them up into something sweet and tasty and that's just what I did - a casserole full makes two meals of dessert- it's really better chilled when the spices and raisins have a chance to jell.

November 16, 1972

Neighbors crowding to the polls…apple-picking-ups at Berryville…fresh patches of poison ivy…a surprise party for Joan Wilt – these were the Bluemont dispatches this week.

Election Day, dawned so bright and clear, it looked like a good day to get some apples for sauce making – the Johnsons will probably have the most expensive apple sauce in both counties – between the doctor's office call for Lara's case of poison ivy, those two bushels of apples ran us around fifteen dollars. Beware—apple-pickers!

I hear Diana Brownell has a terrific case too—burning the dried leaves can be dangerous also. In fact, why do we burn the leaves, they are so colorful on the ground and so unpolluting?

Other news over at the James Brownells is that daughter Susan and husband David Vondle are here for a visit before establishing residency in Ft. Campbell, Ky., where Susan is now a lieutenant in the Army Nurse Corps.

Maybe they will still be here to join us for the annual Bluemont Fair dinner to be held this Sunday evening, Nov. 19 at 6 o'clock in the schoolhouse auditorium.

Everyone who worked at the Fair is invited to attend: we all bring a covered dish, silverware and plates and cups are provided.

It was great to see Herb Little passing by today on his way up to his retreat at the top of the hill. I know Herb and I hope the rest of the community will be interested to see my article about the how's and why's of our first Bluemont Fair, appearing in this month's Virginia Cardinal.

If you would like a copy, I have them available here in the shop. Of course, Herb was our script writer for the historical slide shows.

Everyone has done his "own thing" in such a dynamic way!

My father said the model train layout was the best he had ever seen anywhere.

Erroneously identified in the slide show as the farmer who made the train stop at his door was Frank McComb, former owner of Whitehall Farm who celebrated his 80th birthday this week with a birthday dinner at the Glen Lloyds.

Entertaining over the weekend were the G.W. Townshends with guests of Mr. and Mrs. Krehl Stringer of Ft. Wayne, Ind., and Mr. and Mrs. Winston Hyre of Petersburg, Va.

Half the town of Bluemont is brushing crumbs off Mt. Vernon, the University of Virginia and Springtime on the Skyline Drive as the W.S.C.S. finally got their order of attractive Virginia scenes placemats.

I was expecting to sell them at Clayton Hall Book and Craft Shop but I guess I'll have to wait for another order as they are all sold out, and settle for bragging about the apple-head dolls, tree ornaments and darling knitted hats the neighbors are bringing for sale.

Now the way I know about someone surprising Joan Wilt with a party is that I called up about the Brownie Handbook and got the news right in the middle of the happening on Saturday night.

I still don't know where to get the Brownie Handbook but Jennifer and April Wilt from our neck of the woods will be pleased to be "investitured" Monday afternoon.

Too the week began in the most inspiring way when I was invited to substitute for Mrs. Lipps, instructing her fourth grade class down at Loudoun Country Day School.

A discussion of Halloween ensued and suddenly these seven voices were reciting "Little Orphan Annie's came to our house to stay an' wash the cups and saucers up, and brush the crumbs away." And they went on to reiterate, "O The Raggedy Man, He works for Pa; and he's the goodliest man ever you saw!" Shades of Grandma's pieces!

Then I had a day delving into Mrs. Lipps' book of verse with other James Whitcomb Riley poems – a man who knew the country places like Bluemont.

Then I came home to the closest person we have of our Raggedy Man in the Bluemont area – Herbert Martz doing me a good deed sawing up some logs for the fireplace when the VEPCO boys can't quite make it.

"The Raggedy Man – one time when he wuz making' a little bow-'n-'orry for me, says "When your big like your Pa is, Air you go' to keep a fine store like his—'An be a rich merchant – an' wear fine clothes?—An' I says, I' go' to be a Raggedy Man!, I'st go' to be a nice Raggedy Man! Raggedy! Raggedy! Raggedy Man!"

And if our children turned out kind-hearted and vigorous like the likes of these men, could we ask for anything more?

November 23, 1972

There is buzzing, buzzing talk at the general store – "It feels like snow" and so it was predicted by some for tonight.

And as human nature is wont to do, we remind each other of last year's Thanksgiving – no one need to tell me – there's a little one-year old at our house now, born right before the storm last year.

Libby and Bootsie Stearne entertained the girls and Grandmother Johnson for a wonderful turkey dinner while most of the town ate cold ham and I dined on a tray at Loudoun Memorial Hospital.

As our thoughts turn to the festive day, maybe the real meaning ought to shine through and as the wind howled and the rain blew this week I thought it is right to be thankful for the taken for granted blessings like no leak in the roof and the valve on the water pressure tank is working correctly and no major work on the car needs to be done right now.

With an early deadline there is virtually no news except the G.W. Townshends had a marvelous weekend visiting Senator and Mrs. Charles See in Cumberland, Md., Eugene Thayer and sisters at Oakland, Md., Mrs. Thomas Bergdoll and daughter and Mrs. S.R. Dodd and family in Moorefield, W.Va. and the Ray Peters and George Hokes in Rock Oak, W.Va.

We were happy to see Bessie Carter over in the store in Berryville last week: she is doing fine and enjoying her residency there.

Sorry to hear Marvin Watts has a sick raccoon on his hands but Racquell is certainly getting the best of tender loving care from him and Yoko.

We had a great day with Yoko last night at our house, we made her read everything Japanese in the house and tell us what it meant, including some lacquer chop sticks I have in the shop and then I drilled her all day long on her country's customs, the role of women, political problems, and then Barbara Spring treated her to a good ole American Hershey bar.

How wonderful to have people in our community from other lands.

It's the time of year to draw the family in a little closer, make the nest a more cozy spot – we've been rearranging, organizing and "thinking" about painting.

All the apples are in, all the potatoes in a place where they won't freeze (we are indebted to the Andersons and Bob Joneses for a winter's supply).

The Brownie investiture was very nice and Terry Davis of our neighborhood is also one of the new troop members of Number 514.

Then I turned around and saw my old Girl Scout Handbook and wonder of wonders those manuels were up on some things! It told you what vegetables to use for dying threads for spinning. From onion skins you get light brown, yellow and orange; spinach juice – green; beet juice – rose; goldenrod flowers – gold; coffee bean – brown; sumac (leaves – black, berries – red). You steep the plants in water overnight – it's all here and the new Brownie handbook tells you how to make corn husk dolls, and homemade butter and pebble animals!

Now what I'm really looking for is the pattern for making turkey name cards out of pine cones – I'll have to ask Lynn Carbaugh about that. So let your china glimmer, the candles flicker, the warm talk flow about the Thanksgiving table and don't forget to give a hooray for the pumpkin pie!

November 30, 1972

Of feasting and those who feasted – the Thanksgiving story line was unmarred by snow, wind or rain in Bluemont this year.

The day shone bright with snow blanketing the lawn, gone before the guests arrived for the once-a-year gathering.

Lynn Carbaugh came to give a birthday greeting to our Virginia Clayton and was hood-winked into doing the pine cone place cards for us. Thanks to Dot Richard in Lovettsville for giving me the instruction too over the phone.

The William Carbaughs took their usual trek up the hill to the Wesley Carbaughs where "Mimi" performs her culinary miracles. Lynn's favorite being the stewed oysters with hot horseradish sauce. Mmmm!

The Becks usually in Charlottesville went closer to home to Joyce's parents, the Paul Groves in Lovettsville. The first gathering they were able to have for many years due to Mrs. Grove's usual involvement in the serving of the famous Thanksgiving dinner now discontinued by the Lutheran Church there. I'll never forget those delicious noodles I had at that dinner one year!

And believe me, June Lloyd has recovered, she was making cinnamon buns and pudding last Sunday and they had Thanksgiving dinner with Jerry and children, Paul and Ann Wilson and their brand-new baby boy born last week, James Michael, and Judy and Bill Casey with off-spring plus the other Lloyds still at the home base.

The Robert Allders did it up right, beginning on Wednesday Barbara entertained Mrs. Joan Wilt, Mrs. Russell Parks, Sr., Mrs. Mae Swetnam who is having a nice visit with the Martin Wilts, Robert McDonald and Mrs. Betty Pierson.

Then on Thanksgiving the Russell Parks, Sr. came to dinner and Mrs. Gordon Arnett came by in the afternoon for coffee as she had been a dinner guest of the Charles Parks.

Then the great blessing of the day, J.K. called from his Navy base, relating that he had to stand in line for three hours to get a chance to make the call, no turkey dinner that day but he would be home Dec. 24.

We also found there were other occasions to remember. Curtis Budny had a birthday, the Thomas Ogdens – a wedding anniversary, Lawrence Dawson – a birthday and Sue and Sonny Hall – a first wedding anniversary.

The Halls joined the Dawsons, the Michael Hoggatts at Bootsie and Libby Stearne's for Thanksgiving dinner.

Thanksgiving was Bluemont's second big feed of the week – last Sunday night was the Bluemont Fair covered-dish dinner. I still haven't recovered from being distracted from serving myself a piece of cherry pie only to return and find it gone. I'm suspecting Charles O'Brien of the misdemeanor.

A goodly crowd was on hand in spite of the horrible weather to hear the finance committee report (we expect to net about five thousand again this year), and see interesting slide views taken by Tony Carbone of our valley terrain and the marvelous Fair pictures taken by Alec and Tim Walsh.

Then the big "extra" of the evening was Albert Gordon's "light" show. A fantastic display of colors in water projected on a screen was perfectly lovely with accompaniment on the guitar by Bo Leyden. He and wife Jean brought some terrific whole wheat bread too.

And Thanksgiving Day at Clayton Hall was such a joyous occasion. As is our custom, we all bring something and our appetite. We had turkey, mashed potatoes with giblet gravy, oyster dressing, chestnut dressing, cranberry sauce, turnips, baked squash and boiled squash, jello salad, green beans, rolls, two sweet potato dishes, hot cider, mince tarts, pumpkin pie, apple pie and apple sauce cake with the Johnsons, the Porterfields, the Lardies and three cousins I haven't seen in years. The talk was of their experience running a "tea-room" back in Springfield, Mo. years ago.

It all began one Thanksgiving when a bunch of their friends wanted to gather together and pay fifty cents for the meal so Aunt Ivy said, "Come on over: and they had a turkey dinner with all the trimmings for fifty cents.

Another group asked for the same, then the manager of the Country Golf Club called and they were in the catering business – serving 450 Kiwanians hot food in twenty minutes – yes – they did the dishes for me before they started back to Falls Church in the dark, Thanksgiving night!

And next year if we are snowed in – the invitation's good here – Clayton Hall Tea Room, anyone?

We're happy to know Bruce Cochran was able to come home from Eastern Nazarene College near Boston for the holiday.

The only sour note in the week was the Vepco bill again – the April 9.1 increase in my estimation shouldn't make all our bills double. Let's write our State Senator Waddell – this is how a monopoly can control an area unless we resolve to use the only recourse we have to unfair practices.

Another disturbed Bluemonter this week was Col. Teasdale-Smith when he saw the hunters' work of a slain deer hanging on a scaffold down at Loudoun Country Day School. He says he feeds them up near his home on the mountain.

Want to have some fun, meet interesting people, run an ad – this week I sold a desk to a writer, a bed to a psychiatrist.

Hope to see you at the Olde English Christmas Fair at the Valley Community Center; I will go and take some of the neighbors' hand-crafts and my spice tea and the books.

December 7, 1972

The scent of bayberry and strawberry and cinnamon candles mingled with the aroma of spice tea still hangs in the air or at least in the imagination after a day at a booth at the Christmas Fair.

Not many of the Bluemont neighbors gravitated to Purcellville for the Olde English Christmas Fair but there were our friends who like to come to the Bluemont Fair and many who labor long hours helping us, Meg Nichols and Esther Terrill were there.

Santa was there in jolly form along with the magnificent puppet show and as usual, Emma Mann, my good Bluemont neighbor, was my best customer.

Frankly, I'm almost too tired to discuss it but was I glad to see Moselle Anderson from Philomont and then I had a good chat with the Janneys over at their store in Lincoln before hurrying home to throw on the hash here.

If you intend to keep up with the latest local history, Asa Moore and Werner Janney have out a delightful little book. A Composition Book, reminiscences of days gone by in Lincoln and then Spur Magazine this quarter has a nice article by Worthy Caulk on "Lincoln on Loudoun."

Also a Mrs. Verner now of North Carolina and former Bluemont resident writes that she has some fascinating old letters written by citizens of this locale.

Her grandfather was our famed Dr. George E. Plaster – she has his autobiography – he was an amazing man!

Some of the Throckmortons may be interested in her letters written to Sarah M. Throckmorton of Meadow Farm near Snickersville. Call me if you want more information.

In the same field of reference, Mrs. Griffing of Berryville related the story that our Clayton Hall barn was used to winter the animals of a circus years ago. She has more marvelous ties with this place which I want to have accurate before I repeat them.

Ruth Manuel tells me their Thanksgiving dinner guests were her brother known as Sonny to the neighborhood and his family from Baltimore. Then sister Dolly Journell and her husband and four girls came to the Clarence Manuels for an afternoon visit.

The William Ballengers, Jr. entertained the William Ballengers, Sr. and Bill Break from Herndon, Gary Barrbsen and Peter Armstrong from Arlington and John H. Clifton from Pleasant Valley.

The Kenneth Reids had guests too for Thanksgiving dinner: Mrs. Lillie Reid of Pine Grove, Mr. and Mrs. John Smallwood and daughter of Ransom, W.Va. and Mr. and Mrs. Pete Carter and children from Alexandria.

Then too, this week I met Bo Cutter, one of the candidates seeking the seat vacated by Delegate Phillips.

He seemed to have some real game plans to combat the developing of our county resulting in driving out the natives.

Now I made no bones about it, I'm a new-comer to Loudoun, been here just ten years but I know it's a place where there are roots and a life that is rewarding – why don't those of you who have the heritage here give these developers and dollar-crazy investors a fight?

Why give up and say we will have to go elsewhere – put your support behind the candidate who diagnoses this cancer of the land as a disease.

More schools, more services for a growing population – more taxes – it will never end – no more rolling hills, no more fertile gardens – high-rises and a mass of frustrated apartment dwellers vending hostility on their neighbors – that waving dollar-bill will virtually take our breath – our life away.

Now we have all the riches that money cannot buy – comfort, security, adventure, a satisfaction in living – a cosmos small enough where the individual creativity can be expressed.

For four years I have been trying to say it in my own way – life is good here – why let it be spoiled?

Sometimes life brings a pain we feel we cannot bear; so we all feel about the death of the Jim Brownells' beautiful Susan. There is little comfort at a time like this, a young life so vital and sweet gone. How will the mother and father, the brothers, the grandmothers bear it, the close friends of the family. All we know to say is we wish we could ease the pain. Each one in the community will have to find the answer within themselves how they can best express it.

December 14, 1972

The feeling is creeping in like the fog settling over the village now. Across the street a Christmas tree peeks out under the trunk on Jean and Mike Haggatt's car and the Budnys and Hutchins' mothers have let it be whispered that they are mixing up a batch of gingerbread men.

Here at Clayton Hall, it's Christmas in the kitchen but still Thanksgiving in the dining room.

The horn of plenty on the table with George Cochran's pumpkins seemed too pretty to disassemble while the kitchen mantel boasts Barbara Spring's beautiful knitted potholder and Lindsay Hope's wonderful scented candles. Did most of my shopping at home this year, just opened the door, picked some very select gifts and wrote out a check.

Even before I joined the "merchant" marines I preached "shopping at home." Why people want to fight the crowds at these huge shopping complexes, I've never known.

We have everything you would want in Loudoun County and over in Berryville, Sue Mearns and I were exalting the virtues of the Berryville Variety Store again. In fact, every time I shop in Berryville, I wonder why I ever go anywhere else.

I'll have a little open house here at the shop next weekend. I'll brew up the spice tea again and make a big fire on the stone hearth and I'll get some evergreen boughs and I have the bittersweet and pine cones, and maybe we ought to put a red ribbon on "Little Bit" who took a sniffing tour when the door was open this week.

All the Christmas plans are set now.

Our annual community house decorating judging for the contest will be from the hours of 7-9 p.m. on the 22nd and 23rd.

They asked me to get the judges this year and I'm not telling who they are – no bribing them with food and drink, you know?

Anyone living in a two mile radius of Bluemont is eligible or if you wish to be included, please call me.

Clyde Beck will decorate Miss Alley's lovely large tree again in the next week and the Bluemont Methodist Church group will carol on the 23rd while the MYF will present their program on the 22nd at the church at 7:30 p.m.

It is a perfect time to meet your neighbors, full of good health and merriment, at the little old stone church.

We feel a real loss of Mrs. Maud Alton who lived atop our Bluemont hill for so many years. Somehow most of the community did not receive the word until after the funeral.

We have been comforted with Homer Hall's words along with Bill Betts' at Susan Brownell Vondle's funeral. Certainly our prayers should be altered daily for her family here in our community and her husband.

We are sorry to hear Grandmother Chapman has been ill over at the William Carbaugh's while the youngest granddaughter, Pam had a birthday this week.

She was wishing for a sleeping bag, I'm told, telling her mother it would be ideal on cold nights on the top floor.

This all led me to think of almost all our village houses in days gone by being warmed only by fireplaces, wood, or coal stoves.

Jack Bardon brought a genuine coal shovel here for the shop merchandise and I decided that was one purchase I needed to add to my list from Santa, not for coal but SNOW!

But at nights then, I'm told, one just had to curl down under the heavy quilts in order to keep warm. The stoves are generally just downstairs, not in the upstairs bedrooms. June Lloyd says a relative of hers always gave a big quilt and two pillows to the newlyweds. That was to set them up in housekeeping.

Julie Hope, young daughter of Lindsay and Donald Hope near Airmont, had a birthday too this week.

Now the letters have been written to Santa.

Lara was distressed to hear about the deer, Col. Teasdale-Smith, so she wrote "A deer was killed." She thought Santa ought to know about that since he's such a friend and associate with the creatures.

Then Tracey wrote, "I'm not going to ask for much things 'cause I know you don't have much money."

And the decorations that have been made here for the tree – endless scraps of paper on the floor, string must be located and oh the begging from Mother for her tape.

According to our calculations, twice-daily, check with the calendar, it's fourteen days before Christmas as of this writing and as the excitement rises here, it's too much for a Mother to resist the admonition, "you'd better be good, Santa's coming soon, you know."

Eugene Fields knew the custom well, writing his last stanza of "Jest Fore Christmas."

"For Christmas, with its lots an' lots of candles, cakes, an' toys.
Was made, they say, for proper kids an' not for naughty boys.
So wash yer face an' brush yer hair, an' mine yer p's and q's.
And don't bust out yer pantaloons, an' don't wear out yer shoes.
And when they's company don't pass your plate for pie again.
But be thinkin' of the thing yer'd like to see upon that tree.
Jest fore Christmas be as good as yer kin be!"

December 21, 1972

A chilling, biting wind rocked the shutters, incredible icy drafts came in the cracks, around the old windows of the village and countryside houses as the kitchens rendered up the scents of apple sauce cakes and fudge and cookies – so many different kinds – all in readiness for the holiday just ahead.

Out the window could be seen the telephone man scurrying by, the fuel delivery man filling another tank and the siding folks busily tacking up the wonderful red color on the Snow House.

The evergreens and holly are marching in the doors and the lights of the Christmas decorations twinkle brightly now.

Families have their own traditions so we're glad Papa got his oysters from the Bay again and he is coming up this week to make the oyster stew.

Due to the popularity of the decoration judges who had planned to party both nights of the 22nd and 23rd, we've had to change our judging night to the 21st, the first day of winter so the calendar says. Deck your Halls from 7-9 that night, please!

The Clyde Becks extended their festivities this year to a perfect pre-Christmas trip to New York City.

How enchanting to see the dazzling decorations in the big stores, the 70-foot tree in Rockefeller Center with the ice skaters making it a real picturesque scene and to do the rounds of the museums and a few choice restaurants.

With terrible mixed emotions we have learned that Mrs. Barbara Spring has definitely sold her house to the William Miners.

Mrs. Spring has occupied the old house at the crest of the hill for a number of years, being a good neighbor to all.

Her talents are legion, she knits beautifully – afghans, little tree ornaments, bell corsages and her orange marmalade is popular with the city folks.

Everyone in the community says the same, we hate to see her go.

Of course, we will be pleased to welcome the Miners who are searching out old records for a construction date on the house.

The Jack Bardons' off-spring are making Mom and Dad proud again.

Daughter Jeannie, a Senior at Madison College has been inducted into the National Scholarship Society while son Michael has been named to Who's Who Among American University and College students.

The city newspaper enticed no one to have a "Christmas Adventure" at Clayton Hall Book and Craft Shop but into the warmth of the kitchen around the old oak table, Annie Benedum and Glen and June Lloyd chatted while I listened to the most enchanting swapping of the ways of living a generation ago.

The way the neighbors dealt with death, cold, moving, storing of foods without refrigeration, boarding and feeding laborers and traveling salesman (peddlers, they called them) and any of life's crises together was one of the most fascinating pieces of conversations I've ever heard.

I need no other Christmas present this year – their information was a gift they shared enthusiastically making me richer by far than any store-bought item. It was a Christmas adventure.

Two Italian entertainers pointed out this week to the viewing public that the kitchen is the center of the Italian home. One stated that his family even had a sofa in the kitchen – then there would be a stove there with tangerine peelings – a fact I just learned that for a marvelous tangy scent, put orange peelings or cinnamon in the fireplace.

Dr. Joyce Brothers says for all that Christmas is, it boils down that it is a symbol of love – of course, for the Christians, a belief that God showed his love for us by sending his son Jesus Christ.

Funny that I should pop open a usually closed drawer this week to find a poem I wrote at the tender age of 21.

It seems timely, entitled, "I Believe at Christmas."

"I believe Christmas comes at least once a year
To open, perhaps, just one heart
That would remain clinched and tight
If it weren't for a stream of love
That came spilling out and one drop fell on that heart

At Christmas,
I believe every year

There's a Scrooge
Who turns his back on his role
To new life in the Son of God
Who was born in a manger.

At Christmas,
I believe every year
There's a strife-bitten family
Who licks their wounds
Puts self on the shelf
And resolves to practice
Peace on Earth.

At Christmas,
I believe because I'm that clinched heart
That leaps up
I'm the Scrooge who says
May the Spirit be our Spirit.

At Christmas,
Oh, might our prayer be to the One who came
That love, kindness and peace
Might reign in our hearts
All through the year
Rather than just
At Christmas.

My warmest best wishes for a joyous Merry Christmas.

December 28, 1972

Oh, the scurrying, the hurrying, the merriment and good cheer in the village of Bluemont this day before Christmas could be the setting straight out of an idyllic book.

Early in the morning, John and Brad Campbell, brightly-wrapped packages in tote were singing angelic carols (not quite their claim to fame) as they hurried down the street.

We've had our cookie exchange with the Carbaughs and such other delights the neighbors have shared – a package of fresh sausage and homemade bread and Mrs. Townshend's "Nothings" for the tree besides a wonderful plus of Mrs. Ogden's very special gingerbread men for hanging and if you don't believe in Santa, you don't live in Bluemont.

Herbert Martz maybe minus the beard and red suit but nevertheless, was full steam ahead on his tractor with the little cart behind, loaded down with pounds and pounds of mixed candy, tangerines, oranges, and apples for the good little boys and girls on his list.

And the occasions that we can attend seem to get nicer each year.

The MYF program down at the lovely old stone church was beautiful – lit in candlelight with the village children taking a part.

How marvelous to have Bruce Cochran home from college leading the service and to hear a good strong bass from Allen Carter in the chorus with Hope Carbaugh's really outstanding recitation of a poem, "Annie and Willie's Prayer."

Also this year we have a unique ornament for our tree fashioned by Yoko, our new Japanese friend, the paper is sewn with long streamers accenting the oriental flavor.

Great fun this year was my turn to pick the judges for the Christmas decorating contest.

Jack Bardon chauffeured us through the fog atop the mountain as the judges were giving points to those up there who had a good driveway in which to turn around. In fact, an insect light was about to capture first prize, until we got down to the safe little village, as Claire Bardon said.

Anyway, the Becks took first place "simple but beautiful," they said and then everyone whole-heartedly voted the James Walsh's second. The red and blue lights on the pillars of the porch made a magnificent display.

Then third place went to Sarah Campbell and since there were so many worthy displays – the judges wanted to extend an honorable mention to Miss Alley for her doorway decoration, the Lowes' arrangement that they pronounced as cheerful and to the Manuels who had some pretty blue and green lights down the stairs and across the porch railing.

We missed the Russell Pearsons that night but I've heard it was perfect and Judy Casey tells me Bill Kelley has a big blue cross on his silo which can be seen for miles around.

I thought the Loopes' tree was very pretty up at Ginger Hill and I loved the candles in the windows at the Bill Carbaughs.

If I could have the display I wanted – I'd just have a wonderful old-fashioned sleigh – hitched up and ready to go with sleigh bells ringing – I'm determined there will be a sleigh ride in Bluemont someday.

Preceding the whole community holiday fun here was the brightest day over at Lincoln Elementary.

Now I know why Asa Moore and Werner Janney's mother fought to keep the school in Lincoln.

The teachers seemed so extra nice, the children so friendly and cooperative – a real family atmosphere was there.

Mrs. Pearson's third grade (my assignment for the day) shared treats with their classmates, one mother making an elaborate favor for every child to hang on his or her Christmas tree. The teacher gave each child a book and a box of wonderful homemade cookies and then a first for me – they served their own homemade root beer and was it delicious!

Yes, the Christmases get nicer every year!

It was good to know Jimmy Brownell with his wife and two young children were here from Richmond with the rest of the family drawing close at Whitehall – comforted by the love of their friends in the Loudoun countryside.

How wonderful to see J.K. Cornwall in his sailor suit, safely returned to his family, the Robert Allders for a perfect Christmas furlough.

A bit of sad news, of course, was the death of Lillian Allder, age 89 who was staying with Mrs. Campbell for a number of years. She was Mrs. Manuel's aunt – we do extend our sympathy to all her loved ones.

The decoration judges were a philosophical crew, the Jack Bardons, Mary Alice Wertz, Sue Mearns and as we chatted around the kitchen table, we were optimistic, saying that the trend toward ecology and away from alcohol and eventually drugs, and more concern for our fellow-man is bound to make the world a better place in the 70's.

And as the day neared with all that needed to be done, it still seemed the thing to do to sit down and watch a Jimmy Stewart movie.

It was a Christmas story and everything turned out all right of course, but his guardian angel sent a little note – "Remember George, no man is a failure who has friends."

Not a bad thought for 1973.

Happy New Year!

1973

January 4, 1973

IN THE GRAYNESS of winter days with the merriment of the holiday season behind us, January threatens as the most forbidding of months.

February holds out the promise of hearts and flowers for Valentine's Day but a few of us Capricorns protest that January was a good enough month to bring us into the world.

Hope Carbaugh is celebrating next week as I remember well since I have the same birth date and I was interested to hear Richard Nixon was one of us "wonderful" industrious, persistent, practical people.

The more I think about it though, I wonder if being raised by a Capricorn (my mother's one too) didn't have something to do with the traits.

Before the January boredom set, however, the Christmas entertaining was spirited.

On Christmas Day, Mr. and Mrs. Gordon Arnett from Arlington along with the Charles Parks and Russell Parks Sr., Mae Sweatman of Alexandria and Robert McDonald gathered at the Robert Allders who were also reunited with son J.K. home for the holidays from the Navy which incidentally he finds satisfying.

The Martin Wilts have enjoyed Martin Sweatman's visit with them prior to Christmas and Christmas Eve found them at Martin's mother, Mrs. Martha Wilt in Timberville.

All the Lawrence Dawsons gathered at Sonny and Sue Hall's for Christmas dinner in Leesburg while the Wilts had a festive Christmas party about a week before St. Nick arrived.

The Clyde Becks had a houseful of Groves with Joyce's piece de resistance, a fresh-baked coconut cake and here we were proud to serve Mrs. Townshend's banana nut bread with Mr. Peyton's sausage for a wonderful Christmas breakfast, then later we filled the sweet tooth with Herbert Martz's "sweets."

Near the end of the old year, the Budnys and Hutchins at the Snow House threw an open house, inviting us to see the progress they have made on their renovation project.

It's pretty fantastic to realize they have put in new walls, the plumbing themselves with three bathrooms, a kitchen and in April another kitchen to come, the wiring for electric heat, siding on the outside since last March when they found the house mostly in "snow."

As a New Year dawns we are minus one of our Bluemont families, the Leffingwells who have built a new house near Taylorstown. Our best to them!

Now a lot of people have winter projects – I have a few in mind – first of all, I will teach a little class called, "Life in Loudoun Villages" for the Department of Parks and Recreation for Ladies Day Out. If you would like to join the Tuesday morning group, call Alice Lester at the Valley Community Center and secondly, I believe Clayton Hall could be the setting for an old-fashioned quilting bee.

I have some writing projections but when you get right down to my good lazy self – a blissful time would be to have two hours a day to just lie in bed and read.

How I love the magazines, the pictures of beautiful food, settings and interior decorating ideas and the articles, "Why Husbands are Unfaithful" and "Life on a Welfare Check" and "Ali McGraw's public image versus private self" and the books I would read, "Lee's Forgotten General", and "My Life with Everett Dirksen" and "A Portion for Foxes" and "The Hidden Persuaders" (love books on psychology!). That "I Never Promised You a Rose Garden" was something terrific. In fact, believe I'll stop by the Purcellville Library this week – let my neighbors knit or spin, or refinish a mantle (ok – you didn't have to rub it in) – I'll read!

Come to think of it – January ought to be National Book Month.

January 11, 1973

'Tis a cold winter's night…the fires on the village hearths crackle as the cups of hot tea and steam of vaporizers provide the cold remedy to those suffering in legion from the common cold.

The big prediction was snow—at least six inches but so far not a flake is stirring forcing young Christopher Budny to voice in childish desperation that "it might never snow!"

Anyway I ran a gallon of water into a jug, set it down by the sink – dried milk for babies need water, you know. Of course, you can melt snow in a pot over the fireplace!

The last of the fall apples have been turned into apple sauce and still the undecorating goes on and the fight against the pine needles with the vacuum cleaner is a losing one.

This year the Clyde Becks kept me company with late decorations – lighting their porch arrangement through the week and each of us has agreed we will keep up our swags as a cheerful winter display.

Due to the chill of the night the regular Bluemont Citizens Meeting was poorly attended for the second straight month – so make February the one to attend – the first Wednesday at 7:30 at the schoolhouse.

Speaking of schools, the old Hillsboro School is a charmer even with a couple broken windows. How about it Hillsboro – it's your turn to have a wing-ding of some sort.

It's such a perfectly lovely area: Mary Alice Wertz and I had a pleasant winter ride after the fog had lifted about four o'clock last week, discovering the beautiful land around

Plum Grove Farm and Sycamore Springs in preparation for another Ladies Day Out tour "sans" children.

Now the Jack Bardons have celebrated their 31st anniversary, driving this time to West Virginia for a new dining delight.

April Wilt entertained Jennifer in fine style over the weekend and did I tease Joan about the Safeway brand of soap on which I swear – ten pounds for $1.99. You can't beat that, I said! Husband Martin is the manager, you know, and Joan didn't know the soap existed till I asked her to pick me up a box and lo and behold if they didn't make that a birthday present! You can't beat the Bluemont neighbors, I always say too!

Now that the Budnys and Hutchins have joined us in this part of town – the Becks and I have company in the night crowd – shutting down between 12 and 1 while the Dawsons and Allders begin their lamp lighting about five in the morning.

An article written by a doctor pointed out that scientifically we run by different clocks – neither group is more lazy (the American disgrace according to our Puritan forebears, the articles all say too) or industrious, we just jump at a different alarm rhythm!

Now back to some more of those fascinating magazine articles.

Oh, ready for my book review of The Hidden Persuaders by Vance Packard?

It was written in the fifties which definitely hurts it somewhat but he points out merchandising is mostly done now with social scientists studying why we buy the products we do.

Only one in every five women makes up a grocery list with 90 percent of the buying being impulse-buying, bought mainly by the colorful appearance of the package – women buy items in red packages – men in blue.

In fact, my soap had a little red on it, a lot of blue and a little yellow.

Happy 90 percent chance of snow!

January 18, 1973

Bright and cold – the social pace quickens – generally invitations are accepted gleefully – happy is the populace that we are not "snow-bound."

The flu bug is circling the village and countryside as temperatures of eight degrees and seven degrees have been read around old Snickersville.

The good cheer of Christmas seems to linger, the R.M. Peytons report daughter Rosa was home for the holidays from Northern Virginia College while their other daughter Sadie and her husband had a pleasant trip to Texas in December.

The Capricorns did their celebrating – the nicest part of having a birthday the same day as Hope Carbaugh is that she shared a big hunk of her birthday cake with me and then Mrs. William Ballenger, Jr. celebrated her birthday on the 11th.

William Ballenger, Jr. was a patient at Winchester Hospital undergoing eye surgery but is now recovering nicely at home in Pine Grove.

Gordon Ballenger gives us the news that Betsy Jones Moreland fans can view their favorite star again on the show "Bridget Loves Bernie" on Saturday Feb. 3 at 8:30, Channel 9. Mark it on your calendar.

Naturally too, there was hardly a broken-down television on the East Coast this week as the Redskins competed in the Super bowl.

My father claims this is the first winning team the Washington team has had in 30 years and even Safeway put up a big sign, "All Hail to the Redskins" and at this juncture of life I don't get all excited about football but still I found my eyes misting when I saw it! Indeed, All Hail to the Redskins!

In honor of the cold and the season and the broken down television set at Clayton Hall, I found a book on the shelf, Top of the World by Hans Ruesch all about the Northern Eskimos.

There in the Artic with six months of night, they consider 30 degrees below a warm time.

Their customs and survival techniques are fascinating – rubbing blubber over themselves as a cosmetic and warming agent.

The white man has infiltrated there too, however, bringing our horrible diseases and ethics that we infringe upon the trusting native.

One insult that is not to be tolerated by the Eskimos is to refuse "to laugh a little" with his wife explaining, I'm sure, the death of the five missionaries in South America about fifteen years ago.

In this story, the author stated matter-of-factly that the Eskimo couple who already had two children would expose this next expected child if it was a girl.

It was a girl but when they saw it they loved it dearly as it has "hair like sunshine, eyes like the sky and skin white as snow", the white man's child and they were immensely proud of her and especially loving.

Certainly these unsophisticated people have something beautiful to teach us!

Speaking of beautiful things to teach, Loudoun County is going to miss the Christian influence of the Mead family from Hamilton who are departing about a week from now for Erie, Pa.

Matriarch Sally is some kind of an amazing woman, milking a cow every morning, baking bread for the family of nine children bi-weekly, ever-ready, nevertheless, to stop to help a friend in any crisis, beseeching God's goodness for them.

Rare is her gift of love – a lot of us around Bluemont will feel a real void without her.

Pass the half-way mark of January, the winter bite will loosen, with February will come spring fashions in the stores but in a mountain village we know winter has just begin – many long wonderful winter evenings of reading lie ahead. I must start a 500 pager – The Byrds of Virginia and don't forget to feed the other birds of Virginia – peanut butter and corn meal spread on a pine cone – they love it!

January 25, 1973

Birds were chirping gaily in the spring-like weather on Wednesday, then the rains came and a thick fog rolled in, now the wind has howled churning around the corners in the village streets for two days – all in this mid-January week.

"Unseasonable weather," the Biblical literalists proclaim with a glint in their eye for about 2,000 years now.

Spirits fairly sparkled with the fair weather, now a dismal atmosphere prevails with news of long-standing residents leaving us.

In the first place, the Tyson Paynes who made their home on the far corner of town for 17 years are going to Stonewall Trailer Park in Stephens City, Va. about five miles from Winchester where they will be closer to their children.

Mr. and Mrs. Gordon Rust, Jr. and their young two-week old baby will call the old log house now coated with aluminum siding – home.

Then the James Allders are leaving at the end of February for a new home near Berryville, returning to worship in the old stone church in Bluemont on Sundays.

As we moved to Bluemont, one who had married an Allder told me there was an Allder behind most every bush and tree up this way but it looks like they are thinning out. Just about the time I'm getting them all straight too!

At least the Kelleys are still here though one of the youngest, Lance, son of Mr. and Mrs. Bill Kelley, fell during physical education class at Round Hill School this week and broke his arm.

On Tuesday, I spent the day with a crow, a black snake and some assorted mice. No, not at Clayton Hall this time, although we've had our visitations, but these creatures inhabited the biology department at Valley High School.

Oh yes, a few students came during visiting hours, knocking the crow off his perch and treating the black snake to a drink of water and threatening to treat the black snake to a mouse. Somehow I felt a little more secure in the English department last period.

After reading two pages of my book, The Byrds of Virginia, I find my little pun about the spelling wasn't too clever after all as William I, the patriarch of the American strain of the lineage changed the "i" to "y" just prior to sailing here in 1670.

Now I feel as if I'm acquainted with a celebrity as Mrs. Edith Rodgers, Shir Carbaugh's aunt, certainly proved herself a heroine when she alertly turned in the emergency signal about the hold-up man at the Boyce bank where she plays "teller" every day. Good for her and many more "unheroine" days for her in the future!

Wonder how well the inauguration was television-attended as compared to the Redskins game?

We didn't have television for either event but are finding that creating ceramics with the Christmas clay and playing games of "Winnie the Pooh" and "reading" aren't too miserable for a second to the same canned laughter the children have been viewing for the last five years of those dull repeats over and over.

Thinking of the inauguration, though, rarely do we take in the live event, even though, we're so close to Washington.

Only one did I ever attend. It was Harry Truman's. We got seats on the Capitol steps, freezing, "watching the girls go by" in bathing suits in the low temperature weather. We didn't even pack a lunch but it was all stimulating seeing the Clydesdales and all the bands and the Senators of every state in their official cars and then to hear the calliope at the tall-end as dusk fell.

When the kids get a little older, we'll take it in, we might even be lucky enough to see a Democrat sworn in or a woman. We'll pack a lunch too....

Here's hoping it won't rain or "snow" on your parade this week.

February 1, 1973

Gentle...mild mannered...wonderfully bright...A character reference? No, the weather report for a week in January, 1973.

Even the forsythia began bursting their buds. As I recall something similar happened last year and then we had our March blizzard but my – how we are enjoying these days now.

The local scene seemed quiet this week with the children home from school for two days.

Nationally, there were almost too many events for us to take in – the death of an ex-President and the peace negotiation of our country's longest war.

Mrs. Barbara Spring is still with us as January turns to February. She is planning a sale of her household things after the projected February house settlement.

What a magnificent view she has up there from her front porch. Everyone would love her corner cabinet and Rogers silver-plate. Somehow I've always felt auctions were kinda sad.

I decided I wouldn't sell Grandma's dishes after all.

And the virus hit here – three out of four children were sick and unfortunately Mother is still on her feet and moping. Did you ever notice how few mothers of young children get sick?

But somehow that's what makes a mother. Up until the time I had married, I wanted my mother hovering close-by when I got sick.

Life with children can be a drag and or a joy, it seems to be interpreted with the parent's attitude.

Rainy days bring out the philosopher in me and it's raining again – like every weekend someone pointed out.

Clyde Beck has been ailing with the bug but he still obliged his neighbor, struggling with a mammoth wardrobe (no closets in an old house, you know), along with Jack Allder and my father.

The seven foot wide seven foot tall piece wouldn't go up the stairs either so we've had to settle for another piece in the living room and we should strip it right away. Oh, these projects!

Don't forget to see Betsy Jones Moreland this week on "Bridgett Loves Bernie" and next Wednesday, Feb. 7 is the Bluemont Citizens Meeting.

Mary Lou Markle invited a few of us girls up this week to the top of the mountain and it was interesting to know about the pace of life on the other side of the mountain, Berryville way.

Right now, I'm sailing along with Admiral Byrd over the Artic so I haven't gotten the family here to the Shenandoah yet, but soon it will be Harry's turn, mixing politics and apples, and there is bound to be a "saucy" chapter or two to come with the familiar setting in next door Berryville.

Mary Jo Lloyd tells me she has a new pony, Gypsy, and I've learned things are changing about auto driving.

It seems a new tag system is coming into effect. When a person trades or buys a new car, he will buy tags then, receiving a plate that will not be re-issued for five years, only a yearly sticker on the plate will change. April will not be the month for everyone to renew as it is now.

So in December you can pay your real estate taxes and then in January I'll have car insurance and tags due plus inspection of the car. Is that any way to begin a new year? I doubt it!

February 8, 1973

It's bump, bump as the wind blows the closet door where once a window spanned a view in the old house, the plastic on the window rattles and the dog keeps up a protective bark, sure that someone is entering uninvited as the breezes of February bring winter to the Bluemont scene.

Somehow the wind brings refreshment to the earth, drying up the saturated ground of a Friday downpour; icing up the ponds again for skating.

Winter takes its toll on the old folks though. We are so saddened to hear of Mrs. Townshend's sister's death. She was Mrs. Virginia Conklyn Lyddane of Washington, D.C. In addition our dear neighbor, Mrs. H.A. Vincke, mother of Trudy Verloop died on Thursday.

The Vinckes were a wonderfully devoted Dutch couple whose lives had blessed many, having aided escapes from Hitler's terroristic Germany.

Our sincere sympathy to her husband, to her daughter and her family who have so lovingly cared for her those long months she was so ill.

One of the other neighbors who helped at the Vinckes was Mary Ann Carter whose own mother is hospitalized at Loudoun Memorial and of course, we are all concerned about Robert Carruthers who has suffered a heart attack and is in intensive care at Leesburg.

The virus is still making its move about the village, both Mac Brownell and Virginia Woolman have been smitten.

The rest of the village news this week was "good."

Congratulations to Linda Lloyd, daughter of Mr. and Mrs. Glen Lloyd on her engagement to Michael Cake, "a most likeable fellow" all the family say.

Sister Judy Casey and I found we could commute together to Ladies Day Out at the Community Center as she is teaching the knitting class and I have my little course, Life in Loudoun Villages.

As you might expect we began with Bluemont and I told them how wonderful you all are.

This week they will come for a visit here; hope it will be a pretty day so they can see our lovely countryside, there the following week and then conclude with a trip to Hillsboro.

Maxine Fleming from the class brought me up to date on another local history fact, stating that the Loudoun Ketoctin Chapter of the DAR began in Bluemont as Mrs. Frank McComb was its originator.

Delightful too were the addition of two ladies from Sterling Park in a kind of movement of "East meets West" and now each can appreciate the other's lifestyle.

Now we all ought to be proud of our Bluemont Citizens Association president, Clyde Beck, who was cited for an award in restoration by the Chamber of Commerce for his log cabin here and the site of his home but additionally, he earned two more in actuality as he did the work for the Hoffmans on their Bluemont renovation on the farm across from the Throckmorton place and the Christopher Wilson's of Mt. Gilead.

No doubt, what Loudoun needs is a good old-fashioned trading post.

How I would love to find a 8x10 Oriental rug – I could trade two slightly "unfixed" televisions or a slightly broken straight chair or a choice of several Victorian stuffed chairs or a bent electrical can opener. And wouldn't it be great to trade services – like I have a big wardrobe that needs nailing back together and one that needs refinishing and a mantle that needs re-doing and two chairs that need rush-reed seats and about 10 rooms that need re-plastering and painting and a front porch roof that needs "help."

In return I could…babysit? With four children of my own, I'm not too enthusiastic about that. I could…I can't sew or type as the proofreader of this copy can heartily attest.

I could…Well, one time I rendered a service that suited me – I read to a 96 year-old gentleman who was going blind but still had an alert eager mind and wanted to keep up with things but then a 96 year-old man can't refinish, paint, nail, plaster either so there you are!

Watch out I might give a book review of The Byrds of Virginia gratis anyway followed by my present involvement, The Honorable Mr. Marigold.

February 15, 1973

Twelve degrees up on the mountain, Kay Seidenspinner said, seventeen here in the village, Joyce Beck reported – the traditional January weather settled in in time for Valentine's Day, reason enough to hold the cherished even closer.

While the rest of the south, romped with, fumed and cussed the snow, our only flakes were the paper variety stuck to the windows with tape, keeping the potted geraniums company on the windowsill.

Grandpa Porterfield got an early Valentine birthday celebration Sunday. As usual the neighbors helped make the occasion right.

Helen Freedman made up a special cheesecake for the perfect dessert (she could be in the business!) and Lucy Martz measured off a yard or two of the prettiest lace for our trim of red for a fancy table setting with red candles from Mann's Store.

Generally the sentiment in the area is a hope for a warming trend by the time of Mrs. Spring's sale, scheduled for this Saturday, Feb. 17, at 10 o'clock.

The W.S.C.S. from the Methodist Church will serve lunch and that same day, there will be a puppet show at the Purcellville Community Center and rail-splitting at Belle Grove, all to be rescheduled in case of a storm!

Shir Carbaugh is threatening a "snow" dance so…

The week began graciously when my "ladies" came for the Bluemont tour.

Standard now is a peek in the Clayton Hall Book and Craft Shop on with the dollar tour that includes the attic where one can inspect the structure of rock with cedar beams, next is the barn.

The walking tour takes in Clyde Beck's cabin, the Virginia House – a side trip down Susy's lane to the Snickersville Academy, then into the vehicles to see the Bluemont countryside.

The sights in town are pointed out, the old Lake Store, the Post Office, Mr. Iden's Store with its severe drainage problem now, Mountain Shadow, the former one-room school, the old stucco school, a peek inside at the old stone church, then past the Brownell's lane and the old Plaster place.

A turn to the right reveals Pierott's Hill with a fair elevation, then on the curve at the old oak, the old Throckmorton Place with grazing sheep, newborn lambs frolicked for us;

a right at Hickory Corner, past Marvin Watts' tastefully done cabin and the Cochran farm with the wonderful stone fences to the next right for a turn around.

Back-tracking we note the back entrance to the Walsh's Berkley Farm, then by the Woolman's old stucco house, the Parks' farm, with geese swimming on the wide creek and cattle grazing.

Next it's a nod at the Louis Underwood's neat yellow frame home, a view of the mountain to the right – time to mention Mrs. Peyton's strawberries – back to the hard-surfaced road at the yellow schoolhouse a left to the village, past the Lloyds, Kelleys, First Baptist, and home again into the drive, refreshed by the sights of the country.

The Bluemont Citizens got together this week – re-elected last year's officers – Clyde Beck – President, Louis Underwood – Vice President, Libby Stearne – Secretary, and Ellen Jones – Treasurer.

Residents are reminded suggested donations of six dollars per family for the lights are due now and an important organizational meeting for the 1973 Bluemont Fair is slated for Feb. 28 at 7:30 p.m. at the school.

The problem of the drainage heightened by the highway construction was alluded to and the Board of Supervisors' committee, chaired by Jim Brownell, will advise the villagers of what can be done very shortly.

The Citizens voted to sponsor an individual on the Women's Softball team with our advertisement, Bluemont Fair, running around the bases. We all thought a slow runner would be best or better still a bench-warmer, reminding me of Mark Twain's request for a riding horse – "a tired one, a dead one, preferably."

Great news is the formation of the new Craft Club whose members are still debating a name, Mountaineer Craft Club, Snickersville Craft Club, Blue Ridge Craft Club (I told them we could hold a contest!)

They will meet the third Tuesday of every month at 7:30 p.m. with officers Emma Mann – President, Vice President – Mary Lynn Budny; Secretary – Roberta Underwood, and Treasurer – Leslie Hutchins.

The first session Isabelle Dawson instructed in crocheting, and there are some pretty bed-spreads, throws and tablecloths begun.

Sleeping in late Sunday morning? Forget it! Sassy, the goat was butting his head against the front door at 7:30 a.m., setting the dog howling crazily.

Time to organize my forces for picketing – "The Goat Must Go!"

February 22, 1973

The fact was – it couldn't have been a colder day – zero degrees on the mountain, four degrees in the village, went the reports and the wind was brisk adding in the chill factor to probably make it 10 degrees below but the crowds still came to Barbara Spring's sale – how Virginians love their sales!

I couldn't even get a sitter, made it just in time to see the wonderful old wooden box of bottles heaped up go for a quarter but I managed to get a milk-can and two slop jars for 50 cents.

The can has a Bluemont tag on it too – saw Lindsay Hope and the Ogdens who got some cute things. Clyde Beck was adding to his chair collection – got a nice wrought-iron love-seat; they say Glen Lloyd got a lawn mower. The bookcase I wanted went for a good price.

If a piece goes high, you can always say, "See, someone knows quality" and if you get it cheap you can brag to a friend that there wasn't a soul there who appreciated a good piece.

Barbara Allder didn't make it up to the sale either as there was a frantic knock at the front door at 6:30 a.m. Saturday and lo and behold if it wasn't J.K. home from his Navy base for a surprise visit, tanned by the California sun.

Mac Brownell called with chattering teeth as we compared notes about the freezing pipes – my hot water pipe finally succumbed to a blow torch in the hands of one of the handiest of handymen, Roland Baltimore who is plastering and painting in the family room in the same style as the Lawrence Dawsons with their winter indoor projects.

On one of the loveliest brightest winter days of the week, I researched Hillsboro history, having an informative chat with former Mayor Turbeville, the first woman mayor in the state. Then a stroll downtown, I came across the Alton Echols' old stone house which is done in the finest of taste with the most beautiful mountain stream running through the backyard with the mountain shooting straight up – so lovely!

We're so glad to see Dot Givens' new poetry book and I'll have it here at the Shop along with her first book of poetry.

The week was one of those super affairs except that Papa, that's Floyd Johnson of Paeonian Springs suffered a fall about a month ago and the doctors' found a blood-clot had formed on his brain.

He is progressing well after surgery in Winchester Hospital. Floyd's been in the thick of every major organization in which he served – namely the Democratic Party, serving as Chairman for a number of years when Harry Byrd reigned supreme in Virginia. Then the hospital was in a turmoil when he served on that board and now the school board has far too many headaches for any one group of individuals.

Be on the lookout for the Sabol's Lady Bug, a fat black and white furry pony, last seen at the gate of Mt. Weather. Someone said why didn't they take it in the fence and find the rightful owner but then you know what happened with the Trojan horse!

Joan Wilt was sniffling and sneezing with the cold weather but she is still managing to snicker over the ribbing she has been getting from a certain disc jockey on the Herndon radio station who has been kidding her about her loyalty to the Redskins.

Meanwhile, little Miss Deanna Earman of Pine Grove received an autographed picture of football great, George Blanda as they both celebrate their birthday, Sept. 17.

More news from the W.G. Ballengers, Jr. was that they entertained the Thomas Dillows of Harpers Ferry, W.Va. last Friday.

My Friday was spent at Valley High School viewing a good film on water pollution – a real problem, when you consider our Potomac isn't even suited for recreation now. Fifty gallons each one of us uses a day.

Young Kenny Hutchins over at the Snow House turned six on Sunday with a family gathering, cake, ice cream, movies and that warming trend we were all talking about for Mrs. Spring's sale.

But as of Saturday night, here I sit in my colonial night-cap, rather blasé about the cold snap after reading my Eskimo book and The Byrds of Virginia relating Admiral Richard Byrd's adventures with operation deep-freeze at the South Pole – three sweaters, wool socks, boots – it's not bad at all and for amusement – one can order from seed catalogs, Everitt Dirksen style.

March 1, 1973

A lazy winter sun, not warming but encouraging, grazed in the heavens this week, prompting the children to play garden, plotting off a circle within the old hula-hoop on the front lawn.

Those storybook flakes of white came, floating down in a graceful dance reminiscent of the variety seen in the old paper weights, but alas the school buses still arrived in town, toting the children off to school and the dance was done by nine a.m.

Two of the really close neighbors met with a little more than the common cold. Isabelle Dawson fell on the ice, breaking her arm in two places and she has always been so careful to sweep clean immediately after any frozen precipitation.

Then Leslie Hutchins is hospitalized at Holy Cross Hospital in Silver Spring, Md. having undergone minor surgery.

Worst of all this terrible rumor persisted – it's true, it's true. I checked with Shir that the William Carbaughs are moving to Front Royal probably at the end of March with not so much as a "For Sale" sign on their house.

How we will endure without them I don't know.

Their quartet of girls is always on hand, lending a hand to my special occasions here.

They find us a tree at Christmas, decorate it, share treats with us for each memorable event, babysit, catch mice, lug heavy furniture on one end with us on the other and bring all that delightful wholesomeness of country living to our door-step.

Time to get in some last minute goodbyes to Barbara Spring who will be making her home at the Dulles Trailer Court in Chantilly after next week.

So far at least the two Allders side by side are making Bluemont a permanent home, braving the drainage problem.

The Jack Allders have permission to put in a drain field so at least they can live in greater comfort and Agnes and I had the best chat on Saturday night with my getting more of the Allder clan straight.

I certainly didn't know before that Betty Mitchell (Marvin's wife) was Jack's sister.

The Senior Allders, the brothers and sisters in Jack's family lived in Mrs. Spring's home at one time and Agnes and Jack began housekeeping there with the family.

Jack and Agnes announce the marriage of their daughter, Barbara Jean to William J. Breghner. The couple are making their home in Baltimore with a visit here to the family last Saturday.

Now the Craft Club has an official name, Snickersville Craft Club and will meet the third Tuesday at Mrs. Townshend's at 7:30 p.m.

At this stage I almost feel that I should be writing the Hillsboro news, I've been over there so much this week.

Sue Mearns graciously babysat while I went from the world of mother to history researcher and had a marvelous get acquainted session with Mrs. Elizabeth Thompson Williams whose family has owned a really beautiful piece of land, Stoney Point, for four or five generations.

A good hunk of it is on that lovely wooded slope right in town, Short Hill.

Then I had the grand tour at the Muirs, meeting their darling new kids, (the goats, that is).

Another day back with photographer, Howard Allen to get pictures for the Spur Magazine article for the "Spring number" as Kenneth Levi says and this time Ginger Echols had one huge piece of delicious pecan pie waiting.

The Ned Chamberlains had three perfect old post-cards of town scenes and then the Roberts brothers in the store gave me the story of what had been a mill, a tannery, a blacksmith shop and a jail under the store.

March 8, 1973

Some temperatures in the week registered 60 degrees with a slight greening of the grass and everyone was talking that the winter had been so mild as if it was a definite "has been."

Pardon me, but I've lived in the Washington, D.C. area too long not to look for a snow in March.

Gather your crocus if you like, I'm still keeping that wood pile up high.

The James Allders left us this week and the news is confirmed that at least the Carbaugh house will stay in the Bluemont family as Sonny and Sue Hall, the Lawrence Dawsons' daughter and son-in-law will now call the yellow-sided house home.

A decade of Bluemont News

Shir is a little tearful, hoping those tears might freeze with a good snow so she can get a fun sled ride down the hill on the Snickersville Pike one more time.

We were hoping we could get Lynn again to babysit so she made our favorite no-cook oatmeal cookies on Wednesday night as I took in the first Bluemont Fair meeting for 1973.

The big announcement is that this year our theme will be Blue Grass Music with the association sponsoring a contest the two days of the Fair with a lucrative cash prize for the winner. Libby Stearne suggested an all-expense paid weekend in Bluemont!

The committee chairmen have mainly stayed the same and right now there is a need for a place to accommodate a dinner in or near Bluemont. Any ideas can be forwarded to Ivy Cochran.

We want our new neighbors, Joyce and Charles Fishback at the former Nesmith log house and the William Miners at Mrs. Spring's to know they are welcome and needed.

The next Bluemont Citizens Meeting is this Wednesday, March 7 at 7:30 p.m. at the schoolhouse when a discussion of the drainage problem is to be aired and a vote for what route to take A or B. See the Leesburg bypass dispute has nothing on us!

The State Highway Department has agreed to furnish forty-one percent of the cost, this will be matched by the County Board of Supervisors and in addition, the community will put up some of the funds.

The Bluemont citizens wish to thank Russell Parks, Jr. for painting the stairway at the school.

Now it is generally agreed the auditorium needs painting.

It was a big week for students at Valley High School as their basketball team went on to the State Championship games in Charlottesville.

They lost by one point to Culpeper but they still hold the District Championship for the Class A title.

Glad to know the Jack Bardons are back from their winter sojourn and I am going over to get all the story on Monday.

Then Thelma and Leon Brunelle dropped by on rainy Saturday for a spot of tea and a lot of nice conversation.

Thelma is a little too modest to tell me the whole story but she soloes, entertaining for groups, appearing one-time nightly at Blackie's House of Beef about two weeks ago. She sang a few Irish numbers and so she's to go Irish all the way next week in a Maryland spot.

Now for the Hillsboro segment of the Bluemont News.

There are a lot of fascinating people over there at the foot of the Short Hills – the Mearns, the Echols, Muirs, Nettie Painter who covers the weekly beat for the Times-Mirror, the Turbevilles, the Wares, the Thompsons, the Williams', the Hughes, the Chamberlains, the Flemings, the Grims, Rowes, McMullens and the Grubisichs and I even learned Walton Mann's aunt is the postmaster.

When Sue Mearns told me a cute little story of a Hillsboro happening I had this irresistible urge to write it up in the Bluemont News!

The good friends and neighbors the Tom Grubisichs and Richard Mearns had been alternating in each other's basements thawing out pipes and during one of those basement discussions Rick who is an engineer said the hot water pipe always freezes first.

Tom as you may know writes a delightful column for the Washington Post.

He mentioned in his column that his friend Rick Mearns, an engineer and lamp maker said the hot water pipe always froze first.

Thus began the great debate with an avalanche of letters coming to the Post and the Mearns' saying it "ain't necessarily so."

Well, to pursue it further I asked Clyde Beck about it and he said it was true, the vapors present in hot air freeze first.

Well that settles it! Tom Grubisch and I won't be convinced otherwise, we know who we can trust.

Time to be thinking about those jigs and remember a little blarney goes a long way, especially with a woman – we eat it up!

March 15, 1973

Drizzling and foggy, how our mountain neighbors are socked in on such days, thus the week began and then as the days waxed brighter and warmer, caution was thrown in the wind, my Show Me Missourian attitude forgotten – Spring had come!

We were all sure of it, even though the air kept a damp briskness: weren't the excited shouts of the children's discovery of the tulips poking up enough to allay any fears? In addition, Lara said they had seen a bunny in the woods and the snake scare began in earnest as Donna Miner announced her son's find of a shedded snake skin in the basement.

Nevertheless, a call to the old wizard Glen Lloyd has got me speculating, "Anything can happen in March," he said.

Whatever the case, it was time for the County to think of spring clean-up again as Keep Loudoun Beautiful met this week to motivate all the district chairmen.

A goodly number of the hard workers of the County are involved in this organization and the days for clean-up have been set for April 9-23.

I know I can count on the usual marvelous cooperation of the neighbors, I'm asking the same people to serve again with Jim Brownell even volunteering to take a larger area.

Now if the courts would have upheld his proposal of a ban on no-deposit bottles and cans, we might not have such a problem.

Loudoun County placed second in the state last year and since Virginia is the leader in the country in this non-litter program, that means we ran very high in the country.

Part of the award factor is involved in the number of people who participate so everyone please clean up your own property and then help with the rest.

The Bluemont Citizens Association graciously will treat all the youth workers to lunch during the general clean-up of the town, set for the Friday before Easter and up there at the top of the hill, we've all decided the old junk cars must go! Tony Carbone has volunteered to procure the collection bags for us again and everyone should be saving big dog-food bags and feed sacks.

Cleaning out a little on their own, are the William Carbaughs who are holding a sale at the school grounds this Saturday. Lynn says they have beds, dressers, chairs, tables, a television, kitchen utensils, desks and dishes and other sundryy items, the pigs are already sold.

A covered dish dinner in their honor will be held on Sunday at 6 p.m. in the school auditorium on March 25.

Everyone in the community is invited. Just bring a dish, your family and your appetite.

At least Lynn will be a Bluemonter till June as she will stay with her grandparents, the Wesley Carbaughs atop Pierott's Hill.

The little red wagon's been working over time this week, we're hauling the firewood from the porch out by the barn for next year's emergency and Stoney Creek, remember we're talking about that water in a pipe freezing, not in a pail on the porch.

The vapors caught in the pipe freeze first – it's a hooking discussion, no?

And if only I can get that "patriot red" painted on the kitchen door and cabinet, and oyster white the hall wood-work and check the falling plaster in the dining room, I'll be happy!

April 5, 1973

April has arrived traditionally raining but ah, that beautiful deep green mist surrounds the village lawns and pear blossoms are spied across at the Carrington House and the violet plants are poking up in the flower bed.

April Fool's Day has always been a day to mark off the calendar for me expect for the year I was a college freshman and we sneaked in the upperclass dorm for a few of the usual Vaseline on the toilet seat tricks.

Perhaps, on Sunday with the children too young to know what they're missing, life will be free of that menace to mankind, the practical joker!

How we wish the Carbaugh's move was just a joke but the beginning of the week brought their departure to Front Royal.

Lynn came one more time to babysit and I saw Hope in class with a Howdy Doody puppet as she is learning ventriloquism explaining that you have to learn a new alphabet for those letters that you can't pronounce without extending the lips. My deduction is that is why the dolls always have an immature personality!

I can remember that Bob Smith and ridiculous Clarabelle only too well as my youngest brother was always viewing it as I walked in the door from school; nevertheless, the dinner in the Carbaughs' honor was a very nice get together with the Citizens Association presenting them with a farewell gift.

Because the Snow House occupants said they like the scalloped tomatoes, I'll pass on the recipe which has made a varied use of our frozen tomatoes:

1 cup diced celery
½ cup finely chopped onions
2 tablespoons butter or margarine
2 tablespoons flour
3 ½ cups tomatoes
3 slice bread toasted
1 tablespoon sugar
1 teaspoon salt
Dash pepper
2 teaspoons prepared mustard

Cook celery and onion in butter until just tender (this takes quite a while), blend in flour. Butter toast, cut in ½ inch cubes. In 1 ½ quart casserole, combine the onion-celery mixture with tomatoes, half the toast cubes, the sugar, and seasonings. Bake at 350 degrees for 30 minutes. Top casserole with remaining toast cubes and bake 20 minutes longer. Serves eight.

Of course, the big event of the week for me besides finally filing my tax return was the Quilting Bee.

Well, now that I'm an expert on the subject, (Ahem), having read a book on the Romance of the Patchwork Quilt (notice I can read and write on the subject but as for the sewing, just tonight I finished my basting of the scraps on the 10 inch square); I must rephrase the bee to piecing since technically, quilting is the runnings of stitchings made in any materials, three-fold in thickness.

Well, under the tutelage of Charlotte Laing, we arranged scraps on a 10 inch square (an old sheet did nicely), turned down the edges, basted them to the plain square and added the fancy stitches.

Besides the sewing, there was a whole lot of chatting, the savoring of some tasty sandwiches, desserts and chips and a wonderful display of old quilts.

My favorite was Janet Ball's Album Quilt, a pattern that has the signature of those who quilted for the minister and his wife who just happened to be Janet's grandparents.

In addition, Lois Lees of Sterling Park set up a magnificent old quilting walnut frame and now we must set another time for meeting and tying it together as I learned generally a crazy quilt is not quilting since the pattern of stitches on patches would not be appropriate.

All is well at Valley High School these days as the crow with the broken wing is in a wonderful habitat outside under a tree, feasting on a rabbit someone brought to the enclosed court.

The building classes have constructed a handsome pond and the science classes are planting trees, supplying them with labels of the right genus.

Now that's the kind of education that makes sense to anyone!

Dot Heasley reported in with her ever-widening education having attended a maple sugar festival in Virginia over last weekend.

The sap is supposed to be at its running best the second and third weeks of March with cold nights and warm days but it was off this year, however, folks still stood in long lines for the pancakes with maple syrup, ham or sausage. Knowing Dot, they enlisted her help for an eight-hour shift.

The Spring Clean-Up begins this week and very graciously the Potomac Appalachian Trail Club has already organized one car load of workers with bags to help pick up cans along Rt. 601 leading to the trail.

Tony Carbone says there's a dump up there along the trail so maybe that's where the action ought to be!

And someone left a pair of scissors here and here comes Peter Cottontail totting his umbrella!

April 12, 1973

Showers and sun and daffodils still breath-takingly bright in bouquets was the frame of the week.

Somehow it was a lost week here for me; on Monday Carolyn Sabol brought a book, "A Portion for Foxes," a winter project to be marked off the list and so I began.

Now I'm drained, emotionally spent, fatigued as if on a drinking spree, two days, two nights reading – one floor of the house left unclean, confusion, unrest stirring within my psyche – are the characters real people?

On those beautiful undeveloped acres of land in the Middleburg area, are those people really so unhappy, so unloved, visiting the sins of the parents on the next generation?

About it all there is a tantalizing repulsion, and if that doesn't sell another 100 copies, the publisher and writer will have underestimated what the "general" public wants.

Therapeutically the neighbors were caught up in more wholesome endeavors, the Budnys and Hutchins set out flowers and the building walls.

Tony Carbone procured about 40 bags for the clean-up, stacking them under the barn overhang here if you want to get started earlier than the Friday, April 20 effort.

This would be a good week to get started on your own property and then we will have our joint effort later.

Remember too you can take a night off from food preparation by attending the Round Hill Auxiliary's dinner at the firehouse from 5-8 p.m. on Friday, April 13, ham and scalloped oysters featured.

Speaking of food, Annette Scheel brought a wonderful treat to the Quilting Bee, a Quiche Lorraine.

Reading the Sunday papers later, I found it is quite the "in" dish in Washington circles.

It is an unsweetened custard pie which has evolved over the centuries into a first course for a French dinner and now is being served in chic little spots as luncheon fare with a good green salad.

Bacon or ham has been added to the traditional piece de resistance along with cheese.

Annette's was yummy, a great deal like a plain pizza I had once at the home of some real Italians.

And then with the box of loose leaf tea left here by Claire Bardon I showed the children how my great-Aunt Ivy would read the tea-leaves.

With just the leaves clinging to the bottom of the cup, she would turn the cup over, circling the saucer three times and then tap the top lightly three times.

Then gazing into your china teacup she would tell the future, seeing this or that in the shapes the leaves formed, much like cloud-watching.

All I saw was a trip to a group of islands close to the mainland over which hung a voodoo mask. I guess that's enough for a starter!

Two birthdays celebrated in the area were April Wilt's with a young friend over for ice cream and cake and William Ballenger, Jr. whose wife fixed a turkey dinner with all the trimmings.

Agnes Allder is home from the hospital following an operation and Jack in his marvelous way is keeping his grass trim, acting as chef and chief bottle-washer at the same time hoping the rain will let up so their drain field can be completed.

Herbert Martz said the weather was so wet, he hadn't been able to put in anyone's garden yet and that Lucy had been on a little trip to Roanoke with Bud doing the cooking at which he was quite skilled.

The pear tree is blossoming behind the house, the chubby robins are hopping in the grove of trees where the old farm machinery still rots on and a whole chicken reposed on the meat counter for $2.12.

I assume it's still lying there!

April 19, 1973

Saturday was one of those fair days, bright but chilly, bright enough to reflect the luster from the old floors and freshly painted walls and cold enough for the lament to continue about the freeze that had fallen upon the blossoms.

As Monday came, I only projected one event for the week – the plucking of a bough of pear blossoms for the old crock in the hall, but first came laundry and vacuuming and substitute teaching and snow! So the crock is content with the pussy willows and the sprouting forsythia with the dried-up blooms.

This was the week of Cup races and horse shows and pony club meetings in the tradition that best portrays the Loudoun images, all before the nouveau riche bought up the land, developed it and passed a fabulous sum for a bond issue.

And now a word to our supervisors…Apparently everyone on the board has forgotten the good citizenship of the Bluemont Citizens Association who having been granted a large sum of money from the supervisors to install heat in the old school, returned the money, feeling the expenditure was not practical and footed the cost for other improvements to the building and grounds themselves.

Now when Bluemont needs some assistance to correct the severe drainage, no one wants to start a precedence.

I have a feeling it was slightly unprecedented to return a sum in a conscientious manner too.

Bluemont is denied a community school, a voting precinct and a free telephone call to the county seat. Isn't it time we were reassured we are citizens in the fullest measure as enjoyed in other communities?

Twice this week we went to Round Hill to vote and to visit the art display impressively exhibited by the elementary children.

Everyone was saying Justine Beck was following her father's artistic nature with a marvelous stitchery scene of trees and a stream. The media was varied and the techniques edifying.

We were certainly sorry to hear that W. Jasper Rickard of Lovettsville, a dear friend of our community was stricken with a heart attack this week but the report is he is progressing well at Loudoun Memorial Hospital.

The full report on Emma Mann's trip to Philadelphia for a week's duration was that now she and Walton are proud grandparents of a first granddaughter, Cynthia Jeanette born March 13, weighing seven pounds, one ounce to Tom and Ruth Mann.

Snooks Campbell thoughtfully remembered me with a book on the Randolphs of Virginia and Virginia Woolman assures me there is a book about the Mason family of Virginia in the library and with the loan of two books, Great House of America and

The Golden Treasury of Early American Houses from Janet Ball, I feel very rich indeed this week.

Going on this one full day of sunshine, we are making plans for a concentrated clean-up effort for Friday, April 20.

Please meet at the old store (Clyde Beck's studio) at 9 a.m. garbed in old clothes, boots and gloves and armed with canvas, or plastic bags and steeled with energy.

After a good morning's work, lunch will be served to the workers at the school house grounds, courtesy of the Bluemont Citizens Association. Crew leaders are to record their mileage, number of workers and number of bags collected. If it rains Friday, we will work Saturday.

A pleasant afternoon was spent in golden light in a wonderful old home in Berryville on Saturday afternoon when Mrs. Richard Lake and Mrs. John Milleson entertained for their granddaughter and niece, Mrs. Stephen McCauley, the former Mary Elizabeth Walsh, at a gracious tea at the Millesons' home on Smith street.

I do hope some of you ladies will be joining me for the next segment of Life in Loudoun featuring Round Hill, Hamilton and Philomont this time.

The tours promise to be a delight in the anticipated lush of the countryside.

To register, call Alice Lester at the Community Center, 338-4444.

Time is now to get an extra dozen eggs for dying and stop by the shop here to see Kay Siedenspinner's knitted bunny egg covers, dig out the ham glaze recipe and patent leather shoes and think upon the significance of the event.

The Easter message is summed up for me in this thought of Louis Everly's "Suffering."

"To love a person is to inevitably depend on him, to give him power over us. God wanted to have need of us. The passion is the revelation of our terrible power over God. He surrendered himself to us, we had him at our disposal, we did with him what we wanted."

April 26, 1973

Balmy breezes, sunny skies and the earth burst into bloom overnight, so marked the third week of April.

Really you can't know the feel of Spring till you've cleaned up your backyard and picked a bouquet of tulips from the front.

Bluemont's youth clean-up on Friday accomplished both when after our wiener roast on the old school grounds, Jennifer came running with a "pocketful of posies," yellow ones and violets blown on the breeze on the schoolyard's front lawn.

Joyfully we picked and picked and filled the available vases at home, presenting Ruth Manuel a bunch as she gave her best to the clean-up by caring for the babies while Ruth Lee Holler and an imported friend from Purcellville loaned a gloved hand.

The effort would have been lost, however, without Jim Brownell who contributed truck, bags, personnel and knowledge of campfire building on the project.

Up on the mountain road, the Potomac Appalachian Trail Club headed by Ruth Blackburn combined with Tony Carbone's enthusiasm gleaned 25 bags from the road and trail entrance.

The Lloyd Loopes did their share earlier: not all the returns are in but I have Kingfish Everhart's promise to pick up the two dead autos in our back woods and Tommy Reid says he will finance the clearage of those at the top of the hill.

Revolting, nevertheless, is the accumulation of trash in the middle of town, degrading out beautiful spot of earth already too long.

Now that the clean-up is over, I'll tell the Lloyds' snake story.

Most of the mile strip was accomplished by June herself and Dorothy Dawson, a hard worker, but two weeks ago when they started, daughters Mary Jo and Ann Wilson lent a hand.

Mary picked up a can containing a wiggly specimen, pronouncing it a snake but Ann thought sure it must be a worm until out came the two-foot long creature.

They determined to save it for Hope who might want to take it to biology class as Ann ran in the house and got her mother's best pan and they sealed down the lid by the side of the road, leaving to pick up the school children.

June began to worry about her pan but Ann assured her if a woman picked it up and saw that snake, she would put it back again.

Finally Hope scoffed at the idea of taking it to school, so the two-foot garter is free in the area for the next picker-upper who cares to relate a similar tale.

Still on the subject of the Lloyds, the birthdays are legion in April. Hope, Jamie and Kelley, the Glen Lloyds' children all celebrated and then they added granddaughter Dawn Marie to the month-long cake making and candle-blowing times.

An expert in the kitchen, June made our Easter perfect with a made-to-order lemon meringue pie which grandparents Johnsons and Porterfields and the five Johnson girls relished here at Clayton Hall.

The day's beauty brought visitors to the hillside.

Over at the Snow House, the Budnys entertained a couple with their little "teeny" baby so young Chris said and the Hutchins have their nieces there for a wonderful week of playing house down by the creek.

Staying up at the Brunelles were the William Rays, Mrs. Ray was interestingly telling me of her once-existing quilting shop in Georgetown.

The David Freedmans now have their mothers with them from New York joined by daughter Evelyn and her family, the Tom Cunninghams of Lothian, Md. for the Easter celebration.

The Freedmans too are pleased to announce their Renaissance Romany is now a champion earning his points in the Great Pyrenees category at The Mason Dixon Kennel Club Show in Hagerstown last week.

Now the news of the Herbert Martzes: everyone was buzzing over the sale of Mr. Martz's tractor and his absolutely beautiful tulips now at their peak when news came of son Bud's accident on Friday evening.

Having pulled up the truck by the side of the house on that grade there, he reached over for the kitten he had left on the seat and accidentally released the brake which resulted in the vehicle catching him and dragging him down the hill.

He is now a patient at Newton Baker Hospital in Martinsburg.

Sad too is the fact that Bessie Carter had just resumed residency in Bluemont when she had to be hospitalized at Winchester with a chronic flu condition.

We were so glad to hear from our friend Sally Meade and are anticipating her visit back to Loudoun County in June.

Meanwhile back in town, Bob Bayliss, Bluemont's favorite plumber, proceeds with the Allder's long-awaited drain field. We are watering our treasured peach tree from J.J. Heinemann and awaiting the tractor battery from Whitmore and Arnold when down will do the dandelions but not before we try the dandelion wine recipe.

Best of all we know we'll see the pair of cottontails prance again as they did all day Sunday on the waving "hair of uncut graves!" (Walt Whitman, you know).

May 3, 1973

Dandelion Wine Time

Around Bluemont this week, the word is discouraging as the skies are cloudy all day but the native rosebud in its peak still blushes against the dark background.

Anyway the dandelion wine is in the works and after three weeks of ripening, the decanters will be filled in hopes that a pleasant brew will mellow into a fine Snickersville blend.

You think there is a lot of dandelions out there on the lawn until you seek to gather four quarts? I had to send the children over to the field while I scanned the by-ways.

Now I'm ready to try the "Stalking the Wild Asparagus" approach hoping to savor the dandelion greens and Swiss something or other that Grandma knew all about.

Sue Mearns' mother from New York came for a visit in all this rain and knew all the answers to such questions and fascinatingly she is going to paint the back of her house in a quilt pattern as she is obviously the quilt lady of her town, having organized a Quilt Show about three years ago which was highly successful with the Congressman's wife sending five antique family quilts for display.

Yep, you guessed it! Anyone for a Quilt Show for the 1974 Bluemont Fair?

Reminiscing with us at the beginning of the week was Mrs. Elizabeth Entwisle, mayor of Round Hill when she gave her interesting talk on the history of the settlement for the Ladies Day Out session of the Life in Loudoun series at the Community Center.

I just loved the old post card that pictured the Kuhlman House, Elizabeth's parents' home that served as a boarding house in fine style offering "ice, a bathroom and clean country air."

We are pleased to welcome the newcomers, the Marvin Steeles to Bluemont as they now are to occupy the former James Allder house. Really not strangers, they moved from nearby Unison and Marvin was part of the Blue Ridge Express music group who performed at the last two Bluemont Fairs.

Now if you want to complain about the weather hold on a minute.

Roberta Underwood said they called their daughter Rhonda and her husband Jan Marcus in Montana on Easter Sunday when here the temperature was 82 degrees and Rhonda reported it was 20 degrees with two feet of snow on the ground there.

Jan's parents, the William Marcuses, were down from Pennsylvania for a visit to the Lucien Reeds over the Easter holiday.

The community was stricken to hear that Mike Haggot, Jean Dawson's spouse received word that his brother was killed in a construction accident in Mississippi on Friday. We extend our heartfelt sympathy.

The local news has really taken a back-seat to the national furor with the Watergate incident.

And I'm about to ask the journalistic question "why" here too.

Why is the old store front in worse condition now than when we started the clean-up?

Maybe it's time to enforce a law that would fine the polluting pedestrians and squatters as well as drivers and riders in vehicles.

Well, happy drying out days so happy planting and gardening days can come and all hail to a glimmering emerald green mountain-side!

May 10, 1973

Bright and chill with green grass wildly growing. May day baskets were delivered to a few of the neighbors – wild mustard and lilac over-flowing the poorly-glued construction paper.

Wisteria hung from the old Empress tree in the Lawrence Dawson's yard while elsewhere in the village the tulips were spent, the violets still bravely liked happy faces.

The lament continued, "Who would plow the gardens now that Herbert Martz's tractor was gone?"

Just before April brought her last shower, the Earl Idens celebrated their 65th wedding anniversary with an open house at the Earl Virts'.

Their two daughters, Mrs. Earl Virts of Bluemont and Mrs. Howard Sprague of Purcellville entertained about 50 friends and family in the Idens' honor.

Two of the three grandchildren including Dr. Earl E. Virts, Jr. and Mrs. Marshall Fleming were on hand for the festivities and most of the eight great-grandchildren.

The Keep Loudoun Beautiful clean-up was accomplished with 164 bags collected in Bluemont, including 61 people in 11 miles of road and so far, Kingfish Everhart has promised to pick up seven dead autos for us and we're working on more.

The Bluemont Citizens Association meeting was a very congenial gathering even though the new coffee pot wasn't plugged in in time for refreshments.

Linda and Don Corley are going to see about reinstating the sign, "Closed to through traffic" on the Snickersville Pike Hill.

The Ponytail League has officially been sponsored, taking on the Women's team in a practice game on Wednesday night.

The summer meetings will begin at eight o'clock rather than 7:30 during the daylight saving time.

The publicity committee for the 1973 Bluemont Fair will meet Wednesday night at Clayton Hall. Give us your suggestions.

Although Bluemont claims Bob Bayliss as its favorite plumber after last week's picture in the Times-Mirror we're not too sure the feeling is mutual.

A nice chat with Terry Bell of Hamilton at the Keep Loudoun Beautiful luncheon satisfied my point about the unpretentiousness of the average Loudouner.

We girls were all terribly impressed that she had entertained the Soviets while Terry was very nonchalant saying the Chamber of Commerce gave the dinner and she just supplied the house.

"Well, what did they serve?" we asked.

"Beef Burgundy," Terry replied, "my kids call it beef stew."

The Brownie Hike on Saturday afforded the most wholesome of experiences with our guide, Thomas Baber and then when I read the 1934 Potomac Trail Club pamphlet my appetite was really whetted as it spoke of the popular excursion from Harper's Ferry to Moreland's.

Well, we all know that Moreland's was right up here at Snicker's Gap on the spot Betsy Jones Moreland loved as a child.

The bus fare was $2 from Chevy Chase Circle and the dinner at Moreland's 50 cents.

Now just what was that all about?

Who can tell me?

The Bluemont news wouldn't be complete without the animal happenings.

I have observed that Cinder Beck has taken up with young Kenny Hutchins now that Brian finds himself unable to play during school hours.

Dinner here on the front porch is a real fiasco.

I go with Gretchen's dinner dish while the Dawson's big gray cat walks just inside the gate, backed by their dog Shamrock checking out what's left.

The cat again sits stealthily watching in the deep grass behind the house and the sparrows and goats inspect the incinerator periodically for burnt offerings.

And next Sunday, Jennifer has promised to take some of her 12 dollars from her savings account and treat us to a pizza at Bentley's in honor of Mother's Day.

Yes, all hail to us wonderful creatures!

May 17, 1973

The humble bees menacingly whirled around our heads warning us away from their next under the barn over-hang, furtive with activity as the humans of Bluemont whirled in like manner.

It was a week of plowing and planting and woodcutting, visits, quilting, hiking, touring and dining with the family for Mother's Day.

The first task of the week here was to get the pile of wood from the front porch to the barn over-hang, then on with the golf swing on the weeds.

Now the most popular activity for Ladies Day Out is tennis: I could give them practice with their forehand swing right here outside the stone wall. Frankly, I'm suspicious. When a woman wants a day out, she wants it with a man – Eugene Scheel is the instructor, you know.

The ladies in our Life in Loudoun class got a masculine tour of the Loudoun Milling Company, Hamilton, oldest operating mill in the county.

It was delightful. It smells like they are cooking breakfast all the time.

No wonder – here's the recipe for the Loudoun Supreme Tasty Texture Dairy Feed – wheat bran, flaked whole corn, crimped oats, cottonseed meal, soybean meat, peanut meal, corn gluten feed, dried beet, pulp, corn distillers dried grains, hominy feed, cane molasses, dicalcium phosphate, salt, calcium carbonate, potassium iodine, iron oxide, cobalt carbonate, copper carbonate, zinc carbonate, and Ferry Mango phosphate.

Then we had a peek at Jane's Kindergarten and the Cowarts' lovely recently re-done old home – fun in Philomont is coming next.

I thought I'd take my own Bluemont tour over to see Bill and Judy Casey's new home and I was just in time to find Judy with a hatchet in hand, contemplating whether to whack a big black snake perched on the azalea bush her father, Glen Lloyd had planted at the front door.

Well, since the baby had just been sunning on the porch and these creatures have a way of joining the family in the house, she came down with a mighty chop, just nipping a small branch in the process.

He was still wiggling when we left an hour later.

The weeds are high too over at Ebenezer church so they are having their annual clean-up for the Memorial Day Service.

Please help out if you can on May 19. The rain date will be the following Saturday. The workers will be treated to lunch by the Unison Methodist Church women.

The once-a-year service will be held May 27 at 2 o'clock with the Rev. Mr. Betts of the Philomont, Bluemont, Round Hill Methodist Charge bringing the message.

Jeannie Bardon, daughter of Jack and Claire Bardon knows the way to go, hiking from Snickers Gap to Harpers Ferry, about 13 miles on the Appalachian Trail which any of us could easily do in a day.

After seeing these beautiful sights, she will graduate this week from Madison College in Harrisburg with top honors.

The Bluemont Fair plans are in earnest now; the Finance Committee and Publicity Committee both met Wednesday night.

Curt Budny is working on posters; Ken Hutchins will contact the Trade Magazines for the Blue Grass Country Music aspect of it. Jack Bardon will spread the word to the groups he will see in 14 engagements before our third weekend in October date. (Imagine, Jack rushed home from the meeting to a piece of Claire's freshly-baked rhubarb pie!)

Marvin Watts will cover the Washington scene. Donna Miner will handle the miscellaneous leads and I'll try to get the attention of the local area.

Also anyone in Loudoun and Clarke County who wants a little publicity for an upcoming event: if they know two months in advance, I will see that it gets to the Virginia Cardinal Magazine published in Vienna for Northern Virginia.

Blue Grass groups who want to enter the cash-award contest at the Bluemont Fair are to contact Jack Bardon at 955-1874.

And today, Mother's Day, I feel every inch a Mother just like I feel every day. At twelve p.m. the baby was still rocking in her crib, the dog was wincing (let's face it we're just a human Mamma to these pets!) when I came down to soothe her and get a bottle of milk for the baby and you know what I stepped in in the dark?

I've told Tracey to sit up straight at the table, Jennifer to comb her hair and yelled at them all to quit yelling but today, my daughters brought me breakfast in bed and each made up her own bed without my usual harassing.

Now ain't life grand?

May 31, 1973

Now as spring weather rotates with days of chill, there's an intoxicating fragrance in the air – it is the full blossoms of the locust trees spreading their sweet nectar over the village.

Cinder Beck routed out two turtles for the children in the field across the way while the weeds keep getting taller and we are wondering when the highway department will find its way off Rt. 7 with its long blade.

With an early deadline – news seemed at a premium but we were glad to hear of the up-coming Loudoun Sketch Club's exhibition opening on Sunday, May 27 from 3-6 o'clock at the County Office Building in Leesburg with the show to extend from Monday through Saturday 10 a.m.-6 p.m., closing on Sunday, June 3 from 1 p.m. to 6 p.m.

The list of exhibitors begins with our Clyde Beck and goes out to Dagmar Wilson who will bring some of her works to the Bluemont Fair this year.

I was glad to see Julia Lea's name on the list as she had the most fetching herb article and sketch in the garden section for Historic Garden Week of the Times-Mirror.

The sketch was removed from the article so I clipped them and put them side by side on my refrigerator with a little shading of colored pencil and as soon as I can find some of those ingredients, I'm going to whip up a batch of those brews.

Lois Lees is talking of "stalking the wild mild-weed" this week but I'm not sure my palate is that adventuresome.

Speaking of adventures we're planning, however, is our hike on the Appalachian Trail, hopefully with Thomas Baber. If interested, call me.

A wonderful kind gesture was Barbara Dillon's loan of the book, The Appalachian Trail.

We were all laughing at Mary Alice Wertz's concern about the existence of bears but from my reading, I found the lean-tos in the Great Smokey Mountains have the open side installed with heavy wire as protection against the bears.

For once it's the human looking out at the animals instead of vice-versa.

A day at Valley High School put me in my place – near the grave according to the 18 year-olds. I asked, "Could the plastic yo-yo's be as good as the wooden ones?"

Well, how would they know – they weren't that old!

Jacks had been the "in" thing weeks ago and a card game called Tonk is very popular now.

I found out a certain student's great-grandmother makes quilts and that one of the students had a wreck over the weekend, blaming it on joy-riders. In the faculty room it was revealed Mr. Crossman had beautiful iris for sale and that royalties on a play run 100 years.

Yes, there's a liberal education there for anyone.

Summer plans are beginning as Curt Budny has designed an attractive post-card for the "members of the band" who might want to enter the cash award contest during the Bluemont Fair.

The beach robes came out here as the children begged for the portable pool from the attic and indeed, this is the beginning of the beach-comber's bronze-colored days but here in Bluemont we just reflect green.

Tomorrow the weeds!

Miss Ruth Alley has been distinguished again with a special award never before given for her outstanding volunteer work with the patients at Newton Baker Hospital, Martinsburg, W.Va. Congratulations!

On Tuesday we found out Hamilton's heritage with a marvelous lecture on the subject by Mary Lou Raymond who was instrumental in encouraging members of the Hamilton Book Club to do research which resulted in a fascinating scrap book kept at the town office.

The mountain "gossip" so Harold Robinson says is that he had a distinguished party of guests for Mother's Day at his "Old Red House."

They were the Honorable Dr. Alvano Rizo and his family including his mother, Mrs. Simeon Rizo along with Mr. and Mrs. John Lowery. The doctor is the minister-counselor with the Embassy of Nicaragua.

And John Campbell gave us some marigold seed which have gone in next to the shop door.

Yes, just why isn't the marigold – the national flower?

And the dandelion wine proved to be a reasonably fine blend with a little more kick than I anticipated.

Limit – one wine glass full – here's to you!

June 7, 1973

With temperatures climbing to the 80's and a cessation of school bells' ringing – summer was declared official in Bluemont this week.

The reassuring cycle of the season had returned with Mrs. Peyton announcing she had the strawberries again so down we went for our view of the mountain and a swing on the front porch and tonight we feasted on vanilla ice cream topped with those rich berries.

It was the right time to catch up with the family: last Sunday their son and his family from Harrisonburg came for a visit and daughter Sadie and her husband came over Memorial Day weekend from Winchester where Sadie finished out her first year of teaching.

She mentioned the elderberries and blackberries would be coming on next for jam-making and yes, she made chow-chow every year. "You put cabbage, tomatoes, green pepper, onions in it but have to be careful in preparation so those strong juices don't make it bitter – you put in sugar, you know."

When the academic award assembly at Valley High School was presented, I was there, impressed with Bruce Hopkins' and Charlotte Porter's achievements particularly.

Jim Brownell was on hand to give the VFW award for anticipation in the "I Speak For Democracy" oratorical contest and I have to give him and Mr. Baber my preference of those who appeared on the stage – I'd say they could win some kind of oratorical contest themselves.

Hope Lloyd was honored for her activity as a majorette and Lisa Cornwell received a student service award.

Bluemont has its share of graduates this year and if I leave anyone out, let me know.

They are Allen Carter, Betsy Lemon, Belinda Dawson, Randy Ballenger, Jamie Lloyd, Joanne Dennis and Judy and our former Bluemonter, Ethel Leffingwell.

The community extends its warmest congratulations to these young people, wishing to assure them we are here to help them in any way we can.

I was glad to see Lynn Carbaugh that day, she gave me the news that the Welcome Wagon in Front Royal had given her parents a weekend trip to Skyline Drive so Shir was to celebrate her birthday there last weekend.

She still is claiming loyalty to the Bluemont Fair although Front Royal has decided to hold its fair the same weekend this year.

Activity was the order of the day at the Round Hill Elementary School this week too.

Our village children participated in Mrs. Remsburg's usual super musicals.

Our neighbor, Shirley Lynn's third grade class put on a smashing "Peter Pan" with Gary Ross as one of the lost boys. His sister Pam was in the chorus.

I saw Scotty Casey in a clown suit and Chip Lloyd was a lion for the first grade presentation.

John Campbell and Brian Beck were outstanding as two of the three drummer boys in "The Princess and the Drummer Boy" while Jennifer Johnson disgustingly was just an "American Child."

If I missed some of the other village children, forgive me – an extremely active bouncing baby girl on my lap took most of my attention.

With the highway department's ignorance of the Bluemont drainage problem, the town may want to legislate for a new name – Snicker's Ford – as the creek on the fringe of Clayton Hall property is overflowing across the main thoroughfare with the rain five days in the past.

Though the day was ugly weather-wise, last Sunday we had the most delightful visit with Mrs. Sue Ray of Georgetown and our Thelma Brunelle from up on the mountain.

We were talking quilts and spreading out scraps and Mrs. Ray passed on the secret of washing the beauties.

Wash in cold water detergent, put in dryer. For an old quilt, soak in cold water detergent in the bath tub for two hours, then rinse in cold water three times, just squeezing dry instead of wringing out and transfer to dryer.

Over at Mann's Store which will celebrate its 25th anniversary in Bluemont on June 6, a lot of learning can be acquired by conversing with the proprietors, Walton and Emma Mann.

They said an old saying was that with this abundant blossoming of the locust trees, the corn crop would be good.

Lester Underwood said he would agree but you had to get the corn in the ground first and that hadn't been possible with all this rain.

Anyway we're hoping the recent sunshine will be the perfect ingredient for rendering some beautiful arrangements at the annual Purcellville Garden Club show to be held this Saturday, June 9 from 2-4 p.m. in the St. Peter's Episcopal Church parish hall.

The weatherman calls for only a 20 percent chance of showers today and tomorrow – so tomorrow it's back up the Appalachian Trail.

My blisters and I will give you the story later.

June 14, 1973

Sizzling waves of intense heat hit the east coast this week and after a round trip to Philadelphia, I was still wondering where were the cooling mountain breezes of Bluemont on Sunday evening when I hit the gravel driveway here.

Even before the suitcase was carried in, I was calling for Curt Budny with his trusty crow-bar for a go at the windows, how Sue and Rick Mearns survived here for a weekend with the Johnson four plus prevailing weather conditions, I'll never know.

At the beginning of the week, Thomas Baber had led our merry band of ladies on a day out up on the Appalachian Trail and there in the woods on marginal slopes, the heat seemed remote, the peonies at the haunted house ripe for picking with their divine scent and full blooms.

Much thought is now on the up-coming Fourth of July event.

This was discussed at the Bluemont Citizens Association meeting but since it fell on the night of graduation and some of the regulars were elsewhere, it was decided that the next meeting would be held on June 27 since the usual meeting date comes on the Fourth.

There are hopes for country music again, the balloons are here and all signals are go on the usual homemade ice cream and cake.

The serving will begin at 7:30, Wednesday the Fourth of July on the old Bluemont schoolgrounds.

Jim Walsh interestingly gave the background of the beginning of the Association at the Wednesday night meeting.

He said in 1962, the Bluemont school was vacated, not having been replaced by another for the first time in the county's history and since the building and property were donated by local people, the Board of Supervisors lent the use of the property as a community meeting place to the newly formed association which wanted to see the building maintained for the common use rather than individual gain.

Since then the community has spent much time and money on the property as it did when it was functioning as a school.

At this same meeting a lengthy discussion ensued about the notorious drainage problem and we are now pursuing legal avenues to make our requests known to the highway department.

Curt Budny presented his preliminary drawing for the 1973 Bluemont Fair poster which will be silk-screened again.

With energy at a low ebb, what better way to spend productive leisure hours than in reading? So, the bookmobile will be combining with the Parks and Recreation program at the school grounds on Tuesdays starting July 3 from 11:30-12:30.

We were delighted to see Bud Martz had returned from the hospital and Allen Campbell had met a woman who remembered Bluemont as a resort spot and who is probably still fantasizing about these cool mountain breezes.

Right before my Friday's departure, I got the nicest artistic note in the mail from Julia Lea who enclosed some herbs for brewing. I had not known before that it was she who operated a really charming gallery in Waterford. The Peaceable Kingdom with herb mixtures and currently silk-screens of old quilt patterns.

June 21, 1973

Summer wound its way down the country lanes, smiling at the daisies, offering green grass to the Holsteins in the meadows who were basking in the blue haze here at the foot of the Blue Ridge.

A tourist stopped to ask directions to the Appalachian Trail and the summer nuisances of mosquitoes and poison ivy bothered a number of us here in the village.

Most of the upper end of the town seemed to be involved in the Snow House projects over the weekend.

Bill Miner related the find of an old iron fence still standing in front of a house that had already been taken by a road extension and Curtis and Ken managed to haul the wonder here for the front of the house which will closely resemble a fence erected there early in the country as documented by Mr. Foster, a former owner now residing in Richmond.

Then on Saturday the men up this way, Don Corley and Bill Miner, helped with the hauling of cement for the footings of the new addition on the Snow House.

Lots of work has been accomplished indoors too – painting and wallpapering.

At the other end of town, the Thomas Ogdens were mowing and clipping, discouraged over the loss of tomato and flower plants from vandalism.

Pam Carbaugh came from Front Royal for a nice visit with Justine Beck and we found the trip to Skyline Drive was a gift from a thoughtful husband rather than Welcome Wagon for Shir's birthday.

The Carbaughs are planning to join us here on the Fourth.

The gasoline shortage won't bother us as long as we can get enough to take bi-weekly jaunts close-by to see our good neighbors.

We had a great chat with Glen and June Lloyd on Friday evening about spring houses and ice houses and root cellars and last week we inspected Johnny Carter's garden which is always in super-shape.

How embarrassed I was to ask Scott Brownell if he went to graduation and he said he had graduated.

He has plans for college next year but he will give us the final word later.

A blond – fair with blue eyes full of health and vigor – Scott is what youth should be to me and how encouraging to know he and Mark both want to study agriculture.

I have a good feeling to know the generation gap didn't exist for a young friend of mine who brought her newly-minted husband to Clayton Hall for several days of visiting and seeing the countryside.

Joe and Judy Fine from Richmond toured us in their Volkswagen bus over to Harper's Ferry, a spectacular trip with that rugged scenery.

Especially impressive now in the park section is a living museum of an old town pharmacy with beautiful walnut cabinets on loan from the Smithsonian. Old tins are labeled with drug names and a knowledgeable young man in colonial garb and modern long locks demonstrated pill-making in the old-fashioned way.

Up at Harper House, young women were quilting as we did with our square and a road-side stand near the tavern grounds had patch-work pieces, machine-stitched, single-bed size for $21 and in comparison I have an absolute beauty with the little sun bonnet girl and overalled boy for $40.

Next we went on the Clarke County tour to Old Chapel (Stuart Brown's history certainly makes the trip more meaningful), a stop by Coiner's Department Store with the marvelous old cable carrying the money to the cashier, a picnic and swim in the Shenandoah at Watermelon Park and a disappointment that the Daniel Morgan mill at Millwood is only open to the public on weekends and holidays.

We didn't make it by to see Jack and Claire Bardon who share Joe's interest in ham radio operating but tonight an Airmont ham with a certain call number gave me a telephone message from the Fines as this must be one great fraternity.

Claire Bardon, not exactly fraternity material, is distinguished as a female ham and on one occasion she did a broadcast from her hospital bed in Washington, making news with pictures in the Washington papers.

Incidentally, she and her daughter, Jeannie, have just returned from a trip to California for a family reunion, broadcasting all the way, I suspect.

And as June reaches the high-water mark, let us not ignore the fathers and the grandfathers and the uncles – we love them all – Happy Father's Day!

June 28, 1973

Lightening is flashing, thunder is rumbling as a glorious summer storm is threatening.

Summer is such a magnificent time in Bluemont with tourists dropping by with memories of when the "street car" ran up here.

Perfectly mature now are the tiger lilies, snow-balls and daisies-most everyone has a vase sitting in the kitchen.

A jelly glass rally doesn't do them justice, however.

For a tall arrangement an old crock is my favorite and they are sweet in a low bowl with great clusters of heads bringing fullness to the arrangement or a mug makes a cute container with again just the heads protruding above the edge.

Speaking of flowers, "Mama Mac", a term of endearment somebody in the family coined for Mac Brownell was pleasingly surprised by a beautiful bouquet of long-stem roses sent by her son Scott's friends as a token of appreciation for allowing them to have a room of their own at Whitehall for parties.

Hey, the lights just went out. Is that nay way to run a summer storm?

More parties in the vicinity was David Earman's tenth birthday celebration at his home in Pine Grove with his young friends Harry, Jr., Ronald, Charles and Jenny Dodge also of Pine Grove.

Sunday the family observed the real birthday falling on Father's Day with step-father, William Ballenger, Jr.

The Lloyds and Neffs are up in reunion time again. Glen's side of the family, the Lloyds got together last week at the horse-show grounds in Berryville and this week June's side the Neffs will feast there.

Daughter Judy and husband Bill Casey will miss this week's clan gathering as they are having a week-end at Tangier Island on the Chesapeake Bay where they have been promised some mouth-watering seafood.

Another picnic coming up is the annual Bluemont Methodist Church get-together at Camp Highroad on July 8.

Bluemonters are to meet for lunch about one and swim about two on Sunday afternoon.

Justine Beck isn't "talking" big meals yet with a sore throat due to a tonsillectomy.

Jennifer and the twins are glad to welcome her home as is her brother Brian and neighbor Kenny Hutchins.

The other half of the Snow House bunch, Curtis and Mary Lynn Budny are on vacation to Mary Lynn's mother's in Georgia.

Gene Lehman is thinking of the younger set by inviting them to a free play school on Tuesday and Thursday mornings at the school and she needs some toys which will be returned.

Of course, the County Parks and Recreation program begins on Monday at the school, mornings only and the Bookmobile comes on the third.

Now we are mighty worried to hear Donna Kelley is confined to Loudoun Memorial Hospital and I'm sure this active gal would appreciate company and remembrances.

The Jack Bardons took in the State Folk Festival in Glenville, W.Va. last week even though Jack has injured his foot.

Daughter Jeanne was a bridesmaid in a Takoma Park, Md. wedding a week or so ago and now is aiding flood victims in Elmira, N.Y.

Now a news item in the paper makes me worry.

Why did the Board of Supervisors so readily pass the Broad Run Farms feasibility study "while Bluemont is flooding" and the Supervisors are talking of setting a precedent with Bluemont?

Although I'm not the most astute political science student around, I believe I know what has happened having lived in both communities.

The residents of Broad Run got on that phone and made their request known to their supervisor.

We have only ourselves to blame for not making our feelings known to Jim Brownell.

Jim is anxious to know your views, personable and friendly and I hope he will stay that way when I just state for the record, I like you better as a "No" man when it comes to a tax increase but thanks anyway for Betty Stowe's appointment to the School Board.

Remember to write or call Betty too, she is here to serve our end of the county.

It's pretty exciting to be part of a working democracy, why not try it?

Off the soap-box and onto the ladder-there were three of them resting against our cherry tree this week as Leslie Hutchins and Ken Hutchins (bless their good neighborly hearts) stretched for the tantalizing ones on the edge of the limbs beyond their grasp.

I had big plans to make us all a cobbler until the kids ate up all but a quart and this week the birds are bound to stagger after feasting their weight in over-ripe delicious yellow cherries. Darn it!

Well, in two more years, we'll have peaches, thanks to J.J. Heinemann's gracious gift.

Now we're back full circle to the annual Fourth of July celebration in Bluemont.

Country music, homemade ice cream and cakes, balloons and fireworks – the merriment will begin at 7:30 at the old Bluemont School grounds.

An offering for the display is appreciated.

July 5, 1973

Thirty gallons of ice cream promised was Ivy Cochran's report on the readiness of the Fourth celebration at Bluemont while the heavens again are pouring out their water problems here. Like the washing of a car, this column writing seems to trigger a rainstorm.

More of the Fourth first, The Bluemont Citizens Association voted to buy a set of horseshoes for recreational purposes at the Wednesday night gathering for the flag waving occasion.

At the early-called July Bluemont Citizens' meeting the escalating water problem was reviewed with the resolution on the part of the Citizens' Association to back the citizens who have retained an attorney to relate to the State Highway Department that they intend to pursue the matter into the courts to get satisfactory action.

It was to be a leisurely stay at home week for us, but Monday I set out to Berryville wanting to see Tom Lennon and Coiner's Department Store about some paint and paper and we were virtually in city traffic; big trucks were roaring through town and vans were unloading as in a teaming metropolis!

Tuesday started quietly enough, Gene Lehman had the tots down for her morning session at the school and great things are happening there, refreshments, finger-painting and a sand box!

Gene is doing it all by herself so maybe we could take turns with refreshments at least.

The girls thought they would sunbathe before lunch when Lara came screaming at the door her foot spurting blood – finally we found the cause – a broken bottle at the front door hidden in the grass.

I told Dr. Towe that we saw his fine new quarters a little earlier than expected and six stitches later we were back to the tranquility of Bluemont.

Tranquility indeed! Summer's hard on kids even harder on their parents' nerves and to think I'm fighting the 12-month school plan!

In addition, big sister sprouted out with a new bicycle, joining the cycling set in town. Motorists please slow down!

Next day, over we went to Mr. Horning's black raspberry patch.

By 10:30 others were there, our foursome had picked 23 quarts in two hours. We got six, saw a sparrow's nest laden with six robin tiny blue eggs, got a bite on Tracey's eye that gave her a toad effect and berry stains on champion picker Jennifer, that resembled an Indian Warrior's battle paint.

Some country ways were learned that day, first you have to brag about how many berries you picked and then how many jars of jam you put up.

Tuesday and Wednesday night, I canvassed the homemakers of the community, Ivy Cochran, Emma Mann, Lucy Martz.

They couldn't tell if it was cheaper, but it was sure a lot better than the store-bought article.

Hooked by Watergate, I strained an ear across the threshold and stirred black raspberry jam and figured the ingredients.

In the freezing method where you add water to the berries, three cups of berries and two pounds of sugar, one package of Sure-Jell, I figured I got three pints for the price of one store bought jar.

The cooking method required more berries, paraffin and more sugar so it's cheaper to use your freezer if you have the room.

Of course, the babysitter cost me, but somehow you have to figure that "work" recreation and if it isn't wild fruit, that cost will send the price higher, but those berries of Mr. Horning's are out of this world!

This is a real novice's report on the event (my first time and we haven't sampled the jam yet!) but when it says to remove the foam, we froze that and decided it would be a perfect topping for ice cream.

Like the Hutchins' beets, they can eat the tops now for greens and then the beets later.

Up till this week, I felt I just didn't have time to sit and watch the Watergate hearings.

The vacuum needed running, the children watching, the weeds cut, but with a few projects in the kitchen I can still lend an ear to what should be the concern of every citizen in this country.

Secret lists of enemies of the Administration – this is pretty heady stuff!

I've found that once I get the baby down for a nap, I can quilt too.

We all need this recess. Ah, ten days to get the bathroom papered and painted, the attic cleaned.

Then – see you "Set-side!"

July 12, 1973

The lazy, hazy days of summer are rolling along in a big ball, where the days go, no one knows.

In my sub-conscious I know I must deal with the problem of the fuel shortage now, perhaps, shutting off part of the house, or like the freezing grasshopper who went to the ants with the refrain, "you were right, I was wrong," there will be much chattering of teeth in the only too near future.

But now let's dance and have some fun while the countryside and village yards are lush.

I have heard of more gardens this year than ever before, I inspected Al Serber's down at the "Waldrop's place" it is struggling along behind a screen, keeping out Cottontail who we spotted on an evening stroll.

Up the lane we could see beautiful clumps of petunias in the Fishback's, and then back down the hill; I believe Sonny and Betty Colbert get the blue ribbon for the prettiest neat garden in town.

Indeed isn't that one of life's noblest projects – to grow a garden.

The spontaneous efforts of people in Bluemont never cease to amaze me.

Just simply because there was a need Gene Layman started the pre-school play school. In a big city, there would be a great question of funding.

Gene says she is having a great time, joined by husband here, Bo who made the sandbox and was fashioning paper ducks for everyone the day I visited.

She says she is getting what she needs with her bringing chocolate goat milk for the children.

Then Wanda and Thomas Ogden donated a big watermelon for the Fourth of July celebration, and the Hutchins are helping me paper my bathroom and even treated Jennifer to a shampoo, a job I dread each week.

Next Marvin Watts and Yoko came with the most beautiful basket of lettuce, and put the rope on the bell for ringing for the Fourth.

And the Fourth, it was glorious!

Lou Robey had an outstanding trio who put just the right tone on the occasion, as one of the Skyfields residents relaxing in the grass, tapping his foot to the rhythm, will attest.

Harold Robinson arrived in force with a bicycle pump lent by the new neighbors up at the Deale's for a busy balloon concession.

Yoko came in her native Japanese dress and looked just darling, and then on the way home after the fireworks the homes of the Virts, Halls and Miners' were lovely with their flags waving in the breeze that cooled off a very hot night.

The Brownells gave their donation too, chocolate mix for the ice cream, which was churned the night before in a pre-Fourth party complete with fireworks at the Snow House.

Lots of vanilla this year, but very little chocolate.

The Brownells, Jim, Scott and Mark have been busy pouring cement for a new milking parlor with a handsome stone front.

Sorry to hear Frances Ballenger was in the hospital this week and that Bessie Carter must return.

The Louis Underwoods are back from a marvelous trip to Montana to see daughter Rhonda, her husband and their new grand-child.

Accompanying them was their darling other grandson, Rusty, with his parents Russell and Beverley Powell.

Claire and Jack Bardon took in a pre-retirement party for a long-time Navy friend who chose to relax at Van Winkle Drive, Sleepy Hollow, Falls Church.

Jack gave out with a little of his special Trinidad Steel Band music which was appropriate since most of the guests had met several years ago in Trinidad.

"Faraway places with strange sounding names" prompted me to bid on a nice little trunk with great shipping labels at a sale to settle the estate of the late Mary Agnew up on Rt. 601 on Saturday.

Her husband, Wing Agnew, who was with the Bureau of Mines, appears to have led an intriguing life. The other neighbors came – the McClures, Carolyn Sabol who sadly gave me the news of the sale of their place – they would still like to find acreage close by. The Glen Lloyds went home with a truck load – a nice walnut bedroom set for daughter Judy Casey, a sideboard for daughter Ann Wilson.

On the other side of Rt. 601, the Dave Freedmans' Great Pyrenees Renaissance Kennel welcomed a litter of pups this week, three males, three females.

The Parks and Recreation Program is in full swing from 9 a.m. – 12 noon, Monday – Friday with instructors, Linda Phillips and Barbara Fitzgerald.

The William Ballengers, Jr. were entertaining again, William Brake from Chillicothe, Ohio and Mrs. George Davis, Bill's aunt from McLean last Sunday.

John Campbell gave me the news that his mother, Brad and himself took in a Baltimore Orioles game on Saturday at Baltimore.

Another exciting discovery this week was that there is a log cabin under the boards on the back addition of the Snow House.

And the green beans are in – snaps – the natives call them!

July 19, 1973

At twelve midnight, it's the long, hot summer with hardly a breeze stirring yet from the green of the mountains.

Across the street the neighbors keep the rhythm of the ice cream freezer going, beating the heat with finger dipping in the ice water then later consuming the rich mixture of two batches, peach and chocolate.

The younger set of boys, Brian Beck, Kenny Hutchins and guest Mark with the Jersey accent are the coolest yet camped in a tent around the corner of the house out in the cool grass.

Fireflies send greetings to one another in the haze of a full moon, the dogs howl, tempers flare – it's the long, hot summer.

The only real way to get the body temperature down it seems to be by immersing in cool water and we were fortunate enough to be invited to lake and pool side this week.

I had just about decided those days of sun-bathing, consciously attempting to secure a tan were behind me – after all wasn't that frivolous at best?

Then over at Greenbriar State Park as a guest of J.J. Heinemann, we noted even the tubby figures look better in a tan.

Naturally, J.J. looked terrific so I reconsidered, maybe I ought to try to get all of my freckles to blend together.

Sun-bathing, anyone?

Actually, though it's sort of a cosmopolitan thing, you know.

Now berry-pickers in the country aren't out for a tan – they're clothed in long-sleeved shirts, long pants and big, floppy straw hats and later ignoring the heat they slave over a hot stove, stirring those berries into jam.

Leslie Hutchins joined the pickers this week and says Mr. Horning has the luscious blackberries now.

Overnight guests either fumed or relished our weather according to the climate from whence they came out last weekend, but last weekend Tony Carbone's parents from Naples, Fla. and his sister and brother-in-law from New York had a great time with the Carbones whipping up some gourmet cooking in the kitchen of Whitehall Farm treating all the Brownell clan and their families.

I met a neighbor of Tony's on Saturday.

Mary Lavendis in the red hot heat took a jaunt down from No. 601 stopping to chat and linger for some lemonade and I found she had covered the Vienna scene in the same manner as your correspondent, for three papers down that way.

Two extroverts met – that's about the size of it!

The William Miners entertained friends from Pennsylvania and were taking them to all the area sights.

More guests of the William Ballengers, Jr. were Mr. and Mrs. William Hamilton and son Bill, Mr. and Mrs. Donald Kline, son Pace and Richard Smith III.

The history of Hillsboro is out now in Spur magazine and I will be getting copies for interested readers, hoping to make my deliveries to Hillsboro next week.

For two weeks now I've known now the other three-fourths (maybe 96 percent) of humanity live without a clothes dryer. (There are very few in Bluemont, I've noticed).

First getting a rope to span two trees is no easy task as it sags, unknots and now with a limp wet line from a morning shower, the rope, naturally full of a late night's wash is really sagging.

The bud count in a basket of dried clothes is fairly high, three spiders, one Japanese beetle, one and three other unidentified crawling things, plus about a peck of grass.

But, ah the fresh clean smell of the laundry that all needs ironing!

Mr. Fix-it, please hurry!

A stop off at the Purcellville Library is always a good experience and the great feature there is that Jean Curruthers has almost always read the book of your interest.

Now I'm into The Wyeths by N.C. Wyeth (his letters spanning his life as a young man to maturity).

Jean said it was fascinating reading and it is.

The Bookmobile (Old Ironsides, Jean calls it) will try again this Tuesday for Bluemont and will park at Mann's Store from 11:30-12:30.

Best of all was the call from Grandmother Johnson that the early apples were in so after a delightful swim with Annette Scheel we hasten.

First, we provided the pony over the fence a few and then relished Papa's surprise – a watermelon.

Papa told us in his boyhood days in Southern Virginia, they picked them by the wagonload from their fields and after partying, he would take his turn watching the tobacco curing, feasting on the heart of the melon, picked cool in the late evening hours.

They gave us an amplified knowledge of spring houses too, relating that generally troughs were built down in the spring waters where the food was set and the shelves above in a two-storied affair were for canned foods.

So laden with little green apples, we anticipated fried apples, baked apples, apple sauce, apple crunch, apple cobbler in the long, hot summer.

July 26, 1973

The days hasten one into another, one seemingly fuller than the last.

The big news in Bluemont is the gardens are ripe unto picking, cucumbers are flourishing, the lettuce continues on, the squash is in, green beans are abundant and all the talk is that it won't be long before the tomatoes are here.

Mrs. Overton favored us with some delights including swiss chard which Tracey agreed was delicious and lo and behold, I may have the greens garden to top you all as Mrs. Overton says that poke in my flower bed is still perfect for eating, up until the time it blossoms.

At last I've found someone to identify the plants, she knows them all and has promised to take up on a spring-time walk and stalk the various wild edibles.

Thelma Brunelle came with a surprise, herbs in plastic balls all complete with a bunch of directions.

Considering my non-plus ability at gardening, Thelma decided to take them on back to her "Homestead" where we will plant for a Fair project.

Fair projects are the order of the day, my prediction is that with the price of food soaring, these homemade preserves of all sorts will go better than ever.

Glad to hear that Lucketts will venture forth with their second annual event in August.

Lots of happenings are winging by: Jack Bardon armed with our Bluemont Fair propaganda took in the Championship Contest in Berryville for the weekend.

Heard he won a prize as the picking and singing went on into the wee hours of the night.

Then the Bardons' other interest, from radio-operating took them to an annual picnic in Urbanna, Va.

From a membership of about one hundred from Florida, west to Tennesseee, Ohio and north to New York to the Atlantic Ocean, twenty-five came with their families for the best time ever.

These are all early birds as they converse from 5-7 a.m. each morning.

Jack acted as a judge for Mobile Contest which he explains is for the best set in a vehicle like our friend, Joe Fine, has rigged in his Volkswagen bus.

Joe and Judy were back from Richmond with some great pictures of our visit together previously and were braving it all with another couple for a camping-out experience after a heavy rain down by the Shenandoah.

About twelve midnight they chugged back in the drive, drenched and ready for the indoor comforts of a hot shower and a dry bed and the next morning, did we have a breakfast!

Nancy Rae, a Southern gal, fixed us pore bread with milk gravy, a first for my palate and marvelous!

Entertaining abounded as people savored a time with friends and relatives.

Last week the Earl Virts had dinner guests of Mr. and Mrs. Lloyd Cooper from Orlando, Fla. (Earl's sister and husband), Mrs. Mabel Virts from Hillsboro and Mrs. Earl Virts, Jr. and daughter Elaine from McLean.

Then I found out Mrs. Virts had broken her leg, now mended, without even falling

Justine Beck celebrated her birthday this week with some kind of giggling camp-out in the backyard.

She and Pam Carbaugh seem to be keeping the road warm with visits back and forth from Front Royal.

On Sunday they took in the Farm Craft Days at Belle Grove and had a grand buggy ride.

Then Donna Miner reported she had two sets of guests, the Pennsylvania folks, followed by a California bunch and on Wednesday, her father arrives from Texas.

It was great to see Jan Woolman over at the store across the street with the news that she had graduated from Nursing School and was on her assignment at Loudoun Memorial, working in the emergency room.

The William Ballengers, Jr. were still welcoming guests, Mr. and Mrs. George C. Davis of Langley on Sunday.

It was a good week shop-wise as I met some more of the neighbors.

Barbara Ahlgren from up on Number 601 came by and promised to try to make it to the quilting bee down at Moselle Anderson's on Tuesday.

We'll be quilting on the lawn and happily I can contribute two more patches to the half-finished article.

More quilts are coming in to the Clayton Hall Book and Craft Shop too.

Mrs. Mabel Thomas has brought some fine old hand-stitched ones and some sweet new sun-bonnets.

And the Hillsboro history in Spur Magazine with Howard Allen's fine pictures are a must for Hillsborians.

Hope to see you on Thursday with a picture on the cover of Secretariat, the first Virginia-bred Triple Crown winner!

The hearings are as interesting as ever, I'm told but the projects here have been legion.

Leslie Hutchins is a real wonder and could be hiring herself out as a professional wallpaper hanger.

I've always said you can tell the class of a restaurant by a visit to the restroom and here at this former Inn we were on Duncan Hines minus list but thanks to Leslie and a painted blue floor, we're high class!

Gretchen, the dachshund absolutely barks half the night with all the sound of a teeming metropolis to disturb her which is alright up until one o'clock but this six o'clock business is too much!

August 2, 1973

A breeze flutters through the open windows promising a break in the 90 degree temperatures as the frantic pace of a week slows in the late July hours now turning into August.

The fire-flies have been caught, the bicycles parked and the popcorn consumed for another long summer's evening.

In the children's society, Pam Carbaugh is back for a visit with Justine Beck, Robin has joined the Hutchins' household, acquiring a beautiful new blue bicycle the first full day of residency and John Campbell is nicely bronzed from the sun and a big swimming pool is being added to the Snow House complete.

Another bronzed specimen in town is pretty young Sandy Mitchell returned from a vacation to Myrtle Beach.

She baby-sat along with Debbie Carter while Barbara Algren and I took in the quilting bee down at Moselle Anderson's in Philomont this week.

We had a super time there joined here first by Claire Bardon and Judy Spring who we are pleased to welcome to Bluemont. She and her husband Millard have acquired the former Langer place and Judy already has a healthy garden and has made some jelly pronounced great by my children.

We were off to the lush of Moselle's porch, complete with hanging baskets of petunias. At the side of the house a waterfall flowed into a pond inhabited by two marvelous serenading bull frogs and as usual the most delightful of Loudoun County company attended.

Annette Scheel dropped in with her mother-in-law visiting from New Rochelle, so our folksy pastimes here are gaining attention and Moselle in her best literary manner interviewed each guest, got their name and address straight, their husband's occupation, the number of children begot and their own most compelling life's goal.

Best of all the quilt is progressing beautifully with lovely bright colors and some fine stitching.

It's almost time to embroider on names and give credit where credit is due.

We will need to get Janet Ball's signature, as much to our sorrow her charming Stoneledge on Rt. 690 between here and Purcellville is on the market and they are anticipating a move to the cool of New Hampshire.

She could receive our most congenial quilter award too!

Got a little more news on the Bardens that day. Daughter Jeannie, recently graduated from Madison, has procured a teaching position right at home in the Clarke County public schools.

Observing some moving-in operation across the street at the Dawson's, I found daughter Libby and husband Bootsie Stearne will be staying there until their new house is completed, if all checks out right on the lot next to Allen Campbell.

In like manner, the Wesley Carbaughs are coming back down to their pink house in the village from residency on top of Pierrot's Hill.

And I was glad Mrs. Dawson told me the news of Sandy Sisk's delivery of a baby boy born July 27.

On Thursday, the children and I struck out for Hillsboro armed with Spur Magazine.

After depositing the children with Sue Mearns, she endured incessant squabbles and a bumble bee attack on Lara, I merrily chatted with Mrs. Williams who has many more tales to recite than space afforded in the article and called on the former Evelyn Turbeville who is married to Major Turbeville.

Then I got the Hillsboro tour, just had a wonderful time at the Grimms, while Mrs. Rowe, the artist, sent me on my way with a bouquet of the best-smelling herbs and Joyce Hopkins let me see the house that became an inn that became a house.

Both the antique shops were open, Mrs. Bell's and the one in the former old Methodist Church.

The traffic whirled by Hillsboro on Route 9 but inside each home, that world seemed far away, their world was mine until I was back in the street to a car whose electric windows had jammed.

Naturally the air-conditioning has been broken for a long time – so I thought I'd patent the moving machine as a great reducing innovation.

Pounds would be shed in a sort of moving steam bath machine.

While enjoying the scenery, ones' mind could be distracted from the ordeal of the heat, but Janet Bell said it wasn't practical and with the fuel shortage maybe she's right!

And Hillsboro – how about an event called the Backyards of Hillsboro – lawn party style?

August 9, 1973

It's absolutely one of those perfect days, the cadence of the crickets keep a cheery tune running – butterflies are basking in the warm, not hot, sun on the front porch while a breeze rustles slightly in the trees. All's right with the world until an inevitable screaming child flies through the door or another black snake makes his way up an interior wall.

So much has transpired in a week while I just keep reading the letters of N.C. Wyeth, while Jean Carruthers says that it's a shame better writing is passé, but I'll keep on writing this letter to you, "dear readers," Victorian vintage style each week if you can stand it.

First of all there are several snake stories that can top mine – Hershal, the lovable Basset Hound of Don and Linda Corley – was bitten by a poisonous snake while frisking near their place on the hill and John and Linda Postelle up at the Deale's on the mountain killed a rattlesnake this week.

Then a mouse jumped out from my kitchen drawer on Friday and Mrs. Dawson says they know it's time to come in when August dawns.

The summer days are mellowing toward fall as the softball season winds up: our Debbie Carter was chosen for the All-Star Girls' team in the position of pitcher.

Sorry to hear that Bill Martz, coach of the women's team is back in the hospital.

With the ringing of the church bell this morning, the girls quickly skirted into an occasional dress and sandals and came back with the news that the Sisks were there with their new baby, done up in a pretty blue blanket and that Eric Anderson and Belinda Dawson were celebrating birthdays this week.

Some of our families took a little breather from the chores of lawn mowing, canning and cleaning to travel to some inspiring relaxing spots.

The Robert Allders got a day in last Sunday to nearby Cacapon, the Milton Hollers took Brian and Ruth Lee's brother, Charlie Everhart, from Lovettsville to Hershey for a fabulous day's outing and Mark Brownell in the family camper got up Vermont-New Hampshire way for a week.

Then again Alice and Lloyd Loope did some high mountain backpacking in a remote area called Dark Canyon in Utah, much like the Grand Canyon, Alice says.

They were out to see sons Walter and David and their daughter Amy stayed on for an extended visit until school will begin only too soon.

The Walton Manns went down to Highland County, Va. for a visit with the Maple Sugar man and his wife who again will be seeing us at the Bluemont Fair.

The Manns' new little granddaughter Cynthia Jeanette was christened here at the Bluemont Methodist Church several weeks ago when Tom and Ruth Mann were down for a visit from Philadelphia.

We had a Philadelphia visitor, Miss Jalna Schuler, this week – we only got as far as Waterford and Leesburg for sightseeing but it was nice; and Grandmother Beck was here from Charlottesville for the weekend with the Clyde Becks.

The Snickersville Craft Club is meeting the third Tuesday of the month with toto-painting being the feature.

And shades of 1920, 30, 40 came off Saturday evening in the cool of the mountain atmosphere in the house where Jane King had established her famous boarding house.

Mrs. Robert Beeton said Jane was the Moreland referred to in the Potomac Trail Club excursion pamphlet printed in 1939, as she later married a Moreland.

The house now owned by the Deales of New York is being enjoyed by Linda and John Postello this summer who were our gracious hostess and host, with Harold Robinson showing his superb slides of his trip to England, Scotland and Wales.

Those other travel series have got nothing on Bluemont, Harold was a wealth of information providing a stimulating sociable evening with the mountain residents who are all pretty traveled people themselves.

We had the Verloops, just returned from three sun-tanned weeks in Nags Head, and Herman Vicke back from his trip to his native land, The Netherlands.

Alice and Lloyd Loope and Alice's mother, Mrs. Smith, were there, joined by the Leon Brunelles and their guests, the William Rays and son Bill from Washington; the Robert Bakers retired now in their beautiful, rustic home on Rt. 601 and Peg and Tom Holmes, world travelers, who could answer a question that had stumped five other audiences.

So there it is another week in Bluemont as a screaming child has just hit the front door – gather your butterflies while you may – summer fades fast!

August 16, 1973

Animated conversation in the street, a dog howling in the background, traffic whirling by on the hill, and the constant racket of the katydids – these sounds coming through the open window late on a summer evening mark Bluemont as something less than its previous reputation as a sleepy little mountain village.

And the Bluemont news – all week I've pounded the pavement so I've hardly known the goings and comings here.

Charles and Kathryn Hoge of Ft. Myers, Fla. are up for a month in the Brunelles' resort spot on the mountain and will be entertained by Charles' sister, Mildred Shackleford of Purcellville.

The William Ballengers, Jr. of Pine Grove took their son David up for a two-week visit to Mathias, W.Va. for a time with his cousin, Brian and aunt and uncle, the Roy Mathiases.

What a week – Monday – Ginger Echols and I had a ride out to that most beautiful of properties – Chestnut Hill; Tuesday, J.J. Heinemann and I called on the Irvine Gallery in Paeonian Springs which incidentally is loaded with terrific art, art, art; Wednesday, Sue Mearns and I took a Winchester shopping trip; Thursday, I managed to put up six pints of blackberry jam thanks to Mr. Horning's generosity and he will have berries for another month in his patch on Rt. 719, Friday, Janet Ball and I had a great day in Centreville with Janet's friend, Ann Beresford whose marvelously varied interests have already scheduled two bus tours of senior citizens to the Bluemont Fair, and Saturday, the Heinemann and Johnson girls took in the Brunswick, Md. Potomac River Festival hoping to have a ride on a train to Harper's Ferry.

By 11 o'clock Saturday morning they were sold out to the three scheduled rides for the day.

It's that time of year – Fair time with the 4-H event just over at Clark's Gap and at Berryville and the approaching Lucketts Fair, Aug. 25, 26 and plans crystalizing for the Bluemont Fair, Oct. 20, 21.

Armed with our Bluemont Fair cards hot off the press, I chatted to the exhibitors at Brunswick.

There was our cotton candy man, eager to publicize for us and with a good planning session this week we are in full swing.

Everyone had great news to report – Jack Bardon says it looks good for Bluegrass Music interest, and Don Corley comments many are signing up for the Flea Market space; and we will build a stage for the music performers and put doors on the shed for the dried arrangements and produce, with no plants being accepted this year.

We will have the slide shows and model train display again.

The Methodist Church will sell country ham sandwiches and we will have the usual chuck wagon offerings.

In addition to the craft demonstrations the popular musket shoot will be repeated, and new this year will be an exhibit of the work of five outstanding artists who all reside in Loudoun County's Mt. Gilead district.

Corn meal will be ground again, and the Arnold Grove ladies will stir up a big kettle of apple butter.

Best of all to me is the opportunity for a tour of the Brownells' new milking parlor and a ride out to their fields on the hay wagon.

Mark Brownell says he will come home for the weekend from VPI to do the honors.

And since we were disappointed that we didn't get a train ride in Brunswick perhaps, we can count on a hayride in October right at home in Bluemont on another iron horse, the tractor.

And this week the best news of all is that everyone has tomatoes; Herbert Martz is keeping us supplied.

What's better than a tomato sandwich with lots of mayonnaise?

And tonight I start the dill pickles.

August 23, 1973

"You know and I know that the dog days are just behind us when snakes are practically blind and now with renewed sight they are out looking for winter quarters."

Thus Marion Kerrick gave me an explanation for the black snakes frequenting the exterior walls of my old stone house and basking in the sun on the front porch.

He and his wife were store-keeping while the Walton Manns were on a deserved excursion to Cumberland Gap coming back by way of Kentucky.

The general store still offers a generous liberal education if one had the time or inclination to avail himself of it but somehow the days got shorter and fuller with their passing and canning and storing up for winter time is prime.

Herbert Martz said Lucy in her hay-day had put up 1300 quarts by summer's end, this included meat – sausage, cooked down and spare-ribs reduced to jar size.

The month of July and August seem ripe with birthdays too.

Our Jennifer celebrated on the 17th, Willa Colbert on the 18th and Chris Budny on the 19th.

The celebrations go on and on with the neighbor children and the grandparents with more cake and ice cream and good dinners of corn and tomatoes.

Brownie Camp interfered with our guest list, April Wilt attended and Susan Allison but Susan came from Round Hill on Saturday for more games of Old Maid and Slapjack, finger painting, water coloring, card sewing and Don't Fall in the Ice.

We had to schedule dinner with Mary Alice and the younger Wertzs of Purcellville later, who all went camp-side too this week at Lucketts.

The James Brownells had week-long house guests from North Carolina last week while we welcomed El and Claire Shoemaker from Bowie, Md. who left home out of defense from continuing summer-long visitors.

Their children Brenda and Doug are all ready to come back for the Bluemont Fair.

Jean Lehmann carried on with the Play School, culminating this week as she will be joining our other Bluemonters, Joyce Beck and Shirley Lynn at the Round Hill School on the 27th with teacher pre-school workshop.

The code of bureaucracy has struck again, slaying our good neighbors, the Hutchins and Budnys who in an economic measure and for the sheer joy of doing have wired and done the plumbing of the 17-room house themselves.

The law insists that if two families live together, it must be a commercial venture with one renting to the other so VEPCO wants to charge commercial rates and Loudoun County wants to insist they hire a professional plumber for their kitchen addition.

They just can't believe two families would buy together a 17-room house.

Somehow it is much more logical that Nellie Powell lived there alone without central heat and no plumbing.

"Sing a song of seasons!
Something bright in all!
Flowers in the summer,
Fires in the Fall!"
-Robert Louis Stevenson.

A quilt will be comforting tonight.

August 30, 1973

The majority of the days waxed cool and mellow, the nights crisp – these glorious late summer days linger.

Our neighbors, the Clarke Countyans bid summer a farewell in a last fling with their traditional Fair and Bluemonters, the Hutchins and Leslie's folks, the Goodwins of Cherry Hill, N.J., took in the event before closing night.

The Clyde Becks returned after a refreshing week in the New England states and the William Ballengers, Jr. with three of their children, made the annual pilgrimage to the Jousting Tournament at National Chimneys Regional Park last Saturday.

The Jack Lightners too are back after a two-week respite in South Carolina where they golfed and swam.

Forgot to mention last week that Andrew and Rosemary Murtaugh won 13 ribbons with their goats at the Loudoun 4-H Fair and were competing again this week in Berryville.

When I finally got in a walk with Ginger to the post office this week, I was sorry to hear Mrs. Townshend had been ailing with a vertebrae problem, but she says she is doing quite well now.

Where, oh where, has the summer gone is the lament of most everyone.

We've had lots of visits and day excursions, and now people in the country have no time for frivolity.

The days and nights are for putting up and laying aside for the winter.

As of this week, we will have some tomatoes, some squash, some apple sauce, some peach, plum, and blackberry preserves in the larder and I know the ladies like Ivy Cochran and Mac Brownell are at the kitchen sink and slaving over the stove most of the day and into the night.

What was accomplished in these sunny days?

Well, I can't say for sure like most everyone, but I had a month with the Wyeths.

For 18 cents on an overdue book, I read N.C.'s account of the children's growth, the planting of crops, the canning and storing for winter and a life-time of commissioned painting and illustrating and it all went very fast. I'll pass up the temptation to philosophize.

The J.J. Kelleys were pleased to have their former Loudoun friends, Lois Perenteaus and her children from Palm Springs, Calif. for a visit, and Gail says the new neighbors at the former Pierson House are so nice, they are the Michael Hickmans with five children coming here from Woodbridge.

It's time to tell everyone the Bluemont Fair will be one of the most pleasant of events they ever attended, and there will be $500 given away in cash prizes for the country music contest.

We're a-buzz here and can talk of little else except the high cost of living.

Remember the Bluemont Citizen's Meeting this first Wednesday of the month, 8 p.m. and Mary Lynn Budny says the soy-bean hamburgers are quite tasty at 89 cents a pound.

September 6, 1973

The heat sputtered, pounded and reverberated while the populace sprouted on the cool lawns in the evenings and stayed inside away from the sun's rays in the days.

The first day of the onslaught we took it silently, not quite comprehending the shock that it was really this hot in Bluemont, the second day we merely suffered but by the third day we mapped out our strategy early in the morning.

The girls would buy popsicles for the afternoon and concoct Robin Myer's invention, a half paper cup of water allowed to stand in the freezer, then after a half-hour, add some flavored drink on top, more freezing and real refreshment stood early.

Then for the evening after a cool shower, we would have our sherbet just before retiring and by jove, we did it, we did it! It has all been quite bearable.

What a reception, however, for Ken Hutchins' father and sister from Merritt, N.H.

They are down enrolling Andrea in Maryland University which Ken says now has 10,000 students outflanked by few others in the country.

We met in a hurry when Tracey, hot, bothered and bewildered was attempting to fill the little wading pool, bucket by bucket from the kitchen sink.

She turned the faucet too far and I broke it off and couldn't get all the wonderful cold gushing water stopped until the neighbors came to the rescue.

When summoned they were helping Mary Lynn get her car started.

It was all in a day's work of being a good neighbor, I guess.

Marvin Watts and Yoko were back picking their ever-producing garden after a short escape from the country duties and the children are reluctantly counting the days till school.

Yvonne Allder, Kenny Hutchins and the twins will be our young new first graders.

It's a big step for them and what's a mother to do with only one child at home?

The whole fall schedule will begin. The Ladies Day Out class is starting again on the 11th.

This time in Life in Loudoun we will spend six weeks in Leesburg investigating the history and preservation efforts, the local government, the court system and the press.

Had a nice visit with Suzanne Anderson who is studying for a degree in Recreation but taking some interesting courses about the stock market and I'm starting Gailbraith's The Great Crash.

You see I have great faith in this Republican President. Now that ought to get me on the enemy list. I can't afford to have my reputation ruined by being left off.

September 13, 1973

Now the golden days are upon us and everywhere on the roadside and in the meadows are the yellow flowers – what sheer delight to pick and pick and pick bouquets to be arranged in the old crocks for the halls and downstairs rooms.

Then a nosegay will spill upstairs to my Van Gogh gold-painted walls and "all will be right with the world!"

The earth is still yielding its magnificent bounty, corn and tomatoes by the bushels, with the neighbors remembering us, and the freezer is filling fast while the apples and pears plunge to the ground from the old gnarled trees on the lawn.

Most of the village children are school-bound on the big orange bus these mornings and there is time at least for straight-forward projects to be accomplished and important telephone calls for the Bluemont Fair, Oct. 20 and 21, to be brought to fruition.

The planning goes on in deep earnest now, the posters are to be out by the weekend, the programs are mapped out, the tickets to be delivered shortly, and the first registration for exhibitors set for Sept. 21 from 1-5 p.m. and Sept. 22 from 10 a.m.- 5 p.m. at the old corner store.

The fee will be fifty cents again to defray the cost of the tags.

All signals are go for the hayride over at the Brownells, any adult interested in helping to supervise the ride, please call me.

Dot Givens from McDaniel-Kent Realty gives me the word that our new neighbors in Frances Ballenger's former house are the Flemings.

Judy Casey tells me her aunt, Esther Rose, from Round Hill won a new Datsun convertible while taking in an event near the home of her sister Lillian Keister.

Autumn is the time of year for Bluemont to bloom with Howard Bass and John Marlow to give a program of lute and guitar duets combined with Albert Gordon's light show Sept. 29 at the school-house.

In addition, Al Serber and Clyde Beck are opening up an antique shop in Clyde's studio building, the old store; and the Miners are furnishing their living room with saleable objects, combined with Clayton Hall Book and Craft Shop as the "Shops of Bluemont!" How exclusive can you get?

Then too, the weekend before the Fair one of our Bluegrass Contest judges from the Smithsonian Institute will present a concert and five Mt. Gilead artists will have a pre-Fair opening of their exhibit.

Two rich anecdotes came to my ear this week. The Brownells with their acres of corn lost their sweet corn planted somewhere in the middle, so my mental picture of Mac Brownell standing over gobs of cobs in the kitchen was all wrong.

Secondly, at the time of Mr. Nesmith's death, the Becks took in his cat, who was all of the family he really had, and this week the cat sensing apparently its end was near returned to the old Nesmith place with the Fishbacks reporting a stray cat found dead at their door-step.

But as Tom Taylor said about former Lincoln residents, 'they're not dead, 'cause they still live in my memory."

You can't get a much better tribute to a man's life, now can you? Or a cat's life either for that matter!

September 20, 1973

Dazzling lights in the direction of Berryville, glimmering in the clearest of atmospheres was the Bluemont scene from the foothills of the Blue Ridge as Autumn and the natives renewed their seasonal romance this week.

Plans were afoot for entertainment and refreshments in a pre-nuptial celebration before the Bluemont Fair, Oct. 20, 21.

On Sept. 29 at 8 p.m. Howard Bass and John Marlow will return in a program of lute and guitar duets along with Albert Gordon's fantastic light show.

Charles Anson, our British friend, who frequented Bluemont for several years is back for a visit from the Isles and will be on hand at the program to see old friends.

The Miners say they will call their antique shop, the Ice House Lot, as they feel certain the marvelous structure in their backyard was the icehouse for Clayton Hall. For years the pit was used for refuse and now they are down to the 1920's collection.

Son Brian is becoming a real bottle expert. He and Andy Kelley from Round Hill are wheeling and dealing, and took in the bottle show at Winchester this weekend.

Glen Lloyd explained the whole spring-house, icehouse phenomenon to me one evening.

Only the most affluent families in town had icehouses, he said, in all of Paris – just over the mountain, here where he grew-up, there were only three.

Generally they cut the ice from their own pond, sometimes from the river when it was zero weather, as otherwise the warmer temperatures made the blocks of ice stick to one another and to the clothing of the ice-gatherers.

A wonderfully kept icehouse is down at the Redwines, the old Parks' Place, and the farm extending across the road now, with a different owner, still has the spring house, the original barns and the smokehouse.

How lucky J.J. Heinemann and I were to get a tour while we were following the path of the yellow flowers.

We were both photographing and she is painting so year round we can reconstruct the beauty of these wild flowers that seed to sticky nuisances.

Thelma Brunelle and I noticed there were none past the Loudoun County line when we took in Boonesboro Day, just up Rt. 340 into Washington County, Md.

It was a grand affair, the scenery on the way was worth the trip alone.

They had jousting, Revolutionary War garbed soldiers, the Second Maryland and Infantry reenacted, with plans for bigger and better things next year in their charming municipal park location.

I invited the singer, tole-painter and potter to join us, and they just might do it.

It's wonderful to see these communities come alive with pride in their heritage.

Our former name preserved by the Craft Club, Snickersville Craft Club, will be redoing chair seats in reed rush and caning. The course will be taught in January by Evelyn Pierson and orders for the materials should go in this week. If interested, call Emma Mann.

So when's the last time you went to an old-fashioned song-fest around the piano?

Well, our visiting friends, the Hoges, up at the Brunelles hosted such an affair Saturday night with Mr. Hoge's sister, Mildred Shackleford of Purcellville, accompanying us with Thelma's strong soprano lead in "Daisy, Daisy," "Down by the Old Mill Stream; and "T'was from Aunt Dinah's Quilting Party, I was seeing Nellie Home."

We will quilt again at Clayton Hall on the 26th, card-tables, finger-foods and quilters welcome.

It's all coming back with the big picture hats decorated with artificial cherries and flowers. You'll see!

September 27, 1973

The first official days of Autumn brought a chill this week while most everyone reported he or she had a fire in the fireplace mornings and evenings and some even admitted to turning on the furnace.

I'm with Mary Lou Markle who says her projection date is Oct. 15. Besides I'm still waiting for a furnace cleaning and a thermostat moving.

With the coolness came a new vigor and the publicity for the Bluemont Fair is moving briskly.

The beautiful posters are here.

Curtis Budny is certainly a perfectionist in his art work; everyone appreciates his hours of time on the project.

This community ever amazes me when you consider the number of citizens who devote hours and hours to the endeavor every year.

Truly that's what the Fair is all about, a joint effort to provide a day of enjoyment in the country both for the host and our guests.

It's all getting very exciting with the promise of State Senator Charles Waddell's coming to MC the Music Contest and add to the festivities by giving a solo or two.

Charlie is a man of many interests, one lesser known perhaps is that he is a Civil War buff.

The nicest thing I remember about Charlie being our neighbor in Broad Run Farms, other than his doing all the work of our mutual garden for two seasons, was his accompanying my class of U.S. History on a field trip to Gettysburg.

He was a marvelous guide informing the students of the military personnel involved, the positions of battle-lines drawn and in addition, he had a great selection of Civil War marching songs on record for lending too.

Bet he will love the musket shoot!

The Loudoun County Museum has a lovely slide show now of spots and places to visit in Loudoun County and after the Parks and Recreation Class had learned of the preservation efforts on a county-wide basis from Mrs. Raflo, I felt very proud of Bluemont.

We were the first to have a book of our history, the only community to have a documentary slide show of our history and the first community after Waterford who began their Foundation in 1946, to have any kind of annual event. Of course, we were followed closely by Lincoln and Lucketts who we applaud. It will be marvelous to be able to take in the Lincoln Tour this year since they won't be happening the same weekend.

The Rev. Melvin Steadman, former Loudoun pastor, has written a terrific history of Leesburg in his "A Walking Tour of Leesburg."

This week the Life in Loudoun class will go out to Ball's Bluff, the smallest national cemetery and how I wish I had time to read Gen. Patch's history of the event before going.

When I called the Star about an ad, the advertising department asked me if we were near Purcellville as she had just gotten a nice ad from a man with pumpkins.

Naturally I knew who she meant – George Cochran's and Charlie Brown's Great Pumpkin Patch is aglow again.

What a fantastic sight to spot, that hill of orange to the side of Rt. 7 by Mr. Kirk's where Mary Lou Markle got an oriental rug this week for $30. I'm sick!

Herbert Martz says the grass will need just one more cutting this season, right before the Fair as he handed me the last of the summer posies, an absolutely beautiful bouquet of dahlias.

"Where the neighbors are the dearest and the best-Bluemont."

Why doesn't someone write an original ballad for the contest? There's the richest kind of subject matter here just waiting to be plucked.

October 4, 1973

A fast-paced week settled into a full weekend as the sky hung over-east and the excitement of a candidate coming to town drove the dogs, the children and a sprinkling of adult voters to the general store on Saturday morning.

What vote commitment was accomplished in Bluemont, one can't say but the children of the village were utterly smitten with the great mobile rig called "The Cannonball" and "The Governor, The Governor," they continued to chant.

John Campbell told the Allders he couldn't vote but people ought to vote for Howell "'cause he was giving out papers to everyone!"

Yvonne Allder said she wanted to vote for Nixon but after the Johnson girls said he wasn't any good, she said, "Well, then I'll just vote for the man who came here!"

It was all very exciting, the van drove in with the Singing Senator Charles Waddell's ballad coming across on tape and he and his wife Marie were here in the flesh.

It was great to see them again and what a wonderful way to give your children a living history lesson. Jennifer, my third grader, had already gotten the Howell thrust against the tax on food and medicine.

Now if he can communicate with the registered voters as well as the children of Bluemont, he might do alright!

Then that night a shower fell for the Marlow Bass concert but a pleasant evening of good music transpired at the old school.

Now music lovers were anticipating the other concert before the Fair at the Brownell's Whitehall Farm on Sunday, Oct. 14 at 4 p.m. with James Weaver, one of the country's leading harpsichordists.

The quilters gathered for another bee at Clayton Hall this week and it was kind of the Springers to send their friend, Bernie Boston, chief photographer for the Washington Star here to take some pictures. He even found my old photographic equipment in the shop of interest.

It was delightful when Miss Florence Maitland came calling in time to spend the day with us as she is up for a several weeks visit at the Waldrops from her Florida home.

How marvelous to hear again the old Bluemont stories, the likes of which I haven't heard since Mr. Nesmith's death.

Frolicking on the still warm Ocean City, Md. beach last weekend were Ruth Lee and Milton Holler, getting away at last for a little vacation.

The William Ballengers, Jr. entertained at a birthday party for their daughter, Deanna, last week with guests, the William Hamiltons.

Joe and Helen Deale from Dumont, N.J. are up on the mountain now for a week's visit and she and all are grieving with Kay Siedenspinner on the loss of her dear mother, Mrs. Townshend who loved coming to Bluemont and had many craft items in readiness for the Bluemont Fair.

October 11, 1973

Thinking about the Snickersville Academy sampler, the gem owned by the J.J. Kelleys, I called up and found out son Sam would be home for this weekend from boarding school in Maryland.

News of another of our younger generation is that Junior Wade, son of the Eugene Wades celebrated his birthday this week with two cakes, one coming from his friends at the doctor's office.

It was a stormy Tuesday morning but the Loudoun County Board of Supervisors met with "business as usual" and if you want your faith in the American political system renewed, you should sit in on a session.

I was terribly impressed, we have chosen some mature, conscientious men who refuse to vote on an issue until they can get constituent reaction.

Certainly this is local government at its best with even a youth having his full say for 20 prolonged minutes with the board providing the kindest manners and respect to his opinions.

And of course, our own Jim Brownell was the greatest!

Our own little Bluemont Citizens meetings are satisfying too with everyone acting very congenial, volunteering their best in the final plans for the Fair.

Louis Underwood will clean up the school grounds and Walton Mann, the main street with Mr. Tinsman picking up trash piled by the incinerator on the school grounds by the 16th.

There is an awful lot of litter down the road to the mill.

All our exhibitors are to realize they must get a new number this year and they can still register and bring their items for sale on the 17th and 18th from 10 a.m. – 5 p.m. at the old store.

The Halloween Party was set for Halloween night and the Fair dinner date is to be Nov. 11.

Oh, the delights of the projects transpiring in town now – the Budnys and Halls are painting window frames, the Hutchins are putting in their new kitchen, Clyde Beck and Al Serber are sprucing up the old store for a grand opening of their antique shop, the Bluemont Trading Company, while Donna and Bill Miner are finishing up their arrangement in their new shop, the Ice House Lot all to open this weekend along with an art exhibit and a concert.

October is the fun month in Bluemont!

October 18, 1973

Life seemed especially good this week with just enough bright days to accomplish the weed-cutting and trash collecting for the Bluemont Fair.

Trees had actually sprung up on the fence row which stubbornly resisted my whacks with the sickle until the children rescued me after school.

John Campbell is a wizard with a hatchet.

With all the cleaning about and the turning colors on the mountainside, we will be sparkling for our guests as we all anticipate the best Fair ever.

The best story of the week concerns Herbert Martz who typifies the Bluemont I love so. Spying six baby copperheads sunning in a pile, he simply danced on them, destroying them before they provided a menace to someone.

Almost equally exciting was Trudy Verloop's news that she and husband John are grandparents.

Daughter Emily and husband John Thomas became parents of a first-born, a boy in Baltimore where John is associated with the McDonough School.

It was a real fun weekend here with the Mt. Gilead artists bringing their works on Saturday and a reception in their honor that evening.

They are so talented and I especially enjoyed my chat with Dagmar Wilson and June McAdams.

Then on Sunday we saw Dagmar again over at the Brownell's with a cluster of chestnuts in tote after the concert. She and her English husband were both explaining the game children played with them, tying them on a string, then whacking at the opponent's string hoping to break his best striker. It was all clear when I thought of my generation and their trusty shooter in a game of marbles.

The harpsichord and lute program was filled to over-flowing with Howard Bass and Jim Weaver being most informative along with their fine musical talents.

The Shortridges from down the pike had finished a beautiful harpsichord for the occasion with flowered decorations on the keyboard done by a young woman who was represented by her mother!

It made for a lovely pleasant weekend in such a marvelous setting and it was great to see the Brownell young men home from college for the weekend. Scott from Alfred in New York State and Mark from VPI. Now back for a hayride and dairy tour next weekend at the Bluemont Fair.

October 25, 1973

After the Fair I'll wash my hair…after the Fair I'll bring in the geraniums…after the Fair the girls can have an overnight guest…after the Fair I'll make apple-sauce, but just several hours after the Fair I wonder if I'll have energy even to get the debris off the front lawn tomorrow.

The consensus is – it was the best Fair ever – the sun beamed on us in Bluemont and the people came in droves to hear the Bluegrass music and take a magnificent hayride up the pasture land into the hills.

There was lots of talk of what's for rent out here and what's for sale out here and what a wonderful place to raise children.

Not only were there the daily guests but most every house was over-flowing with overnight guests who pitched in helping with the duties of entertaining the daily guests.

Jack Bardon and Charlie Waddell are talking about holding this Bluegrass Contest every year, and I have to admit it was a wonderful two days of picking and singing.

The top money went to the Southern Sounds of Grass from Martinsburg, W.Va. Then in second place were the Bluegrass Country Boys and third was the Blue Ridge Mountain Buddies.

The Grass Reflection, known formerly as the Spence Kids of Herndon took two firsts and a third – Karen Spence first for female vocalist, Steve – first for banjo and Kevin – third for guitar.

Another crowd favorite was John Henry Alger of West Virginia, a fiddler who held the Virginia State Championship in 1968, but was beat out here by Dave Goldman of Falls Church, third for fiddler was our local friend, Louis D. Crosen.

First in male vocalist went to neighbor J.D. Dawson from the Bluegrass County Boys, Joe Payne of the Southern Sounds took second, and third was Randy Walker of the Bluegrass Dispatch.

Second on banjo was Douglas Knowles who came with partner Random Cayon from Ithaca, N.Y., claiming a special award for the band coming the farthest.

Third in banjo was Linnum Wharton of the Blue Ridge Mountain Buddies from Marshall.

Back to female vocalist was our own Jeanne Bardon as second with former Madison College roommate Brenda Latimer in third place.

On guitar first was Pudge Warfield of Southern Sounds, David Baker, Jr. of The Bluegrass Mountain Buddies, second.

Keith Morris of Southern Sounds took the one mandolin prize.

In the miscellaneous category Johnny Castle got a first for his bass, Jeannie Bardon and Brenda Latimer – a second for their duet and third went to Elliot Jenkins for harmonica and guitar.

Then Charlie came through with his promise to sing, even getting in the Howell Cannonball – much to Jim Brownell's good-natured grimace and Jack Bardon rendered his harmonica without holder, guitar number.

It was all absolutely marvelous fun with Ginger Echols and Mrs. Stanley Greene arriving here this afternoon to help me, decked out in the most super costumes.

The antique dolls are gone, the three chairs, one quilt, the antique wash pitcher and bowl, and tomorrow's time enough to put back the displays and drain the last of the spiced cider from the stone crock, maybe the folks will come again to linger and chat – after the Fair!

November 1, 1973

And suddenly there's an orange tree aflame in the sunlight in the backyard and the neighbor's spotlight focuses on a golden maple, and the days still wax warm and unbelievably gentle as the calendar runs out of October morns.

Time now to summon up some ghosts and goblins and be prancing off to the Halloween party down at the school house at 7:30 p.m. Halloween night, the 31st.

There are always prizes for the costumes and there are cake walks – one of the Johnsons has managed to bring home a chocolate cake each year so here's hoping.

The fun of the Fair still lingers with everyone in town just aglow with the success of it all.

Jim Walsh and his finance committee will have their report for us at the Fair dinner Nov. 11 when everyone who was part of it is invited to bring a dish and rehash the event by sampling each other's cooking.

The Fair never fails to bring out the poet in guests and I received two guests' creations this year.

I like the sentiment in Robert Lewis', a Bluemont native whose father was the postmaster here from 1913-1924.

"The living was simple, the people were plain
Everyone was a neighbor, regardless of fame;
And the hearts in these bodies left no one in doubt
That God planted kindness,
'twas no doubt about."

A short time in the settlement establishes the truth of the goodness of the people.

A big thank you to my former neighbor, Charlie Waddell, for his two days participation as MC of the Bluegrass Music Contest and his great renditions.

In connection with him, thanks to the gentleman who wrote the letter to the editor about my mistake connecting Jimmy Davis with the state of Tennessee rather than Louisiana.

Another one of our favorite people thought of us this week, Betsy Jones Moreland called the Becks from Hollywood sending her love to her fans in Bluemont.

Wouldn't she have loved that hayride?

Finally when I think of Betsy my thoughts turn to the goats as she kept one in Hollywood and my report is that the illustrious goat, Sassy, is now a resident of Clarke County having been vacated by some bruised-up neighbors on the mountain.

But his portrait remains, done expertly by June McAdams and was on display at the special exhibit during the Fair.

Speaking of portraits, Virginia Woolman is back in the business of painting and hopes to have a show shortly at the Purcellville Library where she assisted librarian Jean Carruthers for several years.

Bluemont is to have another social event this Saturday evening, Nov. 3 at 8 p.m. The talented Washington Madrigal Singers will return for a concert in Clyde Beck's studio with light refreshments following.

Folks did come back to linger and to chat this weekend, and it was especially nice to see Miles Rassiga and his wife Molly now living near Ashburn.

Miles was my 6'5" eighth grade student way back when and he has grown a couple inches since along with similar political views of his old history teacher.

Your chance to record what you think is coming soon, election day, Nov. 6 for Governor of Virginia.

And yes, I got my hair washed and the girls too, but the geraniums are still outside basking in the mellow autumn sunshine.

November 8, 1973

The thousands of pumpkins in the patch shone in the early darkened afternoon on Tuesday and thus began the Halloween caper.

Seven-thousand had been sold already was the report by Russell Powell's sister who was inviting pickers to choose any one for a dollar.

J.J. Heinemann and I sent four of our nine children into the vast field and you guessed it, Jennifer had to have a look at them all before she made her selection.

Then as we hit the front door the knives were whipped out and there were three quickly carved up (or should I say chopped up?) Jack-o-lanterns waiting for candles and de-seeding by Yep, you guessed it again – Mother!

As they glowed on the porch's ledge, dinner was slung onto the table, the dirty dishes were whisked off and it was time to dig out the costumes for the Round Hill Elementary School contest.

Lara found an old clown suit in the summer trunk, "Thank heavens that would do for her" and long ago Tracey and I decided the old apple lady would be her costume.

An antique basket loaned by Ginger Echols, now to be purchased from Ginger Echols since it collapsed under the strain of a school bus ride to Round Hill and back, offered apples – five cents and positively no one could have one since she had to carry the same specimens to the Bluemont community party that night.

Finally Jennifer settled on my old Flapper costume with an education of the term and instruction in the basic Charleston step. Of course, I had to add a biographical note that her mother's high school classmates threw money when I sprang into dance.

Then while the kids paraded at school, I brewed up the oatmeal cookies for the party – alas – a few boxes of raisins were back on the shelf and at the school Karen Underwood won the ugliest with an awful set of false teeth and with the gong of 4 o'clock p.m., it was almost time for the annual festivity trick-or-treating.

Many came this year, some I didn't know, not only the faces in the masks were new but the voices. We handed out our sweet-tarts and the rain started.

Between the drops, we scampered up the long stairs to the abandoned school auditorium where the traditional cake walks were beginning.

And you know the Johnsons didn't bring back a chocolate or even a white cake this year. By this time, Lara had changed to her milk-maid outfit and the bucket was weighing her down so she passed it on to Mommie.

Of course, there are some kids who have all the luck. Mike Richardson, Greg McCauley, April Wilt, Brian Hughes, John Campbell, Beecher Hope, Billy Sanford, Donna Tray, Susan Potts were cake winners with Scotty Casey winning his own mother's cake.

Besides the lucky kids, the adult winner was Mary Sleeter, who captured the cake door prize.

Naturally by this time my youngest Ginger was setting track records and with the judges' selection of the funniest – Jeff Fletcher, a boy in a wig; the best witch – Cathy McCauley (they always have a winning costume each year in that family); Brad Campbell as ugliest (what a mask!); to best ghost Kenny Hutchins (now last year his mother spent hours making an elaborate costume while this year a sheet with clothes hanger antennae did it) to most original – Mary Jo Lloyd – a gypsy (now has she ever failed to get a prize?) I was ready to skip the cider and cookies and head for home to the then pounds of Halloween treats.

So it went – another Halloween caper in Bluemont!

The Madrigal Singers were back on Saturday night in a light-hearted repertoire and the Jack Bardons have big news – they are grandparents for the first time. Son Michael and his wife Neva are parents of a girl, Rebekka Lynn born Oct. 21.

Equally exciting, Beverley, daughter of J. and Gail Kelley was crowned Homecoming Queen at Bridgewater College last weekend.

And the Grace Episcopal Church Ladies of Berryville are making great plans for their annual Christmas Bazaar on Nov. 15, 7-9 p.m. and Nov. 16, 10 a.m.-3p.m. with a delightful sit-down turkey luncheon being served on Saturday starting at Noon and there is even a nursery!

In addition, this is the week of the Fair dinner, Sunday, Nov. 11 at 6 o'clock p.m.

All those who helped at the Fair are urged to bring a covered dish and see the Fair slides and hear the finance report.

Lastly a nice stole was left in my kitchen during the Fair. I think it belongs to one of Abe Lincoln's daughters!

November 15, 1973

"Going to be three snow storms in November according to the Hagerstown Almanac," a native quipped and Joan Wilt said she watched a caterpillar cross the road last week with a dark shade on his head and tail and a light shade in the middle which meant a severe beginning to winter, ending up the same but a mild one in the middle and with several mornings and afternoons of flurries this week it was time to get the wood next to the house and the storage food bins full.

Most of us are apprehensive about the fuel shortage looming on the horizon as the old houses leak and are hard to heat and there is much stove buying and emergency measures being taken in the area.

Each week of this autumn has brought a new delight, topped perhaps, by this week's hike on the Appalachian Trail.

Having digested the book on the subject, I concluded that one of the loveliest parts of the entire trail was right in our own backyard over Harper's Ferry way and Mr. Baber, a veteran hiker of the trail asserted this was true.

Wednesday morning, a cold one, found five of us (fifty percent of the original number) springing along on top of the ridge starting at Keyes Gap just above the road that leads to Harper's Ferry from Webb's Corner.

Sue Mearns, Janet Ball and J.J. Heinemann had promised to drive us home from the end of the trail that bisects Route 340 which Mr. Baber showed us earlier in a vehicle.

Our gait was steady up by a trailer park in the lunch break (four of the five brought two sandwiches, one three sandwiches, two – an apple for dessert and one a piece of candy and sharing we had a hot drink around). We hadn't come for the lunch that day, only for the expedition!

Our map told us we were approaching Loudoun Heights, a look-out used during the War Between the States. Nevertheless, nothing prepared us for one of the most magnificent views any of us had ever seen.

There below was the churning river, the peaks, the town all quaint and perfect with Jefferson Rock far below and for a bonus a long freight train whistled through the mountain tunnel seemingly just for our edification.

With each hill we questioned was this Mr. Baber's hill as he had warned about wearing tight shoes for this part of the journey.

Each grade became worse with one of our band who prefers to remain anonymous sliding on her posterior as a pair of sneakers, her only suitable shoes could not manipulate the slippery rocks coated with leaves that form a narrow ledge over-looking a bluff.

Bears up there? No, we spotted three birds and a dead quail, whose features we plunked.

Several are going back soon with their families and next week Brother James of the monastery has promised to show off his finds from the Battle of Cool Spring there on the property as we relish life in our own backyard.

On this Saturday eve all is in readiness for the Fair dinner tomorrow night and the women of Grace Episcopal Church are roasting their turkeys for the annual Christmas Bazaar on Nov. 15 from 7-9 p.m. and Nov. 16 from 10 a.m. – 3 p.m.

Jim Walsh will have a more detailed report on the Bluemont Fair later but at the Bluemont Citizens meeting Wednesday night, he affirmed that we net close to $16,000 with almost $7,000 in gate receipts, $1,500 in dried arrangements, $1,673 in crafts, $2,900 in baked goods, jams and jellies, $240 in cider and $2,419 in chuck wagon offerings.

Now all thoughts skip ahead to our traditional family holiday, Thanksgiving, and don't be fooled, our handling of our nation's troubles prove we are still well and strong, striving to keep this an honest country as sanctioned by those early settlers who somehow survived.

Be ye thankful!

November 22, 1973

Now a pile of crumpled gold covers the backyards and there are showery breezes of fleeting leaves as the eve of Thanksgiving gathers together while the last digits of the November calendar flip by.

Finally it has dawned on some of us, who are caught in a whirl of other activities that the family will be here again this week on Thursday for the inevitable turkey, cranberry sauce and pumpkin pie. And of yes, here at our house, my mother must bring her specialty – the oyster dressing!

The churches of the close communities of Round Hill and Bluemont will join together in a combined service at the Round Hill Baptist Church Wednesday evening at 7:30 p.m. Everyone is invited to attend and give thanks.

With a real energy crisis acknowledged by the White House, nature seemed particularly kind this past week offering days and days of beautiful Indian summer weather. A crock of geranium shoots still remains fresh in the open air.

The ideal weather provided a marvelous backdrop for our adventure Tuesday at the Holy Cross Abbey near the Shenandoah Bridge where Brother James gave the most splendid moving account of the Battle of Cool Springs that took place on the grounds there July 18, 1864.

His magnificent enthusiasm in sharing his finds (my favorite a small silver tea-pot without a handle, which he presumed to be lifted by a solider from a home) is terribly catching. He has an aerial photograph of the property on which are plotted the location of the troops and the slaughter of the Federalists who were trying to ford the river at Parker's Ford, which just happened to be the lad of the same Judge Parker who sentenced John Brown at close by Harper's Ferry, W.Va.

Then a walk out in the beautiful fields, now planted with grain, reveal the river with white trunked sycamores where the Union was crossing to the natural setting on the hills of rock outcroppings that made them the strategic position for the Confederate line.

The sight of the beautiful blue peaks, trimmed in somber autumn colors, now fading, was a picture recorded for memory's restful moments.

How kind it was for Brother James to share their history with us, who live just over Snicker's Gap, from thence reinforcements could have come, 15,000 strong of Early's men.

The Fair dinner was a pleasant affair so I'm told with duets by Jack Bardon and daughter, Jeannie, and some wonderful slides taken by Jim Walsh and Bill Miner.

The Johnsons (four of the five) were down with the virus, the bug, the flu – you name it – as were the four Budnys.

Nevertheless as ever the neighbors brought help.

Judy Casey came and took Ginger to the Lloyds for their family Sunday dinner and brought the ailing, ginger ales, soup, crackers and even medicine!

When we asked Isabelle Dawson for a tray of ice, she sent a ten-pound bag. So even when you're sick it's a more pleasant experience in Bluemont!

And before the old bird can get in his last gobble, Judy Casey is whipping up Christmas cookies!

Happy Thanksgiving!

November 29, 1973

Although the trees stand like skeleton sentinels against the darken skies, the face of autumn still lingers on the countryside as the month of December finishes off the year of 1973.

With the new year, there is some trepidation as a bitter winter and the energy crisis could leave us chattering next to the fireplaces and wood stoves, but for now it was time to give thanks at least in the East for the mildest autumn recalled in many moons.

And the family gatherings were festive occasions, here we had both sets of grandparents and my brother for some really delicious fare and Mark Brownell reported 17 sat down at Whitehall for the occasion with he and Scott coming from their respective colleges and brother Jim down from Richmond with his wife and two children.

The Brownell young men were gathering in the college crowd for a get-together there on Friday night. At least for now, everyone was still traveling about if somewhat at lower speeds.

Harold Robinson entertained four straight days at his Old Red House on top of the mountain with an impressive list of guests and a real groaning board of meats and main dishes whipped up by Harold himself.

The Lawrence Dawsons had all their family at their place on Thanksgiving and our dinner was complete when Mary Lou Markle brought us a loaf of homemade whole wheat bread and the Lloyds sent along a bottle of good rich country milk great for mashed potatoes.

Herbert Martz has even out-topped himself this time. He not only lent me a neighborly hand with the wood chopping but paid my children to put my wood on the porch!

He and Lucy were pleased as punch to go see their new granddaughter of their youngest son's, Bonnie in Manassas last Sunday.

The hunting season came in with Jeannie Bardon tagging a big buck right at early morn but the whole hunting experience has been spoiled for us in Bluemont when we got the news that Clay Radcliff had been shot in the arm by what appears to be a madman. Having left the woods he was heading for home and was in the clearing when a man atop the ridge shot at him. Clay is the dearest young man in the world always helping with the spring clean-up here and now he may have to face life with only one arm. He certainly needs our prayers.

It may be time to talk about what to spend our money on and whether to light or not to light for the annual Christmas Contest, but won't the tree look pretty in strings of popcorn?

December 6, 1973

It's creeping in, around, about, below, beneath in the best prepositional manner – the infectious spirit of Christmas.

Already Sue and Sonny Hall traversed the streets laden with brightly wrapped red and green boxes and a few bagged items have been whisked from back-seats and trunks to special hiding places as Santa continues to put in an appearance here and yon.

Most of the communities seem to be browning-out some of their usual Christmas decorations and private citizens all talk about their cutting back on spending this year and slyly I'm smiling to myself as it has now become fashionable to live as frugally as I have done for years.

Powhatan Shop in Berryville on Thursday morning with their special Christmas toys sale was a picture of mad, happy women shoppers on the track of the best bargains you can find anywhere.

It was a real holiday mood with people helping one another in locating the goodies – in the nickel box were metal and wooden toys!

Then on Saturday, Purcellville hosted its annual Old English Christmas Fair at the Community Center with the usual highly entertaining puppet show and booths of Christmas eatables and stocking stuffers and my own choice – a beautiful pine-cone and nut wreath. Perfect for my shop door.

Brian Beck always gets a birthday in this time of year with an all-stag party and thinking of the neighborhood children, did I see a heart-warming sight! Glancing out my kitchen window one incomparable sunny afternoon the Hutchins and Budnys and Johnsons and Becks were arm in arm in a game of Red Rover.

Now is there anything finer for a child to be doing than playing Red Rover? The caption under my high school picture read, "You haven't lived until you've played Red Rover on top of Sugar Loaf Mountain!" The love for Red Rover and a mountain and I go way back.

Ah, how these cycles go round as we all tramped about in our saddle shoes. Anybody for a revision of white bucks? I think I might have a pair in the attic. And with a plastic shortage threatening we might get some nice metal and wooden items back again.

For sure we'll miss the Carbaugh girls in Bluemont this Christmas but assuredly they will make their new home, Front Royal, a festive place.

Our neighbors, the Rockwood Fosters from up on the mountain have announced the marriage of their son, Reginald Candler to Karen Christie with the young couple making their home in Cambridge, Mass.

More follow-up on Clay Ratliff is that his arm will be saved with an expected operation on the upper part of the limb to be performed on Monday.

Too, he was heroically rescued by friends of the Jim Scotts. The two fellows had just turned off the motor of their truck when they heard his shout and they took off immediately to him, carrying him quickly to medical help. Later they were to call at the hospital.

Mm! The first week of December – time to start the Christmas baking. My! Ginger Echols' treat of lunch at The Inn in Purcellville was fine – savory chicken pot pie and pecan pie! It was almost as good as Harold Robinson's!

December 13, 1973

"It's beginning to look a lot like Christmas
Everywhere you go."

So blares our old Perry Como and Bing Crosby records as Joan Wilt says she has her tree up already.

I haven't baked or decorated or cleaned but we're receiving greetings from some of our neighbors and friends and we like to put them on the kitchen mantle where we can think about the warmth behind the messages.

Harriet Murtaugh sent a card with the painting of the Peaceable Kingdom print on it including the group of Quakers in the background which supposedly was inspired when the artist visited the nearby Quaker settlement, Lincoln.

Loudouners were featured in two national magazines this month – Julie and Douglas Lea whose shop in Waterford just happens to be called The Peaceable Kingdom were in the section called Lifestyles in Woman's Day and secondly our springtime quilting bee with the Times-Mirror pictures made Women's Household.

The most divine scents have filled our nostrils all day since Mrs. Thornton from Hamilton brought some marvelous rich-red candles for the shop in bayberry and strawberry smells.

They are just in time for the exciting project some of us Bluemonters are going to undertake to light the outside of our homes for Christmas.

Donna Miner explained the Spanish lighting which is accomplished by putting a candle preferably in a jar in a pile of sand and in a paper bag, when the candle is lit the bag glows sending off a lovely non-fuel fed light.

And at the Bluemont Citizens Meeting, it was decided to have a house decorating contest of front doors in the daylight. At last I can compete – I'll get my spruce and long needled pine from Dr. Jackson's farm, find the red velvet bow in the attic and…

The decorations should be up by the afternoon of the 23rd when the judges will make their rounds.

Citizens are urged to attend the January meeting when we will elect officers and decide about a horse show and see the Bluemont Fair slides again and talk about how to spend the Fair monies. How's that for a full agenda?

The Snickersville Craft Club had a nice little Christmas party on Tuesday evening up at the Miners with a gift exchange and holiday punch.

Next month they say they will pursue the fashioning of Christmas decorations when the prices are at bargain rates. Suzie Anderson and Leslie Hutchins already started on some quilling which would make sweet snowflakes for the window panes.

And I've got in my toys for myself, that is. Over at the Powhatan Shop there was a metal wind-up crow in the nickel box – the kids found my treasures and Lara has already complained that the crow bit her finger and for my special friends, I let them play with my kaleidoscope. It's fantastic what it does with the red kitchen curtains and the blue bottles on the window sills and the plates on the mantel and somebody said it might snow this week!

December 20, 1973

According to our figuring as of this writing, it's nine days to Christmas.

Nine days to bake a batch of pumpkin bread from Kay Seidenspinner's recipe, an apple sauce cake, some toll-house cookies, some brownies. Nine days to get the tree, decorate it, line the mantels with greens, fashion the sprays for the doors, try to imitate the center piece at Morven Park. (It was boxwood stuck in Styrofoam in a cone shape accented with highly polished apples).

Nine days to do a little more shopping like for all the adults on my list, make up the teacher's gifts and feel guilty about not sending out cards to our dear neighbors and friends. With the Leesburg history assignment pending and another column before Christmas plus teaching and cleaning and laundry.

And we got such nice remembrances from both Allders, the Andersons, the Becks, the Butlers, the Brunelles, the Carters, the Lloyds and Manns, the Martzs, the Ogdens, the Rosses and all the college crowd sent family photograph cards.

'Twas good to hear from our biographer Jean Smith who sends word that she had returned from her government agency and is working on a new project, the history of a church there in Ohio.

No doubt, Christmas is here, Mrs. Townshend has delighted youngsters up our way with her thoughtful "nothing" ornaments. Our favorite is the bird almost in a gilded cage. The cage is two plastic berry baskets meeting each other upside down with a pipe cleaner perch and a little feathery figure sitting there.

Although preparations are frantic, nothing will keep us, however, from our finest traditional custom of attending the annual Candlelight Service at the old stone church. The young people of the Bluemont Methodist Church will present a service on Friday evening Dec. 21 at 7:30 p.m. It's a lovely inspiring ceremony. Plan to attend.

Nine days to keep up with the Las Luminarias plans. Leslie Hutchins says she will make the candles (I have lots of jars for her) to line the path to the crest of our hill and Emma Mann says she will see that we get the three-pound bags (that's the size we'll need). The sand pile is in the Snow House side-yard and there's to be a children's party Friday afternoon.

At least I have something festive to wear. Suzie Anderson whipped me up a forest green jumper for Christmas Day.

Oh yes, I must purchase some of the dinner ingredients and if you want to serve venison over the holidays Claire Bardon gave me the recipe and the venison to go with it. The meat should be marinated in this sauce before roasting. Combine 5/8 cup of soy sauce, ¼ cup of vinegar, sprinkle on some garlic salt and ginger. This should be roasted slowly. I tried 250 degrees, served it quite rare and all of the children asked for seconds.

And would anyone be interested in an almost new electric can opener? No one is going to call me un-American!

Merry Christmas!

December 27, 1973

Last week's snow bothered, baffled, confused, bewildered and delighted all at the same time as Christmas shopping slowed to a halt and school children gaily slung snow in one another's faces.

With twelve inches blanketing the earth's grassy crust our sets of new neighbors were thoroughly initiated to the Bluemont winters.

There seemed to be at first real delight over at the Snow House since that's how it got its name, but then Ken Hutchins, found the weather so foreboding, he spent Monday night in Washington rather than return home in the flurries.

Likewise, the Miners recently moved here from California, found the weather so hazardous for driving while returning from a Sunday antique show in Washington, they were forced to stop in a motel in Sterling for the night.

The village children, Suzie Anderson and myself and all other non-skiers stayed put until the end of the week when the rains came and mainly the snow served to draw us closer. The Hutchins children were overnight at the Becks, Jennifer was at the Hutchins, the Miners passed a snow-bound evening with the Fishbacks and Suzie Anderson was our dinner guest while her husband Jim was clearing the county roads.

Over at Mann's Store, deliveries were late but finally the Monday eggs came on Wednesday and the baking proceeded and we had snow cream made with Mr. Horning's blackberries fresh from the freezer and before the plows came, we quickly got a sled ride down the Snickersville Pike.

It's a curious thing about this newspaper and magazine business. In January one writes of spring flowers, in spring of autumn glories and a week before Christmas one writes about after Christmas.

Here's hoping everyone had a blessed time. Glad we were that J.K. Cornwall could be home for a thirty-day leave from the Navy. After trips to Hong Kong, Hawaii and the Philippines, next he will go to Australia from San Diego, Calif., his home port.

Got a glimpse of Mark Brownell home for the holidays and it will be nice to see Bruce Cochran at church again from his Boston college.

Our sympathy to the loved ones of Daisy Ballenger who passed away this week. She and I had a fine chat one day at which time I judged her to be a very courageous woman.

Our thanks to Leslie Hutchins for her endeavor of candle-making for the Las Luminarias and to Donna Miner who was the brain child of the idea.

Now it seems time to wish each of my kind readers and dear neighbors a bright New Year. May our friendship sustain us through the prospects of some troubled times in 1974.

1974

January 3, 1974

AND SOMEONE WISHED us a grand Christmas and somehow the Christmases get grander and grander every year in Bluemont.

The second snow of last week assured a dirty, white Christmas with a goodly number of villagers and backroaders breaking out of the drifts for the first time on Christmas Eve.

Up our Snickersville Pike hill the Los Luminarias glowed gloriously and it promises to be an annual event. After the bags went up, there was caroling and a stop by the Becks for refreshments and then I did a little house touring.

The Snow House was done up in fine style with lovely pine cone wreaths and greens down the bannister and there were three trees.

The Becks' tree was lovely and Clyde's usual swag of greens with fruit even boasted a parrot.

The Miners topped all, winning first prize in the decorating contest. Their front porch sported lovely red and white ribbon accented with antique baskets and greens and pine cones and inside stood a magnificent tree draped in red bows. Divine!

The Martzs captured second place with several nice wreaths on their door and here at Clayton Hall, Karlton Monroe's holly and Ann Wilson's delivery of the red velvet ribbon from Leesburg just before the second snow helped us get the third prize.

Even the Carbaughs, though removed from the village last winter to Front Royal, returned with some of their delectable fudge with the news that they had won second prize with their gingerbread man fringed in lollipops.

Herbert Martz was making his usual candy deliveries – this is his 50th year of playing Santa with Demory's selection.

How our friends remembered us – Ginger Echols just showered us with everything – cheese and wine, fruit and cookies, decorations and dishes (Blue Willow, at that!). The Brownells said Merry Christmas in a very special way and the Becks sent dolls, the Hutchins – bread and the Budnys – fruit cake and then Thelma and Leon Brunelle (bless their hearts!) reinforced our Friday night institution with a popcorn popper!

There were yummy cookies from Sue Mearns and Claire Bardon and a festive coffee ring from the Heinnemanns. That was quite enough even before the grandparents got here with the dolls and doll clothes and doll furniture and the oyster stew and oyster dressing.

The Bobby Allders had a marvelous large tree and Sonny and Sue Hall had some pretty touches on their newly purchased old home while the Dawsons displayed two fine door decorations as everybody went non-electric.

Better than the holly on the front door, the best sight in town was the three snowmen fashioned by Justine Beck and Robin Myers, Mommy, Papa and Baby were decked out in carrot noses, jeweled necks and ears and capped appropriately in the most cunning way.

I know the Underwoods were glad daughter Rhonda and that new grandchild could be here this Christmas.

Now as a fog envelopes the village like a security blanket, one can count the blessings of the past year. Paramount perhaps, is the gift of good health with no real hardships developing during these last storms of 1973. As 1974 dawns, grateful can we be for the flame of hope that brightens each day no matter what – adversity must be encountered.

January 10, 1974

Somebody casually mentioned snow and within the hour I was out scanning the yard for the fallen branches with the refrain of another casual remark heard long ago. "Sister said they are so good for starting a fire."

The survival game (beating the elements) is on but thus far Southern States and Clayton Hall are still a cooperative while VEPCO is keeping on the current but raising rates.

About this time of year I generally indulge myself in a little editorial comment but it will have to wait as this wasa newsy week in Bluemont.

First of all, the burden is on us all for our helpless feeling in acknowledging the death of Billy Hindman in a hunting accident. His brother Clinton and his wife make their home here on the farm of his aunt and uncle, Ivy and Ralph Cochran. For all those involved in the accident and loved ones remaining, we fruitlessly offer you our sympathetic thoughts and prayers.

Still on the mournful note, Lucy Martz had a slight heart attack last Sunday but seems to be improving well at Loudoun Memorial Hospital.

On the other hand, there was much good youth news. Willa Colbert just returned to Madison College for her last semester after her Christmas vacation with her parents, Sonny and Betty.

Donna Kelley, daughter of the J.J. Kelleys and Linda Lake, daughter of the Richard Lakes of Airmont have been accepted for the fall term at Longwood College in Farmville, Va.

Jerry Lloyd took his children, Dawn and Chip on a fabulous post-Christmas trip to DisneyWorld and it was wonderful to see Clay Ratliff at church on Sunday evening and all the fine participants in the postponed candlelight service.

Our guest for the night was a surprise sister, Mrs. Ruth Browning, a one-time Bluemonter occupying the James Allder's house now occupied by another family.

She stopped in, searching for a lost glove and stayed to afternoon tea with Brother James and Brother Michael of the Holy Cross Abbey, then stayed to dinner and spent the night before her return trip to McLean.

Since she had once directed the MYF at the church, she was pleased to return and see old friends.

J.K. Cornwall was still home and the Robert Allders Jr. had a nice gathering for Christmas dinner with the Gordon Arnetts of Arlington, the Russell Parks, Sr., the Charles Parks of Round Hill, Mrs. Mae Swetnam of Alexandria and Robert McDonald of Round Hill.

The Charles Parks also entertained Mr. and Mrs. Charles McGhee of Arlington during the holiday.

The family and friends didn't have their usual New Year's Eve party this year but Joan and Martin Wilt had a grand time in Leesburg when April saw '74 in with Jennifer as I pecked out the Leesburg history on the typewriter. It's wrapped up for Spur Magazine now which will publish next in February.

Meanwhile it's time to glean the facts from Helen Hirst's Purcellville history for a lecture on that topic when Parks and Recreation begins its Ladies Day Out on Tuesday morning, Jan. 22.

More local personalities have been featured in national magazines. Rosemary and Andrew John Murtaugh, children of Harriet and Tom Murtaugh are the subject of an article in the January issue of Organic Gardening. The children's project of goat-herding is praised, noting that such a discipline develops self-reliance.

If you can read this on Wednesday, please attend the Bluemont Citizens Meeting, an important session for election of officers and postponed decisions at 8 o'clock at the schoolhouse.

We do hope Jim Walsh can join us but it may be questionable as he had a fall and is suffering with broken ribs.

And last night was the nicest Twelfth Night I've known. Donna and Bill Miner threw a Twelfth Night party for the neighbors on the hill and the hours passed quickly with Ken Hutchins' quips.

'Cause if there's anything you cherish in a neighbor, it's a sense of humor!

January 17, 1974

The old metal clock loudly ticks off the minutes, the room is cozy with a fire on the hearth and Jim Birchfield's calendar with a Purcellville farm scene pictures January half-spent.

January, the coldest month, heralds the flitting of beautiful cardinals down the country lanes close-by and their feeding in brilliant reds on the Becks' patio joined by the merry red-headed woodpecker drumming on the old apple tree.

Likewise, it is the month of cold birthdays of warmed little Capricorns entering the world and with two sevens in my birthday, I added another seven on the seventh joined by Hope Carbaugh turning sixteen in Front Royal and who remembered me with a lovely cardinal card and on the same night the cake and ice cream was dished up at the Fishbacks where young Rusty turned three.

The snow was gone by Wednesday evening when the monthly meeting of the Bluemont Citizens was assembled.

Nominations from the floor were accepted for Vice-President, Secretary, and Treasurer and a nominating committee was appointed to bring a choice of candidates for the President in the next meeting.

The now Vice-President will be Clyde Beck, the outgoing President, the Secretary elected was Mary Lynn Budny, and Ellen Jones remained as Treasurer.

Nominations from the floor for President as well as the nominating committee slate are in order for the February meeting at which time the expenditure of Fair profits will be determined.

A Fair Chairman, Donna Miner, was elected for the proposed '74 Bluemont Fair.

In addition, the Bluemont Citizens Association voted to sponsor an Open-Class Horse Show in late March with Stanley Kelley and Tommy Marland, Co-chairmen reporting to the group at the next meeting what personnel, funds and arrangements will be needed.

Hopefully, we can draw out the many back-yard ponies in our scenic Bluemont countryside.

The next meeting time will be Feb. 6 at 7:30 p.m. when the new President can set-up another refreshment committee for the meetings.

We congratulate Glen Horning on his being named to the Dean's List at VPI, Blacksburg where he is a third year engineering student.

I am just getting the news from Mrs. Overton that she had a marvelous trip to a seminar held at Oral Roberts University in Tulsa, Okla. at the end of November.

Some of the nicest memories I have of our area is of winter visits when the warmth of the fire crackling in a fireplace enhanced friendship.

I hope some of you will want to join the Loudoun Towns class at the Valley Community Center starting on the 22nd for some of those fireside chats or maybe you prefer to join Kay McDonald and the ghosts of Waterford.

Something is certainly amiss with the telephones these days-blame it on the spirits if you like, but sorry we can't accept the explanation, "A cow stepped on the cable."

Don't despair of calling, I have a new number, 334-8448 and now Judy Casey and Diana Brownell can have their four-way conversations. When it rains or snows at the time Judy gets a call she may hear Diana in the background talking with another friend. And when are we going to be able to dial Leesburg, our county seat free of charge?

If you are moaning over the high cost of food, I found a really inexpensive meal you might wish to try. It all came about a month ago when visiting the chow mein counter. I remarked to another shopper that this used to be a cheap meal but the can of fixings was now close to a dollar. She advised me to buy just a can of noodles and a can of Chinese vegetables and use left-over meat and make my own fixings.

I found a recipe in my Cutco cookbook. Use any leftover meat (beef, pork, chicken). Ingredients – 2 c. of meat, 2 c. thinly sliced celery, 2 tablespoons butter, 1 ½ c. sliced peeled onions, 1/8 teaspoon pepper (I added cut-up green pepper instead), 2 c. meat broth (save this from the meal before, stretch with water if necessary). 1 can mixed Chinese vegetables (or bean sprouts), ½ c. of canned mushroom caps (didn't have any but this would make it), 2 tablespoons corn starch (flour will do), 3 tablespoons soy sauce, 1.5 oz. can fried noodles.

Brown meat in butter, add celery, onion, pepper, broth. Cover, cook until vegetables are tender. Add drained Chinese vegetables, mushrooms, bring to a boil. Mix corn starch to soy sauce, add to hot mixture, stirring constantly.

Simmer 2 minutes or until slightly thickened. Serve on noodles and with rice if preferred. Makes six servings. Combined with a green salad accented with vinegar and oil dressing and some hot bread makes for even company fare.

January 24, 1974

The dullness of the day blends with the already dull mind as a few English sparrows chirp on the window sills and the energy crisis flickers on, lighted by the burning electric lights in the gloom of the house and if sleep could only be a few light minutes away.

Now into the second week of the horrible night-time rising, the children have adjusted perfectly. They are back to their routine, of slumbering long on school mornings and rising early on weekends while the parent waits for the truth from the song, "The Other Generation" to be enacted, "I hope our grandson gives his father – Hell. Can't wait to see it. I hope our grandson gives his father – Hell!"

"Why can't they be like we were – perfect in every way? Oh, what's the matter with kids today?"

Winter – the longest of seasons – it's the time of year when mothers here console themselves with reminders of the enduring women who were forced to hole up in a pioneer cabin with five or six kids for the durations while the husband was off with the fellows for a little hunting expedition, somehow survived. Of course, Sue Mearns adds some were carried away in fits of hysteria, too.

This all leads me to give my comment on the 12-month school plan.

For years now someone has gotten a rumor going that most learning comes within the four walls of a classroom. As a teacher, I am in a position to refute that.

Anyone learns more when he is personally involved in an experience. It's a rare family who can afford winter pursuits that enrich the lives of their children to a great extent whereas summer projects are legion. There are gardens to be nurtured, structures to be built, trails to be hiked, streams to be explored, butterflies to be caught.

In like manner, in a rural area like ours, the farmer must rely on his school-age children for help. Summer is also a time long enough for an employer to consider a student employee.

And everyone knows the value of on-the-job training.

True, it does seem wasteful that the schools are vacant for three months but perhaps more creative thought could be given to a better year-round use of the facilities.

The cost of air-conditioning could be prohibitive and in my estimation no teaching could be accomplished without it. Even in a class of highly-motivated teachers in a summer extension course one scorching July, it became clear that one's mind fairly fizzled when the air-conditioner faltered.

That's about all I want to say editorially for January, 1974 except it seems the American people have never been so confused with all the contradictory statements being made about everything – "there is oil," "there is not oil" – "there's a toilet paper shortage," "there's not a shortage of toilet paper," but maybe Rick Mearn's is right – "the American people have never been so informed." Maybe that's why we're so confused.

With all the national events whirling around us – to be rationed or not be rationed – our main concern, nevertheless, was with the Dawson family, who lost their husband and father, Lawrence, this week.

Death came suddenly after a day of work before he was able to reach home to his loved ones. We are so glad individual members of the family are close to comfort one another.

The Rev. Mr. Betts said that death is part of life which is a hard statement to accept but when six-year-old Lara saw the neighbors carrying in food she said, "They're taking the food to say they're sorry." Yes," I said, "sorry they are hurting."

And I was grateful for my child's lesson learned that day. Death had taught a pretty important lesson in life in our dear little Bluemont.

January 31, 1974

Now with January gone, there's a stirring. The walls here look especially grim and I just must find a plasterer to stop the deterioration of my dining room wall and then with a coat of light yellow paint – divine!

Likewise, Ginger Echols says she wall-papered a bathroom today at her abode in Hillsboro and J.J. Heinemann kept at an amazing painting schedule of four rooms, and a hall even before Christmas.

No doubt it's the time of year, Senator Everett Dirksen would have had his best romps through the seed catalogs and while Bill Harrison writes of planting fruit trees, my suburban-based brother and I are plotting a potato patch.

No news is good news, they say and I know absolutely no news here so here's hoping…

It's the time of year for thought and reflection and schemes being hatched up for another day. My best projects unfold while vacuuming and with a very dirty house and even worse attic of discards, I decided Spring would be the time for a soap-making demonstration, flea market and rummage sale here on the lawn.

Other friends are dwelling on preservation projects and after a realization that two of Purcellville's oldest homes have been taken, it's time for action in that direction.

One of the oldest was Exedra built by Dr. James Heaton in 1800, removed for the present Loudoun Valley shopping center.

The oldest was the big stone house just lost this past year which stood at the rear of the new medical building. It was built in 1793 by Stacy Taylor, a descendant of Mahlon Kirbride who received an original grant from Lord Fairfax between the years of 1741-1748.

Two other early homes remain. In 1830 Valentine Purcell for whom Purcellville was named paid $500 for two acres of land and improvements to Stacy Taylor. This dwelling was the home of the just recently deceased Miss Frances Gaver located adjacent to the town office.

Just down on Rt. 7 and two houses from the library is the fine home of Mrs. William Holmes Brown established as Asa Moore Janney's wheelwright shop in 1847.

Bluemonters might want to think about our own responsibility for preservation of our landmarks when we receive reports back from a special committee at the monthly meeting of the Citizens Association to be held Feb. 6 at 7:30.

A new president must be elected, there is sure to be much talk of the up-coming horse show and proposed fair money expenditures.

There have been viruses about and actually there hasn't been a full week for all the children to be in school for over a month.

Susie Anderson is crocheting a beautiful blue and white rug while Ken Hutchins had two days of a business trip in New York this past week and the Brownies and Girl Scouts went roller skating in the old building that was once known as the Tabernacle of the famed Bush meetings of Purcellville beginning in 1876 and when I can get back to Helen Hirst Marsh's book, I'll let you know how many years they continued.

Yes, when I get back to that book, I'll let you know and when I finish the Foxfire Book II, I'll tell you about that and so far I can't make the report on the Great Crash or the War of 1812 'cause I haven't finished. Then Kitty Slater's Hunt Country of America looked so fascinating the other day, I just had to pick it up.

February 7, 1974

Rain and quiet times brought in February, there virtually seems to be no news.

The darkened-morning arising continues and no clock is needed other than the first initial sounding of the alarm as the glow of electric lights at Mann's Store tell it's 7:30 a.m. or after.

Mrs. Dawson's lighted lamp tells it's five or after and when the reverberating of the Beck's car begins, the children must fly out the door or the school bus will be gone.

Thinking about our taken for granted electricity, the Loudoun Towns class met Mrs. Moncure Lyon this week whose husband was responsible for beginning the Loudoun Light and Power Company in Purcellville in 1918. Until that time all these farms and homes in the Round Hill, Purcellville, Bluemont and Lincoln areas endured without Ben Franklin's discovery. In addition to generating the power, they manufactured six tons of ice daily, eliminating typhoid fever epidemics spread from germs in ice cut off ponds and rivers close by.

Mrs. Lyon shed more light too on the Bush Meeting phenomenon, explaining that the Quakers were largely responsible for the up-lifting programs and that even William Jennings Bryan spoke at the site on the occasion.

To have met Mrs. Lyon is one of life's warmest experiences and cordially she holds out the promise that we must come again, particularly if we like, at the time the daffodils smile a welcome in her wooded glen.

I had the pleasure of chatting with Mrs. Ruth Schulke this week too who told me of her days of teaching in Bluemont, first at Mountain Shadow and then at our stucco edifice. Linda Corley's grandmother was also there and with another friend from Leesburg they gave me the fine advantages of cooking on a wood stove. Really with young children bustling about, I'm not game for that one. Think I'll stick with Mr. Lyon's electricity.

Still on the subject, Bluemont has a little in joke on the street light situation here. Behind my house, I had noticed certain nights, the street light burned, others it didn't.

I had accused Clyde Beck of having a controlling switch in his house until Donna Miner told me the secret was that if you wanted it lit, you just went over and kicked it. Her son Brian amused a passing hiker from the Appalachian Trail with this feat.

February 14, 1974

There are always a few things I like to have accomplished before a big snow.

I feel more secure with a half-gallon of water drawn in a jug (well, I had that), I like to have the laundry up-to-date, the house clean and wood in and dry just in case the electricity might falter.

I did manage to put in a load of clothes and slice up a few apples into a prepared pie shell and think about getting the upstairs mess straightened when something hit me after bringing the car out to the end of the drive, I realized the flu bug had flown in with the snow.

Lying two days in bed is unreal for a mother of young children – surely every woman knows that unwritten code arrives with the blessed event. Thou Shall Not Be Sick!

Into the night the gay sledding continued down our Snickersville hill and hearing the sounds, I became a little paranoid. "They don't care that I'm sick!" But at least Jennifer was engrossed in that activity which only left the twins and Ginger to slam the refrigerator door, the oven door, the family room door, the front door and then appear at sick bed announcing it was time I got up and fixed a meal.

Somehow the crisis passed and with the children away for the day, I'm folding up laundry, glad that Tracey's wish over the wish-bone came true, "that Mommie get well."

Before the surprise snow and flu, the Loudoun Towns class had a real treat in visiting the home of the Clarence Halls on Main Street. Their house built in 1914 is a marvelous rambling brick Victorian holding an extraordinary collection of antiques.

Mr. Hall is a real expert and gave us a little education as we went from room to room. He explained the English pieces used oak in the interior. He noted the English pieces were the Queen Anne with the curved leg, the Sheraton with a round leg and the Hipplewhite with a square leg.

He expounded on kinds of china saying the unmarked pieces were the oldest, on craftsmen, explaining that most of the real dealers were craftsmen who did restoration work. He had many fine examples of his own beautiful work. There was a trundle bed and quilts and Waterford rockers and a Grandfather clock owned by the founder of Peoples Bank, Leesburg and a perfect spinning wheel – it was magnificent!

He even remembered a book, William Nutting's "Furniture Treasury."

And then it was home to the Bluemont Citizens Association Meeting.

Ken Hutchins was elected President of the Association and Ring Master all in one evening.

The first Bluemont Horse Show is slated for March 31 at the Bluemont Quarterhorse Farm in Frogtown.

Now if you don't know where Frogtown is, it's on the road Rt. 606 that turns left off Rt. 7 right before the Shenandoah Bridge.

Now I've never been to Frogtown, least if I have, I haven't been aware of it. I don't know if I should expect frogs to chorus a welcome or just what but when they mentioned they needed help in dishing up some chili, that captured my imagination.

It will be a schooling and fun show, a class for everyone, even lead arounds.

Found out Pat Walsh, the James Walshes' youngest, had a birthday last Wednesday and now the most beautiful icicles etch the village roofs.

February 21, 1974

As I was saying, I like to have the house clean, the laundry up-to-date, a big pot of home-made soup brewing on the back burner when a snowstorm is threatening and somehow I managed it all – even had the trash carried out when the flakes started down on Saturday, but alas, it didn't amount to much.

Not much but just enough to scare the Brunelles off from a visit, arrange for Brian Miner to get a one-way trip to the Valentine's Dance in Purcellville and send Jennifer scurrying home from a Round Hill overnighter.

And speaking of the houses and the children, everywhere I go in the countryside, it's the same, the children have scattered their toys to the uppermost corners of the house, the dogs and humans have tracked in great gobs of mud and there is much wailing on the part of the housekeeper who lured by other more interesting projects has a simply frightful-looking house, so the story goes.

One place that looked spotless, nevertheless, was the comfortable farm house of the Fowlers in Lovettsville. There within marvelous view of the mountains, the corn crib offered a subject for a Wyeth painting and the piglets grazed on a frozen field while we were warmed by home-made biscuits and local lore.

Lovettsville was a Union stronghold during the Civil War as it was settled in the 1730's by Germans migrating from Pennsylvania.

And then Valentine's Day skipped off the '74 calendar with the twins' Mrs. Bruce making darling red construction paper baskets trimmed with a lovely paper doily for her classes. Now they brighten our red outfitted kitchen.

Even though we are tuned into a winter holiday, someone is thinking of spring, Larry Allder gives notices that any woman who is interested in being a member of the Bluemont Women's Softball Team, should report to the Pine Grove Church on Monday, March 4 at 7:30 p.m. You are eligible if you are 18 years of age or older and reside or work in Loudoun County.

Right over there by Pine Grove, I'm sorry to report I gave the wrong name to the proposed Bluemont Horse Show grounds. It was sold about a year ago and is now known as Tiernoch Farm. There they raise thoroughbreds and hunters and they have exactly two quarterhorses.

The only horses I know anything about are two specimens the family acquired at the Marshall sale.

Were we surprised to see that number stamped in the thoroughbred's mouth and when he got his health back, he ran like the wind. Red, the Morgan, was my favorite, a horse with a wide back, she would walk – now that's my speed! Well, not really – my speed is sitting in the arm chair here reading Black Beauty to the kids.

I'll take a dog any day as a choice in a pet and Stanley Kelley says their new Irish Setter pups are doing alright. They took the six of the new litter to the Dog Show in Marshall on Saturday and got first, second and third in male and second and third in female.

And on snowy Saturday I was thinking summer as I got my Lawn mower fixed by a new-found youthful fix-it man, Robert Combs. He says he can do a little carpentry too and when Jerry Hummer patched the living room ceiling this week, I knew the soft-yellow walls could not be far away and soon Mr. Sisk must be called for discing for the potato patch and I'll call on Johnny Carter to give me some helpful hints and then we have Herbert Martz, a man for all seasons for lawn care and wood chopping and tulip cultivating.

It's so comforting to live in a village where people specialize.

February 28, 1974

The sky was scattered with gray clouds, the wind whipped by the bushes and trees and only the most bleak of landscapes presented itself or so I thought until the morrow's warmth brought forsythia shoots waxing yellow against a backdrop of brown grass.

February is sometimes called the cruelest month and thank goodness it's gone.

Though short, its fury was spent these last two weeks in the critical gasoline shortage. Tensions mounted for station owners and attendants and customers who were just trying to get to work. Friends are driving the road from Leesburg to Winchester to Charles Town looking for gas while the wife of one couple we know makes the rounds in the day so her husband can siphon the gas out at night so he can get to work the next morning. The lines are incredible – three hours people waited in line on Saturday in Purcellville. It seems unreal and most everyone feels there is foul play. I've got my letter off to Charlie Waddell myself in Richmond. He presently is waging war against a bill that would limit the journalistic freedom in our state. His address is Senator Charles Waddell, Room 520, Eighth Street Office Building, Richmond, Va. 23219. Monopolies and monarchs have something in common besides a beginning letter you know.

Meanwhile our class managed to get one car load of gas over to Lovettsville to Bollington as guests of Mrs. Fred Hoetzel. That house with the earliest part erected in the 1730's has superior lines, a beautiful log structure beneath all the roofing and genuine outbuildings of a toll house, a rendering station, a spring house and a magnificent barn. It's story – it will be demolished if a certain route for a Lovettsville sewer line is pursued.

Because of this very problem, a group of concerned citizens are beginning a preservation society for Loudoun County. Not definite yet on what all our purpose should encompass, we will meet again on March 14 at 8 o'clock at the Purcellville Library. Anyone interested is cordially invited. Other Loudoun organizations with like purposes have been asked to share projects and goals for a concerted effort. Eventually all Loudoun communities will be asked to form chapters to the main body. Now may not be soon enough.

There's a restlessness stirring that sent Judy Casey with paint brush in hand to her front door and I'm following suit with my soft yellow in the living room and Judy and I are both muddling over whether we like the change.

We were glad to hear the joyous news that Norma and Clinton Hindman have a new arrival, a baby girl born this week.

Another birthday boy was Kenny Hutchins who invited the after school crowd in for cake and ice cream and all signals are go on the first Bluemont Horse Show for March 31 at Tiernoch Farm.

Just to encourage everyone to come there will be no gate charge and interested entries can call Tommy Marlin at 554-8132 or Stanley Kelley at 554-8484.

And that little bumper sticker, get a horse, might be the up and coming thing!

March 7, 1974

One day merged into another as March smilingly entered the scene.

There was a little more gas to be had for several trips to Round Hill and several more to Purcellville before the gauge fell to a quarter of a tank again and that knowledge came that one more trip out better turn up the liquid gold or there could be no more turns out of the home driveway.

I was glad to hear John Allder got to have his say about the crisis in The Washington Post. Charlie Waddell assured me by return mail, they were doing their darndest in Richmond about alleviating the Northern Virginia shortage.

Bless Ginger Echols' heart, she saved back her gas so we could breeze over to Lovettsville one more time. There as guests of the Charles Dobbins we saw a spectacular before and after project. In a farmhouse that literally was falling down, they had the vision to take off the front porch, build a brick patio, take out partitions and then discover marvelous old logs. Underneath the frame was a beautiful log house, underneath the plaster was a beautiful stone fireplace! Tres magnificent!

Then Bobby George met us for a tour down the road dominated by George properties. He pointed out Camp Field where a skirmish occurred during the Civil War, told us about the buildings that existed on the scene at the time, where the Yankees had buried their dead and in a human interest vein, gave the account of a budding romance between a solider and one of the George ladies who lived up the road nearby.

Back to Bluemont Susy Anderson lent a hand with the painting and in my dreams I just keep seeing yellow and lots and lots of trim.

More and more of the women neighbors are joining the workforce: Mary Lynn Budny is a secretary for a Leesburg church and Mac Brownell finds her full-time work with the volunteers at the Loudoun Memorial Hospital satisfying.

And some are able to get away from it all for trips – Diana Brownell will arrive home shortly from a grand trip to Europe. Joyce Fishback had a respite from the domestic round in California recently and it won't be long before Hope and June Lloyd embark for Spain under the auspices of the Spanish Program at Valley High School.

Bluemont Fair plans are simmering on the back burner though the event is some time off and the monthly meeting of the Bluemont Citizens will be held this week at the school on Wednesday at 7:30 under the leadership of our new president, Ken Hutchins.

Sunday afternoon brought a deluge of Democrats to Bluemont to meet Dennis Gregg, candidate for Congress from the 10th District. Hosting a reception for him were the Clyde Becks. It was a fine time to meet some of the new neighbors and renew greetings with the natives over a cup of punch.

And can a Democrat win in '76? You bet he can!

March 14, 1974

Suddenly the landscape was greening, bulb flowers were shooting up and red buds were engulfing the oak in the center of the drive.

Spring vies with winter but hearts are lighter as the red-headed woodpecker continues his rhythmic dance up the old tree in the front yard.

Herbert Martz sprung into action one warm day this week. Anticipating the mowing season, he sharpened up the blades on the tractor and he tells me now is the time for putting in the potato patch.

The income tax deadline rolled around again but everything must wait here until we give Janet Ball the proper leave-taking with a Monday luncheon. She and her husband, Dana are departing from their cozy home, Stone Haven on No. 690 for the northern charms of New Hampshire.

The Loudoun Towns class won't be the same without her geniality and intelligence and as Charlie Brown says, "What we need is more hellos and less good-byes."

Meeting the deadline Susy Anderson and I stretched for the high trim on the ten-foot walls, climbed down for the trim on the mantle, then with the weekend I scraped the paint from the window panes, washed the windows, scraped the paint off the floor, waxed the floor. Back went the furniture. Polished was the silver and all the tables and all the time I wondered why women need exercise. It was all there for the hips, the arms, the waist.

The children pursued their usual activities as the project ensued, on Saturday, Ginger stuck gum in the dog's fur and cracked a hole in the trunk lid.

Not everyone is so foolish to paint before they have the gang over. Joyce and Clyde Beck had a fabulous array of munchables for Sunday afternoon when they invited the neighbors to meet Dennis Gregg, candidate for Congress.

It was especially nice to meet Karen and Peter Levendis who have built a new house up on No. 601 and Winston and Ann Johns who are restoring the stone house at the end of the Tyroler's lane. It was built as a hunting lodge by a Supreme Court judge in the early 1900's. Naturally his name eludes me whereas Carolyn Tyroler has his biography all straight. She's fabulous that way. Sorry to learn she had broken her arm this year.

It's always great fun to see the Loopes and Verloops – they were there along with Mrs. Redwine and Emma Mann.

Dennis is somewhat of an expert on solar energy, claiming the reason we haven't come further with that is because the big companies haven't figured out how to "cash" in on the sun and rain as yet.

Our sympathy to Martin Wilt and his family on the loss of his mother this week. Praise be, she was making plans for her garden with a neighbor just before her sudden heart attack.

There were birthdays at the Snow House – both Mary Lynn Budny and Ken Hutchins celebrated.

Community projects were the focal point at the Bluemont Citizens meeting. The Health Department is acting on our request to demand better sanitation. Efforts in some of the rentals and the drainage problem is still being pursued with our good neighbor, Attorney Don Bowman bringing it before the right personages.

Again there has been a denial that the new highway initiated the crucial situation. Our supervisor James Brownell is acting in our behalf and Charles Waddell, our State Senator has written Wayne Witham, State Secretary of Transportation and Public Safety to assure him that the building of the new highway agitated the flood problems.

April 1-15 has been set as the annual Spring clean-up. Citizens are expected to clean their own properties and after this week, I'll make the rounds again to recruit crew leaders for our usual designated clean-up route.

The Horse Show nears, set for March 31. Sponsors are needed for class awards.

And tomorrow we will pluck the spreading forsythia for arranging in vases that will heighten the beauty of a soft-yellow freshly painted wall. The temperatures may differ but the fever has come. It's Spring!

March 21, 1974

So again Mother Nature was up to her usual practical jokes in March. One day the air was balmy, the lovely forsythia and daffodils shone bright yellow in a perfect sunny sky

Evelyn Porterfield Johnson

and the next evening a downy snow covered the lawn. Since then the days have been chill, the wind now is blustering, swaying the climbing ivy against the cold stone exterior walls.

Most of us find ourselves, in a bustle every day and when the rains came this week, I envied those who have the leisure to watch the forces of nature enveloping the earth.

At least there were a few moments to watch the blue jays and woodpeckers battering with a net bag of suet up at the Levendis' on the mountain road. Karen invited me up for some of her famous homemade onion soup and in their log home with lots of marvelous windows, one can drink in the sights of nature without stopping the daily routine.

Nevertheless, Clayton Hall is a little better looking place now unless I go out the side door and see the rotting step or out the front door to the porch that is fast decaying.

Now the newly painted windows are graced with new hall fringe country curtains, expertly hung by Ginger Echols and Esther Brown.

Our luncheon was a fine success with Alice Reed's shrimp salad, Lois Lees' special tossed salad, Susie Anderson's waldorf salad with peanuts, Irene Quinn's jello salad, Sue Mearns' broccoli casserole, J.J. Heinemann's spinach casserole, Mary Lee Smith's scalloped potatoes, my scalloped tomatoes and the standing rib roast and hot rolls and dry and sweet wine, and can you believe Ginger Echols made three pecan pies for dessert?

Janet Ball liked the remembrance of the copy of the Yardley Taylor map and the book, Northern Virginia Heritage, a fine edition of Loudoun County homes, quite a few of which we had visited on our sojourns.

Those pictured are still standing but for how long? Hoping to meet the threat of demolition, the group of would-be preservationists met with incident at the Purcellville Library this week.

Gathering at a darkened library, Mary Alice Wertz first scurried to call Jean Carruthers for the key. Being uninformed we should have picked it up before the zero hour. Jean, her husband reported, was at Mass just a half block up the street at the delicate chapel. Somehow I was elected to tip-toe in before the proceedings – there like a head from Salvador Dali's disciples in his painting of The Last Supper, Jean knelt.

Summoning up my courage and thinking it was all quite like a scene from a low-budget movie, I whispered, "the key, do you have the key?"

After one false start she fished it out, gave me my instructions and we were back at the library door. The storm doors were locked, then around the building we went, trying the other locks, into the pretty formal garden behind, silvery in the street light with boxwood and then back to the front steps.

Shall we adjourn to Bentley's, to the community center? Then Lois Lees took a final fumble at the storm doors and they opened. She's fabulous that way! Meeting at the library? Bring your own secret weapon.

Though the wind blew, all the talk everywhere was of gardens and plantings. Helen Brown whose science club at Valley High School was selling pretty cuttings told me geraniums don't need much water. I concluded that's why mine fared well – no special tender loving care.

March 28, 1974

Over at the Snow House the garden plot has been plowed and disced. Milton Holler was calling for CapLloyd's services while I was plotting the same and Louis Underwood and Andrew Sisk are also keeping their motors running.

One friend already reports his peas and onions have been in for three weeks so again the delightful cycle of seasons brings the "time to plant."

Unfortunately, the flu virus too is growing. High fevers, sore throats and coughs blended with a generally weakened state are the symptoms.

Meanwhile the strong went on with business as usual.

Highlighting the week was the Board of Supervisors recommendation to the State Highway Department to give top priority to the problem of drainage in the Bluemont community.

Robert Connock, resident Highway Engineer heard the complaints of Loudoun residents.

Our lawyer, Don Bowman, made a fine presentation and now he, supervisor James Brownell and Clyde Beck, past president of the Bluemont Citizens Association will meet with Wayne Whitman, Secretary of Transportation and Public Safety to hopefully resolve the problem.

State Senator Charles Waddell was also on hand at the meeting. He told me the state delegation meets in Richmond for 60 days normally unless they are called back for a special session. Citizens with road complaints, he explained, really should contact their state representatives in matters of this kind rather than their state's representatives to Congress.

And so Senator Scott reports his meeting with President Nixon as cordial. Hmm! Conservationists too can see the smoke signals in the sky. Virginia first claimed tobacco as king, then the South hailed cotton and now the nation crowns the automobile, meanwhile the earth is more than subdued, it's ravaged. And Senator Scott says he voted to amend the Clean Air Act to permit the burning of coal rather than oil in factories during the national energy emergency.

At least in Bluemont there is still enthusiasm for our yearly Spring Clean-up.

Already all the Reids – Tommy, Hawkeye, Popeye, Buck and the other close kin have done a fantastic job of cleaning up the debris on the hill. The cars and cans are gone and they have even installed a container for "dead" beer bottles. Our grateful thanks to them!

Over in my woods I found a dump and those junk cars hopefully will go in the next several weeks. Clyde Beck has a lead on a hauler. Almost daily a truck passes with a decayed wreck. It is a welcome sight.

How wonderful was the news that Miss Alley's mother, who is now here with her, celebrated her 95th birthday with congratulations sent by President Nixon and the new Vice President Gerald Ford.

The Snickersville Craft Club will engage in the perfect Easter project after Easter at their next monthly April meeting the third Tuesday. They will weave baskets. Donna Miner in describing the inflationary prices of old baskets has convinced me it may be an heirloom by the time the grandchildren come along.

And nature smiles again our way with the Bluemont Horse Show anticipated as a great day of fun.

It is this Sunday, March 31 at 9 a.m. at Tiernoch Farm which is located four and a half miles down No. 606 which turns right off Rt. 7 just above the Shenandoah Bridge.

There will be lots of pony classes and Leslie Hutchins says there will be signs to mark the way. I'd sure hate to get lost while I'm still in Bluemont.

April 4, 1974

The sky was gray, clearing some as the day made midway when a huge two-horse van turned here at the corner.

I was to have taken in my first horse show observing the social mores that accompany such an event while dishing up the chili but alas I was bedside with the worst infected throat of a lifetime.

Penicillin, that wonderful discovery and Dr. Frazer's aspirin with his kind prescription "for rest and comfort" and all four children at the Johnson grandparents for the weekend, would have me back on the homebound teaching road by Monday but for now it was fitful naps and the sound of the wind stirring in the still bleak trees.

Looking back on the week, I had two solid cleaning days to my credit. Mrs. Townshend and Mrs. Dutrow said they were doing the same, sorting out drawers and straightening closets.

I even got in a day in the shop when the warmth of the day took the chill from the old stone walls. Pleasantly I met Mrs. Foxhall Taylor who has an old log house built in three sections near Unison and later a neighbor of hers of way back, Monroe of Monroes of Virginia chatted about local history. He is a collector of books on Mosby.

It was good to talk to Mr. Horning who had just flown back from California on Monday, reporting snow covered states of Tennessee, Alabama and parts of West Virginia.

Nevertheless, spring cleaning is continuing although the season keeps bringing back a day of winter. A terrific clean-up job was accomplished behind Iden's Store. It is now buried and hopefully the area will remain unlittered.

The annual spring youth clean-up day is set for April 12 at 10 a.m. We will meet at Clyde Beck's old store. Usually the MYF and other students meet to clean the center of town down to Rt. 606. Someone has already collected their debris and put it at the school house where everyone is to put their refuse from whence the state highway department will carry it to the landfill.

I will be grateful if the same people who took certain designated areas would do so again, being sure to keep track of the number of bags collected and the number of people involved. Most important this year, if anyone has dead autos on their property which they would like to have hauled away, call me. I will make our list for Mrs. Barbara Evans-Smith, Chairman of this year's clean-up campaign.

Some of our students are home from college for spring vacation. Out of the window I could see Mark Brownell frequenting Mann's Store.

And a chat with Bennie Lightner revealed that the last time I saw her, March 5, she had just become a grandmother and didn't know it. We exchanged greetings on the library steps when she went in to the DAR meeting and got the news by telephone that she and Jack's first grandson, William Cooper Bowen, III had arrived in Newport News. Congratulations to Mrs. Esther Terrill, the great grandmother, too!

Sorry to hear two of our dear ladies are still in the hospital. Mrs. Baker Bayles and Mrs. Herbert Martz and my potato patch still hasn't come into existence while magazine articles are warning of the coming world famine. Wonder how soybeans would do in that soil?

April 11, 1974

Wind and rain coupled with a landscape greening and garnished here and there with flowering trees was April's comment this week.

How the populace longed for warm bright days, days for planning and laughing in the sun but there were none – bravely the little peach tree dressed in delicate pink tossed in the bitter wind.

Sickness still continued to fell inhabitants, our birthday girl April Wilt (when else should a girl named April be born?) had to postpone her birthday party until another "weller" day.

Worst of all, word came that Mrs. Susy Neal who resided in the old Snickersville Academy died over the weekend. Susy was a dear, refined and gentle, sharing her home one summer with her granddaughter and 10 great grandchildren. And she had the finest manners, any token of attention brought a written thank you and in her soul lurked a poet. Her last communique at Christmas read: "It makes my heart rejoice that you would think of me."

Young Gary and David Ross were faithful to the end too, checking on her every day and bringing her water.

It all spells the essence of Bluemont as June Lloyd and Dorothy Dawson with no reminder have already accomplished their usual clean-up down Rt. 734. J.J. Kelley hauled two pick-up truck loads to the schoolhouse for them. In like manner, Lance Kelley had been collecting cans on his own, four bags full to date.

All the young people are urged to meet at the old store at 10 o'clock for the usual youth clean-up on Friday, April 12. In case of rain, we will work the Monday after Easter instead. The Bluemont Citizens Association will treat the workers to lunch.

And now hopefully, June and Hope Lloyd are enjoying a spring fling in Spain along with other Spanish students and teachers from Loudoun Valley High School.

A place that really is decked out for spring with a marvelous new yellow paint job is Mrs. Hottie Ashby's down in Airmont. It looks so pretty!

On the warmest day of the cold week was the monthly Bluemont Citizens Meeting. The last meeting's minutes revealed a fine addition to this year's Bluemont Fair will be a Children's Fair where all kinds of activities, painting, crafts, games, rides will be provided for our young guests. This is to take place in the Snow House field.

A report on the horse show showed that all went well, visitors said it was well organized and participants were pleased with their trophies and ribbons. The state road No. 606 took some entries down near Dulles Airport so they never made the scene at Tiernoch Farm, Bluemont. It was generally concluded that if these 15 entries had found their way, the financial picture would have left everyone in good cheer.

Stanley Kelley especially should be thanked for even acting as one of the judges when the one had car trouble and never arrived.

Our local winners were the Kelley children with a first, two seconds. Phillip took first place in Walk, Trot. Julia Second. Phillip got a second on the Stafford's pony, Cinnamon in the Halter class which was won by Lisa Symons of Grassland Farm.

Lisa in the large pony category got a first in over-jumps and a second in under-saddle.

Relying on the memory of the spectators, the John Orrisons' son took first place in Lead-Line with Geoffrey Dawson taking third with the Stanley Kelley's horse.

The Kranst son took first in under saddle and with large ponies and second in over-jumps in large ponies. Tommy Martin took third in the boot race. If this information is not correct, please call me so I can include all the local Bluemont winners.

The major part of the meeting was consumed in the report by Mr. Cox and Mr. Montgomery of the Loudoun County Health Department who reported on their findings as determined by a survey taken last October.

Bluemont being classified as a foot slope community has 79 buildings as observed in the survey sample. Seven of those building had no water supply at all and nine houses were on a spring system. According to their health standards 74 percent of the homes were unsatisfactory and 46 were severely contaminated.

It was their recommendation that a liaison-type committee be set up by the Bluemont Citizens Association to meet with the Health Department. They further stated we might wish to consider a feasibility study for public water and sewage.

As far as the drainage problem, last week's meeting with the highway officials with Bluemont represented by Supervisor James Brownell and lawyer Don Bowman revealed we are right back where we started, the Highway Department will only admit to 50 percent of the damage. Don Bowman is expected to come to the next Citizen's meeting to make his recommendations to the group.

After all the discouraging news, Walton Mann relayed a message from a Bluemont visitor that he has a film available that his father made of the scenes along the track of the W. and O.D. railroad which might be for our enjoyed viewing. And so we adjourned by eating up leftovers from the food concessions of the Bluemont Horse show.

And Lara says to tell everyone she and Tracey saw two bunnies today up near the woods – they were cottontails. Word is Peter is coming this week and I'm hoping for a chat with Harvey. Happy Easter.

April 18, 1974

The wind blew and the rains came and then there came a day in the sun and the neighbors sat and laughed in the backyards soaking up the sun and the youth gathered the debris left by the careless and then dined on hot dogs and doughnuts in the sun.

Good Friday dawned clear and bright and so began the annual youth Bluemont Clean-Up. Jim Brownell and his crew arrived early and with the bags generously donated by Whitmore and Arnold and the Hamilton Mill and an unknown benefactor who I believe had a maroon pick-up truck, we hit the high spots in the center of town.

Sandy Mitchell came with her friend, Suzy Dennis and Kenny Hutchins and Robin Myers represented The Snow House and then the Parks, the Holmes, the Combs and the Whirleys helped. Sonny Hall did a super job behind the house, hauling out a pick-up truck load. Route 626 still needs help.

It was good to talk to the men of agriculture while making my rounds. Gordon Welsh at Whitmore and Arnold said he had given up his hogs, they just weren't bringing anything. They were down to 30 cents a pound when they had been 60. Then over at the mill, they told me a large tract of land behind them was to be subdivided and no one could have a better neighbor than the farmers.

Jennifer and I were to accompany the Brownies and Mr. Baber in the usual spring rite of a hike on the Appalachian Trail but Saturday morning was only stormy. Clearing later the sun shone brightly but it was pouring in Clayton Hall. When I was having a few minutes conversation with Joyce Beck in the backyard, Ginger slipped to the upstairs bathroom turned on the sink faucet and the rains came tumbling down through the plastered ceiling into the hall beneath. And now the little darlings are waiting for the Easter Bunny to come while my good dime-store oriental rug mildews on the front porch.

Brian Miner with his friend Robin Laing were to have spent an overnight on the Appalachian Trail too.

Then this week Bob Jones, our beloved mail carrier had a major operation on his hip and is doing fine while Patsy Arthur is stuffing the boxes. Friends may write Bob at Room 265, Winchester Hospital, Winchester.

We were sorry to hear Lucy Allder was taken to the hospital this week.

The Upper Loudoun County Midget Football League is sponsoring quite an event on Friday, April 19 at 8 o'clock at Loudoun Valley High School. The Washington Redskins will play the Virginia Sportsman who are the 1974 Industrial League Champions in basketball. Tickets are $1.75 for adults, $1 for students available at Nichols Hardware in Purcellville, the Virginia Sportsman in Leesburg and at the door. Profits will go to the Midget League.

Another nice event coming this week is the spiritual music group from Shenandoah Conservatory of Music called the Koinea Group providing a service in music during the Sunday School hour from 9 o'clock on Sunday April 21 at our own Bluemont Methodist Church. The community is invited to attend.

One of our musical young people, Bruce Cochran is presently touring with his acapella choir from Eastern Nazarene College from the New England area to Virginia. Bruce, a bass and a sophomore is the choir's chaplain this year. He is the son of Ivy and Ralph Cochran.

Word was that June Lloyd, mother of eight and grandmother of at least six looked stunning as she departed with daughter Hope on the Spanish trip. Her young friend, Lisa Symons had presented her with an orchid corsage for the occasion.

Leslie Hutchins' sister, nephews and nieces were on hand from New Jersey for the long weekend and Miss Florence Maitland, former Bluemonter was on her way up from Herndon for the Easter service at the little stone church and Granny was bringing the lemon meringue pies whipped up by Susy LeMarr from Round Hill, the Bunny knew it was time to tip-toe about the living room finding the choice hiding spots for the colored eggs and for some reason the words of St. Francis of Assisi came to mind, "Lord make me an instrument of thy peace, Where there is hatred let me sow love."

April 25, 1974

Magnificent blooms of tulips and daffodils flowering beauties of peach, apple, cherry and woodland gems of violets, May apples and redbud heralded the long-awaited spring this week.

The rakes and brooms came out, the sled was silently stored in the attic and the wood stacked afar from the house, as there was talk of sunburns and the return of the bees, flies and ticks.

Jennifer and I had the pleasure to accompany Thomas Baber and the Brownies on the usual spring trek up to the Appalachian Trail and there the yellow violets dazzled and the views were perfectly clear and Mr. Baber's tales were better than ever. Such a marvelous memory, Mr. Baber has and such stamina. He would stand while the rest of us would gladly sink to the ground in a rest period when he told how George Washington met Lord Fairfax when George was looking for a horse to buy cheap.

George surveyed along the trail in his younger days and then too, Mr. Baber pointed out how the trail was used by the Indians going to council meetings, the revolutionary soldiers for camping and the civil war recruits for travel and lookout positions.

After we had come from the haunted house, there were the Round Hill Boy Scouts. Among their leaders was the Rev. Mr. Betts, minister of the Bluemont, Round Hill and Philomont charge of the Methodist Church.

Welcome back home to the Jack Bardons who have wintered in Hawaii, Mexico and other exotic spots and who upon entering Virginia, quickly left again for North Carolina for another festival.

Mary Lou Markle is back too from Ohio where she visited her daughter and son-in-law and brand new granddaughter who she just has to admit is perfectly adorable.

Sorrowfully we read of the Kulgren's son's death. His many years at Miss Ruth's Home made them intimate members of our Bluemont family.

Word was received from Janet and Dana Ball that they have found a house in Concord, N.H., a 'forty's' Cape Cod, but upon arrival they landed in a snow storm followed by the flu attack and were marooned in a motel room with three lively dogs.

Former resident, Mrs. Ruth Browning, who the children adopted as grandmother after her over-night stay at Clayton Hall some months ago, celebrated her 80th birthday on Sunday with a surprise party given by her daughters in McLean.

And Herbert Martz in true good-neighbor fashion, tidied up my lawn and did the first mowing with the tractor this week and the children are happy to pick the dandelions for dandelion wine again this year, but I still have a half-gallon of last year's brew.

Just to set the record straight, Sue Mearns reports that a part of Loudoun County was struck by the tornadoes as it ripped shutters off their sturdy stone home in the former Salem Church near Hillsboro, up-rooted three trees in the woods and took a strip of roof from the neighbor's barn.

The clean-up still continues and the greatest news is alas I no longer have the remains of a Laundromat in my barn and Newsweek reports that bills are to come before the U.S. Senate to extend the Oregon Plan of returnable containers to a nationwide basis. A study in Oregon shows there was an 88 percent reduction in containers ending up as litter and energy-wise the needed gasoline to produce the 56 billion containers thrown away by Americans each year is two billion gallons. Perhaps, we had better get those letters off to our Senators.

Now in the weeks ahead the girls will be counting the days till the Little Miss and Mister Fashion Show for Multiple Sclerosis. It will be a luncheon affair at Quality Inn. Tickets will be $5 with a door prize of $100 being given away. The Johnson girls are to curl their hair, practice their best smiles and indulge their Leo personalities.

And gloriously next weekend will be the Clarke County Garden Tour, if it is as lovely as two years ago, it will be a memorable occasion.

May 2, 1974

My head ached, my limbs throbbed and my stomach was slightly jumpy as the bright light flooded through the sliver in the curtains. In the old days, B.C. (before children) I would have succumbed to that sick feeling but as the household and neighborhood awoke, somehow experience dictated to sling the covers aside and remember again that week-ends mean less sleep, rather than more.

First, the day began at 6:30 a.m. with the barking of the dog. I gave up, tip-toed down the long stairs, got her a drink and hoisted her back up on the sofa. Two aspirins later, the neighbor's truck began to purr and by seven o'clock the twins had shuttled in twice and at 7:10 they sprang open Ginger's door for her. She gaily began to walk her mechanical dog, Snoopy. You've all seen them and heard them, quack, quack, quack. An incomparable Spring day had dawned!

Seemingly, no one could remain indoors and the lawn mowers winced and the rakes crawled over newly worked soil as the Snow House bunch toiled on their backyard.

Jean Leyden has sent her third grade class members home with radish plants and nothing would do for Jennifer but to get them quickly in the ground. In with our zinnias and marigolds went dill and parsley while the Becks' lettuce and onions were already mature.

There in their backyard a new patio and rose garden combined with perfect red tulips at the side of the white board fence, afforded a garden tour in fine style for Bluemont.

Justine had gotten a new back-pack and there was talk of an overnight hike on the trail after their friends, B.J. and Leonard from New York City arrived for the weekend.

The last of the Spring clean-up was accomplished last week with Don Corley, Gene Wade, Brian Miner, Mike Willett and Clyde Beck cleaning the long hill. Earlier the Reids and Mr. Wolfe had seen that five dead autos were removed.

Sonny Colbert helped load the dry cleaning units on their bye-bye journey from the barn and Karen and Peter Lavendis enlisted the aid of their guest from New York, Peter's brother, and wife and Mrs. Levendis for a good clean up on No. 601.

The statistics I have been able to determine are as follows: 50 people involved, 99 bags collected, 10 miles of road cleaned and to set the record straight, the Bluemont Citizens Association was the host of the lunch for the youth workers on the school grounds. I was just the chief hot dog roaster and disher-upper.

The Bluemont Citizens will meet this Wednesday night for its regular meeting at the school-house and a Fair meeting of department heads and anyone interested in working with the Fair will be held May 6 at 8 o'clock p.m. at the school, according to Chairman Donna Miner.

Also this week Howard Bass will bring another of his fine concerts of classical lute and guitar music to Clyde Beck's studio this Saturday, May 4 at 8 p.m. Everyone is invited to attend.

We are so grateful to know that Larry Cochran escaped either death or severe burning while a freak accident happened on Saturday. He was filling a tractor with gas when it suddenly burst into flames. He was between it and the shortage tank but somehow evaded disaster. The fire department responded promptly. Now Ralph is without a tractor and a bush-hog during a very important season but the important thing is that Larry was spared as his mother, Ivy said.

Happy Birthday to Wendy Kelley.

The Loudoun Towns class roamed the graveyard at old Ketoctin Church, oldest established Baptist Church in the county and perhaps in the state. We saw two revolutionary soldiers' graves and the 1854 brick building, the third structure in the church's history, was very similar to the Ebenezer Church at Bloomfield with the painted mural on the wall. Though the wall is straight, the painting of the Greek columns gives a decided curved illusion.

Thinking of churches and their ministers, I went to school with quite a few and they and their wives were my best friends. Many times I have thought that a politician and a minister must have the same attributes. They must both be dedicated to their cause, be a dynamic enough speaker to persuade people of their convictions and generate trust and rapport with their fellows. In like manner, the wives of both must be above slander, smoothing the rough edges of the husband. And after meeting Rufus Phillips and his wife, Barbara this week, I say that if he should tire of the Congress, if elected from the Tenth District, or wish to forsake his planning occupation, he could apply for a ministerial position. I was very impressed – this man who has a background as a farm boy in Charlotte County would do alright! The Bluemont Church would love him!

And after the coffee in his behalf, we quilted and ate egg salad sandwiches, egg salad with crackers, and deviled eggs and topped off the occasion of seeing a Democratic candidate with a piece of Ruth Lee Holler's cheesecake from the "Watergate" bakery!

And tomorrow is the Clarke County Garden Tour!

May 9, 1974

A full moon smiles down on a just a-bit chilly earth as trees unfold their now full shadows on the moonlight.

At the top of the hill, a dog howls, breaking the serenity of a still Spring evening. It has been a full and delightful week. Howard Bass has just concluded another fine concert with a goodly number of concert lovers in attendance at Clyde Beck's studio.

The past week was the second National Historic Week to be celebrated nationally, having been voted into effect by Congress last year for the first time.

And since we live in a veritable green belt of historic properties, I indulged myself and let the house cleaning go.

The sun shone bright and warmly for the Clark County Garden Tour, the azaleas and dogwood were at their prettiest – most everyone says the dogwoods this year are the loveliest in years. Tomorrow I have promised myself a stroll up to see Herb Little's marvelous array before their inevitable decline.

Next, the Loudoun Towns class had a rare treat as we were escorted by Emma and Doug Myers about the National Registrar's Historic town of Waterford.

Doug, whose father had a tin shop in town, grew up in the village and he knows the nooks and crannies and changing property rates. They ranged from $700 to $10,000 from $2,000 to $70,000 in a 30 or 40 year span of time. The Myers have a beautiful sloped pasture land behind their home which shows Waterford's wisdom in wishing to keep scenic easements.

Then on Saturday, Wilbur Hall's little red Mt. Gap School at Oatlands was dedicated in a ceremony made possible by Washington and Lee University, the National Trust for Historic Preservation and the Wilbur C. Hall estate.

The late Mr. Hall, a Leesburg attorney and alumna of the little school house had carefully collected old texts and marvelous double wooden desks plus a pot-bellied stove in recreating the scene of learning in his formative years. And lo and behold – there on the platform with the celebrated personages was our own Mrs. Barbara Spring who just a year ago sold her home to the Miners in Bluemont. She had been a teacher in the one-room structure before her marriage, boarding up the road from the school, she said, and teaching first through eighth grades there. Now, I know why her hands so nimbly create such cute crafts for the Fair and shop.

Between sizzling heat and rain and moderate weather, Milton and Ruth Lee Holler soared off into the blue to the tropical scene of Jamaica and the Eugene Clarks swelled the population of Bluemont by one, having welcomed a new baby girl.

Snakes were making their presence known as Harriet Murtaugh and Sue Mearns will attest and Billy Carter, Donna Kelley, George Reid, Sandy Lake and Clay Ratliff's thoughts are upon their upcoming high school graduation.

Louis and Roberta Underwood said their daughter Rhonda and husband and baby were happy now settled in Pennsylvania after Jan's release from the Army.

Remarkably, the Earl C. Idens celebrated their 66th wedding anniversary with a small family dinner party in their home here in Bluemont on Monday, April 29.

The William Caseys entertained for the Noel Laings of Purcellville in a farewell gesture as the Laings will be moving at the end of the school year to a farm near Warrenton. Their going-away gift was none other than a real live pig from neighbor Bill Kelley's pen. Dubbed P.P. – the Purcellville pig, he can greet all Loudoun visitors whether in the barnyard or on the table. Come to think of it, wonder where Judy got that turkey she served?

And Don Bowman, our able attorney neighbor, brought his recommendation on the problem of the Bluemont drainage to the monthly Bluemont Citizens Meeting this week. He urges individual citizens to write Gov. Mills Godwin who had sent word to solve the problem at an April meeting between county and state officials and the mission was unaccomplished. The Highway Department continues to admit to only causing damage that will amount to 50 percent of the costs of alleviating the problem.

As taxpayers we have every right to ask that they treat us more fairly than they have. Some pictures are available for enclosing in your letters. Call Clyde Beck for these. Happily, Loudoun County resident engineer, William Wiggins who was once the State Highway Engineer supports us in our stand that the new highway caused the overwhelming flow of water into the village streets, basements, and wells.

When Richard Wilson said, "Let Bluemont bloom" we were with him but no one mentioned "boom" or "flood." "Dear Gov. Godwin…"

May 16, 1974

Bouquets of posies, flower plants tenderly nurtured in a paper cup and a coke served up to me with lots of ice were my rewards for being a mother on Mother's Day.

As mothers were being remembered all over the nation this week, the Dawson girls, their husbands and brother Larry had their usual get-together across the street with their fine mother.

The calendar was so full of special events this week and next week offers more of the same.

Jean Leyden returned to her classroom after a terrible bout with flu, cold and the mumps and delivered promptly the Little Mister and Miss Fashion Show posters made by her third grade class. The luncheon fashion show is this Saturday at 12 o'clock at the Quality Inn, Leesburg and will benefit Multiple Sclerosis. Tickets are available at the door. Our own John Campbell designed a real cute poster, now on exhibit at Mann's Store and the Children's Wardrobe in Purcellville is supplying some darling fashions which little blondes of mine are only too happy to show off.

On the same day of the luncheon, May 18, the usual grounds clean-up day for Ebenezer Church at Bloomfield is being held. Volunteers are asked to bring a sandwich for lunch, beverages will be furnished. The annual service will be held May 26 at 2:30 p.m. with the Rev. Mr. Betts of the Round Hill, Bluemont, and Philomont Methodist charge bringing the message. A clean-up rain date will be May 25.

At the last meeting of the Bluemont Citizens Association, the membership voted to give $150 toward the cost of restoration of the murals in the church. A special story on that will come later.

Citizens met twice this week with a Fair meeting on Monday night as well. Some of the added attractions this year will be the Children's Fair to be handled by the Skyfields neighbors, the hayride again by Curtis Budny, square dancing with guest participation and a blue ribbon quilt show.

Another special meeting of the Bluemont Citizens Association has been called to present the Board of Supervisors report on the drainage problem. It will be May 29 at 8 p.m. at the school. Those who have unusual amounts of flooding on their property particularly should be there. Let's hope this can now be solved.

Scotty Casey gained a year this week with this family over for dinner which isn't too small a gathering taking in the Glen Lloyd clan.

Tuesday was a marvelously fun day for me. First our "Loudoun Towns" class was given a grand tour through a really true garden tour house in Waterford. Jan Kitselman and her daughter Ella were such lovely hostesses in the home that served as the miller's house, a beautiful old brick perched on the top of a superbly landscaped hill. Everything was just perfect and then kindly, Mrs. Marie Hilton welcomed us in the oldest known standing structure, her charming cottage with a beautiful terraced backyard boxwood garden. No one can take anything from Waterford, it's a unique period town, with its beginning in 1732.

Then back to the community center, the Senior Citizens taught me how to make butter. It was the most fun a lot of us have had in a long time. The old glass churn did the best job. June Lloyd sent the cream, Betty Colbert patted out the beat on the piano and Mrs. Colbert from St. Louis kept the rhythm going with the churning announcing this was "her bag." They poured the un-churned cream away from the butter, then padded it with a spoon for lack of something better, continuing to pour off the excess milk. Then adding ice cubes for hardening, pouring off more milk, they added some salt and moulded it into a round mound. It was a bright yellow, they all told me that was because the grass was so green now. Now I know just what my generation missed.

The rain changed our other plans. Mrs. Overton was to have taken us girls on a weed hunt or edible plant find but we're re-scheduling for this Thursday. The confectionary violets sound divine and most everybody has had a "mess" of poke by now.

Surprise! Jean Heron Smith writes. Our village biographer has moved to Fairhope, Ala. 301 South School St. 36532 just two miles from her and our former neighbors the Sam Joneses. Jean reports Ingrid is active with the DAR and League of Women Voters while Sam is busy writing a book.

Lucky for us too, we've got Miss Florence Maitland back on a permanent basis. She is now a Bluemont citizen again residing in her home near the Gilbert Dawsons on the Snickersville Pike.

Now there's a great Mother's Day story. Florence, a maiden lady at a time when it just wasn't done, adopted three children and raised them and now those adults think she's the grandest mother ever.

So here's to all you grand Bluemont mothers. Have the message of love, a sweetened violet.

May 23, 1974

The summer green landscape glimmered in patches of white as the locust trees spread their fragrant blossoms to the balmy breezes.

Temperatures soared while folks flitted here and there rejoicing in the warmth of the sun and the special occasions that marked it's shining.

In the first place, this was Senior Citizens Week in Loudoun County and two of our finest neighbors took part in the festive picnic and fashion show. Styles of old and present were shown by the senior citizens models at the Purcellville Community Center with Jim Brownell announcing the prize winners and Thelma Brunelle rendering some songs in her long blue gown with the song, "In my dear little Alice Blue Gown" commencing the show.

Thelma, the children and I topped off the day with a tramp up to the pond by their house on the ridge where we were delighted to find a variety of wild flowers.

Then over at the Welshes' in Lincoln, the well-established Hamilton Book Club begun about 60 years ago as the forerunner of the lending library met. After they treated me to lunch at the Inn, they served the best punch I have ever had anywhere. It was fabulously refreshing. It had a banana mashed up in it, they said, with crushed pineapple, frozen, thawing as one sipped.

My subject of books on local history and I find there are fifteen so far with hopes that several more will appear as part of the bi-centennial celebration.

Peggy Holler had entertained the Loudoun Towns class that morning, showing us the two magnificent six-foot fireplaces in her home and then we had a marvelous walking tour of Waterford. Oh, the houses are such treasures there!

Then at last the sun shone for a plant hunt. Mrs. Overton led our merry band over by the Murtaugh's flowing creek, onto the field with the goats where the essence of goat-hood exhibited itself. One of the sociable creatures quickly helped herself to Lois Lees' paper bag. In about four gulps, it was gone. The find was nil but I found the water fine. What's better than a wade in a tumbling mountain creek? I know not!

Finally Saturday arrives, the day of the Little Mister and Miss Fashion Show for Multiple Sclerosis. There are a lot of cute kids in the area, at least that's what a lot of doting grandparents and parents thought.

Back at home, we were glad Sandy Mitchell's mother was home from Winchester, neighbors seemed to be out mowing the lawns.

Mrs. Ray, our quilt lady friend from Washington who was visiting atop the mountain, dropped by for a visit, bringing a Yo-Yo quilt for showing. This is made by turning up the edges of a small circle in a gather, then the abbreviated circles are stitched together and then quilted to a backing.

Hopefully she can help us with the quilt show for the sixth annual Bluemont Fair in October. Clayton Hall barn with the high ceiling is a perfect square for hanging if we can only convince the pair of pigeons to move.

May 30, 1974

A week of opening peonies and strawberry picking in local patches heralded the beginning of June and the almost denouncement of school days.

Especially delightful was the annual spring sing at the Round Hill Elementary School with this year's presentation called "A Visit to Library Land" under the very talented Mrs. Remsburg's direction.

Of course, we were all doubly proud of our Bluemont stars.

The second grade class presented The Billy Goats Gruff with Jondra Wilson, Scott Casey, Junior Wade and Debby Ross.

Next Miss Rokus' first grade class recalled The Three Little Pigs. Jay Wilson took part as did Elizabeth Hickman, Kelly James and Beecher Hope.

Mrs. Bruce's first grade class hopped along with the "tale" of Peter Rabbit. The lettuce, turnips and cabbages were Yvonne Allder, Kenny Hutchins, Lara and Tracey Johnson, George Owens and Stephanie Schronder.

Then the beloved character, Winnie the Pooh made his appearance in the third grade rendition.

Brian Beck made an awfully cute owl. Jennifer was a tree with just her face sticking out and Pam Ross, John Campbell with a solo, April Wilt, Kevin Hickman and John Ramey all sang along in the chorus.

Then the upper grades took over strumming ukuleles and playing recorders and it was rather difficult to see everyone. Please forgive if I missed your child and some of them are growing so fast. I'd hardly know them. They were Justine Beck, Karen Underwood, Kitty Lowe, Lance Kelley, Chip Lloyd, Philip Kelley, Julie Kelley, Gary Ross, Katrina Wilt, Chip Wilson, Jill Hickman, Tammy Dawson, Christine Ramey, Robert Holmes, Brenda Holmes and Brad Campbell.

While there I got the official word that Lindsey and Donald Hope had moved down the lane nearby their other house to a log house and are very happy with it.

The sad news came that Bob Jones's mother, better known as Granny Jones died at the age of 95 on Wednesday. She had been able to spend most of her days with Ellen and Bob in their Bluemont home until about a year ago. She was dearly loved here in the village.

Then too, our heart goes out to Mary Jo Lloyd who fell off her bicycle Sunday and chipped her two front teeth. Mary Jo is a fourth grade student at Loudoun Country Day School.

More youth news was that the Brownie Troop had their annual Mother-Daughter tea this week where they welcomed new recruits for next year. Looks like we might have enough from Bluemont to have a pretty good rotating car pool!

Mrs. Overton celebrated Mother's Day and her birthday this week all in one treat when her son and daughter-in-law took her to the Maine Society dinner. The menu was just too much! Shrimp cocktail, New England clam chowder, Maine lobster with Maine baked potatoes as the main entrée and blueberry pie for dessert!

And for two days I have been trying to track down those important busy farmer-lawyer supervisors, Don Bowman and Jim Brownell for an official word on the Bluemont drainage question.

The special meeting of the Bluemont Citizens accomplished a motion that our Association would contribute $2,000 to be paid over a three-year period when the work was completed for the construction of drainage ditching to alleviate the flooding problem. As well, we wished to stipulate that work could not be started that would not be finished by the third weekend in October, traditional date of the Bluemont Fair. Sometimes I think I'm the last person in town to get the news!

May 30, 1974, additional feature article
MAKING MEALS FROM WOODLAND GREENS, STALKING THE WILD POKE IN BLUEMONT

By ten o'clock the sun was glaring. The day smelled of summer, and armed with paper bags and Foxfire Book 11 with its chapter on wild plant foods, we traipsed out into the sunlight on a weed hunt led by Nettie Overton of Bluemont.

First at the doorstep was the plantain, rich in vitamin A and C. This broad leaf based plant kept the French alive after World War II. Mixed with other greens is the preferred rendering, or the leaves can be boiled alone with fat meat until tender.

There too, on the lawn was the dandelion, good in a wild salad, cooked with other greens or used in concocting dandelion wine.

Mrs. Overton was a perfect leader. Under the tutelage of her mother she had learned the plants at a young age in the pastures on a farm near Knoxville, Tennessee.

Her favorite green, she said, was the dry-land cress which she likes to cook with a ham bone or seasoning meat recalling her mother cooked it with a "streak of lean, and a streak of fat."

"Cook your meat a little first then add the greens. It takes longer than the poke, between a half hour and hour or until tender."

Actually it was a little later for many of the plants. The violets had flown and we had so hoped for a tossed salad with violet leaves and then dessert was to be the sweetened violets. The Foxfire book gave a recipe to be saved, I suppose, for another spring. Cook two cups sugar, one-half cup water, a dash of cream of tartar. Stir until sugar grains. Dip fresh violet blossoms (free from stems) and place on platter to dry. Others added the information that these can be frozen and used for decorating cakes.

Next we found the narrow leaf dock, good in mixed greens, cooked up into a mess with poke, probably one of the most abundant edibles in Northern Virginia. All these plants must be gotten young, Mrs. Overton tested them by gently tearing the leaf – if it tears easily, it is not too tough.

Poke is the plant that bears the "poisonous berries" every child has been warned about. Nevertheless, the leaves, not the root are tasty in a two rinse cooking. First, prepare the leaves in a hot water boil for several minutes, then pour off the water, begin with fresh water and cook till tender, like spinach, serving with butter or vinegar.

Then we found a lone piece of pepper plant, its leaves are good in mixed greens and the tiny white flowers are followed by flat, peppery seed capsules which can be used as a substitute for pepper.

Of course, everyone knows the wild onion plant, not only by sight, but by smell. We found mild clusters. Mrs. Overton says she cooks them in bacon grease not quite browning them, then scrambles in her eggs for a flavorful breakfast.

We searched vainly by two streams for watercress which is marvelous in salad or in petite sandwiches with a delectable sauce. Harriet Murtaugh commented that the experts who forage off the land carry flour, salt and pepper with recipes intact for gravies and sauces which are the makings of culinary delights.

Mint can be easily found, I know of a spot – which makes the vital point that to be successful in finds, one must know where to hunt each year.

The neighbors across the road discovered early the wine-berry plants, and down by the creek we found a hearty specimen. Mrs. Overton says they are native to these foothills of the Blue Ridge, their being unknown in Tennessee. They are good in wine and jelly and just chilled with milk and sugar, resembling very closely the bigger wild raspberries.

I had hoped we might brew a pot of sassafras tea, but there was no time. You simply shave the bark, drop into boiling water and add sugar or honey.

Lois Lees quoted a nature lecturer who stated one family had to have a radius of 50 square miles in order to "live off the land."

So we cheated a bit – we had cultivated asparagus from Mrs. Overton's patch, poke with butter, dandelion wine filled in with a Loudoun County grown piece of beef!

The guests rushed off to meet the school bus or to keep a dentist appointment as Mrs. Overton lamented, recalling perhaps, a time when the pace was slower, when a full day could be given to a walk in the sun and Thomas Wolfe's words echoed, "Of time and the river, how swiftly they go by."

June 6, 1974

Showers, showers, this week with only one truly fine day and it was ours to walk down a country lane, inhale the luscious nectar of the honeysuckle, observe blue skies and view the Bluemont hills in the distance.

In the grandest style, the Loudoun Towns class met for the final session doing the cottage tour in Mt. Gilead.

Since neighbor Clyde Beck has spoken of his renovation efforts there, I have been intrigued so last week Alma Newitt in her charming cottage served tea in the cozy kitchen with tones of red and Linda Dowling gave us the tour of her lovely log cabin while this week Dagmar Wilson and Margaret Marks related history, showed their paintings and studios and Clyde Beck's ingenuity in working on their weekend places now turned permanent dwellings. A real treat too was the visit to the Bortman's house made from a handsome barn. As Miss Maitland would say, they were all "loves" of places.

Mt. Gilead, like so many other quiet Loudoun County spots, expected to be at the threshold of the world's door. In an 1835 Gazetteer a writer markets the area with these words, "The prospect from this place is most varied and extensive. To the east and south is a beautiful rolling mountainous country. But it is on the west side of the village that the curious may behold the finest scenery in nature. It contains at present, one mercantile store, one handsome school house, an infirmary, two boot and shoe factories, one copper shop, two cabinet makers, and in the vicinity a large and spacious house of worship (Baptist)", (North Fork, I presume)' "Population – 62 persons, one of whom is a practicing physician."

Then on we went to the Brownie Fly-Up where meeting Barbara Kelley, I found out their Irish Setter, Jennifer, had 15 puppies last week. They took a second at a specialty show in the Greater Richmond area with their Michael, Duke of Erland.

Wednesday we ran through rain drops to a coffee in Irene Quinn's home at Durette Upton's lovely home outside of Hillsboro. Irene and her family are moving to a 90-acre farm in West Virginia and while there I got the official word that Sue and Rick Mearns will be leaving soon for New York State where Rick is to work at Corning Glass Works.

Thursday we girls took our leave of Jeanne Brown at a special luncheon at Red Fox Tavern in Middleburg, second oldest tavern in the country. Helen Gray, Jeanne's and my former neighbor in Leesburg, was an inspiration, having grown up in the burg now gone to very worldly with sophistication and millionaires.

Helen said almost every child kept a pony in their backyard then on the two main streets, front street and back street. The middle of the road was paved but the side was kept in dirt for a bridle path. Only one little unpainted store resembled the look of the town she remembers in the twenties. Once a café where her husband had waited tables in his teenage years, it now served as a place of shortage while across the pike the new French restaurant and the Red Fox Tavern exhibit their beautiful architectural lines and lure "lunching" ladies.

Back home in Bluemont, the news was that the chicken pox is raging. Yvonne Allder has been stricken and frankly I'm holding my breath that we might finish out the school year without an attack!

Lynn Carbaugh sends her graduation commencement from Warren County High School. Our very best to her!

Mrs. Peyton had a few strawberries in her patch while Ivy Cochran is going commercial this year. You can pick your own. If you want to give her a buzz.

The Peytons' son, Ralph is confined at the hospital having undergone minor surgery and daughter Sadie is finishing up her second year of teaching in Winchester.

Jack Bardon is back from a trip to Detroit, having received news earlier in the week that he was named the Single Performer Champion at the Old Time Fiddlers Convention in Union Grove, N.C. with his banjo and harmonica act.

Claire Bardon turned down our invite to one of the best entertainments I've seen in a long time at Valley High School last Saturday night. The students presented "Hello Dolly." It was a terrific show with the performers enjoying themselves so, the audience couldn't help but catch the fever.

Directing, the English teacher, Ike Stoneberger, an enthusiastic young man who managed good choreography, darling costumes and "an all-together highly entertaining evening!"

The long weekend brought some visitors to our one time resort village. Mrs. Overton entertained four of her grandchildren and daughter-in-law while Leslie and Ken Hutchins had Leslie's sister and her son and Leslie's parents and son all from New Jersey.

Meanwhile Curtis Budny just kept hammering and shaping their new chicken coup and for four days straight I sorted our winter and summer clothes from small from large as other women about the countryside.

Mr. Horning jet-setted to his nephew's wedding in San Francisco this weekend; the new granddaughter of the John Markles came for a visit to the Virginia mountainside and away goes the page of the calendar into summer.

June 13, 1974

Activity was at a maximum – lawn mowers roared, dogs howled, children propelled themselves into happy sports and the hammering continued on the chicken coop as the sun shone on the village in weekend stride.

All the craft and antique shoppers had apparently directed their steps to the Harper's Ferry Craft Festival so there were uninterrupted hours for sorting of clothes, toys and gadgets for an end of the month June sale here.

With the promise of the end of the school duration, perhaps the pace would slacken but citizens should be warned of the high incidence of summer accidents.

The Glen Lloyds have had more than their share – this past week, an exploding spray can of paint caught Kelley afire but with good sense he rolled on the ground to put it out but nevertheless he was hospitalized. Then several days later, June Lloyd caught a wire in her foot which required a hospital stay and this was June's birthday week, too.

Of course, the death of Jack Garrison of Round Hill who was the son-in-law of our fine Roy Santmyers was a shock to the upper Loudoun community.

Fortunately, the days had their bright side too, the first grade of Round Hill school had a day at the Washington Zoo and the Heinemann and Johnson gals extended our history tours to Charlottesville to see Jefferson's "Little Mountain," Monticello. Certainly his inventiveness was on a genius level but I still will quibble with him over the lack of the central staircase which he omitted, saying it took up too much space. And when the guide pointed out, our dignified statesman was a redhead with freckles, I giggled.

Hurrying back late to the Bluemont Citizens Meeting, they had already discussed the good piece of legislature enacted by our board of supervisors granting money to ease the drainage problem. Mr. Bowman had been kind enough to call that morning with the news. Now it is up to us to cooperate to the fullest so perhaps, the work can begin by July 1.

This date brings us to the glorious Fourth and Bluemont's usual celebration. Ivy Cochran declined her yearly organizing jog so Mary Lynn Budny volunteered.

The old-fashioned homemade ice cream festival will begin at 7:30 p.m on the Fourth with Ken Hutchins to find some country music for the occasion.

Then the citizens went on to approve a big painting project of the school auditorium, hall and floor sanding to be begun in the next several weeks.

It's good to see the Hatchers back on the mountainside again from Florida.

And Restoration and Preservation and Commemoration have come of age in Loudoun County.

Two weeks ago the Bi-Centennial Committee met, inviting guests and encouraging communities to think of the best way they can celebrate their heritages and I hope Bluemont will show another face, other than the one shown at the Bluemont Fair. How about a house and farm tour?

Then this week, the Restoration Society whose main project is restoration of the very old log cabin that initially served as a silversmith's shop, met in Leesburg.

Adopting by-laws and electing officers and a board of trustees, they are on their way.

And never write off miracles. Today after the dog quieted with a drink of water at 6:30 a.m., this household didn't stir till ten o'clock. The simple explanation – the twins spent the night with their friend, Stephanie.

And as wee Ginger would say, "Happy Day," Fathers!

June 20, 1974

"Roll out those lazy, hazy crazy days of summer," accompanied by a player piano – the feet pat, the countenance lights up and that all-over happy feeling comes with the season.

Picnics at the beach and band concerts mingled with the sea breezes in an honest-to-goodness band shelter were the "working your way through college" routine but in Bluemont it was cooling mountain vapors and swing bands, all before my time, but maybe, maybe they can be revived.

Anyway, the summer guests format is continuing up at the Brunelles. Mrs. and Mrs. Joseph Deeley spent some marvelous days and nights here on the mountain accompanied by their friend, Mrs. Joseph Matat from New York City while they hail from Dumont, N.J.

It was good to hear the Jersey accents again as my summers at the shore were in Ocean Grove, N.J. at the "Seaside Hotel."

While on the mountain top they renewed acquaintances with Mrs. Elizabeth Legg who celebrated her birthday this week and Helen Deeley served cake and tea garnished with Thelma Brunelle's prize "Peace" roses.

Another party thrown in Bluemont this week was Brian Miner's farewell gesture to Robin Laing of Purcellville. Dr. Laing and his family will be missed by those of the dog, horse-loving set joined by the craft enthusiasts on Charlotte's side. They are moving to a farm near Warrenton.

J.J. Heinneman and I mentioned it as we made our way through the area to Charlottesville last week – whatever their new address might be, we will vote for "Summerduck." Doesn't it make you feel poetic, artistic and lazy.

A decade of Bluemont News

It was such a delight to have a brief chat with Miss Maitland who in her usual zest for life way described her activities of the week. She was a guest along with her daughter, Georgia to a plush spot at Rehoboth Beach for several days, then she and Miss Miley joined the Senior Citizens for a trip to Baltimore later in the week, sandwiched in with a bus trip through Falls Church, Reston and Tysons Corner after a visit to a school from which she had retired ten years ago.

The State Treasurers Convention at the Quality Inn in Leesburg turned out to be a nice affair and gave the children an opportunity to meet their great-uncle Johnny Johnson, Treasurer of Roanoke.

He said he had been re-elected six times which tied right in with Rev. Steadman's explanation for the uniqueness of Loudoun County's records being kept intact as the Binn family were Clerks of the Court for about a hundred years span.

As I recall, it was one of the Binns who loaded all the records up in a wagon and kept moving them away from danger during the Civil War.

The Rev. Mr. Steadman, a great lover of Loudoun County and relative of most of the most prominent settlers, returned on the occasion of the 200th anniversary date of the Loudoun Resolves. The Resolves, which most of the counties of Virginia adopted in 1774 made clear their intent to support the Boston compatriots in their rebellion against the British who closed their port.

The fifty-one signers were obviously great men of courage as they had much to lose for their moral stand in resisting the mighty King of England.

The Rev. Mr. Steadman who has an incredible retention capacity gave genealogical connections to the two main drafters of the Resolves, Thomas Mason, brother of George Mason and Leven Powell, founder of Middleburg.

In true preacher style, he gave an inspirational thought that it is up to us to see that Loudoun continues its unique independence in preserving our heritage.

Certainly the first order of business is for citizens to band together to stop the ridiculous "watery demise" of Taylorstown. The idea that a whole settlement can be wiped out for a public works reservoir for a city that "might" let Loudoun have some water for emergency use is absolutely absurd.

People get embroiled over a slight to a group of amateur players but seemingly let "the water roll-off their back" on far-reaching issues like honesty in government and preservation of old homes and historic structures.

We were sorry to hear Tom Ogden had injured his back while he was consumed in another project on Mountain Shadow and Wanda Ogden's recommendation that the Citizens Association purchase a pet mongoose to do in the numerous snakes in the village, may have merit.

I've already had one in the kitchen and after several other encounters with the black variation, one completely blocked her entry into the house today, coiling around the door knob.

Nevertheless, the contradiction in Bluemont attitudes has always been perplexing to me.

Now Earl Bealle, the former owner of Clayton Hall, said the natives scorned anyone who would harm a black snake while Betsy Jones Moreland recalled that in her summers here, they were given the healthiest respect with children hardly daring to play in their yards for fear of a chance meeting. Meanwhile, the city folks visiting on the ridge, walk out even on the wooded paths in the night, without fear.

Even in citified Round Hill, one fell to the sidewalk last week so maybe you'll want to mimic Mary Alice Wertz's custom. She wears boots when she comes for a summer visit.

"Those days of soda and pretzels and beer." And the lightning bugs are flicking in the tall green grass again.

"Roll out those…"

June 27, 1974

Steamy days of sun, cooled by late afternoon showers, the hustling of pedestrians and vehicles around the corner of the two main thoroughfares spell the summer pace in Bluemont.

Traffic meanders up the stairs and through the slamming screen door of Mann's Store for refreshment from the soft-drink cooler and weeds and grass soar higher only to be attacked again by the populace.

The work projects continue, Curtis and Mary Lynn Budny said their hundred baby chicks were to arrive this week, regardless of whether their coop was ready so they may have to be kept in the workroom until their house is ready in center field. All I can picture is the "I Love Lucy" action. Maybe Curt will think to take movies of it all. Now there would be some entertainment for home movies night.

The first association that comes to mind when you say chicken and coop is a flash I see of a Model T Ford from the movie, "Cheaper By The Dozen" that is painted yellow and is stenciled with the words, "Chicken, here's your coop."

Back in the placid fifties, young women like myself at that point in history were designated as "chicks" and somehow it is still all wrapped in humor and affection for me. Being called a "cool chick" was the ultimate compliment.

All these little associations reared their pretty little heads as I continued my attic clean-up of the clothes for the rummage sale which were scattered amidst letter from former boyfriends, now Grandma calls them my "beaus."

Others continue the same schedule, setting out and finding treasures to be passed on to others and the WSCS of the Church will sell baked goods and lemonade and there will be antiques and baby equipment, household items and tools and Hazel Payne's crafts and we can all take a lesson from Sandy DiFlippo on how to turn our cooking drippings into soap. All hail to a sunny Saturday.

Claire Bardon had a beautiful day Tuesday on which to entertain her garden club from Falls Church for a picnic at their home near the beautiful Shenandoah.

On the same day a group of Sue Mearns friends assembled at the Salem Churchhouse in Neersville for a pot luck luncheon as a farewell gesture to her, then we were glad she and Andrew could join us the next night here for dinner before their departure to settle with Rick who is an employee already of Corning.

Sue is one of those rare persons who possesses a sparkling wit and thus enhances those lives with whom she comes in contact so the sunshine will just be transferring to another part of the country.

Already the neighbors are on summer sojourns.

Joyce Beck and the children Brian and Justine hurried along to Roanoke for a visit with Joyce's sister and family and Kenny Hutchins and Robin Myers departed even before school was out for days of sun in New Jersey with the aunts, uncles and grandparents.

And life seems somehow to be a struggle of sorting priorities. Time-wise should I run the vacuum over this filthy rug or iron some clothes in which to greet the summer throng – save this dress or trade it off – contribute my time to Multiple Sclerosis or to the Preservation Society? Should these days be devoted to the family or community affairs? And the answer is never the same in the unending juggling priorities process.

Right now I have reason to be smug while others are healthier and younger looking in suntans, my lily white limbs will age less quickly – all according to an article I read last night by a dermatologist who said the ultra-violet rays of sun were responsible more than any other factor for the leathery-wrinkled look. Of course, I guess advancing age has a little something to do with it. Sun bathers, eat your heart out!

July 4, 1974

Will the Fourth be glorious?

It has never failed to be anything but glorious in Bluemont since I've been privileged to call the village my home but then the rains may come down but the plans are proceeding on schedule with high hopes as usual for a marvelous celebration on the schoolhouse lawn.

Doris Allder and Mary Lynn Budny are making the rounds to the area cooks, recruiting cakes and gallons of home-made ice cream. Doris says she will make her usual banana and I guess we'll stick to chocolate and the music committee has arranged for music, Tracey McClaughry and a group called The Players with leader Jake Mills from Hillsboro will entertain.

And of course, there will be the climax of the evening, the fireworks set off from far out field to remind us all its pretty great to be an American – that we have a heritage that's worth fighting for either on the battlefield or in the courtroom.

Sue Mearns and I have just had one of our analytical talks and we decided by living in a small town with everyone knowing each other, has a way of keeping people honest and pretty loving and tolerant too.

Early July is a time too of hanging macramé baskets created by Karen Levendis for a sale here on the lawn and generous neighbors sharing their yield of salad fixings with the neighbors whose thumb not only didn't turn green with the thought of a garden but withered instead behind a pencil and an open magazine.

So much of our interesting news is of our young people. Really I thought Jackie Legard would never announce her engagement to our special Mark Brownell. I've sat on the story for months! They are both in summer school now hurrying their way through education towards a happy future together.

Our best wishes to Guy Woolman who has acquired a wife and a new career in Alabama.

And then it was good to see Janice Hall, the daughter of our former beloved pastor and his wife, Homer and Ethel, presented a nursing scholarship to Madison College for next year.

Willa Colbert is wheeling a new car along with her college diploma.

At the Fair pow-wow held this week, it was revealed that the Skyfields folks are creating an original puppet show for the Children's Fair, there may be a civil war battle reenactment in a nearby field if the hayride can be switched to Hatcher's field where I love to look down on the roofs of the village houses and pretend I am Emily of "Our Town."

Mrs. Hatcher, incidentally, is industriously putting the old Snickersville Academy back in shape for an ideal summer abode.

The days continue to bring surprises and pleasures – tonight I have a new step at the my door, shutters at the windows and cement patches in cracks of stone just because Bill Powell of Round Hill heard I needed a few projects accomplished and this evening we ventured over to the Chamberlains to find another of Loudoun's stone treasures with a six-foot fireplace in an original Quaker dwelling.

We express our sympathy to the grieving neighboring town and their loss in Hillsboro of Major Turbeville and somehow we are especially grateful for the close-knittedness of these communities where each life counts for so much.

So maybe perhaps, the Fourth this year, will have a little of Thanksgiving rolled up into it!

July 11, 1974

A cool breeze played tag in the glossy green of the full shade trees when the mountain village of Bluemont played host to the western Loudoun neighbors on the Fourth.

The rock band belted out its best and as a full moon lingered after the blast of fireworks, natives felt a real surge of pride that this little spot in the road was our home.

The week of the Fourth had been a marvelously full one – there were picnics, and hikes and visitors and wedding and reunions and meetings with the heat never burning long enough to spoil that all-together glorious feeling of aliveness.

On Sunday evening, Mrs. Prendergast's daughter, Dr. J.J. Wilson gave a sparkling lecture and slide show on Great Women Artists, which are extracts from a book to be published in September by Harper and Row.

The next evening, the Committee of 55 met in a briefing of plans for the bi-centennial celebration by various committee chairman and later members made additional suggestions.

On behalf of the Historical Society, John Lewis made mention of a number of publications that are being compiled by that organization for a written heritage record.

The Tourism Committee reported it hopes to have an architectural tour of 200 years that would include the fine old homes as well as the best examples of good modern architecture.

Ben Lawrence, Chairman of the official Loudoun County Bi-Centennial Committee emphasized that the Bi-Centennial celebration was a birthday party to be for Loudoun County by Loudoun Countyians with the major thrust now concentrated on the tourist trade.

Their main project will be an enactment of the August Court Days that were held on the courthouse lawn, better known as Watermelon Court as Emmitt Jackson will quickly tell you.

The committee wants to involve school children in plays, concerts, pageants and a fine idea has been to have memorial tree planting of dogwoods along country lanes, town streets and major thoroughfares.

Mrs. Hawthorne said the D.A.R. wanted to make local history live. They are marking churches, the Janney House, and the Aldie Mill as well as graves of extraordinary soldiers. One of their suggestions was to sponsor a colonial tea.

Bobby George representing the youth of Loudoun proposed seminars to teach local history. Youth groups are already making plans to do extensive clean-up of historic sites.

Col. Mare's suggestion of a colonial costume ball has already been picked up by the Junior Women's Club and more evening plans are expected to come from every community across the county.

Back in this corner of the world, the managing and coaching staff of the Women's Softball team wishes to thank the ball players for their outstanding performances, which now places them in a tie for first place with a 5-0 record.

On the Fourth, the Lloyds were able to introduce their daughter, Linda and her husband, Bill Cates to the neighbors. The newlyweds were honored at a marvelous family party on Sunday.

At the Fourth gathering too was our former Bluemonter, Ethel Leffingwell who has joined the Army as a MP and she looks absolutely terrific.

Peter and Karen Levendis took in an Italian wedding in New York last weekend and then over at the Snow House the 17 rooms are filled to traditional Bluemont boarding house style with the Budny's entertaining Mary Lynn's mother and step-father, and the Hutchins playing hosts to Leslie's relatives from New Jersey again.

The young people in charge of the Recreation Department program remind the village children of the ages five to 12 to enter morning program from 10 a.m. to 12:00 p.m. Monday through Friday. They will include swimming and hiking along with crafts and games sponsored at the school.

And one of the most fun things of the whole week was the grand Reed reunion at Lewis Reed's Reed's Roost up here at the top of the hill.

They came as far as North Carolina for the event, everyone bringing delicious food. Marvelous drinks were served to the music of the Blue Ridge Mountain Boys music. This country music group was one of our winners at the last Bluemont Fair contest and Bud Canard who married a Reed picked a mean banjo in the lineup.

And after 26 years of opening the door of the general store promptly at 7:30 each morning and lingering for a late customer in the evening, Emma and Walton Mann have sold the last lollypop and piece of bubble gum in Bluemont. Just as a small gesture of love and appreciation for all their extra tender care of store keeping, the Bluemont Citizens Association will sponsor a covered dish dinner in their honor at the school house on Sunday. July 14, at 6:00 p.m. all you residents of the community and patrons of the store, "You all come!"

July 18, 1974

The hour grows late but still there are quiet murmurings from neighbors sitting in the outdoors on lawns, front porches, or patios and the traffic groans on the Rt. 7 hill above the village as lightning bugs flash in the mating game.

Already folks are saying summer is far-spent and with the budget fuel plan arriving in the mail today, it seems so true.

Surely though there are many social delights before the briskness of the breeze heightens to October's song and all the village will flow with cups of streaming cider and gambling guests who may venture a turn around the pasture on the hayride at the Bluemont Fair. Ah! I can hardly wait!

This is the season of green bean canning and pickle-making and jelly stirrings. Mac Brownell was off to the bean patch in the twilight sun after her usual contended day at Loudoun Memorial Hospital where she conducts the volunteer services. And though I'm late in acknowledging the hospital dedication, a real lump came to my throat and a tear to my eye when I read the reminiscences of a patron who recalled a bushel of grapes left at her front door for jelly making for hospital patients.

Speaking of jelly, Mr. Horning's blackberries are back in abundance but expediency always dictates that those first quarts are sugared and served well-chilled with milk.

Glen Horning, a junior at VPI has performed superiorly again having made the dean's list for the last semester with his major in electrical engineering.

The Hoges are doing their usual relaxing on our mountain from their winter home in Florida while Ruth Lee Holler is still anxious about the loss of her little white Pomeranian. Anyone seeing the dog, please call her immediately.

Meetings combine sociability with constructive results as last Thursday the board members of the Historical Society met, the Taylorstown Alliance, the Restoration Committee and the Preservation Society assembled all on the same evening.

Ginger Echols entertained us Preservation people in her beautiful Hillsboro home as we drew up committees with the next step being to call on all you preservationist in every community in Loudoun.

Also in the same historic vein, Brother James from the Holy Cross Abbey will use the Bluemont Slide Show on Snickersville 1864 as a commemorative presentation on the 11th anniversary of their battle of Cool Springs which took place on July 18, 1864. Bluemont is very flattered by the attention and maybe after Brother James breaks the bread, writes the book, gives the lectures; he can make a slide show on the subject.

Then tonight my news observation will be put to its best test as I try to recall the tidbits I'll hear at the Bluemont Citizens Appreciation dinner for the Manns. Won't it be fun to get the Bluemont family together again!

July 25, 1974

The days wax dry and hot but mostly at even-tide the nights cool in Bluemont as even now, one window went down against the chill of the night.

William Powell warns of snakes coming closer to civilization for water due to the dry spell and the natives and nature kinsmen all back him up. Be on the look-out!

The top of the week found Brother James and Father William here for a look at the Bluemont slides and after few technical difficulties they were readied for showing at the monastery. Now Sally Veise will give the presentation to the Loudoun County 4-H Clubs who are studying civil war action in the county.

Then on Tuesday Jennifer and I went on the Brownie Hike at Moss Ridge.

My assignment was the hike up the Appalachian Trail which unhappily follows the hard surface, No. 601 here above us for a long ways. We began on the other end above

Paris on Rt. 50 until we came to the logger's path that took us back to the Moss Ridge Girl Scout Camp.

It was my pleasure to accompany the Cadets and Juniors mostly from Leesburg along with Dr. Priscilla Oliver who is pretty fantastic. Her knowledge of plant life put my little Foxfire chapters to shame and then the coup of the day was our meeting the mowing man at the side of the road who had just killed a rattler up the pike and had several rattles to prove it which to my surprise rattled without the tail to rattle them.

The find of the wine berries was rather fine too, as was Mrs. Butt's special watermelon treat with the leaders taking rind home for pickling.

Frankly though, I was bushed – not so much from the hike as from the driving to Round Hill twice to pick up the girls, to Philomont twice to pick up the babysitter and then on that terribly treacherous road 606. There the Henry Tumblins kindly waited to bring us home after a Sunday accident – two boys on a motorcycle flying around a curve hit the car. If there was only some way to convince youth of the follies of poor judgement before…

Things quieted down a little as the week lengthened. Across the street young Christopher Budny was off to his grandmother's for a summer visit to Georgia and I watched fascinated as the Hutchins loaded the trunk of their car for a trip to Boston. Finally Ken sat on the lid and everything stayed in.

Well, things were almost quiet till Justine Beck's birthday slumber party on Thursday night. Through the open windows drifted the squeals of young girls and rock music playing on the radio and why they ever called those affairs "slumber parties" is a mystery to me.

The summer viruses have been making the rounds with young Eric Hoggett, Mrs. Dawson's grandson, running a high temperature.

Ruth Reed looking happy and well was home briefly when her uncle held the family reunion several weeks ago and it was good to have a visit with Mrs. Kulgren of Round Hill who stopped by briefly last week.

Our fairly new neighbor, Gail Hickman has been named Multiple Sclerosis chairman for Bluemont and hopefully she will be a car-pooling Brownie mother too for next year.

With the excitement of planning ahead for colonial balls and preservation teas, the best of the week still seems to be in hanging out the wash in the serenity of the morning before the children have awakened and having a piece of chocolate cake in Mac Brownell's kitchen.

August 1, 1974

Summer is half-spent, some lament while mothers urge the returned tolling of the school bells.

The children continue their frolic in the dry grass topped by the weeds that flip into an easy sling-shot once you know the trick.

As the days lengthen, the children become more abusive and an honest discussion with several other mothers revealed that we are all cussing like a bunch of "damn" sailors. Sorry I have to band with Mark Twain when he said, "Profanity offers a relief known equal only to prayer."

This is the birthday season and here the townschildren came for the twins celebration on Thursday and the grandparents came for a fine summer picnic party on Wednesday. They were two "chocolate days" combined with far too many trips over to the Bluemont General Store for treats bought with money gifts and right now they probably have the cleanest teeth in town all because Heather Budny brought that delight of delight, a Snoopy toothbrush to them.

And to think I have to repeat this whole process in three weeks for Jennifer's birthday.

Barbara Allder is playing it smart – Yvonne will celebrate her seventh birthday with the family at a great outing at close-by Cacapon Park on Sunday.

And Bluemont has become a tourist town again with visitors stopping to see the shop and having a tour of the house and everyone is excited already about the Bluemont event – the Bluemont Fair slated for Oct. 19-20.

We are talking publicity and quilts here and hayrides. Remember children under 12 are free.

Some of the populace escaped to the seashore, the most popular spot being Ocean City. Now that is a terrific place. Scott Brownell and his college roommate from New York City, one of those real-life natives – were taking in the scene there as were Ruth Lee and Milton Holler this week.

I knew I was missing Leon and Thelma Brunelle's wonderful visits, when Sue Ray wrote to tell me Leon had been in the hospital for treatment of an ulcer. Our warmest wishes for a quick recovery. Mrs. Ray was full of quilt news and Kathryn Chamberlin told me of a show I had missed in Hagerstown, Md. recently.

There are some marvelous activities going on for Senior Citizens at the Valley Community Center in Purcellville, Mrs. Barbara Andrews reports. Go for lunch any day at 11:30 at the Country Kitchen, inspect the craft shop there and join the R.S.V.P. program that makes regular visits to the Lare School, the nursing home and Loudoun Hospital. We all know in giving of ourselves, we receive a double blessing.

Speaking of giving – my mother came this week – giving, giving – everyone in the family got a gift at the party – even me! It was bar of Old English Lavender Soap! Heavenly! Now there's a bi-centennial gift – it has been on the market since 1760 and kept "women in hot water since." I like that.

And then she brought the magazines – I've read Billie Jean's story, Lana Turner's, Cher's. Now I figure I've got a pretty good story too so does Mrs. Ruth Browning herself who came by for a visit this week in her marvelously entertaining way. Now all we have to do is get to be a celebrity so someone will want to read it.

August 8, 1974

It's a lazy summer evening – a full moon caresses the village and mountainside hung with dark shadows of full-slung trees while the crickets keep up a quiet lullaby and a few soft sprinkles of rain spatter gently on the glossy leaves.

The little green apples are back on the tree at the drive and soon enough some of the village youngsters will ask for a bag full and it will be good to fry them again with plenty of sugar and cinnamon for a culinary delight at breakfast time.

Sometimes a restlessness breathes its spirit into the atmosphere and one feels it is time for singing and dancing and fun and games and there have been games in the area.

The Round Hill Junior Pony Tail League won the county championship over Lovettsville in a hard-fought battle ending in the score of 3-2 after extended innings. Our Bluemonters playing on the team were Tammy Dawson, Christine Ramey, Karen Parks and Sharon and Susan Lemon. Their managers were George Price and Ralph Mitchell.

Likewise, the Bluemont Women's Team had an important game in Purcellville on Saturday evening.

While talking to Grace Dawson, I also gleaned from her that her daughters, Debra and Tammy Dawson had a marvelous trip with their relatives, the Truman Hawes of Philomont up to Hershey, Pa., New York State and Canada a week ago.

And the birthday parties continue. Ginger had her social debut at Kristen Scheel's luncheon-sandbox side affair last week. There I took mental notes of the sociological mores of three-year-olds' birthday parties but those superior observations can hardly be contained in a weekly column.

And I conquered more of the accumulated newspapers and magazines this week which included several 1964 Times-Mirrors. There was Frank Raflo and Frank Orrison showing off the Red Cross Fund thermometer on the courthouse lawn and Connie McElhinney was featured by Jean McDonald while Cochran Cowart was writing the Hamilton news and Lillie Darnes was writing the Ashburn column and it was refreshing to know that some of the same newsmakers were with us yet written up by the same news writers.

I was pleased to know that Mrs. Harold Pillow, who is now visiting her mother, Mrs. Ruby Davis and aunt, Mrs. Louise Huyettin, Berryville caught our news each week in California via the Clarke Courier. Mrs. John Markle of our mountainside entertained them for lunch this week.

Unfortunately some of the summer restlessness has brought increased vandalism at the school grounds and on personal property and street lights. Children are cordially invited to attend the County Parks and Recreation Program at the school-house but asked not to report before the designated ten o'clock time as there is no supervision until that hour.

Citizens are reminded of the usual monthly Bluemont Citizens Meeting this first Wednesday of the month at 7:30 p.m. at the school.

And finally when Sally Veise called about showing the Bluemont slides to the 4-H Clubs, it was just the right excuse to have a little party. I mixed up some frozen daiquiris, called on Bobby George to come for a preview since he has graciously promised to show them during the Bluemont Fair, called Lewis Reed and his friends and two of my favorite people, J.J. and Jack Heinemann, along with Sally's husband, Tim, Donna Miner, and Heidi Heinemann for a little film festival saved at the last minute by Tony's Carbone's tape recorder.

Lewis has the nicest friends, they brought laughter and music (Lee Bryant's guitar rendering of country songs was great) and fun to Bluemont and as Mrs. Browning declared on her latest visit here. "You are known by the company you keep."

August 15, 1974

Frankly, Bluemont is quite raggedy around the edges – the weeds have taken over – mixed with the blue flowers which I thought was the chicory.

The days are cooling and darking sooner while the activity mounts as summer flings its last few weeks away.

August traditionally is the month for lining up the final plans for the Bluemont Fair and all the committees are making contacts for new features and expanded fun for the '74 event.

The school house has the most beautiful new plastering and interior paint job and with the completion of the sanding of the auditorium floor, folks ran visibly to see where their admission fee went. Our thanks to Louis Underwood and Charles Dawson who did volunteer labor on the project.

Walton Mann as Chairman of the Fair Finance Committee recommended to the Bluemont Citizens Association that a Fair treasurer be chosen. Curtis Budny was duly elected.

Also relating to the Fair is the change in hours of exhibit days to 1-7 p.m. on Wednesday and Thursday, rather than the 10 a.m. – 8 p.m. stretch.

The Bluemont Citizens are sponsoring a clothes exchange on Saturday, Sept. 7 from 12 to 4 p.m. at the school house. Clean articles of clothing including shoes, boots, gloves with size markings if possible can be brought to the Bluemont General Store now where they will be stored until the September date. This is for community members, and those who have articles they need transported or would like to volunteer can call Leslie Hutchins at 554-8341.

Then at the monthly meeting we were entertained with a film Mr. McCurtize of Arlington brought which showed one of the last runs of the Washington and Old Dominion Railroad which only went to Purcellville in that year of '43.

He recalled the car would hardly make it at times as the current was generated as far away as the Bennings Power Plant in Washington at 15th and H Streets. He said the big stops on the line were Herndon and Leesburg.

Of course, the big news anywhere was the resignation of the President. Some have felt that since this could happen our country has been indicted, but I find the greatest strength in the transaction. Truly our form of government, democracy has been revitalized just before its 200th birthday.

It was a grand week for berry-picking and jelly-making as Mr. Horning's berries are at their peak and the visits and trips have been legion.

The Becks took a few days off for a visit with Grandmother Beck, Sandy Mitchell is tanning beautifully, I know, at Myrtle Beach with her aunt and uncle's family, the James Allders.

The J.J. Kelley children took turns flying for visits with their sister, Gwen who now lives in Windsor, Ontario. First Glenn and Sam went, taking in a ballgame in Detroit during their week there and this week, sister Donna flew up.

When Donna returns it will be nigh on to orientation time at college in Farmville.

Glen Horning entertained two of his college friends several weekends ago here. Lola Coulson of Austinville, Va. and Pamela Farmer from Hillsboro are juniors at VPI in Blacksburg.

Too, Dr. Fleming and his wife Tish had friends from England last week and Miss Maitland said the Flemings graciously treated the village youngsters to lemonade everyday at the Parks and Recreation program.

A big welcome to the new minister and his wife of the Methodist Church, Robert and Dale Forest.

In the sports round-up, the Bluemont Women's Team won the first round of the final tournament against Hamilton this week and the Upper-Loudoun All-Stars Little League team were playing in the District III Championship with Glen Kelley representing Bluemont.

Then we are always grieved when our dear friends are hospitalized. Glen Lloyd has been at Winchester Hospital this week for tests and Leon Brunelle fell while painting which caused internal bleeding on top of his ulcer trouble and our young friend, A.C. Echols from Hillsboro has been at University of Virginia Hospital all week for tests.

Our community's prayers and thoughts are with these very special people.

August 22, 1974

The sun rays are still most intense but somehow, perhaps in the sound of the katydids' song there is a hint that summer's days are numbered.

The county fairs are winding down again with the Murtaugh children collecting their usual amount of blue ribbons for their champion goats.

A fiddler's contest in Warrenton several weeks ago drew our Jack Bardon who found his picture in the local paper there after the gala event. Sorry to learn Jack now is convalescing at Bethesda Naval Hospital from illness.

C.W. and Lucy Spring made their usual trip up from Texas to see the Virginia kin-folk and as always Lucy comes up with a reasonable answer for a perplexing problem. She says if moth balls are put on the pigeon's roost out in the barn, they will leave 'cause they object to the smell. Now to get a ladder and to go to work!

And the Leos continued in fine style, Jennifer celebrated here with April Wilt and Heather Heinnemann for lunch while Christopher Budny turned six on Monday.

It was good to see Glen Lloyd who was able to come home over-night but still remains at Winchester Hospital for more tests and painful traction. Also, A.C. Echols III must undergo an operation this week at University of Virginia Hospital.

Well next week by this time again two Loudoun officials' families will be joined in holy matrimony as Mark Brownell, son of supervisor James Brownell of Whitehall Farm, Bluemont will be wed to Sheriff Legard's daughter, Jackie of Lovettsville. And I hope to be there to throw some rice at one of my favorite young Bluemonters.

We had to bid farewell to our former Leesburg neighbors, Sonny and Jeanne Brown who have been very much involved in civic projects in Loudoun County. Sonny has taken a new position in Richmond so we grilled-up twenty-seven hamburgers, invited Jack and J.J. Heinemann and some of their offspring and mourned that the Jr. Women's Club, the Bells and Beaux and Keep Loudoun Beautiful would be a lot poorer and so would a few dozen friends around the countryside with their moving.

Jeanne was helping us with the new Preservation Society who wishes to invite all interested persons in the county to a film showing for "A Future for the Past" released by the National Trust for Historic Preservation at the Oatlands Carriage House on next Tuesday evening, Aug. 27 at 8 o'clock. Here hopefully neighbors can meet to form committees in the twenty major communities of the county to give serious thought to what should be saved in our own backyards.

We dare not delay any longer, encroachment is upon us! And our Clyde Beck has promised to make up some of his marvelous wine punch for the social evening.

The cycles of the seasons turn around again as I'm suffering with the annual poison ivy. After Kelley Lloyd and Herbert Martz got the edges and lawn trimmed with the machines, I could stand it no longer until I got into the weed crop on the wall and there

I found two turtles, an orange butterfly with black spangles, a piece of blossoming Sweet William and apparently a whole lot of poison ivy! And with the Grandparents coming tomorrow for the family birthday picnic, there isn't a drop of water in the house. Ken Hutchins has diagnosed it as the pressure pump with Bob Bayliss promising to come first thing in the morning.

August 29, 1974

Sizzling, sultry, hot – this summer bore down its full oppressive weight as teaching staffs returned this week to pre-school planning sessions with the children to follow on their heels right after Labor Day.

Fans whimpered at the "old" New Jerusalem Lutheran Church on Saturday as Mark Brownell and Jacquelyn Legard exchanged wedding vows. As might be expected there were a number of distinguished guests on-hand for the nuptials at the old church with a fascinating graveyard called the Lovettsville Union Cemetery established on Dec. 19, 1879 according to the arched iron-frame work.

I won't forget the occasion for a while since my old '64 Lincoln took me there but refused to make the trip back to Bluemont. The old car hasn't gotten such attention in a long time – Supervisor Costello and State Senator Waddell hovered over the engine and once a good neighbor, always a good neighbor, Charlie and Marie brought me back to Bluemont. Now Mark and Jackie had the right idea, they took a cab from the scene to their get-away car.

It was the second old church I had frequented in the week as graciously the Loudoun-Fauquier Garden Club invited me to speak of the new Preservation Society and we assembled first at the old Ebenezer Church in Bloomfield.

There the program chairman, Mrs. William Grayson gave historic notes that the "new" church, now adorned with the Lucien Powell paintings was built in 1855. The adjoining old stone church was supposedly the scene of a division of money among Mosby's men from their spoils with Mosby declining to accept a portion. Whereupon his men collected a purse and bought him a favorite steed. It was a new Mosby tale to most of us and we all enjoyed it. After the formal meeting, Mrs. C.P. Jones in her beautiful home near the church laid a lovely refreshment table.

And aren't we all bursting with pride with our Bluemont Ladies Fast Pitch Softball Team?

The coaches were Bill Martz, Johnny Seace and Larry Allder who gave many enthusiastic hours for the 9-4 record of the team.

The outstanding players who were unified in the effort were Peggy Bemusdoffer, catcher; Joan Wilt, first base; Alice Hayes, Glenda Knutson and Doris Allder on second base; Terry McNob as shortstop; Shelia Tapscott as third base; Geneva Hummer in left field; Linda K. Knutson in center field; Joyce Martz in short field with Frances McDavid and Brenda Smallwood in right and the winning pitcher was Eleanor Anderson.

More and more interesting events are raising their attractive heads, a preservation film, a time with the Rev. Melvin Steadman at the Restoration Society meeting this Wednesday night, and not least, a meeting with our helpful lawyer neighbor, Don Bowman about the plans for an improved drainage plan for Bluemont. Who could ask for anything more?

September 5, 1974

Big, thick cumulus clouds are painted on a light blue sky but even as they pour out their showers, the August sun burns its way into September morns and continues unbearably hot.

Linda and Don Corley have kindly let the children refresh themselves in their backyard pool on these hot afternoons and as the long last weekend of the summer approaches, the neighborhood gang is caught up in soap-box derby-making. First the base was an old ladder with two boards nailed on and now they have progressed from "foot" brakes in a more sophisticated invention.

Brian Beck and Brian Minor took to the Appalachian Trail last weekend for a campout and had just settled down in their sleeping bags without the tent when the evening rain came.

The J.H.H. Verloops are back from island-hopping off the coast of Maine where blueberry bogs abound, Trudy says, and not a bit of commercialism. You can't even buy a jar of home-made jam – the natives have no interest in that all-mighty tourism dollar. Ah – what they could teach Northern Virginia.

The Becks are home after a week exploring the rustic charm of West Virginia and young couples are making final plans for two September weddings.

Jan Woolman will wed Sept. 14 at Trinity Church to the well-liked Jock Pumphrey's son of Leesburg and Jeanne Dennis and Clayton Ratliff, our Bluemont twosome will take their vows on Sept. 21.

The worst blow to come to our community in some time was the sudden death of John Markle who suffered a cerebral hemorrhage on Wednesday night. Our deep-felt sympathy to the family, Mary Lou, her son and the two daughters, Sally and Molly who always came in time for the Bluemont Fair.

And it's that time of year again – it's time to tie-up all the strings on the Fair. The postcards and posters are here and bless be – the pigeons just seemed to migrate away from the barn so the quilts can hang ungarnished.

Citizens should be sure to attend the monthly meeting of the Association this Wednesday at 8 p.m. at the schoolhouse where a lot of Fair business needs to be discussed.

And with all the preservation activity this week, the Preservation Society of Loudoun County had a grand time at the Carriage House on Tuesday night meeting other interested preservationists and seeing the film which convinced us that we were going in the right direction, I got a real blow.

The Highway Department says my beautiful spreading maple so full of shade in the summer, so radiantly glowing in the fall, so magnificently etched against the dark sky in the winter must be taken down in order for the road to be widened and the drainage ditches laid for Bluemont.

Something tells me I should fight for the life of that beautiful living thing and John Lewis points out that our lives are really planned by highway and sanitation departments rather than planning commissions. John also says that if the Taylorstown dam goes through, there will be only one mill out of the remaining three from the original seventy-seven in Loudoun County left and the Aldie Mill has the only dual-wheel in Northern Virginia.

Is it worth the fight? You bet it is!

September 12, 1974

Gone were the scorching days of a heat wave, in came rain and chill with a threat of more in severity with a hurricane hovering off the coast.

Friday seemed to be the chiller of them all but instead of mournfully following the rain-drops from window to window at home 37 tourists who make their home in Loudoun County took a touring bus to four pre-revolutionary homes.

The Loudoun County Historical Society was the host and with 10 volunteers at Emory Plaster's kind invitation our Ladies Day Out class joined in the delightful day.

The first stop was at a log cabin near Leesburg on the site of the first probable patent from Lord Fairfax in Loudoun in 1731. The cabin's erection was in 1734 and during restoration an English coin was found that is exhibited in the wall.

Out onto the back roads of Loudoun, the bus proceeded by Purcellville to the lands of the Nichols and Dillons to a beautifully restored and decorated house with marvelous outbuildings called Cherry Grove built by the Osbornes in 1770. Next we lunched at Plum Grove near Hillsboro where Emily Barbee had every perfect touch with an original part of the house dating to the 1730's.

Mrs. Alice Whitley offered the revolutionary fact that Williams who was one of the captors of Col. Andre who was delivering dispatches to Benedict Arnold who in turn relayed them to Gen. Howe resided in Plum Grove.

Another interesting inhabitant was Emory Plaster's great-grandfather who the story goes: covered his barn with foliage hiding his grain supply from the pillaging Yankees and the whole community subsisted on that supply through the winter due to this clever idea.

The last stop brought us to the Little Fortress near Sunny Ridge of the Appalachian Trail near Round Hill. It was a fortress against the Indians in 1718 – the James family have roots there and during the civil war the house served as a tavern.

Then we came on down by Owen Thomas' property which to me is one of the most beautiful lays of land in Loudoun County. There we noted the little stone missionary Baptist Church and school house that served as the residence of the first David Thomas, the preacher, Owen I, was his son and the land hasn't left the Thomas family since. Touring Loudoun in rain or shine nothing could be nicer.

Back home that evening Ruth Lee Holler invited us for dinner and it was lucky we accepted as the electricity was off here for three hours. Arriving home in the dark about 8 o'clock, we started a fire and were about to try popcorn with the shaker over the fireplace when that welcome hum returned so we promptly plugged in the electric popcorn maker.

Other news this week was that the Snickersville Craft Club was making pressed flower pictures and Jeanne Bardon says she is offering an Adult Education class in drawing and painting sponsored by the Clarke County School System for 10 weeks starting on Sept. 16 from 7-10 p.m. on Monday evenings. The cost is $10 plus supplies.

The Bluemont Citizens met this week with a lot of Fair business. Most of the features seem to be in workable order. Installing lights in the barn may be too costly but we can just open wide the doors and pray for beautiful weather like last year. Charlie Waddell and Kenny Rollins wives have already promised me a quilt to exhibit from their mother's and grandmother's handiwork.

There may be taffy pulling and a corn husking along with a farmyard animal display and puppet show at the Children's Fair and a Glue-in (If you want to find-out what this is, you'll have to come and see!)

And Mr. Duncan down the road here has removed the old junk cars from my woods and life is joyous again as the yellow flowers embrace the fields.

September 19, 1974

The scent of apples that need attention fills the kitchen while the luke-warm sun invites a stroll down Susy's lane up to the mountain pasture lane as the bees buzz about our heads in their most frolicsome play of the year.

The telephone rings seldom now, traffic is thick on the highways as residents delight in the best of all seasons to me.

About all we can talk in Bluemont is the Bluemont Fair – posters and cards are going out in every direction and with the barn being readied it's time for me to gather in the quilts for exhibition. If anyone has an unusual, beautifully stitched quilt she would be willing to exhibit, please contact me at 554-8448.

Our Preservation Society of Loudoun County is moving ahead with involving each community to think about the uniqueness of their own backyard and this Sunday, Sept. 22 Bluemont will have its own Preservation party.

Anyone in the community interested in Preservation is invited to the schoolhouse at 7:30 when we will see the film previously shown at Oatlands, "A Future for the Past." Afterward, we will adjourn to the Becks for refreshments and committee volunteering. It's promised to be a fun time. Please come!

Jennifer and I had a fun time taking-in Uncle Jim's wedding at the University of Maryland Chapel yesterday.

Then on the way to the reception I was deploring the sheer ugliness of growth in the mushrooming area when we came upon a lovely stone mill and miller's house at the side of road and lo and behold we turned into the drive for the reception. It was a good example of adaptive use as the Parks and Recreation Department has converted it into a community center. The young cousins and I explored all the floors but it did seem a shame to see the big wheel solidified in concrete, no longer free to turn and the mill-race was no more. It was quite a contrast to our glorious turning water-wheel at Millwood Mill.

The weekends have been filled with dog shows for the Stanley Kelley's and they have been doing very well. Last Saturday, Michael, their Duke of Erland took first in the puppy class at the Bichon Frise Club Show at Marshall and Meadowlark's Jim of Erland took first in open dogs, first in novice and best of breed and second of all dogs.

Then on Sunday at the Potomac Irish Setter Show, Meadowlark took second in open dogs and Michael took first in puppies, best puppy in a match and the coveted owner-breeder class prize for the Kelleys.

The children are pleased to see their neighbor, Miss Willa Colbert in the assistant librarian post at Round Hill Elementary and the Bluemont Post Office is expanding. The carpenters are building a new front for the interior.

All of us are saddened by two deaths in our Bluemont family.

Willie Littleton who lived atop our mountain for many years, actually over the West Virginia line, they say, passed away. He was a kind person and hard worker.

Secondly, our sympathy to Leslie Hutchins and her family as she lost her father in a heart attack last week in New Jersey. He and his wife made many trips to our village, helping us churn the ice cream in the summer on the porch, taking beautiful pictures of our Bluemont Fair last year which we are using for our publicity this year.

Then some nice ancestors of the John Herefords whose grave was marked by the DAR last week in Leesburg came by. These Alabamians are looking for the grave of another Hereford, Thomas Ammon, who died in 1840 at Bloomfield.

See you at the Preservation party and we'll talk genealogy, folk tales, properties, land-use and such!

September 26, 1974

Everywhere there are smiles on people's faces and laughter on their lips and reflected in their eyes for the world loves a countryside turning to autumn.

People are turning out meeting each other, happy to have an excuse to gather together.

I've just returned from Alice and Jim Powers nuptials party when it poured on their buffet supper tables on the lawn but none of the spirit of the party was dampened. There were live musicians there, a saxophonist and accordionist and I've concluded musicians are a wonderful breed, they just want everyone to have fun.

And our great Bluemont party is fast-approaching with Ken Hutchins reporting a lot of music of all kinds. Isn't it great to have our friends over for the Fair with good times for all?

The Skyfields people in charge of the childrens' fair, a brand new feature, are asking that neighbors contribute buttons, old beads for jewelry-making, plus they need yarn, pieces of fabric, spools and scraps of wood for the craft projects. These can be brought anytime now to the Bluemont General Store.

Of course, the really big news of the week is that Don and Linda Corley are proud adoptive parents of a darling baby girl. My girls were just ecstatic with the news and they already have calculated that they can babysit for the Corleys when they are fourteen.

In was good to get back for a day of teaching at Valley High School. There on the track field with the boys, I got a magnificent view of the blue mountains.

And the river beckons too this week. A segment of our Loudoun Towns class churned across the Potomac via White's Ferry. Driving in the Maryland countryside we noted scattered housing that somehow blighted the interest of the flat land broken by that lovely Sugar Loaf Mountain. There in its shadow, I spent my teenage years, enjoying many a picnic on its slopes.

At the foot of the mountain we had a fine lunch at the Comus Inn and then took in the terrific antique shop.

Back across the river we all summoned up thoughts of Huck Finn lazily floating down on his raft but the ferry is guided by a cable on either side and propelled by a marine diesel engine that is reversed by pushing a button as the craft nears the opposite shore.

Then too we ruminated on the losses of Ball's Bluff below this crossing during the War Between the States, although our skipper said the water was just about seven feet at that expanse.

And finally I reflected on the swans that swam so freely here in 1774 according to a young Englishman who kept a journal about his stay in Leesburg and if Spur Magazine would ever publish my piece on the history of Leesburg, everyone could read my poetic ending to the article, "And the swans are gone from the river forever."

October 3, 1974

With a tinge of orange showing on the tips of the oak tree leaves and apples and pears showering down from over-loaded branches, October bid a lusty hello to the countryside again in the intoxicating change of seasons.

Activities were absolutely legion, especially over the weekend.

The Multiple Sclerosis Tea at Shadow Mountain was a lovely affair as the sun broke through on Saturday afternoon, and what a treat to be entertained by the upcoming super-star, Terri Gregory and The Haymakers. It was nice to meet her energetic manager, Gina Alexander, from nearby Philomont too.

The Dirt Roads Tour at Lincoln was going strong and I planned to avail myself of the rare opportunity to see America's favorite artists, the Wyeth family's works in exhibit at a rescued landmark, "Confederate Hall" on the Mills' Farm, Hickory Tree. Preservation, scenic beauty and art, could there be a more pleasurable combination.

Then as the weekends lengthen into October, the long-established Waterford Foundation will delight visitors at its approaching Craft Fair and Home Tour. This year, Taylorstown will also accommodate the public on Oct. 12 winding up with our Bluemont event on Oct. 19, 20 right before Halloween says goodbye to October.

Emma Mann has done an outstanding display at the Loudoun Museum in Leesburg – try to take it in when you can. Emory Plaster has sent me a beautiful "Grandmother's Flower Garden" patterned quilt with the finest of stitches from his family's collection, signed and dated 1853.

The usual meeting of the Bluemont Citizens Association will be delayed until Oct 9 due to our President being out of town. By that time only the last minute touches should be made on the Fair.

The local high school is into the excitement of the football season, hosting a heart-breaker to Handley by one point on Friday night. Stanley Kelley is becoming a world traveler with trips to Italy and Germany this month while Barbara keeps the dogs going to the shows.

Leslie Hutchins had a snake in the house this week and smugly I feel the Johnson five are in the "fittest" category having survived last week's cold snap with no costly oil furnace running and in fact only did I lay a fire one night.

Of course, we retired early those evenings under the heavy quilts that aren't just for admiring, you know.

October 10, 1974

The temperature dropped as shivers went out over Northern Virginia and there was frost on the pumpkins and persimmons.

I thought I'd shoot for Oct. 31 as furnace starting day or maybe relent on Oct. 15, but come Thursday morning, I was frozen through.

Harriet Murtaugh had laid a wigmam fire that day for us that finally caught to the old logs by nightfall and then we jogged upstairs to the icy sheets.

I began the night in flannel pajamas and housecoat, a pair of knee socks and Betty Walsh's hand-knitted slippers under a blanket and heavy quilt but by 3 a.m., still being sleepless from the chill, I added another pair of socks, two sweaters and my Bluemont Fair colonial cap and when the 7:00 a.m. alarm rang I was glad to be up, dressed and on my way out to the warmth of the car heater.

Ginger Echols chauffeured my Ginger and me over to Brookmead to collect a lovely Grandmother's Flower Garden quilt done by Bill Crossman's great aunt and as we hit the main entrance a wild flurry of snowflakes descended. Another year of a snow before the Bluemont Fair – we don't need it!

Nevertheless, with the weekend the Indian summer weather returned when it is so glorious just to walk into that special sunlight. Jamie Wyatt captured it in his "Bale of Hay" painting. A terribly plump jack rabbit scurried from my path when I made my way to the barn to inspect again the swept-out floor. And from all the ceiling space the quilts can hang beautifully.

This week, I'll collect John Costello's quilt from his mother at Waterford, Charlie Waddell's, Kenneth Rollin's and hopefully Phil Bolen's, Paul Walstad's, Don Devine's. Henry Stowers and Frank Raflo didn't have a quilt but sent a book instead. It wasn't quite what I had in mind but was interesting anyway.

Raflo's Department Store put out its own little history in 1961 with pictures that showed a 1915 photograph of Leesburg with unpaved streets.

I'm always a sucker for a book – hand me one, if it's not too lengthy, I'll tackle it before bedtime.

The Conefreys have been very generous to us, endowing us last week with all the treasures of some Nancy Drew mysteries, some Bobbsey Twins thrillers and then they even threw in a rock collection, Jennifer now has a new hobby.

Sarah Campbell too showered us with some interesting readables – Blondie and Dagwood and a book on Indians which now sits bedside.

Reading a book is really not where the action is these days, however. It's out touring our countryside or washing windows or sorting clothes – two trunks down, two to go, or brewing mulled cider and snipping golden rod for bouquets, but "Claudia, the Story of a Marriage" 1939 vintage is a little much to lay aside.

See you at the Bluemont Fair!

October 17, 1974

Ah! Blissful Indian summer. On a coke I'm absolutely intoxicated with our glorious autumn.

The dry weather has made the leaves, now fast changing, particularly beautiful this year.

And what wonderful views we all can see over our lovely countryside but especially at the James Dietzs of Taylorstown on Saturday.

Lots of people had turned out for the first Taylorstown tour and I have to admit it was my first visit to the perfectly charming spot. Every house, cabin and barn on the tour was a pure delight and most of them were very early in comparison to the rest of the county and general eastern area of the county.

Every place seemed to date to the 1700's. It was a marvelous idea to bring the people there to see what would be lost if the dam project was carried through. Particularly terrific were the heavy stands of trees everywhere and the house dressing at that turkey dinner was delicious!

After going on such a sojourn it's always great to come home and hang another dried arrangement by the kitchen hearth in a gesture of appreciation for the opportunity to be creative in your own surroundings.

When I arrived back in late afternoon, Sonny Hall was busy with the clippers on the hedge across the street while Larry Allder was using the mower, keeping his parents' place in usual perfect trim and the children were talking of collecting trash on their school holiday, all in anticipation for the Bluemont Fair.

I thought by this writing my lawn would be neat but the run-down battery on the tractor made Herbert Martz's and mine best laid plans go astray.

Nevertheless, my timing was right on another matter. While I was gone, a small snake frequented the front hall with Curt Budny kindly rescuing Sandy Mitchell and the children. Yep, at last year's Fair some enterprising young man was selling his freshly caught specimen for pets to the city folks.

The best part of my week has been tracking down the quilts for the quilt show for the Fair.

I had a lovely time meeting John Costello's mother near Waterford who lent a beautiful piece with a quilting pattern in between the squares dating probably to 1860.

Then a stop at the Leesburg Museum turned up a crazy quilt from Charlie Waddell and a log cabin from Kenneth Rollins and another Grandmother's Flower Garden from Paul Walstad. That pattern has got to be the favorite of all time and no wonder, it is so beautiful!

With ten collected, I wanted another five and Diane Gavura rounded up another four unusual pieces and there are promises of more. Won't we quilt buffs have a good time! I noted a beauty at Anna Hendricks' fetching Hunting Hill too.

The men of the village cleaned out the rooms of the school today so all is ready as the exhibits come in on Wednesday and Thursday from 1 to 7 p.m. at the schoolhouse.

Keep in mind that a visit to the Ebenezer Church is possible during the two days of the Fair also.

At the town meeting this week, we planned ahead to the annual Fair dinner held in November when we have a time to socialize and hear the report of the finance committee. Everyone who works at the Fair is invited to come. The covered-dish dinner will be held on Sunday evening, Nov. 10 at 6:30 p.m. in the school house auditorium. Department chairmen should be sure to invite their workers.

Since, of course, Halloween follows on the heels of the Fair, we planned ahead with Mary Lynn Budny and Doris Allder organizing the event that will be held Halloween Eve at 7:30 p.m. in the school auditorium.

The P.T.A. at the Banneker School is sponsoring a Halloween party too that evening from 6 to 9 p.m., with costumes, cake walks and games. This will be a fund-raiser for some much needed projects.

Jack Bardon is back after a swing down South America way and just catching his breath, he and Claire were off again to a cheese festival in Ohio and a fall event in Elkins, W.Va. where the trees turned over night into rapturous hues.

I can feel it in my bones – we're going to have more fun this year than we've ever had – talking quilts and local history, swaying to the music, taking a hayride, seeing the new puppet show…See you at the Bluemont Fair!

October 24, 1974

There was a nip in the air but when the sun shone, it was delightful as the trees showed off their lovely colors on the first day of the Bluemont Fair.

At ten and eleven o'clock there were few milling around but by noon everyone had shown up and the children particularly were having a grand time at the Children's Fair.

The day had begun at seven here: out we went to the barn for the quilt hanging and while everyone complained of the chill, I noticed it not by dressing in layers and by moving. And there was plenty of moving to be done – books to be carried out, ladders and chairs to be moved and quilts, quilts to be hung. Frankly, after this weekend I won't care if I never hang a quilt on a clothesline again.

As the clock creeps toward midnight, one glories in the enjoyment of the day but realization dawns that there is a whole lot of work involved.

A new contribution here which I have had scant time to review is a book by our former historian, Mrs. Ingrid Jewel Jones on the life of Edward Snicker for which the burg, gap and ferry were named at one time.

Mrs. Jones might be pleased to see the old name now posted on the former Mann's Store now operated by the William Miners.

I haven't made the Children's Fair yet but the most fun of all so far has been a terrific hayride that crossed two fords, climbed into the high pasture land that afforded a great view in every direction and then concluded with a greeting exchange with the Brownell men, Jim, Mark and Scott.

It's always fun to see any of my former students from Herndon High School who have now matured into handsome young men like Steve Croson. Maybe Miles Rasigna will be along tomorrow.

The camera buffs were out swapping turns of views through each other's lens and taking close-ups of that lovely Plaster quilt. An anonymous donor of an exquisite hand-knitted spread in off-white will be glad to hear of the compliments paid the piece given to the local Methodist Church. Sealed bids are being taken and if anyone is interested they may call Mrs. Ralph Cochran or Mrs. Walton Mann of Bluemont.

Had a country ham sandwich today too and was the hot cider going…

You may say you want the recipe? To a gallon of cider, add a half cup of brown sugar (the darker makes it richer), some cinnamon (about four shakes from the can), some allspice (about three shakes), and two to three slices of lemon, squeezed into the mixture and then allowed to simmer in the pot.

Here's to you, from Bluemont Fair side!

October 31, 1974

The time for gathering in the wood was now as the buzz saw echoed and re-echoed across the countryside this week.

Over at the Robert Allders in the village, the John Carter family had joined in the task which inspired me to sort out the pile under the barn overhang. It's a big job to transport it to the handy front porch, especially now that the little red wagon is without tongue but must be done, for in the country winterizing is a seasonal way of life.

Mary Lou Markle has been coping with the job, pulling up the dead roots of the garden and chopping wood. Someone suggested that Bluemont is rather matriarchal and maybe it is.

All of us ladies shudder to think how we would manage without the help of Herbert Martz whose wife Lucy (another hard worker) has suffered a heart attack and is recuperating in Loudoun Memorial Hospital.

Another friend to the helpless is congenial Clyde Beck whose family is enjoying a weekend in Charlottesville with his mother.

Isabelle Dawson is unique this week in that she became a grandmother to two new babies in a week's time with her daughter Jean adding a granddaughter, Julie Michelle Hoggett on

Tuesday while daughter Sue Hall gave birth to a boy, John Keith on Wednesday. Grandson number one Eric Hoggett was very pround to show off the brand-new baby sister – so very sweet!

The next social event for Bluemont will be the annual Halloween party sponsored by the Bluemont Citizens Association on Halloween night at 7:30 p.m. at the schoolhouse auditorium. All the Bluemont children and parents are cordially invited.

Thinking of who will be there, it's great that Dr. Martin and Tish Fleming have joined our Bluemont family with Tish helping as department head of the dried flowers at the Fair this year. Martin has the most smashing outfit for winter with a Sherlock Holmes hat that is perfectly complimented with his English accent.

Speaking of fashion, the latest items is what is called a pants apron, a midi-length bibbed apron worn with a top and pants, is especially nice for the coming holiday entertaining.

A nice visit with a charming gal from Aldie revealed that a cottage industry of creating these designs was started in Maine under her leadership.

I'm looking forward to showing the children at Cooley Elementary School in Berryville the fun of crazy quilting at their worthy Virginia Heritage Day in November. Trudy Verloop will be there too, demonstrating her skilled craft of spinning. She will be taking in a week's seminar prior to her demonstration.

The Life in Loudoun class got back on the road again with a tour to the Bluemont backyard of Bloomfield to the two Ebenezer Churches side by side. The day was perfect for strolling in the warmth of the sun-kissed graveyard when I conjured up Walt Whitman's thought that "grass is the beautiful uncut hair of graves."

And I'm going to dare to say it – Lucien Powell's grandson has ruined the original painting. The sense of perspective is gone, the muted colors are now an ugly brown but perhaps, a lesson has been learned. A painter is not necessarily a restorer.

Would be preservationist – beware!

Although the Ebenezer Cemetery Company has been working on it, a wonderful project for some group would be the reclaiming of the oldest part of the cemetery, hidden now in weeds. No doubt, that is where the last Hereford lies in repose at that lovely spot with blue mountains fanning out in every direction.

After seeing a film on school bus safety last week and then receiving a call from a concerned neighbor, it seems time to draw attention to a dangerous practice of the school buses approaching the Bluemont exit off the dual-lane highway.

The buses wait till they get to the crest of the hill, then they pull over from the slow land across the fast lane to the exit. The proper approach as practiced by drivers of individual vehicles is to move to the fast lane at the bottom of the hill, signaling your intention and if others wish to pass, they can move up the slow lane and onward.

There are sixteen school bus accidents a day in this country and with most of us sending our children together on these buses, virtually our families could be wiped out. I hope others concerned will call the proper school board authorities.

Also the one stop at the top of the fog-laden mountain with a full bus load of children seems unnecessary.

Around the corner is Election Day and the fair dinner and Thanksgiving with walnuts and persimmons thudding to the ground and it's all as it should be in the golden glow of autumn.

November 14, 1974

As darkness envelops the village in late afternoon now, it is comforting to pull the family members in near the oven warming dinner and as the soft lights catch the glow of the red paint on the old kitchen cabinet, the coziness of the season turning to winter is relished.

Most exciting of all the week's events was Election Day! I can't hardly believe it but at last my vote went to the winner! Having a fireside chat with Joe Fisher during the Bluemont Fair, I'm convinced a vote for him was a vote for preservation and a concern for the farmer's plight. Certainly wholesale land development as practiced by his opponent is bound to undermine the serenity and friendliness of the lifestyle we enjoy here. In addition, development here will take some of the richest farm land in the country in a world now starving. It will be sacrificed to another sprawl of three bed-room brick ramblers flashing with television antennas.

All of these weighty matters were before the Board of Supervisors this Tuesday when I went to plug the Preservation Society of Loudoun County. It is interesting to note that Supervisor Frank Raflo will be leading a seminar on "How to Reduce Your Taxes" at the Loudoun campus of the Northern Virginia Community College.

The morning had been a unique experience as the Life of Loudoun class had toured the magnificent Aldie Mill. Ned Douglas, Jr. was a wealth of information, even supplying us with copies of a history he had done of the mill. The most beautiful picture presented itself at the back of the mill where the race came through the water wheel. Although the day was cloudy, still the scene with the brilliant plumage of the ducks relaxing in the stream had a dazzling effect on the viewer.

On Wednesday evening the too few Bluemont citizens met with Sheriff Legard to discuss the alleviation of vandalism in the village and particularly on the schoolhouse. He encouraged citizens to call in complaints so they can crack down on the offenders.

The December meeting will be an important one as discussion of changing the date of the Bluemont Fair will be decided and the setting up of the annual Christmas decorating contest will be arranged.

Of course, tomorrow evening is the traditional Bluemont Fair dinner for all those involved in the Fair. A big vote of thanks to this year's chairman, Mrs. Donna Miner.

After the usual two days of house cleaning there, Friday brought the Virginia Heritage Day at Cooley Elementary School in Berryville.

They had some very interesting craftsmen there. I took in our crazy quilt and talked about quilting bees with the children who had grandmothers and mothers who quilted in the library with the potter who "threw" about twenty pots that day while my square still needs a lot of fancy stitching.

There was a lady there with plants used for medicines and a shoemaker carrying wooden shoes and Mrs. Barbara Byrd sketching and a lady fashioning apple-head dolls and Mrs. Forsythe, the librarian has promised to send me a Yo-Yo doll made in the same manner as the Yo-Yo quilt where small circles are gathered together in the middle and then sewn together. Our Trudy Verloop was there with her marvelous spinning and weaving demonstration and the teachers and staff were exceptionally pleasant so it was great fun to go "to the other side of the mountain to see what I could see."

November 21, 1974

The nip of the frost in the night air sends the children from the outdoors in early eve and down the slope of the year, the time advances.

Families are thinking ahead to the holidays when there will be fine gatherings of aunts, uncles, cousins, grandmas and grandfathers around the festive board, heaped perhaps, not so high as usual this year.

Inflation has taken a greedy bite from the good times and especially from the foods upon the table. The grocery bill is one any family tries to cut first as the utility and housing costs have to be met.

Life is never without hope, however, and perhaps our new Congress will be able to deal with the global troubles.

Locally two meetings were held that dealt with at least preserving some of that open space and farm land for feeding the world's hungry.

The Preservation Society of Loudoun County met at the Purcellville Library with community chairmen who in turn are to encourage their neighbors to think about what should be presevered in their own backyard. A registration form for recording these structures or natural items will be forwarded to the chairmen so a grand Loudoun County register can be drawn up.

In like manner, the Open Space Committee reviewed the beginnings of an environmental resources inventory being prepared by the excellent Piedmont Environmental Council which will be for the benefit of the county planning staff.

A marvelous series of maps showing wild life habitats, flood plains (I think downtown Bluemont could be that one), steep slopes, surface water, septic tank suitability, ground water resources, unusual geological formations, scenic areas, historic districts and historically significant structures, open space areas, population density and critical environmental areas will be prepared.

Others in the county are planning for times of fun as a Round Hill neighbor, George Noland would like to hear from any organization or individuals willing to participate in an old-fashioned Christmas celebration to be held on the courthouse lawn in Leesburg. Any bell-ringers, carolers, puppeteers?

The Bluemont Citizens said they would like to have their Los Luminarias again this year with caroling after the lighting.

Our thanks to Miss Ruth Alley, a RSVP volunteer. The group meets regularly at the Purcellville Community Center and our Leslie Hutchins is now the director of the program. She notes that Miss Ruth gave forty-five hours of volunteer work in October visiting nursing home patients and helping at the Bluemont Fair. Of course, we all know Miss Alley has spent many hours of work in visiting with the patients at the Veterans Hospital in Charles Town, W.Va. also.

One of our dear Bluemont neighbors is at the convalescent home in Hagerstown now. Mr. Townshend went last week while Mrs. Townshend continues on as our beloved postmistress but they have decided to put their charming house up for sale. Our prayers are with them in this time of adjustment.

Then the nicest surprise came when I opened the door to find Sue Mearns standing on the doorstep. She, Rick, and Andrew came for a visit to Rick's parents in Front Royal so she ran over for a couple of stops in Loudoun. Sue looked absolutely marvelous and is breaking into the New York social picture with a few of the Virginia recipes like hot cider. They are in the Finger Lakes area near Watkins Glen which is a fascinating spot. It was wonderful to see her again.

And with just two lights burning and the heat turned back to 65 degrees, it is still quite comfortable as the village recedes into its weekend sleep.

November 28, 1974

The wind in icy gusts whirls around the house leaking through the sundry cracks, swaying inside doors and curtains.

On the eve of Thanksgiving the days are somber, overcast with dark clouds and ever the threat of snow looms on the horizon.

Here at last the woodpile has been transferred from the barn overhang to the front porch, requiring many trips as the little red wagon is in disrepair, like the little red tractor, like the leaking pipe under the sink.

Unemployment is creeping over the land but still people are giving hours of their time in volunteer work.

A group I particularly admire are the Taylorstown folks who quickly banned together in the Catoctin Valley Defense Alliance to fight the proposed dam that would flood hundreds of beautifully scenic and historically significant acres.

The Life in Loudoun class had a stimulating session in reviewing Admiral James Dietz's maps of the damage to be done. Then we feasted our eyes on the Short Hill Mountains at the Dietz's home and then were treated to a tour of the Ray Cheronis home. One side of the house was moved there from another location with paneling from the old Stacy Taylor house in Purcellville. It's all perfect with terrific paintings, some done by Mrs. Cheronis, a country kitchen that is adorable to a bathroom with a tin tub. How sunny everything seems when one is touring the mellowness of these old homes in perfect rustic settings.

Mrs. Betty Davis of Round Hill is inviting Bluemonters interested in joining a new chapter of the Home Demonstration Club to a meeting on Tuesday, Nov. 26 at 1:30 p.m. at the Round Hill Fire Department. For further information, she can be reached at 338-4637.

How glad I am to have met the invincible Chauncy Brown before his peaceful death last week. Frankly, I didn't know how famous he was; I just knew he made a memorable evening for all the guests of Jim and Alice Power when they entertained at their nuptial party this September.

I didn't know he had played his special brand of jazz for the guests of Washington society; I only knew his music made me happy and he was happy playing.

"Sweet Georgia Brown" had been a special rendition of a girls trio I had sung in in high school and I never would have guessed his age as high as 78.

I just knew he was a darling personality and so I had just suggested to Peggy Adams that we might try to get his trio for the reception for Joe Fisher at her house on Saturday night. I'll keep his card, "Brown's Society Orchestra" with fond memory.

Now Bluemont citizens, don't forget the Dec. 4th meeting of the Association at 8 o'clock at the schoolhouse.

And the menu plans are being drawn for Thanksgiving. How happy we will be to have our family at Clayton Hall, especially the boy cousins so close in age to the girl cousins.

Steak for Thanksgiving? Never. Mother will bring the turkey and oyster dressing and I'll make the baked squash and scalloped tomatoes and mashed potatoes and giblet gravy. Now the art of gravy-making is tricky. Some expert once told me you must first combine the flour with the drippings with a spoon, not a fork and then add the right amount of water for proper thickening.

And the snow storm can wait! Happy Thanksgiving!

December 5, 1974

December is no lady. Here the first day of her arrival, she's in a rage, beating the slender branches of the old hemlocks to the ground, scattering the birds to small huddling places in the stone wall of the house.

When she's brutal this way it's time to take a quick inventory. The wood pile seems scant already but we'll lay another load of logs in the fireplace for readiness. There's water in a jug beside the red cabinet in the kitchen and I have a big can of tuna fish, two cans of tomato soup, some apple sauce and home-canned peaches, only one and a half loaves of bread, a few scattered potatoes but there's turkey soup in the making, some remains of turkey salad and eggs with heavy skillets for frying over the fireplace.

She battered the soft wool blankets on the clothesline, soaking them with ice and snow and the lights have flickered five or six times already so beware...

Oh, I know she's known for fun and games and smooches under the mistletoe and songs and laughter around a bowl of nog, but she's been known to cancel a few of those little festivities too.

If she would but do her gentle snow dance in Bluemont, we'd like that.

November, however, brought some good times before she left.

Thanksgiving was cold and clear, sending families into each other's arms out in the countryside.

The big attraction in Bluemont was Mr. Butler's gravel pile where the cousins romped all with his permission, the children claim.

The Becks traveled to Joyce's sister's for the day and most of the Lloyd family took off for Tennessee to spend the vacation with daughter Linda and her new handsome husband. Glen held down the fort here with Jerry cooking Thanksgiving breakfast and then daughter, Ann and son-in-law Paul Wilson and grandson Michael in Berryville were his hosts for Thanksgiving dinner.

Mary Lou Markle is back after a pleasant sojourn to South Carolina with her daughter Sally and husband for the Thanksgiving holiday.

The Life in Loudoun class went back to Taylorstown mill, now the lovely home of Sandra and Phil Ehreneranz. It's such a joy to see creative people make a charming setting for themselves in these rich historic structures. Sandra told us of the multiple goodness of their neighbors when Hurricane Agnes sent volumes of water into their home. How ironic it would be if they could reclaim their treasures and serenity from nature's flood, but be sunk by man's proposal of a dam that would flood a mill, the oldest stone dwelling in Loudoun and a town.

Over at the backyard of the Robert Allders was a terribly picturesque scene. They had a leaping fire going under a big iron pot. Soap-making, apple-butter rendering? Too late for those. The children said they were cooking the coons Bobby had hunted. I'll have to find out more about that – anyway to beat inflation sounds like a grand idea.

And on Wednesday, I almost shimmered for joy. There at Valley High School, the students put on a music program for an assembly with the drama club presenting an impressive skit, the choir singing some pretty selections, "The Autumn Leaves", (that was Ben's and my song) and the band, the band came out with the big band sound! It was all Glen Miller-ish and fifty-ish and the kids, I could tell, they wanted to get up and jitterbug! It's all coming back and maybe December will bring a party or two and someone will suggest we jitterbug and even do the Charleston!

December 12, 1974

Was it but a week ago, a big mechanical bird fell out of the sky atop our village?

So many sights, sounds, thoughts, actions and sensations have been jammed into that week that seems so terribly short, yet so terribly long, too.

Now I can say I've been trying to tell you how very special the people in Bluemont are and now quite a few more people know. Countless citizens, friends from Pine Grove, Philomont, Purcellville way sent food, mammoth pots of chili, boxes of sandwiches, homemade cakes and finally breakfasts of eggs and bacon and chicken dinners ordered from two local restaurants, Holly Farms and Kentucky Fried Chicken in Winchester.

No one expected any pay or even any thanks. Workers called and thanked me for asking them to help. Certainly it was an experience that reinforced an observation of mine that basic to human nature is a desire to give and if the receiver can accept graciously, it becomes a beautiful experience for both.

The Federal Investigators, the officials of TWA, insurance agents and rescue workers were extremely grateful. Undoubtedly, it kept up their moral to smell bacon and eggs cooking in the morning at the old schoolhouse.

Sociologically, a disaster provides for a unique study of human relationships. People were actually hurt if they hadn't been asked to help and they identified with the operation in individual ways. One said she always wanted to be a nurse, so she didn't mind working with the medical aspect of it. Another enjoyed the clerical work involved. Another was glad to be part of the food preparation and though I went to great lengths to avoid any sight of broken bodies, I noticed the marvelous order and organization of the rescue endeavor. These were precise, top-notch men, accurate and sensitive.

Now we need to comfort our own. The Parks family with nieces and nephew, Betty Pierson, and Russell Parks, Jr. lost their aunt on Saturday morning from a sudden heart attack. This is their father's sister, Nellie of The Plains.

And our dear Mrs. Townshend fell and broke her hip on Monday and is now at Winchester Hospital – she would love to hear from her neighbors.

And about that front wall of mine – please don't laugh, I need sympathy.

I pulled in the drive the other night, turned off the radio, heater and lights, switched off the key and apparently left it in gear. After making my way in front of the car to the sidewalk to gather ups Suzy Dennis, my babysitter for her return home, I turned to see the car rolling forward, bumping into my old stone wall, resulting in only a dent or two to the bumper of the car but alas, the wonderful Clayton Hall wall! Maybe the Reids will be kind enough to give it a quick repair.

Out of town last weekend were Bill Wolfe and Lewis Reed who spent the holiday in Staunton and at the Bluemont Citizens Meeting on Wednesday night the majority decided to change the Fair date to the third weekend in September. I really didn't have the heart to fight with my neighbors that night, but I believe it's a big mistake. How about a referendum on the issue?

December 19, 1974

Clyde Beck says it's supposed to snow and he's chopping wood and carrying it into the storage space adjacent to the house.

Even though I hated to do it, my hand slipped up to the thermostat and turned it two degrees higher and evergreens are marching again in living rooms in town.

Most everyone says that he or she hasn't done much shopping this year, somehow it seems unsound to go further into debt when there are already existing unpaid bills but that special Christmas feeling is stealing up the two streets of Bluemont, nevertheless.

The Milton Hollers have lit a pretty outdoor tree and over on Owen Thomas' road, the Potts have a sparkling display around the roof outline.

The community will draw closer this year with a special lighting of the Las Luminarias from the Bluemont Store corner down to the little stone church. This will begin at 6:30 with the meeting place being the store and then the traditional candlelight service will be held at the church at 7:30, all on Christmas Eve.

Later a get-together will be held in the old school auditorium decorated in holiday finery under the supervision of Emma Mann.

The Bluemont Citizens will provide a drink and the rest of the guests are asked to bring along a favorite Christmas goodie to share.

It will be good to have this time together with our neighbors that we love so dearly. Early we will depart for Christmas in our own homes that evening.

And frankly my children's attempts at Christmas creativity have reached the point of holiday distraction to me.

On Friday a well-meaning elementary teacher sent home a recipe for plaster of paris decorations for the tree so while I was catching a paragraph or two of Newsweek upstairs, they were busy in the kitchen.

There I found heaps of flour on the floor, six cups of water on the table, two overflowing bowls of mixture sticking to spoons, dish clothes and placemats and an empty box of salt. No the decorations didn't turn out, except out the door.

Then Sonny and Jeanne Brown kept our annual tree decorating event together coming all the way from Richmond where they had moved for an over-nighter and the children removed all sixty of the candy canes brought for trimming the tree!

Nevertheless, some children at least, looked angelic this week at Jane Rogers' annual Christmas program at the Hamilton Church. Her kindergarten children went through the usual darling antics of song with our own little newcomer, Heather Lamond participating.

Another children's outing was the Round Hill School's second grade trip to the National History Museum of the Smithsonian Institution. Our Gail Kelley drove them in the big orange school bus and Van had his magical jewelry display at Clyde Beck's studio on Saturday after which we cruised up to the plane crash site. All of the rubble of what was left of the plane is gone now but the charred rocks and splintered trees are a ghastly reminder of the disaster that so easily could have claimed the lives of our own citizens if the plane had come down on the many nearby homes.

Then last night the Jack Bardons had the best party ever with a group of local musicians bringing guitars, ukuleles, a bass fiddle, banjos and Jack's harmonica for five steady hours of good ole country music.

And was I proud of the true old pro, my next-door neighbor Lou Robey who just rolled into one song after another on his electric guitar.

More of life should be given to such good times and here's a recipe for hot wassail I found this week: 1 cup of sugar, 4 cinnamon sticks, 3 lemon slices, 2 cups pineapple juice, two cups orange juice, 6 cups claret wine, one-half cup lemon juice, 1 cup dry sherry.

Boil first three ingredients with one-half cup water for five minutes. Heat remaining ingredients. Do not boil. Combine with syrup. Garnish with lemon slices and serve hot. Serves 20.

It might be worth trying.

And the Reid boys, bless their hearts, say they will fix my wall!

December 26, 1974

The whispering of the wind in the pine, spruce and fir on lots about town announces the enchantment of Christmas and most everyone in Bluemont seems ready.

As of this writing Clayton Hall has a tree standing with no lights, no greens have been gathered, the bittersweet and Indian corn still grace the doors, no cookies have been baked or apple sauce cakes but there's a turkey in the freezer and a few assorted country items for gift baskets and after all, I do have a whole cold craft shop of my own in which to shop.

Meanwhile, at the Snow House, things are in readiness with Leslie Hutchins and Mary Lynn Budny entertaining the Snickersville Craft Club for their annual Christmas party this past Tuesday night.

Since the Bluemont Citizens Association had neglected to decide about the annual decorating contest, the ladies made the arrangements.

They will ask Clyde Beck to secure some out-of-town judges, it will be a no lights contest again this year and the judging will take place on Sunday, Dec. 29, after Christmas.

Clyde Beck has up his usual sway and I heard hammerings going on at the Herbert Martz's the other day as their usual interesting display went up. There is a nice miniature sleigh at the post office atop the file cabinet but the cheery greeting of Mrs. Townshend is being missed. She is now home from the hospital at her daughter's in Maryland.

A new addition at the general store this year is the tripod with a hanging pot for donations for the Salvation Army.

Considering their particular kindness in Bluemont during the airplane disaster, I'm sure we will all want to contribute.

Too, there are new store hours at the Bluemont General Store. The store will not open until 9 o'clock in the morning instead of 7:30. It will remain open until 6:30 in the evenings.

All of the magic of Christmas will begin in earnest next week and especially on Christmas Eve when we will have a chance to give a warm greeting to our neighbors at the Candlelight Service at the Methodist Church at 7:30 and then we will adjourn to the school for refreshments.

So to all you dear neighbors who in sundry ways have given my family the great gift of contentment in finding a comfortable place for nesting, my warmest best wishes for a Merry Christmas!

Photos

Photo credit: Part of an interview with the author (she's dressed in Colonial garb for the Bluemont Fair) as appeared in the Loudoun Times-Mirror newspaper, Thursday, September 28, 1972 edition, courtesy of Loudoun-Times Mirror.

Photo credit: Bluemont column as appeared in the Loudoun Times-Mirror newspaper, Thursday, September 25, 1969 edition, courtesy of Loudoun-Times Mirror.

A decade of Bluemont News

Photo credit: Mrs. Sam M. Jones, Mrs. Johnson, Mrs. James Brownell and Mrs. Walton Mann as appeared in the Loudoun Times-Mirror newspaper, Thursday, March 5, 1970 edition, courtesy of Loudoun-Times Mirror.

Photo credit: Lara Johnson, daughter and Evelyn Porterfield Johnson, 1991, by Tracey Johnson.

A Note from the Author's Daughter

For a number of years I'd been encouraging my mom to publish her weekly Bluemont News columns in a book mostly because I wanted to read them myself, but she was always either too busy and/or would say to me, "who would be interested in reading my old columns?"

I knew the columns were good because growing-up she had readers who lived in other states, and would receive fan mail sometimes. One letter read: "Keep up the good work - I enjoy reading it - even if I don't know anyone!"

Bluemont attracted great people and for that I'm deeply grateful, in looking back it was an "idyllic childhood."

To all Bluemonters, in body, mind or spirit, may we always embrace "love your neighbor."

-Lara Johnson, Bluemonter and compiler of this book

www.ingramcontent.com/pod-product-compliance
Lightning Source LLC
Chambersburg PA
CBHW080910170426
43201CB00017B/2277